# THE BESIEGED SCHOOL SUPERINTENDENT

A Case Study of
School Superintendent–
School Board Relations
In Washington, D.C., 1973-75

## Nancy L. Arnez

UNIVERSITY
PRESS OF
AMERICA

Copyright © 1981 by
**University Press of America, Inc.**
P.O.Box19101, Washington, D.C. 20036

All rights reserved

Printed in the United States of America

ISBN: 0-8191-1635-1(Perfect)
0-8191-1634-3(Case)

Library of Congress Number: 80-69044

I dedicate this book to children, all of whom are different and talented and deserve justice.

"A potential Charlie Parker or Charles Drew, could be born at 10th and U Streets in the District of Columbia, and be overlooked by the public school system.

"However, where a structure accommodates student differences, ballet, violin, piano lessons become a reality and are no longer dependent on family affluence, a big variable in the success of educational programs. Tutoring services would be available as well as medical, food and clothing services. Students with emotional, psychological and other problems, could be helped by the regular on-going educational program instead of being relegated to programs for those who are not 'normal.'

"What we need is an educational system for people, all of whom are different instead of one for people who are assumed to be alike. All talent, then becomes significant in an institution, where there is justice for all."

                Barbara A. Sizemore
                Superintendent of Schools
                    District of Columbia
                Citizen's Salute
                Barbara A. Sizemore on her First
                    Anniversary as Superintendent of
                    D.C. Public Schools
                The New Brookland School
                Washington, D.C.
                October 23, 1974

PREFACE

This book examines one urban superintendency, that of Barbara A. Sizemore in Washington, D.C., and tries to untangle the power struggles, ideological differences, role confusions and racial and sexual conflicts that beset the relationship between Mrs. Sizemore and her school boards in an effort to provide insights applicable to other urban school systems.

Therefore, the book is concerned with the process by which policy was established in the District of Columbia Public School System (DCPSS) between 1973-75, the factors impinging on the decision-making process engaged in by the school board and superintendent, and how this decision-making unit responded to these factors. Because superintendent and school board relations are often conflicted, the study also examined the nature of conflict as an important problem in this relationship. As a sub-category of such a conflict, we examined the factors that led to conflicts in D.C. Public School superintendent-school board relations prior to 1973 to provide a point of comparison with the 1973-75 period. The study also investigated the exercise of power, in maintaining control of the school system, raging around the divergent values of the conflicting parties as they related to change and/or the maintenance of the status quo. The essential questions considered were: "What is policy-making within the framework of superintendent-school board relationships?", "What is administration within the framework of superintendent-school board relationships?", "What factors precipitated conflict between the policy makers and the central administration of the DCPS system?", "What policy evolved?", "How was the conflict resolved?", and "What were the outcomes of the change in policy?"

To answer these questions it was necessary to construct the outline of a theory of political conflict which defined the traditional educational decision-making structure (superintendent-school board) as the unit of analysis because policy decisions determine the direction in which a school system moves in terms of maintaining the status quo or making changes. But decisions are not made in a vacuum for they are molded by both external and internal factors which cause conflict in the relationship between school superintendents and school boards.

Therefore, it was hypothesized that the combination of <u>external environmental factors</u> of (1) governmental dominance and resulting financial constraints, (2) sexism, (3) racism, (4) classism, and (5) group pressure; and <u>internal organizational factors</u> of (1) change in school board membership, (2) authoritarian leadership behavior, (3) role conflict  (4) motivation of board members, (5) structures, and (6) functioning of boards of education in terms of goal setting, hiring and terminating superintendents, and (7) problems in authority hampered the introduction of change in a racially changing urban school system resulting in conflict in school board-superintendent relations. Chapter 1 concerns itself with an explanation of this paradigm.

The balance of the book devotes itself to utilizing this design for analyzing the conflicted relationship between District of Columbia superintendents and their school boards with an in-depth focus on the 1973-75 period.

Our method was the case study approach. The semi-structured interview was used as the primary method of data collection. This was buttressed by the analysis of tapes, transcripts, minutes, agendas of District of Columbia Board of Education meetings, and related documents, and the observation of the decision-making process in operation at school board meetings and at administrative conferences.

The book reveals that by the mid-1960s both the national and local climate were charged with vitality as Black people saw some positive movement in their lives. This led to continued agitation to establish more real than illusionary gains. But, racism and classism were entrenched in D.C. as attested to by the selection in 1954 of moderate desegregation attempts, the employment of a track system which relegated poor Black students to the lowest track and efforts to thwart the equalization of resources for the poor. Further, it was not until 1966 that the nine member DCBOE became majority Black, due to community pressure, for a school system majority Black.

The city itself was also majority Black and although a Black mayor was finally selected in 1967, he was almost powerless in that his term of office was coterminous with the U.S. Presidents; he could be removed from office at any time; and he was without an electoral base and therefore handicapped in the exercise of power within the city and before the Congress. Funds to run the city have to be petitioned by the mayor as funds to operate the public schools have to be petitioned by the school superintendent before the D.C. subcommittee of the appropriations committees. These committees were the model for the school board committees as was their adversarial relationship with the mayor and school superintendent, the model for how the school board reacted to the school superintendents. Even after the Elected School Board Act was signed into law in 1968, the lack of power of city fathers and school board members was still in evidence. This sense of powerlessness affected how the city fathers reacted to the superintendent in terms of the delegation of authority to make certain kinds of decisions.

Thus, the inadequacy of funds for the city, and therefore, for the school system precipitated many problems that strained the relationship between D.C. school boards and superintendents. Despite the financial problems, efforts were made to set system-wide goals to raise the academic level of the students in the DCPS system through various academic models, none of which were totally acceptable to the superintendents, various board members and some community leaders and members. Also, board priorities shifted due to changes in board membership and school superintendents.

Barbara A. Sizemore, a female and an outsider, with many supporters and indeed many critics, was selected in 1973 as the second Black superintendent of the D.C. Public Schools. Her selection was made by the school board after an exhaustive and conflicted search and screen process. Superintendent Sizemore, also, tried to positively effect the delivery of services aspect of the school system through administrative reorganization and major responsibilities of management services, and introduce a viable educational program to positively affect the learning of the majority Black student population as well as the minority white. Policy decisions made prior to her taking office hampered her moving ahead with her plan to decentralize the school system, and to institute a multi-lingual, multi-cultural, multi-modal educational plan. External factors in the form of racism, sexism, classism, community pressure groups and the unique relation of the school system to the Congress; and internal factors of rapid board changes, role conflict, goal setting, function, and structure established through rules, regulations and laws for setting policy and operating the school system, as well as the authoritarian leadership behavior of board presidents and the political motivation of board members interfered with her efforts to make the school system more responsive to the needs of the 96 percent Black and 70 percent poor student population.

Hence, conflict in the relationship between a superintendent, who desired to make changes, and school board members, who desired to maintain the status quo, mounted. Both elements struggled to influence the decision-making process. In this regard, the microscopic lens of external and internal factors is used to examine three specific policy decisions: The D.C. Youth Orchestra Program Controversy, The General Counsel Dispute and the Budget/Management Controversy; which merged into the Administrative Hearing, climaxing as it did, near the end of school year 1974-75. Subsequently, Sizemore was fired on October 1, 1975 due in large part to extreme community pressure from the white business interests in the city through their news organs, the Washington Post and the Washington Star, both of which unduly influenced the policy setting majority on the D.C. Board of Education (DCBOE).

Seven crucial decisions made after Sizemore's termination were also analyzed. The information presented followed actions begun during the Sizemore administration and continued or discontinued during her successor, Superintendent Vincent Reed's administration. Reed is a male and an insider. The purpose of this analysis was to reveal the state of superintendent-school board relations after Sizemore's termination.

Finally, it is our sincere hope that this publication may help this and other school systems to (1) recognize the force of politics in the educational enterprise, and deal with it realistically, (2) examine the roles and responsibilities of the school board and the superintendent in order to deal with how the ambiguities inherent can be removed, (3) stabilize school board membership, (4) clarify ambiguous statements in the superintendent's contract and (5) clarify school codes in statements indicating that the board will run the schools to mean set policy for rather than administer the schools from day-to-day and adjust conflicting concepts in both so that neither school codes nor superintendent contracts provide a natural scapegoat for school board decisions.

Nancy Levi Arnez

ACKNOWLEDGEMENTS

There is no way possible that I could have completed a study of this magnitude in a year's time without considerable encouragement and help from family, friends and associates. Therefore, I shall take this opportunity to thank as many of them as I can.

First, I thank Barbara A. Sizemore for allowing me to study her superintendency and for sharing all of her personal papers and the draft copy of her doctoral dissertation with me from which I used liberally throughout my study.

Secondly, I thank H. Thomas James and Spencer Foundation for providing me with the economic means which enabled me to take a year off from my teaching assignment at Howard University in order to engage in this study. Therefore, I also thank Howard University officials for granting me a year's leave of absence to conduct the study.

Also, thanks is extended to the American Association of University Women who made it possible for me to begin the collection of data during the summer of 1977.

Naturally, I wish to thank my mother, Ida R. Washington, a retired twenty-nine year veteran teacher, my sisters Doris J. Levi and Emily L. Ford, both school administrators, for their helpful advice and criticism. Additionally, thanks is extended to critical readers of Chapter I: Acklyn Lynch, political scientist, University of

Maryland; and Ronald Walters, political scientist, Howard University, who also assisted with the schema and critiqued the entire manuscript. I also thank Charles Martin, editor, <u>Journal of Negro Education</u>, Charlotte McIntyre, <u>historian</u>, Old Westbury; Gerterlyn Dozier, social scientist, formerly of Bernard Baruch College; and Bertha Hudson, U.S. Justice Department, who read and critiqued several portions of the manuscript.

Others were also helpful to the conduct of the study: Jeanne King, former administrative officer to former D.C. School Superintendent Sizemore; Ruth Goodwin, concerned citizen; Dwight Cropp, executive secretary, DCBOE, Betty Brooks, DCPS; Barbara Simmons, member, DCBOE; Joe Green, former <u>Washington Post</u> news reporter; Joyce E. Bonaparte, secretary and financial administrator to the project; Melvin Davis, graduate assistant, Howard University; Mary Hunter, DCCBPE; John Fargus, D.C. Citizen, who helped obtain political contribution information; and Theresa Rector, Associate editor, <u>Journal of Negro Education</u>, Howard University.

Special thanks is extended to the interviewees who provided me with insight into the conflicts between boards of education and superintendents. These persons who include present and former school board members, and superintendents as well as citizens are: Charles Cassell, Richard Prince, Gilbert Diggs, Luther Elliott, Therman Evans, Gary Freeman, Ruth Goodwin, Kenneth Haskins, Julius Hobson, Jr., Elizabeth Kane, Raymond Kemp, Margaret Labat, Napoleon Lewis, Floretta McKenzie, Virginia Morris, Delores Pryde, William Rice, Vincent Reed, Hugh Scott, William Simons, Barbara Simmons, Barbara Sizemore, Conrad Smith, Mattie Taylor, Bardyl Tirana, William Treanor, Evie Washington, James Williams, and John Warren.

TABLE OF CONTENTS

SECTION I
INTRODUCTION

CHAPTER                                                          PAGE

I.  INTRODUCTION................................  1
    Need for Study..............................  3
    The Approach................................  7
    Techniques and Methods of Data
    Collection..................................  7
        The interview...........................  7
        Observations............................  8
        News clipping file......................  8
        Library sources.........................  8
        Personal files..........................  9
        School board files......................  9
        Board of Election and Ethics............  9
        D.C. Citizens for Better Public
        Education (DCCBPE)......................  9
    System of Data Analysis..................... 10
    The Structure of the Study.................. 11

SECTION II
THE IMPACT OF SELECTED EXTERNAL AND INTERNAL FACTORS
FOR SCHOOL BOARD SUPERINTENDENT-
SCHOOL BOARD RELATIONS

II. AN OUTLINE OF A THEORY..................... 17
    Introduction................................ 17
    Points of Analysis.......................... 20
    The Setting................................. 25
        Decision-making......................... 25
        Authority............................... 26
        Composition............................. 27

xvii

|      |                                           |    |
|------|-------------------------------------------|----|
|      | Structure and function...............     | 27 |
|      | Motivation..........................      | 27 |
|      | Superintendents.....................      | 28 |
|      | Role conflict.......................      | 29 |
|      | Politics............................      | 30 |
|      | Influence and pressures.............      | 31 |
|      | Racial conflict.....................      | 31 |
|      | Class conflict......................      | 34 |
|      | Sexism..............................      | 35 |
|      | Propositions..........................    | 36 |
|      | Summary...............................    | 37 |
| III. | RACE, CLASS, SEX, AND COLONIAL STATUS..   | 43 |
|      | Introduction..........................    | 43 |
|      | Race and Class Factors................    | 46 |
|      | Ward 1..............................      | 48 |
|      | Ward 2..............................      | 48 |
|      | Ward 3..............................      | 51 |
|      | Ward 4..............................      | 51 |
|      | Ward 5..............................      | 52 |
|      | Ward 6..............................      | 52 |
|      | Ward 7..............................      | 52 |
|      | Ward 8..............................      | 53 |
|      | General Comparisons...................    | 53 |
|      | Population..........................      | 53 |
|      | Income..............................      | 53 |
|      | Education...........................      | 54 |
|      | Desegregation.........................    | 55 |
|      | The Track System......................    | 57 |
|      | The Issue of Equalization.............    | 58 |
|      | School Board Appointments.............    | 60 |
|      | Race as a Factor in All Affairs.......    | 61 |
|      | Sexism................................    | 62 |
|      | Colonial Status.......................    | 64 |
|      | Summary...............................    | 77 |
| IV.  | AUTHORITY, FUNCTION, STRUCTURE.........   | 85 |
|      | Introduction..........................    | 85 |
|      | Authority.............................    | 85 |
|      | Board authority.....................      | 85 |
|      | Superintendent's authority..........      | 87 |
|      | Appointment.......................        | 87 |
|      | Authority.........................        | 87 |
|      | Functions.............................    | 87 |

|      | Board functions....................... | 87 |
|---|---|---|
|      | Superintendent's functions........... | 88 |
|      | Structure............................. | 88 |
|      | Composition of the board............. | 88 |
|      | First elected DCBOE............... | 89 |
|      | Filling vacancies................. | 90 |
|      | Committee structure.................. | 92 |
|      | Board of education staff............. | 106 |
|      | Superintendent's staff--1973-75...... | 108 |
|      | Executive staff.................... | 108 |
|      | Selected members of the administrative team..................... | 109 |
|      | Board meetings....................... | 112 |
|      | Agenda............................. | 118 |
|      | Summary............................... | 119 |
| V.   | SELECTION AND TERMINATION PROCESSES -- 1967-73................................. | 127 |
|      | Introduction........................... | 127 |
|      | Superintendent Carl Hansen's Termination........................... | 128 |
|      | Superintendent William Manning's Selection and Termination............. | 129 |
|      | Superintendent Hugh Scott's Selection and Termination...................... | 134 |
|      | Superintendent Search and Selection, 1973................................... | 142 |
|      | Superintendent Barbara A. Sizemore.... | 165 |
|      | Sizemore's Educational Philosophy..... | 168 |
|      | Summary................................ | 172 |
| VI.  | GOAL SETTING........................... | 181 |
|      | Introduction........................... | 181 |
|      | The Track System....................... | 182 |
|      | The Clark Plan......................... | 184 |
|      | Decentralization....................... | 190 |
|      | The Model School Division (MSD)..... | 191 |
|      | The Morgan Community School (MCS)... | 194 |
|      | Adams Community School (ACS)........ | 197 |
|      | Anacostia Community School Project (ACSP).............................. | 198 |
|      | Fort Lincoln New Town (FLNT)........ | 200 |
|      | Spingarn Instructional Unit......... | 202 |
|      | The Pupil Personnel Field Centers... | 203 |

|      |                                                    |     |
|------|----------------------------------------------------|-----|
|      | School-by-school budgeting..........                | 203 |
|      | Principal selection.................                | 204 |
|      | Citizen's decentralization plan.....                | 205 |
|      | Equalization........................                | 207 |
|      | Summary.............................                | 212 |
| VII. | BOARD PROFILE, MOTIVES, LEADERSHIP STYLES, ROLE CONFLICT, MEMBERSHIP CHANGES....... | 223 |
|      | Profile of D.C. Board of Education Members, 1973-76..................... | 223 |
|      | Selected socioeconomic characteristics of D.C. board members.......... | 237 |
|      | The Motives of DCBOE Members..........              | 238 |
|      | Politics of the DCBOE...............                | 241 |
|      | Analysis of school board campaign contributions - 1971-75............. | 245 |
|      | Leadership Styles....................               | 256 |
|      | Role Conflicts.......................               | 267 |
|      | Membership Changes...................               | 277 |
|      | Summary.............................                | 284 |
|      | External factors....................                | 285 |
|      | Internal factors....................                | 290 |

## SECTION III
## DECISION-MAKING PROCESS

| VIII. | CASE STUDIES OF THE DECISION-MAKING PROCESS -- 1973-75..................... | 309 |
|-------|-----------------------------------------------------|-----|
|       | Introduction........................                | 309 |
|       | Case One: The D.C. Youth Orchestra Program............................... | 310 |
|       | Introduction.......................                 | 310 |
|       | The problem.......................                  | 311 |
|       | Sequence of events.................                 | 325 |
|       | June 14, 1974 board meeting.......                  | 331 |
|       | July 2, 1974 special meeting of the board........................ | 334 |
|       | July 8, 1974 board meeting........                  | 336 |
|       | August 1, 1974 board meeting......                  | 342 |
|       | August 13, 1974 board meeting.....                  | 345 |

Case Two: The General Counsel
Dispute............................... 353
  Introduction........................ 353
  The problem........................ 353
  Sequence of events................. 355
Case Three: Budgetary/Management
Problems.............................. 360
  Introduction....................... 360
    Philosophy....................... 360
    Organization..................... 361
    Management....................... 362
    Budget........................... 365
    Personnel........................ 366
  The problem........................ 368
  Sequence of events................. 371
    September 5, 1973 special board
    meeting.......................... 372
    October 25, 1973 special board
    meeting.......................... 373
    September 30, 1974............... 377
    Mayor's freeze................... 390
    October 22, 1974 special board
    meeting.......................... 393
    December 2, 1974 special board
    meeting.......................... 396
    December 6, 1974 committee meet-
    ing, emergency meeting and board
    meeting.......................... 397
    Task team........................ 402
    February 19, 1974 stated board
    meeting.......................... 405
    March 19, 1975 stated board
    meeting.......................... 408
    AHSA speech, April 4, 1975....... 409
    April 7, 1975 emergency meeting.. 410
Case Analysis and Conclusions......... 413
  Introduction to case analysis...... 413
  The D.C. Youth Orchestra program
  controversy........................ 416
  The General Counsel dispute........ 421
  The budgetary/management controversy 422
Conclusions........................... 426

| | | |
|---|---|---|
| IX. | GROUP PRESSURES ON THE DECISION-MAKING PROCESS -- 1973-75..................... | 445 |
| | Introduction.......................... | 445 |
| | Some influential community groups... | 447 |
| | The United Planning Organization (UPO).............................. | 447 |
| | The Federation of Civic Associations........................ | 447 |
| | The Metropolitan Washington Board of Trade.................... | 448 |
| | D.C. Citizens for Better Public Education, Inc. (DCCBPE).......... | 452 |
| | Eugene and Agnes E. Meyer Foundation........................ | 455 |
| | Friends of the D.C. Youth Orchestra Program (DCYOP)......... | 455 |
| | An Analysis of News Coverage of the Superintendent-School Board Controversy -- 1973-75..................... | 461 |
| | Conclusion............................ | 499 |
| X. | TERMINATION PROCESS, 1975............... | 511 |
| | Introduction.......................... | 511 |
| | Threshold of the Hearing.............. | 519 |
| | Chronology of the conflict.......... | 522 |
| | First Hearing......................... | 535 |
| | Second Hearing........................ | 544 |
| | Analysis.............................. | 560 |
| | Selected specifications............. | 560 |
| | Specification 1 - Equalization.... | 560 |
| | Specification 2 - Quarterly Safety Reports.................... | 564 |
| | Specification 3 - Personnel Hiring Controls................... | 565 |
| | Specification 4 - Position of Director of Buildings and Grounds........................... | 565 |
| | Specification 5 - Selection Procedure for Regional Superintendents................... | 566 |
| | Specification 6 - Federal Grant Proposals........................ | 566 |
| | Specification 9 - Questions on FY-1975 Financial Plan............ | 566 |

   Specification 10 - Status
   Reports on Expenditures........... 567
   Specification 11 - Quarterly
   Financial Reports................. 567
   Specification 12 - Quarterly
   Personnel Reports................. 568
   Specification 17 - Report on
   Declining Enrollment.............. 568
  The Former Deputy Superintendent of
  Management's Analysis................ 569
   Personnel control.................... 569
   Director of buildings and grounds... 572
   The status report on expenditures... 573
  Summary.............................. 574

## SECTION IV
## SUMMARY AND CONCLUSIONS

XI. SCHOOL SYSTEM OUTCOMES.................. 591
  Introduction......................... 691
  An Acting Superintendent............. 593
  Superintendent Selection Process..... 596
  Curriculum........................... 599
  Equalization......................... 601
  Decentralization..................... 602
  Budget............................... 605
  Personnel Control System............. 608
  Summary.............................. 614

XII. SUMMARY AND CONCLUSIONS................ 631
  Introduction......................... 631
  What is policy-making within the
  framework of superintendent-school
  board relations?..................... 633
  What is administration within the
  framework of superintendent-school
  board relations?..................... 634
  What factors precipitated conflict
  between the policy-makers and the
  central administration of DCPS
  system?.............................. 636
   Dependent relationship............ 637

|  |  |
|---|---|
| Racism | 637 |
| Sexism | 639 |
| Pressure and influence | 639 |
| Role conflict | 640 |
| Motives | 641 |
| Outsiders vs insiders | 642 |
| What policy evolved? | 642 |
| How was the conflict resolved? | 643 |
| What were the outcomes of the change in policy? | 643 |
| Alternative Strategies | 649 |
| Elect the superintendent | 649 |
| Clarify roles and responsibilities | 650 |
| Eliminate ambiguities between school codes, the chief executive's contract and actual practice | 653 |
| Stabilize board membership | 654 |
| Remove ambiguities within the superintendent's contract | 655 |
| Clearly define "control" of the school system | 655 |
| EPILOGUE | 661 |

APPENDICES

| | | |
|---|---|---|
| I. | EVALUATION DOCUMENT | 667 |
| II. | SUPERINTENDENT'S RATING | 707 |
| III. | INTERVIEW SCHEDULE | 721 |

| | |
|---|---|
| BIBLIOGRAPHY | 729 |
| INDEX | 771 |
| ABOUT THE AUTHOR | 787 |

## LIST OF TABLES

| TABLE | | PAGE |
|---|---|---|
| 1. | Population of the District of Columbia by Races, 1940-1976 | 45 |
| 2. | District of Columbia Public School Population by Races, 1950-1977 | 49 |
| 3. | The Distribution of Percentages of Selected Demographic and Socio-Economic Descriptors in District of Columbia Wards | 50 |
| 4. | The Number of DCPS Principals - 1975 | 65 |
| 5. | D.C. Board of Education Closed (Executive) Meetings | 115 |
| 6. | Selected Campaign Contributions and Expenditures | 253 |
| 7. | D.C. Youth Orchestra Program Financial History (School Year Program Only) | 322 |
| 8. | Estimated FY 1976 Costs for Selected Administrative Offices Affected by Decentralization and Reorganization | 394 |
| 9. | Group Pressures | 458 |
| 10. | Mason's Recommendations Which Evolved Into Charges | 517 |
| 11. | Charges | 520 |
| 12. | Second Hearing | 544 |

LIST OF ILLUSTRATIONS

Figure                                                    Page

1. Model of Superintendent-School Board
   Conflict................................... 18

2. Public School of the District of Columbia
   Decentralized Regions...................... 283

3. One Year Dropouts from Preparatory
   Strings.................................... 313

4. Origin of 67 String Players, Youth
   Orchestra, January 1970.................... 314

5. Organization Chart, D.C. Public Schools.... 383

6. New Organization Directing Line............ 384

7. New Organization Administrative Team....... 385

8. Public Schools of the District of Columbia
   Functional Chart, 1976..................... 604

9. Design of Theory of Reoccupation........... 662

# SECTION I

# INTRODUCTION

# CHAPTER I

## INTRODUCTION

### Need for Study

For the past several years, school superintendents in some major cities have come and gone with great rapidity. Many place-bound superintendents resigned or were terminated in the mid-1960s and another wave of them left superintendencies vacant in the early 1970s. By 1975, at least ten urban areas saw new superintendents come in to administer the schools -- Chicago, Detroit, Boston, Philadelphia, San Francisco, St. Louis, Ft. Worth, Buffalo, Baltimore, and Washington, D.C. No particular pattern seems established as to the reasons for the rapid turnover in superintendents since some resigned, some retired and others were terminated after intensive controversies. Two in particular drew national attention and debate -- Roland Patterson in Baltimore, and Barbara A. Sizemore in Washington, D.C. In both cases, the issue was conflict in superintendent-school board relations, but the underlying issue racism also surfaced. Ironically, in the case of Baltimore, the board was majority white while the superintendent was Black. In Washington, D.C., the board was majority Black and the superintendent was Black.

In both situations, school board membership changed frequently, and conflict is thought by some to be due to the diversity of big-city boards and the overwhelming problems faced by them. Others accuse board members of being racists and interfering in school administration.[1]

Because of the problems apparently involved in being a superintendent in a big city, it is necessary to study some of the situations closely in order to arrive at some reasons why the position of urban superintendent seems to be an untenable one. A case study of one of these situations can be the beginning of a future effort for making comparisons across school districts embroiled in conflicts between superintendents and school boards which may evolve into an eventual solution to this perplexing problem in educational administration.

Therefore, this present research will be an analysis of the conflict in school board-superintendent relations in the District of Columbia from October 1, 1973 through October 9, 1975, including a view of the situation from an historical perspective and a brief view of the aftermath of the termination of the superintendent's contract.

In a wider sense, it is important to the field of educational administration for us to examine the following issues:

- the uniqueness of a board of education created by Congress.

- the role of the board of education and the role of administration.

- who should make policy and who should carry it out and what in the D.C. school situation caused irrevocable conflicts in this regard?

- why did the school board change so much and what effect did this have on relationships between the superintendent and school board?

Other issues which become revealed in this study are:

- power relationships
- broadening the decision-making process
    - flattening the administrative hierarchical structure
    - use of the administrative team
    - abolition of the positions of vice superintendent, and deputy superintendent
- the bifurcation of management services and education services
- contracting out large sums of school funds to certain institutions for services
- renewal of the contract for D.C. Youth Orchestra
- opposition to and defense of an age-graded, monolingual, monocultural structure
- decentralization of the school system using PACTS (Parents, Administrators, Community, Teachers and Students - Communication Flow)
- development of curricula to reflect
    - multilingual, multicultural content
    - four symbol systems - notes, words, numbers, images
- superintendent's evaluation
- hearings on termination of contract.

According to Getzels there can develop role conflicts between a board and its chief executive

since their responsibilities sometimes overlap in
that most school codes give the board the power to
operate the schools and certainly in most states
the legal responsibility to do so rests with the
board.[2] As in the case of the D.C. public school
system, Gross[3] also found that board members and
superintendents frequently disagree regarding their
roles. The problem is not a small one and therefore it needs constant study, for, as Getzels
further points out potential conflict between board
members and the executive exists in the value orientation of the community and the organizational
expectations, the role perception of board members
and the executive, the fact that the legal language
does not precisely describe the board practice of
delegating much of the operation of the school
system to the chief executive, and relationship
with groups in the community and the school system
which the board and the executive have. These
factors, then, preclude the development of the
necessary effective working relationship between
the two -- the school board and the superintendent.[4] The D.C. public school situation needs to
be examined to see if, in fact, there was role
confusion. It is often said that the board makes
policy and the superintendent executes it, but in
practice, as Getzels notes, it seldom works this
way. According to a study made by Allison[5] in
1965, board members seek the help of the superintendent in forming policy through furnishing
information to the board and recommending policy.
Furthermore, it is reasoned that since the board
is the policy-making body which is required to
legitimize administrative decisions, it cannot
remain completely out of the administration of
policy. Of course, a problem presents itself when
there is no clear distinction between policy and
administration. Getzels also suspects that
reference-group conflict and self-role conflict can
also obtain in that board members must decide
between actions representing their personal interests and preferences and those that seem to be
necessary to maintain a healthy organization, for
example the use of a place on the board as a step-
ping stone to a political career.[6]

## The Approach

The research approach is case study. The case study approach was used in this research because it allowed for greater flexibility in the choice of factors to be studied and allowed for the generating and testing of new hypotheses in the course of the study. Further, it allowed for an intensive examination of the decision-making process, providing a wealth of information which could be summarized, categorized, and compared.

Additionally, the case study approach provided data on the sequence of events from which a cause was inferred. The chronological ordering of these events led to a clearer understanding of the decision-making process, that is, the "if... then" formulation of causality. Of course, the inferences derived may not hold for most organizations. Understandably, generalizations cannot be made on the basis of a single case. But the "generalizations" arrived at can begin an accumulation of knowledge which can then be compared with other case study data of the decision-making process in other school systems.

## Techniques and Methods of Data Collection

This section of Chapter I describes the techniques and procedures used in the collection of data for the project.

### The interview

The semi-structured interview was used in this study. General type questions guided the interview although more specific questions were used when certain information was not obtained through general questions. Some respondents seemed reluctant to speak freely, thus more probing kinds of questions were used. In other situations, respondents spoke quite freely. In these instances, fewer guide questions were necessary.

The selection of respondents was done on the basis of their participation in policy-making. Therefore, all board members who wished to be interviewed were interviewed in a formal interview situation either in their homes, in their school board offices, or at their places of business. The recent past superintendent, the superintendent subject of the study, and the current superintendent were interviewed, as well as one deputy superintendent, one associate superintendent, one executive assistant, five regional superintendents, fourteen board members, one community member, the union president, and a Washington Post newswriter who covered school news. Most interviews ran from one hour to one-and-a-half hours although a few were shorter.

Observations

Observations were done by the writer between April 1, 1973 and October 6, 1975 in all D.C. regularly stated school board meetings. The board meets twice a month, on the second and fourth Wednesdays at the District Building, the Board of Education Building or in one of the public schools. In addition, the writer was present during various press conferences called by various school board members, two union meetings and several administrative team meetings. Notes were taken on only a few of these meetings since the observations were made prior to the undertaking of the research study.

News clipping file

A more or less comprehensive news clipping file of local news accounts, editorials, and letters to the editor appearing in the Washington Star and the Washington Post during 1973-77 was maintained by the writer.

Library sources

The Martin Luther King, Jr. Public Library Collection and the Library of Congress Collection were used for background information, especially in preparation of Chapter I and Chapter IX.

### Personal files

This writer had complete access to the files of Mrs. Barbara A. Sizemore, former superintendent of the D.C. public school system (DCPSS) as well as access to the draft copy of her dissertation, which was used liberally in this study.

Additionally, Dr. Hugh Scott, former superintendent of the D.C. public school system, shared material from his files as did Mrs. Barbara Simmons, School board member, Mrs. Ruth Goodwin, concerned citizen, Mrs. Jeanne King, former administrative officer to Barbara Sizemore, Mr. Dwight Cropp, executive secretary to the DCBOE, and Ms. Betty Brooks, principal, DCPS.

### School board files

School board minutes and transcripts were reviewed, school district budgets were studied, as were past studies of the District school system done by outside agencies.

### Board of Election and Ethics

Records of contributors of elected board members, two elected city council members, and the mayor for the last two terms were studied at the Board of Election and Ethics located in the District Building, the Federal Building, and the Munsey Building, where original copies are filed.

### D.C. Citizens for Better Public Education (DCCBPE)

Mary Hunter, of the D.C. Citizens for Better Public Education, allowed the writer free access to the files of the organization. Much useful information on the organization's involvement with the public school system was culled from these files.

## System of Data Analysis

First, minutes, transcripts, and correspondence were examined to see what issues came before the board during 1973-75. Second, a list of twenty-seven issues was compiled and interview questions relating to the issues were constructed. Third, interviews were held with selected school board members and superintendents. They were asked to select from the list of twenty-seven issues those which caused the greatest conflict in superintendent-school board relations. Fourth, interview data were analyzed to see which issues were selected by most of the respondents. Fifth, the ten issues selected were examined for related elements. Sixth, the ten issues were categorized under three major headings: (1) educational programs, (2) personnel, and (3) management/budget. Under the category of educational programs was placed an alternative educational enterprise: the D.C. Youth Orchestra Program. Under the category of personnel, was placed the General Counsel Dispute, a controversy which arose out of the D.C. Youth Orchestra Program dispute. Under the category of management/budget, was placed the Fiscal 1976 Budget/Fiscal 1975 Financial Plan which incorporated several related issues: (1) opening of school problems; (2) teacher payroll problems; (3) mayor's freeze; (4) over-hiring/budget deficit; (5) Hobson Task Force dispute; (6) the AHSA Speech; and (7) decentralization dispute. Seventh, board minutes, transcripts. correspondence and interview data were re-examined to see how these issues led to conflict in superintendent-school board relations. Eighth, the facts of the selected issues were arranged sequentially. And finally, the researcher integrated and compared the information with interview data to see how the variables intervened to disrupt the decision-making process which resulted in conflict in superintendent-school board relations leading to the termination of the superintendent.

## The Structure of the Study

The study is divided into eleven additional chapters: <u>First</u>, an outline of a theory of political conflict is provided. <u>Second</u>, the external factors of <u>racism</u>, <u>classism</u>, <u>sexism</u>, and the <u>colonial status</u> of the District government are examined for conflict elements. <u>Third</u>, the internal factors of <u>authority</u>, <u>structure</u> and <u>functioning</u> of the school board and superintendent's offices are explored. Emphasis is on two important functions of the school board: selection and termination processes. <u>Fourth</u>, another vital function of the board of education: <u>goal setting</u> is examined for elements of conflict. <u>Fifth</u>, an analysis of the internal factors of <u>role conflict</u>, <u>motivations</u>, <u>leadership style</u> and <u>membership changes</u> is provided in order to see how these factors impinge on superintendent-school board relations. <u>Sixth</u>, these case studies of the decision-making process engaged in between 1973-75 provide an intimate view of the conflict on a day-to-day basis. <u>Seventh</u>, we examined the external factor of <u>group pressures</u>, especially during 1973-75, the period of the study, to see its impact on superintendent-school board relations. <u>Eighth</u>, Chapter X considers the internal factor of another school board <u>function</u>: termination -- in light of the evaluation of the superintendent's performance. The <u>next to last</u> chapter, (XI), explores what became of the innovations put in place or proposed during 1973-75. The <u>final chapter</u> summarizes the findings and presents recommendations for avoiding the pitfalls which hampered the effective functioning of the decision-making process during 1973-75.

There are <u>four basic thrusts</u> to this research. <u>First</u>, we shall study the dynamics involved in the decision-making structure and processes. The <u>second</u> emphasis is the study of change dynamics in the decision-making unit and how this shook the school system. The <u>third</u> concern is the study of conflict processes. Of special concern is the type of conflict that develops when interest groups try to influence policy decisions and procedures. The

<u>fourth</u> thrust offers a brief overview of the dissolution of the conflict including a comparison of the 1973-75 administration with the subsequent one.

FOOTNOTES                              Chapter 1


1.  "Big-City School Posts:  Can Anyone Hold the
    Job?"  Education U.S.A. 17 (21 July 1975): 259.

2.  Jacob W. Getzels, James M. Lipham, and Roald F.
    Campbell, Educational Administration as a
    Social Process-Theory, Research, Practice (New
    York:  Harper and Row Publishers, 1968), pp.
    349-350.

3.  Neal Gross, Who Runs Our Schools? (New York:
    Wiley, 1958), p. 139.

4.  Getzels, p. 352.

5.  Howard D. Allison, "Professional and Lay
    Influences on School Board Decision-Making,"
    (Doctoral dissertation, University of Chicago,
    1965).

6.  Getzels, p. 356.

SECTION II

THE IMPACT OF SELECTED EXTERNAL AND INTERNAL
FACTORS ON SCHOOL SUPERINTENDENT-SCHOOL
BOARD RELATIONS

CHAPTER II

AN OUTLINE OF A THEORY

Introduction

The outline of a theory of political conflict constructed for this case study specifies the traditional educational decision-making structure (superintendent-school board) as the unit of analysis because policy decisions determine the direction in which the school system moves in terms of maintaining the status quo or making changes. But decisions are not made in a vacuum for they are molded by both external and internal factors which cause conflict in the relationship between school superintendents and school boards.

Therefore, it is hypothesized that the introduction of change in a racially changing urban school system is hampered by the combination of (A) external environmental factors of (1) governmental dominance -- the Congress, the city council, the mayor and the courts -- and resulting financial constraints, (2) sexism, (3) racism, (4) classism, and (5) group pressure, and (B) internal organizational factors of (1) change in school board membership, (2) authoritarian leadership behavior, (3) role confusion, (4) motivation of school board members, (5) structures and (6) functioning of boards of education in terms of goal setting, hiring and termination of superintendents, and (7) problems in authority, the result of which is conflict in school board-superintendent relations.

The above factors, then, are the twelve points of analysis in the model (see figure 1).

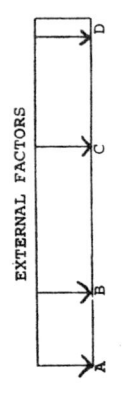

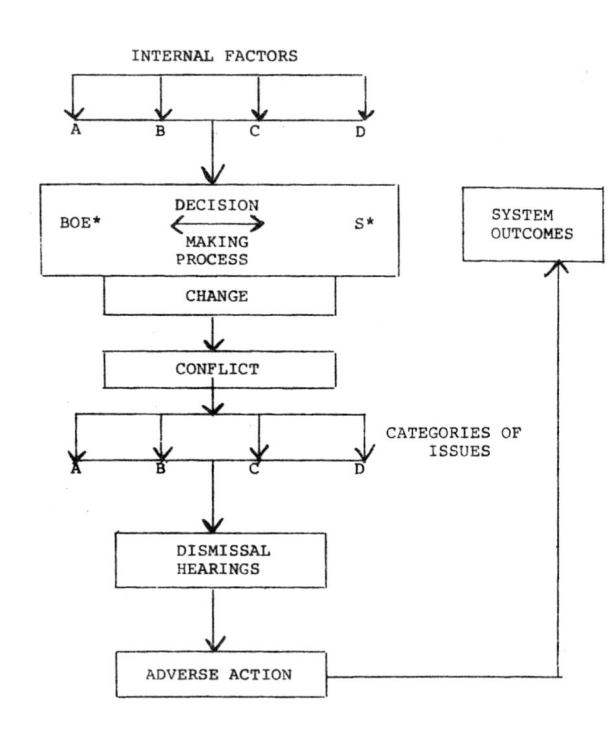

\* BOE - Board of Education
\* S   - Superintendent

FIGURE 1.

MODEL OF SUPERINTENDENT-SCHOOL BOARD CONFLICT

The Model of Superintendent-School Board Conflict pictorially indicates the impact of external factors and internal factors on the decision-making process involved in by the board of education and the superintendent. The external factors are shown at the side of the diagram. They are represented by the letters "A" "B" "C" and "D" defined as government dominance, sexism, racism, classism and group pressures. Thus the external factors are environmental factors outside the domain of the school system which cause disruptions in the relationship between the board of education and the superintendent. The arrows show that these factors impact on the relationship. The internal factors, shown at the upper portion of the diagram, are represented by the letters "A" "B" "C" and "D" defined as change in school board membership, authoritarian leadership behavior, role conflict, motivation of board members, structures and functions of the board of education and authority. Again, the arrows show that these factors also impact on the school board-superintendent relationship. The internal factors are defined within the relationship between the school board and the superintendent and cannot be specified apart from the general nature of the interaction which is represented by the decision-making process engaged in. This process is represented by the large box in the diagram. Both the external factors and the internal factors serve as points of analysis and are independent factors since neither defines the other.

The interplay of external factors and internal factors entering into the decision-making process engaged in by school board members and the superintendent may be regarded as cause of the call for change in the school system. Thus, the smaller box under the large rectangle represents the factor of change. Aspects of the change process may be regarded as impinging on the relationship between the school board members and the superintendent, thus causing conflict.

The impact of change is represented by the arrow leading from the box representing Change to the box representing Conflict. Conflict, then represented by the box under Change, developed from several categories of issues represented by the letters "A" "B" "C" and "D" which consisted of school board decisions concerning, for example, educational programming, personnel, and budget/management.

Disputes about the method of handling the issues which arose between the school board and superintendent evolved into dismissal hearings as the arrow leading to the box representing the Dismissal Hearings indicates. The box containing Adverse Action with the arrow leading from the box representing Dismissal Hearings explains the result of the hearings as being the firing of the superintendent by the school board. The right angle arrow on the right hand side of the diagram connects to the box representing System Outcomes which resulted from the school board action to fire the superintendent.

In summary, we have pictured in the model inputs in the form of both external and internal factors which impinged on the decision-making process engaged in by the school board and the superintendent leading first to the desire for change and then change itself which caused conflict to evolve around decisions about certain issues. This conflict resulted in dismissal hearings. Consequently, the dismissal hearings resulted in a board decision to fire the superintendent. This action led to certain types of outcomes in the system because of the resulting change in policy.

## Points of Analysis

The five external factors are explained as follows:

1. <u>The Unique Relationship between the Congress, the City Council, the Mayor and the Courts</u>:

Federal and local governmental dominance provided a unique financial arrangement with the District school system and stimulated conflict in superintendent-school board relations. Also, pressure for improvement in D.C. schools emanated through legislative and judicial court orders including Bolling v Sharpe (1954), the local school desegregation case; Hobson v Hansen (1967) which affected tracking, the assignment of teachers and other resources in schools located in rich and poor areas of D.C.; the elected school board act (1968) and modified home rule which brought about a change in the political position of the District of Columbia. We will examine this factor at a later point.

2. Racism: A sharp change in the demographic characteristics of the city and its schools occurred in 1960 when the District became predominantly Black. In 1973, Washington, D.C. was a city approximately seventy-two percent Black with a school system approximately ninety-five percent Black. Historically, there has been a struggle by Black people in the District to participate in decisions about them and their progeny and eventually to try to gain some control over decisions made about their destiny. This citywide struggle, coupled with the national effort, resulted in points of conflict between superintendents and school boards. Therefore, this study will also examine the race factor as an aspect of the clashes between D.C. superintendents and school boards.

3. Classism: Notably, most of the D.C. school board members were both college graduates and occupied professional and managerial positions. Thus, there may have been a conflict in how they viewed their role in relation to their class interests vis-a-vis the needs of some of their less affluent constituents. Thus, the model accommodates the factor of class in its design to allow a close examination of this element.

4. <u>Sexism</u>: Then, too, the factor of sex may have influenced how board members reacted to the superintendent administering the D.C. public school system between 1973-75, since the District of Columbia was the first large urban school system to hire a female superintendent. Thus, the study will provide an opportunity to examine sexism as a possible contributory factor in the conflict in superintendent-school board relations.

5. <u>Group Pressures</u>: The two daily local newspapers in the District pointed up, with some consistency, the various points of differences experienced by the school boards and the various superintendents of the District of Columbia public schools. Generally, these two dailies represented the point of view of monied interests in the District about the direction the school system should move. Therefore, we will examine the effect of the influence the newspapers had on the decision-making activities engaged in by the superintendents and the school boards in the District. Additionally, we will analyze how various community groups and the courts brought pressure to bear on the process of decision-making and the decisions made as a result of these pressures.

The seven internal factors are explained as follows:

1. <u>Changes in Board membership and Superintendents</u>: In the District of Columbia, the school board membership changed four times in the approximately twenty-two months of one superintendent's tenure, possibly resulting in changes in philosophy and direction of school policy as new school board members came on board. Interestingly also, Washington, D.C. had five superintendents and two acting superintendents in the ten-year period from 1967 to 1977. Some were outsiders, a factor which may have impacted on the relationship between school superintendents and their boards.

2. <u>Motivation</u>: The motive behind the decision to seek membership on the school board may have been politically inspired as several school board members did campaign for other elected positions in the city government.

3. <u>Role Conflict</u>: Citizens function as a member of the school board, representing their Ward or At Large constituents and as a representative of some special interest group. This sometimes causes role conflicts. Tied to the above factor of role conflict are the factors of role confusion or role usurpation in relation to being a policy maker or an implementor of policy. These two factors will also be studied for their possible impact on the relationship between D.C. superintendents and school boards as perhaps adding to the conflict.

4. <u>Leadership Behavior</u>: Some superintendents and board members may have been concerned with social and educational inequality and developed a belief that change is possible. Hence, they struggled for power and control to effect change. Others may have struggled to maintain the status quo. Therefore, leadership behavior of school board presidents and superintendents will also be examined as another possible conflict point in their relationship.

5. <u>The Structure and Function of the Office of School Board and Superintendent and Authority</u>: In juxtaposition to the above, we will examine other organizational dynamics: the structure of the school board, the functions established by law and practice, including the functions of goal setting, hiring and terminating superintendents, the process of arriving at decisions and the authority and prerogatives defined by statute and perceived by board members and the various superintendents. These factors will be analyzed for trends and compared across time to see if they led to conflict in superintendent-school board relations.

To summarize, this study is concerned with the process by which policy is established in the District of Columbia Public School System (DCPSS), the factors impinging on the decision-making process engaged in by the school board and superintendent, and how this decision-making unit responded to these factors during the period studied. Because superintendent and school board relations are often conflicted, the study will examine the nature of conflict as an important problem in this relationship. As a sub-category of such a conflict, we will examine the factors that led to conflicts in DCPS superintendent-school board relations prior to 1973. This study will also investigate the exercise of power, in maintaining control of the school system, which rages around the divergent values of the conflicting parties as they relate to change and/or the maintenance of the status quo.

The essential questions considered are:

1. What is policy-making within the framework of superintendent-school board relationships?

2. What is administration within the framework of superintendent-school board relationships?

3. What factors precipitated conflict between the policy makers and the central administration of the DCPS system.

    a. Who were the major actors in the conflict between the superintendent and the board of education?

    b. Out of what educational issues did the conflict evolve?

    c. What intervening social, political and/or economic factors compounded the conflict?

        d.  What external <u>pressures</u> impinged on the decision-making unit to compound the conflict?

    4.  What <u>policy</u> evolved?

    5.  How was the <u>conflict</u> resolved?

    6.  What were the <u>outcomes</u> of the change in policy?

The Setting

<u>Decision-making</u>

    For some sociologists, "decision-making" relates to power. For example, Kaplan, C. Wright Mills and Bierstedt seem to feel that power is inherent in the ability to make decisions which have major consequences. Obviously, making a policy decision commits the organization to a certain course of action which speaks to how funds will be used, which programs will be supported, who will be hired, how staff will be deployed, what equipment and materials will be purchased, and so on. The ability to influence the lives of 130,000 children and the adults working with them in this fashion, as is the case in Washington, D.C. is not only a grave responsibility but a powerful position in which to be.

    For purposes of this study, the definition of the decision-making process will follow Simon's definition of the term decision. Simon uses this term to mean "choice" which he views as the process by which alternatives for each moment's behavior are selected to be carried out.[1] As he explains it, there are three steps involved in the process:

    (1) the listing of all the alternative strategies;
    (2) the determination of all the consequences that follow upon each of these strategies;

(3) the comparative evaluation of these sets of consequences....[2]

A further breakdown of the elements of decision-making is provided by Cunningham, when he says:

> Decision-making behavior of school boards can be explained in part by their flesh and blood composition, by their discretionary powers, by their internal organization, by the behavior of their superintendents, by their meeting places and times, by their community relations postures, by the competence of their chairmen, by their agenda-building practices, and by the number of meetings they hold.[3]

## Authority

Barnard and Simon define authority substantially the same, that is, authority is an order accepted by a member of the organization as governing his actions within the organization.[4] Simon explicates the concept of authority further when he says that:

> A subordinate may be said to accept authority whenever he permits his behavior to be guided by a decision reached by another, irrespective of his own judgment as to the merits of that decision.[5]

Authority to make policy decisions is usually vested in boards of education, although this is a somewhat ambiguous concept.[6] In contrast, administration usually focuses on processes and methods of getting the job done.[7] It is evident though that, operationally, decision-making involves both deciding and doing,[8] thus making a perfect conflict point for boards of education and superintendents.

Composition

Individuals who run for the school board expend great effort and often large sums of money in getting elected. Generally, the board members are not paid for their services, even though a small stipend for expenses is sometimes allocated.

Structure and function

In each local community, there is a board of education whose members are either elected or appointed through a political process. Broad powers have been delegated to these local boards of education by their state legislatures. These powers enable the local boards to organize and operate public schools in their communities. Most local boards of education which have legal control of education are composed of lay persons.

In large urban areas, boards meet several times a month -- in regular and special meetings of the whole as well as in committee meetings. The agendas are often long and require preparation in order for board members to feel comfortable about their participation. In some cities, such as Washington, D.C., membership on the school board provides the first chance for some to become visible to the rest of the community. They, then, become targets for pressure and influence by other persons and groups in the community.

Motivation

Some school board members may see the school board as a steppingstone to other political offices. A number of former school board members have moved into positions on city councils, state legislatures, salaried positions in city or county government, or to the Congress of the United States. For example, Louise Hicks, a former Boston school committee member, became well known as a school board member and later competed for other political offices.[9] Similarly, Marion Barry and

Hilda Mason both moved on from school board membership in the DCPS system to D.C. city council membership. McCarty's study on motives of school board members specifically discusses this normal and usual dynamic found in the political arena.[10]

Superintendents

Superintendents, on the other hand, serve at the pleasure of their boards of education, which are usually composed of lay persons. Some of these lay persons have little in-depth understanding of the process of teaching and learning. The superintendents are charged by these boards to develop and operate educational programs which are subsequently evaluated by these lay persons for effectiveness and efficiency. In addition, the superintendents, with the help of staff members, must make careful study of current conditions and must continuously examine the goals and structure of the school system and make recommendations for improving it through changes, as well as recommendations for operating it through policy. Because board of education members do not always understand the need for change in the status quo, they sometimes feel superintendents who function in this manner are moving into their area of making policy.

Likewise, superintendents sometimes feel that boards of education are infringing on their rights when boards, in an effort to maintain the status quo, move into the implementation phase of the decision-making process. This infringement is examined quite fully in the discussion of the D.C. Youth Orchestra controversy in a later chapter. Certainly, then, the difference in how school boards and superintendents perceive of their functions have caused conflicts in their relations.

In addition to the above, the superintendent fulfills a political role. This political role can be seen as the superintendent attempts to fulfill the demands of strong community interest groups such as are represented by big business interests or white or Black professionals (whose interests are generally the same), and the usually less-highly-organized, powerless, poor people who have often been shuttled from one area of the city to another. It is especially significant to note that even in a city that has a majority Black city council, and school board members, a Black mayor, and a Black superintendent of schools, the power structure remains the same in the city and in the schools. Decisions which are allowed through the decision-making apparatus are still made in favor of the most influential people in the community.

Role conflict

Roles represent positions, offices, or status within an institution. Status is a collection of rights and duties. When a person puts these rights and duties into effect, he is performing a role.[11] School board members occupy roles both inside and outside the school system; that is, they represent their constituents (voters) and they also make policy for the school system which affects the children in attendance. Conflict in role can develop when the most influential interest groups have a value orientation different from that of the needs of the children in the schools.[12]

Two ways of understanding role conflict of school board members are: (1) through a study of the individual's reasons (motives) for seeking membership; and (2) a study of the mechanism (board operation) used by the board to reach decisions. McCarty found (1) that there is a wide range of motives for seeking board membership, and (2) the greater the role conflict, the greater may be the frictions in board operation.[13]

The superintendent, too, is exposed to role conflict in terms of the expectations held for the superintendency by the incumbent and those held by various groups, including the board of education. Conflict can arise between the board and superintendent if the board of education expects the superintendent to carry out board policies, regardless of whether or not the superintendent agrees with these policies.[14]

Conflict also ensues when school board members and the superintendent disagree on their respective roles, when the roles are confused, or when one group tries to usurp the other's role. Thus, some school board members feel they have the right to administer the policy decisions of the board[15] and some superintendents see themselves as playing a major role in board decision-making.[16] Further conflict results when some board members have the need to dominate and find it difficult to delegate authority to the superintendent.[17]

Politics

Rosenthal refers to politics as "the methods by which social values and resources are allocated for different purposes and among different people."[18] To be more precise:

> School district decisions to hire a new superintendent, decentralize control, alter district boundaries, accord collective bargaining rights to teacher groups, or establish compensatory education programs are ... political. They, too, involve the distribution of social value and resources by public agencies.[19]

Therefore, the school system can be studied as a small political system, with interest groups and conflict points centering around decision-making processes which set the goals and develop the strategies for obtaining the goals and plans for the future. Since policy decisions are crucial to organization maintenance and development, people inside and outside the school system try to influence decision makers in the direction of their special values and interests. Thus, policy is a major point of conflict and the studying of policy decisions is crucial to an understanding of school system conflict and change.[20]

Influence and pressures

Influence, as defined by Simon, "...is the means...of securing the values that are desired.[21] Influence is exercised when a decision made by one person governs the behavior of another."[22] Certain powerful people and groups in a community influence decisions of school boards and superintendents in line with the ideas they value. In speaking of values, Staples says, "The values of a group refer to what it defines as the desirable and undesirable from a set of options used to guide behavior."[23] Because so many people and groups have so much influence on educational policies, the question has often been asked: Who runs our schools? This question was even used as the title of Neal Gross' significant study of superintendents and school boards and of the support and opposition schools face.

Traditionally, pressure groups abound in our society. These groups influence important decisions on every level of government. Local school districts are no exception to this.

Since group pressure is such an important aspect of the decision-making process, the present study will make reference to community organizations, groups, and individuals who try to influence school decisions.

Racial conflict

The previous discussion introduced the elements of authority and influence into the decision-making process and discussed the roles of the major actors involved in the process, the superintendent and the school board. It was suggested that role conflict is a disruptive element in this relationship. The situation is compounded when race becomes an added factor.

Racial conflict is a fact of social life due to the differing basic interests in the American society.[24] Whites want to keep the power and status resulting from control of resources. Blacks want to share that power and control and the resulting resources. Thus, social conflict is inevitable.[25] It is an ordinary condition of life in this society.[26]

Many divergent groups such as rural and urban, rich and poor, foreign-born and native-born, reflect divergent and clashing interests; so, too, should white interests and Black interests be recognized as divergent interests which cause social conflict. This is normal and ordinary and, as suggested by Himes, should be accommodated in the established practices and norm structure of our society[27] in order for these conflicts to lead to resolutions acceptable to Blacks as well as to whites.

According to Himes, racial conflict is an aspect of social conflict[28] and as such can be studied in relation to the Black community vis-a-vis its relationship to white America. Racial conflict is the "aggressive struggle of blacks by available means for legitimate goals."[29] The notion of opposing forces with opposing interests, as a structural condition, and with the opposing forces having different amounts of power and status resources, constitutes the elements of social conflict.[30] Such conditions are met when we consider the white and Black situation in America. Thus, as Himes further defines the concept of racial conflict, it refers to:

> (1) the deliberate use of social power by collective conflict actors, (2) who are cast in the two-party power and status - unequal structural setting, and (3) who engage in overt activities ranging in intensity from calmness to frenzy and in violence from trivial injury to annihilation (4) for the purpose of maintaining or gaining an advantage in power, status, and their socioeconomic correlates.[31]

Traditionally, it was thought that the schools could and should be separated from politics. Educators now realize that education does not exist in a political vacuum. It includes a political dimension. As Sestak and Frerich (1968) point out, "Educational policy is public policy, and only the citizens can make public policy in a democratic way."[32] But for Blacks, maintained in a colonial position, education, according to Staples, "...acts as a formidable instrument of political power in its role as a transmitter of goals, values, and attitudes...."[33] "Further, the educational system selects those values and attitudes favored by the ruling class and teaches them as universal truths."[34]

What education has done in this country is to teach "the exploited and the oppressed people to virtually love the system that is exploiting and oppressing them."[35] Further, it designs the curriculum so that it does not reveal the racist nature of society.[36] It teaches white people's definitions and descriptions, thus controlling the minds of Black people. Education is indeed political.[37]

As more and more Black people began to understand why school systems paid little attention to their demands, they moved to mobilize people power again to get Black people in upper-status positions within the school system, hoping that this action of theirs would cause schools to become more responsive to the needs of their children. In Washington, D.C., this power was manifested in the election of Black people to the school board and the eventual selection by those school boards of Black superintendents of schools. Implicit in this action was the hope that these superintendents would use the educational resources to do a better job of educating poor children than had been done in the past. Washington, D.C. appeared to be just the place to test this hypotheses since the city was 72 percent Black, the school system was 95 percent Black, the school board was 63 percent Black, and the superintendent was Black.

The superintendency in Washington, D.C. has been a revolving-door job for Blacks in that city. For example, in 1970, Hugh Scott, an outsider, became superintendent; in 1973, Barbara Sizemore, an outsider, became superintendent; and in 1975, Vincent Reed, an insider, became acting superintendent and superintendent in 1976. Thus, over that six-year period, continuity was destroyed and any progress in the educational system increased at an agonizingly sluggish pace. This situation has developed into retardation in the educational process and has delayed true acquisition of educational gains of Black and poor children.

Class conflict

The actions of some Black school board members can be characterized as following a middle-class outlook, that is, those who follow an opportunistic policy. They attempt to accommodate the demands of the Black poor for better education to their personal interests which are tied up with the political machines, which in turn are geared to the interests of the white power structure.

In his seminal work, Black Bourgeoisie, E. Franklin Frazier insightfully analyzes the behavior, attitudes, and values of the Black middle-class in terms of its economic condition and social status, with special attention given to the education of Blacks who shaped the political orientation of this class. In concluding his study, Frazier states:

> Because of its struggle to gain acceptance by whites, the black bourgeoisie has failed to play the role of a responsible elite in the Negro community....
>
> When the opportunity has been present, the black bourgeoisie has exploited the Negro masses as ruthlessly as have whites. As the intellectual leaders in the Negro community, they have never dared think beyond a narrow,

opportunistic philosophy that provided a rationalization for their own advantages.[38]

In this study, one concern is with the Black elite who have internalized white middle-class values to such an extent that they, too, participate in the subjugation of poor Black people -- as illustrated in their support of the status quo (power structure) which denies Blacks their rights and privileges to self-determination (power resources). This elite also sustains and reinforces racial stratification among Black people.

Black leaders in D.C., depending upon white financial support to their campaigns, submitted to what is known in the field of colonial administration as a system of "indirect rule." Some Black leaders have supported, on the whole, the ideas of their white benefactors concerning educational questions.

Sexism

Using Geneva Gay's definition of racism[39] as a model, we can say that sexism is any activity, individual or institutional, deliberate or not, predicated upon a belief in the superiority of males and the inferiority of females which serves to maintain male supremacy through the oppression and subjugation of females.

Sexism is endemic to our society, and our schools reflect sex stereotyping. Some may ask the question: Is sexism in society really a problem? The answer is an emphatic "Yes." Significantly less than half of America's brain power is being used when we have so few women in positions of decision-making. Sexton reports that:

> Male dominance in school leadership ensures that: Males make almost all the important decisions in the school system, decisions that undoubtedly perpetuate and extend sex stereotypes and inequalities;...[40]

In 1971 Friedan and West[41] documented that 75 percent of elementary school principals were males and 96 percent of the secondary school principals were males, nationwide. In another nationwide study conducted by AASA[42] in 1970, it was found that among the over 14,000 superintendents in the public schools, less than 1 percent were women. The results of such studies may lead to the false assumption that men perform these duties better than women do. In response to this concern, mention can be made of some studies which indicate that female administrators are as good as male administrators in their work. Wiles and Grobman[43] and Grobman and Hines[44] found that female principals were more democratic than male principals. In a journal article by Dale,[45] she cited a study done by Helen Morsink[46] which indicated that women high school principals were as effective as men. A study by Hemphill, Griffiths and Frederiksen[47] also found that female principals possessed somewhat better administrative characteristics than did the men.

## Propositions

1. If the school board has a dependency relationship with an agency of higher authority, it will establish an adversarial relationship with the superintendent and use rules and regulations to maintain control of school superintendents.

2. If there are drastic changes in the socio-economic condition of the student body resulting in rapid changes in superintendents and school board members, goals will shift causing strain in superintendent-school board relations.

3. If school board members see their loyalties as being with big business interests in the community, they will succumb to these pressures and make decisions acceptable to big business interests rather than to their historically powerless poor constituents, even when they are of the same racial group.

4. If school board members view their school board position as a steppingstone to higher political offices, they will make political decisions rather than educational ones.

5. If school board members are confused about their role, they will usurp the prerogatives of the superintendent and interfere with the day-to-day operation of the school system rather than focus on making policy decisions.

6. If change is desired, school board members will select superintendents from outside the school system. Conversely, if maintenance of the status quo is desired, school board members will select superintendents from inside the system.

7. If there is sexism in the school system, school board members will require more from a female superintendent than from a male superintendent.

## Summary

In this chapter, an attempt has been made to outline a theory of political conflict by using the school system decision-making structure as the unit of analysis. Twelve factors -- five external and seven internal -- were isolated as the points of analysis to be used to examine conflict in superintendent-school board relations.

The setting gives the background of the argument which is then focused in the list of propositions. These propositions will be expanded upon in the succeeding chapters.

FOOTNOTES                          Chapter 2


1.  Herbert A. Simon, *Administrative Behavior - A Study of Decision-Making Processes in Administrative Organizations* (Glencoe, Ill.: The Free Press, 1957), p. 67.

2.  Ibid.

3.  Luvern L. Cunningham, *Governing Schools - New Approaches to Old Issues* (Columbus, Ohio: Charles E. Merrill Publishing Company, 1971), p. 128.

4.  Chester I. Barnard, *The Functions of the Executive* (Cambridge, Mass.: Harvard University Press, 1968), p. 163; and, Simon, *Administrative Behavior*, p. 12.

5.  Simon, Ibid., p. 22.

6.  Jacob W. Getzels, James M. Lipham, and Roald F. Campbell, *Educational Administration as a Social Process-Theory, Research, Practice* (New York: Harper and Row Publishers, 1968), pp. 350-352; Thomas R. Bowman, "The Participation of the Superintendent in School Board Decision-Making," (Doctoral dissertation, University of Chicago, 1962); Neal Gross, *Who Runs Our Schools?* (New York: Wiley, 1958), p. 5.

7.  Simon, *Administrative Behavior*, p. 1.

8.  Ibid.

9.  Cunningham, *Governing Schools*, pp. 136-137.

10. Donald J. McCarty, "Motives for Seeking School Board Membership," (Doctoral dissertation, University of Chicago, 1959), pp. 54-57.

11. Getzels, *Educational Administration as a Social Process*, p. 61.

12. McCarty, "Motives," pp. 53-62.

13. Ibid., pp. 109-114.

14. S. P. Hencley, "A Typology of Conflict Between School Superintendents and Their Reference Groups," (Doctoral dissertation, University of Chicago, 1960), p. 140.

15. Hencley, "A Topology of Conflict."

16. Getzels, *Educational Administration as a Social Process*, p. 361.

17. Ibid.

18. Allen Rosenthal, *Governing Education* (Garden City, New York: Anchor Books, 1969), Introduction IX.

19. Ibid.

20. Victor Baldridge and Terrence E. Deal, *Managing Change in Educational Organizations* (Berkeley, California: McCutchan Publishing Corporation, 1975), pp. 436-437.

21. Herbert Simon, *Models of Man* (New York: John Wiley and Sons, Inc., 1956), p. 69.

22. Simon, *Administrative Behavior: A Study of Decision-Making Processes in Administrative Organization* (New York: The Free Press, 1959), p. 222.

23. Robert Staples, *Introduction to Black Sociology* (New York: McGraw-Hill Book Company, 1976), p. 76.

24. Gerhard Lenski, *Power and Privilege* (New York: McGraw-Hill, 1967), pp. 24-42.

25. Ibid.

26. Robert E. Park and Ernest W. Burgess, *Introduction to the Science of Sociology* (Chicago:

University of Chicago Press, 1921), pp. 574-76.

27. Joseph S. Himes, *Racial Conflict in American Society* (Columbus, Ohio: Charles E. Merrill Publishing Company, 1973), pp. 191-201.

28. Ibid, p. vii.

29. Ibid, p. 1.

30. Ibid., pp. 6-7.

31. Himes, p. 7.

32. Michael E. Sestak, and David D. Frerich, "The Principal's Role in School-Community Relations," in *Selected Articles for Elementary School Principals* (Washington, D.C.: Department of Elementary School Principals, National Education Association, 1968), p. 118.

33. Staples, *Black Sociology*, p. 36.

34. Ibid.

35. Eldridge Cleaver, "Education and Revolution," *The Black Scholar* 1 (November, 1969): 46.

36. Ibid.

37. Hans Morgenthau, *Politics Among Nations* (New York: Alfred A. Knoff, 1966), p. 29.

38. E. Franklin Frazier, *Black Bourgeoisie: The Rise of a New Middle Class in the United States* (Glencoe, Illinois: The Free Press, 1957), pp. 235-236.

39. Geneva Gay, "Racism in America: Imperatives for Teaching Ethnic Studies," in James A. Banks, ed., *Teaching Ethnic Studies: Concepts and Strategies* (Washington, D.C.: National Council for the Social Studies, 43rd Yearbook, 1973, p. 30.

40. Patricia Sexton, Women in Education (Bloomington, Indiana: Phi Delta Kappa Educational Foundation, 1976), p. 57.

41. Betty Friedan and Anne Grant West, "Sex Bias: The Built-in Mentality that Maims the Public Schools", American School Board Journal, 159 (October 1971): 16-20.

42. Russell T. Gregg and Stephen J. Knezevich "The Superintendent: What Makes Him What He Is?" American School Board Journal, 159 (October 1971): 12-17.

43. Kimball Wiles and Hulda Gross Grobman, "Principals as Leaders", Nations Schools, 56 (October, 1955): 75-77.

44. Hulda Grobman and Vynce A. Hines, "What Makes A Good Principal?" The Bulletin of the National Association of Secondary-School Principals, 40 (November 1956): 5-16.

45. Charlene T. Dale, "Women Are Still Missing Persons in Administrative and Supervisory Jobs", Educational Leadership, 31 (November 1973): 123-27.

46. Helen M. Morsink, "The Leader Behavior of Men and Women Secondary School Principals", (Doctoral dissertation, Central Michigan University, 1968).

47. John K. Hemphill, Daniel E. Griffiths, and Norman Frederiksen, Administrative Performance and Personality: A Study of the Principal in a Simulated Elementary School (New York: Bureau of Publications, Teachers College, Columbia University, 1962), pp. 332-336.

## CHAPTER III

## RACE, CLASS, SEX, AND COLONIAL STATUS

### Introduction

This chapter will deal with the impact of the external factors of race, class, sex, and the colonial status of the District government and the school system on superintendent-school board relations.

It was over a hundred years since the Emancipation Proclamation and this country was still in the grips of poisonous racism in the 1960s. The bombing of a church in Birmingham, Alabama, in 1963, in which four little Black girls were killed, epitomized this sickness as did the hoses and the vicious police dogs and clubs let loose on Black marchers. It was a time when the Kennedy brothers finally spoke out against some forms of injustice. It was the time of the March on Washington when 250,000 citizens descended on the nation's capital, on August 28, 1963, to protest injustice and violence. It was also the time of the assassination of President John F. Kennedy. And after the death of Kennedy, it was the period when then Lyndon B. Johnson, a southerner, called in favors owed him by legislators and pushed through the Civil Rights Bill of 1964. This was the time also of the "King hate campaign" of J. Edgar Hoover -- the McCarthy of the 1960s. Indeed, it was a continuation of historical negative ethics of some white people, until the powerful glaring white light of television revealed their evil acts to the world.

Martin Luther King, Jr. was murdered on April 4, 1968, after his stand on the Vietnam War and his fight with J. Edgar Hoover. H. Rap Brown and Stokeley Carmichael agitated the Black populace into a different kind of push for justice. No longer was the Black movement focused on nonviolent supplications; it had shifted to demands and retaliatory behavior, especially in the northern and western urban areas. This shift in tactics impacted on the colleges and seeped down into the high schools, translating itself into demands for Black studies, Black teachers, jobs, housing and other rights enjoyed by the majority population, which was actually the minority population in terms of numbers in the District of Columbia.

This, then, was the national climate. The local climate was just as charged with vitality as Washingtonians saw some positive movement in their lives -- socially, economically and educationally. This national climate was reflected in the D.C. public school system (DCPSS) and caused great agitation among school people and citizens alike.

In the nation's capital, Blacks now outnumbered whites. As the population of Blacks increased (see table 1), their gain in power did not. Blacks manned the lowest positions in the federal and District governments. The majority of Blacks still clustered in poverty around the lower rungs of the social ladder. And, in most cases, those Blacks with the large salaries had settled for money but no power.[1]

Underemployment and unemployment were rampant as were low wages which accounted for the generally low-quality living conditions, high crime, and delinquency. In a 1965 report discussed by Constance Green in her book, titled <u>The Secret City</u>, it was stated that in "an area near the Capital 41 percent of the families earned less than $3,000 a year, 9 percent less than $1,000." Some people believed that what the District of

TABLE 1*

POPULATION OF THE DISTRICT OF COLUMBIA BY RACES -- 1940-1976

| YEAR: | 1940 | 1950 | 1960 | 1970 | 1975 | 1976 |
|---|---|---|---|---|---|---|
| Black | 187,266 | 280,803 | 411,737 | 547,238 | 559,100 | 538,800 |
| White | 474,326 | 517,865 | 345,263 | 209,272 | 162,700 | 169,100 |
| Total | 663,091 | 802,178 | 763,956 | 756,510 | 721,800 | 707,900 |

Source: Data for 1940-1960 compiled from Constance Green, The Secret City: A History of Race Relations in the Nation's Capital, New Jersey: Princeton University Press, 1967, p. 200.

Data for 1970 and 1975 taken from 1975 Population Estimates City-Wards-Anc's Census Tracts for Washington, D.C. Government of the District of Columbia Municipal Planning Office, Walter E. Washington, Mayor, May, 1977, p. 1. See also: U.S. Bureau of the Census, Current Population Reports, Series, P-23, No. 67. Population Estimates by Race for States: July 1, 1973 and 1975, Washington, D.C.: U.S. Government Printing Office, 1978, pp. 11 and 13.

Data for 1976 taken from 1976 Population Estimates Provisional City-Wards for Washington, D.C. Government of the District of Columbia, Walter E. Washington, Mayor. Washington, D.C.: Municipal Planning Office, November, 1977, p. 1.

* Tables 1 and 2 were prepared by Melvin Davis, Graduate Assistant in the Department of Educational Leadership and Community Service, School of Education, Howard University.

Columbia lacked was a locally elected government that could respond to local wishes -- a persistently voiced feeling held by many Washingtonians. Thus, some saw progress in the appointment in 1961 and reappointment in 1964 of John Duncan, a Black man, as one of three District commissioners. None saw this as a solution, though, believing that as long as committees of Congress acted as the city council, the District of Columbia would be at a distinct disadvantage.[2]

### Race and Class Factors

The phenomena of race and class plagued every aspect of life in the District of Columbia. Politics and education were especially susceptible. Blacks were a majority in the District and in the school system. Between 1960 and 1970 there was a decrease (1%) in the District's population, from 763,956 to 756,510, probably reflecting the "baby bust." From 1970 to 1976, there was a net migration of 10.2 percent with the 1970 total of 756,668 and the 1976 total at 707,900.[3] There was a sharp decrease to 690,000 in the District's population by 1977, the lowest since 1940 which was 663,091.[4]

By 1960, large numbers of whites had fled the District making the percent decrease in whites 33.3.[5] The decline was from 517,865 in 1950 to 345,263 in 1960. By 1970 the white population had decreased to approximately 27.9 percent at 209,272. Contrastingly, the Black population had increased in 1960 to 411,737 from 280,803 in 1950. This was the first time the Black population exceeded the white population in the District, making it the first major city to have a Black majority. By 1970, the Black population increased to approximately 71.1 percent at 547,238 out of a total population of 756,510. It began dropping in 1976 (approximately 71.9 percent), from 559,100 in 1975 to 538,800 in 1976 while the white population showed an increase from 26.7 percent, that is, 162,700 in 1975 to 169,100 in 1976. The median educational level of the total population was 12.2 percent. The median family income was $9,583 with females comprising almost half of the civilian labor force. Singles made up 21 percent of the District's population. Only 26 percent of the District's population are homeowners with the vast majority as renters.[6]*

The increase in student population in the District schools paralleled the increases in the District population. Student enrollment increased from 92,810 in 1940 to 94,716 in 1950. In 1960 it had increased to 122,879 and to approximately 146,224 by 1970. A decline in student population set in in 1972 (140,000) and continued to 1977 (120,672).

During the decade of 1940 to 1950 Black student enrollment began to show an increase over white student enrollment. In 1940 Black student enrollment stood at 36,263 while white student enrollment stood at 56,547. But by 1950, Black student enrollment had increased to 47,980 while white student enrollment had decreased to 46,736. From this narrow majority, Black student enrollment in the District schools steadily increased to 138,207 by 1970, while white student enrollment steadily declined to about 7,555 in that same year. By 1971, though, a decline had set in in the Black student population. It dropped to 136,256 and has steadily declined ever since. By 1977 it had decreased to 114,418. As whites began moving back

---

*Percentages were obtained from U.S. Bureau of the Census, Current Population Reports Series P-23, No. 67. "Population Estimates by Race for States: July 1, 1973 and 1975," (Washington, D.C.: U.S. Government Printing Office, 1978), pp. 11-14. Figures were listed in this report as follows: Black population, 537.9; white population, 211.4; total population, 756.7 for 1970; Black population, 511.4; white population, 189.8; and total population, 711.5 for 1975. The listing is in the thousands.

into the city, they began enrolling their children
in the public schools so that by 1974 the white
student population stood at 5,997 and steadily
increased each year. By 1977 it was recorded as
6,254. A slight dip in white enrollment can be
seen between 1975 (6,234) and 1976 (6,222).

Finally, the Black student enrollment in the
D.C. public schools increased from 64.0 percent in
1955 to 79.7 percent in 1960. By 1966 it had
reached 92.8 percent and steadily increased to 95.4
percent by 1972. By 1976 the Black student enrollment had dropped to 94.1 percent following the drop
in the total enrollment of 126,587 (see table 2).[7]

There are eight wards in the District of Columbia. Since all of the wards figure prominently in
the discussion to follow, all will be examined
briefly (see table 3).

Ward 1

In 1970, Ward 1 had 79.5 percent Black and
20.5 percent white population. The percentage of
families with incomes between $10,000-$24,999 was
28.1 percent (1969), and those with incomes between
$0-$9,999 was 66.8 percent. The poverty population
stood at 22.6 percent. Also, Ward 1 had the highest
percent of unemployment (9.7%) in the city in 1975.
Twenty-nine percent of the households were headed
by women in 1975. The percent of non-high school
graduates, eighteen to twenty-four years old, was
below (34%) that of the District as a whole (36%).
One of the lowest proportions of home ownership
(16%) was in Ward 1.

Ward 2

The population by race in Ward 2, in 1970, was
56.8 percent Black and 43.2 percent white. Family
income, in 1969, was 59.6 percent making between
$0-$9,999, 30.3 percent making between $10,000-
$24,999, and ten percent making $25,000+. Almost
24 percent of the population in the area in 1969

TABLE 2

DISTRICT OF COLUMBIA PUBLIC SCHOOL POPULATION BY RACES -- 1950-1977

| Year: | 1950 | 1960 | 1970 | 1971 | 1972 |
|---|---|---|---|---|---|
| Black | 47,980 | 97,987 | 138,207 | 136,256 | 133,651 |
| White & Others | 46,736 | 24,982 | 8,017 | 7,155 | 6,349 |
| Total | 94,716 | 122,879 | 146,224 | 143,411 | 140,000 |

| Year: | 1973 | 1974 | 1975 | 1976 | 1977 |
|---|---|---|---|---|---|
| Black | 130,321 | 126,309 | 124,451 | 120,365 | 114,418 |
| White & Others | 5,812 | 5,997 | 6,234 | 6,222 | 6,254 |
| Total | 136,133 | 132,306 | 130,685 | 126,587 | 120,672 |

Source: Data for 1950-1960 taken from Membership at the end of the First Advisory prepared by the Division of Research and Planning, District of Columbia Board of Education, December 2, 1960, unnumbered.

Data for 1970-1977 taken from Pupil Membership in Regular Elementary and Secondary Day Schools, by Schools, by Grades, by Race, by Sex, and by Regions, prepared by Division of Research and Evaluation, District of Columbia Public Schools, 1970-1977. See also Data Resource Book, Division of Research and Evaluation, Washington, D.C.: D.C. Public Schools, 1976-77, January 1977, p. 7 for data for 1975-1976.

TABLE 3

The Distribution of Percentages of Selected Demographic and Socio-Economic Descriptors in District of Columbia Wards

| Descriptors | Total | Ward 1 | Ward 2 | Ward 3 | Ward 4 | Ward 5 | Ward 6 | Ward 7 | Ward 8 |
|---|---|---|---|---|---|---|---|---|---|
| **A. Pupil Enrollment by Region** [1] | | | | | | | | | |
| I | 24.3 | --- | --- | --- | --- | --- | 14.0 | 8.4 | 77.6 |
| II | 11.1 | 17.0 | 28.4 | 50.0 | --- | --- | 4.6 | --- | --- |
| III | 19.3 | --- | --- | --- | --- | 16.1 | --- | 83.9 | --- |
| IV | 13.6 | --- | 17.4 | --- | --- | 16.4 | 66.2 | --- | --- |
| V | 15.5 | 46.6 | 15.2 | --- | 35.5 | 2.7 | --- | --- | --- |
| VI | 16.2 | --- | --- | --- | 40.1 | 59.9 | --- | --- | --- |
| **B. Population by Race, 1970** [2] | | | | | | | | | |
| White | 27.2 | 20.5 | 43.2 | 95.3 | 16.6 | 10.6 | 14.6 | 6.6 | 8.9 |
| Black | 72.8 | 79.5 | 56.8 | 4.7 | 83.4 | 89.4 | 85.4 | 93.4 | 91.1 |
| **C. Population Change by Race** [2] | | | | | | | | | |
| White | -22.3 | -27.5 | -23.2 | -9.0 | -30.9 | -33.0 | -47.1 | -61.9 | -48.8 |
| Non-White | +2.2 | -0.5 | +5.8 | +8.9 | +3.9 | +4.0 | +1.0 | +1.1 | +2.6 |
| Total | 4.6 | -6.1 | -7.1 | -8.1 | -2.3 | +0.1 | -6.0 | -3.1 | -4.1 |
| **D. Population by Age, 1970** [2] | | | | | | | | | |
| 0-4 | 7.9 | 7.4 | 5.7 | 4.0 | 6.2 | 7.3 | 8.7 | 10.2 | 13.7 |
| 5-14 | 17.0 | 13.3 | 11.8 | 8.8 | 15.6 | 19.3 | 20.2 | 23.1 | 23.9 |
| 15-24 | 19.2 | 20.4 | 20.5 | 18.6 | 17.9 | 19.0 | 18.4 | 18.4 | 20.1 |
| 25-34 | 14.9 | 15.7 | 17.7 | 12.8 | 12.8 | 11.6 | 15.1 | 14.3 | 19.2 |
| 35-44 | 11.2 | 10.9 | 11.4 | 9.7 | 12.7 | 12.4 | 11.2 | 11.4 | 9.9 |
| 45-64 | 20.5 | 21.0 | 22.3 | 27.0 | 24.7 | 22.2 | 19.1 | 17.4 | 9.2 |
| 65+ | 9.4 | 11.2 | 10.3 | 18.9 | 10.1 | 7.8 | 7.4 | 5.1 | 4.0 |
| **E. Population Change by Age,** [2] **1970-75** | | | | | | | | | |
| 0-4 | -11.8 | | | | | | | | |
| 5-14 | -9.1 | | | | | | | | |
| 15-24 | -11.1 | | | | | | | | |
| 25-34 | +13.1 | | | (Not available by Wards.) | | | | | |
| 35-44 | -4.0 | | | | | | | | |
| 45-64 | -15.3 | | | | | | | | |
| 65+ | +1.1 | | | | | | | | |
| All Ages | -4.6 | -6.1 | -7.1 | -8.1 | -2.3 | +0.1 | -6.0 | -3.1 | -4.1 |
| **F. Decrease in Elementary School Enrollment (1969/70 - 1974/75)** [3] | -22.7 | -24.8 | -26.0 | -24.1 | -23.4 | -21.6 | -27.8 | -20.5 | -17.5 |
| **G. Family Income, 1969** [4] | | | | | | | | | |
| $ 0 - 9,999 | 52.3 | 66.8 | 59.6 | 20.7 | 41.3 | 51.5 | 61.2 | 57.0 | 66.2 |
| $10 - 24,999 | 39.7 | 28.1 | 30.3 | 46.7 | 50.7 | 45.3 | 36.7 | 40.0 | 36.6 |
| $25,000+ | 8.0 | 5.1 | 10.0 | 32.8 | 7.9 | 3.0 | 2.1 | 2.9 | 1.1 |
| **H. Poverty Population, 1969** [4] | 16.2 | 22.6 | 23.6 | 6.3 | 8.7 | 15.8 | 19.1 | 17.7 | 15.9 |
| **I. Unemployment, 1975 (est)** [4] | 7.5 | 9.7 | 7.8 | 4.8 | 5.9 | 7.1 | 8.2 | 7.5 | 9.0 |
| **J. Households Headed by Women** [5] | 25.0 | 29.0 | 29.0 | 15.0 | 21.0 | 24.0 | 27.0 | 28.0 | 29.0 |
| **K. Non-High School Graduates** [6] **18 - 24 years** | 36.0 | 34.0 | 41.0 | 28.0 | 29.0 | 36.0 | 47.0 | 38.0 | 35.0 |
| **L. Owner-Occupied Housing** [4] | 28.2 | 16.0 | 10.7 | 39.0 | 50.8 | 43.2 | 28.6 | 33.5 | 10.3 |
| **M. Housing Units, Construction Permits, 1970 - 75** [4] | (6,154) | 1.9 | 36.5 | 13.5 | 0.5 | 16.7 | 3.6 | 17.8 | 9.4 |

[1] "Pupil Membership in Regular Day Schools on October 21, 1976 By Schools, By Grades, Ey Race, By Sex, and By Regions." D.C. Public Schools: Division of Research and Evaluation. November 1976. (Only memberships of neighborhood schools were included.)
[2] 1975 Population Estimates. District of Columbia: Municipal Planning Office. May 1977. Pages 1 and 6.
[3] Demographic, Social, and Housing Data: District of Columbia and Council Wards. District of Columbia: Municipal Planning Office, February 1976. Table 6.
[4] Demographic, Social and Housing Data. (Ward Data Summary.)
[5] District of Columbia Data. District of Columbia: Municipal Planning Office. December 1976. Page 72.
[6] District of Columbia Data. Page 78.

"Demographic and Socio-Economic Descriptions of Regions." Comprehensive Education Plan-School Year 1977-78. D.C. Public Schools: Division of Research and Evaluation. July 1977.

was poor. Unemployment stood at 7.8 percent in the area. Twenty-nine percent of the households were headed by women. The percent of non-high school graduates between the ages of eighteen to twenty-four years in the ward was 41 percent. Additionally, less than 11 percent of the residents in Ward 2 owned their homes.

Ward 3

Only 4.7 percent of the population in 1970 in Ward 3 was Black while slightly over 95 percent of the population was white. Almost half (46.7%) of the families, in 1969, were in the $10,000-$24,999 income bracket; and 32.8 percent made at least $25,000. As few as 6.3 percent of the population of Ward 3 lived in poverty in 1969. By 1975, only 4.8 percent of the ward residents were unemployed. And, no more than 15 percent of the households were headed by females. Further, only 28 percent of the residents did not have a high school education. Also, 39 percent of the residents owned their homes.

Ward 4

Ward 4 had a Black population in 1970 of 83.4 percent and a white population of 16.6 percent. Family income for the area was 41.3 percent making between $0-$9,999; 50.7 percent making between $10,000-$24,999; and 7.9 percent making $25,000+. Only 8.7 percent of the population was considered poor. Ward 4 had next to the lowest unemployment (5.9%) in the District. The District's percentage of households headed by women was 25. In comparison, three wards were lower: Ward 3 at 15 percent, Ward 4 at 21 percent and Ward 5 at 24 percent. Non-high school graduates living in Ward 4 stood at 29 percent, far less than for the District as a whole at 36 percent. More Ward 4 residents owned their homes (50.8%) than did residents of any other ward in the city. Note that the majority of the people who lived in the ward were Black (83.4%).

Ward 5

Ward 5 had the third highest percentage of Blacks (89.4%) as compared to Ward 7 with 93.4 percent and Ward 8 with 91.1 percent. In 1969, the level of family income was 51.5 percent making between $0-$9,999, 45.3 percent making between $10,000-$24,999, and 3.0 percent making $25,000 or more. At least 15.8 percent of the ward residents were living in poverty in 1969 and by 1975 unemployment stood at 7.1 percent. Twenty-four percent of the households were headed by women as compared to 15 percent in Ward 3 and 21 percent in Ward 4. In addition, 36 percent of the ward residents between the ages of eighteen and twenty-four were non-high school graduates. A little over 43 percent of the residents owned their homes.

Ward 6

In 1970, a little over 85 percent (85.4%) of the residents in Ward 6 were Black. Over 38 percent of the residents made between $10,000-$25,000+ with 61.2 percent making from $0-$9,999. Poverty in the area stood at 19.1 percent in 1969. Unemployment was 8.2 percent in 1975. Twenty-seven percent of the households were headed by women, making the area the fourth lowest in this regard. Ward 6 had the highest percent of non-high school graduates (47%) than any other ward in the area. Approximately 29 percent of the residents owned their homes.

Ward 7

In 1970, Ward 7 had a 93.4 percent Black population. Fifty-seven percent of the workers in the area made between $0-$9,999; 40 percent made between $10,000-$24,999 and 2.9 percent made $25,000 or over as compared to Ward 3 (32.8%). The poverty population in 1969 stood at 17.7 percent. Unemployment in 1975 was 7.5 percent. Twenty-eight percent of the households in the area were headed by women. Thirty-eight percent of the 18-24 year old residents were non-high school graduates in 1975. Over 33 percent of the residents owned their homes.

Ward 8

In 1970, Ward 8 had next to the largest percent of Blacks (91.8%). Ward 7 had 93.4 percent. These two wards show a considerable contrast to Ward 3, west of Rock Creek Park, with 4.7 percent Blacks. Significantly, only 1.1 percent of the population made $25,000 or over and well over half of the families (66.2%) made between $0-$9,999 per year. The poverty population in 1969 was 15.9 percent. Unemployment in 1975 was 9.0 percent, next to the highest in the District. In Wards 1, 2 and 8, 29 percent of the households were headed by women.

## General Comparisons

There are some obvious general comparisons which can be made from the data even though the dates are not consistent.

Population

1. Ward 3 has the smallest percentage of Blacks.

2. Wards 1, 4, 5, 6, 7 and 8 have between 79.5 percent and 93.4 percent Black population.

3. Blacks comprise a little over half of the population in Ward 2 (56.8%).

Income

Income-wise, the wards can be ranked thusly:

1. Ward 3 -- 79.5 percent with incomes between $10,000-$25,000+.

2. Ward 4 -- 58.6 percent with incomes between $10,000-$25,000+;

3. Ward 5 -- 48.3 percent with incomes between $10,000-$25,000+;

4. Ward 7 -- 42.9 percent with incomes between $10,000-$25,000+;

5. Ward 2 -- 40.3 percent with incomes between $10,000-$25,000+;

6. Ward 6 -- 38.8 percent with incomes between $10,000-$25,000+;

7. Ward 8 -- 37.7 percent with incomes between $10,000-$25,000+.; and

8. Ward 1 -- 32.2 percent with incomes between $10,000-$25,000+.

In summary, Ward 1 is the poorest ward. Ward 8 is the next poorest ward. Ward 3 is the richest ward with Ward 4 next in line. Not quite 50 percent of the residents in Ward 5 make between $10,000-$25,000+.

Education

The wards can be ranked in the following manner in terms of the lowest percent of non-high school graduates:

1. Ward 3 (28.0%);

2. Ward 4 (29.0%);

3. Ward 1 (34.0%);

4. Ward 8 (35.0%);

5. Ward 5 (35.0%);

6. Ward 7 (38.0%);

7. Ward 2 (41.0%); and

8. Ward 6 (47.0%).

In summary, Ward 3 has the highest percent of high school graduates. Ward 5 ranks 5th. Ward 6 has the lowest percent of high school graduates. Almost 50 percent of the residents in Ward 6 have not graduated from high school.

## Desegregation

Many of the problems which arose in the D.C. public school system, and impacted upon the relationship between superintendents and school board members, stemmed from years of racism as attested to by a segregated school system and city. Several incidents serve to illuminate this fact.

For one, Marian Anderson, a famous Black singer, was denied the use of Constitution Hall and Central High School in 1939.[8] A second illustration is the furor surrounding the development of an Intergroup Education Handbook in 1947. The document received extensive press coverage and threats from one congressman to reduce appropriations for the District schools.[9] A third situation was the maintenance of a segregated school system where, in 1950, white schools were half empty and Black schools were overcrowded in the same school districts.[10] In connection with this third event, the first sit-in occurred when, on March 31, 1952, Reverend Smallwood Williams brought his son to underenrolled white Wheatley Elementary School to enroll him. Reverend Williams faced opposition but refused to leave for several hours. Carl F. Hansen, who became school superintendent in 1958, blocked Reverend Williams' entrance into the school the next morning.[11]

Other protests followed and culminated in the Supreme Court decision in <u>Brown v Topeka Board of Education</u> and the District's case, <u>Bolling v Sharpe</u>, which abolished school desegregation on May 17, 1954. This action was a decisive factor in modifying the problem described above. The White House, the Congress, the courts, the District government and the D.C. board of education (DCBOE) to some degree supported the school desegregation decision. With this diverse support from the power structure, Washington, D.C. was not pressured to move rapidly to desegregate its schools. Nevertheless, the D.C. board of education did approve a desegregation plan which was a moderate attempt to desegregate the public schools without disruption of school boundaries and a great amount of shuffling of staff and students to increase racial mixing. Hence, by October 17, 1963, 18,882 of 19,956 white pupils were attending schools with Black students and 100,517 out of 119,200 Black students were attending schools with white students.[12]

One cannot infer from these figures though that all went well in desegregation. As time passed, white parents sought ways to circumvent desegregation. One such method was the use by white parents of various school policies to have their children transferred from high-density Black schools to those of low Black enrollment. As it became known that health was a useful factor on which to request a transfer, many white parents presented statements from their doctors and psychiatrists regarding the harmful effects for their children of attending schools with a predominantly Black student enrollment because there they could not participate in social events. Another ruse white parents used was to request that their children be transferred to a school outside their neighborhood because their own school did not offer courses their children wanted.[13]

A fourth incident which occurred around the same time serves to illustrate the impact of race as a disruptive factor impinging on the school system and beginning to make a dent in superintendent-school board relations. The incident involved a racial altercation, at the stadium on Thanksgiving Day, November 22, 1962, between football players from St. John's Academy, a predominantly white Catholic college preparatory high school, and Eastern Senior High School, an all-Black public high school. Following this incident, Superintendent Hansen appointed a committee to investigate what had occurred. Parts of the Committee's report, titled "Report of the Special Committee on Group Activities of the District of Columbia," relate most particularly to this study. The incident was started when a St. John's player elbowed an Eastern player in the face. The Eastern player retaliated and was removed from the game. Eastern players and fans became incensed by this action, and fights on the field and in the stands ensued. Some board members -- Dr. Preston K. McLendon, Dr. Mordecai W. Johnson, and Colonel West A. Hamilton, in particular -- resented the implication in the report that one of the main problems in the D.C. public school system was the need for more discipline due to the large influx of Black students. Thus, they resisted Superintendent Hansen's recommendation to delete the rule which prohibited corporal punishment.[14]

### The Track System

The report also contained an indictment of the track system, designed by Hansen, and introduced by Superintendent Hobart M. Corning (1948-58). Further, the track system was described in the *Passow Report* as having become the "'dumping ground' for hundreds of Negro youth, who are consigned to inferior instruction, far too large classes, and a complete lack of training to fit them to become employable citizens of tomorrow."[15]

Therefore, the report focused attention on this unpopular educational plan put in place after desegregation of the schools in 1954 to provide remedial and compensatory education for Black students. Notably, the racial implications of the track system were a bone of contention between some Black and liberal white board members and the white superintendent. These board members felt that the track system was a new segregation approach since the basic track contained many Black students.

## The Issue of Equalization

One outgrowth of the racial incident on Thanksgiving Day at the stadium appeared to be a presentation to the DCBOE on June 23, 1964 regarding "Integration and the Washington Public Schools" by the Washington Urban League. The implementation mechanism proposed to assist in integration was the establishment of a permanent Advisory Council on Integration directly responsible to the board of education and the superintendent of schools. In expressing his non-support for the establishment of the advisory council, Hansen indicated that he felt the council would be a kind of second board of education to deal specifically with questions of racial implications, and therefore it was unnecessary. Thus, he recommended that the board not support the proposal. Therefore, no action on the proposal was taken at this time.[16]

In the March 17, 1965 meeting, board member Dr. Mordecai W. Johnson stated what appeared to him to be a seemingly deliberate policy of the city imposed by those in control of the city on those in control of the schools. Thus, he said:

> Now, number one, let us take a look at the elementary schools. There are eleven elementary schools which have very significant inter-racial enrollments.... We can see what has happened. The great white population of the city has, not without reason, has fled this school system. They have gone to the suburbs and put their children in the kind of schools that they have been used to for the last one hundred years, because they have never been taught to have any faith in any other kind. What has happened with the School Board is this: seeing that there is fear among the white population, they have, without discussing it publicly, done their very best to keep those whites who have stayed here, as segregated as possible. That is a fact. I

> could take my pencil and delineate to you the
> carefully cultivated segregated white areas
> in this city... they are there, and they are
> there because this Board or those who are
> behind this Board have planned it so. Some-
> times I have a feeling that this Board is not
> the organization that controls the policies
> that affect the schools. There are plenty of
> signs to me that there is a body behind this
> Board which is making decisions purposefully
> and implementing them effectively and is manip-
> ulating this Board....[17]

Further, Dr. Mordecai Johnson raised an issue which was to become the basis of Hansen's most difficult struggle with the board in July 1966 in the <u>Hobson v Hansen</u> case and which eventually led to his retiring from the system. That matter had to do with the amount of money being spent on Black students:

> ...there are 32 elementary schools in the
> first quartile of financial support which are
> being educated anywhere from $10,500.00 up to
> $29,949.00 per group of thirty students... all
> those schools except three have from 82 to 100
> percent either white students or black stu-
> dents....
>
> We are now educating thousands of little Negro
> children at six to seven thousand dollars for
> a group of thirty students per year. We are
> educating select groups of 98 to 100 percent
> white schools and 98 to 100 percent black
> schools with financial support ranging from
> $10,870.00 to $16,911.00 per year for thirty
> students. I ask you this question: is this
> done purposefully in order that we may make a
> demonstration here in Washington that the
> schools that get along the best are the ones
> that stay segregated? If that is true, then
> what we see in that first quartile is a de-
> liberate effort to break the purpose of the
> government when it passed the law to introduce
> integration.[18]

School Superintendent Carl Hansen was under considerable attack by some members of the D.C. board of education (DCBOE) and by civil rights groups; and he was the defendant in a federal suit with the board of education, brought by a Black man, Julius Hobson, Sr., attacking discrimination against Black children in general and, in particular, the track system -- a form of ability grouping which relegated many Black children to the lowest track. Therefore, Hansen agreed to a study by an outside agency, which could be viewed as a delaying tactic, and suggested the National Education Association (NEA) based in Washington, D.C. Apparently, distrusting his intentions and the impartiality of a group of public school educators, which made up the group's membership, liberal groups rejected his proposal. D.C. Citizens for Better Public Education, an influential group in the District, helped arrange for A. Harry Passow of Teachers College, Columbia University, to conduct the study in 1966.

During this time there was a drive on to reform the schools which white children were leaving in droves as their parents fled Washington, D.C. In 1950, the white student population was about 46,000. By 1970, the white student population had decreased to about 8,000 (see table 2).

Meanwhile, however, in June 1967, just prior to the submission of Passow's preliminary findings, Judge J. Skelly Wright decreed that the superintendent and the board unconstitutionally deprived the District's Negro and poor public school children of their right to equal educational opportunity.

## School Board Appointments

One write-up in a local newspaper in 1967 pointedly expressed the view of some citizens in regard to race as an issue in the District and the school system when it said something to the effect that it was now time to give the school board a Black majority.[19]

Race was indeed an issue in the selection of school board members in 1967. In this connection, U.S. District Court Judge George L. Hart, Jr. said he would make no attempt "to establish a racial quota for board members despite growing demands that the board be composed of a majority of Negroes" in view of the fact that the present racial composition is five whites and four Blacks.[20]

Nevertheless, a Black was appointed. Now, for the first time in the history of the D.C. public school system, the nine member DCBOE was majority Black with Dr. Benjamin Alexander, Dr. Euphemia Haynes, and the Rev. Everett Hewlett joined by Anita Allen and Julian Dugas, who were appointed by a panel of three federal judges from the U.S. District Court under pressure from the community to have a board which reflected the composition of the city and the school population.

## Race as a Factor in All Affairs

Carl F. Hansen put in proper perspective the question of race as a factor in all affairs, educational ones included, in the nation's capital when he said:

> It is a rare happening in the Washington public schools that is free of racial considerations. This is hardly surprising, considering that at the last count nearly 93 percent of the school's 150,000 pupils are Negroes, as are nearly 79 percent of its teachers and administrators. Five of the nine school board members, including the president and vice president, are Negroes ....[21]

Here we viewed how the issue of race and, later, class began to develop as disruptive forces between Superintendent Hansen and the school board as some members began to reject a grouping plan which relegated Black students to the basic track.

Superintendent Hansen seemed insensitive to the concerns of those five board members, which exacerbated a growing rift in his relationship with the board. The matter of equalization of resources for the poor widened the split in superintendent-school board relations.

## Sexism*

Sexism in educational administration is not a new trend. On the contrary, it has existed for many years in various states and school systems in the United States. This negative societal attitude toward women has been evident in the administration of the D.C. public school system over the years. Past records of the administration of the D.C. public school system and its administrative directories[22] reveal data supporting the fact that women had been discriminated against. In 1969 the superintendent of schools and his vice and deputy superintendents were men. Out of a list of 22 administrators, which included the superintendent, assistant and associate superintendents, and assistant to the assistant superintendents, 17 of them were men and only 5 were women. Of the five women three were assistants to the assistant superintendents and the other two were assistant superintendents. Also in 1969 there were 12 male senior high school principals and no females; 18 male assistant senior high school principals and 15 females. In the junior high schools, there were 21 male assistant principals and only 8 female principals; 31 male assistant principals and 29 female assistant principals. From the above data one can see that the positions considered important were occupied by men and women were relegated to the secondary positions. It is important, however, to find that on the elementary school level, the pattern

---

*This section was prepared, in part, by Subuola O. Doherty, student in the Administrative Behavior and Theory class at the School of Education, Howard University, Fall 1978.

changed. In 1969 there were 101 female elementary school principals and only 35 males. The same pattern was evident with the assistant elementary principals; 41 females and 11 males. On looking at these figures, one should not be too hasty in concluding that since there were more elementary schools, it then follows that the total percentage of female principals is comparable to that of male principals. Elementary school principals were paid at a lower salary.[23] Although all principals belong to class 6 according to the Teachers and School Officers Salary Schedule (TS-6), the class is further subdivided into three groups according to their qualifications. Within each group are four pay levels. The level of each principal is determined by the following factors: (1) number of employees to be supervised; (2) number of students in school; (3) involvement in extracurricular activities. The higher the number of the above factors, the higher the salary level of the principal. According to the way the schools are set up, most senior and junior high school principals are in levels III and IV which are the highest paid positions. They earn between $27,271 to $34,656 per annum. Elementary school principals who are mostly women are concentrated in the level I with very few on level II. Salary levels I and II range from $25,626 to $33,006.

When seeking information from the administrative offices of the D.C. public school system through formal channels, one finds that the only available data such as EEO reports[24] are compiled in such a way that no valid deductions about the existence of sexism in the system can be made. For example in the formal records for the year 1973, it was documented that there were 88 male administrators and 89 females. In 1974, 91 males and 66 female administrators were reported. No distinction was made between superintendents, administrative aides, or secretaries.

However, in a more detailed analysis of the number of public school principals for 1975 significant figures were compiled by an employee in the division of research of the D.C. public schools for her own personal use (see table 4).

## Colonial Status

On November 3, 1967, the District government changed from the three-man commission to a commissioner (mayor) council form of government. The mayor and deputy mayor were made responsible for the administration of legislation enacted by Congress and by the city council, and the city council was authorized to assume the quasi-legislative functions formerly assigned to the District's board of commissioners. Therefore, the District of Columbia now had a mayor and a deputy mayor and a nine-member city council nominated by the U.S. President and confirmed by the U.S. Senate. This system of governance gave the President more direct control over the District government than before. For one thing, the mayor's term of office coincided with the President's, making him subject to reappointment as presidents changed. Secondly, the President could remove the mayor from office at any time.[25] Without an electoral base, the mayor was handicapped in the exercise of power both within the city and before the Congress.

Legislative authority over local affairs is generally exercised by the U.S. Congress similar to that of a state legislature over its unit of local government. Nevertheless, the District of Columbia has some attributes of statehood while being neither a state nor a territory. It participates as a state in interstate compacts, while it is treated as an agency of the federal government in budgetary and auditing procedures.

Congress works primarily through committees -- the Senate committee and the House committee. The membership of the House committee for the last twenty years has been dominated by southerners. They represent rural districts rather than urban areas. The Senate committee is not much more

TABLE 4

THE NUMBER OF DCPS PRINCIPALS - 1975

| Type of School | No. of Principals | |
|---|---|---|
| | Male | Female |
| **Senior High Schools** | | |
| Principals | 8 | 4 |
| Assistant Principals | 24 | 16 |
| **Vocational Schools** | | |
| Principals | 4 | 1 |
| Assistant Principals | 4 | 1 |
| **Junior High Schools** | | |
| Principals | 22 | 8 |
| Assistant Principals | 41 | 33 |
| **Elementary Schools** | | |
| Principals | 40 | 83 |
| Assistant Principals | 15 | 47 |
| **Special Education Schools** | | |
| Principal | 1 | 3 |
| Assistant Principals | 1 | 3 |

SOURCE: Compiled by Employee in DCPS Division of Research for personal use. From the data, the pattern of women being concentrated in elementary schools, while men are concentrated in secondary schools, is again evident as in the 1969 records.

representative of the interests of the District.

The D.C. subcommittees of the appropriations committees of each House share jurisdiction over the District. Only in Washington, D.C. are the appropriations separated from the legislators who have surveillance over revenue and legislation.

Although the District is treated as an agency of the federal government in budgetary and auditing procedures and all general federal laws apply to the District and its agencies unless changed by special provisions, its status before Congress is inferior to that of other federal agencies.[26]

It was not until September 22, 1970 that District citizens were granted the right to elect a non-voting delegate to the U.S. House of Representatives. In December 1973, the D.C. Self-Government and Governmental Reorganization Act (Public Law 93-198) was enacted, giving the District government certain limited legislative prerogatives. District residents went to the polls on May 24, 1974, and accepted the charter. In September primary elections were held, and a general election was held in November. The first elected government officials were sworn into office on January 2, 1975.

The Congress retained for itself (1) the right to enact legislation affecting the District, (2) the right to review and disapprove within 30 working days any legislation enacted by the mayor and the city council, and (3) the right to review and approve the expenditure of all District funds through the enactment of annual appropriation laws. Among the powers not granted to the District government were legislative authority over several local matters such as (1) the organization and jurisdiction of the D.C. courts, (2) the revision of the criminal code, and (3) the taxation of personal income earned in the District by non-residents.[27]

Home rule was a long time coming to the District and when it came to this predominantly Black city, it came in a modified form. The budgetary control retained by Congress still permitted it to make political and educational policy for the schools. As the Strayer Report (1949) indicated, there was a unique relationship between the District school system and the Congress since the city board of education was also the state governing educational agency -- unlike the situation in other cities of the nation where the local board operates under a state educational agency. Citizens in the District had no voice in the selection of members of the board of education or in any phase of the educational process.[28]

In 1967 the board of education consisted of nine members appointed for terms of three years by the Justice of the District Court of the United States for the District of Columbia. Five years of residency immediately preceding their appointment were required. The Organic Act of 1906 set forth in general terms the powers and duties of the board of education to the effect that "the control of the public schools of the District of Columbia is hereby vested in the Board of Education" which "shall determine all questions of general policy relating to the schools." However, the board of education had a dependent relationship to the District commissioners, and basically the reorganization on August 11, 1967, of the District government to one commissioner and city council left intact this dependent relationship. Nevertheless, the board did have power to set policy and to develop new programs. Previously, it primarily confirmed the school superintendent's recommendations and did not exercise its full powers.[29]

Junior members of the court were given the responsibility of appointing board members. Not having the time to evaluate the qualifications of incumbents or new nominees, they usually automatically reappointed incumbents. In 1967 a bill was introduced by House District Committee Chairman

John L. McMillan to give the District an elected eleven-member board of education.

As an outgrowth of that action, on April 22, 1968, the Elected School Board Act was signed into law and the first elections were held in November 1968, under Public Law 90-292.[30] The elective process provided for eleven board members -- eight to be elected from wards, and three members to be elected at large.

The colonial relationship of the District government to the Congress had negative repercussions on the relationship of the mayor and city council to the DCBOE. Congress still had the major power and was unwilling to provide adequate funds to finance the District government. This, in turn, negatively affected the relationship between the District government and the board of education, for what little power the local government had, it held tenaciously.

An editorial in the Washington Star of January 1968, during Superintendent Manning's administration, pithily pointed to the lack of power of the school board when it indicated that not only does the District school board suffer from dissension and confusion but, in addition, it is hampered by a super superintendent in the sense of Judge J. Skelly Wright's decision about equality of educational opportunity, a new superintendent and a new city council which is telling it how to spend its money.

The editorial continued by saying that Mayor Washington should reject this council action because it usurps the board of education's responsibility in that it rejected a $2.9 million request from the board to set up a pre-kindergarten program and the funds should be used for other school expenditures chosen by the council. Furthermore, the editorial emphasized that the pre-kindergarten program was recommended in the Passow Report and supported by the school board and professional administrators in the school system and probably had broad public support.[31]

Additionally, the editorial called attention to what this would mean in terms of powers the school board had. In this regard, it indicated that if the council could make programmatic decisions, then there was no need for the board of education.[32]

Also, the Council was unable or unwilling to finance the educational enterprise adequately. This left the first elected body -- the school board -- constantly struggling to gain power and funds from its oversight body -- the District government. The constant anxiety over financing translated itself into conflicts between the board of education and the superintendent. The budget-preparation period was an especially trying time.

Several incidents will illuminate the erosion in superintendent-school board relations due to the colonial status of the District government and the school board during the budget crisis faced by then Superintendent Hugh Scott.

Due to the cost factor involved in implementing court decrees, a viable decentralization design, a projected year-end deficit of over $3 million dollars, and inadequate funding of $146.5 million by Congress, Superintendent Scott faced a multi-problem situation. Thus, budget preparation and revision took priority at a number of meetings during the 1971-72 school year. Six months into his superintendency, Scott made the following observation about the relationship between the school system and the government:

> A significant reason for the shortcomings of the District of Columbia Public Schools is the unique dependency relationship they must maintain with the District government and the Congress....

The final decision regarding District affairs, and subsequently District school affairs, particularly financial ones, belongs to the Senate and House, bodies which by definition are concerned with national affairs. Through their several committees they exert, by legislative action, a categorical influence on the District's operations. For the school system, therefore, negotiating the formal and informal channels of the local and national governments is a time-consuming process that decreases the efficiency of system operations.

The unique method of financing the District schools is one which denies the Board of Education full prerogative to determine educational policy. Because the District is not self-governed, and the fact that school revenues are obtained both from taxes levied by the District and from the annual federal payment determined by Congress, the budget is subject to review and reduction by the City Council and subcommittees of the House and the Senate.

Since educational policy is largely manifested in spending priorities, the school system often finds that the budget as approved by Congress does not appropriately represent those policies and spending priorities which have been established by the Board of Education. Compounding the issue is the Congressionally required procedure of line-item justification for new appropriations. All line-item expenditures approved through Congressional appropriations must be used for that purpose alone, unless special permission is obtained from Congress. Federal aid to education is similarly restricted since only special purpose grants are made.

The applied constraints on the system, manipulating the school budget, produce rigidity such that programmatic changes in response to changing needs are not easily made possible.[33]

A very pointed acknowledgement of a possible conflict in mayor-board of education prerogatives for setting educational policy for the schools was revealed in the board meeting of February 17, 1971. There was a full discussion of this issue in regard to a letter received by the board about the budget submitted to the deputy mayor. The letter delivered on February 12, 1971 suggested, according to board member Tirana: ..."That the Board did not have the right to submit its estimate of needs (budget) to the Mayor and City Council, even though the Board had done so in accordance with Section 104 of the Organic Act of 1906."[34]

The problem arose because the board had submitted a minimum budget of $155 million for FY72. Consequently, it had been directed to withdraw that budget and submit instead a budget of $143 million.

It was the thinking of Mr. Tirana, reporting for the Committee on Rules, that a fundamental question about the relationship between the board and the city government had been raised by the letter from the deputy mayor. The question raised dealt with the power of the board to set policy or whether the mayor and the city council have that authority through the budgetary process. In light of the understanding of the complete membership of the board that this was indeed a problem, the board voted to retain the firm of Wilmer, Cutler and Pickering, who had offered to serve the board on a <u>pro bono publico</u> basis as advisors to the board on matters of its legal rights.[36]

Another instance revealing the dependent relationship had to do with a projected year-end deficit of $3.7 million. Hugh Scott, an outside selected superintendent, had difficulty finding out "where the bodies were buried," as for instance he could not get accurate figures from his administration since there was a breakdown in the school systems' ability to account for its spending.[36]

A Washington Daily News article of January 21, 1972 detailed the situation as presented in an exchange of memorandum between Superintendent Scott and his budget officers under a headline of large print entitled, "Deficit! School Officials Knew About Mess." The article stated that some 20 memoranda between school administrators showed that financial chaos and deficits had existed for two years so that the system possibly faced an $11 million deficit by the end of the year.[37]

In a second article on the same page, entitled "Hahn May Take Budget from Schools," it was indicated that D.C. City Council Chairman Gilbert Hahn threatened to take the controls of school finances from school officials if matters were not cleared up before budget time. According to this account, Hahn said he was not sure Dr. Scott had the will or capability to correct the situation. It was explained in the article that even though the District budget office has control over school finances, in the past it had only acted to give final approval. Clearly revealed in the article was that neither Superintendent Scott, Board President James Coates or school budget officer Delroy Cornick, had a handle on the budget or personnel systems in the school system.[38] Some portion of both were handled by the District government. This lack of total control over such serious matters seemed to cause frustrations which manifested themselves in conflict in school board-superintendent relations. Another article signals the erosion of school board member/superintendent relations by the headline "Scott, Tirana Clash on Crisis in School Funds."[39]

Subsequently, it was reported that Dr. Scott threatened to resign if the school board did not appoint an assistant to handle management and financial matters neither of which were entirely

under the control of the school system. In a
<u>Washington Star</u> article, Scott asked why anyone
would want to be head of a system which did not
back the superintendent by providing essentials
like a management official.[40] Scott continued by
describing the degree of harrassment borne by him
by indicating that he was often threatened with
being fired.[41]

At the February 14, 1972 meeting of the DCBOE,
Superintendent Scott told the school board committee that he was told by his budget department
staff that it had discovered a $4.7 million error
in his budget request for the 1972-73 fiscal year.
Therefore, $152.5 million would be needed for the
school system rather than the $147.8 million asked
for in January 1972. This extra money was needed
for promised salary raises, increased utility costs
and expenses for opening a new high school.
Needless-to-say, Board President Marion Barry was
not pleased by this disclosure.[42]

Then, at its February 16, 1972 meeting, there
was a full discussion of a projected deficit of
$3.7 million to reconcile. At that time Superintendent Scott saw no way of doing this without
hurting the schools because 86 percent of the cost
was in the schools, with personnel being number
one. In this regard, the superintendent urged the
board not to take the total $3.7 million out of
administrators since there were so few of them.
Based upon this information, board members felt
they should wait for the head count and consider
across-the-board cuts.[43]

Controversy between the DCBOE and Superintendent Scott continued over which top administrators
would be eliminated. The DCBOE plan proposed 100
administrative and supervisory jobs including the
office of Vice Superintendent Benjamin Henley, to
retire in June 1972, and all five associate superintendents so that those salaries could be redirected into the classroom. Superintendent

Scott's reorganization plan proposed to eliminate the vice superintendent slot but retain three associate superintendents. Other cuts proposed by Superintendent Scott might be made in teachers, counselors and aides. In opposition to Scott's proposed cuts, Board Budget Committee Chairwoman Swaim emphasized that the DCBOE was committed to locating maximum authority and resources at the local school level.[44]

The school board voted on June 12, 1972 to cut back next year's spending by $4 million by abolishing 200 jobs of supervisors, administrators, clerical workers and special elementary school teachers in the fiscal year that begins July 1. Of this number approximately 50 of the jobs to be eliminated were administrators and supervisors. In commenting on this, Superintendent Scott said, "The administrative and supervisory ranks are being reduced to the bone."[45]

The budget process as outlined by President Marion Barry was as follows:

> This year [1972] for the first time in many years the Board will vote on a mark before the Mayor sets one. Once the Board votes approval, the document is submitted to the Mayor, after which it is included in the overall District Government Budget, which is then submitted to the City Council. The City Council holds hearings, and can change or accept what the Mayor has recommended. If they change it, the Mayor can veto it. If they wish to override his veto it takes a three-fourth majority to do so.
>
> When the Council and Mayor have a final budget, it goes to the Office of Management and Budget in the President's Office, where it can be changed or approved. Next it is sent to the Congress, where the Chairman of the District Committees hold hearings, some in Executive Session. After a compromise is worked out between the House and Senate

Committees it goes to the President for signature.... However... once the Board of Education sets its mark, the next move is up to the Mayor and it is up to the citizens to deal with the Mayor.[46]

The DCBOE was never quite satisfied with its powers as it understood them in relationship to those of the city council and the mayor. Therefore, the board meeting of November 21, 1972 was significant in that the DCBOE, under the presidency of Barry, approved the establishment of a committee to confer with the board's attorney in connection with the board's autonomy concerning contracting processes.

In reading Organization Order No. 9 from the D.C. Code Supplement, as amended, Mrs. Mason said she found that with some limitations, contracting authority had been delegated to such officials as the Director, Department of Sanitary Engineering; the Director, Department of Public Health; the Director, Department of Corrections, etc. Therefore, she questioned why like authority should not be delegated to the Public Schools. The Board of Education, an elected body should surely have at least as much autonomy to contract as any of those other agencies.

Therefore the motion was made by Mrs. Mason and seconded by Mr. Cassell, that a Committee of the Board be appointed to confer with the Board's attorney, Mr. Herbert O. Reid*, and to propose a plan which would eliminate any delays resulting from actions of the District Government in connection with the contracting process and would give the Board at least as much autonomy as any other agency serving the District of Columbia.[47]

---

*Mr. Herbert O. Reid later became the Administrative Law Judge in the case of <u>Sizemore v. D.C.B.O.E.</u>, 1975.

At the December 19, 1973 meeting of the DCBOE, Mr. Tirana raised a question about the apparent conflict between the city government and the board on authority to reprogram and redirect funds. In pursuit of this point, he said that he thought the board had the authority as far as policy was concerned. That is, that the city government had the responsibility to account for the money the board spent, but it was up to the board to direct how to spend it. Basically, Tirana's concern was with the delay in processing expenditure actions by the administration and the board and that the board did not have the authority that it should have in terms of negotiating teacher salary increases.[48] Tirana felt the DCBOE had power but did not use it. He argued that "The Board had almost unlimited power over the budget. It never fully realized it. Congress was frequently made a scapegoat."[49]

Board member Cassell had the following to say about the relationship between the D.C. government and the DCBOE:

> And it was true in great measure that the D.C. Department of General Services not being under our influence was not that much interested in timely making of repairs.... The duality of responsibility for physical repairs and for construction was a problem we shouldn't have had. The money was appropriated to the school system. The school system should have been able to do its own contracting and it still doesn't. That is a problem that needs to be resolved. There is no reason for the D.C. Government to be doing our construction for us because we still can't monitor the work. We can't monitor the calibre of the work. We can't monitor what they are spending for it.... The whole problem is that we have a colonial government here in which you can't hold your elected officials and the people appointed by the elected officials responsible to do the work and they can always pass

> responsibility off to the funding source
> which is the U.S. Congress. And we do not
> have home rule. We have a sham called home
> rule which is worse than we had before be-
> cause it now pretends that we have some
> control. We now have elected puppets rather
> than appointed puppets.[50]

According to Pryde: "Congress gave the school board no powers. We use to have to do a line by line item budget. We don't anymore, I understand. What the Council isn't doing to us, by the time it gets to the Congress, the Committee of the District of Columbia, they take it [reduces the budget]."[51]

### Summary

In this chapter we have dealt with four external factors: race, sex, class, and the colonial status of the District government vis-a-vis the Congress. We have examined these four external factors to see whether (and, if so, how) they impacted on the relationship between the superintendent and the school board. Our examination of the factor of race revealed that, collectively, the several incidents and situations translate into racism. This factor of racism certainly disrupted the relationship Superintendent Hansen had with his Black board members and some liberal white ones in terms of desegregation and the track system. Elements of classism also entered the picture in terms of the vast number of poor Blacks, in particular, relegated to the lowest educational track. And, sexism permeated the school system, especially in the administrative ranks.

Theoretically, it appeared that the school board was an autonomous body with authority to establish policy for the school system. However, the board was powerless in terms of control of its finances, which really decided which programs would or would not be supported. Budgetary decisions which the board made were subject to review by both the District government and the congressional committees.

The mayor and the city council determined what the school system's budget would be in total dollars. This determination decided the limit of the budget even before it got to the congressional committees. The frustration experienced by the city governing unit seeped down to the school system's decision-making unit, causing conflict, especially in budgetary matters, as was revealed in the case of Superintendent Scott.

In Chapter IV, we will examine the internal organizational factors of authority, function, and structure to see if any of these factors caused conflict in school superintendent-school board relations in the District of Columbia.

FOOTNOTES                                    Chapter III


1.  Constance McLaughlin Greene, *The Secret City-
    A History of Race Relations in the Nation's
    Capital* (Princeton, N.J.: Princeton Univer-
    sity Press, 1967), pp. 3-5.

2.  Ibid., pp. 8-11.

3.  The figure is 756,668 for 1970 and 702,000 in
    the U.S. Bureau of the Census, Statistical
    Abstract of the United States: 1977, 98
    Edition (Washington, D.C.: 1977), p. 3.
    (No racial breakdown provided.)

4.  Lawrence W. Feinberg, "Population in D.C.
    Falls to 690,000", *Washington Post*, 30 Jan-
    uary 1978, p. B1.

5.  Green, *The Secret City*, p. 200.

6.  "The People of the District of Columbia: A
    Demographic Social, Economic and Physical
    Profile of the District of Columbia and Its
    Nine Service Areas" (Washington, D.C.:
    Office of Planning, 1973).

7.  "Summary of Membership for All School Levels
    by Race" (Washington, D.C.: Division of
    Research and Evaluation, 20 October 1960
    through 21 October 1976; Data for 1955-56
    taken from the *Passow Report*, p. 182.

8.  Carl F. Hansen, *Danger in Washington - The
    Story of My Twenty Years in the Public
    Schools in the Nation's Capital* (West Nyack:
    Parker Publishing Company, Inc., 1968),
    pp. 4-7.

9.  Ibid., pp. 7-9.

10. Ibid., pp. 10-11.

11. Ibid., pp. 12-14.

12. Ibid., p. 25.

13. Ibid., p. 60.

14. "Minutes of the Eleventh (Special) Meeting of the Board of Education 1962-1963", Washington, D.C., 21 February 1963, pp. 3-12 and 25-26.

15. "Report of the Special Committee on Group Activities of the District of Columbia", 8 January 1963, p. 22.

16. "Minutes of the Seventeenth (Stated) Meeting of the Board of Education 1963-64", Washington, D.C., 17 June 1964, pp. 96-98.

17. "Minutes of the Tenth (Stated) Meeting of the Board of Education, 1964-65", Washington, D.C., 17 March 1965, p. 71.

18. Ibid., p. 73.

19. "Balance The Board", Washington Post, 19 March 1967.

20. "Early Deadline Passes for New School Board", Washington Star, 25 April 1967.

21. Hansen, Danger in Washington, pp. 1-2.

22. The Public Schools of the District of Columbia, "The Board of Education Administrative and Supervisory Staff Directory", Washington, D.C., 1969.

23. Memorandum from Claudette E. Helms, Director of Personnel, New Salary Scales for TSA and GS Personnel, The Public Schools of the District of Columbia, Division of Personnel, 11 October 1978.

24. Equal Employment Opportunity Commission, "Elementary-Secondary Staff Information" (EEO-5), Washington, D.C., 1 October 1977.

25. Royce Hanson and Bernard H. Ross, <u>Governing the District of Columbia: An Introduction</u> (Washington, D.C.: Washington Center for Metropolitan STudies, January 1971), pp. 16-17.

26. Ibid., pp. 2-13.

27. Walter E. Washington, Mayor, <u>Ten Years Since April 4, 1968 - A Decade of Progress for the District of Columbia - A Report to the People, The District of Columbia</u>, Washington, D.C.: 4 April 1978, pp. 4 and 25.

28. George D. Strayer, <u>The Report of a Survey of the Public Schools of the District of Columbia</u> (Washington, D.C.: Government Printing Office, 1949), p. 2.

29. A Harry Passow, <u>Toward Creating a Model Urban School System: A Study of the Washington, D.C. Public School</u> (New York, Teachers College, Columbia University, 1967), p. 171.

30. U.S. Congress, House of Representatives, Public Law 90-292, 90th Congress, H.R. 13042, April 22, 1968 and <u>D.C. Code</u>, Title 31.

31. "Who Runs the Schools?" <u>Washington Star</u>, 5 January 1968.

32. Ibid.

33. Hugh J. Scott, <u>The Superintendent's 120-Day Report</u> (Washington, D.C.: District of Columbia Public Schools, February 1971), pp. 22-23.

34. "Minutes of the Fourth (Stated) Meeting of the Board of Education", Washington, D.C., 17 February 1971, p. 31.

35. Ibid., pp. 31-32.

36. Irna Moore, "City's School Deficit Put at $5.9 Million", Washington Post, 20 January 1972. See also Confidential Memorandum to Dr. Hugh Scott from Pete T. Ohl, 11 January 1972.

38. Phil Hilts, "Deficit! School Officials Knew About Mess," Washington Daily News, 21 January 1972.

38. "Hahn May Take Budget from Schools," 21 January 1972.

39. William Delaney, "Scott, Tirana Clash on Crisis in School Funds", Washington Star, January 1972.

40. "Scott Retracts Threat to Quit," Washington Star, 2 February 1972.

41. Ibid.

42. Lawrence Feinberg, "Budget Staff Error for Schools Bared," Washington Post, 15 February 1972.

43. "Minutes of the Third (Stated Meeting of the Board of Education," Washington, D.C., 16 February 1972, pp. 36-41.

44. William Delaney, "School Cost Cuts," Washington Star, 9 May 1972.

45. Irna Moore, "City School Budget Cut by $4 Million," Washington Post, 13 June 1972.

46. "Minutes of the Second Session of the Seventeenth (Special) Meeting of the Board of Education," Washington, D.C., 19 July 1972, p. 25.

47. "Minutes of the Thirty-First (Special) Meeting of the Board of Education, Washington, D.C., 21 November 1972, pp. 12-13.

48. Transcript of the Thirty-Second (Stated) Meeting of the Board of Education," Washington, D.C., 19 December 1973, pp. 69-70.

49. Interview with Bardyl Tirana, D.C. Board of Education Member, Washington, D.C., 27 September 1977.

50. Interview with Charles Cassell, D.C. Board of Education Member, Washington, D.C., 5 October 1977.

51. Interview with Delores Pryde, D.C. Board of Education Member, Washington, D.C., 23 October 1977.

# CHAPTER IV

## AUTHORITY, FUNCTION, STRUCTURE

### Introduction

Superintendent-school board relationships are dynamic and complex and therefore cannot be examined in light of a single factor due to the many interdependent influential factors involved. This section attempts to analyze the impact of some internal factors on school superintendent-school board relations. The internal factors to be examined are: organizational structure, legal authority and function with emphasis on educational governance, and policy-making.

### Authority

The term "school board" is used in this study for the local school governmental body within the local school district. The term school board member signifies those persons who are appointed or elected to serve on the local school board.

#### Board authority

Complete control of the D.C. public schools is vested in an elected school board, consisting of eleven members.[1] Section 31-103 of the *D.C. Code* provides that the board:

> ...shall determine all questions of general policy relating to the schools, shall appoint the executive officers hereinafter provided for, define their duties, and direct expenditures... The Board shall

appoint all... employees provided for in this Charter.

The board is authorized to appoint a superintendent for a three-year term "who shall have the direction of and supervision in all matters pertaining to the instruction in all the schools under the Board of Education."[2]

The board is also authorized to "remove the superintendent at any time for adequate cause affecting his character and efficiency as superintendent."[3] Provision is made in the superintendent's contract for due-process protections against arbitrary board action, including notification and opportunity for a hearing when dismissal is considered.[4]

The superintendent is subject to the board's control and policy-making authority in all instances in the case of appointment, promotion, transfer, or dismissal of any...subordinate to the superintendent except where he has the delegated authority to take final action without prior board approval.

Finally, the board has control over the superintendent in the matter of direction and supervision of public school instruction.[5]

Duties of officers of the board as delineated in the Rules include a provision which relates to when the board has authority. It is important to call attention to this rule as it presented problems in superintendent-school board relations from time to time between 1973-75 as well as prior to this period as noted in the Passow Report. As quoted in the Rules, the section reads:

> The Members of the Board shall have authority only when acting as a Board legally in session. The Board shall not be bound in any way by any action or statement on the part of an individual Board member except

when such statement or action is in pursuance of specific instructions from the Board. Any Board member may attend committee meetings and enter into discussion, but shall not have a vote unless he is a member of the committee.[6]

Superintendent's authority

Appointment --

The superintendent is appointed for a term of three years by the board and may be removed at any time for adequate cause affecting his character and efficiency as superintendent by a majority vote of the full board.[7]

Authority --

The superintendent is the chief executive and administrative officer of the board. As such, the superintendent has all executive and administrative powers and duties in connection with the conduct of schools which are not required by law to be exercised directly by the board or some other officer. The board may delegate specific authority for the superintendent to act. In addition, the superintendent has the right to a seat on the board with the right to speak on all matters but not to vote. The superintendent, or his designee, may attend meetings of the board as well as committee meetings with the exception of the meeting when the appointment of the superintendent is being considered.[8]

Functions

Board functions

In addition to other purposes, the board determines questions of general policy relating to the schools. The board appoints all employees except as delegated to the superintendent. Further, the board defines their duties, and directs expenditures.[9] Another section of the

Rules that had implications later has to do with the attorney for the board. It reads: "When legal advice or services of Counsel are desired by the board (or the superintendent) upon matters relating to school affairs, application shall be made directly to the Corporation Counsel of the District of Columbia."[10]

Superintendent's functions

The superintendent may recommend new policy to the board or changes in existing policy. In this regard, the superintendent may inform the board of policy alternatives and their consequences. Pursuant to the establishment of policy by the board, the superintendent may provide the board with regular and timely information on his administration of board policy. Therefore, the superintendent has reserved for him, administrative initiative.[11]

Functions of the superintendent are (1) directing the administration of the school system, (2) being responsible for the progressive development and maintenance of an educational program designed to meet the needs of the community, (3) enforcing the Compulsory School Attendance Act, the Act to Regulate the Employment of Minors in the District, and other laws under the purview of the office of the superintendent, and (4) to recommend policies on organization, personnel, finance, instruction, school plant and so forth.[12]

## Structure

Composition of the board

The DCBOE is composed of eleven members elected on a non-partisan basis with three members elected at-large and one from each of the eight school election wards. The president and vice president are elected annually, by majority vote at the first meeting on or after the fourth Monday in January. Members receive compensation at a rate fixed by the District of Columbia Council.[13]

First elected DCBOE --

In 1968, President Lyndon B. Johnson signed P.L. 90-292 which created a locally elected school board.[14]

The Elected School Board Act established a rotating membership so that five of the eleven seats are held for one year only and once the rotation is in place, elections are held every four years. Therefore, new elections for the five seats were held in November 1969. The members on the first elected board who drew the one-year terms were Hobson, Sessions, Treanor, Rosenfield and Coates.

There were sixty persons who filed for election to the eleven seats on the first elected board of election. Of those sixty, three appointed school board members, Anita Ford Allen, Julius Hobson, Sr., and John A. Sessions, obtained seats on the elected board.[15]

The first meeting of the elected board of education was held in the Department of Commerce Auditorium on January 27, 1969. At the meeting James E. Coates was elected president and Anita Ford Allen was elected vice president. The following shows the breakdown of the eleven citizens elected as DCBOE members:

    Anita Ford Allen - At Large
    Muriel Alexander - Ward 4
    James E. Coates - Ward 8
    Edward Hancock - Ward 7
    Julius Hobson - At Large
    Nelson Roots - Ward 1
    Albert A. Rosenfield - Ward 3
    John A. Sessions - At Large
    Martha Swaim - Ward 6
    Mattie G. Taylor - Ward 5
    John H. Treanor, Jr. - Ward 2[16]

New officers were elected for the second year of operation for the elected board. At its first (organizational) meeting of 1970, Mrs. Anita Ford Allen was elected as president and Reverend James E. Coates was elected as vice president. Newly elected members to the board were Rev. James E. Coates, Mr. Charles I. Cassell, Mr. Albert A. Rosenfield, Mr. Bardyl R. Tirana, and Mrs. Evie M. Washington.[17] Allen and Coates were elected again in 1971.[18]

Before 1971 was out, Anita Allen (at-large member) resigned and her replacement was delayed until after the run-off election on November 23, 1971. Hancock was elected vice president to fill the unexpired term caused by the vice president, James Coates assuming the presidency until noon on January 24, 1972, by a vote of five to two.[19]

In the organizational meeting in January 1972, Marion Barry, Jr. was elected president and Mattie G. Taylor was elected vice president.[20]

Filling vacancies --

In 1968, the provisions for filling a vacancy stated that in the case of a vacancy in the office of the president, the vice president would assume the presidency until the next regular election date for officers. In the case of a vacancy in the office of vice president, the board, at its next stated meeting or at any special meeting called, would elect by majority vote of the full board a vice president to serve for the balance of the term of office.[21]

Vacancies occurring in board membership were filled by appointment until the unexpired term of the office ended. Some members preferred filling vacancies by a special election rather than by appointment by board members. Tirana, for one, in a minority report, stated that witnesses at a public hearing testified that, because of the importance of elections to the District, the vacancy should be filled by a special election, especially since the board of education was the only elected body in town at that time. An alternative suggestion was that the vacancy be filled by two-thirds of the members of the board. The board settled on appointment by a majority vote of those members present and voting.[22]

The DCBOE did have to fill a vacancy in 1973 when Delores E. Pryde, representative in Ward 7, resigned. Five members of the board of education met in executive session on October 16, 1973 for the purpose of accepting the resignation of Mrs. Pryde and discussing the process for filling the Ward 7 vacancy. Those attending the meeting were Marion Barry, Jr., president, Martha S. Swaim, vice president, Rev. Raymond B. Kemp, Hilda Howland M. Mason, and Albert A. Rosenfield. Also attending were representatives of the D.C. Board of Elections and the D.C. Corporation Counsel's office. The group's recommendation that the board of elections conduct a public election to fill the vacancy in Ward 7 was protested by a member of the Ward 7 community who felt that the board should follow its rule to appoint a member of the Ward 7 community to the vacant seat.

Swaim and Kemp, in particular, stated that it was not the intention of the five people to disregard board rules but only to be prepared with an answer from the board of elections in case the constituents of Ward 7 requested an election. The representative from the board of elections present indicated that the board of elections could not respond to the request to hold an election.[23]

Subsequently, on December 4, 1973, Virginia Morris was appointed as the representative to fill the Ward 7 vacancy after two tie votes of 5-5 and a third unanimous vote.[24] Following Marion Barry's resignation, she assumed the role of president of the board of education on July 15, 1974. At the same time, Hobson was elected vice president.[25]

Committee structure

In 1967 the board operated through nine standing committees: (1) Finance, (2) Rules, (3) Legislation, (4) Health and Special Education Services, (5) Complaints Appeals and Employee Relations, (6) District of Columbia Teachers College, (7) Buildings, Grounds and Equipment (8) Student activities, and (9) Personnel. These committees were designated by the president of the board, and board rules spell out the duties of each of the committees. Both the <u>Strayer Report</u> and the <u>Passow Report</u> urged the abolition of standing committees as being obsolete, overlapping in responsibilities, causing repetitive discussion and confusion.[26]

Committees of the D.C. board of education are of two kinds, Ad Hoc and Special or Standing Committees. In either case the president appointed or provided for the election of members to the two types of committees. In recent years, the president of the board of education appoints members to committees.[27]

The following committees were in operation during 1969: Committee of The Whole on Personnel; Ad Hoc Committee on Appeals and Grievances; Committee on Business Analysis of the Operation of the School System; Committee on Dress Code; Committee on Legal Powers; Committee to Serve as Liaison with Boards of Higher Education; Committee for Liaison with Metropolitan Area Boards of Education; Rules Committee; Committee on Safety; and Committee on Teacher Salary Legislation.[28]

At the meeting of February 18, 1970, ten ad hoc committees were set up by President Allen, upon the approval of the board. The committees for 1970-71 were as follows: Appeals and Grievances; Budget and Finance, Career Development Opportunities, Community School Projects, Curriculum and Instruction, Employee Relations, Legislation and Intergovernment, Rules and Administration, School Facilities and Maintenance, and

Student Activities.[29]

In 1971-72 problems with how the president of the D.C. board of education handled the matter of assignment to committees presented a problem for at least one board member. Mr. Cassell objected to President Allen's removal from the School Facilities and Maintenance Committee, formerly known as the Buildings and Grounds Committee, the responsibilities for monitoring the construction and maintenance programs of the school system. He stated that traditionally these were the responsibilities of the committee. He also resented that this action was taken without consultation with him or any rationale given him, as chairman of the defunct committee. Mr. Cassell's motion to have the president restore to his committee its responsibilities to monitor the construction and maintenance program was lost.[30]

The following information shows the list of school board committee assignments made by Marion Barry in 1974. The Education Program, chaired by Hilda Mason, had two subcommittees: Early Childhood to Secondary Education, chaired by Virginia Morris with Barbara Simmons serving as a member, and Adult Education, Career Development and Special Education, with Therman Evans as chairman; members were Mattie Taylor and William Treanor. The Committee on School Finance, chaired by Martha Swaim was divided into two subcommittees: Federal Grants with Julius Hobson, Jr. as chairman, Hilda Mason and Virginia Morris; Capital Improvements Budget with Raymond Kemp as chairman, and Therman Evans. Student Services and Community Involvement had Julius Hobson, Jr. as chairman with Therman Evans, Raymond Kemp and Hilda Mason.

Employee Relations, Personnel Policies and Appeals, and Grievances was chaired by Virginia Morris with Julius Hobson, Jr., Raymond Kemp, Barbara Simmons and Mattie Taylor. Administrative Services had Albert Rosenfield as chairman with Barbara Simmons and William Treanor. Board

Operations, Rules and Policies consisted of William Treanor as chairman, Martha Swaim and Mattie Taylor. External Affairs which dealt with formal agencies of government was chaired by Marion Barry with Therman Evans, Barbara Simmons and Martha Swaim.[31] Thus, we note seven major committees and four subcommittees, none of which were chaired by board members Mattie Taylor and Barbara Simmons, both of whom publicly expressed contempt for Barry's authoritarian and ofttimes undemocratic procedures as board president.[32] Particularly note that Barry appointed himself chairperson of a committee while leaving two members of the board without a chairmanship.

Interestingly, Rosenfield and Taylor questioned the legality of the committees being formed without input and approval of board members. Furthermore, Rosenfield questioned the authority of Barry to appoint himself as chairperson of a committee since under the Rules of the board of education the president is an ex-officio member of all committees. More importantly, Rosenfield protested the type of committees formed in lieu of the fact that Mrs. Sizemore had recommended the type of committees with which she could function. Barry's committees were in opposition to her recommendations.[33]

Under Virginia Morris who served as DCBOE president after Barry resigned, during the superintendency of Barbara Sizemore, the following committees were operative: The Committee of the Whole on Personnel, the Committee on Educational Programs, the Committee on Adult Education and Career Development, the Committee on School Finance, the Committee on Capital Improvements, the Committee on Federal Grants, the Committee on Student Service and Community Involvement, the Committee on Employee Relations, Personal Policies and Appeals, and Grievances, the Committee on Board Operations, Rules, Policies and Legislation, the Committee on Nutrition, Physical Fitness and Health, and the Committee on Special Education.

Virginia Morris was chairperson of the Committee of the Whole on Personnel with Carol Schwartz and Julius Hobson, Jr. as members. Their duties included (1) evaluation of the performance of the superintendent and consideration of the personnel recommendations, submitted by the superintendent as regards such actions as permanent tenure, filling of positions and retirements. The subcommittee of the Committee of the Whole on Personnel was known as the Subcommittee on Internal Board Staff; it dealt with evaluating the executive secretary, operations and organization of the board office, board office resource needs and staff performance, conduct and organization.

The chairperson of the Committee on Educational Programs was Hilda Howland M. Mason with Barbara Lett Simmons, Carol Schwartz, Elizabeth Kane, and William Treanor as members. Their duties included concerns with curriculum from early childhood to secondary education in terms of what was taught and how it was taught. This committee also monitored the implementation of Hobson v Hansen.

The Committee on Adult Education and Career Development was chaired by Barbara Lett Simmons with William Treanor and Bettie Benjamin as members. Basically, this committee dealt with a review of trends in these fields, the number of persons requiring education in these fields and the adequacy of programs in the areas.

Julius Hobson, Jr. was chairperson of the Committee on School Finance. His committee members were Raymond B. Kemp, Hilda Howland M. Mason, Elizabeth Kane and John Warren. Generally, this committee was responsible for the D.C. school budget, non-appropriated federal funds, and private grants. The group also dealt with policies relating to funds raised in school activities. Included in the membership of this committee were also the Federal Grants and Capital Improvements Committee members.

The Committee on Capital Improvements was composed of Raymond B. Kemp as chairperson and Therman Evans, Elizabeth Kane and Bettie Benjamin as members. The interest of this committee was in preparing recommendations for the annual budget in terms of sites, facilities, and equipment.

Elizabeth Kane was chairperson of the Committee on Federal Grants with John Warren and William Treanor as members. This committee was concerned with all aspects of the operation and program management of school system financed by federal grant funds, including budgets, review of program proposals, and the administration of federal funds.

The Committee on Student Services and Community Involvement was chaired by John E. Warren; Hilda Howland Mason and Raymond B. Kemp were members. The concern of this committee was the operations of Pupil Personnel Services, employment opportunities, and the Office of Student Affairs.

Bettie Benjamin was chairperson of the Committee on Employee Relations, Personnel Policies and Appeals, and Grievances. Along with Barbara Lett Simmons, Julius Hobson, Jr., John Warren and Carol Schwartz, this committee dealt with matters relating to collective bargaining, establishing employee-management guidelines, employee-management contracts, reviewing proposed and existing personnel policies and practices and consideration of appeals and grievances affecting the employees of the board which had not been satisfactorily handled by school officers.

The Committee on Board Operations, Rules, Policies and Legislation was chaired by William Treanor, with Hilda Howland M. Mason and Bettie Benjamin as members. Their primary concern was with the legal framework of operation for the school system, and overseeing the implementation of the court decrees.

Therman E. Evans chaired the Committee on Nutrition, Physical Fitness, and Health. Working with him were Carol Schwartz and John Warren as members. Their job was to handle all aspects of the public school system pertaining to the health, physical development, athletic programs and well being of all students. Nutrition and the efficient operation of the Division of Food Services, also came under the jurisdiction of this committee.

There was also a Committee on Special Education under the chairmanship of Carol Schwartz with Hilda Howland M. Mason, Raymond B. Kemp and Therman E. Evans as members. In addition to its other duties, this committee was concerned with monitoring the school system's compliance with Mills v Board of Education, et al.[34]

The two major committees were the Committee on Budget and Finance, which was usually chaired by the Vice president, and the Committee on Board Operations, Legislation and Procedures. Notably, these committees were generally chaired by whites or inexperienced Blacks who had to rely heavily on a white finance administrator as in the case of Julius Hobson, Jr. Significantly, he called the Black Deputy Superintendent of Management, James Williams, on the carpet and by-passed his authority by reaching down to Williams' subordinate Edward Winner for finance information to trip Williams up. This can be noted in the report of Case 3 - Budget/Management Problems analyzed in Chapter VIII. Thus we have the following chairpersons dealing directly with financial matters:

    Budget and Finance
        Coates, Black, 1970 under Allen
        with Swaim as Vice-Chairperson
        Swaim, white, 1974, under Barry
        Hobson, Jr., Black, 1975, under Morris

*School Facilities and Maintenance
   Cassell, Black, 1970, under Allen

*Changed to Capital Improvements
   Kemp, white, 1974, under Barry
   Kemp, white, 1975, under Morris

Federal Grants
   Hobson, Jr., Black, 1974, under Barry
   Kane, white, 1975, under Morris

Board members chairing the Committee on Board Operations, Legislation and Procedures, under various titles are as follows:

   Rosenfield, white, 1970, under Allen
   Treanor, white, 1974, under Barry
   Treanor, white, 1975, under Morris

Interestingly, there were only four whites on the eleven-member elected school board in 1975 when three of the four were chairpersons of major committees.

Except for the Committee on Student Services and Committee Involvement, few Blacks held committee chairmanships with a base for influence and power. Therefore, this is a situation where we have a majority Black school board with white members in control of policy-making since how money is used determines what programs get funded which in turn becomes the policy of school system.

Superintendent Sizemore was represented by her key administrators in board committee meetings. Additionally, committee reports were reviewed prior to board of education meetings and a response prepared for submission to the board.

Hugh Scott, one of the former superintendents of the District schools, felt the DCBOE invaded administrative zones. He remarked in this connection, "The Board tries to run the school system in two ways. One is through the committee structure.... The other thing is direct calls to people, 'I want this report, this information.'"[35]

Generally, business came to the board meeting through the committee agenda, so any time the superintendent submitted any proposal or recommendation, it went to a committee. If the material was submitted to the board directly, the president would give it to a committee. The committee would then hold a meeting and the administration was summoned to the meeting. At that point, matters were discussed and board committees would make recommendations to the board. Then the board would act on the committee's recommendation. The board very rarely acted on a superintendent's recommendation. In fact, there had to be a two-thirds vote in favor of waivering the rules to receive the recommendations directly from the superintendent at the board meeting.

In responding to the question: What procedure did the DCBOE use to execute its function?, board members discussed the following: (1) the committee structure, (2) how committees were set up, (3) how chairpersons were selected, (4) the majority vote process, (5) attempts to arrive at consensus, and (6) trade-offs made for votes on specific issues.

From the answers provided this interviewer, there seemed to be no set policy for arriving at decisions. For example, "...there was a Committee of the Whole on a variety of things especially around superintendent selection time," explained Charles Cassell in reference to Anita Allen's administration. He said further, "There were many, many private meetings of the board, Executive Sessions. At an Executive Session we couldn't take any action that would become policy because the law requires that has to be done in public, but you could conduct a full scale meeting and then do the same thing in public again and make your action policy."[36] Tirana felt that the committee structure was worthless. He said in his interview, "I don't think the committee structure was worth the power to blow it up. Again, the committee structure was a reflection of the Board trying to do too much. The Board is out there to run the school system....[37]

An especially vivid explanation is given by Mattie Taylor who spoke about the committee structure and the political maneuvering of board members during Marion Barry's administration. Mrs. Taylor commented as follows:

> ...quite often things were decided between a certain power structure group and when they went to committee it was a formality of running it through committees so you could get it formally before the board, but the real decisions had already been made in the power structure along the lines of the persons I just gave you....
>
> Committee chairmanships were put in the hands of the people who could deliver what the power group wanted delivered. And if you are thinking that you didn't get any chairmanship if you were not in the in-crowd, you are exactly right.... If you go back and look at the Committee line up then all the major decisions affecting money and what not, were placed in the hands of people who were in the in-crowd.[38]

Julius Hobson, Jr. agreed that persons who did not vote for the president, received no chairmanship of a committee when Barry was president of the board.[39] Hobson, Jr. also explained how board members negotiated with each other to arrive at a consensus during Marion Barry's and Virginia Morris' administrations:

> Barry would call people up and try to get them to come to a consensus on what he thought was an important issue....

> The power rested in anyone who took the time to get six votes to do anything....You look at the issue. You start off by trying to figure out where each person stands on this particular issue, and you look at the pros and the cons of those people. You go to the pros first, who you think will back it and you say, look we've got such and such and will you support it. You try to lock them in early. Then you deal with the marginals to see if you can sway them. If you know somebody is totally opposed, you don't even talk to them.... It's time-consuming though.
>
> Board members use to do this - talking to people and asking will you support me on this issue. And then you have your trade-offs like in the Ballou (Math-Science High School) situation. And finally, the compromise was, I support Ballou if you will support pre-school. That was with Kane and Mason. And that was the only way that go through that night.40

Taylor became even more specific in terms of DCBOE operations and noted a crucial change in procedure instituted by Marion Barry when he became president. She felt that the new procedure was introduced as a mechanism for controlling any power the superintendent may have. She put the matter squarely:

> With the Anita board though, the superintendent would present his policies and procedures and issues directly to the board. And then the board would receive them and assign them to a committee... if it was not prepared to act on them....
>
> But Barry turned that around to make the superintendent bring everything through the board committees... for greater control over the superintendent and to sort of emasculate the office of superintendent.

In other words they had a mechanism whereby the superintendent gave all the reports to the Executive Secretary who gave them to the President who assigned them to a committee, and the Superintendent's Report got brought up through committee back to the board....[41]

Hobson Jr. was also critical about how Superintendent Sizemore was virtually excluded from participating in the decision-making process during Virginia Morris' administration of the board. He noted that:

Sizemore use to complain, and I agree that the superintendent comes to the meetings, reads the retirement, reads liquor licenses, tuition exemptions and unless there's a major proposal, shuts up and the board members fight for the rest of the night. That's got to change...I don't think it's going to change because board members are politicians and are not going to give up that opportunity for public display.[42]

Simmons, especially, had problems with the way executive sessions were used by Morris to force consensus. In this connection her succinct conclusion was that:

...executive sessions were not always taped ...the executive sessions, under the presidency of Mrs. Morris were probably more cloak and dagger than the executive sessions under any other president that I have experienced.

...these were also brainwashing sessions where you try to convince people when you don't have to be responsible for what you say...and felt quite comfortable that they were behind closed doors and could hide.

Technically, the only appropriate time for executive sessions was when we were talking

about personnel issues, when we were
talking about negotiation strategies with
any of the unions with whom we have contracts,
and whenever we were dealing with exceedingly
sensitive matters in terms of perhaps another
city agency, like the Mayor and the City
Council... But...I guess in the final analysis that is all of the sessions Mrs. Morris
had.... The first one, personnel, being
the major reason, 'cause she wanted to deal
with Superintendent Sizemore....[43]

Hobson, Jr. also believed that the Morris board functioned on whim:

I think a lot of board members then and now
make decisions on whims; make decisions on
what they conceive as their own political
well being. The closing of school buildings
is your best example. Everybody recognizes
that we need to close school buildings to
save money but don't close any buildings in
my ward....

Budget - when we had money to move around
which was the first year (1974) I was on the
board, was another time that people made
decisions on whims. It was the FY76 budget
we were working on...I was trying to get all
the money for Ballou's Math-Science High
School so that it could start off with everything that it needed. I was forced to make
compromises with the board on pre-school.
Kane was the leader. Kane has children in
the public schools. I talked to Treanor and
Mason. We had reached a compromise the night
before...and when I gaveled that meeting
open, I got a bomb, which not only happened
to me, it happened all the time. People
promised to deal with issues in a certain
fashion, and when it comes time to raise
hands they go the other way. Who can explain
it? But it happens. Board members are

> politicians...and must look to deal with what their constituencies want..the pre-school people tended to block up everything because they had more votes on the committee.[44]

In summing up board operations during the presidencies of Morris (1975) and Evans (1976), Warren described his perceptions of the concessions made due to political plays, thusly:

> Chairpersons on this board have been appointed at the whim of the board president. Board jurisdictions in terms of areas of responsibility under committees have changed with board presidents. Some have been left as shells. At one time, every board member had a committee--which was ridiculous. Then it was reduced and consolidated. And so you have a situation where a board member no long functions based on his competency but based on politics....I took the Committee on Capital Improvements with no records whatsoever left to me and made...a number of efforts to really shake up the system. In the final analysis, at the end of my first year...I was removed from that office. It obviously had nothing to do with abilities based on what had been done, but it was a part of the agreement made by white members of the board, in part, as a price for reelecting the president that in addition to whatever else he gave them, he had to promise to remove me from Capital Improvements so he did that. So that was a good example of politics being placed above educational programs or competency in a given area....[45]

In reviewing the decision-making process, Therman Evans, president of the board, but who also served under Virginia Morris, had the following to say:

> A great deal of action that the board takes
> in fact most of the action(s) that the
> board takes comes from the administration...
> The administration is...asked to look at an
> idea with policy making in mind. It gets
> researched and introduced to the relevant
> committee. Then the relevant committee dis-
> cusses it with the administration and board
> members present, then it comes to us. Some-
> times the administration wants to see a
> policy in a particular area and will develop
> the research around that suggested or reccom-
> mended policy present it to the committee
> structure then it comes to the board. Most
> policy action that the board takes comes
> from...the administration....[46]

Although administrators sit on the committees, they also testify before the committees. That is, the board committees operate in a similar fashion to the way the congressional committees operate. In fact, the board of education is a mimic of the Congress just as the city council is a mimic of the congressional structure. Operational proce- dures are similar. Both the city government and the school board are subject to civil service rules and regulations with the exception of the teachers in terms of the Teacher Salary Act (TSA). Otherwise, they have the same personnel regula- tions. Actually, the board of education is an arm of the city government which is, in turn, an arm of the federal government.

The way in which the committees operate place the administrators in a "third degree" rather than a cooperative position. This is demeaning and negates development of good will.

It should also be clear that trade-offs are made and negotiations take place, that is, some board members bargain not just for issues to satisfy their constituents' needs like spaces in the D.C. Youth Orchestra in the case of Julius Hobson, Jr.,[47] but also perhaps, as conjectured by Warren, for issues that satisfy their own needs.[48]

Notably, Marion Barry was very concerned about obtaining consensus and diligently spoke to board members individually by phone and collectively in committee meetings in an effort to arrive at this point prior to the monthly public meetings. Likewise Julius Hobson, Jr., vice-president of the Morris school board, spent a great deal of time conversing with fellow board members.[49]

Taylor alluded to the machinations of cliques and their maneuvers to push through their programs as did Hobson, Jr.[50] Cassell noted that there were often conflicts in regard to issues handled by the Committee of the Whole on Personnel.[51]

It can also be noted that some board members felt that the school board became more political when Marion Barry became president and remained so during Morris' presidency.[52]

The D.C. boards of education operated with similar committees under Allen, Barry and Morris. During Evans' administration, changes were made and committees were combined, reducing them in number to five or six with an increase in the size of the committee. Hence, each board member no longer chaired a committee. Those without a committee served as vice-chairpersons.53

Board of education staff

In 1967, the DCBOE had virtually no supporting staff to provide it with the quantity and quality of information necessary to make policy decisions. Generally, the board heard the school superintendent's proposals and supportive information, asked some questions, exchanged some points of view, and then took a vote. For this reason, the <u>Passow Report</u> recommended that the board staff be enlarged to include research assistants or aides and additional secretarial staff assigned to the board rather than to individual board members.[54]

At the October 20, 1970 meeting of the board of education, objections to the increased board staff were raised by some board members. This issue was of particular concern to Mattie Taylor who questioned the need for two research assistants, GS-12, to be funded out of Title V which she felt could be better used for positions on the superintendent's staff. Her objection was underlined by Superintendent Scott's stated position that there was no substitute for a superintendent and that directions coming from any research assistants to the board which required reports from his staff were not to be adhered to unless the superintendent approved it. Notwithstanding these objections, the board voted its approval of additional board staff.[55]

In 1972, the DCBOE approved a plan to reorganize the board office to provide three basic services: (1) Board Operations; (2) Board Member Support; and (3) Planning Research. The plan as explained by Mattie Taylor, chairperson of the Committee on Internal Board Affairs could be implemented with existing budget and staff resources and FY73 budget projections, if realized, would assure complete implementation. Therefore, the DCBOE proposed a staff with a GS-4 Clerk Typist, GS-3 Clerk Typist, a special assistant to the president, a While Actually Employed (WAE)* employee in the area of planning research, an assistant stenotype reporter, and an executive secretary.[56]

On December 6, 1973, the board approved the appointment of David A. Splitt as special assistant (general counsel) to the board of education.[57]

---

*WAE (While Actually Employed) indicates payment for time actually worked as in the case of part-time employees.

## Superintendent's staff -- 1973-75

Superintendent Barbara A. Sizemore and her key administrators administered the D.C. public school system between 1973-75. In this section of this report, a selected number of key administrators is described briefly. Included also are areas of administrative responsibility within the system, biographical background, and relationship with each other.

### Executive staff --

Kenneth Haskins, a caseworker and administrator at the Wiltwyck School for Boys in New York from 1951 to 1961, became principal of the Morgan Community School in Washington, D.C. in 1967 where he served until 1969. During this time, Hilda Mason, who later became a school board member, was his vice principal. In 1973, he was appointed vice superintendent of the DCPS by Superintendent Barbara A. Sizemore.[58]

In 1974, Haskins found himself caught in the middle of an argument between two friends, Sizemore and Mason on the issue of how the DCPS should be decentralized. He supported Mason in her move to obtain Meyer Foundation funds to support her Citizen's Plan for Decentralization. Fearing he had lost the support of the superintendent, Haskins resigned effective September 1974.

Floretta Dukes McKenzie was a teacher and counselor in Washington, D.C. and Baltimore, Maryland from 1957 to 1967. In 1967 she became the director of Opportunity Project for Education Now in Washington, D.C. where she served until 1969. From 1969-71, McKenzie was executive assistant to the superintendent in charge of secondary schools and became acting deputy superintendent for instruction in March 1972, serving until July 1972. Subsequent to that position, she was special assistant to the superintendent for administration of School Units and Educational

Programs from July 1972 to February 1973. In February 1973, Floretta McKenzie became deputy superintendent, Educational Programs and Services, where she served until July 1973 when she became acting superintendent of schools from July 1 to October 1, 1973. She was appointed deputy superintendent, Educational Programs and Services, by Superintendent Sizemore, and resigned effective July 12, 1974.

James L. Williams held several teaching and administrative positions in the Chicago public schools from 1958-68 and from 1970-73. During that time he became the director of administrative services, Chicago Board of Education, Department of Government, where he worked with a budget of over two million dollars. At Mrs. Sizemore's request, he left that position and was appointed deputy superintendent for Management Services in the Washington, D.C. public school system.

Luther Elliott, Jr. worked as assistant to the director, State Office of Economic Opportunity, Office of the Governor of Oklahoma, Oklahoma City, Oklahoma, from 1965 to 1967. During 1967-72, Mr. Elliott worked as a project developer and manager, Serial Development Corporation in Washington, D.C. Subsequently, he was director, Education Policy and Information Center, at the National Urban League in D.C. and in 1972, Elliott became director, Government Relations, A Better Chance, Inc., Washington, D.C. In 1973 he was appointed an executive assistant under Superintendent Sizemore.

### Selected members of the administrative team --

In July 1974, six interim regional superintendents were appointed by Superintendent Sizemore who formed a part of the administrative team along with executive staff members. These six regional superintendents were: Mr. William Rice, Region I; Dr. Dorothy Johnson, Region II; Mr. Napoleon Lewis, Region III; Dr. Margaret Labat,

Region IV; Mr. Gilbert A. Diggs, Region V; and Dr. Gary Freeman, Region VI.

Mrs. Sizemore appointed Napoleon Lewis regional superintendent of Region III on July 1, 1974, and he remained in that position until July 1, 1977. Prior to this appointment, Mr. Lewis was a junior high school mathematics teacher and then an assistant principal at Elliot Junior High, 1963-64, at Douglass from 1964-67, at Langley from 1967-68, and then at Kelly Miller. He was acting principal at both Kelly Miller and Douglass. Then he was appointed principal at Kelly Miller. From there he became principal at Woodson Senior High School which he described as his greatest experience. His principalship at Woodson was from 1972 until 1974 when he was appointed regional superintendent. When he left the District, Mr. Lewis served as an administrative assistant to the East Oak Cliff Sub District in Dallas, Texas.

In September 1954, Dr. Margaret Labat was appointed as a teacher at the Langley Junior High School just prior to the desegregation effort. She became an assistant principal in 1961 at Paul Junior High School located in upper northwest Washington. At the time she was assigned, the population was approximately 98 percent Jewish and 2 percent Black. She served in that position as the first Black administrator at the school and remained there for five years. In December 1965, Dr. Labat was appointed principal at Garnett Patterson Junior High School. Subsequent to that position, she took a leave of absence to complete her doctorate and worked at Fordham University. When she returned to D.C. in 1973, she resumed her position of principal at Garnett Patterson. In March 1974, Dr. Labat accepted a position of director of staff development under Superintendent Sizemore. Later she was appointed to the Decentralization Committee which was to implement the decentralization process and as of July 1974, she was selected by the superintendent as regional superintendent for

Region IV, which encompassed Dunbar High School and Eastern High School. The understanding was that this would be an interim position until such time that the board approved the superintendent's 120 Day Report. When she left the District, Dr. Labat was superintendent of the Evanston Township High School District, in Illinois, having been appointed to that position on January 10, 1977.[59]

William Rice first became a city school principal in 1960. In 1969 he was appointed assistant superintendent and served in this capacity for nine years. Later, in 1974, he served as regional superintendent in Region I located in Anacostia until his retirement in 1977. Prior to his administrative experience, Mr. Rice served as a high school teacher. In his discussion of the issue of the DCBOE's involvement in administration, Rice compares the three boards under which he served -- the Allen board, the Barry board, and the Morris board -- and indicates that the Allen board was the least interfering and the Morris board the most interfering. He attributes the latter to the fact that the board president felt complimented that someone said she had administrative ability, as she told him on one occasion.[60]

Gary Freeman became a teacher in the D.C. public school system in 1955 where he taught special education for four and a half years and physical education for the same period of time before he became an administrator in the system. In 1969 he became an assistant to the assistant superintendent for Pupil Personnel Services. Later, he served as the assistant superintendent for Personnel Services before being appointed by Superintendent Sizemore as regional superintendent in Region VI.

Vincent E. Reed was born March 1, 1928, in St. Louis, Missouri, where he attended the public schools. He also attended Iowa University, West Virginia State College, and Howard University where he received the master's degree.

In 1956, Reed joined the D.C. public school system as a teacher of industrial arts, mathematics and family living at Jefferson Junior High School. He was appointed counselor at Cardozo High School and then was transferred to Anacostia High School as counselor and ninth grade administrator. Soon he returned to Jefferson Junior High School as a counselor and was promoted in July 1964 to assistant director of the Manpower Development Training Program for the D.C. public schools. From this assignment he went on to become assistant principal of Dunbar High School, then to Woodrow Wilson High School as assistant principal, and later served as principal. In 1969, Reed was promoted to assistant superintendent of Personnel and later to head of the first Security Office until 1971 when he became assistant superintendent of Secondary Schools. When Mrs. Sizemore created the Office of State Administration in 1973, Reed served as associate superintendent in that office.

In October 1975, Reed was appointed by the DCBOE to serve as acting superintendent of the D.C. public schools and on March 17, 1976, he became superintendent of the D.C. public school system.

Board meetings

The board holds three kinds of meetings: stated, special and community. Stated meetings are held monthly during the school year and others as necessary. At these meetings the board acts on proposals, resolutions, or other items presented by the superintendent of schools, members of the board, or citizens of the community. The meetings are open to the public except closed meetings which may be held to deal with appointment, promotion, demotion, suspension, transfer, or termination. Further, the board may close to the public any meeting (or part) dealing with other matters as long as no final policy decision is made. By majority vote of all members, the board may hold additional meetings for persons or organizations desiring to be heard. These meetings must be scheduled far enough in advance to allow for public participation.

Special meetings are called by the president or in response to a written request by at least three members of the board. Written or verbal notice must be given board members by the secretary at least 48 hours before the special meeting. Emergency matters may be considered in special meetings called upon shorter notice. The public must be notified of the time and subject of the meeting through the media or by written notice to persons and organizations on the mailing list, if time permits.

Community meetings are held on a stated schedule or as deemed appropriate by the board. Generally, these are held once a month in various sections of the city. The purpose of these meetings is to hear from persons who desire to address the board.

Public hearings are held by the board or a committee of the board on policy questions relating to the public school system. The board must approve the hearing date before it is fixed.[61]

In 1968 concern was expressed by Dr. Euphemia Haynes, who felt the actions of the board, which is the business of the public, should be handled in public with the exception of closed sessions on personnel matters. She said: "To hold closed meetings is a very, very dangerous thing...."[62]

In 1970 in connection with a motion to hold a closed conference on priorities of the board and the selection of a superintendent, Mrs. Taylor also expressed concern about the increasing number of closed meetings. In this regard, she moved that the conference be open; it lost with three members voting Yes and seven members voting No.[63]

Table 5 shows that there were nineteen closed sessions held in 1969, ten held in 1970, eight held in 1971, and thirteen held in 1972; between 1973 and 1975 from Superintendent Sizemore's selection and termination, approximately twenty-four closed sessions were held. Interestingly, other closed sessions reportedly were held as pointed out by board members Warren and Simmons, in particular, when plans were laid for firing Superintendent Sizemore (around November 20, 1974) and during April and May of 1975 after the African Heritage Studies Association speech as subsequent discussions will reveal.

Special emphasis was placed on the fact that the D.C. Board of Education uses the committee system in carrying out its responsibilities, the results of which are brought to public light at board meetings. At this juncture, the concern expressed by board members Haynes and Taylor regarding closed sessions was noted. Haynes' concern was highlighted because she revealed very clearly the problem as she saw it. From this observation, then, one can infer that one assumed deficiency of closed meetings is that the holding of too many secret sessions by a public body, whose actions are the business of the public, is felt to be dangerous by some. The act of secrecy could easily be construed to mean that the board is acting in an outlaw fashion, and wishes to keep its actions outside of the scrutiny of the public which elected it as the body to represent the public's interest rather than each board member's own individual interest. Evidence of the significance of the concern, as expressed by some board members, is clearly illuminated as we focus in on the processes used to arrive at certain board decisions.

TABLE 5

D.C. BOARD OF EDUCATION CLOSED (EXECUTIVE) MEETINGS, 1969-1978

| Date | Subject of Discussion |
|---|---|
| **1969** | |
| 3/25/69 | Closed |
| 3/27/69 | Closed |
| 4/17/69 | Closed |
| 7/30/69 | Confidential |
| 8/11/69 | Conference with Superintendent (no reporter) |
| 8/14/69 | Task Force on Desegregation Committee (no reporter) |
| 8/25/69 | Briefing on Operations (no reporter) |
| 8/26/69 | Conference (no reporter) |
| 8/27/69 | Conference (no reporter) |
| 9/3/69 | Conference (no reporter) |
| 9/15/69 | Special Projects (no reporter) |
| 9/16/69 | Committee of the Whole on Personnel (no reporter) |
| 9/18/69 | Committee on Legislation (no reporter, no tapes) |
| 9/18/69 | Conference Administration & Teachers Union (no reporter, no tapes) |
| 9/25/69 | Committee Liaison with Board of Higher Education (no reporter) |
| 9/25/69 | Metro Area Boards of Education (no reporter) |
| 9/30/69 | Committee on Rules (no reporter) |
| 10/6/69 | Closed conference |
| 10/24/69 | Closed conference - 1970 Operation Budget |
| **1970** | |
| 1/8/70 | Committee of the Whole on Personnel |
| 1/12/70 | Conference on Safety (Closed) |
| 1/19/70 | Conference on Safety (Closed) |
| 1/20/70 | Committee of the Whole (Closed) |
| 1/28/70 | Closed Conference of Board |
| 2/12/70 | Committee on Budget (Closed) |
| 3/1/70 | Closed conference of Committee on School Facilities and Maintenance |
| 3/13/70 | Committee on Curriculum & Instruction (Closed) |
| 3/31/70 | Closed on Budget |
| 7/25/70 | Executive Session - Committee on Superintendent Selection |
| **1971** | |
| 1/15/71 | Closed |
| 4/29/71 | Closed, Student Activities |
| 4/29/71 | Employee Relations |
| 6/4/71 | Executive Session on Wright Decree |
| 6/24/71 | Superintendent Board Conference |
| 7/2/71 | Executive Session - Committee on Employee Relations |
| 8/11/71 | Executive Session |
| 9/2/71 | Closed Conference on Teacher Reassignment |
| **1972** | |
| 1/26/72 | Closed |
| 2/28/72 | Closed on Financial Management |
| 2/25/72 | Employee Relations |
| 6/7/72 | Closed Conference on Budget |
| 6/27/72 | Committee on Employee Relations (Closed) |

| Date | Subject of Discussion |
|---|---|

### 1972 (continued)

| | |
|---|---|
| 9/18/72 | Closed Conference with Mayor |
| 9/21/72 | Closed Conference Board, Principals and Superintendent |
| 9/21/72 | Closed Conference |
| 9/22/72 | Closed Conference |
| 9/24/72 | Closed Conference |
| 11/10/72 | Closed Conference |
| 12/1/72 | Closed Conference |
| 12/4/72 | Closed Conference |

### 1973

| | |
|---|---|
| 7/24/73 | Closed - Superintendent Selection Committee |
| 8/6/73 | Executive Session on Selection |
| 10/16/73 | Executive Session |
| 12/3/73 | Executive Session to receive recommendation for Ward VII Vacancy |
| 12/10/73 | Executive Session |
| 12/19/73 | Closed Conference |

### 1974

| | |
|---|---|
| 2/21/74 | Executive Session |
| | Board-Superintendent Washington Teachers Union (WTU) Contract |
| 3/6/74 | Executive Session regarding Negotiations |
| 3/27/74 | Executive Session on 120 Day Report |
| 3/29/74 | Emergency Executive Session |
| 5/3/74 | Emergency Session ESEA |
| 5/29/74 | Closed Conference ESEA |
| 7/25/74 | Executive Session |
| 10/1/74 | Executive Session |
| 12/11/74 | Board Conference with Superintendent -- 6:30 pm - 3:30 am |

### 1975

| | |
|---|---|
| 1/23/75 | Executive Session - WTU Contract |
| 2/28/75 | Executive Session - WTU Contract |
| 3/17/75 | Executive Session - Union Negotiations |
| 4/28/75 | Executive Session - Board and Superintendent |
| 4/30/75 | Executive Session - Board and Superintendent |
| 5/1/75 | Executive Session - Board and Superintendent |
| 7/28/75 | Executive Session - Briefing by Judge Benn |
| 7/31/75 | Executive Session |
| 9/18/75 | Closed Conference - Board and Executive Committee on Teacher's Union |
| 10/21/75 | Executive Session - Board and Superintendent |
| 10/24/75 | Executive Session |
| 10/31/75 | Executive Session |
| 11/19/75 | Executive Session |

### 1976

| | |
|---|---|
| 3/1/76 | Executive Session |
| 3/23/76 | Executive Session |
| 3/25/76 | Special Executive Session |

| Date | Subject of Discussion |
|---|---|

**1976 (continued)**

| | |
|---|---|
| 11/1/76 | Executive Session |
| NOTE: | On March 15, September 8 and December 8, 1976, the Board held open Conferences with the Superintendent |

**1977**

| | |
|---|---|
| 1/6/77 | Executive Session |
| 6/13/77 | Executive Session |
| 11/22/77 | Executive Session |

**1978**

| | |
|---|---|
| 1/23/78 | Executive Session - Washington Teachers' Union |

Source:  Desk file maintained by Dwight Cropp, Executive Secretary, D.C. Board of Education, July 20, 1978.

Agenda --

Agenda items are sent to the secretary for inclusion in the board's portion of the agenda. The secretary advises the office of the superintendent fourteen days prior to a stated business meeting of the items to be included. The agenda is prepared by the office of the superintendent and includes reports in the board's portion of the agenda, the Superintendent's Report and a list and summaries of all other items submitted to the board according to the Order of Business.[64]

Conduct at meetings --

In 1970, people at board meetings were felt to be getting out of order by board president Anita Allen. Therefore, she used the city police force to maintain order. Cassell challenged her on this procedure. The following exchange provides some of the flavor of the situation:

> Mr. Cassell stated that he had attended many Board of Education meetings but there had never been need for police; he had never seen police on the first floor and this caused him concern. Mr. Cassell requested that every policeman leave the room, basing his request on the fact that there had never been demonstrated the need for policemen with guns. Mr. Cassell had counted seven police on the first floor and seven guns in the Board room.
>
> In reply to this request, President Allen stated that it was the responsibility of the Chair to control the meeting of the Board of Education so that the business of the Board could be conducted in order and decorum, and for that reason the Chair requested the assistance of the special officers who were present.[65]

Police were also frequently used by President Virginia Morris during 1975 at the time of the termination hearings for Superintendent Sizemore, as the account in Chapter X will show. At that time also, a number of board members expressed concern about the treatment of board members and citizens by the police at public meetings.

## Summary

In the foregoing analysis, an attempt was made to examine the internal organizational factors of authority of the school board and school superintendent, their functions, and the structure of the office of the school board and the office of the superintendent. Points of possible conflict were presented as a basis for studying the relationship between the school superintendent and school board members.

In the section on board authority and also the section on superintendent authority, it was revealed that by law the board had control over the public schools, determined general policy, and appointed a superintendent. The superintendent was designated as the chief administrative officer to whom the board could delegate specific authority.

The section on functions of the board and the superintendent pointed out that the board dealt with policy matters while the superintendent handled the day-to-day operation of the school system.

The structure of the board and the superintendent's office was handled in the third section of the chapter. First, the composition of the board was provided. Here, we examined the first elected board and how vacancies were filled since these two elements recur in our discussions. The committee structure was fully covered because it presented problems for both Superintendents Scott and Sizemore. Likewise, staffing of the board office was reported on as these also caused conflict in school superintendent-school board relations for Dr. Scott and Mrs. Sizemore. The superintendent's administrative team was introduced at this point since some members figure prominently in later sections of our study and also because some of their responses to interview questions helped to illuminate factors which caused conflict in school superintendent-school board relations.

The implications of how the board was structured and how it functioned in relation to two fundamental processes: selecting and terminating superintendents, will be explored in the following chapter.

FOOTNOTES                          Chapter IV

1.  D.C. Code, Par. 31-103(a) (1973 Ed.).

2.  Ibid., Par. 31-105.

3.  Ibid., Par. 31-108.

4.  D.C. Public School System, Superintendent's Contract, 6 September 1973, Par. 2.

5.  D.C. Board of Education, Rules of the Board of Education, Chapter II, Part 200, Section 200.3 (Washington, D.C.: D.C. Public Schools), 1971, p. 23.

6.  Ibid., Chapter I, Part 1, Section 1.7, p. 5.

7.  Ibid., Chapter II, Part 200, Section 200.1, p. 21.

8.  Ibid., pp. 21-22.

9.  Ibid., Part 1, Section 1.6, (b), p. 4.

10. Ibid., Chapter 1, Part 1, Section 1.8, p. 6.

11. Ibid., Chapter 1, Part 2, Section 2.1 (a and b), p. 6.

12. Ibid., Chapter II, Part 200, Section 200.3, pp. 22-24.

13. Ibid., Chapter I, Part I, Section 1.2, p. 1.

14. U.S. Congress, House of Representatives, Public Law 90-292, 90th Congress, H.R. 13042, April 22, 1968.

15. Pamela Howard, "Split School Board Elections Asked," Washington Daily News, 1 September 1967. See also A Compilation of Laws Relating to Elections, Election Campaigns,

Lobbying, and Conflict of Interest in the
District of Columbia (Washington, D.C.:
District of Columbia Board of Elections and
Ethics, Office of General Counsel, District
Building, April 1977), p. 89. See also
Mary R. Hunter, "Looking for a Superperson,"
Bulletin Board, April 1977, pp. 8-9.

16. "Minutes of the First (Organization) Meeting of the Elected Board of Education," Washington, D.C., 27 January 1969.

17. "Minutes of the First (Organizational) Meeting of the Board of Education," Washington, D.C., 26 January 1970, pp. 1-4.

18. "Minutes of the First (Organizational) Meeting of the Board of Education," Washington, D.C., 25 January 1971, pp. 3-5.

19. "Minutes of the Twenty-Third (Stated) Meeting of the Board of Education," Washington, D.C., 17 November 1971, p. 3.

20. "Transcript of the Thirty-Seventh (Stated) Board Meeting, Board of Education of the District of Columbia," Washington, D.C., 17 January 1972, p. 123.

21. Rules of the D.C. Board of Education, p. 2.

22. "Minutes of the Sixteenth (Special) Meeting of the Board of Education," Washington, D.C., 30 July 1970, pp. 15-20, Enclosure 1.

23. "Transcript of the Twenty-Sixth (Stated) Meeting of the Board of Education," Washington, D.C., 17 October 1973, pp. 102-113.

24. "Transcript of a Special Meeting of the Board of Education," Washington, D.C., 4 December 1973, pp. 52-53.

25. "Transcript of the Fifteenth (Special) Meeting of the Board of Education," Washington, D.C., 15 July 1974, pp. 23 and 26.

26. Passow Report, pp. 175-176.

27. Rules of the D.C. Board of Education, Chapter 1, Part 3, Section 3.1, pp. 8-9.

28. "Minutes of the Thirty-Seventh (Stated) Meeting of the Board of Education," Washington, D.C., 16 October 1969.

29. "Minutes of the Fourth (Stated) Meeting of the Board of Education," Washington, D.C., 18 February 1970, Enclosure 4.

30. "Minutes of the Eighth (Stated) Meeting of the Board of Education," Washington, D.C., 17 March 1971, pp. 30-31.

31. "The School Board - Who Does What, Why, and With Whom," The Bulletin Board, Vol. 5, No. 4, May 1974, p. 3.

32. "Transcript of the Stated Meeting of the Board of Education," Washington, D.C., 15 May 1974, pp. 59-60.

33. Memorandum to Mr. Dwight S. Cropp, Executive Secretary, from Mr. Albert A. Rosenfield, re: Committee Structure, 25 March 1974 and 26 March 1974. See also "Transcript of the Seventh Stated Meeting of the Board of Education," Washington, D.C., 17 April 1974, pp. 28-40.

34. D.C. Board of Education, Committee Structure, mimeographed, Washington, D.C., 1975-76, pp. 1-24.

35. Interview with Hugh Scott, Superintendent of Schools, on November 22, 1977.

36. Interview with Charles Cassell, D.C. Board of Education member, Washington, D.C., 5 October 1977.

37. Interview with Bardyl Tirana, D.C. Board of Education member, Washington, D.C., 27 September 1977.

38. Interview with Mattie Taylor, D.C. Board of Education member, Washington, D.C., 6 October 1977.

39. Interview with Julius Hobson, Jr., D.C. Board of Education member, Washington, D.C., 28 September 1977.

40. Ibid.

41. Interview with Mattie Taylor, D.C. Board of Education member, Washington, D.C., 6 October 1977.

42. Interview with Julius Hobson, Jr., D.C. Board of Education member, Washington, D.C., 28 September 1977.

43. Interview with Barbara L. Simmons, D.C. Board of Education member, Washington, D.C., 20 September 1977.

44. Interview with Julius Hobson, Jr., D.C. Board of Education member, Washington, D.C.; 28 September 1977.

45. Interview with John Warren, D.C. Board of Education member, Washington, D.C., 27 September 1977.

46. Interview with Therman Evans, D.C. Board of Education member, Washington, D.C., 19 October 1977.

47. Interview with Julius Hobson, Jr., D.C. Board of Education member, Washington, D.C., 28 September 1977.

48. Interview with John Warren, D.C. Board of Education member, Washington, D.C., 28 September 1977.

49. Interview with Julius Hobson, Jr., D.C. Board of Education member, Washington, D.C., 28 September 1977.

50. Ibid., and Interview with Mattie Taylor, D.C. Board of Education member, Washington, D.C., 6 October 1977.

51. Interview with Charles Cassell, D.C. Board of Education member, Washington, D.C., 5 October 1977.

52. Interview with Charles Cassell, D.C. Board of Education member, Washington, D.C., 5 October 1977, and Mattie Taylor on 6 October 1977.

53. Interview with Julius Hobson, Jr., D.C. Board of Education member, Washington, D.C., 28 September 1977.

54. Passow Report, p. 178.

55. "Minutes of the Twenty-First (Stated) Meeting of the Board of Education," Washington, D.C., 20 October 1971, pp. 38-41.

56. "Minutes of the Tenth (Stated) Meeting of the Board of Education," Washington, D.C., 25 May 1972, pp. 57-59.

57. "Minutes of the Thirty-First (Community) Meeting of the Board of Education," Washington, D.C., 6 December 1973, pp. 13-14.

58. "Minutes of the Twenty-Fifth (Community) Meeting of the Board of Education," Washington, D.C., 3 October 1973, p. 2.

59. Interview with Margaret Labat, Regional Superintendent, Washington, D.C., 18 November 1977.

60. Interview with William Rice, Regional Superintendent, Washington, D.C., 21 September 1977.

61. <u>Rules of the D.C. Board of Education</u>, Chapter 1, Part 4, pp. 10-13.

62. "School Board Bill Attracts," <u>Washington Afro-American</u>, 30 March 1968.

63. "Minutes of the Fourth (Stated) Meeting of the Board of Education," Washington, D.C., 18 February 1970, pp. 25-26.

64. <u>Rules of the D.C. Board of Education</u>, Chapter 1, Part 4, pp. 13-14.

65. "Minutes of the Fourth (Stated) Meeting of the Board of Education," Washington, D.C., 18 February 1970, p. 2.

# CHAPTER V

# SELECTION AND TERMINATION PROCESSES -- 1969-73

## Introduction

Two very significant decision-making functions engaged in by the DCBOE are the selection and termination processes. In these respects the board's power is not subject to the whims of Congress, the courts, the city council, the mayor, or community groups, although sometimes these groups try to bring pressure on the board in an effort to influence the decisions made. Nevertheless, the board is powerful in these two respects as granted to it by the D.C. Code as follows: "The control of the public schools of the District of Columbia is vested in a Board of Education to consist of eleven elected members."

Section 31-103 provides that the board, "shall determine all questions of general policy relating to the schools, shall appoint the executive officers hereinafter provided for, define their duties, and direct expenditures.... The Board shall appoint all... employees provided for in this chapter."

Section 31-105 authorizes the board to appoint, for a three year term, a superintendent "who shall have the direction of and supervision in all matters pertaining to the instruction in all the schools under the Board of Education."

Finally, paragraph 31-108 provides, "The Board shall have power to remove the superintendent at any time for adequate cause affecting his

character and efficiency as superintendent."[1]
This section parallels paragraph 2 of the superintendent's contract with one exception. The contract confers explicit due-process protections against arbitrary board action and requires that the board give notice and an opportunity for the superintendent to have a hearing when dismissal is contemplated.[2]

In the case of both Superintendents William Manning and Hugh Scott, the Superintendent Selection Process engaged in by the elected board was fraught with the vagaries of confusion and strife between board members and with community groups which impinged on the relationship of superintendent and school board, causing conflicts.

Neither Superintendents Carl Hansen, William Manning, nor Hugh Scott were fired. Each, in turn, though, left the superintendency under pressure.

### Superintendent Carl Hansen's Termination (1958-1967)

Superintendent Hansen met considerable opposition among board members in relation to his track system of ability grouping and in relation to his attitude about the Hobson v Hansen case.

Dr. Euphemia L. Haynes, president of the board in 1967, voiced opposition to Superintendent Hansen's reappointment in a statement to the press. The Washington Star reported:

> Dr. Haynes, a frequent critic of Hansen, noted that the superintendent's contract expires May 21. Before that date, she said, the board should review Hansen's record of service, philosophy of education and program for the future....
>
> Dr. Haynes denied she was personally hostile to Hansen. However, she added: 'I have had grave doubts about many of the programs

which Dr. Hansen has installed and defended.'[3]

Subsequently, the conflict in superintendent-school board relations during the Hansen administration, arising from racial and class factors impinging on the relationship, reached a turning point. Hansen's insistence on appealing the decision, against the DCBOE's wishes, caused a severe split in his relationship with the majority of school board members.

The DCBOE voted not to appeal the court's decision and so ordered the superintendent, who felt this (in a sense) also ordered his dismissal. At a press conference on July 3, 1967, he said:

> This action in effect orders my dismissal from the school system. This is so because my refusal to accept this order places me in direct insubordination in relation to my employers. If I chose to observe my contractual rights with the Board of Education under these circumstances, the Board would have no alternative but to order my dismissal for cause. I choose to spare the Board of Education the embarrassment of such a debasing spectacle. The Board's action also relieves me of any further sense of obligation for the Board of Education.[4]

On July 3, 1967, Superintendent Hansen submitted his resignation from the superintendency, as of that date, with his retirement effective as of July 31, 1967.

### Superintendent William Manning's Selection and Termination (1968-1970)

During the time between Superintendent Hansen's resignation and the appointment of a predecessor, several events initiated under Dr. Hansen's administration continued to be moved forward. Among these were: the establishment of an Executive Study Group to study the recommendations of the Passow Report; the decentralization thrust through the Morgan Community School project; and the Fort Lincoln New Town project. Two individuals served as acting superintendent during the interim: John H. Riecks, June-July 1967, and Benjamin J. Henley, a Black man, July, 1967 - October, 1968.

A week after the new board was sworn in on July 2, 1967, its president, Rev. Everett Hewlett, selected Dr. Anita Allen as chairman of an ad hoc committee, consisting of Benjamin Alexander, John Sessions and Ann Stults, to formulate a superintendent selection process. The board agreed that race, nationality, background, religious affiliation and sex were not factors to be considered in selecting a new superintendent. Providing assistance to the selection committee was a panel of consultants headed by Dr. Francis Ianni of Columbia University. Approximately 140 organizations on the school board's mailing list were to submit names. Eventually, 81 nominations were screened by the Ianni panel.

The list was narrowed down to six by August 9, 1967.[5] Finalists were Wilson C. Riles, a Black man who was director of compensatory education for the state of California; Gordon O. McAndrew, former superintendent of Gary, Indiana public schools and director of the Learning Institute in Rougemont, North Carolina;[6] Carl Dolce, superintendent of the New Orleans public schools, Leslie Dunbar, executive director of the Field Foundation and the only non-educator; William Manning, superintendent of the Lansing, Michigan public schools; and Neil C. Sullivan, superintendent of the Berkeley, California public schools.

Even though Acting Superintendent Henley was proposed by some community groups and citizens, he preferred not to be considered and wrote a letter dated October 16, 1967 to the board indicating this.

At this time, an elected school board act

was then in conference[7] and though some board members and some candidates felt uncomfortable at the possibility of making a selection before the act was passed, others felt that in face of the uncertainty of its passing, a selection needed to be made so that implementation of the Wright Decree (Hobson v Hansen) and the Passow Report could proceed. Meanwhile, Riles and McAndrew withdrew from the competition and the report from Lansing on Manning was highly favorable.[8]

Nevertheless, problems occurred because some board members, especially Haynes and Hobson, felt that the community had been excluded from the selection process. Thus, they filed a suit to overthrow the Manning appointment. The case was thrown out of court.

Subsequently, Hobson led a group of citizens into a public meeting set up on October 27, 1967, for citizens to question Manning. The group disrupted the meeting and called for Henley's appointment.[9] Later, when the demonstration ended, board members voted 4-2 to appoint Manning, with Sessions and B. Alexander switching from abstension to a Yes vote to make it unanimous. Both Haynes and Dugas were absent from the room when the vote was taken.

All board members were not united in the matter, however. This portended future conflict in school board-superintendent relations.

Thus, Manning came into the office of superintendent during turmoil, and turmoil remained the order of the day. On February 23, 1968, the erosion in superintendent-school board relations erupted publicly when Allen, Manning's chief supporter during the selection process, publicly criticized him for failing to bring changes and innovations to the D.C. school system.

The elected school board act was signed into law in April 1968 and the first elections were set for November 1968. This might have been the catalytic agent which precipitated open confrontations between the school board and Superintendent Manning as board members began considering whether or not they would run for office and how their stand on issues would set with voters. Board members did ask Manning to resign in July 1968, but he held on until 1970.

Meanwhile, the dispute sharpened between Superintendent Manning and his severest critics on the school board, namely Allen, Hobson and Sessions, who won seats on the expanded elected school board.

Though Hobson claimed he should be president of the board because he was the only candidate that won a plurality, Allen challenged this and was voted in as president. From this point on, their clash of wills was a dominant factor in most school board meetings. Along with the board's running clashes with Superintendent Manning, these factors disrupted educational progress in the District schools.[10]

In a letter to Superintendent Manning from Mrs. Anita Ford Allen, dated February 21, 1968, she expressed the sentiment of board members about having a superintendent from outside the city and, in a sense, her displeasure with his slow progress in changing the school system. Her letter included the following:

> What I am trying to say, Mr. Superintendent, is that we have now perhaps our last chance to upgrade the system. That sufficient changes and planning can be made by school officers long a part of the system you must prove. I would add that at least a part of the thinking behind bringing in a superintendent from out of the city was that the radical reshuffling and creation of new ways of doing things could be done best by one with no commitment or defensiveness about the past.[11]

A local news article expressed the drama of events concerning the board's dissatisfaction with Superintendent Manning. It stated that four of the DCBOE members have urged Superintendent Manning to leave before the fall election campaign so that he will not become an issue in it. Manning indicated that he had no intentions of leaving after six months. Nevertheless, among those anxious for him to leave were Mr. John A. Sessions, who was not happy about Manning's superintendency and Dr. Benjamin H. Alexander, who felt he was a good man, but not good for the city.

Among the narrow majority in support of Manning were Rev. Everett A. Hewlett, president of the board, who felt that operating the schools was a shared responsibility; board member Albert A. Rosenfield, who felt that people were trying to make a scapegoat of Manning, and board member Euphemia Haynes, who felt that Manning had not been given a fair chance.[12]

Finally, on July 30, 1969 the Hobson faction united with the Allen faction to approve a motion to relieve Manning of his duties. Therefore, he was given a contract to make a study.

At the December 17, 1969 meeting, the board accepted the resignation of Dr. William R. Manning. The information conveyed to the group at the meeting by Mr. John Sessions was that on December 11, 1969, Dr. William Manning presented a letter to him, as chairman of the committee which the board had appointed to oversee his work. The letter indicated that Dr. Manning resigned as superintendent of schools for the Washington, D.C. public school system, effective March 1, 1970. Board members accepted Dr. Manning's resignation.[13] Manning's letter indicated that he would be employed by the Xerox Corporation as chairman, Education Board of the American Education Publications Company.[14]

Deputy Superintendent Benjamin J. Henley was

again appointed acting Superintendent of the DCPS. He served from April 1970 to September 1970.

Meanwhile, Coates, Rosenfield, Hobson, Treanor and Sessions came up for re-election. Obviously, the in-fighting was not lost on the public as citizens declined to vote Hobson back in office and Sessions and Treanor decided not to run. Both Rosenfield and Coates were re-elected; Cassell and Tirana joined them on the board as at-large members.

### Superintendent Hugh Scott's Selection and Termination (1970-1973)

Under the leadership of Acting Superintendent Benjamin Henley, the DCPS system pursued its course for educating the children in the District of Columbia. But some members of the DCBOE felt that change was necessary in order for the school system to take a giant step forward toward the dream of a quality education program. Therefore, the board proceeded to plan for a nationwide search for a new superintendent.

The meeting of March 12, 1970 was called for the purpose of discussing and acting on a report of the ad hoc committee on steps for selecting a superintendent. Consisting of Reverend James Coates, chairman, Mr. Charles Cassell, and Mr. Nelson Roots, the committee developed a process similar to that used in 1967 but included community involvement. The steps were approved, as amended, with Mr. Bardyl Tirana voting No. Therefore, the following board members were appointed by the chair to serve on the Selection Committee: Reverend James E. Coates, chairman, Mr. Charles I. Cassell, Mr. Nelson G. Roots, Mrs. Evie Washington, and Mr. Albert A. Rosenfield.[15] On May 27, 1970, the board adopted the job description and Desirable Criteria for Selection proposed by the committee, which indicated it was looking for a person with inner-city experience. This signalled that a Black superintendent may be selected in the

city with a 70 percent Black population and a
school system 95 percent Black. At that same
meeting, the board received from the Citizen's
Panel chosen to assist in the selection a request
to make separately and independently the initial
screening of candidates for the position of superintendent. Since most members of the board felt
that the screening should be done jointly by the
board's 5 members and the 11 community members
appointed to the screening committee, the request
was denied with Rosenfield, Roots, Hancock, Coates,
Allen and Alexander voting Aye (for joint screening) and Cassell, Swaim, Tirana and Washington
voting No.[16]

The next high point of the selection process
occurred in the July 24, 1970 meeting of the
DCBOE, at which time 21 citizens voiced their
objection to the superintendent selection process.
In addition to the above, when the citizens' panel
eliminated Rhody McCoy as a candidate, Charles I
Cassell (board member) filed suit, entitled
<u>Charles I. Cassell, et al. v Board of Education,
et al.</u>, to obtain a restraining order which would
halt the process.[17] Nevertheless, the board
approved continuation. Members had been informed,
in executive session by Corporation Counsel
Mullaney, that there were no strictures on the
board or its committee from proceeding with the
scheduling and conducting of interviews, so long
as the board did not take action to advance one
candidate or limit the list of twelve remaining
candidates. The motion was put and carried with
Mr. Tirana and Mr. Cassell voting No, and Mrs.
Taylor and Mrs. Swaim abstaining.[18]

Later, the court found that the procedure of
the Committee on Selection of a Superintendent was
proper and that it had been faithful in its discharge of responsibilities and had provided
opportunity for community participation.[19]

In August, Coates stated that the selection
committee had voted to interview three finalists:

Robert Wheeler, assistant superintendent of Urban Affairs in Kansas City, Missouri; Hugh J. Scott, assistant superintendent of a region in Detroit, Michigan; and George Rhodes of New York. The board eliminated Rhodes and the contest was between Scott and Wheeler. Finally, after several conferences and visits with the two contending candidates, the Wheeler faction, supporters of Anita Allen, lost one member and the winning votes were cast for Scott.

At 6:30 p.m. on August 31, 1970, at a special meeting of the DCBOE, board members met as a Committee of the Whole on Personnel to receive the report from the Committee to Select a Superintendent. During that meeting the Committee of the Whole recommended to the board of education Dr. Hugh J. Scott of Detroit as superintendent of schools for the District of Columbia. Reverend James Coates made the motion to appoint Dr. Hugh Scott, and it was seconded by Mr. Charles Cassell. In speaking on behalf of the motion, Rev. James Coates mentioned the opportunity of being provided a well-trained, dedicated dynamic Black by the D.C. public school system as an example to the nation; and the contribution of the citizens' panel in screening seventy-two applications and preparing the list of candidates to recommend to the board. Other board members also expressed pleasure at the selection with even Mr. Cassell saying he considered Dr. Scott to be equal to the candidate for whom he worked so hard in the beginning. Thus, Dr. Scott received a unanimous vote to the position of superintendent of the DCPS.[20]

A marriage between the DCBOE and Scott was consummated with a vote of confidence and support from each member of the 1970-71 DCBOE. On September 24, 1970, Dr. Scott signed a three-year contract to serve as superintendent, effective October 1, 1970.

Dr. Scott, a Black man born in Detroit, Michigan, was married with two children. He was a graduate of Wayne University in 1956. His M.A. in Education was received from Wayne State University in 1960 and his Ed.D. in Educational Administration was received from Michigan State University in 1966. Scott began his career in education as a teacher in social studies, grades one through eight, in the Detroit public schools from January 1965 to June 1965. From there he became assistant to the director of the Detroit Great Cities School Improvement Project (June to September 1965). Then he became an instructor in the School of Education, Michigan State University. In September 1966 to September 1967, Dr. Scott served as an elementary school assistant principal in the Detroit public schools and moved from that position to that of assistant to the deputy superintendent of School-Community Relations. Later, from 1968 to 1970, Scott served as region assistant superintendent in the Detroit schools. Following that position, he was selected as superintendent of schools for the District of Columbia public schools. He served in that capacity from October 1, 1970 to September 30, 1973.

A Memorandum of Understanding was adopted by the superintendent and the DCBOE on March 15, 1972. Items included in the memorandum were: standard operating procedures, budget, personnel practices, and additional top priority matters such as the Wright Decree Compliance by April 1972. The point of the document was to set down for both groups -- the policy makers and the policy implementers -- as well as for local field personnel and the community, a schedule for implementation of priority goals and guidelines for board-superintendent relationships. For example, item 1E stated that "The Superintendent will be routinely consulted on all matters before Board action." To emphasize the significance of this step to the parties involved, the board and Superintendent Scott agreed to hold a press conference on the Memorandum of Understanding. In addition, a motion was approved to hold a series of nine meetings to discuss with all staff at the ward level about the Memorandum of Understanding, with Rosenfield and Cassell voting No.[21] (It is important to keep in mind at this point that Mr. Marion Barry was soon to run for a city council seat; press exposure at this point would be helpful.)

By March 31, 1972, as stated by Superintendent Scott in an interview, there had been calls for his resignation by school board members but never from citizens' groups. Seemingly, he had some confrontation with one board president:

> Scott's frequent confrontations with the board last year centered on his clashes with former board president Anita F. Allen. Mrs. Allen was defeated for re-election last November by Marion Barry, who based his campaign in part on a theme of 'give Scott a chance.'
>
> His relations with Barry and the other members who were sworn in with Barry in January have been publicly harmonious. Scott said he feels 'much better' in his private dealings with board members because 'there's more respect for this office now.'[22]

In September 1972, Superintendent Hugh J. Scott again requested that the DCBOE decide whether or not it planned to renew his contract for the fall of 1973. At the request of Marion Barry, board president, he withdrew his request in order for the board and superintendent to present a united front at budget hearings in their efforts to obtain additional funds for the school system. At the time of this latest request for a decision, Scott stated that it would be easier to make plans for the school system if he knew whether or not he was going to be retained.[23]

Scott had annoyed some board members in regard to the implementation of an equalization process.[24] Beyond this, the Allen faction of the DCBOE was not happy with his implementation of

Kenneth Clark's Academic Achievement Plan.[25] Also, problems arose in regard to Scott's handling of management[26] and budgetary matters.[27] In the midst of this, the issue of special education was pushed forward on the board's agenda by the Waddy Decree handed down in August 1972 in Peter Mills, et al. v Board of Education, et al. Their dissatisfaction crystalized in the issue of decentralization.[28] All of these issues were perceived by some members of the DCBOE and by Superintendent Scott as test cases of whether the superintendent could implement the board's policy without the board's interference into administrative matters. Obviously, the majority faction of the DCBOE felt there was sufficient need to involve the board into some aspects of the day-to-day operation of the school system due to their displeasure with Superintendent Scott's administration. Therefore, by January 9, 1973, Dr. Scott withdrew his request for a one-year extension of his present contract.

By January 19, 1973, the DCBOE, with Superintendent Scott, set up Ten Priority Goals to be accomplished by June 1973. Great concern was shown by some members of the board, namely Mrs. Taylor, Mr. Barry, Mrs. Swaim, and Father Kemp, in the area of the Ten Priority Goals over the matter of giving the superintendent the authority to act on the goals once they were approved by the board without paralyzing him by having documents keep coming back to the board or putting other goals ahead of the agreed upon Ten Priority Goals in the remaining months of his contract. Mr. Cassell and Mr. Barry had problems with the proposal to give the superintendent authority to reprogram or redirect funds in this regard. They felt that without the board's prior knowledge, it places itself in a position of having to defend an action within its realm of authority and for which the public will hold it accountable. In further clarification of her point, Mrs. Taylor explained that the board needed to stop doing business as usual, which is non-implementation as in the cases of the Strayer Report, the Passow Report, the Clark Plan and all other reports, and change its way of operating. To emphasize this point, Superintendent Scott asked again for full authority to move personnel and create interim positions to get people working on the ten goals. He further explained that he wanted to be able to move ahead without having to come back to the board fifteen times a week or that kind of thing.

Parents and some citizens were not as silent on the issue of race as were many people in the District. Some felt Dr. Scott was being given a hard time because he was Black. Mr. Lewis Anthony, a citizen testifying before the board, brought up the subject of race in the following manner:

> Historically for Black people in this country they have received inferior education, the worse kind of leadership, and the reason has been made to the fact that we had a Board of Education that was predominantly white that did not and could not understand the needs of Black children. But as I stand at this microphone tonight I see a portrait of ebony only fringed with alabaster, but our children are still in the same predicament that they have been and which they will be in until you decide between politics and children's needs.[29]

Another speaker, Mrs. Theresa Jones, a parent, also testified about race as a factor in decision-making as she said, "I am not politicking for Dr. Hugh Scott. But if you can give a President... another chance, why don't you Black people get together and give your man a chance'...."[30]

Response from board of education members was generous with Mrs. Taylor, Mr. Rosenfield and Mr. Barry speaking in support of renewing Dr. Scott's contract or extending it for another year.

During the meeting several members referred

to the fact that the issue of the superintendent's contract had come up several times since the spring of 1972 at which time the superintendent asked board members to give him some definitive answer since (1) he wanted to fill the coterminous-administrative positions, whose staff must leave when he leaves, and (2) he wanted to plan for continuity of the system. The issue came to a head on December 9, 1972 during an all day meeting. Subsequently, Dr. Scott received a 6-5 vote of confidence which he felt was insufficient support for him to continue at the helm. Thus, in a press conference, he announced that he would leave in June 1973.

Significantly, Mrs. Ruth Goodwin, a community leader, firmly called attention to the fact that white men were given years to obtain expertise and perfection in a job and that Dr. Scott had been given only two years. She noted also that half of the DCBOE had been seated three to five years whereas others had been at the job for only one and a half years. Her final comment was an emphatic No to Dr. Scott's leaving and reminder that if the DCBOE did not listen to the community, they may find themselves unseated.[31]

After additional discussion clarifying board members' positions on the matter, the ten members present voted Aye for the motion that the Board tonight agree on the ten items listed here in terms of categories and areas of priorities for the next six to nine months for the board of education.[32]

On February 7, 1973 at the DCBOE's second community meeting for the year, Dr. Scott discussed a document titled: <u>Superintendent's Identification of Tasks, Resource Needs and Prerequisite Actions Associated with the Ten Priority Goals of the Board of Education</u>. In presenting the document, the superintendent stressed that the comprehensive nature of the priority goals and tasks was such that other board considerations and demands on administrative resources had to be curtailed and, in this regard, he requested a two month moratorium on board requests directed to the administration and said that to the extent that the moratorium was observed, was the extent that the administration would be able to concentrate on the goals and the tasks involved.

Again some board members were reluctant to commit the board to the acceptance of the superintendent's report on the Ten Priority Goals and the transcript is unclear as to whether or not the superintendent received sanction to go full speed ahead on the implementation of the goals.[33]

Evidence of the board concluding its conflict with Superintendent Scott consisted of two specific actions. The first was to grant leave to Superintendent Scott, in accordance with his contract, effective July 1, 1973. The second matter concerned the board's approval of the board of education's Superintendent Selection Process.

### Superintendent Search and Selection, 1973

The third superintendent search in six years began quietly and orderly. On February 21, 1973, the DCBOE approved the Superintendent Selection Process. A five-member board Selection Committee was appointed by President Barry. In explaining his selection of members, Barry stated he had (1) talked with all eleven members of the board about the committee, (2) had taken their feelings and concerns into consideration, (3) had put together a committee composed of members whose terms expired in January 1974 and members whose terms expired in January 1976, and (4) taken into consideration a geographic, racial, and socio-economic balance. Thus, Barry selected two white members, Mr. Rosenfield and Mrs. Swaim, and three Black members, Mrs. Mason, Mrs. Taylor and himself, to serve on the committee. It is interesting to note that his selection consisted of three women and two men.

Mrs. Taylor declined the honor saying she did not have time to devote to the activity and also that she felt it was stupid to be searching for a superintendent at that time. Mr. Barry then chose Reverend James Coates to serve, tipping the balance in favor of the males. At this point Mr. Cassell argued for his inclusion as an enthusiastic volunteer. Mr. Barry reiterated his selection criterion and assured Mr. Cassell that he, Barry, was not prejudiced against him. Subsequent events hinged on this initial action of Barry's.

The primary responsibilities of the Selection Committee were to (1) develop the superintendent's profile, (2) prepare an announcement brochure, (3) seek out possible candidates, (4) narrow the field down to five persons for interview with the full board, (5) make a final recommendation to the board, and (6) other duties felt to be necessary.

During that same meeting (2/21/73), the DCBOE established a seven member Citizens' Superintendent Selection Resource Commission composed of three members and two alternates selected by board members. The procedure used to select the at-large members, as explained by Barry, was that each board member would make one or more nominations and three members and two alternatives would be selected out of this group. The following nine persons were nominated: Mrs. Barbara Simmons, president of an educational consultant firm, by Mrs. Mason; Mr. Joseph Danzansky, president of Giant Food, by Mr. Rosenfield; Mr. John R. Kinard, director, Anacostia Smithsonian Museum and formerly of the Peace Corps, by Reverend James Coates; Mr. Cleveland Dennard, president of Washington Technical Institute, by Mrs. Martha Swaim; Ms. Margo Weaver, student at Washington Technical Institute, nurse and mother, by Mr. Charles Cassell; Mr. Oliver E. Brown, by Mrs. Mattie Taylor; Dr. Andrew Billingsley, vice president of Academic Affairs at Howard University, by Mrs. Hilda Mason; Judge Harry T. Alexander, by Mr. Charles Cassell; and Ricardo Byrd, by Mrs. Evie Washington. The result of the secret balloting was Mr. Danzansky - 6; Mr. Kinard - 5; and Mr. Cleveland Dennard - 5. The alternates were Mrs. Barbara Lett Simmons - 4; and Judge Harry Alexander - 3.

In an effort to have strong citizen input, as indicated in the document entitled, "The Board of Education Superintendent Selection Process," the above-named persons were to assist the board Selection Committee in: (1) identifying potential candidates; (2) narrowing the field down to fifteen applicants; and (3) consulting with the board's committee concerning rationale for their fifteen choices. The citizens on the resource commission were to be residents of the District of Columbia. Additionally, they were instructed to meet separately, to report to the board's committee and if they so choose to sit ex-officio (speak but not vote), in meetings of the board committee. In addition to those three citizens and two alternates selected by board members, the resource commission was composed of four other members: one selected by the Student Advisory Council; one selected by the Congress of Parent Teacher Association (PTA); one selected by the Washington Teachers' Union; and one selected by the Council of School Officers.

Notably, the process also called for the new superintendent to be on board by the first week in June.[34]

When the board met on March 7, 1973 at its fourth (community) meeting of the year, a very prominent member of the community and former board member, Mr. Julius Hobson, Sr., spoke on the superintendent's selection process. His desire was to involve other community groups in the process, such as the Federation of Civic Associations, and to protest what he felt to be the delegation of the board's responsibility in the selection process to the Citizens Resource Commission. His special objection was to Mr. Danzansky, head of Giant Food Stores, being included. In this regard,

Mr. Hobson said that he had spent three years in front of Danzansky's store battling to try to get him to hire Black people, and, further, that he is a member of the Board of Trade, the Murchison Manufacturer's Association and every other organization that have fought the social advancement of Black people. Therefore, he could not understand how Mr. Danzansky was placed on a commission to select a superintendent for a 90 percent Black school district. In fact, Mr. Hobson felt so strongly about this that he threatened to take it to court and try to get a restraining order to really make the superintendent selection process a broad-based community participation effort. Furthermore, he felt that DCBOE should exercise its prerogative and responsibility to pare down the list of applicants and make the final selection of the superintendent. In this connection, Mr. Hobson further stated:

> We have the only elected body now with some power -- people who do not have to cater.... Nobody can take your job away as a result of your exercising your prerogative...
>
> So...since we have a Board with limited powers that gets batted around by all kinds of committees, when we do have an opportunity to exercise that power I think that we ought to do it exclusively... Please do not pass it on to the Board of Trade....

In response to Mr. Hobson, President Barry indicated that board members had spent the previous day reviewing their Superintendent Selection Process document, and had thus arrived at the conclusion that every applicant's credentials would be reviewed by the entire board. In answer to Mr. Hobson's concern about the inclusion of Mr. Danzansky on the commission, President Barry explained that each board member had a chance to nominate a citizen, and that Mr. Danzansky received the majority of votes.

With incredible perception and in utter amazement, Mrs. Taylor made these very telling remarks about the ideological direction of the majority of the board members:

> We find as alternates Mrs. Barbara Simmons and Judge Harry Alexander. Mrs. Simmons' record and history of concern and investing her time and her talents in behalf of the public school system is known to everyone who works with the schools, either in an employment or volunteer capacity. It was that very Judge Harry Alexander who swore in the six board members who were last elected to the Board. I find it most puzzling to me as one main individual to understand how persons who have given most of their adult life to concerns for the schools, for the students, and for this city and its residents, could draw so few votes. I was personally amazed at the popularity of the candidates that drew the highest number....

Mrs. Mason's concern was that no woman was selected on the Citizens Commission as she had nominated Mrs. Barbara Simmons, who received only enough votes to be an alternate.[35]

Mr. Cassell also voiced his opposition to Mr. Joseph Danzansky's presence on the commission. In his interview, Mr. Cassell stated:

> Danzansky was proposed as a member of the Superintendent Selection Committee. He was a member of the Board of Trade. He was President of Giant Foods. My position was (that) we have a Black school system, 96 percent means it is a Black system to me. We have extensive problems of negligence regarding the people who control that system, most of them were white. I mean people who have some influence on the board and on the administration. We had committed ourselves to strong community involvement for people's kids who

were going to the schools. I saw no indication prior or afterwards of any interest on Mr. Danzansky's part in the public schools. It didn't make any sense at all to me, any more than if you should bring Nixon in. The thing is he was a prominent businessman and Mr. Barry felt we needed the businessmen. We needed the business community. I couldn't understand how we needed them. We were always having budget problems. They didn't give us any money. So I opposed him because there was no basis for it. He was not a member of our community. He was not active in our community. He wasn't interested in our community so the only reason for bringing him in is to have a relationship with him which might be of benefit later on to the person who proposed him. So I opposed him very strongly and I asked for justification, why Joe Danzansky?

Now, why does Mr. Danzansky want to be on the Superintendent Selection Committee? Purely to pick up some credits as an active person in the Black community doing some stuff for the folks. Mr. Danzansky was appointed. He came to one meeting and we never saw him again. That one meeting he came to was not one where there was work done, but simply to get organized and decide how we would function. We never saw him again, which proved my point. But if you talk to him now he will use that as a credit. He was a member of the Superintendent's Selection Committee and I opposed that, catering to white folks just because they've got big names....36

    Another citizen, Mr. Nelson C. Roots, a former Black school board member and chairman of the Education Committee of the D.C. Federation of Civic Associations and the Federation of Citizens Associations, spoke at the March 7 meeting about the desire of the associations to have representation on the Superintendent Selection Advisory Committee, stating that the federation, with 67 member associations, had the largest membership of any organization in the city.

In line with the above, the DCBOE at its March 14, 1974 meeting, enlarged the Citizen's Resource Commission by three representatives, one each from the Federation of Civic Associations, Federation of Citizens Associations, and Home and School Associations.

Also, at this meeting, the DCBOE outlined the method to be used by the citizens' groups to select their representative. The method was to directly name their representative or submit to the DCBOE three names from their group, one of whom would be selected by drawing.

In spite of pressure from Mr. Cassell to change the process for the board's selection of three individuals to the Citizens' Resource Commission in order to eliminate Mr. Danzansky, there was no change made in the process as Barry, Rosenfield, Washington, Swaim and Kemp voted No to a change.[37]

Despite the dissension presented by citizens who objected to the superintendent selection process, progress was made. At its meeting of March 21, 1973, Mr. Barry reported that a drafting committee had been named to prepare the brochure which should be ready by April 6. The search was expected to consume six weeks, from April 6 to May 18, and the field would be winnowed down during the three-week period between May 18 and June 15. Also, the committee for the selection of a new superintendent voted to hire Mrs. Barbara Simmons as staff director (she agreed to withdraw as an alternate on the Citizens' Commission) and Mrs. Ruth Pearl as administrative aide and secretary to the committee. Subsequent to this, Barry announced that a public meeting would be held the next night in order to hear citizens' views on what they thought the board should look for in a superintendent in the areas of management skills, and educational and administrative qualifications.[38] The next major action was the board's authorization to distribute the brochure.[39]

The progress report of the Committee on the Selection of the Superintendent at the May 16, 1973 meeting, as received from Barbara Lett Simmons, Superintendent Selection Coordinator, noted that of the 72 candidates under consideration: 4 were women; 23 were school superintendents; 2 were deputy superintendents; 7 associate or assistant superintendents; 4 supervising directors; 5 principals; and 31 others who represented local and federal government administrators, college and university administrators, professors and local school administrators on leave, completing doctoral residences, corporate officers and managers, educational consultants, human resource agency administrators, and professional organization executives from within and outside the school system as well as from all sections of the country. It was also at this meeting that recommendations were approved to have current operating heads and the Citizens' Resource Commission to provide questions for use when interviewing candidates.[40]

Since the school year was drawing to a close and the superintendent, Dr. Hugh Scott, had been granted leave from July 1 to September 30, Mrs. Floretta D. McKenzie was named acting superintendent in the June 4, 1973 meeting of the DCBOE,[41] until a superintendent was appointed.

By June 20, 1973, applicants for the position of superintendent had swelled to 98. Then the list was narrowed down to 15 names. Mr. Barry suggested he be sole spokesman to the press on the candidate selection process, and that no names would be revealed to protect the candidates. However, the names of the three finalists would be made public.

Mr. Cassell spoke in opposition to this board adopted policy not to make public the names of the applicants, and indicated that he would discuss publicly the 15 candidates unless they had expressed a desire to remain unnamed. After further clarification of the policy, Mr. Cassell indicated that he would abide by it.[42]

This action of Cassell's, nonetheless, nudged Mr. Barry to name 12 of the candidates. Earlier, Cassell had made known to the public that Kenneth Haskins, former principal of the Morgan Community School, George Moody, from Wilmington, Delaware, and Barbara Sizemore, associate secretary of the American Association of School Administrators, were finalists. Interestingly, Haskins' name appeared on the list released by Barry, but Moody and Sizemore were omitted. Immediately this revealed that the superintendent selection was not to go as smoothly as it appeared on the surface.

About this time, a controversy arose as to the role of the Citizens Resource Commission. According to the procedure outlined, its job should have been completed after designating the 15 semifinalists, but the members asked to participate in the selection of the five finalists. The board granted the request. Thus, on July 22, 1973, the Commission named the five finalists to be Barbara Sizemore, Harriette Jenkins, a California educator, Kenneth Haskins, John Minor, a former superintendent also from California, and Charles F. Kenny, a California superintendent and the only white candidate. When Barry added Andrew Donaldson from New York to the list, the issue of favoritism erupted since Donaldson, who was originally rejected, was the uncle of Barry's close associate, Ivanhoe Donaldson. It took several meetings to resolve the problem. Barry explained the problem as a misinterpretation on the part of the commission as to its role in the selection process.[43]

Not all citizens were happy about the direction the DCBOE was apparently taking in its selection of candidates. Some wanted a local administrator, others had wanted Dr. Scott to remain, and some spoke vehemently in favor of their special choices from among the out-of-towners.[44]

By the July 25, 1973 board meeting, the list of finalists had been narrowed down to 3. Thus, at this meeting three significant board actions took place:

1. The Board approved inviting members of the acting superintendent's Executive Council to attend the interviews as non-participating observers.

2. The board voted not to invite the news media to conduct interviews of the final three candidates.

3. The board voted not to hold interviews of candidates on separate days for citizens and the news media.[45]

The above board decisions were shortlived ones, for commission member Kinard threatened to bring a group of supporters for open sessions to the meetings; whereupon, the board rescinded its original decisions for closed sessions and decided that the interviews would be open to the public and members of the commission could question the candidates.

Board members in 1972-74 were much concerned with decentralizing the D.C. public school system. Therefore, their questions probed candidates for their views on operationalizing this concept. Although aspects of decentralization could be seen in the school system in school-by-school budgeting, principal selection and three sub-systems (Model School Division, Adams-Morgan-Antioch College project, and the Anacostia Division), some board members still had great concerns about how to handle the decentralization of the entire system. Thus, they pressed each of the three finalists for an answer to this overwhelming concern.

John Minor's interview was held on July 28 and 29. In the interview, he discussed administration, community involvement, and decentralization. His preference was for community involvement rather than community control; thus he advocated a consortium of teachers, administrators, citizens, students, and parents who would share power and also decide what kind of decentralization they desired.[46]

Donaldson spent nine hours in interview sessions on July 30, at which time he discussed: political decentralization, where local boards had authority and power; standardized tests; career education; and a structured school system. His detailed plan for decentralization involved several phases: administrative decentralization; establishing local boards; and decentralizing decision-making to local boards. He proposed three years to complete the process.[47]

Notably, Barbara Sizemore's plan for decentralizing the school system was similar to Donaldson's in that she proposed to use the feeder school plan. But, more importantly, Sizemore's plan involved more sweeping systemic changes than did the plans of the other two finalists. It included nongrading, team teaching, a K-12 integrated structure, curriculum changes and the administrative team concept and related them to decentralization through the PACTS process involving goal setting and planning. To help her bring this about, she proposed to invite Kenneth Haskins into the administration as vice superintendent.

But more than any one else, Sizemore's articulation of how to educate the poor and the Black youngsters in the city strongly influenced the citizens and some board members who had reservations about her paper qualifications for managing a large urban school system, and she was propelled into first position. Her philosophy in this regard compelled most of them to select her as superintendent. Ideas such as the following captivated her audience:

> I don't think education is ever literal, and it is always political. The history of education in any country you would like to cite indicates that it has generally two purposes, a socialization purpose, and a purpose for providing information, knowledge and skills, that that particular culture considers necessary for operating within it....[48]

She further intrigued the audience when she expanded her philosophy by saying:

> I believe that a student is a learner, and teachers can be students, administrators can be students, board members can be students. A student is a learner, in a teaching-learning situation, and in an effective teaching-learning situation, a two-way dialogue appears between the teacher and the student. So that both are actors in the process, because learning is an aggressive activity.
>
> And, therefore, when the teacher is teaching, he or she is also learning. And when the learner is learning, he or she is also teaching. So that it is a two-way dialogue that occurs, and a person who is teaching at that moment is the subject actor, and the learner is the actor subject.
>
> But in a real teaching-learning situation, there is no object. There's no person to whom one is imparting information, to whom one is giving information. It is a continuous dialogue....
>
> The schools have really been successful in their failure, because of the purpose of education to prepare some people to be consumers and some people to be distributors.
>
> The other side...is that the schools have

failed to carry out the activity for which they can say they should be responsible, such as teaching reading, writing and arithmetic.

Now, when you look at the matter of teaching skills, we find that the schools seem to be unable to teach skills to certain kinds of students. Children who come from families that are poor, and children who come from certain minority groups.

With respect to this observation, I believe that the reason for it is because we use methods and tests that are not compatible with certain living styles and certain cultural differences....

I think that...we could look at the whole matter of testing, so that we can get more information about our students, and then can design the kinds of methods that will expedite the talents and insights that our children bring to the teaching-learning situation.[49]

She proceeded with:

> I think that the exigencies of certain hostile environments make people approach problem-solving in very different manners, and that the way one approaches problem-solving in a family of affluence, accustomed to approaching problem-solving with conceptualizations and abstractions which need not be duplicated in the real domain, may cause one to solve problems in a decidedly different manner than a person which requires a real-life approach to real problems at an early age.
>
> I am not satisfied that we spend enough time unearthing and discovering the things that are necessary for assessing a child's manner of solving problems, and I think this might give us better clues to solve the problems for certain kinds of children.[50]

Notably, Mrs. Sizemore gave specific examples to explain her ideas and concluded this thesis with:

> It just may be that we are using the wrong tests to find out what the problem is. And so, the test tells us the problem is X when it's really Y, and we don't have the tools to decide what Y is, so we keep doing A because A solves X, but not the problem.[51]

Each point was stated, well-documented and developed following along the lines of the discussion above. It was no wonder, then, that there were cheers and applause throughout her interview from people who probably had never before heard an educator speak in such a clear and descriptive manner about educational problems which had confounded them in the past.

Further on in the interview, in a prophetic way, Mrs. Sizemore predicted what needed to occur, and did in actual fact occur, if the board members who posed specific questions in this regard wanted to see change brought to the DCPS system when she said:

> There is always comfort in what is, somebody always has an investment in what is, so when you change what is to something else, the people who have the investment in what is are going to complain, and this is only human. This is natural, that's why whenever you want to talk about change, you have to talk about conflict.[52]

But conflict did not wait for the change agent to begin to make changes; it began even before Mrs. Sizemore was selected. Up to this point, there was conflict over (1) the process of the selection of the Citizens' Resource Commission, (2) Mr. Danzansky's membership on the commission, (3) the role of the commission in the final stages of the selection process, and (4) Mr. Donaldson's name on the list of finalists for the superintendency. The selection of Mrs. Sizemore as the people's choice for school superintendent now added a fifth source of conflict to the list.

Several external and internal factors impinged upon the final selection which caused the conflict. First, the national social unrest peaked the consciousness of board members to the need for viable citizen participation in the selection process and to the consequences, politically, in a city new in the election process if their choice ran counter to that of the vocal populace. An illustration from the minutes of August 7, 1973 will illuminate this point:

> Mrs. Pryde stated that after hours of careful examination of the qualifications of the three final candidates, probably the most overriding factor in making the decision to support the motion came from the intensive feedback of her community, Ward VII, which favored the appointment of Mrs. Sizemore.[53]

Second, the fact that the people's choice was female rather than male ran counter to the traditional choice in terms of the sex of big city school superintendents. The quotation below is an interesting illustration of the impact of sex as a factor on board members:

> Mason, Cassell, Tirana, Swaim and Mattie Taylor were the liberals. From time to time, some of those people would move over to the conservative side. Those of us who remained steadfast to a progressive position were Mason and myself. In many instances we found ourselves acting alone and especially for Mrs. Sizemore. We were the only two people who wanted her, who fought for her, who organized a strong community movement to challenge the board's carrying out that interviewing process in secrecy. We forced the board to open up that process and gained for Mrs. Sizemore extensive publicity -- radio, TV, newspaper reports and so on and so we had

kind of a heavy landslide movement within
the community, and it was after the board
finally reacted and appointed her as superintendent. Most of them didn't want her
because she was too militant. She was Black
and she was also a female which are the very
reasons we did want her.[54]

Third, some board members preferred the appointment of someone from inside the school system as superintendent. So the insider-versus-outsider factor surfaced. Although she voted for Sizemore, Pryde, in particular, had a problem with the fact that Sizemore was from outside the city. Her comments on this factor were as follows:

I think she was wonderful. I knew what she
wanted for the Black kids of this city, but
number 1, I was for someone in the system
because it takes too much learning for the
process of getting education done in the
District of Columbia for somebody coming in
out of the city.[55]

Fourth, the factor of management ability versus educational leadership was of concern to other board members. They emphasized the school system's need for a manager rather than an educational leader. Swaim said in her eight page letter to board members on August 7, 1973:

I would enjoy having a superintendent who
talks like Mrs. Sizemore. I really would.
She is brilliant, her ideas are right on the
mark.... But I do not feel that we can
afford the luxury of hiring a philosopher....
The children I represent do not need any more
on the job training for Superintendents.
They need a system for getting rid of those
incompetent teachers NOW, a sensible
decentralization NOW.[56]

Pryde also had some problems with this aspect of Sizemore's qualifications. In retrospect, she said, "I voted for her, but it was a difficult decision because she had no management training at all."[57]

The following discussion offers further insight as to how important the factor of management ability was to some board members. During the initial superintendent search interview with Mrs. Sizemore, the following transpired:

Question:

We've encountered some administrative problems in our school system, and I think it's caused us to be very much concerned about getting a good manager and a good administrator.

In our discussions, Board members have said that what they think we need at this point is a very efficient manager, because they see the school system essentially as a business. Because of the amount of money that we spend, and the similarity between the business operations of the school system and other kinds of businesses, as those people see them.

Others feel that an educational institution is perhaps a bit different, that it has a different kind of mission. It doesn't merchandise, it doesn't sell, it has a kind of service to provide, which takes it somewhat away from that particular arena....

Could you say a few things to us that would persuade those of us who are very much concerned about administration as opposed to education?

Ms. Sizemore:

Well, I really don't think you can separate the two, and I guess that's what I've been arguing here, in my statement.... I am not in agreement with a separation of management from education.

> I believe it is an integrated function, and you have to have a reason for a budget....
>
> In addition, it must happen to decide what you're going to take up and what you're not going to take up, what you're going to do again and what you're not going to do again. And this is determined on the assessment of the educational process. What your gains are and what your losses are.
>
> So I don't see administration separate from educational leadership, but that's what I argue in the papers that I write and the presentations that I make, in that, you cannot in public school administration, you cannot separate them like doctors do in hospitals because that's a pathological model that deals with the fact that something is wrong that the doctor has the expertise and diagnosis, et cetera.... so the hospital administrator has to make the hospital available for the doctor to do whatever he has to do.... but in public schools they're not that way. Because the administrator has to be able to assess the teacher's performance. The administrator of a hospital doesn't do that for a doctor.[58]

Fifth, the approach to making changes in the school system also loomed as a factor in the selection process as evidenced by Martha Swaim's comments in her August 7, 1973 statement and letter to board members regarding the selection of Mrs. Sizemore. She wrote:

> I supported...a candidate who in my view had a record of successful accomplishment in the areas of work needed in D.C.,... who had a problem solving approach that achieved quite radical goals without major conflict....[59]
>
> Mrs. Sizemore...state[s] flatly that change requires conflict...

> I agree that change will always involve some conflict, but I am only interested in necessary conflict. D.C. is not Chicago....[60]

Nonetheless, there were some board members who were interested in change. One of these who felt the need very strongly was Cassell. Thus, he stated:

> I wanted substantive change, structural change, philosophical change, personnel change. I wanted to see a completely different orientation from that left or inherited from Carl Hansen. There were other board members who felt an obligation to protect the interest of the system as it was. I tended to identify with Mr. Hobson's views of a complete change and whatever it took to make that change was significant in the interest of the students rather than the people who have been there for so long and done rather well moving up the ladder without giving quality education...[61]

So, in addition to Cassell, enough other board members accepted the challenge posed by Macchiavelli in The Prince:

> There is nothing more difficult to take in hand, more perilous to conduct, or more uncertain in its success, than to take the lead in the introduction of a new order of things.

and hired Mrs. Sizemore as superintendent.

In spite of their voiced commitment to change, Kenneth Haskins, for one, felt that the board was more conservative in terms of making changes than it appeared to be during the superintendent search interview. His response during his interview for this study was that:

> The Board...really ended up being very conservative when it came to Barbara and I doing anything that made for drastic kinds of changes even though...we were interviewed and

hired...with the tone that the Board was ready to see even some disruption in the system, if we really were going to make some major changes. So that in some ways, the Board sort of choraled us into functioning in a style that was different from what either of us had anticipated. So that they really didn't function, from my point of view, any different from any other Board. There were some things they were doing that were positive like their insistence upon minority vendors being given certain kinds of things. They would take nice stands on issues like Martin Luther King's birthday. But as far as really doing things to seriously change the structure of the school system, it really wasn't there....

A lot of things that we did without really the Board's saying, 'Go ahead.' Like the decentralization that was done without the Board...saying, 'That's exactly what we want - go ahead,' and be supportive 100 percent.[62]

Interestingly, three out of four white school board members did not vote for Barbara Sizemore. This fact could lead to a conclusion that race was also a factor in the superintendent selection process. Martha Swaim, in particular, keenly felt the pressure of race as is evidenced in her letter of August 7, 1973, in which she stated:

> I hope to prevail upon my fellow Board members to make their decision on the basis of the actual performance record of the candidates, rather than on the bandwagon effect.[63]

Notably, at that point in time, no Black females had ever been given an opportunity to administer a large urban school system. Therefore, an argument such as the one posed by Mrs. Swaim would naturally eliminate all Blacks and females from the competition.

In the second paragraph of her letter to the board, Swaim emphasizes race as a factor again when she says:

> In February, the Citizen's Commission, which we set up for strong input, elected Ellis Haworth (white) chairman after most other members declined. Haworth represents the one organization in town recognized by no one except the <u>Evening Star</u>. It is probably the most <u>segregated</u> association in D.C.[64]

Swaim continued with:

> But Charles (Cassell) was the canker, the rub, and everything he did, from yelling and making his tapes of all the sessions, to going to the press was designed to intimidate not the white members of the Board but <u>all</u> the members of the Board, and the Citizens' Commission. He certainly succeeded.[65]

And, finally, by page 7 of her 8 page letter, Swaim actually says what she was leading up to all along, that the only really qualified candidate was a white male. First, she said, on page 5: "The problem with William Kenny is that he is white, and traditional."[66] She reemphasizes this on page 7 when she states:

> Few members on the Board are willing to argue that even though decentralization is a necessary condition for radical change, we should consider a white candidate who has decentralized.[67]

Swaim's approach to the superintendent selection process then would have moved the board backward to the traditional kind of selection made in 1967, that of a white male as superintendent of a school system now 96 percent Black. Fortunately, there were enough forward thinking members of the DCBOE to prevent this turn of events.

Pursuant to her interview, Barbara A. Sizemore was appointed as superintendent of the D.C. public school system at the August 7, 1973 school board meeting.[68] The motion was made by Taylor and seconded by Mason, who was later to regret her decision. Washington abstained because she felt all of the candidates were second best. Cassell voted Yes with reservations regarding the conditions placed on the selection in terms of a contractual agreement and a memorandum of understanding. Mason voted Yes after listing 14 reasons why she supported Mrs. Sizemore's appointment. Rosenfield felt that administrative leadership was very important and of the highest priority and for this reason, Mr. Minor was his choice. Therefore, he voted No. Both Tirana and Coates voted Yes. After giving his reason why Andrew Donaldson was the best qualified of the final three candidates, Kemp voted No. Pryde voted Yes. Swaim mentioned that she had supported a candidate who had a record of successful accomplishment in the area of work needed in D.C. in the areas of recruitment, management, and reading instruction -- and who had a problem-solving approach that achieved radical goals without major conflict. Therefore, she voted No.

Swaim expanded on her opposition to the appointment of Mrs. Sizemore in her eight page letter to the DCBOE sent just prior to the voting. In the letter she enumerated several points in opposition to Sizemore's appointment. Point 11 was that "Mrs. Sizemore, and most of the Chicago people who supported her, state flatly that change requires conflict."[69] Swaim further stated:

> Now it is true that we learned about problems with all of the people we considered. John Minor had a financial crisis two years into his contract at Ravenswood that would not have occurred had he fired the business manager. Andrew Donaldson is domineering, traditional, very public relations minded. The problem with William Kenny is that he is white, and

traditional.

On the other hand, nothing that I heard in Mrs. Sizemore's interview showed that my earlier assessment was incorrect. Her apparent claque for her candidacy gave me pause, for a job that required a certain amount of conflict resolution.[70]

Thus, Swaim proposed as two possible solutions: (1) to appoint John Minor, or (2) to appoint Floretta McKenzie for one year and continue the search.[71] In conclusion, Swaim summarized her dilemma as follows:

I agree that change will always involve some conflict, but I am only interested in necessary conflict. D.C. is not Chicago. D.C. is not a strong union town - just a civil service procedures town.

In summary, then, I believe that the Board is faced with an unhappy choice between a brilliant teacher of a philosophy about education which I agree with 100 percent and two candidates who lack that brilliance but show a record that they could decentralize the authority to the local school. Since I believe that change in D.C. Schools can only come at the local school, and that no amount of fire from the top can substitute for that, I must support John Minor. I urge you to do the same.[72]

The letter in its entirety can lead one to believe that Swaim wanted a white superintendent and, in lieu of this, a Black who did not project himself as a Black nationalist.

To recapitulate, the countdown, then, was as follows: Cassell, Taylor, Tirana, Mason, Pryde, Barry and Coates voting for Sizemore as superintendent and Kemp, Swaim and Rosenfield voting against Sizemore, with Washington abstaining.[73]

As a result, seven board members made history by hiring the first Black female superintendent of schools in a large urban area.

## Superintendent Barbara A. Sizemore

Mrs. Barbara A. Sizemore, a Black woman born in Indiana and mother of a girl and two boys, one adopted, is a graduate of Northwestern University. She was a classic language scholarship student, majoring in Latin, who graduated with a B.A. degree in 1947. In 1954, she received an M.A. degree from the same university. Mrs. Sizemore received her Ph.D. degree from the University of Chicago in 1979.

Mrs. Sizemore has been actively involved in public education over a span of 28 years. Initially, she taught English and reading to the educable mentally handicapped and Spanish in an elementary school; 7th and 8th grade English, reading, and Spanish in a junior high school; and 3rd and 4th grade students in another elementary public school in Chicago. She then became principal of the Anton Dvorak Elementary School (K-6 Nongraded) in 1963 and principal of the Forrestville High School in 1965. By this time, Mrs. Sizemore's creative spirit had reached its stride as she initiated efforts to turn Forrestville from a gangland oasis into an innovative hiatus for the creative energies of her students, using the arts as a vehicle for learning the basic skills. In 1969, Mrs. Sizemore became director, district superintendent of the Woodlawn Experimental Schools Project, a Title III ESEA program, funded under Public Law 89-10 for three million dollars. Meanwhile, she was an instructor at the Center for Inner City Studies, Northeastern Illinois University -- an innovative multi-disciplinary, multi-ethnic graduate school program -- located in a poverty area on the south side of Chicago. When the money ran out, in 1971, for the Woodlawn "community control" project experiment, Mrs. Sizemore became the coordinator for Proposal

Development, Department of Government Funded Programs for the Chicago public schools. In 1973, she left the Chicago public school system for a job as associate secretary, American Association of School Administrators, in Arlington, Virginia. Subsequently, after a controversial selection process and a gruelling 11 hours of public interviewing, Mrs. Sizemore became superintendent of the D.C. public schools on October 1, 1973. She served in this capacity until her firing in October 1975.

At its August 7, 1974 meeting, after Mrs. Sizemore was appointed superintendent of schools (conditional upon a contractual agreement for her services and a memorandum of understanding), Board President Barry appointed a committee of five, consisting of Mrs. Mason, Mr. Cassell, Mrs. Taylor, Reverend Coates and himself, to negotiate a contract and memorandum of understanding. Consequently, at this meeting the board discussed meeting with the newly appointed superintendent to work out goals. Later, in connection with the goal statement, it was agreed that the submission of this document be postponed until after Mrs. Sizemore had officially come aboard and had had an opportunity to look at the system. Furthermore, it was agreed that Mrs. Sizemore would evaluate previously agreed upon goals and board directives and make proposed recommendations to the board as to goals for the coming years.[74] This decision was in keeping with Section 2.3 of the board Rules which reads, in part:

> The Superintendent shall submit to the Board within 120 days of his appointment, his initial program for the improvement of the public schools and his recommended timetable for its implementation.[75]

A motion to follow this procedure was made and carried during the August 7, 1973 meeting of the DCBOE.

At least three points made in the contract should be noted since they surface in the conflict which ensues later. Item two is of particular significance:

> Throughout the term of this contract the Superintendent shall be subject to discharge for adequate cause affecting her character and efficiency as Superintendent, provided, however, that the Board does not arbitrarily or capriciously call for her dismissal and that the Superintendent shall have the right to written charges, notice of hearing, and a fair hearing before the Board. If the Superintendent chooses to be accompanied by legal counsel at the hearing, she will assume the cost of legal counsel.[76]

Item seven should also be noted, for aspects of it consistently surfaced and exacerbated the conflict in superintendent-school board relations that ensued:

> The Superintendent will have complete freedom to organize, reorganize, and arrange the administrative and supervisory staff, including instruction and business affairs, which in her judgment best serves the District of Columbia Public Schools. The responsibility of selection, placement, and transfer of personnel shall be vested in the Superintendent subject to approval by the Board; and the Board, individually and collectively, will refer promptly all criticisms, complaints and suggestions called to its attention to the Superintendent for study, action, and/or recommendation.[77]

Finally, an item which undergirded this whole investigation was discussed. It reads:

> The Board shall provide the Superintendent with periodic opportunities to discuss Superintendent-Board relationships and shall

provide for an annual conference for the purpose of discussing the performance of the Superintendent.[78]

Mrs. Sizemore had now begun her official duties as superintendent of the D.C. public school system. In her opening address to the community, she clarified her position in regard to the involvement of community people by referring to the PACTS process. She stated:

> She would hope that in the future the speakers at community meetings would at least give equal time to what goes on in the buildings between the people there, the teachers and the students, the maintenance staff and the administrators, the parents and the community who must work together in order to improve education. She had suggested the establishment of what she called PACTS [for Parents, Administrators, Community, Teachers, Students] in each local school community in order to begin a meaningful dialogue between the various groups. This would require working together very hard and very conscientiously. Therefore, she asked that energies be used positively in the creation of a meaningful dialogue between those groups rather than to spend the time destructively blaming each other for why the quality of education did not improve. She pledged her best efforts in that direction and could only do that -- her best.[79]

## Sizemore's Educational Philosophy

Barbara A. Sizemore was selected as superintendent of the D.C. Public School System because of her philosophy of education and her record of implementation as principal of an elementary school and a high school as well as a district superintendent in Chicago. The philosophy which brought her to the forefront nationally had as its basic tenet educational justice for all students. Therefore, Mrs. Sizemore believes that the organizational structure, called the teaching and learning environment, must be changed. She postulates that change is necessary so that schools are compatible with the way human beings grow and develop. She persuasively argues in many of her articles that "human beings do not grow at the same rate at the same time for the same reasons with the same materials in the same way" and therefore we must provide for human variation in the student population. Mrs. Sizemore feels that any parent who watches his or her children grow knows that each learns to do things like walking, talking, feeding him or herself at different rates and are free to explore and learn in the open space environment of the home. From this, she concludes that human beings are different in how they acquire knowledge, order knowledge and receive knowledge. Hence all people are different. Black people are different. All can learn equally in general only as they can learn differently. This being the case then, Mrs. Sizemore asserts that the school system does not deal with Black people's gifts and talents. In other words, it deals with the norm and talents of some other group. As proof of the above assertion, she suggests that the educational system in this country is structured along mono-lingual or monocultural lines while the population is multi-lingual or multi-cultural. Therefore, she insists, if we want to design a teaching/learning environment that is compatible with the way human beings grow, then it has to be re-constructed so that open space is an option; and it must be multimodal (that is, containing children of different colors, ages, sizes, etc. within the group), multi-lingual and multi-cultural.

Furthermore, Sizemore believes that human beings process knowledge through four symbol systems: words, numbers (Mathematics), notes (as in musical instruction) and images (art, pictures, etc.). She explains that we teach children to handle only one symbol system, maybe two, when in the 21st century knowledge will be disseminated as much by art and music as by word and number. She asks us to consider, then, whether or not art and music are frills or basics. Actually, Sizemore is opposed to placing emphasis on any single symbol system as a method of helping students understand and feels that a child should be exposed to each method in order to help him reach his full potential. Additionally, she believes that language, mathematics, music and art should be developed into skill units where mastery is acquired through performance tasks with direct feedback.

Thus, she insists the acquisition of procedural knowledge (skills on how to do something like read, write, etc.) is just as important as the acquisition of propositional knowledge, that is, knowledge in and of itself. Both are necessary for solving problems, she explains.

Sizemore further informs us that the structure of public education in this country is based on white Anglo-Saxon Protestant affluent male norms which ignore the individuality of each person and his unique patterns of growth and development. In this regard, she tells us that the average person is a fiction of someone's imagination. Growing out of this fiction, she feels, is our insistence on using norm-referenced tests geared to a norm-referenced curriculum based on an Anglo-Saxon value system and talents imposed on other people as the only culture. In essence, Sizemore is concerned that these tests are used in our society to sort human beings into two basic groups -- those with experiences most like Anglo-Saxon Protestant males with money (the most successful) and those with experiences least like Anglo-Saxon Protestant males with money (the least successful). They are not used, she feels, as tools for learning what special services or extra resources each child needs to meet his special "growth rates, development patterns, learning styles, cultural heritage and sociolinguistic experiences." In this connection, she suggests the use of criterion-referenced tests based on set criteria and learning experiences designed to help students reach the criteria.

In order to accomplish the above, Sizemore was to restructure the D.C. public school system into six administratively decentralized regions with six regional superintendents, each in charge of similarly sized regions. Programmatically and budget-wise, she hoped to incorporate the following other changes in support of her philosophy of educational justice for all students in the school system:

1. To structure a pre-kindergarten through 12 system which provides for multi-age, multi-level grouping in individual classrooms and in open space.

2. To decentralize the school system using PACTS* and to flatten out the administrative hierarchy by broadening the decision-making responsibility of staff through the concept of the administrative team.

3. To develop curricula to reflect:
   - an emphasis on procedural and propositional knowledge
   - multi-lingual, multi-cultural content
   - changes in conceptual framework of content organization
   - a combination of like disciplines
   - flexible time sequences
   - emphasis on concepts instead of facts
   - an integrated approach to special education and career education

4. To establish a facilities planning unit which will provide the mechanism through which data will be secured, compiled and disseminated.

---

*The PACTS process is a method of collective decision-making among parents, administrators, community persons, teachers and students to set and achieve educational goals in an orderly fashion.

5. To improve management services.

6. To increase the capacity for research, planning and evaluation.

7. To provide a humanistic approach to security and safety.

8. To create an Office of Communication.[80]

### Summary

As the arguments advanced as this chapter suggests, three superintendents -- Drs. Hansen, Manning and Scott -- who preceded Mrs. Sizemore, had conflicts with the DCBOE. School superintendent-school board relations in all three cases were such that Hansen resigned; Manning was relieved of his duties and allowed to resign; and Scott's contract was not renewed. One could ask the questions: Will a new superintendent be allowed to administer the DCPS without undue interference?; Will the new superintendent be allowed to make significant systemic changes?; or will the new superintendent also become embroiled in the politics in the city and the school system?

Chapter VI focuses on another significant internal organizational factor, goal setting. The review of three educational programs and priorities growing out of goals set for the school system provide insight into how goals changed as board membership and superintendents changed. It also reveals how these goal changes caused conflict in superintendent-school board relations.

FOOTNOTES                           Chapter V


1.  *D.C. Code*, Par. 31-101 (a) (1973 Ed.).

2.  D.C. Public School System, "Superintendent's Contract," 6 September 1973, p. 2.

3.  "Hansen Critic Asks Study of Others for Job," *Washington Star*, 25 January 1976.

4.  Hansen, quoted in *Danger in Washington*, pp. 228-229.

5.  "School Board Will Interview Lansing Man," *Washington Star*, 4 October 1967.

6.  "Hobson Has Candidates for D.C. School Head," *Washington Star*, 1 October 1967.

7.  John Matthews, "School Board Majority Leans Toward Manning," *Washington Star*, 25 October 1967.

8.  "School Board Will Interview Lansing Man," ibid.

9.  "Fireworks Explode," *Washington Afro-American*, 2 October, 1967.

10. Mary R. Hunter, "Looking for Superperson," *Bulletin Board*, April 1977, pp. 7-8.

11. "Minutes of the Twenty-Seventh (Stated) Meeting of the Board of Education, 1967-1968" (Washington, D.C., 21 February 1968), Enclosure F, p. 2.

12. L. V. Anderson, "4 on School Board Suggest Manning Find Another Job," *Washington Post*, 6 July 1968.

13. "Minutes of the Forty-Fifth (Stated) Meeting of the Board of Education," Washington, D.C., 17 December 1969, p. 14.

14. Ibid., Enclosure 3.

15. "Minutes of the Fifth (Special) Meeting of the Board of Education," Washington, D.C., 12 March 1970, pp. 2-10.

16. "Minutes of the Eleventh (Special) Meeting of the Board of Education," Washington, D.C., 27 May 1970, p. 7.

17. "Minutes of the Fifteenth (Special) Meeting of the Board of Education," Washington, D.C., 24 July 1970, pp. 1-10.

18. Ibid., pp. 12-13.

19. "Minutes of the Sixteenth (Special) Meeting of the Board of Education," Washington, D.C., 30 July 1970, p. 26.

20. "Minutes of the Eighteenth (Special) Meeting of the Board of Education," Washington, D.C., 31 August 1970, pp. 2-5.

21. "Minutes of the Fifth (Stated) Meeting of the Board of Education," Washington, D.C., 15 March 1972, pp. 25-27; and Enclosure 2, "Memorandum of Understanding Between D.C. Board of Education and Superintendent of Schools."

22. Irna Moore, "Scott: Schools Like 'Combat Zone', Washington Post, 31 March, 1972.

23. "Scott to Stress Budget; Will Wait on Contract," Washington Post, 24 October 1972.

24. "Minutes of the Twenty-Second (Stated) Meeting of the Board of Education, " Washington, D.C., 21 October 1970, pp. 15-18; see also

"Minutes of the Sixteenth (Special) Meeting of the Board of Education," Washington, D.C., 12 August 1971, pp. 3-19. "Minutes of the Eighth (Special) Meeting of the Board of Education," Washington, D.C., 25 April 1972, pp. 2-8. "Minutes of the Second Session of the Seventeenth (Special) Meeting of the Board of Education," Washington, D.C., 19 July 1972, pp. 43-44.

25. "Minutes of the Twenty-Second (Stated) Meeting of the Board of Education," Washington, D.C., 21 October 1970, pp. 15-18. See also "Minutes of the Eighth (Stated) Meeting of the Board of Education," Washington, D.C., 17 March 1971, pp. 37-39. "Minutes of the Fourteenth (Special) Meeting of the Board of Education," Washington, D.C., 12 July 1971, pp. 2-12, Enclosures 3 and 4.

26. "Minutes of the Third (Stated) Meeting of the Board of Education," Washington, D.C., 16 February 1972, pp. 44-52.

27. "Minutes of the Third (Stated) Meeting of the Board of Education," Washington, D.C., 16 February 1972, pp. 36-41; see also "The Superintendent's Annual Report: School Year 1971-72", Washington, D.C., District of Columbia Public Schools, p. 9.

28. "Proposed Administrative Reorganization of the D.C. Public School System." Submitted to the DCBOE by Hugh J. Scott, Superintendent, 5 May 1971, in Reorganization Summary. See also, "The Superintendent's Annual Report: School Year 1970-71," Washington, D.C., District of Columbia Public Schools, December 1971), pp. 22-23; "The Superintendent's Annual Report: School Year 1971-72," Washington, D.C., District of Columbia Public Schools, 1972, pp. 11-12.

29. "Minutes of the Thirty-Seventh (Stated) Meeting of the Board of Education," Washington, D.C., 17 January 1973, pp. 28-29.

30. Ibid., p. 34.

31. Ibid., pp. 1-15.

32. Ibid., pp. 69-74.

33. "Transcript of the Second (Community) Meeting, Board of Education," Washington, D.C., 7 February 1973, pp. 1-14. See also Hugh J. Scott, Superintendent of Schools, "Superintendent's Identification of Tasks, Resource Needs and Prerequisite Actions Associated with the Ten Priority Goals of the Board of Education - A Planning Document," (Washington, D.C.: District of Columbia Public Schools, February 1973).

34. "Minutes of the Third (Stated) Meeting of the Board of Education," Washington, D.C., 21 February 1973, pp. 19-20, Enclosure 1, pp. 20-26.

35. "Transcript of the Fourth (Community) Meeting Public Schools of the District of Columbia," Washington, D.C., 7 March 1973, pp. 4-37.

36. Interview with Charles Cassell, D.C. Board of Education member, Washington, D.C., 5 October 1977.

37. "Minutes of the Fifth (Special) Meeting of the Board of Education," Washington, D.C., 14 March 1973, pp. 3-6.

38. "Minutes of the Sixth (Stated) Meeting of the Board of Education," Washington, D.C., 21 March 1973, pp. 19.

39. "Transcript of the Seventh (Special) Meeting of the Board of Education," Washington, D.C., 26 March 1973, p. 39.

40. "Transcript of the Twelfth (Stated) Meeting of the Board of Education," Washington, D.C., 16 May 1973, pp. 43-46.

41. "Minutes of the Thirteenth (Business) Meeting of the Board of Education," Washington, D.C., 4 June 1973, p. 16.

42. "Minutes of the Sixteenth (Stated) Meeting of the Board of Education," Washington, D.C., 20 June 1973, pp. 20-22.

43. Mary R. Hunter, "Looking for Superperson, Part II: Barbara A. Sizemore--1973-75," Bulletin Board, May 1977, pp. 3-4.

44. "Transcript of the Board of Education," Washington, D.C., 12 July 1973, pp. 3-19.

45. "Minutes of the Nineteenth (Special) Meeting of the Board of Education," Washington, D.C., 25 July 1973, pp. 1-4.

46. Tapes of the interview held by the D.C. Board of Education with John Minor, finalist for D.C. Superintendency, Washington, D.C., 28 July 1973.

47. Tapes of the interview held by the D.C. Board of Education with Andrew Donaldson, finalist for the D.C. Superintendency, Washington, D.C. 30 July 1973.

48. Tapes of the interview held by the D.C. Board of Education with Barbara A. Sizemore, finalist for D.C. Superintendency, Washington, D.C. 31 July 1973.

49. Ibid.

50. Ibid.

51. Ibid.

52. Ibid.

53. "Minutes of the Twenty-First (Special) Meeting of the Board of Education, Washington, D.C., 7 August 1973, p. 4.

54. Interview with Charles Cassell, D.C. Board of Education member, Washington, D.C., 5 October 1977.

55. Interview with Delores Pryde, D.C. Board of Education member, Washington, D.C., 23 October 1977.

56. Statement to friends from Martha Swaim re: Barbara A. Sizemore as Superintendent, 7 August 1973.

57. Interview with Delores Pryde, D.C. Board of Education member, Washington, D.C., 23 October 1977.

58. Tapes of the interview held by the D.C. Board of Education with Mrs. Barbara A. Sizemore, finalist for the D.C. Superintendency, Washington, D.C., 31 July 1973.

59. Statement to friends from Martha Swaim re: Barbara A. Sizemore as Superintendent, 7 August 1973.

60. Swaim to D.C. Board of Education members re: Barbara A. Sizemore as Superintendent, 7 August 1973, p. 5.

61. Interview with Charles Cassell, D.C. Board of Education member, Washington, D.C., 5 October 1977.

62. Interview with Kenneth Haskins, DCPS Vice Superintendent, Washington, D.C., 22 November 1977.

63. Swaim to D.C. Board of Education members re: Barbara A. Sizemore as Superintendent, 7 August 1973, p. 1.

64. Ibid.

65. Ibid., p. 6.

66. Ibid., p. 5.

67. Ibid., p. 7.

68. "Minutes of the Twenty-First (Special) Meeting of the Board of Education," Washington, D.C., 7 August 1973, pp. 2-4.

69. Letter to D.C. Board of Education members from Martha Swaim re: Barbara A. Sizemore as Superintendent, 7 August 1973, p. 5.

70. Ibid.

71. Ibid.

72. Ibid., p. 8.

73. "Minutes of the Twenty-First (Special) Meeting of the Board of Education," Washington, D.C., 7 August 1973, pp. 26-27.

74. Ibid.

75. Rules of the Board of Education, Chapter 1, Part 1, Section 2.3.

76. D.C. Public School System, "Superintendent's Contract," 6 September 1973.

77. Ibid.

78. Ibid.

79. "Minutes of the Twenty-Fifth (Community) Meeting of the Board of Education," Washington, D.C., 3 October 1973, p. 3.

80. Opinion expressed by Barbara A. Sizemore, former superintendent of schools in Washington, D.C., in an address ("Quality Education and the Black Community) at the Institute of the Black World, Inc., Atlanta, Georgia, January 1976 (tape on file in the Institute of the Black World, Inc.); "Interview: Barbara Sizemore," Black Books Bulletin 2 (Winter 1974), 50-59; Barbara A. Sizemore, "Education and Justice Through PACTS", Comment, November 1973, pp. 1-8; "The Dysfunctions of Public Education," The Black Child Advocate, November 1974, p. 6; Barbara A. Sizemore, "The Four M Curriculum: A Way to Shape the Future," The Journal of Negro Education, 48 (Summer 1979), 341-356; Amy Billingsley and Pat Nagle, "An Interview with Barbara Sizemore", Bulletin Board, February 1974, pp. 2-4; Barbara A. Sizemore, "Education: Is Accommodation Enough?", The Journal of Negro Education 44 (Summer 1975), 223-246; Barbara A. Sizemore, "A Retreat From Progress: Back to the Basics?", December 3, 1975, pp. 1-7 (mimeographed). Barbara A. Sizemore, "Is There Still Room for the Black School?", (Washington, D.C.: Sixth Annual Research Conference, Howard University, June 2, 1978), pp. 1-24 (mimeographed).

CHAPTER VI

GOAL SETTING

Introduction

The problem of goal setting has proved to be a most difficult matter for the decision-making unit. Settling on goals and establishing priorities have consumed considerable time and energy. Some aspects of the goals set, changed or shifted emphasis with each new superintendent and with each new board.* Constant change and constant redefinition of goals seemed to paralyze any attempts at programmatic continuity, growth and development. Some changes or lack of changes on the part of superintendents caused conflict with some board members.

This section will concentrate on three major goal-setting efforts which helped make conflict between boards and superintendents a routine matter by 1973: (1) academic achievement plans reflected in the Track System, designed by Superintendent Carl Hansen, and the Clark Plan, introduced during Acting Superintendent Benjamin Henley's administration, but left for newly selected Superintendent Hugh Scott to implement; and (2) decentralization, the initial phases of which were introduced in 1964, but left for Superintendent Scott to shape into a system-wide effort, which was actually done by Superintendent Barbara Sizemore; and (3) equalization.

---
*A board is considered to be new when new members join it.

## The Track System

In 1956 the District of Columbia school system began a new program which was to cause conflict eleven years later between Superintendent Hansen, some school board members, and civil rights groups. The new program designed by Hansen was the track system, or "ability grouping." It consisted of four curriculum tracks: honors, college preparatory, general and basic. The objective was to permit students of similar academic achievement to learn together. In 1958, the track system was implemented in the senior high schools for all grades. Shortly thereafter, it was introduced into the elementary and junior high schools. For example, tracking was incorporated in the Amidon Plan which was a subject-centered curriculum initiated by Hansen in 1960 in a 25-room Washington, D.C. elementary school named Amidon.[1]

The track system became a heated issue within the community, and a matter of conflict between the school board and the superintendent. For example, at the April 22, 1965 board of education meeting, Dr. Euphemia L. Haynes made a motion to abolish the track system, seconded by Dr. Mordecai W. Johnson, former president of Howard University. The motion was lost with Dr. Haynes and Dr. Johnson voting Aye, and Mr. Smuck, Colonel West Hamilton, Mrs. Louise Steele, Dr. McLendon, Mrs. Roberts and Mr. Yochelson voting Nay.[2]

Further concern about the track system was shown by board member Steele on May 19, 1965 when she raised questions about the system based on Superintendent Hansen's report entitled, "Improving the Operation of the Track System." Steele questioned: (1) the establishment of a Department of Special Education and teacher training programs in the area; (2) how individualized programming by subject would be implemented; and (3) how the proposal would allow for a flow of new ideas from principals and teachers, a sharing of experiences in other organizational patterns, and use of new materials and programs. Decentralization of administration was suggested by board president Wesley S. Williams as one way to handle the concerns voiced by Mrs. Steele through her questions. Both statements were referred to the superintendent.[3]

Finally, in September 1965, due to pressure from board members Haynes and Steele, in particular, who felt that the track system had overtones of racism because the basic track served as a dumping ground for Black students, the board approved Superintendent Hansen's recommendation that an objective outside agency review the entire school system.[4]

But even subsequent to the above, disagreement about the track system persisted as attested to by Dr. Euphemia L. Haynes' April 20, 1966 statement on the track system in which she calls attention to: (1) criticism lodged by community officials in government and leaders in education; (2) the interchangeable use of the terms "track system," "ability grouping," and "varied curriculum," to misrepresent the facts; (3) the waste of public funds to study a program widely felt to be untenable; and (4) the damage of the track system to large numbers of children. Again, she made a motion to abolish the track system. Her motion lost for lack of a second.[5]

Eventually, though, the outside group chosen to review the school system, headed by A. Harry Passow, Teachers College, Columbia University,[6] made its report. The group recommended abandonment of the Amidon Plan which incorporated the track system since it was too misunderstood to be effective. In support of this suggested course of action, the report enumerated several problems with the track system. For one, it noted that in 1966 only one percent of the total school population was represented in the special academic classes and 2.2 percent of the Black population in the regular plus special academic classes, grades

1-6. Secondly, at the junior high level about 7.4 percent of Washington, D.C. pupils were placed in the special education curriculum which averaged between 2.5 percent white and 7.8 percent Black. Third, indications showed that honors students were mostly white. Further, honors classes were twice as likely to be taught by a white teacher than by a Black teacher and special academic classes were seven times more likely to have a Black teacher than a white one.[7]

### The Clark Plan

In February 1970, during the administration of Acting Superintendent Benjamin J. Henley, the board of education discussed the securing of consultants to work with the DCBOE in various areas. Dr. Kenneth Clark of the Metropolitan Applied Research Center (MARC) was approached about this in March and April of 1970. He agreed to work with the board in terms of raising the academic achievement level of the students in the DCPS system. The board also requested that Dr. Clark furnish a plan implementable within the framework of public school resources by the end of June, 1970.[8]

Dr. Clark's plan was approved by the DCBOE at a July 13, 1970 special meeting. The report was entitled "A Possible Reality, A Design for the Attainment of High Academic Achievements for the Students of the Public Elementary and Junior High Schools of Washington, D.C." Dr. Clark and MARC were asked to continue to serve as consultants to the board for about one year during the implementation of the report.

Dr. Clark, then, explained the essence of the plan. In the area of curriculum it was essential to have specific educational content and requirements per grade that teachers, parents and students understood, that were obtainable, and that teachers would be involved in in setting up the standards and seeing that they were attained. His thrust for teachers was for high and realistic motivation and high professional performance. This carried for other personnel as well. Considered, also, was the DCBOE's responsibility to clarify its goals, and in making the appointments and determining the policies and procedures necessary to attain the goals. Furthermore, a reading mobilization year was suggested, as the heart of the report, which would permit the raising of the average grade of the children in the elementary and the junior high schools to the national norm within the first year.

Also, Dr. Clark explained that not so much was needed in terms of major new resources in personnel or finance as major changes in attitudes and perspectives towards the children. He pointed out, in response to a question by Cassell, that there would be no need for his study had the board implemented the Passow study recommendations.[9] Also suggested were changes in the organizational structure of the schools, in selection and training of teachers, in providing realistic rewards for teaching, and in emphasizing standard English. Some more specific suggestions were: (1) reading teams per building; (2) the completion of written curriculum standards for each grade level; (3) the reorganization of the elementary school; (4) differentiated staffing; (5) heterogeneous grouping; and (6) multiple adults in the classroom. Additionally, Dr. Clark stated that if the board adopted his report, he understood that it would become the policy of the board and he could not concede that the board would elect a superintendent that would be contrary or in conflict with its policy.

The question of policy changes being made by an outside agent was of great concern to some board members, especially as at least one aspect of the policy changes was contrary to present board policy. Swaim, Tirana, and Cassell were especially concerned, with Tirana pinpointing four areas of policy changes and Cassell emphasizing a fifth: (1) ability grouping; (2) the need for additional funding for staff development; (3) differential staffing requiring a change in the entire salary structure for teachers; and (4) a new criteria for selection of a superintendent, namely acceptance of policy implementations in the Clark Plan, not yet articulated to the citizen's panel and community. Cassell's main concerns were with regard to competition among children and with negative views regarding the use of Black dialect. Therefore, all three members urged the board to delay action on the acceptance of the Clark Plan until the board had had time to consider the policy issues raised. Nevertheless, the motion was amended that the board approve the report, request that the services of MARC and Dr. Clark be continued, and that the liaison committee composed of board members Alexander, Hancock and Allen continue to work with Dr. Clark on its implementation. Thereupon, a vote was put and carried with board members Taylor, Swaim, Coates, Rosenfield, Allen, Hancock, Roots, Alexander and Washington voting Aye, Cassell voting No, and Tirana abstaining.[10]

After only one month in office, some board members, namely, Hancock, Rosenfield and Roots (Allen supporters), felt that Scott, the new superintendent, was dragging his feet on the implementation of the Clark Plan. They began to press him for movement. Thus, the status of committee reports on implementation and projected timetable for review of reports were called for in the board meeting of October 21, 1970. Superintendent Scott's replies indicated that he felt the plan had already been initiated before his arrival and was moving forward. He also indicated that a total realignment of the budget was necessary for a program which involved over two-thirds of the school system, and therefore the budget for long-range programmatic changes would not be available by November 13 when other task force reports would be ready. He reiterated that he planned to bring the full resources of the system to bear on the board's stated policy of a design for academic achievement.[11]

The board urged movement; the superintendent stressed involvement.[12] Later it appeared that this difference in approach toward implementation created conflict in terms of the board's number one priority. During the meeting, the board was reminded by Mr. Tirana that it had charged the superintendent with implementation of the Clark report and must set the goals and priorities and allow the administration to act upon these policies.[13]

Two conferences were held with Superintendent Scott, one on February 4, 1971 and another March 11, 1971. Essentially, both conferences dealt with the implementation of the Design for Academic Achievement and that part of the 120-Day Report dealing with same.

Primarily questions put by board members to the superintendent dealt with the (1) superintendent's goals; (2) what was going on in the classroom at the present time that was different because of the Academic Achievement Plan (AAP), (3) steps the superintendent planned to take to raise the level of academic achievement; and (4) recommendations of areas of the plan to discard. Further, Superintendent Scott was requested to submit an initial plan and the implementation timetable in line with the board's agreement with the superintendent that he would submit to the board within 120 days of his appointment his initial program for the improvement of the public schools and a recommended timetable for its implementation.[14]

Notes of the conferences between the superintendent and the board about the implementation of the Clark Plan had been leaked to the press as a pressure tactic. Even while resenting this pressure, Superintendent Scott responded to the implications of the implied criticism of his administration. The superintendent stated that there was a board tendency to: (1) overlook the process to organize to accomplish a conceptual goal; (2) seek instant solutions and immediate success; and (3) hire a superintendent for an instant solution to problems.

In addition, Superintendent Scott expressed the views that: (1) he had tried to communicate to the board that progress was being made; (2) the Design for Academic Achievement offered no specificity in terms of what should happen in the classroom to achieve quality education; and (3) the design called for the establishment of mobilization teams to seek ways to resolve problems of reading and those teams were composed of classroom teachers who may or may not have the expertise.

Furthermore, the superintendent stated that he found two basic problems with the design: (1) there was no specificity as to how teachers were to improve instruction; and (2) how heterogeneous grouping and individualization could be made compatible and how use of minimum floors could guide promotion or student placement.

An acute problem was due to the lack of preplanning prior to the mobilization of forces for implementation such as organization of financial and personnel resources to attack the problem of massive retardation in the acquisition of basic skills. In this regard, particularly, it had been difficult to provide leadership because the board refused to recognize the complexity of the problems.

In summing up his resentment of the board's public attack on his leadership, Superintendent Scott emphasized that he felt it was wrong to circulate notes from a private conference between the superintendent and the board and that he felt he had provided effective leadership to administrators, teachers, and the community. Thus, he no longer wished to be placed on the defensive about the Design for Academic Achievement since he had appropriately responded to it in his 120-Day Report.[15]

The rocky marriage between the superintendent and the DCBOE was steadied, somewhat, after the submission of the superintendent's report on the implementation of the Academic Achievement Plan at the May 19, 1971 meeting of the board. The report was endorsed pending further modifications in some areas. Most significant, though, was the support expressed for the superintendent's leadership as indicated in the following excerpt from the minutes: "Mr. Rosenfield stated that he intended to vote for the motion; that he could guarantee that he knew of eight Board members who wished for the Superintendent the best in bringing about the kinds of change that was needed in the school system."[16]

Mrs. Taylor asked that she be included on the list of those in support of Dr. Scott's leadership, making this a total of nine board members.[17]

A special meeting was held on July 12, 1971 to discuss the Academic Achievement Program. Prior to this meeting, six ward-level meetings were held to secure comments and questions from the community. Conflict among board members, and between board members and the superintendent arose as a result of the submission of (1) a report by Allen which was very critical of the administration's performance, and (2) a minority report from Cassell and two other members of the board. Points in Allen's report objected to by Cassell were: (1) the insistence of board members in telling the superintendent what to do and when to report on each phase of the AAP instead of asking him how he was going to evaluate the program; (2) insistence on the use of and possible misuse of standardized tests; (3) the exclusion of creativity and initiative as components in the process of teaching and learning; (4) the stringent adherence to the graded system; (5) the lock step approach to teaching and learning incorporated in the program; and (6) the narrow definition of quality education in terms of minimum floors and promotion policies. This conflict over the AAP was later to flare up again.[18]

Significantly, the death knell of the Clark Plan AAP occurred at an April 19, 1972 board meeting. In an effort to reconcile a budget deficit of $400,000, the board voted to approve Superintendent Scott's recommendation that the May 1972 testing survey in connection with AAP be eliminated since the test series would cost approximately $369,586. Pryde, Mason, Kemp and Barry voted in favor of the motion and Swaim, Washington and Tirana opposed it.[19]

This decision to partially abandon the Clark Plan came too late to mend relations between Superintendent Scott and the board. Scott shed light on his view of the Clark Plan in the following remarks made in retrospect:

> We had this damn Clark plan which was really highly, highly overrated approach and simplistic-approach to curriculum improvement, and I had to try to get the best out of that.
>
> The union was up in arms because his plan was adopted without their in-put and without the in-put of faculty. It was the president's [Anita Allen] and Kenneth Clark's plan. I tried to make the most out of that. I think we did a fairly good job in that regard.[20]

## Decentralization*

The issue of implementing a decentralization plan for the District of Columbia school system also added to the conflict in relations between several school boards and several superintendents.

---

*A full discussion of the decentralization issue is presented in "Barbara A. Sizemore, The Politics of Decentralization, A Case Study of the D.C. Public Schools, 1973-76," Doctoral Dissertation, University of Chicago, 1979.

This issue did not seem to be as much of a problem with Hansen as was the track system and the <u>Hobson v Hansen</u> case. Superintendent Manning moved too slowly in making changes in the school system; among these was decentralization. The issue of implementing an approved decentralization plan also contributed to Superintendent Hugh Scott's troubles with his boards. A brief history of this decentralization issue, including the implementation of projects leading up to system-wide decentralization, will be presented next, emphasizing in particular those aspects detailing the various conflict points.

The Model School Division (MSD)

Late in 1961, a panelist of educators, headed by Jerrold R. Zeonarias, physics professor at the Massachusetts Institute of Technology, was set up by President John F. Kennedy. The idea proposed by the group was to create a model for the total school system, in a poor area in the nation's capital. The model was to be built around the concept of an experimental sub-system of 20 or more schools, that is, a decentralized unit where local community people would be actively involved in the schools. Money promised in the sum of $10 million never materialized.[21]

At any rate, the concept of a Model School Subsystem Project for the Inner City Target Area was approved by the DCBOE, upon recommendation of Superintendent Hansen. Further, on June 17, 1964, the DCBOE approved the superintendent's recommendation that a committee be appointed to develop and adopt a plan of action to implement the concept. The president of the board, the superintendent and the director of the United Planning Organization, the District's poverty agency, were each to appoint members to the Model School Division Advisory Committee.[22]

The establishment of the Model School Division was not yet a part of a total school system decentralization plan. Therefore, in the June 23, 1965 board of education meeting, Board President Wesley S. Williams reiterated his request that the administration study the question of decentralization. This was the third request made by Dr. Williams, the other two having come in the April 5, 1965 and the May 19, 1965 board of education meetings. His request was based on the complaints coming downtown from citizens because an administrator was not easily available to handle the problems and that there must be some merit in decentralization since other cities were utilizing it.[23]

In a statement presented before Alpha Phi Alpha Fraternity, Inc. on September 2, 1965, Board President Wesley S. Williams (Black) emphasized the significance of considering administrative decentralization for the following reasons: (1) to make the school system more flexible; (2) to facilitate transfers for teachers and students; (3) to test new ideas in education; (4) to tailor school administration to particularized needs of school communities; (5) to promote racial integration of the schools; and (6) to facilitate sharing of activities and curriculum offerings between units. Thus, he proposed a vertical organization "with a comprehensive sub-administration for each decentralized unit, and with like functions in each decentralized unit coordinated or made relatively uniform only at the top, at the superintendent level."[24]

On September 22, 1964, the board of education approved the recommendation of Superintendent Hansen to establish the Model School Division (MSD). This division consisted of 19 schools, as an autonomous geographic (decentralized) district in the geographical area of Cardozo High School boundaries. It was viewed as an experimental program in curriculum development and in the management of the system to improve instruction for so-called disadvantaged children. Operating functions for the schools were to be transferred from the junior-senior high school office and elementary school office to the office of the assistant superintendent of the Model School Division, which was directly responsible to the superintendent and the board of education. Maintenance and business functions were to remain centrally located.[25]

Therefore, in an effort to keep the principal concept of an area of demonstration meaningful in the MSD, the DCBOE, on February 16, 1966, approved an Experimental Model Elementary Division under Title 1, P.L. 89-10 of the Elementary and Secondary Education Act of 1965 (ESEA). Implementation of this experimental program was to be in three elementary schools in poverty areas of the District of Columbia, namely: Harrison, Garrison, and Montgomery-Morse, exemplifying different problems, facilities, and structures.[26]

The Cardozo area was selected as the model system site and a target for intensive community action due to the fact that the four square miles contained a microcosm of the city's ills as defined on the basis of studies made by the Washington Action for Youth, an arm of the President's Committee on Juvenile Delinquency.

In most reports of the Model School Division, its relationship to the agencies named earlier was mentioned as the biggest problem encountered. Disparate objectives of the agencies caused conflicts over personnel regulations, program authorization, authority, and expectations about the role of the MSD. Additionally, within the MSD, problems existed in the areas of poor planning and communication among staff, resulting in inadequate program coordination and duplication of efforts. Funding and related regulations caused a number of major problems also. Later, the DCBOE voted to give the MSD the authority to deploy all specialized teaching and supervisory personnel to insure coordination of activities. In addition, in order to place on record the authority implied in previous documents, the DCBOE voted to give the MSD authority to disseminate experimental programs and curricula of demonstrated validity and applicability throughout the MSD. The purpose of this motion was to eliminate confusion about authority and responsibility of the MSD for its programs.[27]

The DCBOE adopted in 1968 the MSD Reorganization Plan as presented by the new superintendent, William Manning, who stated it could establish a model for decentralized subsystems in the DCPS. Dr. Euphemia L. Haynes pointed out that if the board accepted this plan it would in effect be accepting decentralization. The board, with Dr. Haynes dissenting, voted to approve in principle the Model School Division Reorganization plan.[28]

In 1970, the MSD consisted of about 15,500 students and 800 teachers in 5 pre-schools, 16 elementary schools, 4 junior high schools, 1 senior high school (Cardozo), and 1 city-wide vocational high school. Originally, it had control over programs only; in 1965 it received operating control over its schools; and in 1968, the board approved a reorganization plan which proposed 5 divisions: Instruction, Administrative Services, Community Affairs, Pupil Services, and Planning and Development -- each with extensive responsibilities.

The Morgan Community School (MCS)

The teachers, principal and parents of the Adams School, a white elementary school, and the Morgan School, a nearby Black elementary school, began discussions in 1952 on how to revitalize their neighborhood. Seven years later, when the District government received a federal grant, American University was invited to assist in the plan. This effort brought the Adams-Morgan Project into being. It was short-lived though due to bureaucratic red tape and rising costs. Out of the effort emerged the Adams-Morgan Community Council, established in 1959.[29]

A power struggle occurred between liberal whites and middle class Black parents with the

Black poor which precipitated the dissolution of the Adams-Morgan Community Council. In its place, emerged the Morgan Community Council.

Because of overcrowding at the Morgan Elementary School, which led to half-day classes and the shifting of pupils to other neighborhood schools, the community, with the help of Antioch College, developed a plan for community control. Subsequently, the DCBOE gave Antioch and the elected Morgan Community School Board authority for the organization and the administration of the school, located in Ward 1 in the integrated Adams-Morgan neighborhood.

Problems encountered in the school included (1) the transferring out of teachers, leaving 7 of 17 D.C. licensed teachers with no previous classroom experience, (2) classes taught by Antioch interns, (3) disagreement among staff regarding the use of innovative teaching methods and classroom organization, (4) the lack of discipline, and (5) an unclear relationship between Antioch, the DCBOE and the elected Community School Board.

In September 1967, Kenneth Haskins, a former social worker with no classroom experience, and later vice-superintendent of the D.C. public school system, was brought in as principal-administrator. Soon, the Antioch tie was loosened and the pupil-teacher-community interaction strengthened through the use of parent aides in each classroom. As a result, an increase in pupil reading scores occurred.

Nevertheless, a year later, the program was in danger of being ended. In order to prevent this from happening, some 75 representatives of the Morgan community attended a board of education meeting to lobby for its continuation.[30]

Three significant events occurred at the board's September 18, 1968 meeting which established the fact that the 1968 board wanted decentralization without local control, and that Superintendent Manning wanted decentralization with local control. The first event was a presentation by Manning, titled "A Position on Decentralization and Local Control" in which he stated that he had "weighed carefully the arguments for and against decentralization and local control," and concluded "that the arguments for ... are stronger than those against. It is local control to which I am addressing myself," he stated, "for to have decentralization without local control is a travesty."[31]

He pointed out that the Morgan Community School was one of only four truly decentralized demonstration projects in the country and stated that: "In addition, we do have the Model School Division which is a decentralized unit with limited local control. The Anacostia Community Project is ready to go into operation as a subsystem with some local control at such a time as Congress provides the funds. Other decentralized units will be emerging, including Fort Lincoln New Town."[32]

The second event which pointed at decentralization was the approval of the board of a policy statement on the administration of the Morgan Community School Program in which the local school board was granted "maximum feasible autonomy within the present legal framework." On this measure, Dr. Haynes and Mr. Rosenfield voted No and Mrs. Allen, Dr. Alexander, Dr. Sessions and Mrs. Stults voted Aye.[33]

The third event was the board's approval, with one abstaining vote by Mrs. Allen, of the Anacostia Community School Project, with a request for funds from the Office of Education for continued planning and implementation.[34]

The Policy Agreement for the administration of the Morgan Community School explicitly set out what aspects of the operation of the school were to be controlled by the Morgan Community Board

(MCB). The statement restricted the MCB from: (1) negotiating contracts binding upon the District of Columbia government; (2) directly submitting a budget to Congress; (3) creating its own Board of Examiners; (4) creating rules in conflict with the D.C. Code; and (5) operating contrary to established policies and rules created by the board of education, including this agreement. However, the MCB in agreement with the DCBOE had the power to: (1) operate through the Division of Special Projects (Superintendent's Office); (2) determine the number and kind of personnel that will be hired within allocated funds and will recommend its staff through the Division of Special Projects; (3) have responsibility for curriculum formation and instruction; (4) determine priorities for expending allocated funds; (5) be responsible for preparing budget requests in the new decentralized budgetary project; and (6) receive through the Division of Special Projects complete staff and services support that are available to all other schools.[35]

### Adams Community School (ACS)

Charges of discrimination, harsh discipline, lack of playground space, unprofessional staff conduct, and low reading test scores, led to the formation of the Emergency Committee Parent Teacher Association for Adams School in the summer of 1969. On May 26, 1969, 35 representatives of community groups attended a meeting and formed a more permanent group on June 4, to advise the administration on the needs of the school.[36]

Finally, after repeated meetings with the administration as to the status of the group, the DCBOE held a hearing for the community during the summer of 1969. At that time, Nelson Roots, school board representative from the area, voted against the creation of a local school board maintaining that a referendum should be held because the community was divided.[37]

Superintendent Manning favored an advisory

committee rather than an elected community board. The PTA favored no change in status. However, the DCBOE approved the community's plan. Hence, the community elected a local board. As a result, the principal transferred out and about half the staff requested to be reassigned. Thus, the Adams School opened in September 1969 with some teacher vacancies, and some classes covered by interns, substitute teachers, and unemployed teachers. The administrative coordinator for Special Projects acted as interim principal until January 1970 at which time a principal was appointed.[38]

A policy agreement for the administration of the Adams Community School contained authority: (1) to determine the number and kind of personnel to be hired; (2) to formulate curriculum and decide on instruction; (3) determine priorities for the expenditure of funds normally allocated; (4) prepare budgetary requests for the Adams School; (5) receive the complete staff and services support available to all other schools; (6) operate an evening school if funds are provided through DCBOE budget request; (7) receive funds from federal agencies and private foundations; (8) make available to the public reports and evaluations; and (9) operate under the Division of Special Projects (Office of the Superintendent). This agreement was approved by the DCBOE with Mr. Rosenfield voting No and Mr. Roots abstaining.[39]

## Anacostia Community School Project (ACSP)

The Anacostia Community School Project was one of three significant projects operating in 1968, or soon to be operating, in the D.C. public school system. The other two were: The Fort Lincoln Project (in the planning stage), and the Model School Division.[40]

A proposal for the Anacostia Community School Project (ACSP) was also developed in response to President Johnson's request to Congress for $10 million to develop a demonstration project of excellence in urban education in the nation's capital. Involved in the development of the project were parents, teachers and students who, first, assessed the educational needs of their community and, second, developed programs which would be responsive to those needs. Especially crucial to the project was a mechanism for the continued participation of the community.[41]

The ACSP encountered many problems in the area of finances and shifting from the Bureau of Elementary and Secondary Education, the National Center for Educational Research, the Experimental Schools and the National Institute of Education in the Office of Education. These problems resulted in confusion in policy, direction, and personnel.[42]

A major difference between ACSP and MSD was that ACSP provided for an elected board to set policy, within certain limits, for its 11 schools and 13,500 students. Also, there was an elected board for each local school included in the project. Reverend James Coates, who became an elected school board member and a president, developed the community component of the Anacostia project. Its first administrative officer was Mr. William S. Rice, former director of the Division of Special Projects and later a regional superintendent (July 1975) during the superintendency of Barbara A. Sizemore.

In November 1971, HEW notified the administration that it would terminate the Anacostia project in August 1972. Mrs. Swaim (chairman of the ad hoc committee on community schools), the board of education, the Anacostia board, administrative staff, and Superintendent Scott felt that the HEW action was taken abruptly and that no charges had been made. This they felt to be unfair in light of a favorable evaluation contracted for by HEW. The decision to terminate was given by Dr. Robert Binswanger of the Experimental Schools Division of the Office of Education for Dr. Sidney P. Marland, Commissioner of Education, United States Office of Education.[43]

From the beginning, the project was beset with funding problems. In spite of strong White House interest, Congress voted only $1 million to begin the Anacostia project. Another $5 million was spent on the venture from 1969 to 1971. An appeal made by the school system in 1971 for additional funding was denied by the Commissioner of Education.[44]

In 1972, funds became available for a new project. The new project, in the same area, and assigned to the National Institute of Education, was called the Response to Educational Needs Project (RENP). It emphasized meeting educational needs in perceptual and cognitive skills through instructional activities and community organization.

Finally, the ACSP became a subdivision of the school system under an assistant superintendent.[45] However, the project continued to encounter difficulties and was finally terminated on May 30, 1977.

## Fort Lincoln New Town (FLNT)

Fort Lincoln is located on 360 acres in northeast Washington, D.C. and was originally set up to defend Washington, D.C. from Confederate forces advancing from the south during the Civil War years. In subsequent years, Fort Lincoln was owned by the federal government. At one time it housed the National Training School for Boys. In 1967, President Johnson declared this acreage available to build a "New Town-In Town," conceptualized as building a complete community with approximately 5,000 housing units to accommodate various income levels of a resident population of about 15,000 persons.[46]

Again presidential concern for the quality of education in the nation's capital propelled the DCBOE and the superintendent of schools to hire outside consultants to help them improve the system. This time, however, a comprehensive study of the entire system was not proposed. Instead, a whole new concept of planning an entire new town within the confines of the boundary lines of the city of Washington, D.C. was proposed. The die was cast when President Lyndon B. Johnson expressed concern that the town be more than a housing project; he envisioned a community with a full range of education, recreation and other public services to citizens. It took 10 years to bring this dream to fruition.

In response to Superintendent Manning's request to Mario Fantini, chief consultant to the project, and Milton A. Young, Senior Educational Planner, to plan an outstanding educational system for FLNT, they presented him, on August 15, 1968, with a conceptualization of a new and relevant system.

Administratively, the FLNT would be headed by an administrator, directly responsible for its operation. The organization would be pyramidal, but dynamic with decision-making points at all levels and community involvement in policy-setting through participation in learning activities and the education committee. Students would be organized in the following patterns: 0-5 years, Early childhood level; 5-8 years, Primary school level; 8-12 years, Middle school level; 12-15 years, Junior school level; and 15-18 years, Senior school level. Grouping would be by age for social purposes rather than ability or achievement.[47]

Operations were continuing according to schedule with the exception of the Government Services Administration's hold-up in the transfer of the land to the District government.[48]

Finally, after two months of negotiations, the DCBOE received information from the Redevelopment Land Agency indicating that the Department of Housing and Urban Development had now approved the District's plan for Fort Lincoln Elementary School #1 and that the Redevelopment Land Agency was to proceed with the development of the project.[49]

By now the implementation of the project was extended into the administration of the new superintendent, Hugh J. Scott.

The entire FLNT development was so slow that citizens' attention began being focused on just the school. It appeared to some that the Nixon administration slowed down the process of completing the project. Many people urged the school's completion because schools in the community were overcrowded.

In school year 1974-75 broad involvement of the school community was utilized in planning for the interim use of the new elementary school at Fort Lincoln which was scheduled for completion prior to the arrival of the resident student population. Proposed ideas included use of the school as an educational center to have a pre-kindergarten program, a special education learning center, and a community school component, the Region VI Curriculum/Staff Development Center and for regional activities involving the components of PACTS, Superintendent Sizemore's acronym for the involvement of parents, administrators, community other than parents, teachers and students, implemented during her administration, 1973-75.[50] Unfortunately, at the time of the write-up of this present study, the school at FLNT is still standing vacant.

## Spingarn Instructional Unit

The Spingarn Instructional Unit (SIU) was the prototype instructional unit established under the Five-Year Plan for improving instructional services in the Division of Instruction. The unit was approved by the board in June 1969, as one step in the decentralization of the school system. It was activated in January 1970 with no funding but with the use of deployed personnel. There are within the unit 23 schools located in the far northeast and southeast in Wards 5, 6, and 7. Spingarn High School is the satellite with four feeder junior high schools, 17 feeder elementary schools and Phelps Vocational High School.

Due to the hiring freeze imposed by the Mayor-Commissioner in 1972, adequate staffing was unavailable to the unit and it therefore suffered the possibility of being eliminated.[51]

The Pupil Personnel Field Centers

Pupil personnel services were decentralized to different sections of the city in 1965. Attendance officers, pupil personnel workers and support staff manned each office. In 1974, when the school system was decentralized, one center was developed in each of the six regions. Parents were involved through programs to enhance educational readiness and identify both learning and health problems.[52]

Other planned aspects of community involvement in the public schools included the community meetings instituted in 1967-68,[53] neighborhood participation in school site selection and school design initiated in March 1968,[54] a principal selection process, and local school budgeting. At least two of these efforts involved some conflict in school superintendent relations during Hugh Scott's superintendency.

School-by-school budgeting

Incorporated in the board-approved report on procedure for handling the FY73 operating budget as amended, was a consideration for the preparation of school-by-school budgets, which reflected both regular operating and federal funds available at the local school level reflecting the priorities as established by the local school.

Superintendent Scott voiced concern as to how his staff was going to proceed to implement nearly 180 school units with its present structure on a school-by-school budgeting basis. Thus, he wished to consult with Price-Waterhouse, the management firm hired by the board, on the implementation phase because the present staff could not respond to the specifications of the proposal.

At its January 19, 1973 meeting, Superintendent Scott brought in a report clarifying the problem of full community participation in the budgeting process at this time with the school personnel resources available. Therefore, the board adopted a policy of directing the superintendent to implement a program of local school budgeting phased in on the elementary level beginning in the school year 1972-73, with respect to FY73.[55]

Principal selection

During the 1969-70 school year, a procedure was worked out so that the community could participate in the selection of school officers (principals). It was felt by some board members that there was an urgency for the board to agree on a procedure since there had been many interim appointments to key positions which needed to be acted upon.[56]

At its December 3, 1969 board meeting, board members approved the School Officer Promotion Procedure as presented by Acting Superintendent Henley. In speaking about the policy, Dr. Henley stated that the District of Columbia schools were pioneers in developing a procedure which provided for formal community participation in the selection of school principals. The board vote was unanimous.[57]

A list of goals submitted to the DCBOE on May 20, 1970 by the Superintendent Selection Committee made no mention of decentralization. Instead the goals focused on a well-trained staff, a curriculum development process, the adequate distribution of materials in the area of instruction, a management study and sound administrative policies and qualified administrative staff in the administrative area, and a community involvement and community support from other agencies in the community.[58]

Nevertheless, the goal of decentralization was addressed by the new superintendent, Hugh J. Scott, in the 120-Day Report. He stated:

> A sound decentralized system of smaller organizational units would permit an intense focusing of resources, an improved articulation of programs and policies, and a greater flexibility for program development. The lines of authority would be more clearly defined and very importantly, the decision-making process would be brought closer to unit personnel....
>
> The Superintendent will submit to the Board of Education in the very near future his plan for the decentralization of certain administrative and supervisory functions to a number of regional units.[59]

After almost three years into Superintendent Scott's tenure, the DCBOE finally accepted his decentralization plan.

In his interview Scott indicated that he had difficulty getting his decentralization plans passed by the board because of political motivations of some members. He stated, in essence, that board members did not like the local advisory bodies because they were not sure the advisory bodies would be composed of their forces.[60]

Citizen's decentralization plan

On February 21, 1973, at the DCBOE meeting, the board received from a community group a plan for decentralization, which it referred to the Committees on Curriculum, Special Education, and Education Planning and Student Life and Community Involvement.[61]

Their planning process for decentralization was described as a community effort with people representing a cross-section of the city including professionals, educational and other organizations, parents and interested observers having been involved in the designing of it. Only one phase of decentralization was dealt with in the proposal: the redistribution of central administrative services closer to the schools to be served. The presenter of the proposal, Mr. Jimmie McWilliams, requested the board to receive the document and assign it to the DCBOE and to Superintendent Scott and, in addition, to appoint a steering committee to include some of the citizens who had worked on the document to analyze it and determine available funding sources.

In this connection, both Mr. McWilliams and Mrs. Mason emphasized their hope that the decentralization plan submitted by the community group would be compatible with the plans worked out by the DCBOE and the superintendent. Whereupon, the DCBOE received the citizens' decentralization plan and referred it to the committees mentioned above.[62]

Decentralization remained the major thrust for the DCPS system during the search for a new superintendent, after Scott resigned in 1973.

Mason pushed forward the citizen's decentralization plan during Sizemore's administration. When the plan was rejected by Sizemore because it called for an elite steering committee chosen by the board to structure decentralization rather than broad-based participation in decision-making by poor and rich alike, Mason withdrew her support of Sizemore. From thenceforth, conflict ensued between this once staunch supporter of Sizemore, as the superintendent.

Other goals to restructure the school system propounded by Superintendent Sizemore were (1) multi-lingual and multi-cultural content; (2) curriculum changes which emphasize the four notation systems of language, music, art and mathematics; (3) multi-level grouping; (4) a PACTS process which would allow parents, administrators, community, teachers and students to participate in goal setting; and (5) teacher accountability.[63] These were circumvented by her latest of four boards in two years.

## Equalization

Equalization of the school system became a goal of the DCBOE by court decree in the Hobson v Hansen case. Superintendent Scott ran into conflict with the board in trying to provide a satisfactory equalization formula.

As indicated in the minutes of June 9, 1971, there was concern shown for the implementation of the decree of May 25, 1971 in the case of Hobson v Hansen. In speaking to the motion not to appeal this, the court's second order to equalize expenditures, a number of board members showed great concern and some even appeared to be agitated over this recent court decision. Hancock took issue with a statement in the report regarding intent of the board to discriminate. In addition, he felt the board should appeal the recent decision of the Hobson v Hansen case requiring the school system to equalize per pupil expenditures per school within a 5 percent range based on teachers' salaries to provide a teacher-cost per pupil equalization.

Further Hancock indicated that the decision would cause administrative chaos and that he rejected the idea that young teachers located in the Anacostia area were inefficient and not able to handle the affairs of Black children. Also, he questioned the idea that older teachers west of the park should be transferred out of those schools against their will or that the court order had no effect on the Clark Plan. Thus, he felt it unfair to new Superintendent Scott to superimpose Judge Skelly Wright as the super superintendent of the

D.C. Public Schools. Contrastingly, Taylor stated that legislators and board members in the south had accused the Supreme Court of acting like a super board of education or super superintendent in 1954 when the school desegregation decision was handed down. Rosenfield also expressed the view that equity through the Wright decision would bring the board chaos because it equated longevity in teaching and teacher salaries with quality education. Therefore, he felt that the DCBOE should appeal the decision. In contrast to this view, Coates stated he felt it was quite correct for Judge Wright to relate quality to dollars.

Finally, after extended discussion, the board voted in favor of not appealing the Wright decision, with Hancock and Rosenfield voting No.[64]

The problems involved in the implementation of the Wright decree were enormous and almost overwhelming for a new superintendent. Therefore, Scott secured the services of Thompson, Lewis and Associates and others to form a study team, to plan for the implementation of the Wright Decree which called for the equalization of teacher expenditures per pupil in each regular elementary school building within 5 percent of the city-wide average using only funds from the D.C. budget. Federal funds could not be used in the equalization plan. Three alternative plans were presented, one of which was recommended to the board by the superintendent as being most educationally sound. Nevertheless, a different alternative was accepted by the DCBOE.[65] In a subsequent meeting, Mrs. Taylor, speaking to the same issue, stated:

> Although I regret the Board was unable to see the wisdom of good sound management procedures prior to this crisis, I do urge the Board to let the Superintendent lead us in matters crucial to the operation of the schools, and reject his direction and his recommendations only after we have established that doing it his way is totally incorrect. We have not as

a Board, seen the wisdom of following this
course. I continue to pray and hope that
we will let the Superintendent lead the public
schools and give him full support and backing
in such a fashion that all of the employees
of the public schools, all of the students
who attend our schools, all of the parents of
the students and all other members of the
Washington community know that we are moving
with a single thrust and that the Superintendent is the engineer.[66]

The board reluctantly approved the administration's compliance report on the Wright Decree of
May 25, 1971, as amended with reports received
from the local schools. This was accomplished
after a long discussion about how unrealistic it
was to equalize by the transfer of teachers based
on teachers' salaries as ordered by the court.[67]

Since neither the board nor the superintendent
were entirely pleased with the compliance report,[68]
it took action to utilize the services of Julius
Hobson, Sr. and his group, the Washington Institute for Quality Education (WIQE) to develop
alternative compliance plans.[69]

At the July 19, 1972 meeting of the DCBOE
Superintendent Scott stated that after the year of
implementing the Wright Decree, it was obvious
that the school system had succeeded in equalizing
teacher resources with regard to teacher salaries
and benefits but not in terms of improving the
quality of education since the emphasis had not
been on teacher performance. Additionally, he
stated that the school system was working with
Julius Hobson, Sr., the head of WIQE on the problem of schools being in and out of compliance
during the year due to retirements and departure
of teachers. Therefore, a new proposal was
presented to the effect that equalization be based
solely on class size.[70]

Interestingly also is the fact that the board

hampered the complex equalization process by not allowing Superintendent Scott to transfer teachers on an involuntary basis. In fact Swaim vigorously opposed this: "She said she would like to move, formally, a summary of the recommendations that the superintendent made, but the summary stops short of involuntary transfers."[71]

Superintendent Scott voiced his objections to the motion which included the item about involuntary transfers put by Swaim and seconded by Pryde. He explained that it would restrict him in moving personnel making it difficult to equalize. This in turn might force violation of the court's order. He was not being given the flexibility to do what he has the authority to do which is to transfer teachers.[72]

Finally, it was decided that involuntary transfer of teachers could be used as a last resort.[73]

At the January 11, 1973 meeting, Superintendent Scott presented the DCBOE with the equalization plan for 1972-73. The DCBOE requested the administration to adjust the factor of teachers on leave, having their salaries in that space and use the salaries of those personnel who were filling the vacancies rather than the teacher on leave of absence. A plan was established within the two month time frame that established compliance without having to remove any regular classroom teachers by adding additional salaries from the 125 positions that had been authorized because of negotiated settlements of the work stoppage with the Washington Teachers' Union (WTU). Thus the documentation to be annually submitted to the court was prepared and made available. He recommended that the DCBOE accept the equalization plan and indicate this to the Corporation Counsel so that a statement could be submitted to the judge to make them in a favorable position for the June 15 deadline for contempt.

A motion that the board adopt the

Compliance Plan and forward it to the court was made by Mrs. Swaim and seconded by Rev. Raymond Kemp.

Mrs. Swaim's concern was that last Spring principals were asked for their preferences if they had to lose something. Therefore, some faculties or PTAs decided they would rather lose science than to lose something else.

Dr. Wilbur Millard, Assistant Superintendent of Pupil Personnel Services, explained that this time those decisions were put in the hands of the supervisors of the content areas who had supervision over the people in the schools in which they worked. This would insure that the decisions made could have some relevance to the needs of the local schools.

Rev. James Coates was concerned that Anacostia, a predominantly Black ward located across the river, would have equal amounts of money spent in the schools based on teachers' salaries.

Superintendent Scott felt it would be too disruptive to move teachers around all during the year in order to be in compliance.[74]

Mrs. Taylor's concern was that a different formula be used to compute building capacity which eliminates using the cafeteria, the hallways, the lavatory and the indentations for the water fountain as basis for determining the capacity for students. Finally, the motion to accept the administration's plan was adopted.[75]

1. A date for projected schedule for filling of the vacancies indicated in the report.

2. Plans and options for "in-house" correction of the schools that are near the minus 5 percent.

3. A report on a formula for a new method of arriving at facility capacity.[76]

## Summary

Goals of the school system shifted due (1) to the external factor of group pressures in the form of presidential concern about the Black push for local control of schools, (2) to the desire to raise the academic level of the students in the DCPS system, and (3) to a need to equalize expenditures of DCPS system resources in schools located in rich and poor areas of the District.

Presidential concern about local control of schools was articulated in the form of providing a model for the nation in urban areas. It evolved into a move to decentralize the D.C. public school system.

The concern to raise the academic level of the students in the DCPS system was translated into the Academic Achievement Plan (AAP) of Kenneth Clark.

Court pressure on the school system was exhibited through the Hobson v Hansen decree to equalize expenditures of the DCPS system resources in schools located in rich and poor areas of the District of Columbia.

These three system-wide goals shifted in importance as board priorities shifted due to some extent to changes in board membership. For instance, Superintendent Manning's board tried to accelerate his pace toward decentralizing the school system. Superintendent Scott's first board had as its dominant goal the implementation of the Clark Plan. This priority changed to decentralization and equalization under a new board president and when new board members displaced old ones. Decentralization remained a board priority during the selection of a new superintendent in 1973, but, as we will see, goals shifted again during 1973-75 causing conflict in school superintendent-school board relations. And, even though the real conflict came later, as indicated above, when Superintendent Sizemore actually decentralized the school system, we do now see the beginnings of the build-up for the protracted struggle yet to come as changes in board members continued to occur.

Chapter VII specifically provides a portrait of the board members between 1973-76, and their perceived motives for seeking board membership. Furthermore, an examination of the leadership style of board presidents and superintendents is provided for study for possible conflict elements. A number of instances of role conflict are also provided for examination. Lastly, we examine the effect of board membership changes as another factor impinging on school superintendent-school board relations causing conflict.

FOOTNOTES                                    Chapter VI


1. Hansen, *The Amidon Elementary School - A Successful Demonstration in Basic Education* (Englewood Cliffs, N.J.: Prentice-Hall, Inc., 1962, pp. ix and 3-40; see also "Minutes of the Twelfth (Special) Meeting of the Board of Education, 1964-65," Washington, D.C., April 22, 1965, pp. 3-7; Hansen, *Danger in Washington*, pp. 195-202; Hansen, *The Four Track Curriculum for Today's High Schools* (Englewood Cliffs, N.J.: Prentice-Hall, Inc., 1964).

2. "Minutes of the Twelfth (Special) Meeting of the Board of Education, 1964-65," Washington, D.C., 22 April 1965, p. 7.

3. "Minutes of the Thirteenth (Stated) Meeting of the Board of Education, 1964-1965," Washington, D.C., 19 May 1965, pp. 78-79.

4. "Minutes of the Fourth (Postponed) Meeting of the Board of Education, 1965-1966," Washington, D.C., 22 September 1965, p. 29.

5. "Minutes of the Twelfth (Stated) Meeting of the Board of Education, 1965-1966," Washington, D.C., 20 April 1966, pp. 95-97.

6. "Minutes of the Eleventh (Stated) Meeting of the Board of Education, 1965-1966," Washington, D.C., 16 March 1966, pp. 25-31. See also: "Minutes of the Fourteenth (Stated) Meeting of the Board of Education, 1965-1966," 18 May 1966, pp. 82-90.

7. *Passow Report*, pp. 197-241; 278.

8. "Minutes of the Fourteenth (Special) Meeting of the Board of Education," Washington, D.C., 13 July 1970, p. 2.

9. Ibid., pp. 406.

10. Ibid., pp. 2-11.

11. "Minutes of the Twenty-Second (Stated) Meeting of the Board of Education," Washington, D.C., 21 October 1970, pp. 15-18.

12. Ibid. See also: Hugh J. Scott, The Superintendent's 120-Day Report, Washington, D.C.: District of Columbia Public Schools, February 1971); and Hugh J. Scott, The Superintendent's Annual Report (Washington, D.C.: District of Columbia Public Schools, December 1971).

13. "Minutes of the Twenty-Second (Stated) Meeting of the Board of Education," pp. 30-33.

14. "Minutes of the Eighth (Stated) Meeting of the Board of Education," Washington, D.C., 17 March 1971, pp. 26-27.

15. Ibid., pp. 37-39.

16. "Minutes of the Eleventh (Stated) Meeting of the Board of Education," Washington, D.C., 19 May 1971, p. 13.

17. Ibid.

18. "Minutes of the Fourteenth (Special) Meeting of the Board of Education," Washington, D.C., 12 July 1971, pp. 2-12; Enclosures 3 and 4.

19. "Minutes of the Seventh (Stated) Meeting of the Board of Education," Washington, D.C., 19 April 1972, p. 38.

20. Interview with Hugh J. Scott, Superintendent of D. C. Public Schools, Washington, D.C., 21 November 1977.

21. Carl F. Hansen, Danger in Washington, p. 128.

22. "Minutes of the Seventeenth (Stated) Meeting of the Board of Education, 1963-1964," Washington, D.C., 17 June 1964, pp. 66-67.

23. "Minutes of the Fourteenth (Postponed) Meeting of the Board of Education, 1964-1965," Washington, D.C., 23 June 1965, p. 120.

24. Statement Presented by President Williams before Alpha Phi Alpha Fraternity, Inc., on 2 September 1965. See "Minutes of the Fourth (Postponed) Meeting of the Board of Education, 1965-1966," 22 September, 1965, pp. 130-139.

25. "Minutes of the Fourth (Postponed) Meeting of the Board of Education, 1965-1966," Washington, D.C., 22 September 1965, p. 22.

26. "Minutes of the Tenth (Stated) Meeting of the Board of Education, 1965-1966," Washington, D.C., 16 February 1966, pp. 71, 73.

27. "Model School Division: A Report to the Board of Education," Model School Division, Public Schools of the District of Columbia, Washington, D.C., June 1967, pp. 1-11. See also "Minutes of the Twenty-Seventh (Special) Meeting of the Board of Education," 26 June 1967.

28. "Minutes of the Third (Special) Meeting of the Board of Education, 1965-1969," Washington, D.C., 15 July 1968, p. 9.

29. Constance McLaughlin Green, *The Secret City*, p. 324.

30. "Background for Workshop on Education, School Decentralization and Community Involvement," League of Women Voters, 18 March 1970, p. 13. See also: Barbara A. Sizemore, "The Politics of Decentralization: A Case Study of the D.C. Public Schools, 1973-1976," Doctoral Dissertation, University of Chicago, 1979.

31. "Minutes of the Ninth (Stated and the Reconvened) Meeting of the Board of Education, 1968-1969," Washington, D.C., 18 September 1968, and Reconvened - 26 September 1968," Enclosure 1, p. 1.

32. Ibid., p. 2.

33. Ibid., p. 4.

34. "Minutes of the Ninth (Stated and the Reconvened) Meeting of the Board of Education, 1968-1969," Washington, D.C., September 18, 1968 and reconvened - 26 September 1968, pp. 5-7.

35. "Minutes of the Twenty-Sixth (Special) Meeting of the Board of Education," Washington, D.C., 2 July 1969, Enclosure 1.

36. "Minutes of the Twenty-Fourth (Community) Meeting of the Board of Education," Washington, D.C., 24 June 1969, p. 3.

37. "Background for Workshop on Education, School Decentralization and Community Involvement," League of Women Voters, 18 March 1970, p. 14.

38. Ibid.

39. "Minutes of the Thirty-Second (Stated) Meeting of the Board of Education," Washington, D.C., 17 September 1969, pp. 16-21 and Enclosure 3.

40. "Minutes of the Thirty-Fourth (Special) Meeting of the Board of Education, 1967-1968," Washington, D.C., 25 April 1968, p. 7.

41. William R. Manning (Superintendent), Major Activities (mimeographed), Washington, D.C.: D.C. Public School System, 1968, p. 8.

42. Barbara A. Sizemore, "The Politics of Decentralization: A Case Study of the D.C. Public Schools, 1973-76," Doctoral dissertation, University of Chicago, 1979.

43. "Minutes of the Twenty-Third (Stated) Meeting of the Board of Education," Washington, D.C., 17 November 1971, pp. 5-13.

44. "Minutes of the Twenty-Fifth (Stated) Meeting of the Board of Education," Washington, D.C., 19 January 1972, pp. 29-30.

45. "Response to Educational Needs Report," Washington, D.C., District of Columbia Public Schools, August 1972.

46. Advertising supplement, *Washington Post*, 12 August 1977.

47. Mario D. Fantini, Milton A. Young, and Freda Douglas, *A Design for a New and Relevant System of Education for Fort Lincoln New Town* (Washington, D.C.: Washington, D.C. Schools and Ford Foundation, 15 August 1958), pp. 1-5.

48. "Minutes of the Forty-Seventh (Stated) Meeting of the Board of Education," Washington, D.C., 21 January 1970, Enclosure 2, pp. 1-2.

49. "Minutes of the Nineteenth (Stated) Meeting of the Board of Education, Washington, D.C., 16 September 1970, p. 31.

50. Gary Freeman (Regional Superintendent), *Region VI Progress Report, 1974-75* (Washington, D.C.: District of Columbia Public Schools, July 1975), p. 5.

51. "Minutes of the Third (Stated) Meeting of the Board of Education," Washington, D.C., 16 February 1972, pp. 3-5.

52. "The Superintendent's Annual Report: School Year 1970-71," Washington, D.C.: District of Columbia Public Schools, December 1971, p. 12.

53. Ellen Hoffman, "Board Flunking Its Public Relations," Washington Post, 6 July 1968.

54. "Minutes of the Thirteenth (Stated) Meeting of the Board of Education, 1967-1968," Washington, D.C., 20 March 1968, pp. 3-4, Enclosure 3.

55. "Minutes of the Twenty-Fifth (Stated) Meeting of the Board of Education," Washington, D.C., 9 January 1973, pp. 6-11.

56. "Minutes of the Fortieth (Stated) Meeting of the Board of Education," Washington, D.C., 19 November 1969, pp. 8-13.

57. "Minutes of the Forty-Third (Special) Meeting of the Board of Education," Washington, D.C., 3 December 1969, pp. 2-3.

58. "Minutes of the Eleventh (Special) Meeting of the Board of Education," Washington, D.C., 27 May 1970, pp. 3-4.

59. The Superintendent's 120 Day Report, Washington, D.C., District of Columbia Public Schools, February 1971, p. 21.

60. Interview with Hugh Scott, Superintendent, D.C. Public Schools, Washington, D.C., 21 November 1977.

61. "Minutes of the Third (Stated) Meeting of the Board of Education," Washington, D.C., 21 February 1973, pp. 3-4.

62. Ibid., "Minutes of the Twenty-Second (Special) Meeting of the Board of Education," Washington, D.C., 21 August 1973, pp. 16-19.

63. Barbara A. Sizemore, Superintendent, The Superintendent's 120-Day Report (Washington, D.C.: District of Columbia Public Schools, March 1974).

64. "Minutes of the Twelfth (Stated) Meeting of the Board of Education," Washington, D.C., 9 June 1971, pp. 49-59.

65. "Minutes of the Sixteenth (Special) Meeting of the Board of Education, Washington, D.C., 12 August 1971, pp. 3-19.

66. "Minutes of the Seventeenth (Special) Meeting of the Board of Education, Washington, D.C., 30 August 1971, p. 9.

67. "Minutes of the Eighth (Special) Meeting of the Board of Education, Washington, D.C., 25 April 1972, pp. 2-8.

68. Lawrence Feinberg, "School Board Clears Shifting of Teachers," Washington Post, 26 April 1972.

69. "Minutes of the Eighth (Special) Meeting of the Board of Education, Washington, D.C., 25 April 1972, p. 3.

70. "Minutes of the Second Session of the Seventeenth (Special) Meeting of the Board of Education," Washington, D.C., 19 July 1972, pp. 43-44.

71. Ibid.

72. Ibid.

73. Ibid.

74. "Minutes of the Thirty-Sixth (Special) Meeting of the Board of Education," Washington, D.C., 11 January 1973, pp. 1-32.

75. Ibid.

76. Ibid.

CHAPTER VII

BOARD PROFILE, MOTIVES, LEADERSHIP STYLES,
ROLE CONFLICT, MEMBERSHIP CHANGES

## Profile of D.C. Board of Education Members, 1973-76

Marion S. Barry, Jr., Black, from Mississippi, attended schools in Memphis, Tennessee. He received the bachelor's degree from LeMoyne College, and a master's degree from Fisk University. While pursuing his doctoral studies, Barry in the early 1960s was active in the Sit-In Movement and the SNCC Voter Registration Drives in Alabama, Georgia, Mississippi and Louisiana. He directed the New York office of the Student Non-Violent Coordinating Committee (SNCC) in 1964 and was also director of the SNCC Washington office in 1965.

In 1967, Barry became the Director of Operations, Youth Pride, Inc., a Washington, D.C., self-held organization and Chairman Protem of the board of directors of Pride Economic Enterprises, a Black-owned corporation which operates gasoline stations, landscaping-gardening businesses, and painting services.

Marion Barry was an at-large member and president of the D.C. board of education from January 1972 to July 1974. Barry left the board to run for the D.C. City Council when home rule was granted to the District in 1974. He won a council seat. On January 20, 1978, Barry declared his intention to run for mayor of Washington, D.C. despite advice from City Council Chairman Sterling

Tucker and D.C. Delegate Walter Fauntroy who felt that he should wait his turn. It is interesting to note that Barry declared that in this race he would not accept contributions from large corporations and unions[1] as he did when running for a seat on the school board and on the city council.

     Mattie G. Taylor, Black, attended the Atlanta public schools, West Virginia State College, and George Washington University. She was a policewoman for the Washington Metropolitan Police Department (Youth Aid Division and the Women's Bureau); a social worker for the D.C. Department of Public Welfare, and a community organizer for the Commissioner's Youth Council. Presently, Taylor is a manpower development officer for the D.C. Manpower Administration; U.S. Department of Labor. Her community affiliations include advisor to Baptist Youth Fellowship Council, Inner-City Church Summer Youth Program, and Inter-Agency Staff Committee for Children and Youth. Taylor was elected from Ward 5 to the D.C. board of education, for a term of office from January 1969 to January 1972 in a run-off election because she failed to gain a majority of the votes cast in the first election. In her campaign speech she opposed the Clark Plan. Taylor was re-elected for a term of office from January 1972 to January 1976. She was vice-president of the board of education, during her second term of office. She left because the bill for self-government, passed in December 1973, made it illegal for her to continue when her agency was transferred from the federal government to the D.C. government.

     Also, Taylor was both a Scott and Sizemore supporter. She supported board policies centering on administrative decentralization while at the same time resisting efforts of the DCBOE delving into administrative matters which she felt should be left to the superintendents and their staffs to handle.

Raymond B. Kemp, white, assistant pastor at Sts. Paul and Augustine Catholic Church, located in a Black parish, attended Gonzaga College High School in Washington, D.C., and St. Mary's Seminary and University in Baltimore, Maryland. He was a member of the board of directors of the National Committee on Household Employment, the Inter-Agency Staff Committee for Children and Youth, the Washington Urban League, and D.C. Citizens for Better Public Education. Kemp was elected to the board of education representing Ward 1, a predominantly Black ward, by defeating Nelson Roots, a Black man, in November 1971. He served until his term expired in January 1976.

Kemp supported political decentralization at the local school level. He supported Scott but was opposed to the hiring of Sizemore as superintendent of schools. Kemp was also a supporter of the Hawthorne Alternative School.

Evie Washington, Black, originally from Alabama, attended school in Washington, D.C., and did her college work at Howard University. She is the director-specialist for education at the Community Improvement Corporation, United Planning Organization. Washington was a member of the board of directors of the Model Inner City Community Organization, secretary of the Health Subcommittee for Model Cities, a member of D.C. Citizens for Better Public Education, National Committee for Better Public Education; Board of National Medical Association Foundation, D.C. City-wide Consumer Council; Neighborhood Planning Council for Children and Youth; secretary of the Shaw Junior High School Community Council; chairperson of the Planning Council for the building of the new Shaw; and a member of the D.C. board of education from Ward 2 from January 26, 1970 to December 1973. Washington generally voted with Allen. Along with Cassell, Mason, Rosenfield and Tirana, she was opposed to Scott.

In the case of Sizemore, Washington abstained,

she said, because she had problems with Mrs. Sizemore's view of reading and mathematics as discussed in the superintendent search interview.[2] Notably also, Washington always voted against Barry who defeated Anita Allen whom she supported.

Albert A. Rosenfield, white, born in Argentina, was a graduate of Catholic University of America, and has resided in Washington, D.C. since 1931. Both of his daughters attended D.C. public schools and became teachers in the school system. Rosenfield, a Jewish liquor store owner, was formerly a head basketball coach at Catholic University (1948 to 1952). His affiliations included Adas Israel Congregation, Cleveland Park Citizen's Association, Uptown Lions Club, president of the Cleveland Park Businessmen's Association, president of Norbeck Country Club, Citizens Advisory Council to D.C. Commissioner, and the Touchdown Club of Washington, D.C.

Rosenfield was elected to the D.C. school board in November 1969, from Ward 3, and served from January 27, 1969 to January 1974. He generally voted with President Anita Allen. He supported administrative decentralization in support of the vested interests of his predominantly white constituents in Ward 3.

Rosenfield was opposed to Scott; he voted no for Sizemore for superintendent. Also, Rosenfield declined to be interviewed by this investigator.

Hilda Howland M. Mason, Black, was born in Virginia and is married to Charles N. Mason, Jr., a white former real estate dealer and lawyer. She attended Miner Teacher's College, D.C. Teachers College, Plattsburgh State University and Catholic University. Mason was formerly assistant principal of the Adams-Morgan Community School when Kenneth Haskins, later vice superintendent of the D.C. public schools, was principal of Morgan. In addition, Mason was a counselor at LaSalle Laboratory School, a teacher at Van Ness Elementary School, and a consultant-lecturer at Dunbarton and

Trinity Colleges.

Mason's community activities included membership in the D.C. Education Association; American Federation of Teachers, Women's Political Caucus, and advisor to the Day Care Coalition. She was elected to the D.C. board of education from Ward 4 in November 1971, in a run-off election where she served until 1977.

As one of the board members who supported decentralization at the local school level, Mason sponsored a Citizens' Plan submitted to the board on February 21, 1973. She viewed Superintendent Sizemore's decentralization of the school system into six regions as regionalism, not decentralization, and vigorously opposed the parents, administrators, community, teachers, students (PACTS) concept as she felt threatened that the Black poor might become organized through this vehicle.

Influenced by the April 1975 Washington Star and Washington Post editorials (see Chapter IX) lambasting Superintendent Sizemore for revealing the plan of whites to recover the city, Mason joined the white faction on the DCBOE to terminate Sizemore's contract.

In 1977, Mason was appointed a member of the D.C. City Council to serve out the term of Julius Hobson, Sr., of the Statehood Party, who died in 1977. In a special election held in July 1977, Mason defeated Barbara Sizemore, the former superintendent of schools whom she helped to fire, for the seat by 683 votes.[3] She declined to be interviewed for this study.

Martha S. Swaim, white, was born in Scotsdale, Pennsylvania. She graduated from Oberlin College and Howard University. Her master's degree from Howard was in American History. Swaim was a first grade teacher in Princeton, New Jersey, and a general reference librarian with the D.C. public library. In 1968, she was elected from Ward 6 to the D.C. board of education. She was re-elected in 1971 to serve until January 1976.

Swaim served as chairperson of the Committee on Finance during Barry's presidency and was selected by Barry as his vice-president. School-by-school budgeting was introduced by Swaim[4] as an outgrowth of her support for political decentralization at the local school level. This, apparently, was beneficial to the vested interests of her predominantly white ward constituents in Ward C. As chairperson of the Finance Committee, Swaim spearheaded the severe slashing in administrative and supervisory staff under a budget sub-title "Back to the Classroom."[5] Nevertheless, she, too, was one of Superintendent Scott's supporters but resigned from the board in June 1973, in protest over the selection of another Black superintendent, Barbara A. Sizemore.

A number of school board members interviewed for this study felt Swaim to be one of the most powerful members of the board because of her control over school finances through the Finance Committee. Swaim declined to be interviewed.

James E. Coates, Black, born in Washington, D.C., had four children who attended D.C. public schools. He graduated from Howard University and is currently minister of a church in Anacostia.

Coates was director of Planning and Economic Development of the Near Northeast Community Corporation and director of the Anti-Poverty Programs in Anacostia. He was also president of the Nichols Avenue Elementary School PTA, chairman of the Anacostia Community School Project, and a member of the D.C. Mental Health Association. Coates, who was elected to the D.C. board of education from Ward 8 (Anacostia) in 1969, served as president of the board in 1969 and as vice-president in 1970 under Anita Allen.

Coates was an advocate of community control

but supported Anita Allen in her policies. In 1972, he advocated administrative decentralization and was among those who wanted to renew Superintendent Scott's contract.

Charles I. Cassell, Black, was born in Washington, D.C. He has two children, both of whom attended the public schools in the city. Cassell attended Cornell University and Rensselaer Polytechnic Institute in Troy, New York, where he obtained a degree in architecture. He was chairman of the D.C. School Action Council where he edited their newsletter, "The Activist." In addition, Cassell was: vice-chairman of the Emergency Committee on Transportation Crisis; chairman of the Washington Urban Coalition's Police-Community Relations Committee; President of the GSA Branch of the National Alliance of Postal and Federal Employees. In 1970, Cassell, while living in Ward 1, was elected an at-large member of the D.C. board of education.

In 1970 he went to court to stop the superintendent's selection process. He joined the teachers in the Washington Teachers' Union strike of 1972. Cassell was a supporter of Superintendent Scott until a conflict arose when Scott, as superintendent, insisted that Cassell not organize a demonstration in a school Cassell's daughter attended.[6]

Cassell voted against board President Allen's policies along with Tirana, Swaim, and Taylor.

Bardyl R. Tirana, white, of Albanian ancestry, was born in Geneva, Switzerland, and graduated from Princeton University and Columbia University. He was a member of the law firm of Amram, Hahn, and Sundlun in Washington, D.C.; and a former trial attorney for the Admiralty and Shipping Section, Civil Division, U.S. Department of Justice. Tirana is the director of the Civil Defense Preparedness Agency in the Pentagon, a level 4 executive appointment under the Carter administration. He was elected to the D.C. board of education as an at-large member from Ward 3, located west of Rock Creek Park.

Tirana was opposed to many of Anita Allen's policies. In addition, he supported decentralization at the local school level and believed that the board had "almost unlimited" power over the budget although it never fully realized it.[7] Tirana was not a Scott supporter.

<u>Delores Pryde</u>, Black, a homemaker with children in the D.C. public schools in 1973, campaigned on a platform of community control.[8] Pryde defeated Edward Hancock in the 1972 elections for the Ward 7 seat and joined the group who supported administrative decentralization. Additionally, Pryde was one of Superintendent Scott's strong supporters even though she believed he had not accomplished to her satisfaction the goals of the board.[9] In December 1973, **Delores** Pryde resigned from the DCBOE because of illness and Virginia Morris was appointed by the board to replace her.

<u>William Treanor</u>, white, was the initiator and project coordinator of the National Youth Alternatives Project and was instrumental in the formation of the National Network of Runaway and Youth Services. In addition, he was consulted by the House and Senate staffs and presented written testimony on the Juvenile Justice and Delinquency Prevention Act of 1974. Himself a former delinquent runaway and tenth grade high school dropout, Treanor became a field worker for the Southern Christian Leadership Conference and later received an Ed.M. degree from the Harvard Graduate School of Education. Treanor is the founder and past director of Special Approaches in Juvenile Assistance, which included one of the country's first residential runaway counseling centers, three group foster homes for troubled youths, two free schools, several employment programs, and directed an NIMH-funded national training program for paraprofessional youth workers. Treanor is director of National Youth Alternatives.

He was elected to the D.C. board of education in 1974 from Ward 2 using as campaign manager, David Splitt, who was appointed on December 19, 1973 as the DCBOE's general counsel. Treanor joined the faction of Morris, Hobson, Jr., Mason and Kemp against Superintendent Sizemore.

Barbara Lett Simmons, Black, is currently founder and president of BLS Associates, Inc., a firm which focuses on management leadership training for staff in educational and correctional institutions, and public and private social services agencies. In addition, the firm also offers technical assistance and public relations services.

Simmons was educated at Western Michigan University where she received the A.B. degree. She did graduate work at Wayne State University, the University of Maryland and George Washington University.

In 1968 Simmons was assistant director of the Mid-Atlantic Area Manpower Institutes for Development of Staff. Prior to that, she taught school in Michigan, Montgomery County, Maryland, and Wayne State University.

When Simmons came to Washington, D.C. in 1962, she became involved in the D.C. public schools which her sons attended. She also served on the Vocational Educational Advisory Council for fiscal year 1973 for the school system. In November 1973, Simmons was elected as an at-large member of the D.C. board of education. She supported Sizemore's due process rights so she sought an injunction against the board to cease the Sizemore firing process. She supported Sizemore's programs for structural change in the DCPS for humanistic education. She was one of Sizemore's staunch supporters all during her superintendency. Nevertheless, Simmons cast her vote for Vincent E. Reed as superintendent of schools after Sizemore was fired.

Virginia Morris, Black, is the mother of 8 children, all of whom at one time or another were enrolled in the D.C. public schools. Her school related activities included being president of Phelps Vocational High School Home and School Association, past president of Stanton Elementary School PTA, and Richardson Elementary School PTA; member of various committees at Kelly-Miller Junior High School; D.C. Congress of Parents and Teachers, and vice-president of Area Four Council. In 1968, Morris took court action with other parents, to assure bus transportation for children in the northeast and southeast areas while boundaries for the junior high schools were being changed. Also, she helped to develop guidelines for the selection of principals. Furthermore, Morris appeared before the board of education, city government agencies, and the Congress to request improved and expanded educational programs and facilities.

In addition to the above, Morris belonged to the Washington Association for the Education of Young Children, D.C. Citizens for Better Public Education, the Washington Urban League, the D.C. Chamber of Commerce, and the Republican Party. Morris was appointed D.C. board of education member in the winter of 1973 to replace Ward 7 member Delores Pryde. She was voted president of the board in 1974 and served until her term expired in 1975.

Morris supported administrative decentralization but when Superintendent Sizemore appointed six regional superintendents in July 1975 without the board's permission, Morris opposed her actions and led the board coalition to fire Sizemore apparently against the wishes of her Ward 7 constituents. When Morris ran again in 1975 for the board, she was defeated. Later, she ran for the Neighborhood Advisory Council in Ward 7 and again lost.

Morris was for a strong centralized bureaucracy and, like Anita Allen, was authoritarian in her methods. She fought Superintendent Sizemore for control of the system, quoting from the Rules of the board in this regard. Additionally, Morris believed in strengthening the board through the addition of staff and usurped the superintendent's right to legal counsel for the administration of court decrees and other legal matters.

Julius W. Hobson, Jr., Black, son of Julius W. Hobson, Sr. (a former board member), was a graduate of McKinley High School and is attending Howard University Law School. His work experience includes a job as research assistant for Morris Associates, Inc., Executive Aide and Youth Program Director for Hospitality House, Inc., research assistant for the Civil Rights Documentation Project and research assistant for the Washington Institute for Quality Education. In 1977, Hobson was worked as an editorial assistant at Howard University.

Hobson was elected from Ward 8 to the D.C. board of education in 1974 and served as vice-president of the board. He was chairperson of the Committee on School Finance and was a member of the coalition which fired Barbara A. Sizemore from the superintendency.

Carol Sevitt Schwartz, Jewish, is married to a lawyer and has three children attending schools in the District of Columbia. She is originally from Texas, having graduated from the University of Texas with a B.S. degree in Special Education and Elementary Education. She was a special education teacher in Austin, Texas. In 1965, Schwartz moved to Washington, D.C. and taught school in Montgomery County, Maryland.

Schwartz was actively involved in the Parents Pre-School Council for the Recreation Department. In 1974 she was appointed by the President of the United States to the National Advisory Council on the Education of Disadvantaged Children where she served as chairperson of the Parental Involvement Committee. She was elected to the board of education of the District of Columbia in November 1974 as Rosenfield's replacement in Ward 3, and immediately joined the coalition to fire Superintendent Sizemore.

Therman E. Evans, Black, received his M.D. degree in 1971 from the Howard University College of Medicine. Evans has worked as special assistant to the director of the Office of Health Manpower Opportunity, Bureau of Health Manpower Education, National Institutes of Health, HEW; Program Development Branch, Office of Health Resources Opportunity, Health Resources Administration, HEW; and executive director, Health Manpower Development Corporation. Also, he was national health director of Operation PUSH (People United to Save Humanity).

Evans was elected as an at-large member of the D.C. board of education and served until 1978. He was president of the board from 1976 to 1978. Evans was one of the board members who supported Barbara A. Sizemore and voted against her firing.

Bettie G. Benjamin, Black, is engaged in the private practice of law, having received her Juris Doctor degree from the Howard University School of Law. Both of Benjamin's children attended Washington, D.C. public schools. A resident of Washington, D.C. for over 20 years, Benjamin was active in the Brookland Civic Association, the Judicial Concern for Children in Trouble Committee, the D.C. PTA, a delegate to the National Black Assembly, and the Washington Urban League.

Benjamin's educational activities included membership on the summer 1973 workshop to design a new English curriculum for high school students, the 1974 Summer Workshop on Students' Rights and Responsibilities; United Planning Organization; PACTS Workshop on Decentralization; the Fort Lincoln New Town Citizens Advisory Committee on Education; the Brookland School Replacement Committee of 21; and the board of directors, D.C. Citizens for Better Public Education.

Additionally, she was active in numerous parent-teachers associations.

Benjamin was elected to the D.C. board of education from Ward 5 in 1974 replacing Mattie Taylor; she is very responsive to the interests of her constituents and is currently serving thereon. She also supported Superintendent Sizemore, and was among the four who voted not to fire her.

John A. Warren, Black, received his B.A. degree from Howard University. He is a member of the Conference of Minority Public Administrators, American Society of Public Administrators, the Governing Council National Capital Area Chapter, American Society for Public Administration, board of directors of Reading is Fundamental, Inc. (D.C.) and board of directors, Friendship House. From 1963 to 1966 he served as: staff assistant to the late Honorable Adam C. Powell, Jr., Congressman, U.S. House of Representatives; co-ordinator, Neighborhood Planning Council Elections for Washington, D.C.; co-coordinator, National Policy Conference on Education for Blacks sponsored by the Congressional Black Caucus; vice-president of Election Management Associates, Inc.; research assistant, House Committee on Education and Labor, U.S. House of Representatives; and legislative assistant, House Committee on Education and Labor, U.S. House of Representatives.

Warren was first elected to the DCBOE from Ward 6 in a special election held in November 1974. Since Warren believes in due process, he supported the right of Mrs. Sizemore to a fair legal hearing.

Elizabeth Cooper Kane (known as Betty Ann), white, studied at Middlebury College in Vermont, Yale University, and New York University. In 1965, she was a teaching assistant at Yale University and assistant professor at Catholic University of America. From 1969-73 Kane served as programs assistant at the Folger Shakespeare Library and is currently working as head of Public Programs, Folger Shakespeare Library.

Kane's community activities included service on: the board of directors, Capitol East Children's Center (day care); Capitol Hill Action Group; board of trustees, WETA (educational television station); and board of directors of the Museum Education Roundtable. In addition, Kane was a member of the Women's National Democratic Club, D.C. Women's Political Caucus, Task Force on Health Education, and the D.C. Commission on the Status of Women.

In November 1974 Kane was elected to the D.C. board of education as an at-large member and was re-elected in November 1975. Kane voted to fire Barbara A. Sizemore as superintendent of schools. Kane was endorsed by the D.C. Citizens for Better Public Education (DCCBPE) for a city council seat.

Conrad P. Smith, Black, an emigre from Detroit, Michigan, received a Bachelor of Arts degree and a Juris Doctor degree from Howard University. He has worked for the National Security Agency, the U.S. Department of Labor, and the U.S. Commission on Civil Rights, and currently practices law in Washington, D.C. As one actively involved in professional and community affairs, Smith is affiliated with the NAACP, the District of Columbia Bar Association, the National Bar Association, the Washington Council of Lawyers, the American Civil Liberties Union, the Center for the Study of Democratic Institutions, People's Involvement Corporation, Ward 1 Democrats, and the Metropolitan Citizens Advisory Council.

Smith was elected to the D.C. board of education in 1975 as the Ward 1 representative. He served during Vincent Reed's tenure as superintendent. Smith was elected president of the board in January 1977.

Minnie Shumate Woodson, Black, has been a resident of the far northeast section of Washington, D.C. since 1921. She is a graduate of Miner Teachers College (later known as D.C. Teachers College and now part of the University of the

District of Columbia). Woodson taught elementary school in D.C. for 18 years. Also, her two sons attended D.C. public schools.

In terms of community participation, Woodson was a member of the Northeast Boundary Civic Association, D.C. Congress of Parents, Teachers, and the Right-to-Read Task Force of the D.C. school system, and Commissioner on the D.C. Commission on the Arts and Humanities. In 1977, Woodson was elected from Ward 7 to membership on the D.C. board of education. She also served during Vincent Reed's tenure as superintendent of schools.

## Selected socioeconomic characteristics of D.C. board members

Characteristics of board members have been noted in a number of studies over the years. According to Getzels, et al, people's view of the educational task is affected by their level of education and their occupation.[10] Further, Cunningham states that people serving on school boards represent all classes, races and religions, although they generally come from business, managerial and professional occupations.[11]

In this regard, the D.C. school board is no different from others. Nonetheless, if it is true that D.C. school board members do in fact represent all social classes, it is because the constituents of certain poor wards in the District voted them into office, not necessarily that they are from the poorer classes. Of the 22 board members who served during 1973-75, 19 are college graduates. According to their official biographies, Morris, Hobson and Pryde did not graduate from college.

In addition, almost all of these school board members were drawn from the business, managerial and professional occupations. Two of the three housewives (Pryde, Mason, Schwartz) were formerly teachers (Mason, Schwartz) and one of the two teachers (Mason) was an administrator. Barry, Taylor, Kemp, Washington, Coates, Cassell, Tirana,

Treanor, Morris, Evans, Kane and Mason were administrators in various enterprises. Rosenfield, a businessman, is the owner of a liquor store. Simmons, a businesswoman, is president of her own consultant firm. Benjamin and Smith are attorneys in private practice. Hence, it can hardly be stated that these professionals, managers, and business persons were truly representative of the poor residents in the District of Columbia. This is not to say, though, that none of them were concerned about making structural changes in the school system to assist the learning needs of poor children. It is simply being noted that the membership of the D.C. board of education, as is the membership of most boards of education, is composed of lay people from socioeconomic classes other than that of the majority of their constituents.

## The Motives of DCBOE Members

Why do citizens seek membership on the DCBOE and what are the possible consequences of these motives in the operation of the boards?

We can get partial insight into the general motives of the reasons articulated by board members through their responses to the interview questions. No claim is made that these responses are representative of the total board or that the data is conclusive. It is based upon conjecture or opinion and not upon scientific research since responses to a question of this nature were not solicited but revealed themselves indirectly through responses to other questions. There was no attempt to tabulate responses in a systematic way. Therefore, only a sample of responses are presented below which may give some clues as to the direction other researchers may wish to go since testimonial statements leave many questions unanswered.

One of the early studies dealing specifically with the motives of school board members is Donald J. McCarty's dissertation titled "Motives for

Seeking School Board Membership." McCarty found in his study that the majority of his respondents gave civic responsibility as their main reason for seeking board membership.[12] Another particularly significant example of school board members giving altruistic reasons for seeking public office can be seen in a 1978 study done on Black school board members by Thornton. In it he included a hypothesis relating to the motives for a Black school board member seeking public office. Results of tests of the hypothesis dealing with the public regardingness (concern for their general community that are not exclusively predicated on consideration of private gain) of the 450 participants indicated a medium to very high index on this variable. Data in this regard was secured from questionnaires sent to the participants.[13]

Only seven of the 14 school board members interviewed for this present study revealed their reasons for joining the DCBOE. All seven gave altruistic reasons for doing so. Some representative responses are as follows:

> I wanted to represent the area to try to get the city to realize that because a child is poor, it doesn't mean he can't learn. That was my main thrust on the board.[14]

> I believe in lay control in...public institutions, non-professional control and in accountability to the citizens... It seems to be the best that we have come up with in this country. I see my own role in terms of my constituents is to be particularly concerned about little people getting messed over by the school system.[15]

> And the real reason I got on the board of education in the beginning...[was that] the guy who was on the board didn't share any information... My prime interest was in helping parents and getting the parents organized...[16]

At the time, the D.C. School Board was the only elected body in Washington, D.C. so I not only perceived my job to be that of an elected school board member to deal with school problems but as an elected official who must respond to all kinds of problems brought to us by the citizens in this colonial city who had no representation in their own local government.[17]

I represent my constituents in Ward 6. The city is not concerned about the schools. The present school board race [1977] is a reflection of that. There are four candidates running for two at-large seats -- one Black candidate who is seeking re-election; one Spanish surnamed candidate, one white candidate and one person of Greek ethnic extraction. There is something wrong when you have one Black person seeking one of two seats in a city that has a population still at least 70 percent Black and a school system that is at least 97 percent Black.[18]

As previously stated all seven board members who revealed their motivations for seeking membership on the DCBOE gave altruistic reasons for doing so. That is, each emphasized the service they wished to render to their constituents, thereby confirming this writer's belief that if a direct question had been posed on this issue, there is the possibility that the same sort of replies would have been forthcoming, thus revealing nothing more than what the respondents felt their motives should be or what they felt this researcher wished to hear. One might say then that DCBOE members are inclined to articulate altruistic reasons for joining the board. So it is for the above reasons that this section of the report is offered as exploratory, as a future research question in reference to the motives for seeking membership on the DCBOE. For it does seem strange that the possibilities of a political career would not have been mentioned by board members in the

course of the interview, especially in light of
the fact that Marion Barry and Hilda Mason were
not the only two board members who ran for another
political office between 1973 and 1977 or who
aspired to do so. It can be noted that Swaim ran
and lost. Morris ran and lost. Evans discussed
his political aspirations in the newspapers.
Warren discussed the possibility of running for a
city council seat in a taped interview in the
researcher's class with her students. And Kane
recently declared her candidacy for a city council
seat. It is then for these reasons again that
this writer emphasizes the need for a study focused
on this issue to uncover how this political leaning
of board members actually affects the relationship
between D.C. school superintendents and DCBOE
members. This trend may be one of the factors that
either creates a high conflict board, or tempers
the board as it seeks consensus on issues among
board members, or in support or not of the superintendent's proposals. Obviously, such an analysis
must take into consideration the range of data
mentioned above in determining motive, and not
just questionnaire responses.

Politics of the DCBOE --

School affairs in America at one time were
thought to be separated from politics. This is no
longer true and certainly the DCPS system is an
example of this change in perspective. The school
system in D.C. is a political entity in that it
involves the making of decisions which realistically cannot be isolated from their setting of being
one governmental unit among others in the city
government of the District of Columbia. Nor can
education be separated from the politics in the
District because the DCBOE is an elected body and
its members must declare their candidacy, design
a support system for campaigning (by securing funds
from various factions or individuals in the community), develop a constituency, fashion a plat-
form (usually around some conflict inherent in the
present school situation), and project an electable
image to compel citizens to choose them rather than

another candidate. Thus, we see board members with further political ambitions maneuvering for positions that would make them highly visible to the public.

Politics was noted in board activities as early as 1967. A <u>Washington Afro-American</u> article gave the impression that political maneuvering had become more important than the problem of education.[19]

Reference to political maneuverings was also noted in the minutes of the February 12, 1969 meeting of the board. It was suggested that some members sought personal publicity in connection with Superintendent Manning's deletion of objectionable material from textbooks. The following comments were noted:

> Mr. Roots stated he believed Board Members must learn proper procedures for handling Board business. He stated that he did not think it right to "scoop" certain things for the benefit of personal prestige without the courtesy of going to the persons involved. He stated it was most important that the Board act as a Board and not as individual members taking action to implement certain matters.[20]

In 1973, the political ambitions continued to plague superintendent-school board relations. When the school board and Scott were having some disputes, charges were made that individuals were using the school system as a steppingstone to other political positions. Mr. Anthony, a citizen, spoke to this issue when he said:

> I think the problem is one solely of politics. We have members of the Board of Education that are more concerned about using this as a platform for hopeful political gains [whenever you get home rule in this town], than they are concerned with the needs of children ....The kind of politics that we need in this

city is a politics of purpose and the purpose should be to try to bring forth as much substance of education for our children as is possible.[21]

In line with this, the board on January 20, 1974 recorded its opposition to the provision in the home rule bill which would require that an elected official of the District resign from his current position before running for another office. It was felt that a special hardship existed since the school board is elected in odd numbered years while the other elections are in even numbered years.

Taylor, who served on the DCBOE for five years, saw the Barry years as more political than prior years. She said:

> First was Coates then Anita for two years and Barry for two years. The goals shifted during the Barry years. The Board became highly political. Decisions were made almost in terms of how many votes they would pile up for board members when they later ran for higher offices. That almost became the controlling factor. We were not then talking as much about what, in fact, was good for children as we were talking about what was politically stimulating, what will win me the greatest amount of attention and will build me a following. And we tended to occupy and preoccupy ourselves more with letting our vocal groups who we knew could be counted on to work and give support in a campaign have some expression of their will via the school board. So we moved into the gay liberation question and issue. We moved into the right of dissident groups to come in and hold assemblies. We moved into a great debate over the right to wear anything you want to wear to school and the hairdos, the plaits, braids. All of this became our foremost issues and we stopped talking about educating children and

> we started talking about popular political causes and how can I win brownie points by offering them a forum through the board of education....Mr. Barry and Mrs. Mason made it to the City Council...[22]

Cassell also characterized Barry's behavior as politically oriented:

> Barry became essentially conservative as compared to Mason and myself who were seen as the radicals. Barry was always politically oriented anyway. The school board was sort of an interim thing for him whereas for us the school board is something that you do now, make some changes now. My opinion of Barry is that since it was an interim thing, don't do too much...[23]

Internal board politics also operated in relation to the selection of committee chairpersons. In answer to the question: "How were chairpersons (of committees) chosen?", Father Kemp replied:

> In various times through...a lot of consultation. I think Barry talked to every board member every week. In Morris' time it wasn't that broad consultation thing, but more of a majority approach -- more political -- Virginia kind of rolled certain people out of certain committees...the majority would never get a permanent chairmanship....It's called politics.[24]

According to Evans, internal board politics did occur; certainly he played politics to get elected president of the board. He stated:

> Well, I don't know how it was done in 1973-75. As I remember, when Mr. Barry was president, he did ask people to outline what committees they were interested in. And he tried to assign people to committees based

Walter F. Fauntroy, D.C. delegate, $100.00; D.C. Gazette (Samuel F. H. Smith, a white liberal), $200.00; James D. Hurd, $150.00; Betsy Folger, $200.00; Joseph Wright, Tiny Tots Day Care Center, $75.00; Lionel C. Epstein, $200.00; Albert J. Beveridge, III, $75.00; Census Tasks Force, $75.00; Edith B. Simpson, $110.00; John J. Rigbey, $100.00; Richard England, $100.00; Bernie Burguden, Jr., $100.00; Mr. & Mrs. Lloyd Symington, member, board of directors, D.C. Citizens for Better Public Education, $100.00; Phillip Stern, $100.00; A. Newmyer, $100.00; Ed. Sylvester, $100.00; Dr. Robert T. Lewis, $100.00; Mr. & Mrs. Harry Vincent, $100.00; Walter Kay, Lithogram Inter. Ltd. 1012, $100.00; Ralph H. Dwan, Jr., $100.00; Cornelius C. Pitts, $100.00; and Jean Fitzgerald's fund raising party, $500.00.

Loans to the fund were made by Sam H. Smith for $500.00, Marion Barry himself for $2,000.00, and Jeff Mitchell, chairman of the Friends of Marion Barry Fund, for $400.00.

Additionally, Mr. Barry ran a very high-powered campaign as indicated by the following taken from his campaign report: sums for salaries for 11 people totaled $2,732.00; food costs totaled $510.00; rent $1,175.00; radio and research $6,549.00; campaign materials costing $2,400.00; telephone deposit, $700.00; petty cash, $640.00; sound equipment, $290.00; miscellaneous expenses, $1,414.64; and temporary personnel, $650.00.[28]

From the large sums of money that Barry invested in his campaign, it may be deduced that his eye was on a bigger stake than a school board seat and that this was the first stop toward the mayor's position. Within five years, Barry went from the school board to the city council, and to the mayor.

The Ward 5 Committee for Mattie G. Taylor raised approximately $2,700.00. Most of the contributions were given in small amounts of $5.00 to $25.00 with amounts over $100.00 coming from two receptions, one held on October 16, 1971 ($592.50) and another held on November 20, 1971 ($670.00). Taylor received only a $20.00 contribution from John Hechinger, president of the Hechinger Company.[29]

The Raymond B. Kemp Ward 1 Campaign received approximately $2,000.00. Among the individual contributors who contributed $100.00 or more were: James A. McGuire, $100.00; Areatha Jarvis, $250.00; Michael Whedbee of California, $100.00; David Splitt, who became the board's attorney in 1973, $100.00; Mrs. J. Carter Brown, $150.00; and Mr. & Mrs. William T. Hannan, Sr., $100.00. A $50.00 contribution was made by Polly Shackleton, city councilwoman. Campaign expenditures totaled approximately $2,200.00.[30]

Albert Rosenfield's Report of Campaign Contributions revealed that, for the October 31, 1973 reporting period, Rosenfield received approximately $2,750.00 with expenditures totaling approximately $1,874.78. Board members contributing to the campaign included Mattie Taylor, Bardyl Tirana and Marion Barry. In addition, the D.C. Republican Committee gave $190.00.[31]

The December 10, 1973 report showed a total collection of approximately $120.00 with expenditures totaling approximately $1,048.00, of which $830.00 was paid to the D.C. Congress of P.T.A.'s Shoe and Rubber Fund.[32]

Evie Washington was another board member who received mostly small contributions, with the exception of a $250.00 contribution from the D.C. Republican Committee and a $287.12 contribution from Richard Hurlbut, a school system employee who contributed moderately large sums to several school board members' campaigns.[33]

The November 12, 1971 school board election report of Hilda Howland Mason showed a contribution given by her husband, Charles N. Mason, of

$2,859.00 to the Hilda Howland Mason Campaign Committee. Smaller contributions between $5.00 and $50.00 were given by about 45 people; $75.00 and $100.00 were given by two other contributors. Expenses for this report period totaled approximately $7,800.00.[34]

Mason's November 30, 1971 report revealed a total collected of $1,244.00 with Charles Cassell giving $100.00; Ramond G. Hay contributing $119.00; Barbara L. Simmons giving $100.00 and Samuel Smith giving $75.00. Other contributions ranged from $5.00 to $47.00. Expenses for this period totaled $4,095.09. Thus, according to the two reports found in Mason's campaign folder for the November 1971 school board election, a total of $7,884.33[35] was spent -- considerably lower than the amount of $17,060.64 spent by Marion Barry for his school board campaign of 1971.

Contributions for the 1975 Board of Education Campaign in Ward 4 for Hilda Mason amounted to $2,243.43 for three report periods. The October 10, 1975 report showed contributions from the following sources: Charles N. Mason, $100.00; Richard Hurlbut, $100.00; James Johnson from Louisville, Kentucky, former associate superintendent, $100.00; and $100.00 from Morris Milgram, housing developer and real estate broker.[36] The October 20, 1975 report showed two contributors, Melvin Leventon, builder, c/o Partners in Housing in Philadelphia, Pennsylvania, for $100.00; and Noel W. Kane, attorney, for $100.00.[37] Data collected from a third report revealed contributions from out-of-towners: a lawyer from Philadelphia for $100.00, a person in real estate and housing from Lynbrook, New York, for $100.00, and a person from East Orange, New Jersey for $100.00.[38]

The December 15, 1975 report showed that a contribution was made by Philip R. Newell, Jr., a member of the D.C. Citizens for Better Public Education, who also contributed to Barry's campaign.[39]

Martha S. Swaim's campaign contribution list contained only seven contributions for $50.00 or more: John Hechinger, a lumber yard company president, contributed $50.00; Polly Shackleton, city councilwoman, contributed $50.00; three other persons contributed $50.00 and one $64.00. In addition, a party raised $207.00 and the other 90-odd contributions were between $2.00 and $30.00, totaling $1,107.80. Expenses totaled $1,102.38. A well-known name among Swaim's contributors was Willard Wirtz, who made a small contribution.[40]

Delores Pryde's campaign contributions amounted to approximately $1,183.00 and total expenditures amounted to approximately $1,148.10. The largest contribution, $250.00, was made by Charles N. Mason, Jr., Hilda Mason's husband. Charles T. Cassell was the only board member whose name showed up on the report.[41]

The Citizen's Coalition for Cassell collected approximately $1,600.00 while expenses totaled approximately $5,000.00. Among his contributors were Charles and Hilda Mason who gave $328.00; Barbara L. Simmons who gave $20.00, and Bardyl R. Tirana who gave $100.00.[42]

Virginia Morris ran a very low budget campaign. Her major support came from Charles and Hilda Mason. From Charles H. Mason, Jr., attorney, she listed $100.00 on October 24, 1975 and $100.00 on the September 25, 1975 report from Hilda Mason listed as Howland M. Mason. Morris' husband contributed $100.00, and $100.00 or less was received from three other persons.[43]

William Treanor's campaign committee data for November 1973 showed 88 contributors whose contributions totaled approximately $2,500.00. Expenditures totaled approximately $3,200.00. Tirana was the only board member whose name showed up on the report. However, one of the largest contributions was made by AFL-CIO D.C. Council of Labor (Political Education Fund, COPE) in the amount of $500.00

and only one other sizeable contribution of $300.00 was contributed by an individual.[44]

Dr. Therman Evans' Campaign Fund had total receipts of approximately $6,900.00. John H. Hechinger contributed $100.00 to the campaign, as did six other people. Most contributions though fell within the range of $5.00 and $60.00, with the majority hovering around $10.00 (45) and the next largest grouping around $5.00 (48). Thus, only one amount was given by an immediately recognizable businessman, John H. Hechinger.[45]

Most of the money from October 20, 1974 to January 31, 1975, for Carol Schwartz's 1974 campaign seemed to come primarily from a labor union, $100.00; a government employee, $50.00; Engineers Political Education Committee, $100.00; an attorney, $100.00; her husband and herself, $300.00; and a retiree, $100.00; totaling approximately $1,800.00 according to data in her board of elections folder.[46]

Most of Bettie Benjamin's contributions for her 1975 re-election campaign came from the sale of tickets to parties, totaling approximately $1,000.00.[47]

The 1974 Committee to Elect John Warren reported on October 17, 1974 three $50.00 contributions and 9 other contributions between $10.00 and $35.00, excluding Warren's own contribution of $75.00.[48]

An October 10, 1975 report showed 17 contributions for $25.00 or under; one for $30.00; one ticket sales from a tea for $80.00; and two $60.00 ticket sales contributions.[49] An October 24, 1975 contribution list showed five contributions under $50.00.[50]

Generally, John Warren received small contributions of less than $50.00 -- approximately 53 such contributions. He reported only three contributions for $50.00 or over.[51]

In January 1975, four contributions were received: two for $25.00, one for $10.00 and one for $4.00.[52] In addition, the committee raised $500.00 at a raffle.[53]

Some of the larger contributors to Betty Ann Kane's campaign were Charles N. Mason (Hilda Mason's husband), and Hilda Mason, who contributed $200.00 apiece on October 15, 1975, and William Treanor who contributed $100.00 on July 31, 1975.[54] Also contributing to Kane's campaign was the Drive Teamsters Educational Fund in the sum of $200.00.

Barbara Simmons' campaign contribution report dated December 6, 1973 revealed sizeable contributions of $100.00 to $500.00 from 15 persons, of which Charles Mason provided $250.00 and John Hechinger provided $100.00, and Bardyl R. Tirana provided $100.00. The total contributed for this period amounted to $2,450.00 with expenditures of approximately $7,000.00.[55]

Approximate contributions and expenditures for selected campaigns are presented in table 6. The following table shows that Marion Barry collected and spent more money ($17,060.64) for his school board campaign than any of the other candidates. The next largest spender was Hilda Mason who spent over $7,000.00. Evans spent $6,433.00 and Cassell almost $5,000.00. These sums of money are unusual in Washington, D.C. as can be noted in table 6. Eight of the 17 campaigns cost $2,000.00 or less; five cost between $2,000.00 and $3,500.00, leaving six costing between $3,500.00 and $17,000.00. When comparing contributions with expenditures, one can deduce that at least four candidates strongly desired a school board seat since in some cases (Mason's in particular) private funds must have been spent in the 1971 campaign. Also, in the case of Cassell and Simmons, it can be noted that their expenditures far exceeded their contributions.

TABLE 6

SELECTED CAMPAIGN CONTRIBUTIONS AND EXPENDITURES

| School Board Member | Campaign Year | Ward | Contributions (Approximations) | Expenditures (Approximations) |
|---|---|---|---|---|
| BARRY, M. | 1971 | At-Large | $ 16,000.00 | $ 17,060.64 |
| MASON, H. | 1971 | 4 | $ 5,000.00 | $ 7,800.00 |
| SIMMONS, B. | 1973 | At-Large | $ 2,450.00 | $ 7,000.00 |
| EVANS, T. | 1974 | At-Large | $ 6,882.96 | $ 6,433.03 |
| CASSELL, W. | 1973 | At-Large | $ 1,600.00 | $ 5,000.00 |
| KANE, E. | 1975 | At-Large | $ 4,013.18 | $ 4,112.16 |
| TREANOR, W. | 1973 | 2 | $ 2,500.00 | $ 3,200.00 |
| ROSENFIELD, A. | 1973 | 3 | $ 2,750.00 | $ 2,900.00 |
| TAYLOR, M. | 1971 | 5 | $ 2,600.00 | $ 2,700.00 |
| KEMP, R. | 1971 | 1 | $ 2,000.00 | $ 2,200.00 |
| WARREN, J. | 1974 | 6 | $ 2,000.00 | $ 2,000.00 |
| SCHWARTZ, C. | 1974 | 3 | $ 1,804.00 | $ 1,813.98 |
| PRYDE, D. | 1971 | 7 | $ 1,183.00 | $ 1,148.10 |
| SWAIM, M. | 1971 | 6 | $ 1,107.80 | $ 1,102.38 |
| MASON, H. | 1975 | 4 | $ 2,243.43 | $ 1,117.68 |
| BENJAMIN, B. | 1975 | 5 | $ 1,090.00 | $ 1,039.50 |
| MORRIS, V. | 1975 | 7 | $ 1,236.93 | $ 794.79 |
| WASHINGTON, E. | 1973 | 2 | $ 1,000.00 | $ 700.00 |
| HOBSON, J., JR. | 1973 | 8 | $ N/A | $ N/A |

Total $ 67,922.23

It can also be noted in table 6 that $17,060.64 was spent on Marion Barry's campaign for an at-large school board seat in 1971. In comparison to the average of $5,000.00 spent for other at-large seats, the sum of $17,060.64 does seem unusually large. This is especially true when it is compared to the amount spent obtaining a city council seat. For instance, in the July 1977 city council race, Hilda Mason spent over $14,000.00 of her own money[56] while Barbara Sizemore spent approximately $6,000.00 in campaign contributions.[57]

In summary, John Hechinger contributed $950.00 to Barry's campaign in two amounts of $600.00 and $350.00, according to information in Mr. Barry's folder at the Board of Elections; $20.00 to Mattie Taylor's campaign; $50.00 to Martha Swaim's campaign and $100.00 to Evans' campaign. D.C. Delegate Walter Fauntroy contributed $175.00 in three amounts of $100.00, $50.00 and $25.00 to Barry's campaign; and $25.00 to Evans' campaign. David Splitt, who was sponsored by Treanor for the job of DCBOE attorney, contributed $100.00 to Kemp's campaign. Polly Shackleton, a city councilwoman, contributed to at least three school board campaign candidates: Kemp in the amount of $50.00; Barry, $122.00; and Swaim $50.00.

Another significant point to be noted is that Hilda and Charles Mason, according to the data, contributed money to several campaigns: Cassell, $328.00; Morris, $200.00; and Kane, $400.00, for a total of $928.00.

Interestingly, a Marvin Gerstin of 1150-17th Street N.W. contributed $1,000.00 to Barry's campaign. The D.C. telephone directory (1977) lists a Gerstin Zoslow Advertising Company at the 1150-17th Street N.W. address on the contribution list.

Finally, at least two contributors to Barry's campaign belong to the Metropolitan Board of Trade: Jean H. Sisco and Theodore Hagans, Jr., and a possible third connection is discernible in the name (Mrs.) William Cafritz. At least two members of the DCCBPE also contributed to Barry's campaign: Philip Newell and Lloyd Symington, which points up a link with that organization.

In the political climate of 1977, it might be possible to infer that large contributors to a politician's campaign expect to be able to influence the way that politician votes on issues of concern to the contributors. If this is true, then, there is the possibility that persons who made large contributions to board members' campaigns might have expected to have had some influence over certain board decisions of particular interest to them. In light of this, then, we might view sizeable contributions made to Marion Barry's campaigns by business people in the private domain to have influenced his perception about the use of public monies for private enterprises. Although Barry received approximately $4,000.00 from smaller contributors, it appeared through his actions that Barry's allegiance might have been to the big business interests in the District since at least three of his contributors had connections with the Metropolitan D.C. Board of Trade -- Jean H. Sisco, Theodore Hagans, Jr. and William Cafritz. Also, large contributions to his campaign derived from Hechinger and other monied people west of the park. Seemingly, Barry supported white interests in maintaining board contracts with the Friends of the D.C. Youth Orchestra Program and the Hawthorne Alternative School, the former of which will be discussed at length in Chapter VIII. It can be noted here though that at the July 8, 1974 board meeting Barry, Kemp, Treanor, Mason, and Swaim all voted to maintain the contract which gave over $150,000.00 of public school monies to a private group named the Friends of the D.C. Youth Orchestra Program. This board decision was made in opposition to the wishes of Superintendent Sizemore, who expressed a wish to use these public school funds to help strengthen the public school system's own music department.

As was noted above, Kemp, Treanor, Mason and Swaim were also in receipt of contributions from the business sector, the private sector. Morris who also finally voted to let the contract to a private enterprise received a sizeable contribution from Mason which might have influenced her vote. Despite the speculative nature of these observations, the truth of the matter is that the possibility of undo influence does exist.

## Leadership Styles

The leadership style of school board presidents and superintendents also is a factor in superintendent-school board relations in terms of exacerbating conflict in the DCPS system decision-making unit. Although no specific interview question focused directly on this aspect of the problem, a number of respondents emphasized this in their responses to other questions causing this factor to surface as a significant point in the investigation.

Comments by some interviewees, as well as minutes and transcripts of the DCBOE meetings, clearly reveal that Mrs. Anita Allen and Mrs. Virginia Morris were the two most authoritarian presidents of the board between 1970 and 1976. Just a few examples will suffice to reveal the strong direction the board was subjected to under President Allen. One comment about Evans is included. The case studies presented later in the report will focus on Mrs. Virginia Morris' style of leadership on the DCBOE between 1973-75.

Apparently, the majority of DCBOE members between 1970 and 1972 were pleased with the strong leadership posture of Mrs. Anita Allen, for she was voted back in as president of the board at the January 25, 1971 first organizational meeting for the year. The seven members of the DCBOE who voted in favor of retaining Mrs. Allen as president were Mrs. Washington, Mr. Rosenfield, Mr. Roots, Mr. Hancock, Reverend Coates, Mrs. Allen, and Mrs. Alexander. Those opposed were Mrs. Swaim, Mr. Tirana, Mrs. Taylor and Mr. Cassell (who voted for Mrs. Martha Swaim). However, Mrs. Swaim lost the election for both president and vice-president as Reverend Coates received that office by a 6-5 majority vote.[58]

In commenting about Anita Allen, board member Evie Washington said, "Under the chairmanship of Anita Allen, a lady with a magnificent mind, who had her fingertips...resources, [the board] wanted to bring children up to grade standards, to help them to become merit scholars, to be able to compete."[59]

Mrs. Washington felt positive about Allen's leadership style. Contrastingly, other board members saw the leadership style of Mrs. Allen as more authoritarian than did Mrs. Washington. Cassell said the following: "The president had the authority to assign board members to committees. People were punished if they did not vote for the president. I was punished on a few occasions - under Anita Allen."[60]

Former Superintendent Scott also characterized Allen's leadership style as authoritarian when he said, "Anita Allen ran that board with a far stronger arm than Barry. She intimidated people."[61]

In relation to Morris and Barry, Hobson felt

that both were authoritarian and interfered with the administration of the schools. Thus, he said: "I think again in retrospect Virginia was involved in a lot of things that she should not have been involved in. Same with Marion."[62]

Evie Washington likewise felt that Barry was an authoritarian leader. She said, "He played political games. He gave what he thought was all of the important committees to his friends and those people who voted for him."[63]

Only Hobson spoke about Evans' leadership style. He thought it was positive, as the following quote shows: "I think that a strong board president tends to create problems. Some had assertive leadership. Some examples are Marion, Anita Allen and Virginia Morris. I think Therman's style, some people tend not to say it's leadership but there is a style to it, tends to ease that and tends to make things kind of back off...."[64]

Several board members as well as key administrators spoke about the leadership style of their superintendents. Here, too, we hear echoes of autocratic and democratic strains. Scott's leadership style was highly appreciated by Delores Pryde, as the following quote indicates: "We considered Dr. Scott an ex-officio member of the board and he was available to us at all times. If we had any problems with any decisions that he had made, he could do it collectively or individually."[65]

Quite a number of respondents felt compelled to discuss Barbara Sizemore's leadership style -- some in a positive way and some in a negative way. Treanor said, "Barbara Sizemore wanted to have a dynamic and invigorated school system with a lot of pride and spirit. Her aspirations for the children in the school system was for them to be well and reasonably happy and as adults able to deal with their own personal lives as well as with the political involvements.... Implementation was not so hot."66

Taylor mentioned that Sizemore's leadership style was one of inclusion of other people into the decision-making process. She said:

> Her major goal was to decentralize the school system, and she did achieve that. She had other goals: to change the curriculum thrust so that the child became the center of the learning process so that the focus was always on the learner and this was quite a major goal with her, and that I don't think she was ever able to achieve because of many factors and many reasons not of her own making.
>
> She also wanted to change the power base of where decisions got made, who held the power to affecting how all this money gets spent and how our children get educated. She wanted to bring in some new players to the power table and make those who held the power share it with an ever widening range of people and, of course, no one gives up power without a fight, and I think this is why she found herself in such a heated battle.
>
> She was beginning to move it and I think if she'd stayed she would have, and they knew that.67

The same sentiment about Sizemore's leadership style was echoed by Tirana, although he has a negative feeling about Sizemore's administrative know-how, when he said:

> I believe that Barbara Sizemore was effective and the board in its selection of Mrs. Sizemore. Both were effective in terms of general goals of communicating to teachers in the local building that they were an important part of the decision-making process. And to

parents and to a certain extent children. I think that feeling, notwithstanding all of the effort of the first elected school board, and the second election and the hiring of Hugh Scott, the talk about decentralization, the communication of the feeling did not take place until some place during Barbara Sizemore's term. The implementation of the feeling was frustrated by Barbara's administrative inability and bad political judgment, and weaknesses. But that particular accomplishment was generally unrecognized but it took place.[68]

Evans also believed Sizemore's leadership style was effective educationally:

As I remember, Mrs. Sizemore spoke quite vigorously for making the system much more flexible, much more multicultural, much more multimodal. I think she brought to the school system an excellent experience with respect to public education, or education in general for inner city poor youth and she tried to, it was her effort both through her testimony and interviews and through her experience as superintendent to try to get to make the system more flexible to incorporate or to be more effective with handling the problem or situations that Black young people brought to the school system which was set up and designed for predominantly middle income white students. So I think that was definitely her primary objective and I think that she worked at that quite vigorously. If nothing else, she put it on the minds of a lot of people. There were, of course, many other problems and difficulties that were experienced during that time that did not make the full implementation of her ideas possible.[69]

It was Margaret Labat's impression that Barbara Sizemore was encouraged by the current superintendent among others to take on a confrontation leadership style with the board. She stated:

> I am going back to my comment about the intelligence and manner of the superintendent. I think it was threatening to the board members whose psychics got involved and the manner of speech and the quickness of her responses were frequently misinterpreted. I did have a question, initially. The first meeting I attended with the superintendent was on how X information should be presented to the board. People who were there gave their various opinions. My comment to the superintendent was I had met her outside the district and knew of her reputation, and I was sincere, that if I were in your place, I would not take on an adversary conflict role with the board because as long as I had been here, human beings do not like to be threatened. I much prefer the strategy of trying to persuade and convince and though they may seem like safe strategies its a matter of taking the course so you don't cut off the listening and hearing process. Vincent Reed said that this board has done exactly what it wants to do for so long; its time for someone to take on this board and you are to do it. I made one further comment, and that is it's very difficult to listen to all of the advice you get when you don't know all of the background. Let me share one observation with you. The people who were admonishing Hugh Scott to take on the board are still here and he is gone. I don't think you would take this position as a means of living; I think you would take it out of a desire to have something happen. This superintendent may have decided that she would use the confrontation approach, but it would never work with that board. I just felt that she had too much to offer not to make it available to the children and parents in the District of Columbia, but even from the beginning I saw encouragement to use that approach.[70]

Ken Haskins saw his leadership style and Sizemore's as being quite different and in the beginning he thought that they might therefore complement each other. In the long run though, he reversed his position in this regard:

> I can...talk about myself in relation to the superintendent, because we have different styles and that became an issue. I felt that we might complement each other in that way....
>
> I don't know exactly why, but I have the reputation of relating well to people....
>
> Barbara is one of the brightest people I have ever worked with. I was always amazed at the kind of information she could absorb and work with but she has some problems.[71]

The implication here and further on in the interview is that the superintendent did not always relate well to people, although she was one of the most intelligent people the system had.

Simmons' response is as follows:

> Probably the only notion that I didn't speak directly to is the notion that the superintendent's [Sizemore] leadership style was one that people in the Washington area were not accustomed to. It is a mid-west approach which is frankness and openness and in the cosmopolitan international city capital of the world, diplomacy and tongue in cheek and, if you please, dishonesty is the order of the day here.[72]

In answer to a question, "What procedures did the D.C. board of education use to execute its functions?", one key administrator compared the leadership styles of Sizemore and Reed in the following fashion:

I'll give you an example. You take the situation like Gil Diggs was faced with in this last thing where he was trying to be the regional superintendent of Region 5 again. Well, now, see now, in a situation like that Barbara probably would have kept supporting him, you see, and the board member would have kept opposing it, you see. Well, Vince is not that type, see. He would say, well no point in you keep coming up, I'm not gonna keep taking your name, and he is not gonna support it. Well, Barbara would say well, I will support him 'til hell freezes over. Just a difference in people. So you would have had this confrontation and, of course, she would have been right to do that as superintendent because that board member can't do anything but vote against her but because it's emotionally charged, it always results in a confrontation. Now that's just one example.[73]

Hobson felt less threatened by Vincent Reed's leadership style than by Barbara Sizemore's. He stated:

Any kind of change is fought...if people feel threatened. People have to be kind of prepared for change. I think that the way Vince is preparing people for CBC is an example. It's not what I consider completely successful, but nobody felt anything was sprung on them. It was a two year process of bringing it out gradually. Telling people that this is what we are going to do. This is what we will be moving towards so nobody felt threatened in moving towards it. We've been able to slide in things like teachers having to be recertified every five years; that all teachers regardless of status ought to be rated twice a year, and that if they receive poor ratings, they are to be dismissed. And when you move in that kind of a manner at least within this bureaucracy, it tends to get over better. But to announce a new program that's going to start in September generally gets fought even when people don't know what it's about...maybe sometimes you need to take things a step at a time...

Mr. Reed is quite adept at moving the bureaucracy, moving the administrative management, getting things done that should have been done a long time ago, moving and motivating people to do some things, I think he, too, is quite strong willed and determined and hard nosed about people doing what they should be doing. He's not afraid of the bureaucracy. I think he knows the bureaucracy well, which is an asset that Mrs. Sizemore did not have coming from another city, and I think that maybe put him in a better position to know where he needed to go to get some of these management functions done that had not been done for many years. My own opinion about his philosophical educational assets is that they're good. I think though they do not match those of Mrs. Sizemore, but then, we all have different assets and liabilities.[74]

Treanor said the following:

There were a lot of things we got into by default...I've only been on the board with two superintendents...her and Vince Reed. Reed does not let us get into a lot of areas. He just provides us with the information. He is pretty fast about that. He keeps us out of a lot of areas by satisfying our needs for information or whatever - being responsive and having some give and take in terms of policy or whatever. The board as a whole, not as individual members, but as an entity is not a very activist, intervening kind of a board now. It was much more so, of course, when Sizemore was superintendent.[75]

Mrs. Sizemore's leadership qualities may also be observed in the establishment of a specific program. One such is the use of the Administrative

Team concept as an integral part of the decision-making process in the D.C. public school system. In her effort to help the public schools serve the poor and powerless, she changed the method of governance from an hierarchical form to a participatory inclusive form. Consequently, in conjunction with decentralization, the Administrative Team concept was introduced. The team consisted of the top administrators who interpreted together in a free exchange how best to implement board policy and worked out procedures by consensus. Following this negotiation process, directives were issued and responsibilities assumed by each directing line. Unfortunately, the process was hampered and did not reach the next line down from the Administrative Team since board members whittled away the credibility of the Administrative Team,[76] especially during the financial crisis of 1975. An example of this collusion will be observed in the case study of the budget/management decision-making situation analyzed in Chapter VIII. Three of the six regional superintendents, who were members of the Administrative Team, reacted favorably to the use of the concept in the decision-making realm. Their comments are as follows:

> I really felt that the Administrative Team concept had tremendous possibilities for improving the decision-making process. That it was not given a chance to be fully implemented. Right now, the superintendent [Vincent Reed] has a cabinet of which no regional superintendent is a member. I discussed this with him in an interview and he told me that no way was he going to get people together and engage in all that useless talk. I told him that as a superintendent, he has the right to develop whatever he wants. I just personally regret that the Administrative Team concept has been eliminated.[77]

Gilbert Diggs, another supporter of the Administrative Team concept, stated that:

For example, personnel couldn't emerge without budget. Federal programs couldn't emerge without budget. Regional superintendents couldn't emerge without budget or personnel. So it was an interesting phenomenon that they all had influence and control over one another so that not one could emerge....

It validates the administrative concept to indicate... that it requires the cooperation of all of the major entities in a concerted effort for all of the major entities as a group to elevate the educational achievement of students.[78]

Thirdly, William Rice said:

You take the one on decentralization, it was just sheer grit that we got into that. It wasn't because of the board of education. We just made that work, you know. And I think one thing that made it work [was] the team approach where we were there every week, and almost every day, where Barbara knew what we were doing and we knew. We were... on a day-to-day basis. But now if we had had a centralized administration, it never would have worked because it would have taken too long to get things done. But you see we could run up to Barbara, and say "Barbara such and such a thing," and she could talk to Williams and say, "Get this done," and it could be done right on the spot.... Now that might not be the best way to do things. But under those circumstances where you don't have money and you have to take money from here to make this thing go, and money from here to make that go, that's the only way you can do it. I think that it was really marvelous that it worked with no money... decentralize a system this big and with not a dime.[79]

In terms of the leadership styles of three board presidents, Anita Allen, Marion Barry, and

Therman Evans, and three superintendents, Hugh Scott, Barbara Sizemore and Vincent Reed, only sporadic comments were made by board members. In the case of Sizemore's administration, which is the period of the major concentration of this study, some key administrators also commented. It should be noted that there was no effort made to interview key administrators of the Scott era, nor those operating presently during the Reed era, since neither was the period of concentration. Therefore, in no way can the data be considered conclusive. It can only point toward a direction of the feelings of some informants who felt keen enough about the issue to make comments. In summary, then, no systematic attempt was made to elicit comments about the leadership style of board presidents or superintendents. Comments came in relation to other questions. In retrospect, this investigator feels that this may prove to be a fruitful area for a future investigation of school board-superintendent relations. That is, these observations may provide clues as to some of the interpersonal forces at work in the school political system and thus need further probing.

## Role Conflicts

Gross points out one dilemma in superintendent-school board relations, which occurred time and time again in the D.C. school situation under investigation. He notes that in some school systems school board members deal almost exclusively with trivialities rather than tackle something as crucial as curriculum improvement. Some make decisions which are the board's prerogative, while others as if they are the superintendent and had the right to administer the board's policy decisions. Gross further notes that frequently superintendents and school board members disagree over their rights and responsibilities.[80]

Again the minutes provide a number of illustrations of this dilemma as viewed by some DCBOE members, D.C. superintendents and some D.C. top staff members. A particularly vivid account is presented by Julius Hobson, Sr. as he described how some board members got involved in what he felt to be administrative matters.

His attitude toward the intrusion of board members into administrative matters and what he thought to be Superintendent Manning's attitude about this was made quite clear in a memorandum to the DCBOE under the subject: "The Board of Education Proposes and the School Administration Disposes."

Mr. Hobson stated that administrators were dishonest and the organizational structure obsolete, thus the work of the school board members becomes a full-time job. He further emphasized that he thought Superintendent Manning felt that board members came to their positions with little knowledge of school matters and, therefore, should stay out of those areas which the school administration ran. Nevertheless, Mr. Hobson felt that unless the school administration changed, board members needed to become experts in administration as well as in policy-making. He noted that the board needed a way of finding out how and when its policies were implemented.[81]

According to Dr. Hugh J. Scott, board-superintendent relations are hard to define, that is, there is a thin line between matters within the domain of the school superintendent defined as administrative. The school board has policy and review powers, and the superintendent has the responsibility to administer the schools in an orderly and effective fashion. School board members, as a collective body, are legally empowered to represent the citizens in setting educational goals and policies. Although specific functions ought to be clearly separated for the board and superintendent, their efforts are interrelated and interdependent. Neither should view the other as a rubber stamp. Though there are rules set down for both, the job of the superintendent and the role of the board need better definition in the D.C. board of education rules. In further explaining the distinctions between policy and administration, Dr. Scott provided some specific instances of conflict situations during his administration in school board-superintendent relations which he felt were produced by board interference in matters which were administrative.[82]

One instance had to do with major changes made in a Title I (ESEA) program which had been developed cooperatively by the staff and the Title I Advisory Committee. The board expanded the number of schools to be served by Title I funds in spite of the fact that guidelines from the Office of Education suggested that emphasis should be placed on quality rather than on quantity to maximize the impact of funds.[83] In this regard, Scott felt that board members made political decisions rather than educational ones.[84]

Another case that Dr. Scott discussed in both the article and an interview dealt with the instructional programs which must be reviewed and approved by the DCBOE before implementation. He noted that the superintendent is held responsible by the board for the quality of the curriculum and the implementation of educational programs but that some board members, during his tenure, made major insertions, deletions and changes in the curricular documents presented to them. He, therefore, felt that often the final documents approved by the board were more representative of the personal preferences and biases of board members than the best thinking of educators in the school system.[85] He also attributes this change to political expediency rather than to educational merits.[86]

One particularly appropriate example was the D.C. Youth Orchestra Program. Dr. Scott stated that the school board reduced the support services to the schools in terms of music while at the same time added over a hundred and some thousand dollars to the D.C. Youth Orchestra. Although Scott felt the program was a good one, he said he did not feel that it warranted a shift of funds from direct services to the general population of the school system to students who resided in Maryland and Virginia. In this regard Dr. Scott said the following:

> I lost that because of political influences and that was related a good deal to the influence of Ward 3 and 4. Ward 4 is the most predominantly white ward and the D.C. Youth Orchestra was most heavily white, the jobs went to people who were white. In fact, the director of the orchestra at that time hired a good number of people who were in the U.S. army band who were predominantly white. I once raised the issue as to whether or not we couldn't employ some people who were skilled in teaching or who were minority or who could teach some of the basic instruments. I had a big problem with that. Well, that was a case I think where the merits were more political than certainly educational and certainly not an equitable distribution of the tax dollars to the students and residents of the District of Columbia. Well, I lost that one as a political concern.[87]

Furthermore, Scott stated that the above examples seem to him to represent inappropriate interference by board members in administrative matters or unsound judgments by the policy-making body. He feels that the best relationship "depends on mutual respect and a desire to deal with the task at hand (education) rather than petty differences and personalities."[88]

Some board members also felt that other board members became too involved in administrative matters. Hobson, Jr. saw this happening, especially in the case of retired individuals who became school board members. Thus he was opposed to their appointment to fill vacant positions on the board. He stated that:

board members ought not to be super-administrators or not to be always attempting to monitor decisions that the superintendent makes.... School board members who are retired or who have employment circumstances which allow them a lot of time tend to cause more problems.... Not only when there are things to be done, but when there's nothing to be done, they are looking for something to be done. They tend to visit schools all the time which is not what I think school board members ought to be doing. They tend to start more issues based upon their having more time, and it creates problems. It was for that reason that I had some reservations about the board's appointment of Minnie Woodson when she came on and did not support Victoria Street. Both are retired. And in my observations I saw the same thing with Virginia Morris and with Hilda Mason. And in my own experience I learned that. In the beginning I put in a lot of time and then you find yourself dealing in issues that you ought not to be dealing in.[89]

Tirana felt that because he was white, and elected at-large, he had one advantage over some other board members, in that he was able to bring an objectivity to the job which kept him from becoming involved in the day-to-day operation of the schools. In this regard, he made the following comments:

Since I was white and elected at large, I perceived of my role as critical because I could have objectivity that many of the Black members of the Board could not or did not have.

Example. Many of the Black members tended to get deeply involved in day-to-day operations. They were unable when a crisis or a problem was occurring at a local school level or with an individual child to delineate clearly as

to what they as board members could or
should do. And what they couldn't do or
shouldn't do. I think the board suffered
greatly from trying to do too much and the
individual board members tried to do too much.
The board member who I knew who was best able
to draw the distinction between the band aid
approach to being a member of the Board of
Education and a policy and pragmatic approach
was Julius Hobson, Sr.[90]

Kemp felt that the role of a D.C. board of
education member was to set policy but that policy
can only come about as a result of having consulted with and been on site in the schools, that is,
it involves a great deal of consultation and col-
laboration with one's constituents and one's
school communities. He felt, in retrospect, that
as an activist board member, he was interested in
making sure that the policies established by the
prior boards and the current board were being
implemented. Thus, Kemp did not view the board
as one which became too involved in implementation.
He perceived his role as one to call to the attention of the administration situations that were
not working in the system. Furthermore, Kemp
stressed the monitoring function.[91]

> I don't think I could be a board member with-
> out writing a letter a week about some problem
> or another that had been called to my atten-
> tion and that I had observed. I think that
> got interpreted as messing with administra-
> tion.[92]

In further explaining his position, Kemp stated:

> I think the pressures that were on the board
> from outside, from the constituents, espec-
> ially in crisis situations, parents, were
> often pressures that did not respect the
> difference between policy and administration.
> The board felt the pressure of policy imple-
> mentation or failure to implement policy

before the administration did. If a principal wasn't on her or his job in a local school, I got the impression during the four years that I was on the board that the superintendent or all those top management positions didn't feel that like the board members felt it.... We were the people that were perceived of as those who had to change a bad situation. And I don't think we had the power to effect those kinds of changes, and I don't think we needed it.... When crisis situations developed, our job was to lay those crises in front of the administration, the people they paid their money to to resolve those (problems) and to hold them to some solution. I think we did that.[93]

Martha Swaim, school board member from 1968 to 1973, presents instances where, in her opinion, board members must become involved in administration. Thus, she explained a case where 200 children in special education classes stayed home for a month or so because they had no transportation although the administrators had known about the problem for some time but had failed to solve it. A special meeting was called to discuss the problem and at that time the superintendent was told to solve it. Swaim said that the board became involved because the school administration did not solve the problem.

Swaim also presented a case where parents came to the school board because they could not get results from administrators. Swaim felt that superintendents become annoyed when the board attempts to find out if a policy is being carried out and especially so when the board finds out that a policy is not being carried out; for instance, that some kindergartens do not have teachers and some others are without equipment. Admitting that boards do make mistakes and sometimes propose impractical solutions, Swaim felt that superintendents believe that professionals in the school system know best. Additionally, she said that the board cannot expect to find out what is wrong from people responsible for the mistakes so the board must look for itself and use other sources not on the school management payroll, such as field staff, residents, and the Census Bureau as in the prediction of the size of a new school or whether or not an addition is needed on another school.

Basically, what Swaim was saying is that the D.C. public school system "has not had an administration that solved basic problems for a good many years," and that "anyone who complains about the board 'meddling in administration' usually has something to hide." Finally, she said policy is not only rules, regulations and procedures, but it deals with what is important to people.[94]

The feelings of some citizens about school board interference in administration were revealed in the January 17, 1973 meeting of the board of education.[95] Some of these comments merit mention here.

Mrs. Goodwin, community member, said in relation to the board's reactions to Superintendent Scott: "We do not need another superintendent, and he does not need a board that administers."[96]

Mr. Arthuro Griffiths, president of the Washington Ghetto Industrial Development and Investment Corporation, admonished the board when he testified at that meeting that the board had to decide what its responsibility is, the school board director or the superintendent as an implementor.[97]

Mr. Lewis Anthony, a citizen, also felt that the problem was a question of who is going to administer the schools, the board or the superintendent? He stated:

> The problem is a perennial one. It is a problem which the Board of Education will have to come to grip with.... the question

of who is going to administer the schools? You, or the Superintendent. That has to be clearly made and one is going to come to the determination of what it is.[98]

In commenting about the role of the DCBOE, Dr. James Williams, former deputy superintendent, Office of Management, described the functioning of board members thusly:

I think the D.C. board is different in many respects. It tends to be both policy setting and administrative. The D.C. board tends to want to define how their policy is to be implemented as a part of their role in setting the policy or establishing the policy. They tend to preestablish the way in which the policy will be carried out...without leaving it to administration to decide on the method of implementation of policy.[99]

The present superintendent, Vincent Reed, also feels that the board should not have a hand in the selection of principals and assistant principals -- that it is an administrative function and not a function of policy makers. He stated:

I don't think it's right for the board to be involved in personnel selection at all. I think that the recommendation of the superintendent should go to the board and they can deal with it at that time, but for board members to sit on a panel to select principals and assistant principals and all other school personnel like regional superintendents and regional assistant superintendents, I don't agree with...the board has voted me down on it every time.... I have made it very clear to them I don't agree with it. I think it puts the personnel situation into politics and I don't think that's proper.[100]

The above comments clearly establish that some board members and some community members feel the DCBOE did not define any sharp dichotomy between policy formulation and administration.

The statutory provisions, to which reference was made, in Chapter III, placed the DCBOE in a middle position between policy-making and management of the school system. It is apparent that the board involves itself in letting contracts, purchasing transactions, hiring of personnel, building construction, site selection, safety, and financial transactions, budget crisis situations and student matters. Note, in fact, the reflection of this concern in the names of board committees. Encroachment upon those matters generally considered the domain of the chief administrative officer has been resented by some of the superintendents; note particularly resentment expressed by Superintendent Scott. This reaction hardly seems unreasonable in light of the fact that it is necessary to spend considerable time of administrative staff personnel in preparing material. Likewise, nit-picking and interrogation of administrative staff members interferes with the expeditious handling of matters and diverts both administrators and board members from more substantive transactions and issues presented by the community, students and local school staff through the superintendent. In the case of the DCBOE, this infringement of the board upon routine operations strengthened the board's influence on program and policy matters, and diffused the chief administrator's influence, thus providing board members with more power politically than the superintendent had.

On the subject of role confusion, Getzels indicates that boards of education are often confused about the roles of the superintendent and the role of the board, especially when they are establishing criteria for the selection of superintendents. He feels that although it is commonly thought that boards make policy and superintendents carry it out, it does not work this way in practice since superintendents not only influence policy by supplying information to the board, but he or she also recommends policy. Getzel's feeling seems to be that a board must also administer policy because, by law, it must legitimize administrative decisions made about employing staff, approving expenditures and adopting books.[101]

Interestingly, all 14 board members interviewed said, in essence, that school board members make policy and the superintendent's job was to implement that policy. Obviously, though, some of these same 14 board members had difficulty following their own articulated definitions of the role of board members, judging from the testimony of their fellow board members and some key administrators. Some specific examples of role confusion of some board members will be revealed in the case studies discussed in Chapter VIII.

## Membership Changes

There were seven board changes in membership between January 1973 and October 1976. First, between January 1973 and December 1973, Mrs. Pryde left and was replaced by Mrs. Morris. Second, Mr. Cassell, Rev. Coates, and Mr. Tirana left between December 1973 and January 1974. Their replacements were Dr. Evans, Mr. Hobson, and Mrs. Simmons. Third, between January 1974 and July 12, 1974 Mr. Barry, Mr. Rosenfield, Mrs. Swaim, and Mrs. Taylor left. This left a seven member board. Fourth, in November 1974, they were replaced by Attorney Benjamin, Mrs. Kane, Mrs. Schwartz, and Mr. Warren. Fifth, between November 1975 and January 1976, Mrs. Morris left and was replaced by Mr. Featherstone. Sixth, Mr. Featherstone left between January 1976 and October 1976. Seventh, a 10 member board operated between October 1976 to December 1976.

Of special note is the fact that the board changed three times between October 1973 and October 1975 during the period when Mrs. Barbara Sizemore was superintendent of schools. This, then, means that Mrs. Sizemore had four boards in two years. Consequently, the goals of the board shifted from the priority of decentralization and flexibility in educational planning to facilitate the acquisition of skills by the 95 percent Black student population back to the status quo of maintaining the school system in fact for a student population slowly returning as was noted in table 2.

Another external factor which had negative effects on school board-superintendent relations was the rapidity of changes in school board membership. As the membership changed, goals changed, personalities changed and needs changed. Getzels makes a very significant point about change when he discusses the impact of the technological changes and population changes in a community. He seems to feel that when these type changes come about so too are changes in values exhibited. Naturally, these value changes impact upon the school. Suffice it to say, then, that roles may have to be reexamined. In this regard then, an "insider," one who has moved up through the ranks, may not be selected as superintendent since it is expected that he or she will maintain the status quo and the board is probably looking for a person who will change the status quo. If this is the case, then the selection may be an "outsider" who receives a broad mandate from the board as to goals and is given wide leeway for accomplishing them including redefining role expectations, and adding new staff.

Another aspect of this change in value, suggests Getzels, is a counter-pressure against change by the old guard who refuses to change. Eventually, the change in values loses its support. This limits how fast an administrator can change things for, if he continues, he may be replaced.[102]

Getzels used the impact of technology or a change in the composition of the community as the starting point for change as an illustration of a general phenomenon. In the case of Washington, D.C., one initiating force for change was the shift in the composition of the local population as well as the school community from predominantly white to predominantly Black and from more or less affluent to primarily poor. These changes were brought about by the flight of middle income people, both Black and white, to the suburbs of Maryland and Virginia. Concomitant with the racial shift came a shift in the value orientation of community members, including some board members. Therefore, a clamour for change in the schools followed on the heels of this population shift. After the Hansen administration, the several D.C. boards of education sought new blood (outsiders) to fill the key slot and, subsequently, after the Manning administration they sought not only an outsider but a Black who had served administratively in an inner-city area. So, then, we had Hugh Scott and Barbara Sizemore, brought in by DCBOE members who were seeking change or who purported to have been seeking some change in the status quo. Alas, though, changes in school board membership were rapid and constant with new personality needs, new expectations, and new dispositions, arising and overlapping old ones, causing alterations in relationships and behaviors of school board members and superintendents alike. Consequently, some of those board members who sought change left the board and were replaced by a new group of board members who struggled to maintain the status quo.

Class and racial interests also were factors that impacted on the kinds of decisions made by board members about the education of poor and Black children in the DCPS. Only one board member specifically reflected on this aspect of the problem in an interview, although additional evidence of its impact can be viewed in discussions of specific decisions made about issues between

1973-75, analyzed in Chapter VIII. In speaking about Superintendent Sizemore's strategies for attaining the goals of transmitting broad skills to young people, that is, communication and computational skills, Mrs. Barbara Simmons discussed how the backgrounds of the four replacements on the school board in 1974 caused a change in the board's direction away from its focus on decentralization through PACTS, multi-level, multicultural and multi-lingual strategies proposed to implement the goals.

Simmons' comments imply a shift in direction as Blacks took the place of whites, or vice versa, youth took the place of the seasoned, a legalistic mind set replaced an astute activist type, a social activist male was replaced by a Yankee type white female, and a clearly peasant bent though now rich type no longer sat on the board.[103]

Most board members interviewed agreed that instability in DCBOE membership affected the goals of the system. Treanor felt it was hard for new people to adjust and a lot of skill was lost.[104] Evans felt that constant change had a negative impact on goals.[105] Pryde said that constant change affected the morale of teachers.[106] Tirana felt there was not enough time between different people's tenure on the board to even design goals.[107] Taylor felt that changes in goals paralleled changes in board membership.[108] Hobson said change had a negative impact in terms of the lack of continuity, knowledge of past history of board operations and goals of the system.[109] Morris' comments indicated that she felt rapid changes in superintendents and board members negatively affected continuity in goals.[110]

If we go back to Getzels, et al, we note that the component elements of a social system are dynamic, that each element can alter and exert pressure on other elements. Thus, if the values change as manifested in goal statements, then this initiating change triggers other changes in the system.

Not only did board members who were interviewed reveal how they felt rapid changes in school board membership affected the system, but so, too, did some key administrators. Generally, these respondents also felt the effect was negative. James Williams, deputy superintendent from 1973-75, defined instability in the DCBOE from a perspective different from that of most of the other respondents, by saying:

> I think that the D.C. board is unstable, simply by its political arena and atmosphere, and not unstable because of any changes in board members. I don't think that constitutes instability. I think the very nature of the city and the political forces cause the school system or the board to be unstable as opposed to this interchange of membership.
>
> I think the fact that you're sitting in the Nation's Capital, the whole atmosphere of the system is political, competitive and combatant...board members feel that they must carry on this posture, even when there are no legitimate issues or reasons to be competitive. Consequently, there's an unstableness because there is a jockeying for the limelight, in terms of relating to their constituency in transacting board business as opposed to relating to the needs of the school system and the children in transacting board business....
>
> Board members who came on following the first ones that were elected from the board into the council were literally preparing themselves for the next election to challenge or replace someone on the city council. I'd say it's as if the board was a training ground for becoming a council member.[111]

In speaking about the goals of the DCBOE, Elliott, one of the Executive Assistants to Mrs. Sizemore, alluded to the change in focus as the board membership changed. Although decentralization (see figure 2) was the goal of the first DCBOE which appointed Sizemore, this thrust changed as the boards changed.[112]

Freeman, one of the six regional superintendents, also felt that in 1974, the number one priority of the DCBOE was decentralization, but this priority changed with the changes in board membership and also with the change in superintendents. As he viewed it, decentralization was now taking place primarily in the management field and in personnel. Whereas, before Vincent Reed became superintendent and the board changed again in 1975, personnel coordinators based in the regions handled personnel matters of the regions. Now, the operation is handled in the central administrative office. One explanation for this change which Freeman gave was that due to a reduction in force in 1977, the six coordinators had to be deployed to the central office. He further explained that this change had nothing to do with the fact that the decentralized operation did not work but because the situation had to be viewed from a central point of view, that is, if 12 teachers have to be lost, all 12 would not have to be lost from one region but citywide. Thus, the need for coordination centrally.[113]

Kenneth Haskins, vice superintendent, was ambiguous about the changes in board membership. His focus was on working relationships that needed to be set up but were not due to rapid changes.[114]

Margaret Labat, a regional superintendent, spoke to the change in thrust first toward decentralization and then away from it as changes in board membership took place.[115]

William Rice, another regional superintendent also felt that the rapid turnover in board

FIGURE 2.

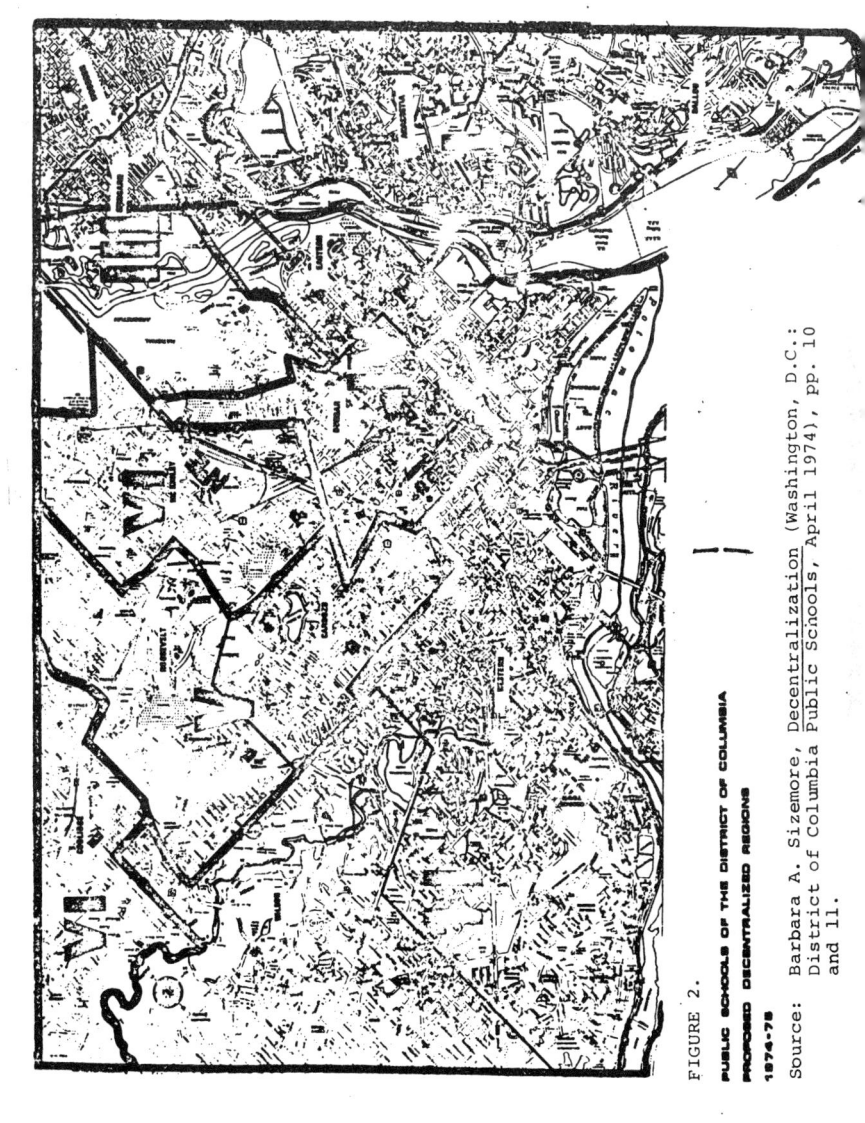

**PUBLIC SCHOOLS OF THE DISTRICT OF COLUMBIA**

**PROPOSED DECENTRALIZED REGIONS**

**1974-75**

Source: Barbara A. Sizemore, Decentralization (Washington, D.C.: District of Columbia Public Schools, April 1974), pp. 10 and 11.

membership had negative effects on the goals of Superintendent Sizemore as presented in the superintendent's 120 Day Report.[116]

The above discussion points up the pervasive effect of changes in board membership not only on the superintendent-board relationship but also on the goals established by previous boards which became modified as new citizens joined the board. Some of these new board members came with new mandates from their constituents. They came with perhaps a different value orientation, perhaps even with new interests, new needs, and certainly with different personality dispositions which shifted the pressure points. In the case of Superintendent Sizemore, the pressure was away from an emphasis on affirmative educational policies undergirded by flexibility in programs which speak to human growth and development needs of children and youth based on positive interpersonal relationships between all segments of the educational community. It shifted to a focus of time, money and energies on straightening out the management mess, as it was termed by several respondents, and hold the line on innovations. So in a sense, the rules of the game changed midstream as the players on the DCBOE shifted. Thus, the career-bound administrator, namely Sizemore, was placed in a position, through budgetary means, to call a halt to her innovations and when she moved ahead in spite of the lack of funds and decentralized the D.C. public school system, for example, she was superseded by a place-bound administrator, as the information further on in this discussion will show.

### Summary

The findings so far are briefly summarized in the following pages.

External factors

All five of the external factors were dealt with. These were: (1) **authority** of the school board vis-a-vis the other governmental units including the Congress, the city council, the mayor's office, and the courts with the elements of the colonial status of the District, modified home rule and inadequate funding precipitating management problems surfacing; (2) **racial conflict** with the problem of how to educate minority and poor children surfacing around the question of the powerlessness of a majority Black population in a city governed by a Black mayor, a majority Black city council, a majority Black school board in a school system with a majority Black student, teacher and administrator population; (3) **class conflict** pinpointed by the flight of middle income Blacks and whites to the suburbs, and currently a reversal of this trend impacting on the type of educational programs proposed; (4) **the sexist nature of our society** generally which put pressures on a school district which appointed the first Black female superintendent of a large urban area; and (5) the fifth factor of **group pressures** dealt with in terms of Scott's administration and will be further dealt with separately in a later chapter since news coverage of the Sizemore administration was so influential in the outcome.

1. **Governmental Dominance**: Since the District had no elected government until 1968, and this came in the form of an elected board of education, there was no history of how to function adequately within this political milieu. In this context, then, elected officials were naive and had to learn as they were doing. Much time was consumed running for office. Added to this was the fact that the school board was the only political game in town until 1974 when the District received modified home rule. Thus, a scramble among school board members for city council seats began pushing educational concerns further from the forefront of activity. In addition to the

above, the Congress retained for itself control of the criminal justice system, the power to veto any legislation within 30 days, and control over the budgetary process; thus, the District government in the form of the city council and the mayor, shared less authority with the school board. This was especially noted by Mason and Cassell in the areas of contracting authority and by Mason in the area of an attorney for the board. It was noted that several board members felt that lack of power hampered board members' authority to effectively and efficiently manage a viable educational system. Contrastingly though, other board members, notably Rosenfield, Tirana and Kemp, felt that the board had adequate power but did not effectively manage that which it had. Nonetheless, it should be noted that the District, a predominantly Black area, has not yet a voting representative in Congress.

The Congress allocated insufficient funds to the District government for providing services to the city and the school system. In addition, funds for education were inadequate and were subject to budget cuts by the mayor, the city council and the Congress on a line item basis which reduced or eliminated programs or the possibility of introducing innovations geared toward the education of the poor and minority children, including the decentralization thrust. Likewise, the management area and the superintendent's office were cut to bare bones by the Budget and Finance Committee under the chairmanship of Martha Swaim of the third elected board, leaving them destaffed and unable to produce the changes needed to create a viable financial and personnel control system as proposed in the Price Waterhouse Report. This was clearly shown to be the case during the Hugh Scott era and, as will be shown, continued into the Sizemore administration.

The President of the United States signed into law in December 1973 the home rule bill for the District of Columbia. On May 7, 1974, citizens of D.C. voted for the charter (bill) which provided for an elected mayor and city council and advisory neighborhood councils.

The bill provided that the new council would have 13 members: 8 elected from the city wards, four at-large (with only two from the same party), and one elected at-large as chairperson. Council members would have staggered four-year terms at salaries of $22,705.00 with the chairperson receiving $32,705.00. Their powers are similar to the powers of a state legislature, including setting taxes, changing criminal laws (after January 1977), regulating insurance, traffic and parking, reorganizing, abolishing or changing D.C. agencies, setting housing standards and imposing rent control, and adopting a city-wide personnel system. Among the things the council cannot do are: tax federal or state property, establish a commuter tax, change the height limitation on D.C. buildings, or change the court system.

Even though the mayor can veto city council actions, the council can override a veto by a two-thirds vote, but the Congress can stop a law passed by the Council if both House and Senate pass resolutions disapproving the law within 30 days.

Thus, the Congress reserved for itself the power of veto, within 30 days, and control of the judicial and budgetary systems. As the law explains it, the President appoints judges from a list of three provided him by a new seven-member D.C. Judicial Nomination Commission, and the Senate approves these appointments. In the case of the budgetary process, after the proposed budget is approved by the mayor and city council, it must go to the President and the Congress for revision and approval much like it was handled before home rule except that the mayor and city council can no longer make line item changes in the school budget. The Council and the mayor decide the total amount to be allocated for the schools, but within the total, the city council cannot make changes. It should be noted that increases in the amount of teachers' salaries must be approved by Congress. In addition, the council sets all taxes and can borrow on the guaranteed federal payment by issuing bonds.

The elected mayor has a four-year term, a salary of $42,000.00, and the power to appoint a city administrator, reorganize city agencies and appoint heads of city agencies.

Only Congress can change the council-mayor structure of the new government although other changes can be made by the city council and then voted on in a referendum (election). Changes ratified by the voters must be approved by Congress within 35 days.[117]

Notably, although the board of education is vested with the control of public schools by the Act of 1906, it does not control such crucial matters as budget, personnel, contracting authority, or legal counsel. Specifically, it must go across the street to the District Building housing the city council and the mayor-commissioner to get personnel authority; it cannot reprogram for more than $25,000.00 which is about the cost for two teachers; and it must use the city's legal counsel to go to court to interpret its authority.[118]

2. Racism: Race was always a factor in the District of Columbia and has remained one, permeating every facet of life in the city and, thus, in the school system. Historically, as Blacks gained in population in the District, opposition to their presence hardened and laws were made to contain them or reduce their numbers, circumscribe their behavior, and hamper their employment during the early days. Nevertheless, Blacks kept on coming into the District of Columbia until their numbers reached a majority in 1965 and in 1973-75 approximated 70 percent of the total population and between 95-97 percent in the school system. As the numbers of Blacks increased, D.C. citizens clamored to have a majority Black city governing unit, a majority Black school board and, indeed, a Black superintendent.

Nonetheless, power of the governing units -- the Mayor, the city council and the school board and superintendent -- evaporated. It followed the people who left the city, the money people. Real power did not remain with the positions vacated by whites because power in this country is money and whoever has the money has the power. The name of the position does not really count. It is simply a label. The label "mayor" has no meaning, no power, if the person in the position has no control over money. The same is true with the city council, school board, and superintendent. Therefore, the budget situation during the superintendency of Hugh Scott caused the hardest fights and the deepest erosion in the relationship between the school boards and the superintendent because of lack of needed funds to run an adequate program. Fighting over the use of inadequate dollars became critical. As the data show, the District of Columbia school system was in a constant state of near chaos due to the constraints of an obsolete funding pattern which did not acknowledge that the District schools were catering to a new type of constituent -- one that had to overcome accumulated deficiencies due to the many years of deprivation based on past discrimination.

The school board reached majority Black by 1968. Soon after, Cassell questioned the non-use of Black architects. Hobson, Sr., in turn, questioned the racial composition of some offices in school administration pointing out the fact that some were all white while others were all Black. Then in 1970 Hugh Scott was appointed the first Black superintendent. For some time, the question had been: Do we continue the status quo in educational programming or do we adjust for the new majority in the schools? The answer for Hansen was tracking. For Anita Allen and imposed on Scott, it became the Clark Plan. So the struggle to answer the question advanced and evolved into a major point of conflict between board members and Scott.

When Scott left, some board members again

sought a Black to administer the majority Black D.C. public school system. It was noted that Martha Swaim felt that none of the Black candidates qualified for the appointment to superintendent, due (she said) to their lack of experience in administering a major urban school system. Interestingly, she did not note the fact that at that point in time few Blacks had been given the opportunity to do so, so there could be no history of achievement in this area. Some, though, had had experience with sub-districts or regions and three of these Blacks became finalists in the competition -- Sizemore, Donaldson and Minor. Sizemore was chosen, which brings us to a third factor which reared its head at this point, sexism.

3. <u>Sexism</u>: Some board members clearly were adverse to the selection of a female for the top slot in the school system. Cassell pointed this out in his interview. Further documentation on this point will be forthcoming as we pursue our study of the Sizemore superintendency.

4. <u>Classism</u>: Classism also permeated the smooth functioning of relations between the superintendent and school board as indicated in the resistance of Hansen at the insistence of the school board that he drop the track system and not go to court to try to have the decision made in the <u>Hobson v Hansen</u> equalization case in favor of poor Black children overturned.

5. <u>Group Pressures</u>: News accounts clobbered Scott repeatedly during his administration and most assuredly in regard to the budget crisis. It is difficult to imagine that the negative coverage had no effect on superintendent-school board relations.

<u>Internal factors</u>

Internal factors impinging on the relationship between school board members and superintendents causing conflict were: (1) <u>changes in the makeup of the school board</u> in terms of race, sex, class, personality, needs and changes in superintendents; (2) __motivations__ of school board members in terms of service to the community, the gaining of knowledge or to satisfy political ambitions; (3) __role conflict__ and role confusion focused on intrusion into administrative domains or representing some special interest group; (4) __leadership styles__; (5) other organizational dynamics, i.e., __goal setting, structure, and function__, in relation to changing them or maintaining the status quo.

   1. __Instability in School Board Membership and Superintendents__: There were many changes in board membership due to the rotating membership set up through the new elective process, the regular elections, illness, job requirements, and the desire to seek a higher city office. Additionally, the socioeconomic characteristics of school board members show them to be primarily from the business, managerial or professional category of jobs, in contrast to the majority poor students in the schools. Some conflicts resulted from differing expectations of school board members, superintendents and constituents. Superintendents Hansen, Manning, Scott and Sizemore were all hired from outside the school system. Each in turn was sought as a catalytic agent to produce changes for the purpose of elevating the achievement level of the student population. Subsequently, each, in turn, for various reasons, found himself/herself in conflict with the prevailing values of the local citizen groups, school board members, constituents, personal inclinations of individual board members or cliques on the various boards which changed in personalities, thus causing shifts in goals, purposes and focus in the educational enterprise. Evidence points to the fact that there was ambiguity among board members as to whether the board should select insiders or outsiders to head the school system. Some preferred insiders who knew the system. Some were fearful that insiders might be hampered through long-standing associations with the current staff or might become involved in the internal politics of the school system. And

yet others sought a definite change in direction and vigorously opposed a local selection. They opted full force for a person outside the system.

Many board members and citizens felt that Hansen faltered in his approach to the education of Black children especially in his design of the track system. Hobson, in particular, felt this so strongly that he took Hansen to court on the basis of inequality in the schools which resulted in the Wright Decree. The ire of the board finally converged on Hansen and this precipitated his retirement. Manning also felt the pressures of the board's displeasure at his performance, especially in connection with decentralization. He, too, resigned. Though Scott persisted for the three years of his contract, he was embroiled in many conflicts with board members, including the implementation of the Clark Plan, decentralization, and equalization which finally culminated in the nonrenewal of his contract.

2. <u>Motivation</u>: Enough board members and key administrators interviewed stressed the political motivation of some school board members for us to draw the conclusion that for some the position was viewed as a steppingstone to higher offices in the city. Evidence shows that it was used as such by Hobson, Sr., Barry, Mason and now Kane who is currently running for a city council seat. Rosenfield and Swaim tried to use it but failed. Likewise, Morris failed in her bid for a Neighborhood Advisory seat. She tried to use the mileage she had gained from membership on the school board for another elected position in the city government.

3. <u>Role Conflict</u>: Discussion about the intrusion of board members into administrative concerns abound throughout the document from the Hansen through the Scott administrations, even though we have so far only touched the tip of the iceberg. More will follow on this point.

4. <u>Leadership Styles</u>: Many board members viewed Anita Allen and Virginia Morris as more

authoritarian than either Marion Barry or Therman Evans.  Several members mentioned that Barry would consistently talk to all board members in his efforts to obtain consensus on issues.  Nevertheless, all three board presidents were viewed by some of their colleagues as power brokers who rewarded members who voted them in as president, by providing them with committee chairmanships which lent themselves to use as platforms for exposure to the citizenry.  This may or may not have been useful in future efforts to seek other political positions in town.  However, Swaim did move from the chairmanship of the Budget and Finance Committee and vice-presidency to run for the city council though she lost; Rosenfield ran and lost.  Mason did move from the chairmanship of the Committee on Educational Programs, ran for the city council and won.  Elizabeth Kane is moving from the chairmanship of the Committee on Federal Grants and running for a city council seat.[119]

Notably the authoritarian leadership style employed by Anita Allen, it can be assumed, did clash with the leadership style of Hugh Scott, as did the leadership style employed by Virginia Morris clash with that of Barbara Sizemore.  In both cases, the cleavages were so great that both superintendents were let go, the former by the non-renewal of his contract and the latter by firing.  But something else comes into play here, too, so it is not enough to say that the authoritarian leadership style was the main force although it seems apparent that it was one of the precipitating factors.

What must also be taken into consideration is the majority vote pattern.  Obviously, no president has the power unless he is on the side of the majority and though it might appear that there is power in the position of president, in actuality, the power rests with the majority.  Either the leader can sway the majority of members to his or her position, as in the case of Allen and Barry, or the majority can sway the president to do their bidding, as in the case of Morris.*

5. <u>Organizational Dynamics of Function, Structure, and Goal-setting</u>: These were dealt with in terms of Hansen, Manning and Scott. Changes in these areas were hampered by inadequate funds which slowed down the setting up of a financial system and a personnel control system as parts of a viable management framework. In the area of goal-setting, board members interviewed remarked how goals changed as board members and superintendents changed.

Chapter VIII will focus on three specific decision-making situations which occurred between 1973-75 in order to illuminate the process engaged in by the board and the superintendent to arrive at the decisions. One case deals with an educational program matter. The second case pertains to a decision about a personnel matter. The third case is a study of how the board and the superintendent arrived at a decision about the budget/management phase of the operation. In these three cases we will not only be analyzing how the external and internal factors influenced how decisions were made but how these factors caused the board to interfere with the superintendent in the implementation of board policies.

---
*An interpretation provided by Mrs. Barbara A. Sizemore in her interview on April 17, 1978.

FOOTNOTES  CHAPTER VII

1. CBS News broadcast, 20 January 1978.

2. Interview with Evie Washington, D.C. Board of Education member, Washington, D.C., 12 October 1972.

3. Milton Coleman's City Notebook, "Barbara Sizemore Leaves D.C. Politics with No Regrets," *Washington Post*, District Weekly, 23 March 1978.

4. Interview with Delores Pryde, D.C. Board of Education member, Washington, D.C., 23 October 1977.

5. William Delaney, "'Weeding Out' Eyed: School Cost Cuts," *Evening Star*, 9 May 1972.

6. Interview with Hugh J. Scott, Superintendent of Schools, Washington, D.C., 21 November 1977.

7. Interview with Bardyl Tirana, D.C. Board of Education member, Washington, D.C., 27 September, 1977.

8. "Minutes of the Second (Special) Meeting of the Board of Education," Washington, D.C., 9 February 1972, p. 38.

9. Interview with Delores Pryde, D.C. Board of Education member, Washington, D.C., 23 October 1977.

10. Getzels, p. 355.

11. Cunningham, p. 120.

12. Donald J. McCarty, "Motives," pp. 54-55.

13. Alvin Thornton, "Black Educational Policy-Makers: A Study of the Effect of Community Racial Composition on Correlates of the Political Efficacy, Political, Authority, and Public Regardingness of Black School Board members," (Howard University, Ph.D. dissertation, 1978), p. 49.

14. Interview with Delores Pryde, D.C. Board of Education member, Washington, D.C., 23 October 1977.

15. Interview with William Treanor, D.C. Board of Education member, Washington, D.C., 28 September 1977.

16. Interview with Father Raymond Kemp, D.C. Board of Education member, Washington, D.C., 21 November 1977.

17. Interview with Charles Cassell, D.C. Board of Education member, Washington, D.C., 5 October 1977.

18. Interview with John Warren, D.C. Board of Education member, Washington, D.C., 27 September 1977.

19. "Re-elect Dr. Haynes," *Washington Afro-American*, 1 July 1967.

20. "Minutes of the Third (Special) Meeting of the Elected Board of Education," Washington, D.C., 12 February 1969, p. 13.

21. "Minutes of the Thirty-Seventh (Stated) Meeting of the Board of Education," Washington, D.C., 17 January 1973, p. 26.

22. Interview with Mattie Taylor, D.C. Board of Education member, Washington, D.C., 6 October 1977.

23. Interview with Charles Cassell, D.C. Board of Education member, Washington, D.C., 5 October 1977.

24. Interview with Raymond Kemp, D.C. Board of Education member, Washington, D.C., 21 November 1977.

25. Interview with Therman Evans, D.C. Board of Education member, Washington, D.C., 19 October 1977.

26. "Voter Information," Bulletin Board, August-September, 1973, p. 1. See also A Compilation of Laws Relating to Elections, Election Campaigns, Lobbying, and Conflict of Interest in the District of Columbia (Washington, D.C.: District of Columbia Board of Elections and Ethics, Office of General Counsel, District Building, Current to April 1977), p. 19.

27. Memorandum to Thornell Page from Marion Barry contained in his campaign folder, Government of the District of Columbia, Board of Elections, Washington, D.C., 16 May 1973.

28. Government of the District of Columbia, Board of Elections, Washington, D.C., Marion Barry for School Board, "Report of Campaign Contributions," 3 December 1971.

29. Government of the District of Columbia, Board of Elections, Washington, D.C., Ward 5 Committee for Mattie G. Taylor, "Report of Campaign Contributions," 20 December 1971.

30. Government of the District of Columbia, Board of Elections, Washington, D.C., Raymond B. Kemp, Ward 1, "Report of Campaign Contributions," 3 January 1971.

31. Government of the District of Columbia, Board of Elections, Washington, D.C., Albert A. Rosenfield, "Report of Campaign Contributions," 31 October 1973.

32. Ibid., 10 December 1973.

33. Government of the District of Columbia, Board of Elections, Washington, D.C., Committee to Elect Evie Washington, "Report of Receipts and Expenditures for a Committee," 7 December 1973.
34. Government of the District of Columbia, Board of Elections, Washington, D.C., Hilda Howland M. Mason, "Report of Receipts and Expenditures for a Candidate," 10 October 1975.
35. Ibid., 23 November 1971.
36. Government of the District of Columbia, Board of Elections, Washington, D.C., Hilda Howland M. Mason, "Report of Receipts and Expenditures for a Candidate," 10 October 1975.
37. Ibid., 20 October 1975.
38. Ibid., 30 October 1975.
39. Ibid., 15 December 1975.
40. Government of the District of Columbia, Board of Elections, Washington, D.C., Martha S. Swaim, "Report of Campaign Contributions," 7 January 1972.
41. Government of the District of Columbia, Board of Elections, Washington, D.C., Delores Pryde for Board of Education, "Report of Campaign Contributions," Accounting period September through 5 December 1971.
42. Government of the District of Columbia, Board of Elections, Washington, D.C., Citizen's Coalition for Cassell, "Report of Campaign Contributions," 1 November 1973.
43. Government of the District of Columbia, Board of Elections, Washington, D.C., Citizens for Virginia Morris, "Report of Receipts and Expenditures for a Committee," 29 October 1975 and 30 October 1975.
44. Government of the District of Columbia, Board of Elections, Washington, D.C., Bill Treanor Campaign Committee, "Report of Campaign Contributions," 1 November 1973, 23 November 1973 and 29 January 1974.

45. Government of the District of Columbia, Board of Elections, Washington, D.C., Dr. Therman Evans' Campaign Fund, "Report of Campaign Contributions," 28 January 1974.

46. Government of the District of Columbia, Board of Elections, Washington, D.C., The Carol Schwartz for School Board Committee, "Report of Receipts and Expenditures for a Committee," 21 October 1974, 30 October 1974, 10 December 1974 and 31 January 1975.

47. Government of the District of Columbia, Board of Elections, Washington, D.C., Citizens to Re-elect Bettie Benjamin, "Report of Receipts and Expenditures for a Committee," 15 October 1975 and 20 October 1975.

48. Government of the District of Columbia, Board of Elections, Washington, D.C., The Committee to Elect John Warren, "Report of Receipts and Expenditures for a Committee," 17 October 1974.

49. Ibid., 10 October 1975.

50. Ibid., 24 October 1975.

51. Ibid., 10 December 1975.

52. Ibid., January 1975.

53. Ibid., 25 October 1976.

54. Government of the District of Columbia, Board of Elections, Washington, D.C., Citizens for Kane, "Report of Receipts and Expenditures for a Committee," 15 October 1975 and 10 December 1975.

55. Government of the District of Columbia, Board of Elections, Washington, D.C., The Committee to Elect Barbara Lett Simmons, "Report of Campaign Contributions," 6 December 1973.

56. Milton Coleman's City Hall Notebook, "Barbara Sizemore Leaves D.C. Politics With No Regrets," *Washington Post*, 23 March 1978.

57. Paul W. Valentine, "Big Donations Scarce in D.C. Council Race," *Washington Post*, 7 July 1977.

58. "Minutes of the First (Organization) Meeting of the Board of Education," Washington, D.C., 25 January 1971, pp. 2-5.

59. Interview with Evie Washington, D.C. Board of Education member, Washington, D.C., 12 October 1977.

60. Interview with Charles Cassell, D.C. Board of Education member, Washington, D.C., 5 October 1977.

61. Interview with Hugh Scott, Superintendent of Schools, Washington, D.C., 21 November 1977.

62. Interview with Julius Hobson, Jr., D.C. Board of Education member, Washington, D.C., 28 September 1977.

63. Interview with Evie Washington, D.C. Board of Education member, Washington, D.C., 12 October 1977.

64. Interview with Julius Hobson, Jr., D.C. Board of Education member, Washington, D.C., 28 September 1977.

65. Interview with Delores Pryde, D.C. Board of Education member, Washington, D.C., 23 October, 1977.

66. Interview with William Treanor, D.C. Board of Education member, Washington, D.C., 28 September 1977.

67. Interview with Mattie Taylor, D.C. Board of Education member, Washington, D.C., 6 October 1977.

68. Interview with Bardyl Tirana, D.C. Board of Education member, Washington, D.C. 27 September 1977.

69. Interview with Therman Evans, D.C. Board of Education member, Washington, D.C., 19 October 1977.

70. Interview with Margaret Labat, Regional Superintendent, Washington, D.C., 18 November 1977.

71. Interview with Kenneth Haskins, Vice Superintendent of Schools, Washington, D.C., 22 November 1977.

72. Interview with Barbara Simmons, D.C. Board of Education member, Washington, D.C., 20 September 1977.

73. Interview with William Rice, Regional Superintendent, Washington, D.C., 21 September 1977.

74. Interview with Julius Hobson, Jr., D.C. Board of Education member, Washington, D.C., 28 September 1977.

75. Interview with William Treanor, D.C. Board of Education member, Washington, D.C., 28 September 1977.

76. Barbara A. Sizemore, "Education: Is Accommodation Enough?", The Journal of Negro Education 44 (Summer 1975), pp. 233-246.

77. Interview with Margaret Labat, Regional Superintendent, Washington, D.C., 18 November 1977.

78. Interview with Gilbert Diggs, Regional Superintendent, Washington, D.C., 30 September 1977.

79. Interview with William Rice, Regional Superintendent, Washington, D.C., 21 September 1977.

80. Neal Gross, <u>Who Runs Our Schools?</u> (New York: Wiley, 1958), p. 139.

81. "Minutes of the Forty-Seventh (Stated) Meeting of the Board of Education," Washington, D.C., 21 January 1970, Enclosure 3, pp. 1-3.

82. "Educators Discuss Board-Superintendent Relations in District," <u>Bulletin Board</u>, December 1974, p. 1.

83. Ibid., p. 2.

84. Interview with Hugh J. Scott, Superintendent of Schools, Washington, D.C., 21 November 1977.

85. <u>Bulletin Board</u>, p. 2.

86. Interview with Hugh J. Scott, Superintendent of Schools, Washington, D.C. 21 November 1977.

87. Ibid.

88. <u>Bulletin Board</u>, p. 2.

89. Interview with Julius Hobson, Jr., D.C. Board of Education member, Washington, D.C., 28 September 1977.

90. Interview with Bardyl Tirana, D.C. Board of Education member, Washington, D.C., 27 September 1977.

91. Interview with Raymond Kemp, D.C. Board of Education member, Washington, D.C., 21 November 1977.

92. Ibid.

93. Ibid.

94. <u>Bulletin Board</u>, p. 5.

95. "Minutes of the Thirty-Seventh (Stated) Meeting of the Board of Education," Washington, D.C., 17 January 1973.

96. Ibid., p. 14.

97. Ibid.

98. Ibid., p. 25.

99. Interview with James Williams, Deputy Superintendent, Washington, D.C., 14 December 1977.

100. Interview with Vincent Reed, Superintendent of Schools, Washington, D.C., 5 December 1977.

101. Getzels, p. 360.

102. Ibid., pp. 151-152.

103. Interview with Barbara L. Simmons, D.C. Board of Education member, Washington, D.C., 20 September 1977.

104. Interview with William Treanor, D.C. Board of Education member, Washington, D.C., 28 September 1977.

105. Interview with Therman Evans, D.C. Board of Education member, Washington, D.C., 19 October 1977.

106. Interview with Delores Pryde, D.C. Board of Education member, Washington, D.C., 23 October 1977.

107. Interview with Bardyl Tirana, D.C. Board of Education member, Washington, D.C., 27 September 1977.

108. Interview with Mattie Taylor, D.C. Board of Education member, Washington, D.C., 6 October 1977.

109. Interview with Julius Hobson, D.C. Board of Education member, Washington, D.C., 28 September 1977.

110. Interview with Virginia Morris, D.C. Board of Education member, Washington, D.C., 11 October 1977.

111. Interview with James Williams, Deputy Superintendent, Washington, D.C., 14 December 1977.

112. Interview with Luther Elliott, Executive Assistant to the Superintendent, Washington, D.C., 20 October 1977.

113. Interview with Gary Freeman, Regional Superintendent, Washington, D.C., 6 October 1977.

114. Interview with Kenneth Haskins, Vice-Superintendent, Washington, D.C., 22 November 1977.

115. Interview with Margaret Labat, Regional Superintendent, Washington, D.C., 18 November 1977.

116. Interview with William Rice, Regional Superintendent, Washington, D.C., 21 September 1977.

117. Walter E. Washington, Mayor, Ten Years Since April 4, 1968 - A Decade of Progress for the District of Columbia - A Report to the People (Washington, D.C.: 4 April 1978), pp. 4 and 25.

118. "Transcript of the Eighteenth (Special) Meeting of the Board of Education," Washington, D.C., 12 July 1973, pp. 67-93.

119. "Betty Ann Kane Announces for Council At-Large Seat," *Washington Post*, 23 March 1978.

# SECTION III

## DECISION-MAKING PROCESS

CHAPTER VIII

## CASE STUDIES OF THE DECISION-MAKING PROCESS -- 1973-75

### Introduction

Chapters II through VII have focused on the conflicted elements involved in the decision-making process in the District of Columbia and the development of a body of background information about the decision-making unit for education. This chapter contains the cases of decision-making in the D.C. public schools selected for study and analysis. What is particularly significant in the discussion of the cases as contrasted with a discussion of these same or similar issues in the previous chapters is the view of the inside machinations involved in the decision-making process of school board members and the administrative staff. This information is primarily revealed through the exchange of correspondence which is not often known by citizens who generally only attend open board meetings.

Three cases which caused conflict in school board-superintendent relations in the public school system of the District of Columbia between 1973-75 are discussed in this chapter in order to analyze how decisions were made. The cases fall under three large categories: educational program, personnel, and budget/management. Each of the three decisions made were enacted during the period of observation for this investigation. Related significant events to the decisions made were studied and reported when this information was necessary in understanding the specific elements

involved in the cases. The D.C. Youth Orchestra
Program (DCYOP) controversy will be examined,
since it falls under the rubric of alternative
education programs. It will be used as backup of
the conflicting points of view about the use of
public school funds for private enterprise ventures
with a limited cultural and value orientation during a period of severe budgetary constraints.

The second case fits into the category of
personnel. It focuses on a dispute which arose
between the school board president and the superintendent in relation to the authority to assign
duties to the general counsel, a controversy which
arose out of the DCYOP case.

Case three falls under the category of management, as it involves (1) a decision to change the
structure of the school system from a centralized
to a decentralized system, (2) the companion problem of implementation in the face of changing
board membership and priorities, and (3) fiscal
arrangements designed to accommodate matters discussed in cases one and two. It deals with the
FY75 Budget and FY76 Financial Plan. Naturally,
there were many other decisions made during 1973-75
and many other issues which illustrated conflict in
school board-superintendent relations which are not
included here. However, those cases selected do
make the point quite adequately and focus on a
number of collateral issues.

Case One: The D.C. Youth Orchestra Program

Introduction

This case study illustrates how a decision-making body decides to refund a music program provided by an outside private agency.

A document, entitled "The D.C. Youth Orchestra
Program and the Morale of the Public School
Instrumental Music Teachers," reveals information
concerning the evolution of the DCYOP, a critique
of the DCYOP structure and the state of teacher

morale as of 1971. As indicated in the document, the District of Columbia Youth Orchestra Program was started within the Music Department of the DCPS system in 1961 as an enrichment program to provide selected children of promising ability a chance to play in a symphony orchestra. Qualifications for admission to the orchestra were developed by the teachers and orchestra conductors, including the rule that only students selected by their instrumental teachers in the school could become members of the Youth Orchestra.

In 1964, a group of parents organized the Friends of the D.C. Youth Orchestra, to provide scholarship aid for private lessons, and clerical functions. Thereafter, the scope and direction of the organization changed and expanded. Thus, preparatory classes were begun, department teachers were consulted less on policy, and outside teachers were hired.

By 1968, the name was changed to the D.C. Youth Orchestra Program (DCYOP). The structure, supported by the supervising director of music, Mr. Paul D. Gable, but not the majority of the department teachers, assumed the character of a private music school with students at all levels, extensive preparatory classes, ensembles and bands and orchestras from beginners to advanced, a full-time director, an assistant director, committees, an office with a secretary, and a large faculty. Furthermore, extensive publicity techniques were used, and direct appeals were made to the community for support and contributions. Additionally, the DCYOP had its own budget and made direct appeals to the DCBOE for funds in spite of the fact that it had an almost autonomous structure. In line with this, children were openly invited to join the program and no longer needed to be recommended by their department teachers.

The Problem

Under the section designated "Critique of the DCYOP Structure," in the report of 1971, several questions were raised. One question had to do with the establishment of a large preparatory program which music teachers felt duplicated the instrumental music program in the public schools that had served as a feeder program for the original Youth Orchestra. To refute the publicity claim that 70 percent of the Youth Orchestra membership was obtained from the DCYOP preparatory classes, data was secured to show that one-half to two-thirds of beginners dropped out after one year in the DCYOP as illustrated in figure 3. Additionally, the document noted that 73 percent of the students entered directly into the Youth Orchestra rather than from the DCYOP preparatory classes. The string sections of the Youth Orchestra for 1970 were examined for this data. It was noted that in January 1970 there were 67 string players in the Youth Orchestra who entered from the following sources: 19 percent from the preparatory program and 8 percent from an advanced group (the Junior Orchestra) (see figure 4). This, then, confirmed for the investigators that the bulk of the Youth Orchestra instrumentalists were not a product of the DCYOP training program. Thus, the gains realized after four or five years' effort from such great numbers of children were too minimal to insist on the need for a training program within the DCYOP and these children would have developed in their school programs.

Another grievance as noted by the investigators, Barbara White and Rosanna B. Saffran, had to do with the use of professionals on the Switzerland trip which swelled the group from its normal size of approximately 115 to 132 players. Furthermore, it was revealed that none of the specialized instrumentalists (six bassoonists, four oboeists, and two bass clarinetists) came from the DCYOP preparatory programs between 1967 and 1971 in spite of the fact that there was an extensive preparatory program.

A point of great contention at this time, as well as in 1973-74, was the fact that Maryland and Virginia children were included in a program

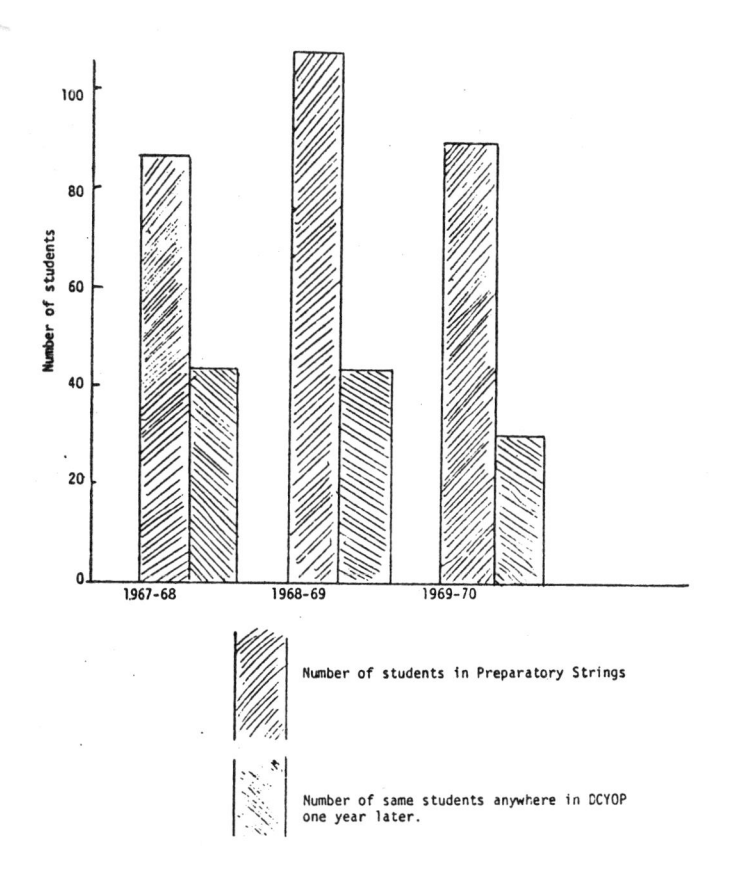

FIGURE 3.

ONE YEAR DROPOUTS FROM PREPARATORY STRINGS

SOURCE: "The D.C. Youth Orchestra Program and the Morale of the Public School Instrumental Music Teachers," to Dr. James T. Guines, Associate Superintendent of Schools from Barbara White, Representative, Superintendent and Rosanna B. Saffran, Teacher, Elementary Instrumental Music Department, July 16, 1971, p. 7.

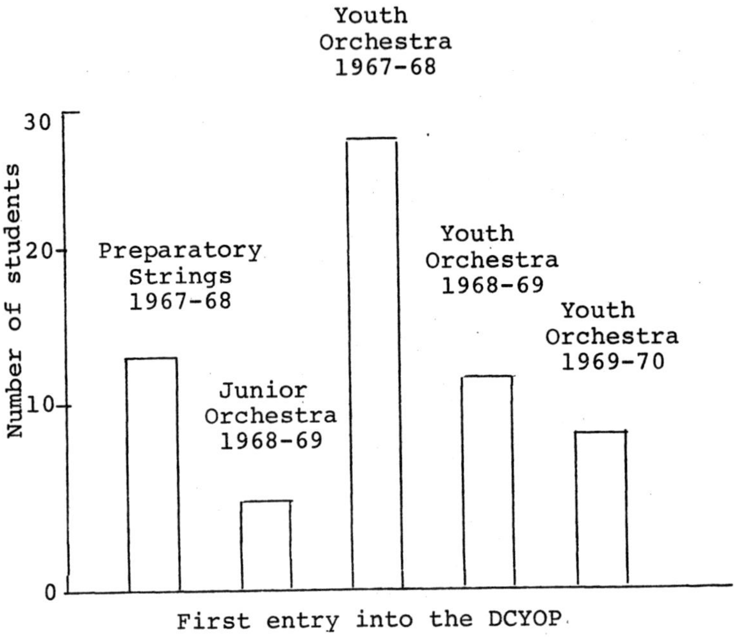
Youth
Orchestra
1967-68
30
Number of students
20
10
0
Preparatory
Strings
1967-68
Junior
Orchestra
1968-69
Youth
Orchestra
1968-69
Youth
Orchestra
1969-70
First entry into the DCYOP

SOURCE: "The D.C. Youth Orchestra Program and the Morale of the Public School Instrumental Music Teachers," to Dr. James T. Guines, Associate Superintendent of Schools from Barbara White, Representative, Superintendent and Rosanna B. Saffran, Teacher, Elementary Instrumental Music Department, July 16, 1971, p. 9.

FIGURE 4

ORIGIN OF 67 STRING PLAYERS,
YOUTH ORCHESTRA, JANUARY 1970

partially funded by the DCPS system. In this regard, the report noted that of the 42 secondary schools in the District, only 28 were represented in the Youth Orchestra while players from seven Maryland and one Virginia schools were in the orchestra, thus depriving inner-city talented District children, in particular, access to the program. Some specific problem areas were noted:

- In November 1970, 164 children out of 735 (22%) were from outside the DCPS;

- In January 1969, only 30 members of the Youth Orchestra were from southeast, northeast and lower northwest, the poorer areas of the city; 78 were from upper northwest, west of Rock Creek, the more affluent areas of the District, and suburban Maryland and Virginia.

- A September 1970 list of graduates showed one from northeast and one from southwest with the remaining 31 from the more affluent sections of the District;

- An undue proportion of white players in respect to the over 90 percent Black population was observed at Youth Orchestra concerts;

- The actual number of students in the DCYOP was much lower than that claimed;

- A comparison of purported summer school attendance of 99.6 percent with regular year attendance in the public schools, a dubious comparison;

- A claimed cost of 42 cents per student-hour when the actual cost per student was $51.00;

- The imputation that college admission is due to Youth Orchestra training when it is common for talented music students to receive scholarships;

- The public was misled into believing that the public school music classes are oversized;

- Emphasis on the "free" nature of the DCYOP program when in actuality intermediate and advanced students are urged to take private lessons and solicited to employ DCYOP staff teachers whereas the public school music program is free and music teachers are forbidden to provide private instruction to their own students.

In regard to teacher morale, the report states that this stems specifically from the following factors:

- The autonomous structure of the DCYOP;

- Duplication of the schools' training functions by the DCYOP;

- Generation of unwanted competition and dispute between DCYOP and the public schools;

- The perplexing attitude of the public school music director, Mr. Paul Gable, who gave carte blanche to the DCYOP and his bias toward the DCYOP at the expense of the regular school program.

Specific grievances were indicated as:

- Accusations at a departmental meeting that DCPS music teachers did nothing for the children;

- Less and less communication with departmental music teachers by the Friends of the DCYOP;

- The location of the program in the northwest making it a hardship for children in the central and distant areas to attend or even know about the program;

- The implication that the students would not have access to a free formal musical education except for the DCYOP;

- Reflections on the professional competence of the department teachers through references to the "specialists" and "professionals" when all regular school music teachers are specialists in some instrument and over half are professional performing musicians;

- Felt harassment during personal contacts and departmental meetings when teachers were accused of being "uncooperative" in not sending children to the DCYOP or of purposely leaving instruments in poor repair before the summer; holding secret meetings and excluding Mr. Lyn G. McLain, the director, from the annual festival;

- Omittance in publicity statements of the teachers' association with the DCYOP;

- A feeling of an eroded relationship with parents and pupils due to the inference in the DCYOP publicity that the school program is inferior;

- A decrease in employment in the DCYOP while outsiders have been employed in increasing numbers as indicated in figure 4.

On the basis of the aforementioned study, the following conclusions were drawn:

1. Although the teachers of the D.C. music department want a Youth Orchestra, they object to the structure of the DCYOP as a traditional music school.

2. The DCYOP is virtually autonomous.

3. The training program duplicates that of the public schools, and it is ineffective.

4. Excessive performances are scheduled which disrupt students' training and school attendance.

5. Solicitation of students at all levels disregards departmental policy.

6. The DCYOP has questionable practices in the areas of publicity, statistical claims, benefits, competition and ethics.

7. Adequate talent is available in the D.C. secondary schools.

8. Places in the DCYO should be first filled from the D.C. public schools.

9. Low morale exists among the D.C. music teachers because of: (a) the duplication of the schools' training function; (b) the autonomous structure of the DCYOP in competition with the schools' music program; (c) the degradation of teachers' professionalism; (d) the music department's lack of control over the DCYOP; and (e) the lack of positive direction by the supervising director of music in solving the problems.

The recommendations included the following:

1. Solve the problem by using an authority higher than the supervising director of music.

2. Retain a city-wide Youth Orchestra with the following conditions:

    (a) Under the de facto administration of the music department.

    (b) Emphasize musical values and education, not the number of performances.

(c) Contain mainly D.C. students recommended by their public school music teacher.

(d) Accept a few other students on a yearly space-available basis.

(e) Have a staff of no more than four from the D.C. music faculties at extra-duty pay.

(f) Periodically rotate the conductor.

(g) Locate at a more central place.

(h) Encourage the Friends to handle their original role of providing needed services and funds for private lessons, transportation, etc.

(i) Utilize community music schools for low-cost private lessons.

3. Dismantle the DCYOP and return children to their respective schools for training.

4. Music programs related to the public schools should be under the clear control of the music department.[1]

Correspondence of August 11, 1969 indicates the beginning of a greater involvement by the DCPS in terms of the funding of the DCYOP. Some historical insight is provided by the following passages:

> The Friends of the D.C. Youth Orchestra Program wish to apply for an allotment of $30,000.00 for the school year September 1969 through June 1970 to be administered as a Negotiated Service Contract in the same manner as our contract...for the period March 1 to June 30, 1969....
>
> Foundations which have supported us are now questioning why, after seven years, the school administration has not yet provided a budget for this demonstrated need and have indicated that our grants will not be renewed....

>If the program is forced to cut back, there will unquestionably be a protest reaction from our large parent-student body.[2]

One can note that this last sentence in the correspondence can possibly be viewed as a form of strong arm tactic. Subsequent to this piece of correspondence, Mrs. Marian S. Banner, president, DCYOP, called Mr. Benjamin Henley, acting superintendent of schools, after being advised by Mr. Delroy L. Cornick, director, Department of Budget and Legislation, that the decision for the contract had to be made by Mr. Henley. A memorandum for the files dated September 17, 1969 indicated Mr. Henley's response to the above request as follows:

>I called Mr. Henley today to inquire about our request for an allotment of $30,000.00 to be administered as a Negotiated Services Contract as described in our letter of August 11, 1969 to Mr. Cornick.

>Mr. Henley asked why we needed a Negotiated Services Contract, 'why can't we just put them on the payroll?' I explained to him that we have a number of teachers who are not in the D.C. School system and we also have an Administrative Aide who is not on a school payroll.

>To this Mr. Henley answered 'In that case the contract is best'.... 'Go ahead, announce registration, get everything going today.'[3]

On the basis of the following objectives, a negotiated contract was let for October 1, 1970 to June 17, 1971:

1. To provide specialized instrumental instruction in the schools with a program of training on Saturdays and evenings by professional, performing musicians, specialists on the instrument they will teach.

2. To prepare students technically and musically to perform in ensembles and all-city performing groups at all levels capable of providing concerts in the schools and in communities.

3. To provide a center for instrumental students structured for class flexibility to maximize development on their instruments.[4]

As will be noted, this cavalier fashion of handling the letting of a contract to the DCYOP in 1971 was to create problems between the school administration and the school board in 1973.

The following table 7 provides a financial history of the funding for the DCYOP. It especially shows the DCPS system financial involvement beginning with the 1966-67 school year and the steady increase of public school funds to support the program. As indicated in table 7, public school funds given to the DCYOP by the DCBOE rose from $5,131.00 in 1966-67 to over $90,000.00 in 1972-73 as enrollment in the program increased from 445 in 1966-67 to between 600-700 students by 1972-73.

Obviously, all was still not well by July 1972, as attested to by Superintendent Hugh Scott's memorandum to the DCBOE in which he pinpoints two basic problems: (1) the DCYOP's relationship with the department of music, and (2) the participation of non-D.C. residents. Thus, Scott tried to provide a new foundation upon which the operation of the DCYOP could go forward. First, he expressed the basic purposes as (1) to provide expanded opportunities for talented students to improve their techniques and skills in instrumental music, and (2) to expand opportunities for students and citizens of the District to hear quality music played by young people. To this end, he provided support for the DCYOP to remain under the D.C. public school system and for its administrative personnel to be staff members of the school system. Secondly, Scott provided support for the idea that the number of non-residents should at no time

TABLE 7

D. C. YOUTH ORCHESTRA PROGRAM

FINANCIAL HISTORY
(SCHOOL YEAR PROGRAM ONLY)

| Year | Enrollment | Staff | D.C. Schools | Foundations | Friends |
|------|------------|-------|--------------|-------------|---------|
| 1961-62 | 80 | 2 unpaid | - | - | |
| 1962-63 | 165 | 4 unpaid | - | - | |
| 1963-64 | 250 | 5 unpaid | - | - | |
| 1964-65 | 265 | 6 unpaid | - | - | $110-instruments |
| 1965-66 | 390 | 10 unpaid | - | - | $400-instruments |
| 1966-67 | 445 | 14 | $5,131 | $4,775 | $2,120 |
| 1967-68 | 525 | 25 | $5,131 | $5,000 | $5,013 |
| 1968-69 | 750 | 38 | $14,131 | $23,700 | $13,547 |
| 1969-70 | 750 | 41 | $30,000 | $16,705 | $13,550 |
| 1970-71 | 800 | 56 | $35,000 | $10,000* | $18,000*** |
| 1971-72 | 700 | 34**** | $35,000 | $12,000** | $15,000***** |
| 1972-73 | 600-700 | 36 | $91,500 | - | $15,912 |

\*      Foundation (Cafritz)[a] grant for the purchase of oboes, bassoons, French horns.
\*\*     Foundation (Cafritz) grant for the purchase of violins, cellos, basses - undersized.
\*\*\*    Friends contribution in 1970-71 was the balance of funds raised for the trip to the International Festival in Summer 1970.
\*\*\*\*   Staff reduced in number from previous year, but each member is giving more hours of instruction so that total instruction time is the same.
\*\*\*\*\* Friends contribution in 1971-72 is result of mail fund drive and ticket contributions in connection with Berlin trip.
+       School Board provided total year funding for instruction--$31,500 for Summer Program, $60,000 for school year.

SOURCE: Component B Friends of the D.C. Youth Orchestra Program Proposal for ESAA Grant, 1974-75.

a       William Cafritz is in real estate investments and is a member of the Metropolitan Board of Trade.

constitute more than one-fourth of its membership and that they should pay a tuition fee for the services. Additionally, Scott maintained that the orchestra's first responsibility was to service the residents of the District of Columbia and that the thrust should be participatory rather than performatory.[5]

Following this declaration by Scott, the Committee on Elementary Instrumental Music met on August 11, 15, and 25 with its subcommittee meeting on August 22 and 24 (1972). As pointed out in the meeting notes, the first two meetings produced some sharp and visceral differences related to: (1) the structure of the instrumental music component of the department; (2) the relationship of the department of the Youth Orchestra and the Youth Chorale; (3) accountability of the Youth Orchestra program vis-a-vis the department of music; (4) the music education philosophy as it concerns the teaching of instrumental music; and (5) providing opportunities for instrumental music education to all children in the school system.

The three recommendations which emerged from the subcommittee meetings and which were approved by the whole committee were as follows:

1. That all instrumental music programs come under the administration of and be accountable to the Assistant Director of Instrumental Music.

2. That the $60,000.00 allocated to the DCYOP be administered by the music department.

3. That the music department develop a comprehensive curriculum, K-12, that meets the needs of all students.[6]

Following the above meetings, a comprehensive K-12 music education program was developed at the request of the deputy superintendent, Dr. James T. Guines. The design of the program recommended a spiral progression of cumulative understandings and skills in music.[7]

Soon after the submission of the report but prior to September 1972, Mrs. Hortense P. Taylor was appointed to the position of acting director of music for the D.C. public schools.[8]

Thus, the Fall of 1972 saw an expansion of the Resource Professional Program of the DCYOP into 35 elementary schools servicing over 1,000 students.

Significantly, there was inconsistency in terms of the number of elementary schools to be serviced. On November 3, 1972 at a meeting called by Drs. Scott and Guines with Messrs. Hall, McLain and Bellamy, it was revealed that all elementary schools were to be provided instrumental music experiences using a four-pronged approach as follows:

1. Forty-nine schools to be serviced by the 15 regular elementary school instrumental music teachers;

2. Thirty schools serviced by the junior high school instrumental music teachers;

3. Ten schools serviced by three volunteer qualified professionals; and

4. Forty-six schools serviced by the D.C. Youth Orchestra Program approach for $60,000.00.

One deep concern of the superintendent's was how teachers released during the summer would be involved. The resolution of the problem, as explained by Mr. Lyn McLain, appeared to be that the teachers had been placed in other positions. Subsequently, Dr. Scott questioned the legality of using a negotiated services contract between the DCPS and the Friends of the DCYOP. He raised the questions, "Why the public schools would be paying 'outsiders' to do its job?", and "Since the D.C. Youth Orchestra Program was a part of the public schools music department, how such a contract could be valid?" Further, Dr. Scott questioned how Mr. Wilbur Bellamy, a regular instrumental music teacher on sabbatical leave, could be paid public school funds to coordinate the program.

    Superintendent Scott further indicated that since the DCYOP was an agent of the public schools, the Friends of the DCYOP had no say in the matter. At that point in the meeting, Mr. William Bedford from the budget department said that the DCYOP had been informed for years that such a contract was illegal. Interestingly, the contract had been approved each year by some school system administrators. To date the status of negotiated service contracts with the DCYOP was still unresolved.[9]

Sequence of Events

    A "negotiated Services Contract" between the D.C. board of education and the Friends of the DCYOP was let on September 24, 1973, for which the Friends group was to receive $151,500.00 in return for professional teaching services provided students during 1973-74.[10] The enrollment breakdown for 1973-74 was: Blacks 562; whites 167; others 13; and Orientals 8; making a total of 750 students in the Regular Program and 1262 Blacks, 47 whites, 12 others, 4 Spanish and 2 Orientals, for a total of 1327 in the Resource Professional Project servicing 32 elementary schools; and 602 Blacks, 87 Whites, 7 others and 7 Orientals, making a total of 703 students in the ESAA Project. Total students serviced were 2,426 Blacks, 301 whites, 32 others, 4 Spanish and 17 Oriental students. In addition, the breakdown of students by wards in the regular program was:

| Ward 1.... 21 | Ward 5....163 |
|---|---|
| Ward 2.... 14 | Ward 6.... 67 |
| Ward 3.... 46 | Ward 7.... 58 |
| Ward 4....240 | Ward 8.... 21 |

By states the enrollment figures were:

```
D.C. ......630
Maryland ..100
Virginia .. 20
         750[11]
```

The DCYOP, a city-wide instrumental music training program, provided instruction on Saturdays and evenings for children at all levels of competency. Both children from the District and from outside the District of Columbia were permitted to attend. The 1973-74 enrollment of 703 students was 76 percent Black in a school system about 96 percent Black. The non-minority students came from schools in the District which had white students and from private, parochial and public schools in Virginia and Maryland.

In addition to the above, the DCYOP provided instrumental music training to approximately 2,000 children in 32 of the D.C. public elementary schools during the school day. Interestingly, the Senior Youth Orchestra was only 45 percent Black. In 1972 it was 40 percent Black.

In 1973, there were 29 Black professionals and 39 white professionals out of a total of 68 staff members.[12]

In explaining why there were fewer Black students in the DCYOP, the document, entitled "Component B - Friends of the D.C. Youth Orchestra Program," which was submitted to Region III and the Office of Education, basically said:

> The minority student who begins in the group classes of the Program frequently reaches a plateau in terms of conquering his instrument. If he does not bring a middle class tradition or economic means with him, he is not likely to seek private lessons which the non-minority child sitting next to him has been having from the start. He drops out rather than not be able to keep up.

Secondly, the racial isolation in the regular school program has militated against developing students on the more difficult instruments. No school is able to teach a child to play the French Horn, bassoon, oboe or viola, nor can any one school as a result produce a fully instrumented orchestra. Most of the schools of the city have no orchestra.

Thus the minority student finds himself being surpassed by the non-minority child who has been given private lessons because of the tradition expectation, and economic capability of his culture.[13]

One precipitating incident for investigating the DCYOP's arrangement with the DCBOE by the administration appeared to be a conflict between the Junior Band and the administration of DCYOP. In a memorandum dated February 23, 1974, some Junior Band members outlined a series of grievances against the administration of the DCYOP regarding the lack of instruments, the lack of supervision during practice, the lack of communication, threats of being dropped from the program if they registered complaints, and the firing of the director of the Junior Band. Seemingly, this incident surfaced the issue of control of the music program by a private outside agency or by the school system.[14]

Following this above incident, a series of letters was sent from the school administration and the DCYOP administration and the Friends. Additionally, a series of meetings was held to resolve the problems pinpointed above.

A memorandum was sent February 27, 1974, from Wilbur Bellamy to Lyn McLain, describing a problem which the DCYOP had had during the past 8 months coordinating the Junior Band activities with the rest of the program. In particular, the memorandum focused on Mr. James E. Hall's insubordinate behavior with regard to following policies, and recommended that he be replaced.[15]

Another memorandum received by Mrs. Sizemore from Mr. Hall indicated that the Junior Band was not included in the All City Band Festival because Mr. McLain stated that he had received nothing in writing from Mr. Hall indicating that they were prepared to play. His objection to this was that it was said before parents, and that in previous years he had not been requested to state same in writing. Subsequently, the two had an altercation outside the school. After the fight was broken up by some other instructors, Mr. Hall went down the hall where the Friends were meeting in the Coolidge High School building to inform Mrs. Myrtle Morris of the incident. She rejected his account. In his appeal to Superintendent Sizemore, Mr. Hall noted that of the approximately 30 teachers on staff in the DCYOP, only four taught in the DCPS and that some of the teachers were without music degrees.[16]

On the same day of Mr. Hall's letter to the superintendent, Lyn McLain sent a report of the incident of Saturday, March 23, 1974, which substantially contradicted the statements made by Mr. Hall in his letter. Also contained in the letter was Mr. McLain's intention to terminate Mr. Hall's employment.[17]

Additional statements were submitted by witnesses to the incident to Edgar B. Dews, Jr., security director, who reported his investigation to Floretta McKenzie, deputy superintendent.[18]

As of April 1, 1974, no action had been taken against Mr. Hall as attested to by a memorandum sent to Mrs. McKenzie from James T. Guines, associate superintendent. He stated that he directed Mr. Lyn McLain to take no action relative to Mr. James Hall until recommendations had been given.[19]

An April 4, 1974 letter from Floretta D. McKenzie to Mr. Lyn McLain indicated that Mr. Hall had been dismissed. In that same communication, McKenzie, in confirming statements made during their conference on Monday, April 1, 1974, indicated that after the conference she received a letter from Junior Band parents which stated that all was still not well. Furthermore, Mrs. McKenzie called attention to Article VII in the contract which states: "No changes shall be made in key personnel approved for this project without consent of the Contract Manager and Contracting Officer." She further indicated that, in dismissing Mr. James E. Hall, Mr. Lyn McLain had not observed the terms of the contract.[20]

An April 4, 1974 correspondence from a parent in the Junior Band made reference to McKenzie's letter and indicated a troubled existence for the band, in that the students were locked out of their rooms for 40 minutes, there were no musical scores available, instruments were lacking, and Mr. Floyd Robinson* intimidated the parents and threatened to call the police.[21]

A different interpretation of what occurred was presented to Lyn McLain by Wilbur Bellamy in his April 5, 1974 correspondence. In this regard he indicated that Mrs. Juanita Thompson had initiated the problem.[22]

A full report of the altercation and the subsequent actions taken were reported to Mrs. Sizemore in a memorandum dated April 5, 1974 from Mrs. McKenzie. In closing Mrs. McKenzie recommended the following actions:

1. Sustain Mr. Hall's termination as Junior Band conductor.

---

*Mr. Floyd Robinson was described, in a memorandum to Lyn McLain from Wilbur Bellamy re: Junior Band Rehearsal (April 2, 1974), April 5, 1974, as a parent, President Emeritus of the Friends of the D.C. Youth Orchestra Program and on the Ad Hoc Committee to air grievances of Junior Band parents.

2. Take no action against Mr. Hall relative to his teaching position at Paul Junior High School.

3. Request an audit of the records of the Friends of the D.C. Youth Orchestra.

4. Investigate the internal procedures of the Friends of the D.C. Youth Orchestra.

5. Meet with representatives of the music department to discuss renewal of our contract with the Friends.[23]

Numerous other correspondence and meetings brought the dispute to the point where the administrators of the DCPS began considering whether or not to renew the negotiated contract with the Friends of the DCYOP.

On May 27, 1974, a letter from Myrtle C. Morris, president, Friends of the DCYOP, was sent to Superintendent Barbara A. Sizemore. In this correspondence, Mrs. Morris stated that "On April 23, 1974, I received a letter from Mrs. Floretta D. McKenzie, deputy superintendent, stating that 'serious charges had been made against the Friends of the D.C. Youth Orchestra Program which raises the question of whether or not the Friends had administered properly the contract between it and the Board of Education.'"

Mrs. Myrtle C. Morris continued with the fact that, as a consequence, a meeting was set up between Dr. James Guines, Mr. Wilbur Bellamy and herself for April 29, 1973, at which time Dr. Guines stressed that a contract was no longer desired. The reasons for cancelling the contract were that: (1) public school funds should remain under the public schools; and (2) that Dr. Guines would like to have complete control of programs that he, as associate superintendent of Instructional Services, would be held responsible for. Thus, Dr. Guines pushed for an agreement instead.

Mrs. Morris continued in her correspondence by saying that, after meeting with the Executive Committee of the Friends to determine the feasibility of such a plan, a meeting was scheduled with Dr. Guines for May 20, 1974 to discuss the proposed change. She indicated that the change was not satisfactory, hence her letter to Mrs. Sizemore. In this connection, Mrs. Morris referred to the arrangement set up with Mr. Benjamin Henley, former deputy superintendent of public schools, five years ago, and asked what a meeting with approximately 10 Junior Band parents and approximately 30 Junior Band students had to do with a cancellation of a contract between the board and the Friends. In this regard, she requested to know why the administration was dissatisfied.[24]

Mr. Guines' response to the letter received by Superintendent Sizemore from Mrs. Myrtle Morris stated in substance that "the decision not to renew the contract with the Friends of the D.C. Youth Orchestra Program is primarily related to the desire to strengthen the instrumental music offerings of our school system by having a unified program, operating under the Music Department."[25]

In response to a request from Guines for a program that reorganized the music department to absorb the DCYOP,[26] Hortense Taylor presented this information in a May 24, 1974 communication which he forwarded to the superintendent on May 31, 1974.[27]

Meanwhile, requests were made by the administration for information regarding the non-resident students in the DCYOP and the financial contributions made to the program.[28]

June 14, 1974 board meeting --

On June 14, 1974, the third annual meeting for students was held with board of education members and the key administrators. The issue discussed was whether or not to continue the D.C. Youth Orchestra Program under its present arrangement as a supplemental music program administered by a non-profit private group. At that time, several graduates and students voiced their objection to any change in the present arrangement as did board members Mason, Barry and Kemp. Contrastingly, Mrs. Sizemore revealed that the D.C. Youth Orchestra would become a part of the Ellington High School of the Arts (Western) and that the proposal would be coming to the board. Both Mason and Barry questioned whether the $150,000.00 allotted for the orchestra was in the budget. Mrs. Sizemore's reply was that the money was in the regular budget.

Citizen Alfonso Pollard, who had just testified to the importance of the program, objected to the move of the program to Western High School. Hobson's main concern in that meeting focused on the fact that his ward, Ward 7, Anacostia, Congress Heights, Ward 8, and Ward 6 constituents, all east of the Anacostia River in southeast, complained about the distance that had to be traveled to Coolidge High School located in northwest Washington in Ward 3. In addition, Hobson stated that east of the river, they had been discriminated against and had won several court cases on that basis. Thus the question being asked was, why the program could not be moved to Western High School, which is located much closer to Anacostia, or to Ballou High School, which is located in Anacostia?

Barry's comments were most supportive of the idea of using public funds for private non-public organizations when he said, "I think that it is possible to publicly finance educational programs, so that they can be privately, through non-public organizations, administered."[29]

At the meeting held on June 19, 1974, the board considered a proposal submitted by Superintendent Sizemore for the proposed High School of the Arts, which had two purposes: (1) to provide intensive arts instruction to talented students who are considering careers in the arts; and (2) to become a community resource for developing art activity throughout the city. It was in this meeting that the matter of authority for and control of the DCYOP by the DCPS system was aired for the public starting with a question raised by board member Mattie Taylor as to what was intended with respect to the Youth Orchestra program.

In answering the question, Superintendent Sizemore noted that two phases were proposed: (1) the feeder program for the regions; and (2) the High School for Performing Arts. Continuing, she explained that the original idea was to absorb all music and performing arts programs into the High School for Performing Arts, thereby rendering unnecessary the contracting out of these services. Since that time members of the board had indicated that the board preferred to have these services contracted outside the school system. Therefore, their wishes had been given consideration by the staff. After nudging by Mrs. Taylor, the superintendent further clarified her remarks by stating that if the proposal were accepted as written, it would mean the absorption of the D.C. Youth Orchestra into the High School of the Performing Arts. She added, that if the board continued the contractual arrangement with the D.C. Youth Orchestra, it would not.

At this point in the discussion, Mrs. Taylor asked that the board clarify its position with respect to the D.C. Youth Orchestra before voting on the proposal to absorb it. Thus, she moved "That we clarify our intent with respect to the D.C. Youth Orchestra as it is proposed in the document before us on the page and paragraph that I so cited." This motion was seconded by board member Simmons and voted in favor of by Barry, Taylor, Simmons, Morris, Mason, Treanor, Evans and Swaim. Hobson voted against the motion.

On the heels of this motion, Mason moved, "That we continue our relationship with the Youth Orchestra with a contractual arrangement." Swaim seconded the motion.

After a lengthy argument engaged in by Taylor and Mason, concerning tuition paid by non-residents, Mrs. Morris suddenly made a substitute motion to delete on page 2, paragraph 2, line 1, "the D.C. Youth Orchestra and D.C. Youth Chorale" from consideration as to being absorbed into the High School of Performing Arts. Voting in favor of the motion were Treanor, Taylor, Swaim, Mason, Evans, Morris, Barry and Hobson. Mrs. Simmons abstained from voting on the substitute motion.

Finally, a vote was taken on the 300 slots at Western High School of Performing Arts for September 1975. As interpreted by the chair, the question of the housing of the Youth Orchestra at Western was not a part of the proposal and that it had not been settled. Also, the housing of the D.C. Youth Chorale had not been settled. Therefore, the vote was simply on the 300 slots at Western. Those who voted for the amended proposal were Treanor, Taylor, Simmons, Swaim, Mason, Evans, Morris, Barry and Hobson, making the vote a unanimous one.[30]

### July 2, 1974 special meeting of the board --

A special meeting of the DCBOE held on July 2, 1974 was called for the purpose of getting input from citizens concerning the Youth Orchestra and the D.C. public schools. The basic issue was whether the DCPS system should take control of the program or the school system should continue contracting out music services to the Friends of the DCYOP. Swirling around this basic issue and energizing an emotional climate in Room 500 of the District Building, were concerns about racism, elitism, due process, control, the use of public funds, collusion with power groups, and maltreatment of children.

At the meeting there were 14 citizens who spoke in favor of maintaining the status quo (contracting out the services) and 10 citizens who spoke in favor of a change in status (control by the DCPS). Among the board members present who desired to maintain the status quo were Kemp, Treanor, Mason, and Barry; those who vigorously called for change in control were Hobson, Morris and Simmons. Rosenfield leaned toward change but spoke more vigorously for working out differences.

One particularly strong argument against letting the contract to the Friends of the DCYOP was given by Mrs. Ruth Goodwin, a citizen who has been involved consistently in DCPS affairs:

> I want this entered on the record. Mrs. Louise Malone who is a budget analyst for the D.C. Youth Orchestra is also statistician for the D.C. Citizens for Better Public Education. In 1972 when the budget was written under the auspices of Mrs. Swaim who was chairman of that Committee, Mrs. Malone was loaned to the school system for two months at the admission of the citizens to structure the budget when there was a cut back in mathematics, reading, science, military science, home economics and physical education. But the D.C. Youth Orchestra was tripled treated and both organizations which Mrs. Malone represented and Citizens plucked off a contract..., I am talking about dirty tricks ladies and gentlemen.... I am talking about opening this thing up. I am talking about internal audit.... You have $250,000 funded and $151,000 goes to the D.C. Youth Orchestra and the rest is left for the entire city of approximately 128,000 students and you tell me that's adequate? All I am saying is bring it out. I think you will get a lot more support from the people who question this. Let this community deal with the resources that these people get. A whole lot of us would definitely come and back this, but this is a monopoly.... I think this is the concern of these parents here. This is the concern when a TSA-15 can indeed instigate a fight and then the other person of whom it is afflicted is fired and the TSA-15 remains when no other TSA-15 has that right. These are the inequities we are talking about....[31]

July 8, 1974 board meeting --

The July 8, 1974 meeting of the DCBOE was another very significant one in that major decisions were made about the DCYOP. It was at this meeting that Superintendent Sizemore presented a report on the DCYOP and the Instrumental Music Contract. After recalling the sequence of events that led up to her investigation of the case, the superintendent reported on her assessment of the program. She indicated first that the DCYOP concentrated on the symphony, a western European notation form. In addition, she gave a mini-history of its development, stating that the curriculum emphasized European superiority; therefore, it did not provide white students with another kind of experience such as Oriental music or African music which differs from Western music in many ways. In support of this point, Mrs. Sizemore provided a brief description of Eastern and African music.

She further said that testimony given by students on July 2, 1974 praised the DCYOP for interracial experiences, yet the basic assumptions of the program were racist. To support this contention, Mrs. Sizemore cited the ESAA Project Description which stated that hostilities and tensions increase in a majority Black city and school systems within the integrated program and the school system. She also rejected the premise for locating the program at Coolidge which is not, as the description states, centrally located, making it accessible to minority and non-minority students alike. Additionally, she took issue at the two recommendations in that in them the Black city is described as hostile and unsafe. Also, Mrs. Sizemore noted that the writers of the project appeared to be more interested in non-minority participants from the suburbs and non-public schools than in those from southwest or far northeast. This showed more interest in providing affluent Blacks access to white culture but not the reverse which is another example of cultural arrogance. Further, note was made of the long hours of practice spoken about at the special board meeting of July 2, 1974, inferring that this kind of effort is not expected by students outside of the DCYOP. In this regard, Mrs. Sizemore questioned whether the board felt that the performance of a DCYO student on the violin in an orchestra was better than the performance of a Cardozo student on the saxophone in a stage band, given equal performances. This she gave as only one example of the problem she was having.

Mrs. Sizemore also questioned the fact that students attributed all of their successes to the DCYO, where in actuality some training of some of the students was provided by McKinley Technical High School teachers.

In summarizing her concerns, Mrs. Sizemore noted that the Friends attempted to speak to racial isolation but not to the resolution of the effects of poverty in a city 96 percent Black and approximately 60 percent poor. She clinched her argument by revealing that the public school officials are blamed for the inequities in the feeder program and assigned the task for resolution by the Friends, the parents are blamed for not being motivated enough to reduce the inequities in the Saturday and evening programs, and the Friends are not blamed for any inequities. Based on the above, the superintendent made several recommendations for board approval, namely that: (1) the internal conflicts in the program be subject to arbitration by a board committee; (2) the Friends submit a complete roster of the Friends, including officers, executive committee contributors and fund sources; (3) the Friends submit their rules and regulations including those about student dismissal; (4) they submit a financial report; (5) they submit evidence of due process for Mr. James Hall; and (6) the president of the DCBOE apologize to Mrs. Juanita Thompson for the character defamation issued by one of the speakers at the July 2, 1974 board meeting.

Discussion on the report centered around the mono-lingual, mono-cultural model of the Friends' program and the present goal of the school system to move toward a multi-lingual, multi-cultural curriculum which was one of the thrusts of the superintendent's <u>120 Day Report</u>, approved by the board; a plea not to destroy the DCYOP as it is; and the opinion that some of the items were not addressed in the contract. Thus, the vote for recommendation Number 1 was Hobson, Swaim and Morris in favor and Evans, Kemp, Mason, Barry, Rosenfield and Treanor opposed. A motion was made that Numbers 2, 3 and 4 be approved by the board as questions to be dealt with in the presumed contract negotiations which would follow, which was unanimously approved. The personnel matter involved in Recommendation Number 5 was substituted by a motion to refer the matter to the Committee of the Whole on Personnel which was also unanimously approved. Item Number 6 was likewise unanimously approved.

The second item in the superintendent's report dealt with the letting of the Instrumental Music Contract to open bidding, in compliance with Title 1, Section 808, of the D.C. <u>Code</u>, pertaining to advertising for proposals for purchasing contracts for supplies or services, applications of sale contracting out. The arguments against this issue had to do with a different interpretation of the regulation in favor of sole source contracting.

Barry referred to his July 8, 1974 memorandum in which he mentioned the month-long controversy and debate as spending too much time on the subject at the expense of the other 133,000 students which he felt was necessary since the superintendent was opposed to renewing the present contract.

His recommendations included letting the contract for $151,500.00 to the Friends of the DCYOP with the same control essentially along the same lines as the present contract, consummate the contract by July 31, 1974, and adopt the superintendent's recommendations concerning the tuition for non-residents.

At this point in the discussion, both Hobson and Morris were still opposed to the renewal of the contract without some concessions made to include more students from their wards or accountability from the Friends.

After Mrs. Simmons returned to the meeting, she, too, voiced her objection to the number of hours spent on two of Mr. Barry's favorite topics -- the Hawthorne School and the DCYOP -- which she said was an unbelievable kind of inequitable proportion of time given when we have a student body of 128,000. Thus, she moved to table the action on the DCYOP. Only Hobson, Morris and Simmons voted in favor of tabling the motion, so it lost. At this point, Hobson noted that three of the people that voted against tabling the motion would not be on the DCBOE the following week.

Next, the vote was taken on the superintendent's recommendation to let bids. This motion was defeated with Hobson, Morris and Simmons voting in favor and Kemp, Mason, Barry, Rosenfield, Swaim and Treanor voting against. Following this 6-3 vote, a discussion commenced on the applicability of the D.C. Non-Resident Tuition Act to non-residents enrolled in the DCYOP, but was stifled by a motion by Mrs. Mason to renew the contract with the DCYOP. During the course of much discussion of the motion as regards the legality and the unfairness of it to the administration, a more encompassing motion was made by Mr. Barry:

> That a contract for $151,500.00 be let between the public schools and the Friends of the D.C. Youth Orchestra with the same control essentially along the same lines as the present contract with the Friends of the D.C. Youth Orchestra being responsible for providing instructors for professional teaching services and the public schools responsible for the

selection of 35 elementary schools which provides for some 1300 elementary students being taught.

Kemp, Mason, Simmons, Treanor, Barry and Swaim voted in favor of the motion while Hobson and Morris voted in opposition; Evans abstained. A companion motion setting July 31 as the suggested time for the administration to consummate the contract was opposed by Morris and Simmons. The third related motion had to do with charging tuition which was approved by Morris, Kemp, Hobson, Barry, Simmons, Swaim and Treanor.[32] This action by no means put the issue of the DCYOP to rest.

On July 9, 1974, a Letter of Intent was sent to the DCPS from Myrtle C. Morris, president, Friends of the DCYOP.[33]

A memorandum sent to the superintendent, dated July 10, 1974 from Dwight S. Cropp, executive secretary of the board of education, indicated that the board on July 8, 1974 voted nonapproval of the action proposed by Superintendent Sizemore that the administration will advertise for submission of proposals to provide D.C. public schools with an instructional and performing instrumental music program.[34]

On July 10, 1974, Relford Patterson, chairman, Department of Music, Howard University, sent a letter to Superintendent Sizemore expressing interest by the Department of Music at Howard University in submitting a bid to provide music services for the DCPS.[35]

In following the sequence of events, it is important to note that McLain, director, DCYOP, received a memorandum from Hurlbut requesting a list of non-resident students.[36] He submitted a list of non-resident students in the DCYOP as of July 24, 1974. This list contained 99 names of students, instrument, group or level, parents' names and addresses.[37]

In reply to Sizemore's letter of July 15, 1974 regarding the "Negotiated Services Contract," Splitt outlined the authority for letting contracts for services without first advertising the contract and accepting bids. In doing so, he quoted from the D.C. Code and the U.S. Code, the substance of which was that the law was ambiguous. Therefore, his advice to Superintendent Sizemore was for her to proceed with the contracting process and refer correspondence on the contract to the D.C.Division of Contracts, Bureau of Materiel Management, Department of General Services, for approval, and that in the event of disapproval by them, advertising for bids may be required.[38]

Myrtle Morris' letter of July 29, 1974 to Sizemore emphasized the urgency for the administration and the DCBOE to complete negotiations of the contract by July 31, 1974, according to the board mandate at its July 8 meeting as the DCYO was leaving for Scotland on August 1, 1974, to participate in the International Festival of Youth Orchestras.[39]

The August 1, 1974 memorandum from Sizemore to the DCBOE focused on the issue of inequity in opportunity for instrumental music instruction available to all elementary pupils, which appeared to violate the intent of the Wright decision. Sizemore established that administration was unable to justify a program that limits services to 35 out of 41 schools. She further reiterated her receipt of a letter from the Department of Music at Howard University expressing an interest in bidding on the contract to provide music services to the public schools. Thus, she recommended that consideration be given to them before giving the Friends a sole source contract. Her other suggestion was that schools could be selected by a lottery. A list of schools served by elementary instrument teachers, DCYO personnel, and schools receiving no service was attached along with a contract from the Friends.[40]

## August 1, 1974 board meeting --

The August 1, 1974 meeting is particularly significant because this was the first meeting of the seven member board, since the four members who were scheduled to leave the board, namely Rosenfield, Barry, Swaim and Taylor, had now left. Those remaining were Mrs. Morris, Mr. Hobson, Dr. Evans, Rev. Kemp, Mrs. Mason, Mrs. Simmons and Mr. Treanor. Morris was now president of the board. The following actions relating to the DCYOP were consummated by vote:

- That the superintendent's August 1, 1974 report on the D.C. Youth Orchestra Program be referred to committee. Those in favor of the motion put by Kemp and seconded by Simmons were Simmons, Morris, Hobson, Treanor, Kemp and Evans. Mason abstained.

- That August 13, 1974 would be the time frame within which the committee would take action. Those voting in favor of the motion made by Kemp and seconded by Treanor were Simmons, Hobson, Mason, Morris, Treanor, Evans and Kemp.

- That the board adopt the superintendent's report that the non-resident tuition rates be applied to those students whose cost of education is under the D.C. public funds. Those in favor of the motion made by Hobson and seconded by Mason, were Evans, Kemp, Mason, Morris, Hobson, Treanor and Simmons.

- That the amendment to the above motion be referred to the board's legal counsel for advice. Those in favor of the motion made by Mason were Evans, Kemp, Mason, Morris, Treanor and Simmons. Hobson opposed the motion.

A memorandum from Cropp to Sizemore, sent August 2, 1974, informed the superintendent that her August 1, 1974 report on the DCYOP was referred to the committees on Student Services and Community Involvement and on Educational Programs.[42]

On August 10, 1974, Richard Hurlbut sent a memorandum to Sizemore and James Guines which summarized the meeting of the joint committees on Student Services and Community Involvement, and on Educational Programs. At that meeting, the committee reviewed the superintendent's report of August 1, 1974 on the DCYOP. All seven members of the board were present. The meeting was chaired by Mrs. Hilda Mason. Persons from the administration were also present: James Johnson, Hortense Taylor, and Richard Hurlbut. The action included a motion by Barbara Simmons that the superintendent's draft of the "Negotiated Services Contract" of August 1 be submitted to the Friends for review. Second, that the superintendent promptly negotiate with the Friends in preparing a final draft of the contract to be submitted to the DCBOE by August 19, 1974 for review and adoption.

In addition, the seven DCBOE members present voted three for (Morris, Hobson, Simmons) and four against (Evans, Kemp, Mason, Treanor) advertising the contract. It was noted that the action approved at the joint committee meeting would be brought up again at the next board meeting for formal approval.[43]

Cropp's report included some additional information, as for instance, both Ms. Ruth Goodwin, Black community leader, and Ms. Diane Brockett, white news reporter, were also present. In essence, other aspects of the report were similar with Cropp giving the voting breakdown on the following points: (1) it was moved by Hobson and seconded by Simmons that Task I, Elementary Resources Professional Program, be placed in the Music Department of the D.C. public schools, which motion failed to pass; (2) it was moved by Hobson and seconded by Simmons that the DCBOE put up for bids Task II, D.C. Youth Orchestra Program, which motion failed to pass;

and (3) it was moved by Simmons and seconded by Hobson that Task I, Elementary Resources Professional Program, be put up for bid, which also failed to pass.[44]

Following this latest nudge from the DCBOE for the superintendent to act on the DCYOP contract, Superintendent Sizemore sent another memorandum to the board dated August 13, 1974 entitled "Statement on Contracting." Her major points were first that four board members (Evans, Kemp, Mason and Treanor) ordered the superintendent to negotiate a contract with the Friends of the DCYOP, a private nonprofit organization, to control the music program in 35 schools.

Sizemore's second point was that it was normal in the DCPS system to contract out services as in sole source contracting, thus diminishing the resources controlled by the people. She was saying, in essence, that even in contracting out services, control can be retained if the contractor gives the service, with the DCPS system retaining control over the service or allowing everybody interested in providing the service a chance to apply.

The point made by the rest of the letter is that the control of public monies had been taken out of the hands of parents, that they had no voice in how those monies would be used since there was no bidding, and that the superintendent had no control over the contractors. Furthermore, the superintendent wrote that power was in the hands of the private nonprofit organization and not in the hands of the parents of the children in the 33 schools serviced by the DCYOP.[45]

Kemp's reply to Sizemore's August 13, 1974 letter, entitled "Statement on Contracting" to the DCBOE, was dated August 14, 1974. His letter indicated that he thought personal differences between himself and the superintendent had been ironed out three months ago. He followed with a rebuttal which enumerated his concept of board actions that

had transpired and the superintendent's failure to
implement board action, the forming of the joint
committee, and their recommendation which leaves
the superintendent in control of the contracting
process. He further pointed out that the Friends'
contract had existed for about two years, and that
the board's policy on contracting services had been
to leave such matters to administration, mentioning
that Sizemore's administration had done its share
of sole source contracting. Kemp's third point was
that Hawthorne School was not a case of sole source
contracting. Kemp noted that Sizemore's administration had let $800,000.00 which she reprogrammed
from savings during FY74 for staff development and
other funds, making a total of $949,455.32. Of
that amount, he said $64,456.44 appeared to be to
sole source contractors, and $71,458.24 seemed to
have been bid on by one contractor. In addition,
Kemp posed questions which dealt with: the amount
of the $949,455.32 which was expended; the number
of participants served; the amount of control
exercised by the superintendent; future assurance
of more than one bidder; the expansion of potential
bidder listings until the system had developed an
"in-house" staff development capacity; the number
of contracts developed through the PACTS* process;
the investigating of Mediax, Howard or Antioch for
possible bidding lobbies opposed to the peoples'
control of education in the District of Columbia;
and the administration's evaluation of the contracts, which contracts are outside the power of
the people.[46]

### August 13, 1974 board meeting --

Meanwhile, a board of education meeting was
held the night of August 13, 1974, at which time
the joint committee on Educational Programs and
Student Services and Community Involvement, that
had been given the task of mediating the contracting of music services at the August 1, 1974 DCBOE

---

*Acronym for Parents, Administrators, Community, Teachers and Students.

meeting, presented several actions for adoption. Among these were the following: (1) that the superintendent's draft of the "Negotiated Services Contract" of August 1, 1974 be submitted to the board by August 19, 1974; (2) that the committee refer to the administration and to the School Finance Committee the problem of providing instrumental music instruction at the elementary level to schools not currently served by the regular music program or the DCYOP resource program and to identify funding to provide the service; (3) that the contract would have control established essentially along the lines as the present contract; and (4) that a policy for contractual relations be established which includes that only such services as our own capability does not possess be contracted to any agency, and that the bid process would be adhered to unless sole source can be identified as the agency which singularly possesses that capability.

Board members voting in favor of adopting the report were Evans, Kemp, Mason and Treanor; those opposed were Hobson, Morris and Simmons. Interestingly, item four, which was Simmon's motion, was referred to the Committee on Board Operation, Rules, Policies and Legislation, by a motion made by Rev. Kemp and seconded by Mrs. Mason. The Record of Official Action of the DCBOE reported that the vote by members was not recorded.[47]

A letter dated August 17, 1974 arrived in the superintendent's office signalling that Mr. Edward Maguire, attorney for the Friends, and Dr. James Johnson, of the DCPS, had negotiated a joint draft of a negotiated services contract for the superintendent's consideration and final approval.[48]

On August 19, 1974, Superintendent Sizemore sent a memorandum to the board of education on the subject of the DCYOP contract with an attached draft, dated August 17, 1974, of the proposed "Negotiated Services Contract" between the Friends of the D. C. Youth Orchestra Program, Inc. and the

District of Columbia public schools.[49]

Meanwhile, there transpired a dispute between the superintendent and the board president which revolved around the administration's draft of the contract and changes in the DCYOP contract suggested by David Splitt, general counsel to the board, which the administration felt were substantive rather than technical and therefore unacceptable to the administration. Subsequently, the contract was returned to the administration by the board president for Superintendent Sizemore to have included in the contract the recommendations contained in the general counsel's memorandum to the president of the board dated August 23, 1974. A memorandum to Virginia Morris from the superintendent dated August 30, 1974 emphasized that the board, in a "Report of the Joint Committee on Educational Programs and Student Services and Community Involvement" dated August 12, 1974, assigned the responsibility for the development of the contract to the superintendent of schools and authorized representatives of the "Friends" by August 19, 1974 and that the board did not instruct the superintendent to involve the board's staff in the negotiations. This letter also referred to a memorandum of August 22, 1974 to the superintendent's office from the president of the board on administrative requests to the general counsel, which stated that the general counsel had several other priority assignments to complete and that effective immediately all such requests should be directed to the executive secretary, who had responsibility for establishing board staff priorities. The memorandum followed with a notation that two requests for legal assistance sent by the superintendent to the board's general counsel were returned unanswered. Morris, in a September 4, 1974 memorandum to the superintendent, directed her to include Splitt's suggestions in a final draft of the contract and submit it to the board for final action. A follow-up memorandum from the superintendent to the board president, dated September 9, 1974, indicated that Splitt's references in his memorandum to the board president, dated August 23, 1974, appeared to be directed to the draft contract dated August 17, and not to the August 26, 1974 copy typed on the standard format of the Negotiated Services Contract Unit. Finally, a September 17, 1974 report of the joint committee on Educational Programs and Student Services and Community Involvement stated that the general counsel to the board of education presented two amended drafts of the DCYO contract, Draft A which contained the two modifications with which the administration concurred, and Draft B which contained all of the changes in contract language which the general counsel developed. The committee unanimously voted to accept Draft B. A note was included at the end of the report indicating that no objections were made by Hurlbut, Kimbrough and Margolies, who were present from the administration.[50]

While the matters previously discussed were transpiring, a number of related events took place. For one, the superintendent sent a reply dated August 23, 1974 to Kemp's letter dated August 14, 1974, which was a response to what he termed charges made in the superintendent's August 13, 1974 letter against him and three other board members. Superintendent Sizemore's letter stated that the cause of the problem associated with the spate of contracts is the lack of board policy. In addition, she supplied answers to Kemp's questions, item by item, indicating at the conclusion that the superintendent may request a reactive General Accounting Office audit of DCPS contracts and contracting procedures and an opinion of the corporation counsel about the legality and propriety of letting contracts to organizations and agencies with whom sitting board members have formal affiliations.[51]

Second, Sizemore sent a memorandum to Guines, dated September 3, 1974, requesting a report of the number of students who went to Scotland with the DCYOP and to Spokane with the D.C. Youth

Chorale, the number of Blacks, and the number out of the District. She also requested the cost of the trip.[52]

   Third, Guines' reply dated September 4, 1974 to the superintendent, informed her that 52 Blacks, 54 whites, 2 Orientals and 2 other students went to Scotland out of a total of 110 students, of which 76 were from the District, 27 from Maryland and 7 from Virginia. Students who went to Spokane with the D.C. Youth Chorale were all Black and all D.C. residents. The cost of the Spokane trip was approximately $42,264.80. In answer to the request regarding the cost of the Scotland trip, Guines reported that Mr. McLain refused to provide costs for the trip. Guines said that McLain indicated by telephone that private funds were used by a private organization and, consequently, the cost of the trip was none of their business.[53]

   Fourth, additional information was offered in regard to the DCYOP in a memorandum dated September 6, 1974. This information indicated that 76 D.C. residents, of which 54 attend D.C. public schools and 22 attend non-public schools, went to Scotland.[54]

   Also, on September 18, 1974, the superintendent forwarded another memorandum to the board of education regarding the "Negotiated Services Contract" containing an extensive report of decisions made by the board of education, and subsequent decisions made by the administration to implement board decisions. The superintendent's memorandum stated that the board's approval of the contract ends the controversy but leaves the conditions for the conflict unattended to because there still exists no board policy governing how, when, and why contracts will be let, and the purchase of alternative educational programs by outside organizations. She also wrote that continued inability to differentiate policy from administration and low priority given to developing system capability remain problems. In addition, Superintendent Sizemore

recorded that $4,499,367.21 was authorized for 114
Negotiated Services Contracts and of these 114 or
61.5 percent were competitive. She listed the
categories of the sole source contracts: seven,
dictated by Federal Grant terms; seven, continuing
programs previously advertised; 17, Manpower Training; and 13 others, totaling 44.

The memorandum further reiterated recommendations submitted by the superintendent on May 14,
1974, in a report on board-administrative relationships, regarding expectations of the superintendent
and the board of education, and the separating of
policy issues from administrative issues. Additional recommendations included, reporting out of the
committee on Student Services and Community Involvement, a report titled "Procedures for Alternative
Programs" submitted on June 11, 1974; developing
the capability to provide options for students
within the system; and establishing a policy for
contractual relations. Attached to this memorandum
was a D.C. Youth Orchestra Chronology beginning
July 19, 1972 with Superintendent Scott's involvement and ending September 9, 1974 as well as a
summary of contracts let.[55]

In a memorandum dated October 7, 1974, the
acting materiel management officer, D.C., required
of Superintendent Sizemore corrections for 8 deficiencies found in the "Proposed Negotiated Services
Contract."[56] A memorandum dated November 13, 1974
from the superintendent was sent to the board
entitled "Status Report on the D.C. Youth Orchestra
Contract." It informed them that the proposed
contract was returned to the administration for the
correction of deficiencies. Further, deficiencies
were corrected. The contract was returned to Mr.
Richard E. Wingate, acting materiel management
officer of the Department of General Services, and
finally mailed from his office to the Friends of
the DCYOP for signature on November 8, 1974. In
addition, the administration had been advised that
the proposed contract would be reviewed by the
corporation counsel on November 25, 1974. Attached
to this memorandum to the board was the memorandum

of October 7, 1974 from Mr. Wingate, acting materiel management officer.[57]

A memorandum dated December 19, 1974 from the president of the board of education to the superintendent inquired when the contract would be forwarded to the Friends.[58] Sizemore's reply, dated December 24, 1974, advised Morris that the administration had been informed that the DCYOP contract had been signed and sent by the Bureau of Materiel Management to the Friends of the DCYOP.[59]

There was a remarkable similarity to the responses of both Hobson and Morris to interview questions regarding why, in the final analysis, they switched their positions from opposing a renewal of the DCYOP contract to pressuring the superintendent to consummate the task. In this regard, Hobson said, "An example is the D.C. Youth Orchestra because we never had the votes to support Sizemore. It was very clear from the beginning.... The votes were never there and probably never will be there, in relation to change the funding, to change that contract around...."[60] In this same regard, Morris stated that:

> The D.C. Youth Orchestra controversy was a major problem because of the concerns based upon the children who were involved in that problem and the D.C. school system actually subsidizing it. That was a major concern of many board members including the superintendent.... [You supported the superintendent up until about June that the contract should not be renewed; then you no longer supported the superintendent. What happened?] The thing that I asked was simply this. Whatever you want this contract to say, write it. I was as concerned as she was, but I've always felt if you have a concern and you don't like what is being presented, then give your version of what it should be....[61]

Another view of the matter was presented by Mrs. Sizemore when she said in her interview that:

Mrs. Virginia Morris came on the board in December nineteen seventy-three because Mrs. Pryde became ill and had to leave. Mrs. Pryde had been one of my supporters and I lost her. In the beginning Mrs. Morris supported the programs which I had advanced in the <u>120 Day Report</u>, but she later changed her mind about supporting those programs in exchange for the presidency of the board. That was, she bargained...for the support of Mr. Barry and Mrs. Swaim and etcetera. The bargain was...as it was explained to me by another board member who did not want to be quoted as saying this, Mr. Tirana...was supporting one person. Mr. Rosenfield was supporting one person, and Mr. Barry was supporting a person. Then there was Mrs. Morris. And on the first vote Mrs. Morris did not get the vote but in the second vote she was voted in. Later when Mrs. Swaim and Mr. Barry and Mr. Rosenfield were going to leave the board, Mr. Barry and Mrs. Swaim made a deal with Mrs. Morris that Mrs. Swaim would resign her office as vice president prior to her leaving the board and that they would support Mrs. Morris for that vice presidency providing Mrs. Morris would support the Hawthorne School and the D.C. Youth Orchestra after they left and providing that she would force my compliance with those programs, so they left. So that was the deal that was made for Mrs. Morris to be president.

At any rate, Mrs. Morris became the board president and from that period she found it difficult to support any of the programs that I suggested....[62]

The contract with the DCYOP was finally consummated but this implementation of a board policy did not end the conflict in superintendent-school board relations. The General Counsel dispute which grew out of the DCYOP controversy is presented next.

## Case Two: The General Counsel Dispute

### Introduction

The dispute surrounding the position of general counsel to the DCBOE grew out of the DCYOP case and exploded into prominence during that same general period of time. It, too, helped to erode the relationship between the superintendent and some school board members. And, although neither of the two issues -- the DCYOP and the General Counsel Dispute -- evolved into charges for the termination of Superintendent Sizemore's contract, they certainly were precipitating factors for the antagonistic feelings that subsequently existed. As a matter of fact, though, evidence of the General Counsel Dispute was noted in the exhibits presented by Attorney DeLong Harris to refute charge Number 13 -- Failure to Comply with Board Directive to Provide Fiscal Year 1975 Legislative Proposal.

### The problem

It appears that a basic problem existed in the position description submitted to the District of Columbia government signed by Martha S. Swaim on May 31, 1974 for the position of special assistant.

First of all the description submitted for a special assistant, D.C. board of education, later changed to general counsel, explicitly states on page one that the incumbent serves as special assistant to the D.C. board of education, under the general direction of the president of the board. Note that this put the person out of the supervisory realm of the superintendent.

Secondly, on that same page in paragraph two, the description says that the person "receives assignments directly from the President of the Board who provides extremely general supervision in the form of consultations on special assignments," which reiterates the point that the superintendent had no control over assignments.

Third, on page two of that same document in paragraph one, the first sentence reads: "On behalf of the Board of Education, incumbent coordinates efforts within and for the D.C. Public School System in pursuit of its legislative goals," which again indicates quite clearly that this is a direct function of the board of education through the efforts of the special assistant to the D.C. board of education and not a matter directed by the superintendent nor within the realm of administration although up until this time the coordinating function had been handled by the superintendent through the administrative staff. As the reader will see later, this coordinating function was considered to be a part of administration. Therefore, it was transferred to the state office when it was established.

Fourth, problems also arose due to the interpretation of paragraph five on page 3 which reads:

> Incumbent is responsible for the overall management, supervision, and development of all special legislative projects involved in the Board's innovative planning. In developing proposals, incumbent is designated as principal liaison officer between the Board and the school administration and is relied upon for effective and diplomatic synthesizing of differing approaches toward the result of achieving creative and desirable solutions.

One normal interpretation of the above paragraph must lead one to believe that the administration could contact directly the special assistant (general counsel) for assistance in legal (legislative) matters. Later discourse will dispel this notion through the board president's different interpretation of the paragraph.

And fifth, the first paragraph on page 4 which reads: "In addition, is responsible for coordinating work with the D.C. Corporation Counsel by screening requests for advisory opinions," also led to conflicts in superintendent-school board relations as will be revealed.[63]

At the December 19, 1973 meeting of the DCBOE, the ad hoc committee on Internal Board Staff recommended the appointment of Mr. David A. Splitt, white, to the position of special assistant to the board of education after conducting final interviews with the two candidates for the position, namely Splitt and Mr. Claude Roxborough, Black. Additionally, the committee recommended a GS-14 as a salary placement. During the discussion of the recommendation, it was revealed that Splitt was a lawyer and a member of the D.C. Bar and therefore perhaps could be of assistance to the administration as well. Those board members voting in favor of the recommendation were Coates, Tirana, Washington, Swaim, Mason, Taylor and Barry; Cassell was opposed; and Kemp abstained.[64]

## Sequence of events

At the January 2, 1974 board of education meeting, approval was given to the following recommendation of the committee on Curriculum, Special Education, and Education Planning, "That the Board approve as administrative policy that in the future all matters relating to school system business involving contact with the Corporation Counsel and his office be screened and coordinated by the counsel of the Board; including requests for legal opinions and matters involving litigation."[65]

On May 13, 1974, a memorandum entitled "Referral of Document 'Duties of the General Counsel to the Board of Education,'" was sent to the committee on Board Operations, Rules and Policies consisting of Treanor as chairman, Swaim, and Taylor, from Dwight S. Cropp, executive secretary of the D.C. board of education. Attached to the memorandum was a document which indicated that the superintendent in a letter dated April 17, 1974 requested a clarification of the action taken by the board on January 21, 1974, modifying the board Rules, Chapter 1, Part 1, Section 1.8, to provide for screening and coordination of school system business with the corporation counsel through the general counsel to the board.[66]

In a May 15, 1974 memorandum to the board of education from the superintendent, she explained that she had increasing need for legal counsel. Therefore, she again asked for a clarification of the role of the general counsel to the board as it related to assisting the office of the superintendent in obtaining essential legal services. Further, Mrs. Sizemore requested that the board determine the source of authority, weight, and effect of legal advisory opinions to the board and the superintendent. Lastly, she asked that the board advise her if she was restricted from requesting the corporation counsel, D.C., to give her advisory opinions.[67]

In a September 19, 1974 memorandum to the board president, Mrs. Sizemore emphasized that she and the administrative staff would communicate directly with the corporation counsel when legal advice was required since the procedure laid down by the board president, i.e., to submit requests to the executive secretary for prioritizing before submitting to the board's general counsel, was an obstruction to efficient day-to-day administrative operations. Furthermore, she said that she would interpret failure on the part of the board to act on administrative recommendations, necessary for the day-to-day operations of the school, in a timely and expedient manner as concurrence. Therefore, the administration would proceed to implement recommendations not in conflict with existing board policy after 45 days. Additionally, Mrs. Sizemore indicated that she and the administrative staff would no longer honor requests by individual board members except those matters submitted in a manner consistent with the language of the superintendent's contract since the practice diverts talent, time and skill from activity which could become a positive contribution to the educational program of the students.68

In the follow-up memorandum dated October 3, 1974 to the board of education of the District of Columbia from the superintendent of schools regarding the 1975 Legislative Program, the superintendent indicated that:

> In recognition of the broader concerns involved in the total legislative needs of the D.C. Public Schools the Superintendent has requested Mr. Vincent E. Reed, Acting Associate Superintendent for State Administration and Chairman of the Standing Committee on Legislation, to develop a plan and a process...to commence and maintain effective legislative liaison with Key Committees of the Congress.69

Reaction to this direction for the development of the 1975 Legislative Programs was immediately forthcoming from the DCBOE. Thus, part of the discussion at the October 16, 1974 meeting as regards the general counsel revolved around who would handle the 1975 Legislative Program -- the general counsel or the State Office personnel of the administration? The dispute had to do with the report entitled "Procedures for Legislative Operations," Item "b" under Section III, "Developing the Legislative Program." Superintendent Sizemore's reaction to the section indicated that the administration felt put upon to do the detailed work only to have the general counsel and the board committee on Board Operations, Rules and Regulations mess it up. In indicating this, she was referring to the part which said that, "The legislative background/goal package is referred to the Board Committee on Board Operations, Rules & Policies for review. The Board Counsel provides drafting assistance and counsel to the Board Committee." In relation to this point, the superintendent referred to the DCYOP contract when she stated:

Now if this is going to be the procedure for the Board to follow, then it should be clear that the administration has no responsibility for assuming the consequences of such action as was in the case of the D.C. Youth Orchestra Contract, which was returned to us on October 15th and which we sent to the Board on October 15th to indicate to you that the things we objected to in the document of September the 9th and which were overruled in favor of the General Counsel are now being resubmitted to the administration to redo.

Additionally, the superintendent voiced objection to the recommended role proposed by the general counsel for his office and for the board as compared with the responsibilities listed for Mr. Vincent Reed (State Office), in that they provide for duplication of effort. At this point, she also asserted that the problem with the clarification of the role of the general counsel was still outstanding and that the board had not resolved it.

Mr. Treanor retorted that the superintendent had asked the board to decide and the committee decided that the responsibilities as listed would be handled by the general counsel of the board of education. The superintendent interjected that the issue had to do with where the responsibility for decision-making about what is educationally sound lie in this system. She wondered aloud whether or not it was with the superintendent or with the general counsel. She stated that her concern was that it be a matter of public record so that she did not have to take the consequences for those decisions.

Continued discussion occurred, but the main issue voted upon was the deletion in the report of Item "b" under Section III, referred to on page number 3. Those in favor of the motion to delete were Morris, Simmons, Evans, and Hobson. Those opposed were Treanor, Kemp and Mason. After this vote was taken, the same four voted in favor of accepting the remainder of the report with Treanor and Kemp opposed and Mason abstaining.[70]

Finally, in a March 19, 1975 memorandum to the citizens, Virginia Morris presented a statement on the role of the general counsel to the board of education. The memorandum indicated that the need for this act on her part had to do with what appeared to be a growing controversy in the school system over the role of the general counsel. Thus the communication read, in part:

> The Board, in anticipation of Congressional approval of its request for an independent General Counsel, has appointed Mr. David Splitt to the position of Special Assistant (General Counsel) to the D.C. Board of Education.
>
> Mr. Splitt serves under the general direction of the Executive Secretary to the Board, and he is expected to coordinate his efforts very closely with those of the School Administration....
>
> There should be no confusion on the part of any members of the D.C. Public Schools community concerning the role of the General Counsel to the Board. The General Counsel is a member of the Board staff who has specific legal and legislative responsibilities. He is not expected to administer any educational programs nor directly supervise the implementation of Board policy in the schools. The Superintendent is the Board's Chief Executive Officer. There should be no doubt in anyone's mind that no one has been interposed between the Superintendent and the Board. The Superintendent is a non-voting member of the Board of Education and the chief administrator of this school system. The General Counsel is here to assist the Board and the Superintendent in those specific areas listed above.[71]

The general counsel's service under the general direction of the board's executive secretary really removes him from under the authority of the superintendent. Thus, the superintendent had no legal counsel to advise the administration on such recurring matters as the Waddy Decree (special education) or the Wright Decree (<u>Hobson v Hansen</u>) or suits against the administration. Without free access to legal counsel, the superintendent was hampered in her efforts to efficiently and effectively operate the school system.

Although the general counsel dispute subsided, it was not forgotten and surfaced again in Charge Number 13.

<u>Case Three: Budgetary/Management Problems</u>

<u>Introduction</u>

<u>Philosophy</u> --

The educational philosophy of the DCPS system during Mrs. Sizemore's administration was the following:

> Our public school system must be designed so that educational justice is afforded each child irrespective of ethnic, social, or economic background, irrespective of physical and/or emotional, and/or intellectual handicaps. Every child must be provided equal access to learning situations which build and/or enhance the unique talents, cultures, and languages which he or she brings.
>
> In order to accomplish this, we need a multi-age, multi-level kind of grouping practice, vigorously pursued by those knowledgeable in human growth and development, so that we can begin to accommodate the massive differences in rates of growth and patterns of development which occur in human beings.[72]

Organization --

There were 15 divisions or departments in the school system in 1970-71: (1) Instruction, (2) Elementary, (3) Secondary, (4) Vocational, (5) Special, (6) Adult, (7) Pupil Personnel, (8) Personnel, (9) Staff Development, (10) Administrative Services, (11) Business Administration, (12) Buildings and Grounds, (13) Planning, Research and Evaluation, (14) Budget and Legislation, and (15) Federal Programs. Each was headed by an assistant or associate superintendent or a director. A change was made in the organization of the system in 1973. There were two divisions: the Office of Educational Services and the Office of Management Services. Each was headed by a deputy superintendent. The office of Educational Services was divided into the following divisions or departments: (1) Instructional services, (2) Elementary, (3) Secondary, (4) Model Schools Division, (5) Pupil Personnel Services, (6) Special Education, and (7) Career Development. The Office of Management Services was divided into 8 divisions: (1) Logistical Support, (2) Budget, (3) Finance, (4) Data Automated Information Services (DAIS), (5) Personnel, (6) Buildings and Grounds, (7) Federal Programs, and (8) Employee-Employer Relations (see figure 5).

In an effort to flatten the hierarchy in line with a board mandate to decentralize, Superintendent Sizemore proposed to abolish the office of vice superintendent and the two offices of deputy superintendent.

The 1974 proposal to reorganize the central office was never approved by the board. That organizational plan incorporated the concept of an administrative team consisting of the heads of 8 offices: (1) Regional Administrations, (2) State Office, (3) Bilingual Education, (4) Management Services, (5) Communications and Community Relations, (6) Planning, Development Research and Evaluation, (7) Labor Relations, and (8) Student Development Services. The superintendent and her three executive assistants were to be included on the team, made up of executive or cabinet level staff.[73]

Management --

In her letter of resignation of May 31, 1974, Martha Swaim stated that the D.C. schools' history of poor management began after World War II. From that point on she said, increases in size and complexity contributed to the management problem.[74]

As pointed out by Mr. James Williams, deputy superintendent of management, in his report on the reorganization of management services, the area of management of the DCPS had been given significant attention in a number of other reports. Some were made of the District government, others of the school system. These reports include: The Passow Report, 1967; the Executive Study Group Report, 1969; the Nelsen Commission Report, 1971; the Management Review Report, 1971; and the Price-Waterhouse Report, 1972.

The Passow Report, conducted at the invitation of Superintendent Hansen and the DCBOE in school year 1965-66 and issued in May 1966, was a comprehensive study of the public schools. Its recommendations which had significance for the areas of management included: (1) updating personnel procedures; (2) improving teacher recruitment, selection and retention; (3) separating certification from employment; (4) reorganization of the central office; and (5) creating the position of executive deputy superintendent of schools for management.

The Executive Study Group Report, issued in 1969, was a review of the recommendations of the Passow Report and it stressed the need to implement the recommendations of that report.

The Nelsen Commission Report was a review of the operation of the entire District government. As such, it included recommendations for the improvement of the management functions of the school system. Among these recommendations were included:

    1. The establishment of a position of deputy superintendent of business management to administer all personnel, finance, business management, administrative services, general support, and internal security activities;

    2. The establishment of a position of comptroller under the deputy superintendent for business management;

    3. The establishment of the office of Federal Programs;

    4. The establishment of the office of Audit and Investigations;

    5. A revision of the activity structure of the schools' budget to reflect the resources invested in each teaching activity;

    6. The development of a timetable for the preparation of the FY74 budget that will permit more meaningful participation and deliberation in the budget formulation process and still meet the mayor-commissioner's deadlines for the submission of budget requests;

    7. Develop and institute an effective position control system; and

    8. Establish an office of Safety Management in the personnel department.

    The <u>Management Review Report</u>, issued in 1971, was cooperatively arranged and conducted by the U.S. Office of Education and the District of Columbia public schools to strengthen the management of federally supported programs.

    The <u>Price-Waterhouse Report</u> was sponsored by the Washington Board of Trade and commissioned by the DCBOE to study the management support systems of the public schools. The report issued in 1972 contained major recommendations for structuring an effective management apparatus. Included among the recommendations were:

1. The establishment of an office of deputy superintendent for management;

2. Implementation of an automated control system;

3. Establishment of a financial reporting unit, and various control procedures; and

4. Centralization of preparation for processing personnel action forms.

All of the reports recommended many other procedures for more effective management of the school system. The various studies resulted in some movement in improving management services, including: (1) establishment of the office of deputy superintendent of management; and (2) establishment of the divisions of Automated Information Systems, Budget, Buildings and Grounds, Employee-Employer Relations, Finance, Federal Programs, Logistical Support, and Personnel. A program budget structure was developed to reflect subject areas of instruction. A tentative personnel control system to provide total personnel accounting was designed and partially operational. Further, computerization of the base budget and automation of an allotment system is operating, making available financial accounting data in the area of obligations and disbursements, payroll and status of appropriations.

In spite of the achievements made in the management areas listed above, Mr. James Williams, deputy superintendent of management for the DCPS, felt that the level of management was still at a minimum acceptable level. He stressed in his report that the efficiency of the unit was directly related to the resources provided.75

Budget --

The budget process is long and complicated. A brief description of the process and the problems involved will lay the groundwork for understanding subsequent discussions about the budget.

The fiscal year began on July 1, and ended on June 30 until 1975, while the school year began September 1 and ended August 31. This caused the DCPS and other District agencies to operate on a continuing appropriation which led to financial problems each year.

In the summer of each year, the mayor announced his budget mark (ceiling) for the school budget. He issued the budget call for October 1. Then the budget plan was made for use two years hence.

In 1971 a local school budgeting process was approved. The budget committee set up in the elementary and junior high school was to have the principal or his assistant, two teachers and four community members to be selected by board members representing the wards. Community members for city-wide schools would be selected by at-large board members. Senior and vocational high schools would have, in addition, two students elected by the student government. Available school resources would be identified by these school committees who would then decide on necessary additional resources. The budget proposals of the local committees would be reviewed by review committees in light of the total budget. From these submissions, the budget department would make the superintendent's budget which was submitted to the D.C. board of education.

After the board approved the budget, it was submitted by the board to the mayor, who, after approval, submitted it to the D.C. city council, who, when the budget was approved, included it in

the city budget for submission to the President of
the United States.

Revisions in the city budget were made by the
office of management and budget and submitted to the
Congress to be considered and approved by the House
of Representatives and submitted to the Senate.
After receiving approval from the Senate, the city
budget was submitted to the Joint Senate-House
Conference Committee. Then it was submitted, after
approval, to both houses of Congress for final
approval and subsequently to the President of the
United States for signature or veto.

The 10 line-items for which dollars are allocated in the regular public school budget refer to
the following program categories: (1) elementary
education; (2) junior high education; (3) senior
high education; (4) career development; (5) special
education; (6) continuing education; (7) food services; (8) facilities; (9) instructional support;
and (10) central services and management. The two
ways of changing the expenditure pattern once
approved by the Congress are (1) redirection for a
permanent change, and (2) reprogramming for a temporary change. No change can be made above
$25,000.00 unless it is submitted to the city
council and the Congress for approval.

Personnel --

Personnel control has a direct connection to
school-by-school budget in that specific sums of
money are allocated to each school based on its
anticipated enrollment and therefore need for
teachers. In a sense, schools purchase positions
according to the amount of funds they receive, a
procedure mandated by board action. This procedure
made the full organization of school units unknown
until school units fully identified the amount of
services it purchased from its dollar allocation.

A significant factor in the financial difficulties of the school system was that 85 percent of

the school system's budget was in salaries. Therefore, major budgetary problems were precipitated by the lack of a personnel control system.

The Department of Automated Information Services (DAIS) developed an automated personnel accounting system for the school system in July 1970, which was only used to develop a general personnel data bank. Since 1973, the automated system has been used only to record personnel data fed to it by copies of personnel actions processed through the Department of Personnel. It is therefore an informational file representing employment and distribution of personnel.

This personnel accounting system is not a control system. It does not include a systems process to establish and confirm authorized positions. It does not control the entry of data onto the payroll.

In 1974, the only record of position information was a separate data file, maintained by the budget division, which coded and recorded positions as they appeared in the operating budget. This data file included positions in the general fund, impact aid, and indirect cost. It did not include the additional positions in other federal grants. This information was maintained in non-automated files. This position data file carried positions by total quantity only, but not the location of the position. For example, the total number of junior high school English teachers, but not their distribution among the junior high schools. In other words, the file system was only able to report on information gathered after the fact: (1) the budget has authorized the total number of positions; and (2) the positions have been distributed.

Consequently, the position file and the personnel accounting file could not be linked together. Therefore, if the personnel file contained more positions than authorized, a line-by-line comparison could not be made to determine what positions in the file were unauthorized.[77]

Undoubtedly, the budget is the key to a statement of school plans, for when the board of education approves the budget, it makes decisions on what the goals of the system are as evidenced in the programs it supports.

A persistently recurring problem, which carried over from the Hugh Scott era, was the budget. This problem certainly had an influence on all educational program, personnel and management decisions made by the school board and the superintendent. Therefore, in examining the budget situation, we will look closely at some aspects of it, and at several other related issues that fell under the rubric of management, which emerged in the conflict between Superintendent Sizemore and the school board majority in terms of policy decision-making and implementation. Included here, then, are the following issues: (1) administration reorganization controversy; (2) decentralization dispute; (3) opening of schools problem; (4) teacher payroll problems; (5) mayor's freeze; (6) overhiring/budget deficit; (7) Hobson Task Force dispute; (8) FY76 budget/FY75 financial plan; and (9) Title I Comparability/Wright Decree which occurred between May 1974 through December 1974. Many of these issues later meshed with some of the charges drawn up against the superintendent in connection with the adverse action taken, such as (1) personnel hiring controls, (2) timely annual reports, (3) administrative committee on Non-Personnel Expenditures, (4) questions on FY75 financial plan, (5) status report on expenditures, (6) quarterly financial reports, (7) quarterly personnel reports, (8) declining enrollment, (9) Federal grants proposals, (10) equalization plans, and (11) director of building and grounds.

### The Problem

As could be noted from the discussion about the financial crisis of 1972 (see Chapter III), which focused the attention of the community at-large on the school system's finances, the schools suffered from unauthorized and non-productive positions, duplication in supervisory functions, past and potential deficits, and budget cuts. Furthermore, there were increases in teacher salaries and increases in other costs due to inflation which were not covered by concommitant increases in appropriations. In this connection, Congress had ordered that a part of each pay raise was to be absorbed in the base budget, and the mayor had required that inflationary costs also be absorbed. In order to meet these increased costs, the school administration and the board in June 1971 indicated that it would eliminate 811 positions, some of which were never reduced, creating a projected deficit, according to reports.

Over-laid on this problem was the mayor's order in 1971 for a city-wide reduction in positions of five percent in response to a White House economy order which required a reduction of 154 additional positions in FY72 and 59 in FY73. Additionally, the Appropriations Bill for 1973 passed by Congress gave the schools over $2 million for special education, without increasing the total appropriation by that amount, therefore indicating that new positions for special education had to be balanced by a cut in other positions.

Thus, in summarizing the required cuts, the following was noted:

$152.2 million was requested, FY73
$146.5 million was appropriated, FY73
$142.9 million was the operating budget, FY72

Of the $9.1 million increase requested, $6 million was for mandatories, that is, within-grade salary increases, staffing of new buildings, and increases in non-personnel costs. Therefore, an immediate deficit of $6 million for FY73 was precipitated when Congress gave only a $3.6 million increase over the 1972 appropriation. Buttressing this problem was the position ceiling imposed by the mayor (five percent reduction in positions) necessitating a cut of 333 positions -- namely 154 for FY72, 59 for 1973 and 120 in new special educational positions.

Basically, subsequent events occurred in the following sequence:

- The 811 position cuts were made in teacher positions in January 1972.

- The administration presented the 1973 budget request to the board showing the 154 position economy cuts primarily in teacher positions.

- The new board that took office in January 1972 faced the problem of avoiding a $5 million deficit in the fiscal year ending June 30, 1972.

- At the same time, it was required to present to the city council and Congress a 1974 budget.

- The city council refused to consider the board's request for $155 million for 1973.

- It, therefore, sent up to the mayor a budget figure of $146.7 million.

- In seeking to get a larger amount from Congress, the board suffered a further cut when the increase in special education funds was honored without an increase in total funds.

- The 1972 deficit was resolved in April 1973.

- Thus, the board, through Martha Swaim, chairperson of the Budget and Financial Committee, made an independent study of the budget in an effort, it said, to cut with least harm at the classroom level.

- Cuts totalling 137 positions and over $2 million were made in central instructional and administrative staff positions.

- Elementary teacher cuts totalled 137, 87 of which were in special teacher positions (instrumental music, special reading teachers).

- The major cuts made in secondary education were 50 physical education teachers, 13 military science teachers, and five junior high home economics teachers.

- On July 19, the superintendent submitted to the board a recommended budget level for 1974 of $165 million, based on the 1973 base of $146.5, mandatory increases of $7.5 million including the projected teacher pay raise, and $11 million under the category "New and Improved Services."[78]

Arguments ensued between the board, Superintendent Scott and concerned citizens over the cuts made in the regular school program while an increase of funds was provided for such alternative education programs as the D.C. Youth Orchestra Program, covered previously in this chapter.

## Sequence of events

Obviously, the new superintendent, Barbara Sizemore, inherited a critical budget and management problem when she took office on October 1, 1973, involving problems attended upon two teachers' pay raises and substantial increases in the costs of utilities, supplies, food, equipment, etc., a greatly expanded special education program, ordered by Congress without the addition of new money, economy cuts imposed by the mayor, and the uncertainties surrounding the financial assistance provided by Impact Aid and other federal grant funds and special revenue sharing. Additionally, the superintendent faced a drastically slashed central administration staff to help her manage the system. Joining these problems was the immediacy of presenting a budget to the city administration and the Congress.

## September 5, 1973 special board meeting --

At the September 5, 1973 special meeting of the DCBOE, at which time Acting Superintendent Floretta McKenzie was in office, Edward Winner, the budget director, presented the FY75 Budget Call from the mayor of $163.1 million which represented a reduction of over $11 million from the present level of service. In reaction to the report and what he had read in the newspapers, Rosenfield offered his services to the board budget committee and the administration to sit down with the mayor and discuss their fiscal problems. He stated that his position in the private sector required him to handle a great deal of money so he was atuned to budgetary fiscal problems. Actually, Rosenfield was suggesting that the board engage in some lobbying as other organizations do to achieve some of their goals. President Barry disagreed with this stragegy and a confrontation developed. Into this dialogue Mr. Cassell threw in the power and authority factor.

In his discussion, Cassell focused on the fact that the mayor's memorandum on the budget call was addressed to the head of all agencies whom he appoints and instructs. In this case, the mayor instructed his agency heads to make certain modifications in their budgets, and they had to respond. According to Cassell's interpretation, the DCBOE, an elected body, was not an agency of the government and, therefore, did not have to take instructions from the mayor. Further, he felt that the board of education had control of the public school system and should no longer yield to the mayor's budget process in that elected officials had a little more power than that. Therefore, he suggested that the DCBOE decide on the needs of the system, cost them out, and send the budget to the mayor with instructions that the board expected him to submit their budget to Congress intact.

In opposition to Cassell's approach, Rosenfield said: "When we talk about 'we control the system' how can we control the system when we don't control the dollars? What is control? Who pays for the cost? Where do we get the money?" Despite the agitation between Barry, Cassell, and Rosenfield, the budget discussion ended on a high note with Cassell commenting that he agreed with Barry's concluding point of organizing around strategies to implement the will of the board of education and the community.[79]

October 25, 1973 special board meeting --

On October 25, 1973, at another special meeting of the DCBOE, the report of the committee on Budget and Finance was presented by Mrs. Swaim, chairperson of that committee. The committee recommended approval of the administration's proposed budget of $185,933,400.00 for FY75. The schedule of public hearings on the budget were tentatively scheduled for November 8 and November 12, at 7:30 p.m., for the purpose of discussing the budget. Before approving the report, a discussion ensued wherein Reverend Raymond Kemp queried Superintendent Sizemore as to whether or not the administration was satisfied that there were sufficient funds to institute decentralization proposals. She replied that the proposed plan would use the available resources for four districts with the other districts phased in the following year. After board members were satisfied with replies by the superintendent and Mr. Winner to several other questions, the motion to approve the recommendations of the committee was put and carried unanimously.[80]

In April 1974, a public statement was issued by the D.C. Citizens for Better Public Education, Inc., through its organization's organ entitled Bulletin Board. It provided a succinct statement of the D.C. school budget for FY75 which included the following information. The budget request of $177.4 million was an increase of $9.6 million over the current year's funds; one-half of which was for mandatories and $4.4 million for new and improved services. The school system's budget was 20.1 percent of the total city budget, a decline from 24 percent for 1971 and 20.3 percent for 1974. The projected enrollment drop was about 7,000, primarily in the elementary schools, with a projected enrollment for the following year of 125,700 down from the 1970 enrollment figure of 149,656. The implications here were that as the budget total increased and the enrollment dropped, the per pupil expenditure increased. Thus problems were created since the city budget officials and Congress used pupil expenditures as the gauge to determine the funds the schools would receive.

Mandatory increases of $5.1 million were required to annualize the cost of new positions, to pay within grade increases for current staff, and to staff new facilities.

New and improved services included positions and services shifted from Impact Aid, Emergency Employment and other funds such as community aides in the secondary schools, the Adult Education Demonstration Center, and administrative positions in budget and accounting. Also, increases included special education positions and regional learning centers, building maintenance, staff development and staff for decentralization.

The Capital Outlay request was for $41.7 million.

Significant also is the fact that the D.C. Citizens complimented the school system for the enormous progress made since the crisis year of 1972 in presenting a credible and readable budget and <u>Supplementary Data Book</u> which for the first time provided school finance information in a program format which showed such things as the amount of funds needed to teach mathematics at each level, for counseling services, and for training custodians. Clearly noted also was the fact that the 1975 budget had not as yet been recast to fit the superintendent's program.[81]

In an August 23, 1974 memorandum to Virginia Morris, president, DCBOE, from Sizemore, she responded to questions raised by Morris relating to: (1) the opening of school and (2) local school budgeting. With respect to whether the schools would open on September 5, Sizemore replied that she believed the schools would open on time and indicated efforts were being put forth by regional superintendents, personnel in the warehouse, and those involved in teacher transfers and filling of vacant positions. Mrs. Sizemore also recalled that there were five principalship vacancies and that the division of Personnel had been instructed to follow through on the procedures to fill the vacancies.

The information on local school budgeting was also explained in some detail.[82]

A September 6, 1974 Washington Star news article helped to puncture the at least surface calm which existed at this time by headlining its story on school openings, "Delay in School Openings is News to Sizemore." The story stated that two elementary schools did not open on September 5, 1975 and this delay caught the superintendent's office by surprise. The situation was clarified later in the article by explaining that Birney Elementary would open the following Monday and that the new open space Brookland Elementary would observe a staggered opening schedule according to school policy. Nonetheless, the headline was damaging and appeared to be an effort to cause the public to lose faith in the superintendent.[83]

In a memorandum dated September 4, 1974 regarding 1976 budget proposals, it was obvious that the superintendent was initiating plans for this phase of the operation. The memorandum addressed to the executive staff requested that each member of the staff provide by September 13, 1974 a program/budget statement. Among the items of concern listed was the matter of how to re-direct monies for new thrusts as, for instance, change the $151,000.00 now budgeted for DCYOP to instructional music, for supplies and equipment for regional offices, set up as a part of the decentralization into six regions on July 1, 1974, and for supplies and equipment for the High School of Performing Arts.[84]

On September 10, 1974, the superintendent sent a 9 page letter to president of the board, Morris, in response to her 16 questions concerning FY75 Congressional Budget Reports, dated August 28, 1974, in regard to educational programs, capital outlay, management, student services, and teacher salary increases. A specific question which was to come up later as a charge in the adverse action taken by the board against the superintendent was as follows:

EDUCATIONAL PROGRAMS - Continued

QUESTION #5

The Senate Report indicates that the declining enrollment will release $2.3 million in FY 1975 to fund improved and innovative programs. Do you agree with this statement? If not, will a response be forwarded to the Board and Committee?

RESPONSE

In the testimony before the Congressional Committee, I indicated that approximately $2.3 million would be released due to declining enrollment and that the $2.3 million would fund approximately 161 positions that would be used in implementation of new and innovative programs for FY 1975. I agree with the statement in the Senate Report.[85]

Later, it will be seen that this response was unacceptable to the president of the board. At this point letters and memoranda from some board members posing questions of this comprehensive a nature began to bombard the superintendent and her administrative staff.

September 30, 1974 --

On September 30, 1974, Mr. James Williams, deputy superintendent, sent a memorandum to Mrs. Sizemore regarding the FY75 financial plan to which he attached a copy of the Mayor-Commissioner's Memorandum #74-139. In this memorandum, Williams explained that the financial plan was a budget document which was developed from the appropriation by Congress of general operating funds for the fiscal year which was broken down into a plan of expenditure by object and month allowing the City Accounting Office to measure the school system's rates of expenditure against the plan of expenditures as the fiscal year unfolded. Specific restrictions were referred to such as $16,000.00 for out-of-city travel, $3,000.00 for the office of the board of education, $13,000.00 for the superintendent's office, under Williams, and partial pay increases granted for Wage Board employees. Only the Teacher's Retirement Fund and a small portion of utility costs, it was explained, were chargeable to revenue sharing. Furthermore, he continued, there was a ceiling established by the Congress restricting the total number of permanent and temporary positions. Authority to reprogram was restricted below the $25,000.00 which could be used in previous years with an added restriction that no personnel funds could be reprogrammed without the prior approval of the city.[86]

Mrs. Sizemore's second year as superintendent of the DCPS system was to begin on October 1, 1974. Appropriately then, a special meeting was called on September 30, 1974, at which time the superintendent was instructed to brief the board members and the public on the status of the school system and the FY75 budget and program plan.

In the preamble to her report, Mrs. Sizemore noted that her first year had been challenging and rewarding as well as frustrating and disappointing. The challenge lay in the opportunity to construct a model urban educational system to educate minorities and the poor and the rewards lay in the response of teacher, parent, administrator, citizen and student excitement about the strategies of multi-lingual, multi-cultural, and multi-modal structures. Frustration lay in the obstacles preventing rapid change created by federal agency rules and regulations which prevented flexibility and impeded adaptation in terms of facilitating human growth and development and the rapid discovery of new knowledge to solve problems which prevented the implementation of new approaches. She pointed out that just as a research department was needed by the medical profession, so, too, was there a need for one by the school system and the FY75 budget allowed for inadequate funding to staff the office of Planning, Research, and Evaluation.

Mrs. Sizemore recalled that during the 11 hour interview for the superintendency, in which three members of the present board participated, decentralization and change in the classroom situation were emphasized. Thus, she was impelled to make something happen during her first year. This she did on July 1, 1974, by decentralizing the school system into six regions; and in September by opening the High School of the Arts, the Six Small Schools and Brookland Elementary School, an open space school. Subsequently, this making things happen by sheer will created conflict between board priorities and administrative goals; funds for the DCYOP were designated to help create the High School of the Arts but the board's priority was to continue the DCYOP; and the alternative school programs, which were not subject to federal rules and regulations binding on public school teachers and administrators, were continued by the board. In this case again, rules were not changed and money was given away. Thus, the administration was asked to seek funds for new ideas without changing anything.

Mrs. Sizemore called attention to the fact that study and new knowledge were needed to solve the problems in management services, special education, tenure, and equalization. Continuing, the superintendent stressed that when the board approved the 120 Day Report, it also approved the concept that people have different talents and deficiencies and grow at different rates and according to different patterns. Thus, education must change to accommodate these differences from the traditional way of education according to similarities, using the norm as the criterion. Hence, to accomplish the goals and objectives, to create new structures to keep the approximately half of the children who fall through the cracks from doing so, greater cooperation and effort were needed in the ensuing year.

Following this preamble, Mrs. Sizemore dealt with: (1) problems related to building conditions as they affected school openings; (2) special education; and (3) relocation of TMR (Trainable Mentally Retarded) Career Development Program at Brookland. In the case of delayed openings in Birney and Brookland, referred to earlier in Diane Brockett's Washington Star news article entitled "Delay in School Openings is News to Sizemore," Mrs. Sizemore explained that under regional decentralization, regional superintendents exercise authority over their schools. In the case of Birney and Brookland, the regional superintendents approved the delayed openings for staff development purposes without notifying or consulting the superintendent because they considered that the action was within their prerogative.

Later in the meeting, the superintendent presented a report on the reorganization of the central office which spoke to what the school would be like under decentralization, what would be left in the central office, what the responsibilities of the people would be, and where the old functions that use to be in the Elementary,

Secondary, Model School Division and the Anacostia Division would now be located. The report, titled "Reorganization of Central Office" noted that:

- On July 1, 1974, the six regions created marked the beginning of decentralization, one of the changes described in the superintendent's 120 Day Report, which would bring about most of the other changes in terms of smaller, more manageable units responsive to the needs and characteristics of each student and allow for effective channels of communication and working relationships between school people, citizens and students.

- Total system-wide decentralization was to become operational in four phases:
  1. Physical decentralization
  2. Twelve regions
  3. Delegation of administrative authority to regions
  4. Delegation of policy-making authority to regions.

- The FY75 budget request of $173,500.00 for decentralization was denied by Congress so additional staffing for two regions was requested since existing positions in Anacostia Division, Model Schools Division, Elementary Office, Secondary Office and The Spingarn Instructional Unit were to be used to staff the other four regions.

- Administratively, the school system is a hierarchical structure with goals, directives and information flowing from the board through the superintendent to middle-management on down to the classroom teacher which limits the range of thinking that goes into decision-making and the number of people who can be held accountable. Therefore, the creation of six regions and the appointment of six interim regional

superintendents reduces this distance, thus
rendering the administration more flexible
and adaptable.

- Salaries for the proposed staffing of the
  six regional offices must be found as well
  as salaries for six regional superintendents commensurate with their responsibilities. The list showed that much of the
  superintendent's authority was delegated to
  regional superintendents.

- The office of Planning, Research, and Evaluation was to be expanded to include a
  division of Development.

- The functions of the divisions of Pupil
  Personnel Services, Special Education, and
  Career Development, etc., are to be combined
  under the office of Student Development
  Services.

- The office of State Administration and the
  office of Communications and Community
  Relations would be created by bringing
  together functions dispersed in the former
  organizations.

- The division of Employer-Employee Relations
  will function as the office of Labor Relations.

- The office of Services to the Spanish
  Speaking will include all related programs.

After presenting the above in much more detail
than is here, the superintendent explained the new
kinds of relationships.

In explaining the reorganization design, Mrs.
Sizemore pointed out that figure 5 was the way the
school system was presently organized. Figure 6
showed the directing line in the new organization
with the administrative team setting goals, planning, coordinating and communicating as shown in

the circle arrangement in figure 7. The wheel
design, figure 5, would be used so that the
superintendent, as the hub is to the wheel, could
be held accountable to see that the solutions,
arrived at in the circle with no one to stop the
flow of ideas, were implemented.*

In regard to the above, the superintendent
indicated that she and her executive assistants
would also be a part of the administrative team.
These executive assistants would be hired or detailed by the superintendent for a contractual
term ending no later than the term of the superintendent, according to Section 2.2 of the Rules of
the board of education.

An important point made in the comprehensive
document presented by the superintendent noted that
funding for reorganization and decentralization
needed to occur by redirecting funds used for former offices and positions. Thus, specific positions
were noted for this purpose.

At this point, the board accepted the report
in order to review it in preparation for another
meeting before October 6.

At that same meeting additional budget matters
were dealt with. Mr. Williams presented the information on the FY75 and FY76 budgets. In his presentation, Mr. Williams noted the following changes
in the FY75 budget:

- All but approximately $2 million was ap-
  proved.

- Cuts occurred in the area of special
  education and the transportation for

---
*The figures 5, 6 and 7, used here, are the
more finalized designs found in Barbara A. Sizemore,
Superintendent of Schools, Reorganization of Central
Office, Washington, D.C.: Public Schools of the
District of Columbia, November 8, 1974, pp. 14-19.

**ORGANIZATION CHART**

**D.C. PUBLIC SCHOOLS**

Source: Barbara A. Sizemore, Superintendent of Schools, *Reorganization of Central Office*, Washington, D.C.: Public Schools of the District of Columbia, November 8, 1974, pp. 14-19.

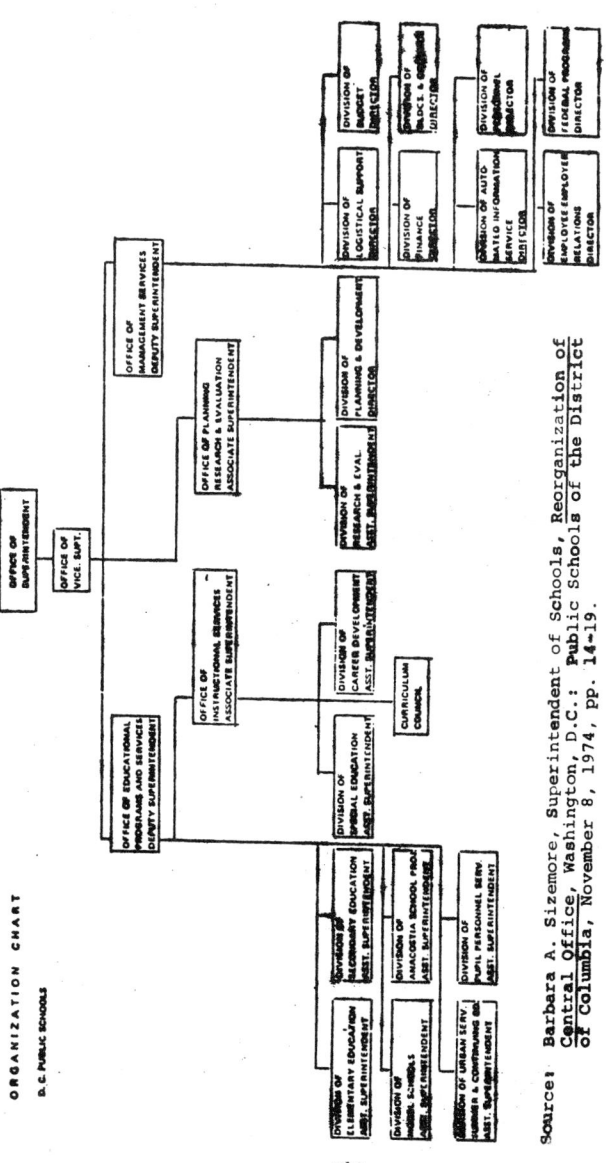

**FIGURE 5.**

ORGANIZATION CHART, D.C. PUBLIC SCHOOLS

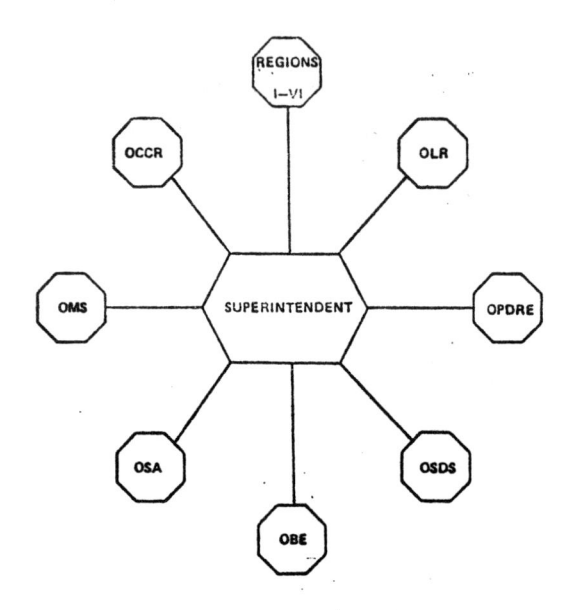

**REGIONS I–VI**
**OBE** — Office of Bilingual Education
**OCCR** — Office of Communications and Community Relations
**OLR** — Office of Labor Relations
**OMS** — Office of Management Services
**OPDRE** — Office of Planning, Development, Research and Evaluation
**OSA** — Office of State Administration
**OSDS** — Office of Student Development Services

Source: Barbara A. Sizemore, Superintendent of Schools, Reorganization of Central Office, Washington, D.C.: Public Schools of the District of Columbia, November 8, 1974, pp. 14-19.

FIGURE 6.

NEW ORGANIZATION DIRECTING LINE

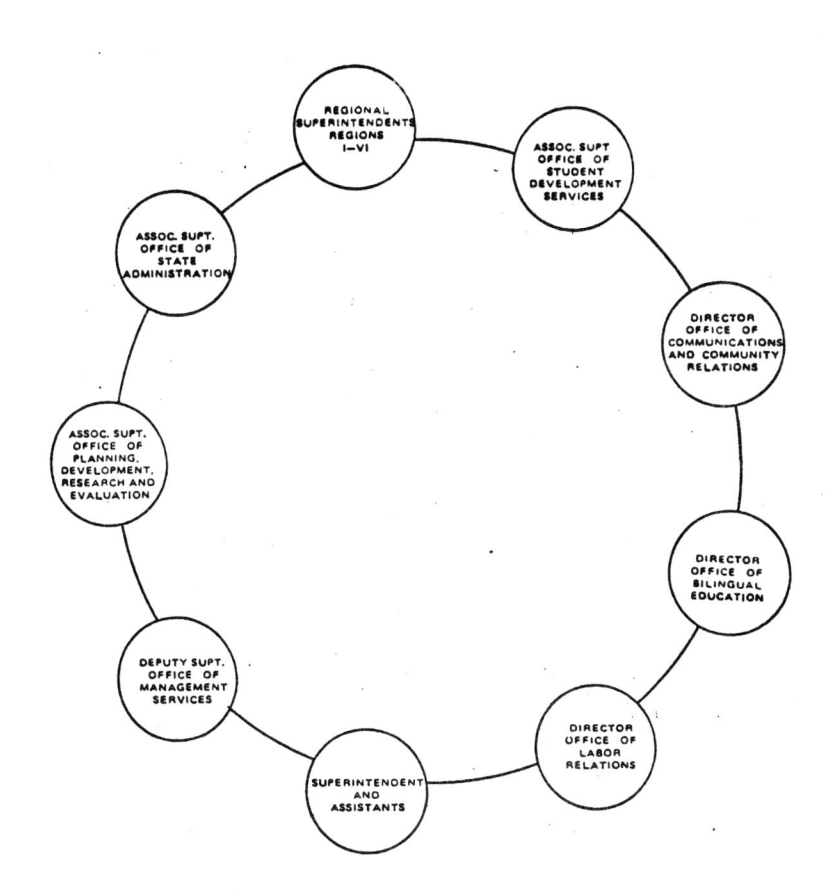

Source: Barbara A. Sizemore, Superintendent of Schools, *Reorganization of Central Office*, Washington, D.C.: Public Schools of the District of Columbia, November 8, 1974, pp. 14-19.

FIGURE 7

NEW ORGANIZATION ADMINISTRATIVE TEAM

special education.

- The six or eight decentralization positions were not allowed.

- $100,000.00 for staff development in connection with decentralization was allowed.

- Approximately 45 management positions were allowed.

- The teachers' raise would be able to be absorbed within the existing salary structure.

It was at this point that the beginning of the budget conflict began to emerge as board members interrogated Mr. Williams, deputy superintendent, about the maintenance of a two percent vacancy rate to cover teacher increases which in the past led to X amount of savings and reprogramming actions that caused a lapse of monies at the end of the year, what bearings it had on pupil-teacher ratio and board-union relations. Thereafter, both Mrs. Mason and Father Kemp requested a report of the organizational structure with the list of authorized positions in the 1975 budget, filled and not filled. Mason followed this with a query about the estimated rate of spending by departments and by regions for FY75. Mr. Williams' reply indicated that due to the construction of the budget in the traditional manner and decentralization coming at July 1, it would be difficult to tease out that information. Therefore, the report could not be made on a regional basis because the system had not changed to a regional budgeting format. However, Williams mentioned that his department was analyzing how to recast the budget in a regional format that would reveal how much money was actually allocated into each region. Additional questions were levelled at Williams by Mrs. Mason which concluded with the prime question. She asked whether or not the board would get quarterly reports of how the money was being spent from the '75 budget. This question dealt with a matter which later evolved into Charge

11: Failure to Provide Quarterly Financial Reports. Mr. Williams replied that he intended that they would get quarterly reports.

Mrs. Mason's next question dealt with whether or not the cost had been computed for the 12 regions with the corresponding reductions in the central office and whether or not it really turned out to be more expensive than the six regions. Mr. Williams' answer indicated that no cost calculation was made for 12 regions, but one was made for the six regions based on an earlier proposed staffing of the regions. Not satisfied with Mr. Williams' responses, after she posed the question several more times, Mrs. Mason referred it to the superintendent. Sizemore responded by referring to (1) additional functions that the board wanted created such as the office of Communications, (2) the office of Planning, Development, Research and Evaluation proposed in the 120 Day Report and agreed with by most board members, and (3) other functions which had fallen through the cracks such as census taking, evaluation of private schools related to the school system, and interagency problems. She continued by stating that an analysis could be made as to which functions needed to remain in the central office and which needed to be decentralized and that administration had problems with reducing central office at a time when some functions still needed to be taken care of. Mason's response indicated that she was interested in a projected time frame for doing this, the cost, and the difficulty of dealing with the concept of decentralizing into six regions instead of 12 costing too much, when she did not know what it was going to cost.

Later in the discussion, Father Kemp quoted from the newspaper the number of students presently enrolled in the public schools. In reply, Dr. Johnson, who was in charge of this area, firmly stated that the membership figure would be available the third Monday of October as usual.

In answer to Dr. Evans' questions about whether funds would be requested in FY76 for the facilities planning unit or office, Mr. Williams indicated that the Facilities Planning Office would be requested again; however, as indicated in the reorganization plan, use would be made of some existing positions and rearrangements since the buildings and grounds operation was abolished. This fact is noted here because Charge 4 (Failure to fill the position as directed by the board of education) referred to the filling of the position of director of buildings and grounds within 60 days of October 16, 1974, a position which the transcript of this September 30, 1974 board meeting indicated was abolished.

Mason then asked a question about the formula used in planning facilities in terms of a new formula which would base capacity only on regular academic instructional space and how this would demonstrate to the board the needs in a particular school situation. In response both Dr. James Johnson and Mrs. Sizemore explained that a new board policy was needed which spoke to the amount of time the space was used and what space was needed for a specific educational activity for specific youngsters. In an effort to illuminate the concern of the administration, Mrs. Sizemore clarified the process of moving toward a new concept for change which the administration was examining called incommensurability. She explained it thusly:

> In trying to find a way to change the structure of the system so that it is more compatible with human growth and development [a] new conceptual framework had to be discovered and developed in order to hang programs on. First you have to have the idea; then you have to develop your programs and activities. What we were given was equalization and equalization didn't work; everybody is dissatisfied with it. So we are searching for a concept that would give us a way to deal

with the differences that human beings exhibit in growth and development.

The scholars at the University of Nebraska happen(ed) to send us a paper...it referred to the concept of incommensurability.... So what we have been doing...is trying to develop this concept which we believe would provide the foundation for this change. So what is going on right now is the discovery of knowledge....

The next thing you have to do is to apply this concept to all of the social indicators and the criteria that you are using to build your programs.... What are some of these criterias? Pupil-teacher ratio. With incommensurability pupil-teacher ratio may be archaic and obsolete because what teacher-pupil ratio tells you is to treat everybody, say 1-25, 1-30. But it is for everybody across the board.... But the more you study incommensurability and you find out as you go through this paper it really is not the right way you do it. So maybe we need to talk about adults per one thousand students and then you can use these adults in any way you wanted to. This would be teachers, teachers' aides, counselor aides, community aides or any kinds of WAE persons.... So what we are searching for right now are new indicators and new criteria for making incommensurability work because it won't work with the old things we have been using.

You may need 1 to 1 relationship or a 1 to 5 relationship; you may need a 1 to 200 relationship in certain kinds of experiences. So what we are trying to do now is to wrestle with the concept of incommensurability and to try to construct the kind of indicators and criteria that the board will need in order to make the thing work when we refine it. That is our problem.

At this point complete endorsement for proceeding in this way was given by only one board member, Father Kemp.

Other budgetary problems touched on were: (1) methods for accounting for capital outlay funds by the District government so that leftover funds could be used for other school projects; (2) the lack of school system control other than by transfer to D.C. General Services the monies that they say are used for maintenance of schools; (3) a monitoring staff to check on permanent improvements and capital projects which was denied funding in the FY75 budget; (4) the development of school system capability to handle the maintenance operation; and (5) the non-delivery or late delivery of furniture to buildings completed during the summer causing late school openings.[87] These and many other similar problems having to do with maintenance and construction were aired which pointed to the lack of control which the school system had in terms of these areas since they were handled for the school system by the District government, a fact little understood by the citizens despite public airing at board meetings such as this one.

Mayor's freeze --

Coming on the heels of the budgetary problems discussed at the September 30, 1974 board meeting was the mayor's freeze which imposed limitations on personnel and other obligations for the remainder of the 1975 fiscal year. Under the heading "Required Reductions," the statement in the memorandum read: "To comply with the limitations imposed, your agency apportionments are reduced $3,834,200 for the remainder of Fiscal Year 1975." Also included was an absorption of approximately $5,000,000.00 of pay increases, totaling close to $9,000,000.00 in budget reductions.[88] So what we have here now is a school administration enmeshed in budgetary consideration for FY75 and FY76 toppling over each other as they struggle to give time also to conceptualizing and working out new structures to effectuate a viable educational program for the elevation of achievement, and handling the day-to-day operation of the public schools -- all at the same time.

At the October 16, 1974 meeting of the DCBOE, Simmons, chairperson of the Committee on Administrative Services, reported on a meeting held on October 3 with Mr. Williams, at which time he indicated that some new positions to implement administrative reorganization had been advertised. Later in the day when they learned about the mayor's freeze, the board realized that the positions were in question. Furthermore, Simmons indicated that according to Mr. Williams, it was not feasible to decentralize management and support services until the total reorganization was in place and truly functioning, and then various departments in management and support services could be considered in connection with decentralization.

Additionally, several other items related to the budget/management area were discussed and board policy adopted over the initial vigorous objection of Mr. Williams, deputy superintendent of management services. He maintained that his office was not staffed to comply. He then finally gave his acquiescence to provide a cursory review of Capital Improvement projects. The items under question which had later implications in the subsequent hearing to fire the superintendent were the following:

  3. That the Board of Education direct the Superintendent to prepare a major legislative and reorganizational package concomittant with the presentation of the FY76 budget to reflect:

    a. Phased in school system control of contracts related to building construction.

    b. Total control of major maintenance and repairs for the school system by the school system.

    c. Positions and costs to implement these new controls.

    d. Such information as is necessary to convince the Mayor, the Council and the Congress that such controls are needed by the school system.

5. That the Board of Education direct the superintendent to place top priority on filling the acting position of Buildings and Grounds Assistant Superintendent with a probationary appointment within sixty days.

The vote on these items was deferred until the November meeting.[89]

    On October 21, 1974, Superintendent Sizemore sent a memorandum to DCBOE members in relation to the proposed FY76 operating budget as developed by the administrative staff. The package contained the mandatory base budget required by the commissioner as the initial submission of the public school system, and a series of additional schedules of the needs of the system. The description included increases because of the inflation of non-personnel items of expenditure in the budget and major changes in the school organization and program: the establishment of an appeals office; the increase of the pre-school program; expanded pupil appraisal function; support of the School for the Arts; increase to regional offices; the development of the Spanish affairs program; and increased funds for staff development proposed for funding by the redirection of elementary school teacher compensation projected to be available due to anticipated reduction in elementary school population. Additionally, new and improved services for program improvement were included.[90]

    On the following day, October 22, 1974, Julius W. Hobson, Jr., chairman, Committee on School

Finance, sent a list of questions to the superintendent regarding the above described package. Included in his list of questions were two which referred to decentralization, one of the main budget issues. One in particular reflected his either lack of understanding or disagreement with the process designed by the superintendent to bring about decentralization. The question expressed Hobson's disagreement with the termination of the position of vice-superintendent.[91]

### October 22, 1974 special board meeting --

A special meeting of the board was called October 22, 1974 to receive the FY76 Preliminary Operating Budget materials as proposed by the superintendent of schools.

As regards Hobson's objection to collapsing the position of vice-superintendent, freed by the resignation of Ken Haskins, the superintendent referred again to her 11 hour interview for the job of superintendent in which she was told to put administrative decision-making in the decentralized regions for the PACTS process to operate. Thus she explained that the reporting process should change. Regional superintendents should now report directly to the superintendent and not to an intervening central officer. And that it was for this reason that she wanted to collapse the position of vice-superintendent.

Meanwhile, additional questions and answers transpired, after which a motion was put by Mason and seconded by Kemp that the budget be received. It was voted on unanimously.[92]

On November 12, 1974, Superintendent Sizemore sent a memorandum to Mrs. Morris, president of the DCBOE, in reply to her request of October 31 of "Estimated FY 1976 Costs for Selected Administrative Officers Affected by Decentralization and Reorganization." Table 8 summarizes those costs.

On October 16, 1974, the superintendent and

TABLE 8

ESTIMATED FY1976 COSTS FOR SELECTED ADMINISTRATIVE OFFICES AFFECTED BY DECENTRALIZATION AND REORGANIZATION

| | Regular | | Current Cost Impact Aid | | Other Federal | | Redirections In | | Redirections Out | | New & Improved | | Total FY-76 Cost | |
|---|---|---|---|---|---|---|---|---|---|---|---|---|---|---|
| | Pos. | Amount | Pos. | Amount | Pos. | Amount | Pos. | Amount | Pos. | Amount | Pos. | Amount | Pos. | Amount |
| Region I | 17 | $328,197 | 1 | $12,858 | 1 | $11,896 | 4 | $106,331 | ... | ... | 1 | $23,470 | 24 | $482,752 |
| II | 16 | 301,569 | 2 | 39,586 | ... | ... | 4 | 106,331 | ... | ... | 1 | 23,470 | 23 | 470,956 |
| III | 10 | 177,897 | 3 | 53,923 | ... | ... | 5 | 131,406 | ... | ... | 1 | 23,470 | 19 | 386,696 |
| IV | 12 | 300,376 | 3 | 49,930 | ... | ... | 6 | 163,011 | ... | ... | 1 | 23,470 | 22 | 436,787 |
| V | 16 | 313,325 | 4 | 63,376 | 1 | 21,525 | 3 | 32,861 | 1 | 20,681 | 1 | 23,470 | 24 | 433,876 |
| VI | 10 | 180,730 | 6 | 104,714 | ... | ... | 5 | 139,561 | ... | ... | 1 | 23,470 | 22 | 448,455 |
| State Office | 1 | 20,681 | 12 | 156,749 | 27 | 465,281 | 4 | 54,771 | ... | ... | 11 | 223,237 | 55 | 920,719 |
| Office of Planning, Development, Research, and Evaluation | 34 | 585,917 | 6 | 99,844 | 19 | 329,206 | 7 | 97,383 | 1 | 25,075 | 67 | 1,118,420 | 132 | 2,205,695 |
| Student Development Serv. (Central Offices) | 59 | 990,800 | ... | ... | 36 | 563,500 | 2 | 64,200 | 6 | 135,300 | 16 | 304,900 | 107 | 1,788,100 |
| Office of Bilingual Ed. | 2 | 34,200 | 8 | 95,000 | 3 | 48,700 | 15 | 209,600 | 13 | 177,900 | ... | ... | 15 | 209,600 |
| Office of Communications and Community Relations | ... | ... | ... | ... | ... | ... | 29 | 450,396 | ... | ... | 8 | 111,484 | 37 | 561,880 |
| Office of Labor Relations | 7 | 142,500 | ... | ... | ... | ... | ... | ... | ... | ... | ... | ... | 7 | 142,500 |
| Additional Available Resources | ... | ... | ... | ... | ... | ... | ... | ... | 64 | 1,214,600 | ... | ... | −64 | −1,214,600 |
| TOTAL | 184 | $3,278,182 | 45 | $675,992 | 87 | $1,440,108 | 84 | $1,605,831 | −85 | −$1,573,556 | 108 | $1,898,861 | 423 | $7,325,456 |

Source: Memorandum to Mrs. Virginia Morris, President, Board of Education, from Barbara A. Sizemore, Superintendent of Schools, November 12, 1974, re: Estimated FY1976 Costs for Selected Administrative Officers Affected by Decentralization and Reorganization.

mayor had met to discuss his request for budget reductions. Thus, in a memorandum of November 13, 1974 to the president of the board, Mrs. Sizemore submitted, in response to the mayor's request and in response to the requirement of the board that the administration identify the funding necessary to provide full support for all program operations for the remainder of FY75, data on the following: (1) summary of expenditures through September 1974; (2) projected expenditures through June 1974; (3) detailed expenditure projections by budget category; and (4) summary of projected expenditure imbalances and additional funding requirements. In this connection, the superintendent indicated that the conclusion to be drawn from the reports was that the school system was expending funds at a rate exceeding the funding available, and did not accommodate the absorption of the school system's share of pay increases of approximately $5 million. In addition, she also revealed that the data showed that there was a serious imbalance in the use of positions, especially in central services and management in which large numbers of vacancies existed and were being maintained because of the freeze. This obscured the magnitude of the overexpenditures occurring in the teaching service.[93]

On November 19, 1974, James Williams sent a confidential memorandum to the superintendent regarding the revision of the FY75 Financial Plan. In the memorandum, Williams referred to a commitment he had made, after the executive staff meeting held on November 18, to review the October 11, 1974 board report proposed for resubmission to the board in compliance with the requests contained in Mrs. Morris' letter dated November 15, 1974. Thus, he recalled that he submitted a report to the superintendent on November 12, which indicated a projected deficit of $5,407,800.00. It also indicated the areas which contributed to the calculated deficit and translated into excess positions the dollars which represented the deficit in the various budget categories. Furthermore, Williams stated that the

excess expenditure was continuing to accumulate
and that, in retrospect, the final decision made in
the November 18 staff meeting did not address the
question of adjusting to prevent a deficit occurring. Therefore, Williams proposed action in
several other areas.[94]

The new board members appointed at the Novem-
ber 20, 1974 DCBOE meeting were Bettie G. Benjamin
(Ward 5), Elizabeth Kane (at-large), Carol L.
Schwartz (Ward 3), and John E. Warren (Ward 6).

Budget business dealt with a statement
presented by Virginia Morris concerning the FY75
Financial Plan and the FY76 Budget which requested
detailed information regarding (a) status of all
personnel slots as of October 31, 1974, (b) copy
of the monthly payroll printout for the last pay
period in October, (c) revised FY75 Financial Plan,
and (d) revised FY76 Operating Budget.[95]

### December 2, 1974 special board meeting --

Then, at the December 2, 1974 meeting of the
DCBOE, the board voted in favor of the recommendation of the Subcommittee on Federal Grants to
approve the superintendent's FY75 State Plan for
Title III. Also, at that same meeting the board
approved the FY75 Financial Plan. The last item
on the agenda dealt with a review of the Wright
Decree Compliance Report forwarded to the board by
the superintendent on November 20, 1974. This was
a plan for compliance with the court's order of
May 25, 1971 requiring the equalization of per
pupil expenditures for all teachers' salaries and
benefits in each elementary school to within plus
or minus five percent of the city-wide mean. The
report accompanied a recommendation from the
superintendent for approval by the board for submission to the court through the corporation
counsel. At this point, President Morris mentioned
that she and other board members had noted some
inequities in the report. Therefore, she moved
"that the Board direct the superintendent to hold
in abeyance the transfer of teachers as required

by the compliance report pending a further study
and review of the data that was previously submitted."[96] This board action later became a part
of Superintendent Sizemore's defense to the charge
that she did not implement an Equalization Plan.

<u>December 6, 1974 committee meeting, emergency
meeting and board meeting</u> --

The Committee on School Finance convened on
December 6, 1974 for the purpose of interrogating
the administrative team about overhiring. Thus,
each member of the team introduced herself/himself
for the benefit of new board members. The superintendent was out of town but all board members were
present. Hobson, chairperson of the committee,
began by saying that the board had received the
previous day an FY75 Expenditure Plan (Revision
III) and that morning a revision of part of that
plan. He inquired as to whether the entire team
agreed with the plan since the board had been told
repeatedly that decisions were made in a democratic
process through the administrative team. Therefore,
the board could never get at the bottom of things.
Hence, the entire administrative team had been
requested to appear before the board to answer
questions and explain how they had reached some of
their decisions.

Kemp pressed hard on the point of the maintenance of the two percent vacancy rate vis-a-vis the
overhiring of personnel and asked for an explanation of this discrepancy, as he saw it, in terms of
decentralization of the hiring function and then
the later recentralization of same. Thus, he asked
Williams to reconstruct what had happened in August
in relation to this move. Williams' reply was as
follows:

> You would have to go back...historically to
> what happened before decentralization...in
> hiring you have a semantics problem, theoreti-
> cally no one is hired until the Board order is
> cut and it is processed through personnel.
> Technically, personnel does the hiring, but

the obligating of positions has been done in the operating office. In other words, the selection of the person, the promise of the position to the person, has been done there. This was before decentralization....

On August 1, in order to try and begin centralizing personnel into a personnel function the hiring of personnel was supposed to take place through the Personnel Office, and a memorandum was sent out to this effect that all positions, all persons to be employed were to be recommended after August 9th, anyone after August 9th was to be referred to Personnel and they would be actually employed there, with the Board Orders...being cut at that point....

That is part of what is still trying to be ascertained as to what has actually happened, and that has not been completed, that we may have at maybe some place overhired.

Kemp asked if Williams could attribute the overhiring at that one entry point or elsewhere. After Williams' response to the effect that the team was still studying the situation, Kemp pressed forward with, "With the information that you have, what we read in the papers and what is vaguely in literature, and some prior reports, can the board assume that after August the 9th there was more than one entry point...?" Williams replied that he had no information to support that conclusion.

Subsequently, Hobson said that was just why he had all persons listed above attend the meeting to tell him if any of them hired anybody? Thus, he asked each member of the administrative team to tell him, one by one, if they had hired anybody since August 9. Hobson's explanation for this procedure was that he had consistently read in the paper that the regional superintendents did this hiring, and some papers said they had not.

Each regional superintendent, in turn, denied having overhired, and insisted that they had followed the position control procedure which included the allocation of a position control budget number on every board order to authenticate the personnel action.

The whole matter of some members of the board misunderstanding or disagreeing with the Administrative Team Concept surfaced throughout this meeting.

Further on in the meeting Kemp again referred to the Washington Star as a source of valid data when he said, "Can we try to get at some of this from today's Star perhaps?"

Kemp proceeded to interrogate Mr. Williams on the information in Brockett's column when Schwartz interrupted to say she would like to know where Brockett got her figures. After which, Kemp continued badgering Williams, who often answered that he did not know the answers, or he could not comment on a number of questions put which indicated a different interpretation or semantic translation by board members of much of the information presented in the December 5 and December 6, 1974 documents from the superintendent.

Then Morris began reading from the Washington Star article and said that "It also talks about 294 teachers and 95 of them unauthorized, etc. So, now if these kind of specifics can be pulled by the 'media,' why is it so difficult for us to get information?"

No specific response revealing Brockett's sources of all of the data contained in the article was made.

Later in the proceedings, Warren also expressed concern that the budget officer was not a part of the administrative team as it deliberated budget matters.

Further discussion centered on when a report would be ready to go to the mayor delineating school system needs for the rest of FY75 and the form of that document, and the preparation of a clearer report form for all budget documents received by board members to date having to do with the budget crisis.

Then Hobson moved that a task team be formed to revise the FY75 Financial Plan. It was approved by the board. After which, Hobson moved that an emergency meeting of the board of education be held immediately to deal with the proposal. The motion passed[97] and an emergency board meeting was immediately convened by President Morris who read into the record the part of the board Rules which was interpreted as covering the procedure about to transpire. Part IV, Chapter 1, of the board of education Rules, Section 4.2 (b) as read by Morris stated:

> (b) Whenever a Special Meeting is called, verbal or written notice shall be served on each Board member by the secretary at least forty-eight hours prior to the Special Meeting. Special Meetings to consider Emergency matters may be called upon shorter notice. The purpose of the Special Meeting shall be stated in such notice. No other matters shall be considered at such Special Meeting.

Interestingly, the above meeting was called at the shortest possible notice, if we consider immediately to mean the same as "upon shorter notice." Hence the recommendation about setting up a task team made at the earlier meeting was put into motion form and carried with Simmons dissenting.[98]

At the December 6, 1974 DCBOE meeting held that night, the Committee on School Finance, which met earlier that same day, reported that they discussed the Revised FY75 Expenditure Plan revised a second time and recommended to the full board for action:

That a Task Team be formed consisting of the
Deputy Superintendent for Management,
the Associate Superintendent for State Administration, the Director of the Budget, Chairperson of the Federal Grants Subcommittee of
the Committee on School Finance, Chairman of
the Committee on School Finance, President of
the Board as an Ex-Officio Member, the Associate Superintendent for the Office of Planning, Research, and Evaluation, the Assistant
Superintendent for Personnel, One Regional
Superintendent, a Representative from the
Washington Teachers' Union and the Council
of School Officers, Representative from the
Council Twenty of the American Federation of
State, County and Municipal Employees.

The purpose of the task team, as described in
the report, was to arrive at a Revised FY75 Financial Plan to include recommendations to avoid the
projected deficit and to establish a firm base for
the FY76 Operating Budget; and a Revised Proposed
FY76 Operating Budget that reflected changes made
in the FY75 Financial Plan. In doing this, it was
proposed that the task team would analyze unauthorized and unallowable positions within the system,
and report to the Committee on School Finance and
the board. The board would approve the financial
plan, and the task team would monitor the plan
until the end of FY75. A motion was put and voted
in by Benjamin, Kane, Mason, Hobson, Morris, Kemp,
Schwartz, and Warren. Simmons opposed the motion,
saying in part that she found the action:

> ...a denigrating and disgraceful step taken by
> this board. I think we ought to indicate what
> it is in precise terms that we want and that
> becomes the responsibility of the legally held
> responsible party for providing it. If they
> elect to use all of these people or more than
> this number or less than this number, the
> responsibility is in fact six. I would want
> it very clear that when the regional superintendents were left out I found this appalling
> and I will not support that motion.[99]

Task team --

Mrs. Sizemore received a memorandum sent on December 9, 1974, from Dwight Cropp, executive secretary of the board, recalling the action taken in regard to the setting up of the task team at the Friday, December 6, 1974 special (emergency) meeting. In addition, he included the note that the president canvassed members of the board, and they felt that the superintendent of schools would also serve as an ex-officio member of the task team. Further, the president directed, in part, that:

> 1. The Superintendent appoint those members of the Administration who have been designated as members of the Task Team and notify these administrators of their appointment by the close of business today;....
>
> 2. Those administrators assigned to the Task Team be relieved of their regular duties in order that they may devote one hundred percent (100%) of their time to the activities of the Team.[100]

A sharp memorandum dated December 12, 1974, then went from Virginia Morris to the superintendent in response to a request for clarification from the superintendent, accompanying a December 10, 1974 document entitled "FY 1975 Budget Reductions." It said, in essence, the DCBOE met in executive session on Wednesday, December 11, 1974, to consider her document, and their response was (1) that the task team shall act in an advisory capacity to the School Finance Committee, (2) the intent of the board was that 100 percent of the time of the administrative staff members of the team will be devoted to the task, and (3) in response to her request to be on the task team, the board granted her request and then in response to her request not to serve, the board accepted that also. Morris continued with:

> This is the Board's response to your request for clarification. It is the complete response. It is not the intention of the Board to spend valuable time quibbling over operating procedures, or over the meaning of particular words in a battle of memoranda.... The Board, in its vote of December 6th, has directed the Superintendent to appoint members of the administration to a Task Team to advise the Committee on School Finance in dealing with this crisis. The Superintendent is contractually required to comply with Board directives. It is expected that this clear directive will be complied with forthwith.[101]

After this sharp reminder to the superintendent of her duties to obey the board, another emergency special meeting took place that night, December 12, 1974. Only 10 members of the board were present at the meeting. The purpose of the meeting was to receive a recommendation from the president of the board concerning the financial crisis of the school system. Thus, Morris made the following motion which was passed:

> 1. That a Special Committee of the Board be appointed to meet with the Superintendent for the purpose of further clarifying concerns expressed by the Superintendent about the Board's December 6, 1974 action.

Benjamin's question about whether the superintendent would appoint the administrators if the issue of 100 percent time was clarified led right into the superintendent's response that she was prepared to do as directed even though she disagreed with the directive, if it came at a public meeting rather than in secrecy at a special meeting.

Sizemore's concern was that if the administrators were relieved of their responsibilities and assigned to the task team 100 percent of the time, then the duties that they must perform for the day-to-day operations of the public schools

would go undone, and for this reason it must be a
formal board action that directs her to do this so
that it will be a board action that indicates
approval of their responsibilities being left
undone.

Morris' response, in brief, had to do with
her recalling that private meetings are common and
that she had heard no outcry about them. Eventually, the board voted unanimously in favor of
the motion reported earlier, on the setting up of
a committee to clarify.[102]

Certainly, it was obvious that the rift
between the superintendent and the board widened
during the DCYOP controversy, almost came to a head
during the General Counsel dispute, and had at this
point developed into a chasm almost too wide to
bridge as they engaged in the controversy over the
FY75 Financial Plan and FY76 Budget. Brockett, of
the Washington Star, who seemed bent on sensationalizing the information she received from school
sources, did not miss this opportunity to widen the
breach. For as it happened, several board members
used her articles and the editorials to guide
their activities, as testified to by Kemp and Morris
during the December 6 school Finance Committee
meeting.

Brockett's article was headlined "D.C. School
Board Issues Ultimatum to Sizemore," and it blatantly proclaimed that the DCBOE issued an ultimatum to Sizemore that if she would appoint her six
top administrators to the task force to solve the
financial crisis she could keep her job as superintendent,[103] implying, of course, that if she did
not they would fire her. These implications
obviously added fuel to the fire.

Special meetings continued to be held during
the month of December as the conflict between the
superintendent and some board members gathered
momentum.

February 19, 1975 stated board meeting --

A very lengthy discussion was held on FY76 budget matters at the February 19, 1975 stated meeting of the DCBOE, at which time all 11 members of the board were present. After the preliminaries were concluded, the superintendent reported on a statement on the FY76 budget which she submitted for the record. The substance of the statement dealt with her concerns regarding the FY76 budget. She said that, in general, the FY75 budget plan represented the system's assessment and programmatic responses of the previous administration with three minor exceptions: (1) decentralization; (2) facilities planning unit; and (3) research, planning and evaluation sanctioned by the board and the previous and current administrations. Two of these were denied. Therefore, the budget was not representative of the goals and objectives of her administration, such as a pluralistic system based on human growth and development. She also said the problem is that the FY76 budget being recommended by the Finance Committee was not her administration's budget. Contrastingly, the budget document submitted by her on October 21, 1974 was based on the current administration's assessment of the school system's needs as stated in the superintendent's 120 Day Report transmitted on March 8, 1974, and unanimously approved by the board on May 30, 1974. Sizemore continued by stating that:

> The budget recommendations of the Finance Committee represent a decimation and rejection of the programs designed to support the realization of those objectives outlined in the 120 Day Report....The recommendations of the Finance Committee represent a strange and unorthodox technique to change established Board policy....the Board of Education did not act in a direct and open fashion to express its desire to change its policy positions and, therefore its priorities and the FY76 budget recommendations do not reflect stated Board policy used by the Administration as guidance

for the establishment of system priorities.

Pursuant to this declaration, the superintendent enumerated all of the programs which her administration introduced to change the system to make it responsive to the needs of the children in the public schools and to therefore effectuate learning, elevate achievement and eliminate discipline as a problem in the public schools which the Committee on School Finance had relegated to the New and Improved Budget Schedule described by her as the not-likely-to-get category.[104]

The result of the new budget priorities meant that decentralization was hampered as the establishment of six TSA-2 positions and salary for regional superintendents in line with their responsibilities was defeated as the board created the executive secretary's position on the board at a higher salary than that of the regional superintendent's.

The PACTS office was abolished. No provision was made for curriculum, testing, or staff development. Also, the board reversed the decentralization of curriculum by maintaining the office of Instructional Services, justifying it by saying it provided direct services to the classroom. Meanwhile, approximately $70,000.00 in administrative cost was being maintained for two positions unnecessary in the decentralized structure, thus creating another layer in the bureaucracy. This also effectively abolished the office of Student Development Services since funds were not available for the positions. Additionally, effective mainstreaming was aborted. Most of the new positions in management services were put in New and Improved Services.

Furthermore, there was extra money provided for the six small schools west of Rock Creek Park in the more affluent predominantly white section of town, while other schools in poorer areas were left in competition with all other schools to fight for their fair share of the pot. Also, in spite of the severe budget crisis, money for the DCYOP was provided.[105]

After several minutes of discussion and debate, Simmons offered a Minority Report in support of matters covered in the superintendent's memorandum. It was signed by Simmons, Benjamin, Evans and Warren. Hence, it was at this point (February 19, 1975) in the conflict between the superintendent and the DCBOE that the seven to four voting pattern was clearly established. The seven non-supporters of the superintendent, namely Morris, Hobson, Jr., Treanor, Kemp, Schwartz, Mason and Kane, became a steady opposition group which persisted throughout the rest of her term of office, through the hearings, and up to the firing.

A motion to substitute the Minority Report for the Majority Report of the Committee on School Finance was lost, seven to four (Simmons, Benjamin, Evans and Warren). Therefore, the items in the Majority Report were discussed separately before a vote was taken. In connection with the issue of retaining the vice-superintendent's position which was released due to the resignation of Kenneth Haskins in June 1974, Evans reminded the board that one of the most controversial and most frequently discussed issues was that of policy versus administration. In this regard, he stated that:

> ...of course, we have all been reminded of the fact that there is no real clear line, but it does seem to me that if we are going to suggest, that down to the point where we even include in the budget a position that he or she has recommended eliminating, but clearly seems to be that we are [delving] into the administration of the school system and going beyond our realm of the policy Board.

Evans supplied this same argument in support of abolishing the position of associate superintendent of Instructional Services which the Committee on School Finance and the board majority supported. In conclusion, most of the changes proposed by the Committee on School Finance were supported by the 7-member majority including Hobson, Kane, Kemp,

Mason, Morris, Schwartz and Treanor with a few exceptions from time to time.[106]

### March 19, 1975 stated board meeting --

At the March 19, 1975 stated board meeting, another recommendation was made by the board which emerged into a charge against the superintendent. Hobson presented the report of the DCBOE's school Finance Committee which focused on the revised FY75 financial plan, noting in particular, that the committee recommended for board action a reaffirmation of its rejection in October of the mayor's cut of $2.6 million in the budget. Secondly, a recommendation was made that the school administration provide the board with the final operating budget report, including recommendations on the non-personnel category. This latter request was later to evolve into Charge 8 - Failure to Comply with Board Directive to Appoint Administration Committee (to review requests for exemptions from, and modifications in, the freeze on non-personnel expenditures). A motion to accept the recommendation was put and carried with Treanor, Hobson, Morris, Kemp, Kane and Evans voting in favor, Simmons and Benjamin voting against, and Warren abstaining.[107]

As mentioned earlier on, in connection with the alleged overhiring, position control appeared to be a problem. Therefore, Mrs. Sizemore sent a memorandum to Mr. James Williams, her deputy superintendent, dated March 20, 1975, to the effect that as they "enter the stage of making 1976 budget allotments to school units and examine procedures for reducing the number of TSA-15 positions to be allotted to schools for the next fiscal year, the question of position control becomes critical." So, she asked him to establish an operational effective position control system which she would bring before the administrative team for discussion on March 31 or April 7.[108] The matter of personnel hiring controls emerged into Charge 3 - Failure to provide and implement adequate personnel hiring

controls and failure to maintain hiring within
fiscally responsible limits.

AHSA speech, April 4, 1975 --

On April 4, 1975 the superintendent made a
speech before the African Heritage Studies Association, an association of scholars of African descent
dedicated to the preservation, interpretation, and
academic presentations of the historical and cultural heritage of African people, on the ancestral
soil of Africa and in the African diaspora. Her
presentation, entitled "Education: Is Accommodation Enough?", provided a penetrating analysis of
racist efforts, internationally and nationally,
from the perspective of the past to the present,
to cripple the creativity and vitality of Black
and other poor people. The thrust of the last part
of the paper focused on Washington, D.C. with its
76 percent Black population, a Black mayor, a
majority Black city council (11 to 2), a majority
Black-elected school board (7 to 4) and a Black
public school system with its 96 percent Black
student population, 86 percent Black teachers and
85 percent Black administrators, including a Black
superintendent. Here, she spoke about the ways
whites tried to rid themselves of Black rule; the
two Washingtons, one Black and one white, described
in the March 1975 issue of Fortune Magazine; the
unfortunate circumstance of having three Blacks
a part of the policymaking majority on the school
board preventing long-range planning for Black
children; the movement of whites back into the city
thus displacing Blacks; and various other actions
or plans designed to decimate the school system.
She described them as: (1) the abolition of
tenure; (2) the contracting out of large sums of
money to white organizations; (3) the election of
like-minded citizens to the board; (4) the imputation of Black inferiority and incompetence; (5) the
rotation of the superintendency to destroy continuity of effort toward the improvement of the quality
of education for the Black poor; and (6) the
prevention of change in the age-graded, mono-lingual,

mono-cultural, hierarchical public school structure which does not benefit Blacks. After this, Mrs. Sizemore presented a sequence of events and board decisions to support her allegations.[109]

### April 7, 1975 emergency meeting --

Undoubtedly, the above presentation did not make Mrs. Sizemore a popular candidate for retention in the superintendency. The shove toward the door preceding the slam of the door to the superintendency came at the April 7, 1975 emergency meeting, called for the purpose of entertaining the report from the Committee on School Finance on the FY75 budget deficit. A motion which included the item below was made which stirred up an instructive interchange between some of the policymaking majority on the board and the superintendent:

> The Superintendent designate an Administrative Committee to review requests for exemptions from and modifications in the "freeze" on non-personnel expenditures; this Committee is to meet on a weekly basis and is to present its recommendations to the Committee on School Finance each week. The Board is to delegate to the Committee on School Finance full power to approve or disapprove the recommendations presented by the Administrative Committee. The Committee on School Finance will meet frequently for this purpose and will review the items included in Schedule 1, column 6, as "mandatory", those included in Schedule 1, column 3, as "processed not obligated", and any new proposals presented by the Administrative Committee for approval....
>
> The Administration provide the Board of Education with monthly status reports at the May and June business meetings reflecting the total expenditures applied against the new financial plan and the appropriate balances.
>
> The Administration should be asked to supply answers to the attached questions regarding

the March 27, 1975, FY 1975 Financial Status Report [Memorandum from Mrs. Mason] and to any further questions which other members of the Committee on Finance or Board may raise.

The interchange in the transcript points to the possibility that the trouble that had been brewing for some time now between the superintendent and the majority on the board was coming to a head. First, the superintendent indicated that there was no need for an administrative committee to review requests for exemptions from and modifications in the "freeze" on non-personnel expenditures recommended by Mason since the school system needed the total amount to operate. This was ignored. The matter later evolved into Charge 8 - Failure to comply with board directive to appoint administrative committee. Second, the superintendent explained that it would be difficult to prepare a financial report and answers to questions posed by Mason for May and June because the entire management staff was working on the Title I report. This item evolved into Charge 9 - Failure to provide responses to the board's questions on the FY75 financial plan. Morris said that the board had never gotten monthly financial reports as requested, to which Mrs. Sizemore replied that the board had said previously that it had received more financial reports since Mr. Williams' tenure than ever before, especially since they had received none during other administrations. Mr. Williams also responded by indicating that his staff of four in the Finance Department had been working 10 to 12 hours a day plus Saturdays for six to 8 months and were completely exhausted. Additionally, Mr. Williams added that:

> ...the changes that we have been put through about the city signing off on it in the final analyses we verified and reverified the same thing that we have been giving the board since last October. The figures haven't changed. The city did sign off;.... So we have been working over the same identical

thing for eight months and the figures have not changed. They have decreased proportionately to the amount of time that has elapsed in which we did not fill positions. There is no change. You take the first report you received from me and add back everything and you will come right back to where we were originally.

This, too, seemingly was ignored at the time, and the motion passed with Kemp, Morris, Mason, Kane, Hobson and Treanor voting in favor and Evans and Warren voting against. Benjamin, Schwartz and Simmons were absent. The issue later evolved into Charge 10 - Failure to comply with board directive to submit status report on expenditures.

Significantly, out of the highly charged atmosphere of the April 7 DCBOE meeting, three days following the superintendent's presentation before the African Heritage Studies Association, four issues arose which evolved into charges at the superintendent's hearing. These were:

Charge 8. Failure to Comply with Board Directive to Appoint Administrative Committee

Charge 9. Failure to Provide Responses to the Board's Question on the FY 1975 Financial Plan

Charge 10. Failure to Comply with Board Directive to Submit Status Report on Expenditures

Charge 11. Failure to Provide Quarterly Financial Reports

The most eventful aspect at the April 16, 1975 board meeting was Mrs. Simmons calling attention to the conduct of board business, specifically the concern about the number of emergency meetings and how they were scheduled.[110]

By April 25, 1975, relations between the superintendent and the board had deteriorated to such an extent that, although budgetary problems were not cleared up, they took a back seat as the board proceeded to evaluate the superintendent as a prelude to firing her.

## Case Analysis and Conclusions

### Introduction to case analysis

The system of case analysis was described in Chapter I. It was stated that external and internal factors impinged on the decision-making process engaged in by the superintendent and school board causing conflicts in their relationship. Among these factors were societal forces and organizational forces.

In the analysis of the three cases included in this study, each will be treated with the factors to see how they intervened to disturb the decision-making process causing conflicts in superintendent-school board relations. None of the factors is discrete for each factor intertwines with those that preceed or follow. Therefore, even though the factors are enumerated in sequence, they should be considered only as elements in a continuum. Thus, the ordering may vary from case to case. The factors used in this analysis are commonly used in social science literature as the microscopic lens to examine the causes and effects of events.

    I.  External (Societal) Factors:

        Racism
        Classism
        Sexism
        Group Pressures
        Colonial Status: Authority and power derived from Congress and the District Government

II. Internal (Organizational) Factors:

    Role conflicts, motives, membership changes, leadership styles, policy versus implementation
    Functions
    Structure
    Goal Setting
    Authority

Although only three decision-making situations were extrapolated for this investigation, it should be noted that other decisions were made during the period of observation for this study. In all of the cases reported, the superintendent chose to become involved in the deliberating but not the bargaining that took place within the decision-making unit; that is, although other administrators may have felt that the stakes were not sufficiently high enough to take a stand in opposition to the proposed policy retention or change, the superintendent pressed for change since the proposed action was at variance with her personal and organizational values. Therefore, all three cases presented are examples of active participation of the superintendent in the decision-making process.

It is important to keep in mind that many policy problems surfaced at the same time so that not all effort is made to solve problems consecutively since a number of problems are under consideration for an extended period of time. An illustration of this is the DCYOP controversy and the General Council dispute.

It should be noted that the literature on the relationship between the school superintendent and the school board concluded that, although it is generally felt that the school superintendent advises the school board and carries out the policy decisions and the school board makes policy, this separation in function does not hold steady in the enactment of roles. Therefore, it may be that those in the field of educational administration

should consider alternative ways for boards of
education and/or superintendents to be selected
and/or function in order to avoid the type of conflicts examined in this case study.

There is no intent in this analysis to pass
value judgments on the behavior of school board
members or superintendent or the staffs of either
in the four cases presented. The cases have
attempted to reconstruct the real situation of the
decision-making process in order to examine the
elements involved that led to conflicts in superintendent-school board relations.

Before the D.C. Self-Government Act was passed,
the board of education was the only elected body in
the District. The District of Columbia had a population that was 71 percent Black, approximately 60
percent poor with a student population approximately
96 percent Black. Yet, neither the community nor
the schools were controlled by Black people. Local
businesses were owned in large measure by whites
who lived in the surrounding suburbs. Many jobs
such as those in the fire and police departments
and the post office were held by white people living
outside the District. At the same time the survival
of many District residents was dependent on the lar-
gesse of social service agencies.

Even though Blacks were in the majority on the
city council, on the school board, and the mayor
was Black, generally money to support a candidacy
for these elected positions was obtained from the
monied elements, that is, the business community
which was predominantly white. Policies which
favored the white power structure were almost always
passed by these elected officials who apparently
were under the influence of these suburbanites who
controlled the District's economy. Therefore, what
D.C. had was an elected board of education with
limited power, home rule with no control over the
budget or the judicial system and subject to a 30
day Congressional veto of all legislation, and a
Congressional delegate with no vote.

In a situation like that described above, the factors of race, sex, class, the colonial status of the District and community pressure groups have to be seen as impinging on the decision-making process engaged in by the superintendent and school board members, especially when the data show that decisions made favored whites, males, and those with money. Likewise, role conflict surfaced in terms of motivations, leadership styles, policy versus implementation, and membership changes on the board along with other internal organizational factors such as goal setting, function, structure, process and authority of the offices of the board of education and the superintendent.

The D.C. Youth Orchestra program controversy

In the DCYOP case, white Virginians and Marylanders were given more favored treatment than were the Black poor in the DCPS system. The data on the regular program revealed that, though Blacks dominated on the beginning level, the number of whites was greater than the number of Blacks at the two highest levels, that is, 89 whites as compared to 77 Blacks. In the discussion comparing the number of students from the lowest income area, Ward 8, it was noted that there were only 21 students. But Maryland had contributed 100 and Virginia 20. Thus, out-of-state white students received more service than did District poor Black students from Ward 8. At this point in the discussion, a curve ball was thrown into the decision-making process when Mason called attention to the point that Ward 3, an affluent section of the District, was next to last in music services rendered by the DCYOP. Of course, she failed to point out that the parents in Ward 3 could well afford private music lessons if they chose, whereas parents in Ward 8 could not.

Related to this issue of differentiated music services for different races was the determination of most white, and some Black, board members to continue the DCYOP at Coolidge High School, located in the northwest section of the District close to an affluent suburban area. Deliberations in a board meeting revealed that the Coolidge location was more convenient for suburban whites and upper income Blacks and was felt to be safer also than the mid-city location of Western High School for the Performing Arts. This, of course, implied that sections of the District located closer to whites were less crime-ridden than those engulfed by Blacks. Here again the racism and classism factors are exposed.

Into this issue dropped another racial bombshell. One board member (Barry) was so anxious to rush through a decision in favor of renewing the contract with the Friends that he vociferously declared in a board meeting that the PACTS (Parents, Administrators, Community, Teachers, Students) concept, previously voted on by the DCBOE as a method for involving the predominantly Black public and others in the decision-making process at the local school level, was rejected as prolonging the decision about whether to incorporate the DCYOP into Western High.

Albeit symphonic music has its attributes, cultural arrogance appeared to be displayed when it was emphasized to the near exclusion of African and Eastern music. Board members were not moved by the superintendent's argument on this issue presented during the decision-making process. Thus, the decision to retain the structure as is was made in the face of a recent board decision to expand the goals to include a multi-lingual, multi-cultural curriculum thrust as proposed in the superintendent's 120 Day Report.

Reference was made in the Friends' ESAA Project description that the racial isolation in the regular school program militated against developing students on the more difficult instruments like the French Horn, bassoon, oboe or viola, implying that the African drum and the guitar were not as difficult as the Western European symphonic instruments.

The majority of board members rejected the superintendent's argument on this issue also in their deliberations.

Note, too, the extraordinary resistance of white board members along with Barry and Mason against the control of the DCYOP by the predominantly Black public school system or even the submitting of bids by predominantly Black Howard University. Noteworthy also was their resistance to the use of the approximately $151,000.00 by the public schools to upgrade its own music department. In these instances also, the majority was led by President Barry and Mrs. Mason to reject the superintendent's arguments in their deliberations to renew the contract with the Friends of the DCYOP.

Swaim, in particular, downgraded the training and music preparation of the predominantly Black teaching force of the public school system in her efforts to extoll the superiority of the part-time military band instructors hired by Lyn McClain, the white director of the DCYOP. In board members' arguments to explain the superiority of these persons, it was repeatedly noted that they were practicing musicians. Undeniably though, the data gathered by some members of the school system indicated that over half of the public school music instructors were professional performing musicians. Deliberations of the majority of board members overlooked these data and therefore was apparently swayed by Swaim's argument. Racial considerations can perhaps be seen in this situation also.

Another racial feature of this case might be seen in the firing of James Hall, director of the Junior Band, by the executive committee of the Friends without observing his due process rights. Intervention by the superintendent and her staff was limited due to the structure of the DCYOP, which denied any authority or control arrangements to the school administration. Interestingly, both Hall and McLain were involved in fisticuffs on school property. Was it incidental that Hall was

Black and McLain was white? Was it incidental that the decision to fire was made by the Friends, an integrated group controlled by whites, which pressured the DCBOE to accept their terms for a contract?

Therefore, not only did the DCBOE make a decision that forced the superintendent to prepare a contract with few even minor revisions to incorporate some of the administration's concerns, but some board members pressured the superintendent to do so speedily. This was particularly true in the case of the president of the board, Marion Barry. Seemingly, in his case and perhaps even in the case of Martha Swaim and Hilda Mason, political ambitions arose to the forefront. Barry planned to leave his school board seat to run for the city council as did Swaim that same year. Barry won; Swaim lost. Mason ran and won in 1977. One might surmise from the transcript data, in particular, that all three were anxious to build up support among the powerful interests in the community. This became more and more clear as one read about the desperate attempts to sway the total school board and the public into an acceptance of the decision to renew the contract with the Friends. It became clear also as Barry assumed a more and more dictatorial posture on the board and disputed with Taylor and Simmons, especially, about his railroading decisions through and his use of rules and regulations to stymie discussion and pivot opposing remarks in favor of his position. Thus, it can be deduced that some board members did view their membership on the school board as a stepping-stone to a higher political office. This was reflected in the decisions they made that favored the money interests in the District.

This case underscored one of the biggest problems for the superintendent in her relations with the majority of the board. The resolution of the alternative school program may have stemmed from the fact that several people on the board made their living or obtained money from alternative educational enterprises -- Mr. Barry with 'Pride,' Mr. Treanor with the 'run away school,' Father Kemp with the Catholic system, Mrs. Morris with the 'United Planning Organization,' 'Head Start,' Mrs. Simmons with B.L.S., a private consultant firm, although she was not opposed to Sizemore's plans, Hobson with Hospitality House, Inc. (see Chapter V), and Mrs. Mason trying to get money from the Eugene and Agnes Meyer Foundation to fund the citizens' decentralization proposal (see Chapter IV). Many of these board members were involved in private agencies and, as a result, they were very prone to give away public school money to private organizations like the DCYOP.

Now, it was very clear from the Ten Priority Goals which Superintendent Scott had left that if Sizemore and the board intended to decentralize the school system, they would have to do it with the resources available. It was also unlikely that Congress would give additional money for this purpose. Therefore, if decentralization and other changes were to occur, they would have to occur within the limitations of the budget. As previously discussed, in 1972, Mrs. Swaim, who at that time was chairperson of the Budget and Finance Committee, had slashed the budget by eliminating one-third of the administrative personnel. This further curtailed the resources that were available for the implementation of the plan that Dr. Scott had submitted to the board prior to his leaving in May 1973. This meant, then, that the administration had to examine the budget for monies and recall all monies in order to reallocate them for the decentralization plan. One way the superintendent and the executive staff thought they could do this would have been to call in all the monies that had been given out to private organizations in order to utilize them for this new purpose. The DCYOP which caused conflicts between the superintendent and the school board, was important, first, because the school system needed the money, and, secondly, it and others like it showed the administration that the board was more committed to private enterprise than it was to public schools. Interestingly, although an alternative educational policy was offered to the DCBOE by Superintendent Sizemore, it was not accepted, and even by the Fall of 1977 it had not been definitized, that is, there is still no stated policy codified in concise terms within the board <u>Rules</u> on alternative education programs.

## The General Counsel dispute

The General Counsel dispute grew out of the DCYOP controversy. Seemingly, the general counsel was employed to erode the authority of the superintendent and also to give the board more staff. Therefore, what the board did was to try to make the superintendent report through the general counsel of the DCBOE to the corporation counsel of the District government. When the superintendent refused to do so, it just aggravated a problem in superintendent-school board relations that existed prior to that, as could be seen in the DCYOP controversy and similar disputes. Two factors in particular can be viewed as blatant evidence of racism and sexism unwittingly or wittingly ingrained in the ideology of some board members. The general counsel, David Splitt, was a white male; the superintendent of schools was a Black female. It may be that Virginia Morris, president of the DCBOE, a Black female who came to view the superintendent as a strong opponent to some of her values, felt the need for a white male to circumvent or thwart the superintendent's long strides toward a successful implementation of her program to change the school system to better serve the children there.

There is reason to believe, as reported in the interview data gathered by Mrs. Sizemore and to be reported in her study entitled: "The Politics of Decentralization: A Case Study of the D.C. Public Schools, 1973-1976," that Virginia Morris was voted into the presidency of the DCBOE through negotiation with white board members and some Black ones. The stakes traded off were the presidency of the DCBOE for control of the superintendent and Morris' vote to let the contract for the DCYOP. It can be noted in the transcripts that Morris rejected the contract up until the time that she became president of the DCBOE in July 1974. Soon after that, she very forcefully pushed the superintendent to prepare the contract for her signature.

Later, it will be noted that the General Counsel dispute came into play during the hearings in Charge 13: Failure to comply with board directive to provide fiscal year 1975 legislative proposal.

The budgetary/management controversy

The budget crisis created many problems. It certainly created problems in terms of management and educational programming. Significantly, these were problems that had existed in the system for over 10 years. Actually, the evidence reveals that the budget crisis provided a convenient cover for a decision which seemed to have been made in December 1975 by the policy-making majority of the DCBOE to fire the superintendent. This was alluded to by several board members in their interviews.

Throughout each of the three cases described, the conflict mounted as the board substituted implementation for policy-making and delved deeper and deeper into the day-to-day operation of the D.C. public school system. The climax came when the board decided to form a task force to deal with the FY75 financial plan and the FY76 budget and removed these tasks from the purview of the superintendent. In doing so, the Committee on School Finance under the chairmanship of Julius Hobson, Jr., through the task force, decimated the structural and programmatic changes introduced by Superintendent Sizemore in the 120 Day Report, a document presenting her goals for the school system.

The FY75 budget document was Hugh Scott's

budget prepared in 1973 to support his goals for the system as approved by the DCBOE. But the FY76 budget was Sizemore's first and, as it turned out, only budget. Nevertheless, her authority to support her administration's programs was removed from her and her budget document butchered by the board's seven member policy-making majority.

Specifically, the FY76 budget was almost unrelated to the goals and objectives established in the 120 Day Report presented in March 1974 and adopted by the board of education on May 30, 1974.

Several examples of media pressure were revealed as Kemp, in particular, and sometimes Morris, referred to news articles or editorials in the Washington Star and the Washington Post for data about the school, almost implying that these were valid sources of such data.

Obviously, Brockett had a pipeline to board sources since, as she admits, the conference to which she referred at one point in an article was "closed." In answer to the interview question: "Who was feeding Diane Brockett information?," Kemp stated that everybody was feeding her information, even himself, and that she had more information than did Sizemore. In fact, Kemp admitted that "Brockett had that whole building wired inside of six months...and she found stuff printed on pieces of paper...and I think she was influential in the whole process."[111] It does appear quite possible that the Washington Star's biased news coverage was a potent factor in the conflict.

Notably, group pressures from the organized organizations in southeast Washington, especially in support of the superintendent's programs, had little or no effect on the decisions made by the board to continue funding the six small schools, the DCYOP and the Hawthorne School or forced the board to support the innovative plans proposed by the superintendent.

Special note was made of the factor of the board's powerlessness in terms of the budget cuts and the freeze imposed by the mayor-commissioner which almost created havoc in the school operations and certainly made its imprint felt in terms of having to set priorities and re-do budgets. This factor also had a damaging effect on superintendent-school board relations as both factions struggled to have its programs receive the higher priority. In the end though, the seven member policy-making majority on the board won out. They changed the superintendent's FY76 budget to fund their pet projects which aborted her efforts to change the school system and make it more responsive to the 96 percent Black student population.

The internal factor of role conflict was evident as the board snatched the authority to design the FY76 budget package away from the superintendent and gave it to the task force (team) recommended by the committee on School Finance under the chairmanship of Julius Hobson, Jr., who appeared to have been influenced by forces in the community other than the people he represented in Ward 8. Erosion of the superintendent's power was also seen during board meetings as her arguments in favor of educationally sound programs and against retaining dysfunctional administrative positions and establishing illogical bureaucratic layers between the community and the superintendent were discounted. Obviously, some board members felt they made better superintendents than the person hired to administer the school system. Board changes, which occurred at the November 20, 1975 board meeting, brought on board Kane and Schwartz who joined Mason, Morris, Hobson, Treanor and Kemp, making up the seven member majority against the superintendent and only Benjamin and Warren to join Simmons and Evans to make the four member minority who supported the superintendent. Thus, changes in board membership did affect the relationship but not the balance actually, as Taylor and Rosenfield who left were supporters, while Barry and Swaim, who also left, were not.

The leadership style of Morris was authoritarian as revealed in not only how she treated the community in board meetings but in how she treated the superintendent. One example was her denial of permission for the superintendent to take her vacation after she had waited until the end of the year to do so. Demands and directives as regards the 100 percent time of key administrators on the task force is another example.

Mason designed four of the charges which derived from the April 7, 1975 board meeting, a few days after Mrs. Sizemore's speech before the African Heritage Studies Association. Was she building a pathway to a city council seat? This is a fair question for speculation as she did run and win in white and middle class Black wards, in particular, over the superintendent in a close contest in July 1977, two years later. Morris ran for a school board seat soon after the hearings but she lost. Then she ran for an Advisory Neighborhood Council seat and lost. Did her poor and Black constituents abhor her obscene rejection of all that was good for Black children? Hobson, Jr. declined to run for his school board seat again stating financial reasons as his excuse. Did he see the handwriting on the wall? Kane recently declared her candidacy for a city council seat. After examining the decisions made by the board on the budgets and subsequent actions of board members, it becomes clearer that some decisions may have been political ones rather than educational ones.

The structure of the system was kept almost intact as the board revealed its rejection of the change to decentralization, curriculum changes, new goals and relationships through the budget process by removing the superintendent's priorities to new and improved services and putting theirs into the base budget.

## Conclusions

As was noted earlier, the social structure of the school system had changed to a vast Black student population. Black school superintendents were hired who had had some experience managing urban school systems. The hands of the first Black superintendent were tied due to a policy decision to accept a curriculum plan made prior to his taking office as well as a plan for re-structuring the school system on the basis of a decentralization plan. This superintendent struggled with the curriculum plan in which he had lost faith and in turn struggled to design an acceptable equalization and decentralization plan. Before he could complete either task, his contract was not renewed. The second Black superintendent was a female of strong convictions about the type of educational program which needed to be implemented in order to positively affect the learning of the majority Black student population, as well as the minority white. Decisions made prior to her taking office hampered her moving ahead with the plan to decentralize the system, and to institute a multi-lingual, multicultural, multi-modal educational plan which spoke to the needs of the students presently in the school system. External factors in the form of racism, sexism, classism, group pressures and the unique relation of the school system to the Congress and internal factors of role conflict, goal setting, function, structure, and processes established through rules, regulations and laws for setting policy and operating the school system, interfered with her efforts to make the system more responsive to the needs of the student population. Hence, conflict in the relationship between the superintendent, who desired to make changes, and school board members who desired to maintain the status quo, mounted. Both elements struggled to influence the decision-making process. The superintendent tried to make it more responsive to the citizens and their children through the introduction of the PACTS process on the local, regional and system-wide levels, and the majority of the DCBOE tried to maintain their control of the process and the way decisions were made in order to make policy decisions in favor of the power elements in the community. Thus, outside pressure on school board members resulted in no major policy revisions that had to do with their responsiveness to the majority constituents in the District. Therefore, all three decisions were apparently more political than they were educational; that is, they were decisions that extended the power and control of the majority on the school board rather than facilitating the learning and development of the student population.

The direction the administration was interested in taking was one rejected by some board members whose bent was focused on developing options and alternatives outside the public school system. Therefore, this became a hotly disputed issue since Sizemore leaned, at this time, toward utilizing the energies, time and resources of public school personnel toward developing alternatives within the public school system. However, this strategy did not rule out using ideas, practices or programs developed outside the public school system. It did though, at the minimum, support the plan of incorporating these outside alternatives if they (1) lent themselves to being useful and supportive of a 96 percent Black and majority poor student population, (2) were equally available to all public school children, (3) would enhance and not destroy the public school, and (4) could provide something for public school children that the public schools were not able presently to provide. This was a large order for school board members who were bent on funneling public school funds into their pet private enterprise projects in order, it appeared, to gain favor with the power interests in the community. Therefore, no such reasonable argument, such as the above put forth by the superintendent, was acceptable to them.

In the case discussed above we see another instance of the withdrawal of the authority of the superintendent to mount viable educational programs coupled with the denial of authority to shop around for the best educational services to be provided by outside agencies due to the constraints imposed by sole source contracting engaged in by the board.

On January 21, 1974, the board "approved as administrative policy that [all] future...matters relating to School System business involving contact with the Corporation Counsel and his office be screened and coordinated by the Counsel of the Board: including requests for legal opinions and matters involving litigation." Further, the board president directed the superintendent to submit all requests to the corporation counsel through the board's general counsel. This position was reaffirmed by the board on a number of occasions. This withdrawal of authority from the superintendent, and assigned to the board's general counsel, obviously impeded the progress of impending court action in the case of school system legal matters including the area of special education. Needless-to-say, accountability mechanisms and control of the general counsel's attendance to these duties was never developed by the board.

The withdrawal of the budgetary process from the purview of the superintendent usurped administrative authority and prerogatives inherent in the position of superintendent of schools and served to render the superintendent without leadership authority. Historically speaking, the superintendent submitted to the board of education on October 11, 1974, November 13, 1974, November 26, 1974, December 5, 1974, and December 12, 1974 recommendations and plans of action to resolve the deficit anticipated in FY75. All five of the reports with recommendations were rejected or ignored by the board. Instead, the board decided to give, on December 5, 1974, the authority to recommend solutions to the problems to a school Finance Committee task team, chaired by Julius Hobson, Jr. Specifically, the task team was given the authority to devise a FY75 financial plan. The task team's recommendations were approved by the board on December 23, 1974. One of these recommendations required the mayor to absorb approximately $10.5 million of the school system's unmet needs. Only $700,000.00 of the $10.5 million was granted. A request from the board's president to the chairperson of the task team to revitalize the team was ignored, reflecting the loss of control of an arm of the board by the president, different, in fact, from the contractual arrangements with the superintendent.

In October 1974, the superintendent submitted to the board a FY76 budget request. No action was taken by the board. On January 8, 1975, the superintendent requested board guidance relative to developing a FY76 budgetary strategy which projected system solidarity. No action was forthcoming. Another request was proferred from the superintendent to the board to expedite the FY76 budget submission of October so that the administration could proceed to develop justification statements in support of the document. No board action was taken. But rather, on January 13, 1975, the Finance Committee did direct the administration not to take any action relative to the submission of justifying statements of the system's FY76 budget request to the mayor. Thus, the superintendent on January 23, 1975 requested the board to reassess its position. No response was forthcoming. In February 1975, the board approved a FY76 budget request document five months after the original document was submitted by the superintendent.

The above brief outline of events points to a serious D.C. superintendent-school board problem involving (1) the withdrawal of authority from the chief executive officer, (2) the giving of that authority to another arm of the board, (3) thus affording the board an opportunity to ignore the superintendent's requests for action on important issues, and (4) the board's subsequent losing of control over its creation, the task team, and (5) finally a submission of the same recommendations originally submitted by the superintendent after a five month passage of time.

Evidence from board budgetary decisions made during Scott's tenure, and Sizemore's tenure as well, point to a board practice of reacting to fiscal crisis by reducing the capability of the central office. Witness Swaim's drastic slash in 1972 and the Sizemore board's slashes in funds to staff the management office while increasing capabilities of board operations by increasing board staff.

These three cases just analyzed clearly point up the basic cause and related side issues of the protracted conflict in superintendent-school board relations in the D.C. public school system during the 1973-75 time span which led directly to the superintendent's hearing and finally to her termination.

Three specific instances of the withdrawal of authority from the superintendent, and the placement of it elsewhere, were documented in detail. These three instances just discussed were the DCYOP case, the General Counsel dispute, and the Budget/Management controversy.

Chapter IX will detail aspects of group pressures on the decision-making unit.

FOOTNOTES                                CHAPTER VIII


1.  Correspondence with attached report, "The D.C.
    Youth Orchestra Program and the Morale of the
    Public School Instrumental Music Teachers," to
    Dr. James T. Guines, Associate Superintendent
    of Schools, from Barbara White, Representative,
    Superintendent's Advisory Council, Elementary
    Instrumental Music Department, and Rosanna B.
    Saffran, Teacher, Elementary Instrumental
    Music Department, 16 July 1971.

2.  Correspondence to Mr. Delroy L. Cornick,
    Director, Department of Budget and Legislation,
    Public Schools of the District of Columbia,
    from Mrs. Paul H. Banner, President, Friends
    of the D.C. Youth Orchestra Program, 11 August
    1969.

3.  Memorandum for the Files from Marian S. Banner,
    President, Friends of the D.C. Youth Orchestra
    Program, 17 September 1969.

4.  Memorandum to Mr. William Bedford, Assistant
    Superintendent, from Paul D. Gable, Super-
    vising Director, Music Department, and Lyn G.
    McLain, Director, D.C. Youth Orchestra Program,
    9 October 1970.

5.  Memorandum to DCBOE from Hugh J. Scott, Super-
    intendent of Schools, re: The D.C. Youth
    Orchestra, 19 July 1972.

6.  Latinee Gullattee, Committee Chairman, "Report
    of the Committee on Elementary Instrumental
    Music," 25 August 1972.

7.  Hortense Taylor, Chairman, Proposal Committee,
    "Toward a Comprehensive Music Education Pro-
    gram of Quality for the Public Schools of
    Washington, D.C.--K-12," 18 July 1972.

8. Petition signed by 22 persons and submitted to Superintendent Scott, Marion Barry, other administrators and some citizens, dated 8 September 1972.

9. Wilbur Bellamy, Coordinator, Resource Professional Program, "1972-1973 Progress Report," Resource Professional Program, D.C. Youth Orchestra Program, Music Department, Public Schools of the District of Columbia, 30 June 1973, pp. 1-19.

10. Contract, Government of the District of Columbia, Bureau of Procurement, Department of Public Schools, Negotiated Services, 24 September 1973, 23 April 1974.

11. Memorandum to Wilbur Bellamy, Assistant Director, D.C. Youth Orchestra Program, from Mr. Lyn McLain, Director, D.C. Youth Orchestra Program, re: Enrollment Breakdown (1973-74) Winter Season -- September-June, 29 April 1974.

12. ESAA Grant Proposal, Component B, 1974.

13. Ibid.

14. Memorandum to To Whom It May Concern, from D.C. Youth Orchestra Program, Junior Band Percussion Section, 23 February 1974; Memorandum to Parents from Wilbur Bellamy, Assistant Director, DCYOP, 24 May 1974; Memorandum to Parents of Junior Band Students from Wilbur Bellamy, Assistant Director, re: Junior Band Rehearsals, 27 March 1973; Flyer, "Grievances of the Junior Band," no date.

15. Memorandum to Mrs. Myrtle Morris, President, Friends of the D.C. Youth Orchestra Program, from Lyn McLain, Director, DCYOP re: Attached memo from Mr. Bellamy, 28 February 1974 re: The Junior Band Situation, 27 February 1974.

16. Letter to Mrs. Barbara A. Sizemore, Superintendent of Schools, from James E. Hall, Junior Band Director, 26 March 1974.

17. Lyn McLain, Director, D.C. Youth Orchestra Program, "Brief Report of Incident of Saturday, 23 March 1974."

18. Memorandum to Floretta McKenzie, Deputy Superintendent, from Edgar B. Dews, Jr., Security Director, re: "Assault-D.C. Youth Orchestra Program, Coolidge High School, 28 March 1974.

19. Memorandum to Floretta D. McKenzie, Deputy Superintendent, from James T. Guines, Associate Superintendent, re: Mr. Lyn McLain, 1 April 1974.

20. Letter to Mr. Lyn McLain, Teacher, from Floretta D. McKenzie, Deputy Superintendent, 4 April 1974.

21. Letter to Floretta McKenzie, Deputy Superintendent, from Juanita Thompson, President, Junior Band Boosters, 4 April 1974.

22. Memorandum to Lyn McLain from Wilbur Bellamy re: Junior Band Rehearsal (2 April 1974), 5 April 1974.

23. Memorandum to Barbara A. Sizemore, Superintendent of Schools, from Floretta D. McKenzie, Deputy Superintendent, re: Altercation at Coolidge High School; D.C. Youth Orchestra Program, 5 April 1974.

24. Correspondence to Barbara A. Sizemore, Superintendent of Schools, from Myrtle Morris, President, re: Friends of the D.C. Youth Orchestra Program, 22 May 1974.

25. Letter to Mrs. Myrtle C. Morris, President, from James T. Guines, Associate Superintendent, re: Friends of the D.C. Youth Orchestra Program, 31 May 1974.

26. Memorandum to Hortense Taylor, Department of Music, from James T. Guines, Associate Superintendent, re: Future Arrangements for the D.C. Youth Orchestra, 15 May 1974.

27. Memorandum to Barbara A. Sizemore, Superintendent of Schools, and Floretta McKenzie, Deputy Superintendent, from James T. Guines, Associate Superintendent, 31 May 1974.

28. Letters to Mr. Richard L. Hurlbut, Chief, Tuition Act Enforcement Branch, from Lyn McLain, Director, D.C. Youth Orchestra Program, 4 June 1974.

29. "Transcript of the Third Annual Meeting for Students, D.C. Board of Education Meeting," Washington, D.C., 14 June 1974, p. 1.

30. "Transcript of the Twelfth (Stated) Meeting of the Board of Education," Washington, D.C., 19 June 1974, pp. 25-83.

31. "Transcript of the Thirteenth (Special) Meeting of the Board of Education," Washington, D.C., 2 July 1974, p. 105; Interview with Ruth Goodwin, D.C. Concerned Citizen, 6 May 1978.

32. "Transcript of the Fourteenth (Special) Meeting," Washington, D.C., 8 July 1974, pp. 7-90.

33. Letter of Intent, Myrtle C. Morris, President, Friends of the D.C. Youth Orchestra Program, 9 July 1974.

34. Memorandum to Superintendent from Dwight S. Cropp, Executive Secretary, DCBOE, 10 July 1974.

35. Letter from Relford Patterson, Ph.D., Chairman, Department of Music, Howard University, 10 July 1974.

36. Letter to Lyn McLain, Director, D.C. Youth Orchestra Program, from Mr. Richard L. Hurlbut, Chief, Tuition Act Enforcement Branch, DCPS, re: Payment of Tuition, 15 July 1974.

37. Mrmorandum to Richard L. Hurlbut, Chief, Tuition Act Enforcement Branch, DCPS, from Lyn McLain, Director, DCYOP, re: Listing of Nonresident Students, 24 July 1974.

38. Memorandum to Ms. Barbara Sizemore, Superintendent of Schools, from David A. Splitt, General Counsel, re: Negotiated Services Contract (74-15), 25 July 1974.

39. Letter to Mrs. Barbara A. Sizemore, Superintendent, Public Schools of the District of Columbia, from Mrs. Myrtle C. Morris, President, Friends of the D.C. Youth Orchestra Program, Inc., 29 July 1974.

40. Memorandum to DCBOE from Barbara A. Sizemore, Superintendent of Schools, D.C. Youth Orchestra Program, 1 August 1974.

41. "Transcript of the Special Meeting of the Board of Education," Washington, D.C., 1 August 1974.

42. Letter to Mrs. Barbara A. Sizemore, Superintendent of Schools, from Dwight S. Cropp, Executive Secretary, Board of Education, 2 August, 1974.

43. Memorandum to Mrs. Sizemore and Dr. Guines, from Dick Hurlbut, re: DCYOP Contractual Agreement, 10 August 1974.

44. Dwight S. Cropp, Executive Secretary, "Report of the Joint Committee on Educational Programs and Student Services and Community Involvement," 12 August 1974.

45. Memorandum to DCBOE from Barbara A. Sizemore, Superintendent of Schools, re: Statement on Contracting, 13 August 1974, p. 1.

46. Letter to Mrs. Barbara A. Sizemore, Superintendent of Schools, from Reverend Raymond B. Kemp, Member, Board of Education, 14 August 1974.

47. Journal, Index to the Transcript of the Eighteenth (Special) Meeting of the Board of Education, District of Columbia, 13 August 1974, pp. 74-20 to 74-21.

48. Letter to Mrs. Barbara A. Sizemore, Superintendent, District of Columbia Public Schools, from Edward Maguire, Chief Negotiator, Friends of the District of Columbia, Youth Orchestra Program, Inc., and Dr. James Johnson, Chief Negotiator, District of Columbia Public Schools, 17 August 1974.

49. Memorandum to DCBOE from Barbara A. Sizemore, Superintendent of Schools, re: The D.C. Youth Orchestra Contract, 19 August 1974.

50. Memorandum to Mrs. Barbara A. Sizemore, Superintendent of Schools, from Virginia Morris, President, Board of Education, re: Administrative requests to General Counsel, 22 August 1974; Memorandum to Mrs. Virginia Morris, President, D.C. Board of Education, from Barbara A. Sizemore, 22 August 1974; Memorandum to Mr. Dwight S. Cropp, Executive Secretary, D.C. Board of Education, from Barbara A. Sizemore, Superintendent of Schools, re: "Transmittal of Draft of Proposed D.C. Youth Orchestra Contract Prepared on D.C. Government Negotiated Services Contract Forms,"

26 August 1974; Memorandum to Mrs. Barbara A. Sizemore, Superintendent of Schools, from Mrs. Virginia Morris, President, Board of Education of the District of Columbia, re: "D.C. Youth Orchestra Contract," 29 August 1974; Memorandum to Mrs. Virginia Morris, President, Board of Education, from Barbara A. Sizemore, Superintendent of Schools, re: "D.C. Youth Orchestra Contract," 30 August 1974; Memorandum to Mrs. Barbara A. Sizemore, Superintendent of Schools, from Virginia A. Morris, President, Board of Education, re: "D.C. Youth Orchestra Contract," 4 September 1974; Memorandum to Mrs. Virginia Morris, President, Board of Education, from Barbara A. Sizemore, Superintendent, re: "D.C. Youth Orchestra Program," 9 September 1974; Report from Committee on Student Services and Community Involvement, Chairman, Julius Hobson, Jr., "Report on the Joint Committees on Educational Programs and Student Services and Community Involvement," 17 September 1974.

51. Letter To Rev. Raymond B. Kemp, Member, Board of Education, from Barbara A. Sizemore, Superintendent of Schools, 23 August 1974.

52. Memorandum to Dr. James T. Guines, Deputy Superintendent, Instructional Services, from Ms. Barbara A. Sizemore, Superintendent, re: DCYOP Youth Chorale, 3 September 1974.

53. Memorandum to Ms. Barbara A. Sizemore, Superintendent, from James T. Guines, Associate Superintendent, 4 September 1974.

54. Memorandum to Mrs. Barbara A. Sizemore, Superintendent of Schools, from James T. Guines, Associate Superintendent, 6 September 1974.

55. Memorandum to Board of Education of the District of Columbia, from Barbara A. Sizemore, Superintendent of Schools, re: Negotiated Services Contracts, 18 September 1974.

56. Memorandum to Barbara Sizemore, Superintendent, D.C. Public Schools, from Acting Material Management Officer, D.C. General Services, Material Management, Government of the District of Columbia, re: Proposed Negotiated Services Contract 0477-AA-NS-5-GA, The Friends of the D.C. Orchestra Program, Inc., 7 October 1974.

57. Memorandum to Mrs. Virginia Morris, President, Board of Education, from Barbara A. Sizemore, Superintendent of Schools, 13 November 1974.

58. Memorandum to Barbara A. Sizemore, Superintendent of Schools, from Virginia Morris, President, Board of Education, re: D.C. Youth Orchestra Contract, 19 December 1974.

59. Memorandum to Mrs. Virginia Morris, President, Board of Education, from Barbara A. Sizemore, Superintendent of Schools, 24 December 1974.

60. Interview with Julius Hobson, Jr., D.C. Board of Education member, Washington, D.C., 28 September 1977.

61. Interview with Virginia Morris, D.C. Board of Education member, Washington, D.C., 11 October 1977.

62. Interview with Barbara A. Sizemore, Superintendent of Schools, Washington, D.C., 17 April 1978.

63. "Position Description," Special Assistant, D.C. Board of Education, Position Control, 31 May 1973.

64. "Transcript of the Thirty-Second (Stated) Meeting of the Board of Education," Washington, D.C., 19 December 1973, pp. 52-54.

65. "Transcript of the Continuation Meeting of 16 January 1974, (Stated)," Washington, D.C., 21 January 1974, p. 13.

66. Memorandum to Mr. William Treanor, Chairman, Mrs. Martha S. Swaim, Member, Mrs. Mattie G. Taylor, Member, Committee on Board Operations, Rules and Policies from Mr. Dwight S. Cropp, Executive Secretary, re: "Referral of document 'Duties of the General Counsel to the Board of Education'" to Committee, 13 May 1974.

67. Memorandum to DCBOE from Barbara A. Sizemore, Superintendent of Schools, re: General Counsel to the Board of Education, 15 May 1974.

68. Correspondence to Mrs. Virginia Morris, President, Board of Education, from Barbara A. Sizemore, 19 September 1974.

69. Memorandum to the Board of Education of the District of Columbia from Barbara A. Sizemore, Superintendent of Schools, re: 1975 Legislative Program: Addendum Number I, 3 October 1974, p. 2.

70. "Transcript of the Twenty-Fourth (Stated) Meeting of the Board of Education," Washington, D.C., 16 October 1974, pp. 168-193.

71. Memorandum to the Citizenry from Mrs. Virginia Morris, President, Board of Education, re: A Statement on the Role of the General Counsel to the Board of Education, 19 March 1975, p. 2; See also Transcript of the Fifth (Stated) Meeting of the Board of Education, Washington, D.C., 19 March 1975, pp. 173-175.

72. Barbara A. Sizemore, Superintendent of Schools, "Become 'Comparable' and 'Equal': Questions and Answers," January 1975, p. 4.

73. Barbara A. Sizemore, <u>Superintendent of Schools Reorganization of Central Office</u>, Washington, D.C.: Public Schools of the District of Columbia, 8 November 1974, pp. 1-19; see "The Politics of Decentralization: A Case Study of the D.C. Public Schools, 1973-76," Doctoral dissertation, University of Chicago, 1979.

74. Letter to the President and Members of the Board of Education from Martha S. Swaim, Member, Board of Education, 31 May 1974.

75. James L. Williams, Deputy Superintendent, <u>Administrative Reorganization and Major Responsibilities of Management Services of the District of Columbia Public Schools -- Part I</u>, Washington, D.C.: Public Schools of the District of Columbia, May 1974.

76. "Minutes of the Fifth (Special) Meeting of the Board of Education, 1968-1969," Washington, D.C., 24 February 1969, pp. 3-7.

77. The Respondent's Answer submitted to the DCBOE in compliance with the specifications of the charges brought against the Superintendent, Barbara A. Sizemore, 25 June 1975, pp. 27-29.

78. "The New Budget What Will Happen to the Schools?," <u>Bulletin Board</u>, September 1972, pp. 1-3.

79. "Transcript of the Twenty-Third (Special) Meeting of the Board," Washington, D.C., 5 September 1973, pp. 2-22.

80. "Minutes of the Twenty-Seventh (Special) Meeting of the Board of Education," Washington, D.C., 25 October 1973, pp. 2-3.

81. Louise Malone, "D.C. School Budget-FY'75," <u>Bulletin Board</u>, District of Columbia Citizens for Better Public Education, Inc., Vol. 5, No. 3, April 1974, pp. 1, 2 and 5.

82. Memorandum to Dr. James Johnson, Associate Superintendent, Planning, Research and Evaluation and Mr. James L. Williams, Deputy Superintendent, Management Services, from Barbara A. Sizemore, Superintendent of Schools, 7 August 1974; Memorandum to Ms. Barbara A. Sizemore from James L. Williams, Deputy Superintendent (reply), 12 August 1974; Memorandum to Mr. James L. Williams from Barbara A. Sizemore, Superintendent of Schools, 16 August 1974; and Memorandum to Ms. Virginia Morris, President, D.C. Board of Education, from Barbara A. Sizemore, Superintendent of Schools, 23 August 1974 with attached memorandum to Elementary School Principals from Ms. Floretta D. McKenzie, Deputy Superintendent, re: Teacher Service Allotment: Regular Budget FY'75, 29 March 1974.

83. Diane Brockett, "Delay in School Openings Is News to Sizemore," Washington Star, 6 September 1974.

84. Memorandum to Executive Staff from Ms. Barbara A. Sizemore, re: 1976 Budget Proposals, 6 September 1974, and 4 September 1974 Memorandum attached.

85. Letter to Mrs. Virginia Morris, President, Board of Education, from Barbara A. Sizemore, Superintendent of Schools, 10 September 1974.

86. Memorandum to Ms. Barbara A. Sizemore from James L. Williams, Deputy Superintendent, re: FY 1975 Financial Plan, September 30, 1974; and Commissioner's Memorandum 74-139 to Public Schools from Comer S. Coppie, Special Assistant to the Mayor-Commissioner for Budget and Financial Management, re: Apportionments and Financial Plans for Fiscal Year 1975 Appropriated Funds, 3 September 1974.

87. "Transcript of the Twentieth (Special) Meeting of the Board of Education," Washington, D.C., 30 September 1974.

88. Memorandum to Public Schools from Comer S. Coppie, Special Assistant to the Mayor-Commissioner for Budget and Financial Management, re: Revised Apportionments and Financial Plans for Fiscal Year 1975, 3 October 1974.

89. "Transcript of the Twenty-Fourth (Stated) Meeting of 1974, Board of Education," Washington, D.C., 16 October 1974, pp. 154-246.

90. Memorandum to DCBOE from Barbara A. Sizemore, Superintendent of Schools, re: FY 1976 Operating Budget, 21 October 1974.

91. Memorandum to Ms. Barbara A. Sizemore, Superintendent of Schools, from Julius W. Hobson, Jr., Chairman, Committee on School Finance, re: FY76 Budget Plan, 22 October 1974.

92. "Transcript of the Twenty-Fifth (Special) Board Meeting," Washington, D.C., 22 October 1974.

93. Memorandum to Mrs. Virginia Morris, President, Board of Education, from Barbara A. Sizemore, Superintendent of Schools, 12 November 1974; Letter to Mrs. Virginia Morris, President, Board of Education, from Barbara A. Sizemore, Superintendent of Schools, 13 November 1974, and Memorandum to Ms. Barbara A. Sizemore, Superintendent of Schools, from James L. Williams, Deputy Superintendent, re: Projected FY 1975 Expenditure Requirements, 11 November 1974.

94. Memorandum to Barbara A. Sizemore, Superintendent of Schools, from James L. Williams, Deputy Superintendent, re: Revision of FY 1975 Financial Plan, 19 November 1974.

95. "Transcript of the Twenty-Sixth (Stated) Meeting of the Board of Education," Washington, D.C., 20 November 1974, p. 210.

96. "Transcript of the Twenty-Sixth (Special) Board Meeting," Washington, D.C., 2 December 1974, pp. 70A-102.

97. "Transcript of the Committee on School Finance Meeting," Washington, D.C., 6 December 1974, pp. R-13; R-33 - R-72; R-140.

98. "Transcript of An Emergency (Special) Meeting of the Board of Education," Washington, D.C., 6 December 1974.

99. "Transcript of the Twenty-Seventh (Special) Meeting of the Board of Education," Washington, D.C., 6 December 1974, pp. 1-3A.

100. Letter to Mrs. Barbara Sizemore, Superintendent of Schools, from Dwight S. Cropp, Executive Secretary, 9 December 1974.

101. Letter to Mrs. Barbara A. Sizemore, Superintendent, District of Columbia Public Schools, from Virginia Morris, President, Board of Education, 12 December 1974.

102. "Transcript of An Emergency (Special) Meeting of the Board of Education," Washington, D.C., 12 December 1974.

103. Diane Brockett, "D.C. School Board Issues Ultimatum to Sizemore," Washington Star, 12 December 1974.

104. "Transcript of the Third (Stated) Meeting of the Board of Education," Washington, D.C., 19 February 1975.

105. Barbara A. Sizemore, "Education: Is Accommodation Enough?", The Journal of Negro Education, 44 (Summer 1975).

106. "Transcript of the Fifth (Stated) Meeting of the Board of Education," Washington, D.C., 19 March 1975.

107. Ibid.

108. Memorandum to Mr. James L. Williams, Deputy Superintendent, from Barbara A. Sizemore, re: Position Control, 20 March 1975.

109. Sizemore, "Education: Is Accommodation Enough?", The Journal of Negro Education, 44 (Summer 1975).

110. "Transcript of the Sixth Special (Emergency) Meeting of the Board of Education," Washington, D.C., 7 April 1975.

111. "Transcript of the Seventh (Stated) Meeting of the Board of Education," Washington, D.C., 16 April 1975.

CHAPTER IX

GROUP PRESSURES ON THE DECISION-MAKING
PROCESS -- 1973-75

Introduction

Outside influences and pressures penetrated the school system, causing a twist in the fate of the students, first in one direction, then in another. Not only did the politics of local constituents influence, reverse and change the ebb and flow of the educational enterprise, but so, too, did the politics and ideology of our national leaders and private business concerns reign supreme over the needs of local students. More than likely, no other school system in the nation has been subjected to such high level scrutiny by the Congress or the White House as has been the Washington, D.C. school system. And, probably, no other school system in the nation has been the subject of as much debate as has been the school system in the nation's capital. Just a brief listing of the various reports is illustrative of this deep and, in some cases perhaps, unhealthy concern.

The Advisory Committee on Education made a study in 1938 titled "Public Education in the District of Columbia." Congress ordered three major probes into all operations of the school system during the 20 year period between 1947 to 1967. These were the George D. Strayer Study completed February 28, 1949 under the auspices of the chairmen of the Senate and the House; the Davis Investigation directed by James C. Davis, Georgia, as subcommittee chairman, in 1956 which was the

Investigation of Public School Conditions by a subcommittee of the House District Committee; the 1966 Investigation of the Schools and Poverty in the District of Columbia by the Task Force on Antipoverty in the District of Columbia of the House Committee on Education and Labor, chaired by Roman C. Pucinski, Illinois; the 1962 Stadium Riot Study by a citizens committee; the <u>Passow Report</u>, completed in 1967; the <u>Nelsen Commission Report</u>, 1971; and the <u>Price-Waterhouse Report</u> in 1972. In addition, there were annual hearings held by the House and Senate subcommittees on Appropriations on the school line item budget requests. Likewise, the court cases have had a penetratingly sharp effect on policy and operations. For instance, <u>Bolling v Sharpe</u> in 1954 calling for school desegregation, <u>Hobson v Hansen</u> in 1967 regarding the equalization of school resources, and the Waddy Decree of 1972 regarding special education.

    This plethora of studies and investigations kept a sharp lens on the local schools and in the minds of many local citizens nudged their feelings that there was something radically wrong with the public schools. This, in itself, may have been a precipitating cause for the stepped-up flight of middle class Blacks and whites from the public schools in the District.

    A political interpretation of the school system must deal with interest groups inside and outside the system. There are strong pressures in the school system that promote the formation of strong interest groups. On the inside the sharp cleavages between the superintendent and the school board make conflict the normal state of affairs. Power groups form on every side to fight for privileges and favors. On the outside there are strong sentiments about the school system and numerous community groups try to influence its operation. Interest groups may take a variety of forms, some calling for stricter discipline, others demanding ability grouping, and still others investigating alleged mismanagement.

## Some Influential Community Groups

### The United Planning Organization (UPO) --

The UPO is the official poverty program funding agency for the District of Columbia. In this capacity it occupies a semi-governmental role in relation to the schools, through the development and partial funding of portions of the Model School Division (MSD) program.

The relationship between the school system and the UPO has been stormy with argument over the MSD program, especially as UPO sought more involvement in programming, and the school system tried to minimize the UPO role in the operation of the MSD.

It is significant to note that in 1967 the UPO was the only example of a direct cooperative relationship between a private agency and the public school system.[1] Later there developed a relationship with the Friends of the DCYOP, another very stormy encounter with a private agency.

### The Federation of Civic Associations --

The federation was formally established on November 10, 1921. It is presently a delegate body of 55 voluntary organizations, 53 of which are neighborhood civic associations representative of a geographical area in the District and two are honorary associations. The primary objective of the organization is to provide a medium for self-improvement of neighborhoods and, secondarily, coordination in overall community projects.[2]

On numerous occasions the federation became involved in school affairs. Nelson Roots, member of the D.C. board of education from 1969 to 1972, was also a member of the federation and after his tenure on the board often spoke in favor of or in opposition to various school board proposals.

Three specific occasions illustrating the

federation's attempt to bring pressure on the decision-making unit can be noted in the minutes of November 15, 1967 in connection with (1) problems at the Morgan School,[3] (2) in the matter of tenure for principals, and (3) in the superintendent selection process of 1973.

According to Hansen, "If there is any single voice speaking for the city-wide Negro population this is it."[4]

The Metropolitan Washington Board of Trade --

The Metropolitan Washington Board of Trade was founded in November 1889 at the invitation of Beriah Wilkins, former representative in the House of Representatives from Ohio, who had bought a controlling interest in the Washington Post. The organization was viewed by many as a small group of self-serving men primarily of real estate speculators and bankers who financed them. The membership also included street railway executives, insurance agents and politicians. Little or no interest was shown in the working man or in Blacks or in public schools.

The organization soon became the most influential group in Washington, D.C. Initially it did not exclude Jews or Blacks from its membership. In fact, in the 1890s the organization included Isadore Saks and Simon Wolf, both Jewish, and four Blacks including James T. Wormley, Dr. Charles Purvis, George F. Cook, superintendent of the Black schools, and Robert Terrell.

In the early 1900s, the board of directors included among its white members Charles Glover, president of the Riggs National Bank, S. W. Woodward, department store owner, Brainard Warner, real estate broker, and well known lawyers, journalists, editors, doctors, and engineers who were also directors of banks and other business enterprises. The bankers and real estate brokers held law degrees, thus, in a sense, illustrating the interlocking interests of the members. The first concern of the board of trade in the early days of its existence was the strengthening of the economic position of the city, but, in addition, its members involved themselves in directing local charities and reform institutions.[5]

Soon the board of trade showed a tendency to identify the welfare of the city with that of the rich and gradually lost its representativeness. Newer members of the board of directors took little interest in strengthening the local community. As the influence of the organization continued to grow, it developed a strong relationship with Congress and members expected to name citizens whom the President would appoint as district commissioners. This influence declined though during President Wilson's administration.[6]

By 1920 white antagonism against Black citizens had mounted to such an extent in the city and within the organization that the Black members resigned.[7] After World War I, the board of trade was accused of profiteering. Additionally, its members resented continued rent controls as a socialist measure so that by 1925 it was on record as opposing social welfare.[8]

As spokesman for the most financially powerful Washingtonians, the board of trade in the 1930s opposed an elected city government. Local business was booming, and for this reason they evidently wanted to preserve the political status quo. By this time these businessmen had tightened their control of the community's economic resources through their interlocking directorates among the biggest of the 77 business corporations chartered in the District. This suggested a concentration of control in the hands of 80 to 100 men.

This opposition to home rule blazed into the forefront of political thinking and maneuvering by the 1940s with the board of trade leading the opposition.[9]

The board of trade seemed to focus on what was good for big business interests as opposed to what was good for the poor in the District or in the school system. One illustration of this point may be viewed through Hugh Scott's discussion of his involvement with the Metropolitan Washington Board of Trade:

> Shortly into my administration, it was October, just before Christmas, members of the Board of Trade came to see me. They said, 'we want you Mr. Superintendent to help us work on the shoplifting problem.' I thought that was rather interesting. I said, 'Yes I'm interested. What do you want me to do?' 'Well, we'd like for you to have your teachers in the elementary schools especially and in the junior highs once a week or twice a week lecture the kids on the evils of shoplifting.' I said, 'I have a problem with that, now let me explain why. If I do that then I am putting the teachers in a position of indicting the kids or making allegations without any evidence that the kids are doing it and some of my research indicates that the greatest shoplifters are white middle class housewives coming from Virginia who come here to do the shoplifting.' I said, 'In all good conscience, I cannot assume that the kids are doing it and I don't want to put the teachers in the role of policemen. I have no objection if a policeman comes because they are use to the role of policeman and talks to the kids about shoplifting. I have no problem with that. I recognize your problem of shoplifting but I don't think the school is the approach I want to use to lambast the kids. They are already condemned of everything. Anyway if any Black kids walk into Woodward and Lothrop, they are going to stop them and keep them out anyway. It's that lady who looks like she can buy something.' I knew then that the Board of Trade and all of them in my office I did not

make a good impression. But I said, 'why don't you start a campaign of bringing the kids into the store, take them on a tour and then talk to them as a part of training.' They said, 'Oh, that's a good idea,' but they never got to it. That's the kind of thing I think a Black superintendent should do. Because I perceive different from them. Their perception was that the previous superintendent would have worked with them - no question.[10]

Generally, it appeared that the board of trade tangentially influenced school board programs in the schools. For instance, the minutes of November 15, 1967[11] stated that Joseph B. Danzansky, president of Giant Food, Inc., and member of the Washington Board of Trade, in a letter dated November 1, 1967 advised that Giant Food, Inc. contributed 144 safety patrol belts and had conducted an intensive advertising campaign at the beginning of the school semester to remind citizens to drive safely now that children had returned to school. Furthermore, Danzansky served on the citizen's council to recommend persons for the D.C. superintendency in 1973, a matter of great controversy between Barry and Cassell. Also, money contributions were made to the campaigns of several school board members by members of the board of trade as shown in a previous chapter.

The board of trade changed back to its initially inclusive character. Today, for the second time in three years, the president is Jewish. Joseph Danzansky was president in 1971 and in 1976, and now in 1973 R. Robert Linowes is president. Presently, there are also at least 12 Blacks or women on the 80 member board of directors. Other changes include the courting of the D.C. city council members and high officials in the mayor's administration to strengthen the link between business and government.[12]

### D.C. Citizens for Better Public Education, Inc. (DCCBPE) --

In 1964, a group of citizens concerned about improving the public schools in Washington, D.C. organized DCCBPE. Originating members included Nancy Harrison, of the Chicago McCormick family, Charles Horsky and Flaxie Pinkett, members of the Metropolitan Washington Board of Trade and the Pepco board (Potomac Electric Power Company). The purpose of the group is:

> ...to study on a continuing basis the problems of public education in the District, to stimulate interest in public education in the District of Columbia, to encourage participation in volunteer programs for the public, and to propose and promote such changes in the organization, management and methods of the public schools as may from time to time be deemed desirable.[13]

In 1965, the group received funding from the Eugene and Agnes E. Meyer Foundation and the New World Foundation, and free rent from the Communication Workers of America. During the year, the DCCBPE employed Helen Morse as executive director. Later she served on the working party under the aegis of the committee on Community and Congressional Relations, Executive Study Group, Passow study.[14] During the year they worked to promote the establishment of Federal City College and the Washington Technical Institute.

In 1966 under the leadership of Mrs. Robert McNamara, the Reading-Is-Fundamental program began. It was a program to provide paperback books to elementary school children.

Also in 1966, the group widely distributed a summary of the Passow study, researched elected school board procedures in other communities, and summarized the 1967 Wright decision in the Hobson v Hansen case for public distribution.

In 1967 the DCCBPE had a membership in excess of 600, its own offices, an executive secretary and other staff.[15]

In 1968 the DCCBPE worked with the League of Women Voters to distribute information about candidates for the DCBOE election and provided candidates with kits of information about the schools. This project began by DCCBPE was incorporated into the public school system.

In 1969 the group developed a career ladder for para-professionals in the D.C. public schools and published a pamphlet on the D.C. school budget called Financing the D.C. Public Schools.

The Clark Plan also came under the scrutiny of the DCCBPE. Thus, they published four issues of their newsletter, the Bulletin Board, on problems surrounding it. In addition, the group prepared a summary of the Clark Plan and distributed 20,000 copies in 1970.

In 1971, the group printed and distributed a summary of the 1971 Wright decision on the equalization of elementary school teachers salaries with ± five percent of the District-wide mean.

Nineteen seventy-two saw the production of a summary of the Waddy court decision requiring schooling for all handicapped children.

Workshops were held on the Nelsen Commission recommendations as another project by the DCCBPE in 1973. Additionally, follow-up reports and workshops were held on the Wright and Waddy decisions. Funds were obtained from the National Institute of Education to prepare a report on the Wright equalization decision of 1971.

In 1974, the group reported on the Teachers Union contract, and analyzed the decentralization plans of the school system.

Additionally, in 1975, the DCCBPE received a

Ford Foundation grant to work with the school system to develop alternative possibilities for the equalization problem.[16]

Chiefly, the group sent representatives to most school board meetings, prepared and distributed reports, done primarily by hired consultants on such issues as decentralization, school finances, and equalization, in an effort to recommend alternatives to existing DCBOE policies.

In spite of all of the above activities reported by the DCCBPE, the Passow team evaluated the group as to its effectiveness by stating that only limited evidence hints at the DCCBPE's influence on school policy or practice.[17]

Nevertheless, there are divided opinions by DCBOE members as to whether or not this group has been effective in influencing school system decisions.

As reported in the minutes of September 16, 1970, personal attacks were made against Dr. Kenneth Clark, a Black psychologist from Metropolitan Applied Research Center (MARC) in New York, during a meeting at Sharpe Health School sponsored by the DCCBPE to clearly state for the public record that they did not support the personal attack. One board member added that if the group did not do so, he would personally go to the civic organizations of the city and also the community organizations in his area and instruct them to cancel their membership in the DCCBPE. This sentiment was supported by some other board members.[18]

Anne (Nancy) Blaine Harrison -- a great-granddaughter of Cyrus McCormick, inventor of the McCormick reaper, and James G. Blaine, former U.S. senator from Maine and twice Secretary of State -- was one of the founders, presidents and executive secretaries of the DCCBPE. She was left $11 million in 1954 by her grandmother, Anita McCormick

Blaine, who also left money to finance the New World Foundation which awarded money to DCCBPE. Further, Nancy Harrison was married to Gilbert Harrison, owner and editor-in-chief of New Republic magazine for 20 years.[19] This information surely ties the DCCBPE to the big business interests of the country and the District of Columbia through partial funding by the Eugene and Agnes E. Meyer Foundation, set up by the Meyers, owners of the Washington Post.

### Eugene and Agnes E. Meyer Foundation --

In December 1944, Eugene and Agnes Meyer, owners of the Washington Post, jointly set up a foundation with funds for donation to community service and development, to the arts and humanities, and to projects concerned with health, mental health, and education. In 1972 the foundation's assets were valued at approximately $25 million and at that time it was one of the largest charitable institutions in Washington. Later, their son, Bill, became a member of the board.[20]

Around June 1948, Eugene Meyer transferred the non-voting stock of the Washington Post Company to the foundation.[21]

### Friends of the D.C. Youth Orchestra Program (DCYOP) --

The DCYOP was started within the music department of the DCPS system in 1961 as an enrichment program to provide selected children of promising ability a chance to play in a symphony orchestra. Qualifications for admission to the orchestra were developed by the teachers and orchestra conductors, which included the rule that only students selected by their instrumental teachers in the school could become members of the youth orchestra.

In 1964, a group of parents organized the Friends of the DCYOP to provide scholarship aid for private lessons, and clerical functions. Thereafter the scope and direction of the organization changed and expanded. Preparatory classes were begun, music department teachers were consulted less on policy, and outside teachers were hired.

By 1968, the name of the orchestra was changed to the D.C. Youth Orchestra Program (DCYOP). In 1971, music teachers in the DCPS system formalized their complaints about the program and the Friends in a report to Dr. James T. Guines, associate superintendent of schools.[22] The complaints evolved into a dispute between Superintendent Sizemore and the 1974 DCBOE around the issue of letting a $150,000.00 contract to the Friends.

Obviously, there are other community groups not so visible who have indirect influence on various school programs and policies through their active participation or through their contacts or with DCBOE members or administrators, teachers or children in the school system.

An analysis of the interview data revealed that the 26 key administrators, school board members and union official who were asked the question: "What community groups had influence on the decisions made by the school board?", had varied opinions. Only three felt that the board of trade had direct influence on the decisions made by school board members. Sixteen felt that the D.C. Citizens for Better Public Education had great influence. Reasons offered by some were: (1) do good research; (2) organized; (3) on top of issues; (4) did their homework; (5) presented reliable data; and (6) there all the time. In contrast, Hobson offered that the research on equalization was full of inaccuracies. Some respondents even mentioned which board members were greatly influenced by the group. Hobson felt Mason and Kane were influenced by the group and Scott felt that Swaim was greatly influenced. In describing the group, respondents stated that the group was composed of either mostly whites, or integrated, or middle class whites and Blacks or Wards 3 and 6 constituents (see table 9).

Nine respondents stated that the Friends of the DCYOP was an influential group. At least four respondents said they were a one-issue group. Another respondent described the group as composed of middle class citizens.

Only three respondents stated that the Federation of Civic Organizations influenced decisions made by school board members. And only one respondent felt that the Washington Teachers Union was an influential group. In contrast though, 13 respondents specifically stated that the press (media) greatly influenced decisions made by school board members.

In terms of other groups felt to be influential, the Parent Teacher Association was mentioned more often (**six times**) than were other groups. Ward 5 was mentioned by one respondent, the Group of 100 Ministers was mentioned twice, Title I Advisory Group was mentioned once, local constituents was mentioned by Kemp, and the Washington Council on Drug Abuse was mentioned by Kane.

Obviously then, the data reveal that the two most influential pressure points in the community were seen by these respondents to be the DCCBPE (16) and the press (13). Nevertheless, a review of the transcript data as presented in this report does show that such groups as the Washington Metropolitan Board of Trade, the Federation of Civic Associations, the UPO, the Meyer foundation, the union and some other groups did become involved in a public school issue or several special public school issues.

Specific in-depth discussions of the influence of these various community pressure groups have been presented throughout this study, as for instance the influence of the Friends of the DCYOP

TABLE 9

GROUP PRESSURES

QUESTION: What community groups had great influence on the decisions made by the school board?

| Respondents | Board of Trade | DCCBPE | Friends of DCYOP | Federation of Civic Assoc. | Union | 100 Ministers | Press | PTA |
|---|---|---|---|---|---|---|---|---|
| Cassell |  | x |  |  |  |  |  |  |
| Warren |  |  |  |  |  |  |  |  |
| Hobson |  | x | x |  |  |  |  |  |
| Morris |  | x |  |  |  |  | x |  |
| Pryde |  | x |  |  |  |  |  | x |
| Washington |  | x |  |  |  |  |  |  |
| Taylor |  | x | x |  |  |  |  |  |
| Tirana |  |  |  | x | x | x | x | x |
| Evans |  | x | x |  |  |  |  |  |
| Treanor |  |  | x |  |  |  | x | x |

QUESTION: What community groups had great influence on the decisions made by the school board?

| Respondents | Board of Trade | DCCBPE | Friends of DCYOP | Federation of Civic Assoc. | Union | 100 Ministers | Press | PTA |
|---|---|---|---|---|---|---|---|---|
| Haskins | | | | | | | | |
| Lewis | x | x | x | | | | x | |
| Labat | | | | | | | x | |
| Smith | | | | | | | | |
| Simons | | x | x | | | | x | |
| Freeman | | x | x | | | | | x |
| Kemp | | x | | | | | x | |
| Kane | | x | | | | | | |
| Williams | | | | | | | | |
| Elliott | | | | | | | x | |
| Simmons | x | x | | | | | | |

QUESTION: What community groups had great influence on the decisions made by the school board?

| Respondents | Board of Trade | DCCBPE | Friends of DCYOP | Federation of Civic Assoc. | Union | 100 Ministers | Press | PTA |
|---|---|---|---|---|---|---|---|---|
| Rice |  |  |  |  |  |  | x |  |
| Sizemore |  | x | x |  |  |  | x |  |
| Reed |  |  |  | x |  |  | x | x |
| Diggs |  | x | x |  |  |  | x | x |
| Scott | x | x |  | x |  | x | x |  |
| 26 Total Responses | 3 | 16 | 9 | 3 | 1 | 2 | 13 | 6 |

on school board-superintendent relations is
thoroughly discussed in Case I in Chapter VIII.
Since the press had such a great influence on
school board-superintendent relations between
1973-75, an extended discussion will be presented
next.

### An Analysis of News Coverage of the Superintendent-School Board Controversy -- 1973-75*

Newspapers in Washington, D.C. play an
extraordinary role in the life of the nation's
capital. Perhaps with the exception of New York
City, home of the powerful New York Times newspaper, no other city is as influenced by the
preponderance and presence of a daily press such
as both the Washington Post and the Washington
Star.

The Washington Post newspaper, with a
national audience and international clout, is not
only read by 500,000 people each day, but much of
that which is presented and read is repeated and
before the day is ended becomes the gospel for most
of those that have seen it or heard of it.

News stories are read by television and
radio assignment editors and they assign reporters
to follow up those stories. So, much of what has
been covered in the Washington Post, a morning
paper, is distributed by other media throughout
the day.

Coverage by the Washington Post, and its
afternoon competitor, the Washington Star, is
consummate. Nothing goes on in the town without
the two papers covering it. Many times, because
of competition between the two, issues and
controversies between subjects are blown entirely

---

*Some of the information reported here was
prepared by Joe Green, former reporter for the
Washington Post.

out of proportion or exacerbated in the media, usually by over-zealous reporters who are bent on getting a story.

In many respects, the controversy between the board of education in Washington, D.C. and the professional educators that it hired to run the schools was no different than controversy experienced in other cities. But in Washington, the controversy became major when the press interceded and became a participant in the controversy. Such was the case in the situation involving Superintendent Hugh Scott, and later, much more pronounced, when Barbara A. Sizemore became head of the District school system.

Sizemore, a volatile and exciting individual, provided reporters with "good copy" because of her alertness and ability to use words, and her unwillingness to compromise on issues when she believed that she was right, or when she believed that the school system was not serving the best interests of poor Black children who are predominant in the District school system.

Also, the press was used as a weapon by certain individuals with vested interests to attack Superintendents Scott and Sizemore. This ploy of using the press is not new or uncommon. Reporters, hungry for information, often have as their best sources persons who have defined and special interests in circumventing or destroying the work of other individuals who usually are their enemies.

The position of school superintendent in the D.C. public school system has never been a safe position, especially for a Black.

Elected school board members, whose actions are greatly influenced by an active, articulate, opinionated and aggressive press, have been in controvention with the people that they have hired to run the system continuously -- particularly when that person was an educator and innovator of ideas, systems, and thought.

Scott, who was the third superintendent to leave the District school system since 1967, said in a newspaper interview that the elected school board, established in 1969, was too interventionist in the daily running of the school system.

Confronted with mounting disgust about school board attempts to intervene in the management of the system, Scott said shortly before his departure that the next superintendent should be an educator rather than a management-type administrator.[23]

Scott said that one element that haunted the District's school system was race. That comment sent reporters scurrying like field mice. It dominated the headlines of both the Washington Post and the Washington Star. Furthermore, Scott indicated that he would not seek another superintendency, since Blacks are not selected for posts where there is anything decent to run.[24]

During the tempest of the Scott superintendency, a Black school board member from a Black district, the Reverend James Coates, accused white board members of being prejudiced and unwilling to rely fully on the expertise and administrative ability of a Black superintendent.

During the session where the Reverend Coates made his accusations, a white school board member, Mr. Albert A. Rosenfield, retorted that it was not true.[25] The incident, like many others involving school board members, community people, and personnel hired by the board, made instant headlines in both Washington newspapers. Any incident involving racial verbage sold hundreds of newspapers in the racially conscious city of Washington.

Scott was not a superintendent who gave the press immediate access. His inability or unwillingness to talk to reporters may have caused him some political problems with copy-hungry writers. So, during his tenure, reporters relied on board members or school administrators for their information. That situation and the headlines were to change drastically when Barbara A. Sizemore became head of the District schools.

In July of 1973, the D.C. board of education, in closed session, began a process which would result in a successor to Hugh Scott, who resigned and left the District school post for a position at Howard University. He later became Dean in the School of Education at Hunter College, New York City.

There were three candidates for the post. They included: Andrew G. Donaldson of New York City, an educator and relative of a political ally of the board president, Marion Barry; John Minor, a systems analyst from California; and Barbara A. Sizemore, a renowned Black educator, former regional superintendent in Chicago and then official of the American Association of School Administrators in Virginia.

From the very beginning, Barry, a Black man with higher political ambitions, lobbied against Barbara Sizemore. The whites on the school board were against her, and Barry, a former president of SNCC, was not persuaded that the whites would forgive him for voting for Sizemore, someone who had a national reputation as being an ardent supporter of Black people and having a keen interest in the education of Black children.

Barry was more willing to go along with the selection of a Minor or a Donaldson who were not perceived as threats by whites and whose reputations did not equal that of Sizemore's.

The director of the Anacostia Neighborhood Museum, John Kinard, a community activist, accused Barry and white school board members of trying to get a superintendent who would allow them to continue to run the school system.[26]

Kinard and other school community activists, who favored the selection of Barbara A. Sizemore, said that Barry and the whites wanted a "safe" school board chief who would rubber stamp school board decisions and would not present the board with any controversial matters that might prove politically embarrassing.

Kinard accused Barry of placing his own political ambitions before the education of Black children in the District. Kinard said also that Barry, who later was elected to the city council, did not want to have a superintendent that held positions at variance with his own, and who would create newspaper headlines.

Barry, Kinard suggested, not only had a Black constituency, but also had to cater to the powerful board of trade which financed political campaigns and to the even more powerful white controlled media.

Richard Prince, a former Washington Post reporter who covered the school board during the time when Barry was President, said that he (Barry) was media conscious and always wanted to be portrayed in the most favorable light possible.[27]

As the drama around the selection of Sizemore unfolded, Kinard's assertions were reinforced by Black school board member Charles I. Cassell, who said during an interview with the Washington Post that Barry wanted a school board president that he could control, who would simply manage the system and would not be a competitor with the media-conscious Barry for newspaper headlines.

Speaking of Barry and a white board member, Mrs. Martha Swaim, Cassell said that they wanted an administrative type they can control and that Sizemore was going to put the focus on education, and bring in all kinds of resources. Cassell felt that Swaim and Barry were jealous.[28]

Cassell's accusations, like those of Kinard,

gained considerable space in both Washington newspapers. The space devoted to Sizemore began to lessen the space usually reserved for other media-hungry politicians. This did not make her any friends in the political community.

Cassell and Barry were the main players in the eventual selection of Sizemore as superintendent. Initially, Barry, a former president of Pride, Inc., a self-help organization, held out, but when community pressure swayed his opinion, Barry changed his vote to join the Black majority on the school board and voted for Sizemore.

Barry could not have voted against Barbara A. Sizemore and avoid offending the gregarious Black support that had mounted for her in Washington's Black community.

It was obvious that if Sizemore were selected, the focus of education in the city would be on her and not on politicians such as Barry and Swaim who had considerable political ambition. It seemed that this shift in the spotlight was terrifying to some board members.[29]

Once Barbara A. Sizemore was selected as school superintendent of the District's schools in late August of 1973, she became its first woman head and the manager of the twelfth largest system in the country. She signed a three year contract for more than $40,000.00 annually.

In order to properly understand the events that would take place during the Sizemore superintendency, it is important to understand the nature of the District of Columbia.

A federal enclave, Washington is a company town with the largest employer being the federal government. The Washington Post is one of the country's two leading newspapers with 350 reporters. The Post hires and retains reporters that are "team players," in the words of Post administrators. They are usually aggressive, assertive, unrelenting in their pursuit of news and conscious of the fact that their employer plays a significant role in the molding of thought in the city, way beyond that of simply being a daily recorder of events.

The other newspaper, the Washington Star, was in 1973 in deep financial trouble. Its ineptly-run family corporation and inbreeding of staff had brought the paper to near financial ruin. Still, the Star, the city's only afternoon paper, had a significant role in the life of the District.

Management at the Star realized that, to attract additional advertising and stay abreast with the Post, the paper had to feature startling stories and eyecatching headlines. During the Sizemore controversy, that is exactly what the Washington Star, through the use of several reporters, attempted to do. The primary objective was to sell newspapers. The secondary objective was the reporting of details and the dissemination of information.

In 1973, Congress had full control over the District of Columbia. Home rule, such as it was called, was limited, with Congress maintaining for itself significant control over the District's budget and veto power over all legislation passed by the District's city council and signed by the mayor.

Representative Charles Diggs of Detroit and Senator Thomas Eagleton of Missouri chaired the two Congressional committees that had oversight over the functioning of the District. Very little of import was done in the District without the knowledge of Eagleton and Diggs. Diggs saw himself as a surrogate mayor, while Eagleton was more concerned with his electorate in his home state. In "company towns" such as Washington, where team playing is vital, individualists or persons who are not inclined to play ball are labelled "dangerous" by those in power, and an effort is made to get rid of them.

When Barbara Sizemore came to town, it was known to many that she was not a team player. Certainly, Marion Barry and white members of the school board who objected to her selection felt this was true. What they did not expect was that she would openly challenge the school board and demand that a majority Black school system serve the needs of Black children, and that curriculum be designed to fit that need.

Sizemore said, upon assuming office, that she wanted a school system that showed children their role in "helping to transform the world." That type of language coming from anyone, and particularly from a Black woman, was foreign and errant to the company town types, the white-controlled newspapers, and the members of the board of education who feared change with the greatest of magnitude.

In the beginning of her tenure, Washington's newspapers, especially the Washington Star, began to follow Mrs. Sizemore wherever she happened to go. They knew the vocal superintendent might say something that would create headlines and sell newspapers for their afternoon broad sheet.

The Washington Star was not to be denied; before the end of the first month of her new appointment, the Star carried a one-inch headline shocking its readers with "Mrs. Sizemore's View of Schools, Sexist, Racist."[30]

Actually the superintendent had talked about American education and how it was dominated by white males, a theory that no measured educator denied. The superintendent had said in a speech that the three things which can be found in all institutions are male superiority, white European superiority, and the superiority of people with money, and that we as women were only taught to catch a man. The Star began early to distort the words of Mrs. Sizemore. In the same speech that made headlines in the Star, Mrs. Sizemore said about the D.C. school system that you did not find any recreational programs that really respond to the needs of girls and that most vocational programs in the District for girls were of a clerical nature.[31]

Sizemore spoke to a *Star* reporter, Diane Brockett, a young white woman who was to feature prominently in the Sizemore affair, about her proposals for changing the system, but the solutions did not find themselves in the headline nor in the lead of the story. In fact, they were appendaged at the rear of the article where most readers' eyes never venture.

It was noted by editors at both of Washington's white papers that Sizemore was "hot copy." She was the type of superintendent that could be counted upon to provide reporters with front page news stories that people would read one day and follow in subsequent editions.

In a *Washington Post* article, the superintendent, who had then been on her job less than a week, was depicted as being an advocate of educational materials which included English that was not standard. The subject matter was a book for first grade students that had been written by a Chicago-based educator named Essie Branch. It had been designed by Miss Branch as a substitute for materials that had been designed for white youths in the Chicago public school system. The book featured characters who used language that is commonly referred to as "street talk" or "slang."[32]

The *Washington Post* article, which ran for 28 paragraphs, did not focus on Miss Branch's creation of Arnold. The major portion of their story concerned Mrs. Sizemore's defense of the material, which she had characterized as an alternative tool for teachers who did not understand the social conditions that many poor youths dwelled in and went home to each day.

It was not until the very end of the story that the article stated that Mrs. Sizemore had said that she would not use the primer if parents objected to it. By this time, no doubt, most readers had already formed their biases regarding the primer (and Mrs. Sizemore) which ranged, because of media angles, from racial paranoid to racial fanatic.

With tarnishing views of the superintendent being presented in the media, Mrs. Sizemore, a proponent of an educational system that was designed to assist Black children evolve, came under heavy attack from white readers of the newspapers who did not approve of her views and who were not sensitive to, or concerned with, the needs and educational dilemmas of Black children.

She began to receive letters of resentment from angry white citizens. One such letter negatively referred to her Afro, big African earrings and her speech. The Ebony article, where the letter from the white detractor appeared, made reference to one of the problems that plagued Mrs. Sizemore throughout her superintendency. Many of her critics, including Blacks, complained about her constant reference to the Black poor during her early days in the Washington school system. It is interesting to note that few of her critics were among the Black poor. They were usually people of means with contacts or alliances in the white community. Race is never an easy subject to discuss in integrated circles. Such was the case in Washington.

Many upper middle class Blacks had followed a pattern established by whites and moved their children out of the District's public school system. Many families placed their children into private suburban schools.

Mrs. Sizemore's positions on the nature of Black children in the District school system was further elucidated in the Ebony article when she explained that she hoped she could construct a just system that would be advantageous to all and open to all.[33]

Comments such as those made in the *Ebony* interview did not endear Mrs. Sizemore to many people of means and influence in Washington. Though most observers would note that the character of the school system was poor in the person of disenfranchised Black students, it was still Washington, and there were many who wanted to eschew the malignant poverty and portray a picture of a school system in the nation's capital that was one of the best in the world, serving one of the nation's most affluent populations. Mrs. Sizemore knew well that this was not the case.

In a three hour interview with editors and writers at the *Washington Post* in July 1974, Mrs. Sizemore was asked to explain further her educational philosophy. She explained her bias in favor of Black students and how she viewed the educational system in Washington and in the country. Her comments about a white male dominated system unnerved some of the editors present who were mostly white, mostly male.

One of the early questions that she was asked during the interview was about test scores. She explained that she had problems using tests which were norm referenced on Palo Alto children who were neither poor nor Black and then fault her children who were Black and poor because they did not perform in the same manner.

In that same interview, Mrs. Sizemore told *Post* staff members that District school children were weary of being taught Abraham Lincoln and George Washington as models to follow in American history. Instead, she indicated, students wanted to learn more about themselves and of the history of Black people and of the contributions that Blacks had made in America.[34]

The Post printed Mrs. Sizemore's interview with her responses to questions concerning the testing and the teaching of American history. The public response was immediate. Many people whose children attended upper middle class schools took exception to Mrs. Sizemore's educational philosophy.

Washington Post columnist William Raspberry, himself a Black, had recently written a column suggesting that the cultural bias charge against the tests was simply nothing but a cop-out by educators such as Sizemore who could not face the challenge of educating students in the District public schools.[35]

The test issue was to become a major issue during the Sizemore superintendency. The Raspberry column and other editorials critical of Mrs. Sizemore were crucial to her eventual firing. Raspberry and other newspaper editorial writers like him had a significant following. That following usually believed most of what the columnists wrote.

Within six months of taking office, Superintendent Sizemore had made enemies in the press, the upper income Black class, and among the upper income white community. The three year contract that she had signed in October became more fragile each passing day as she became an ever-increasing issue in the running of the public school system.

An issue that began early in the conflict between Mrs. Sizemore and the board of education was the renewal of the Hawthorne School contract between the board and the people who ran the semiprivate institution. The school, a private institution, established by Alexander and Eleanor Orr in 1956, had a contract with the school system that dated back to 1972. The contract allowed the Orrs to use a District public school building in exchange for the education of 41 District public school students.

In April of 1974, the board of education voted to renew its annual agreement which allowed the Orrs to use the Sumner school at 17th and M Streets, N.W. for their institution known as the Hawthorne School. In return, the 41 District school children received full scholarships to the institution.

At a board meeting on April 17, an angry Mrs. Sizemore said that the board's renewal of the contract with the Hawthorne School was an affront to the District school system and stated that the board's decision displayed a lack of confidence in the teaching qualities of the District school teachers.

Superintendent Sizemore said that numerous visits and investigations of the Hawthorne School by a group of professional educators had revealed that the school's curriculum was culturally tainted in favor of whites and that school officials had allowed the school to fall into serious disrepair.

One of the white board members, William Treanor, said to Mrs. Sizemore that he believed the investigation that she alluded to had not, in fact, taken place. Treanor said he believed that the performance of the Hawthorne School had been fine.[36]

The Star article made no mention of the Howard University team of educators, which included the editor of the Journal of Negro Education, Dr. Charles Martin, and the Dean of the Howard University School of Education.

The Hawthorne School incident and the coverage of it in the press once again presented Barbara Sizemore as a racial fanatic whose sole purpose was the education of Black school children and the denial of educational opportunities for whites. Yet nowhere in newspaper print did the opinions of the Howard University educators appear. They wrote:

> It seems to us that renewing the lease may be
> a monetary disservice to poor hard working
> taxpaying parents of public school students
> and poor people generally.
>
> We at Howard University are committed to
> Black excellence and we would hope that we
> could be of some assistance to the board in
> creating alternatives for the students in the
> public schools.[37]

The absence of the Howard University letter in print simply reaffirmed what many for so long believed, that the white papers did not give merit to what Black professionals or laypersons had to say.

As stories of declining reading scores and lack of discipline dominated the headlines of the Washington Post and the Washington Star, Superintendent Sizemore was portrayed in the media as the villain who was responsible for the demise of the school system. Particularly detrimental to her was reporting done by the television news media which simply restated what it had read in the newspapers without doing any research of its own or checking for accuracy.

In May 1974, Martha S. Swaim, a white school board member who voted against the initial hiring of Superintendent Sizemore, decided to resign from the school board. She was quoted as saying that the children she represented did not need any more on-the-job training for superintendents. Soon after resigning and making her statement against Superintendent Sizemore, Swaim became a candidate for the District's first elected city council. To some political observers, board members-turned-city-council-candidates used the school system and their feud with Superintendent Sizemore as an issue in the upcoming elections. Marion Barry was later elected to an at-large seat on the council while Swaim was defeated.

Nearly two months after the Hawthorne School issue, the board and Superintendent Sizemore became embroiled in another debate, this time concerning the relationship between another private organization which administered a program serving some District public school children. The incident involved the D.C. Youth Orchestra previously discussed.[38]

Among the alternatives suggested to the school board by Superintendent Sizemore was that students, who were not from the District of Columbia but who took part in the youth orchestra program, pay tuition. She also suggested that the music program could be run by the District school system, which had a preponderance of music teachers, many acclaimed in their fields. None of Superintendent Sizemore's alternatives appeared in either the Washington Post or the Washington Star accounts of the youth orchestra contract dispute.

Going against the recommendation of the person that they had hired to run the school system and to bring innovation to a stifled system, the board, which was heavily lobbied by Friends of the DCYOP, voted 6 to 2 to renew the contract.[39]

During the two years that Sizemore served as superintendent of the District public school system, she received as much newspaper ink as any of the city's politicians who had spent their entire lives in the town. This frightened many aspiring politicians -- Martha Swaim, Marion Barry, and Albert Rosenfield, among them -- who knew that newspaper ink for aspiring politicians in D.C. was like gold in the mint.

As Charles Cassell, a former school board member, had predicted, Superintendent Sizemore did dominate the headlines and some school board members resented it.

One piece of journalism written by a polished female writer for the Washington Star newspaper,

Jacqueline Trescott, appeared in the July 8, 1974 edition of that paper on the front page of the paper's Metropolitan section. The Trescott account depicted Sizemore as a learned educator, who had become in a short while a Washington "public figure." The article informed many readers that Mrs. Sizemore was a student of Russian, French, Greek, and Latin languages. The Trescott account further said that Sizemore was often referred to as the first lady in education in America.[40]

It is interesting to note that while Trescott was doing such a piece on Superintendent Sizemore, the distinguished educator was doing battle with the board of education, none of whose members were acknowledged educational experts. The fact that Superintendent Sizemore could receive such good press and be doing battle with the school board at the same time confused and alarmed several members of the board, particularly those that wanted to see her ousted.

Further, Trescott wrote in her account that after official dinners at which time she is the guest speaker or honoree, Mrs. Sizemore usually is surrounded by parents who all want to talk to her.[41]

Refusing to deny what she considered to be the truth, particularly during a time of turmoil involving issues that were being termed racial by some in town, Superintendent Sizemore told Trescott that the Western world was European-dominated, white-dominated and male-dominated and that she wanted justice for all.[42]

A second article on Sizemore and the school system penned by Trescott appeared the next day. The Trescott articles were to be the last by employees of the Washington *Star* and *Post* that could be considered favorable to Sizemore.

In May 1974, the D.C. school system and the board of education refused to administer a U.S.

Office of Education test that it considered to be racially offensive and an invasion of privacy in the lives of District school children. Among the questions posed in the test was one that asked whether white students were better off in all-white or racially mixed schools. In a Washington Star article dated May 25, staff writer Diane Brockett seemed to imply in her explanation that the test was aimed at helping integration and overcoming educational disadvantages of minority groups.[43]

The article was headlined in half inch letters -- "Face Fund Halt" -- then, in one inch headlines, "D.C. Schools----No On Tests."[44] The Star article mentioned Superintendent Sizemore by name but omitted to mention any of the names of board members. Therefore, the implication of the Star article was that Sizemore had unilaterally arrived at a decision and had then forced her will on reluctant school board officials.

The Washington Post did not give the U.S. Office of Education dispute with the D.C. school system the same prominence as did the Washington Star. Prince, a Black reporter, in a May 25 article quoted Superintendent Sizemore as saying that she was disturbed with questions which asked students about home matters and which are sociologically or psychologically damaging.[45]

The Post article included a comment from U.S. government official Herman R. Goldberg to Superintendent Sizemore about his feeling that ultimate judgments as to the utility of particular questions or the theoretical bases for posing them really rests with the federal government evaluators.[46]

Superintendent Sizemore responded in a fashion that federal officials had not been accustomed to when dealing with District officials. She told Goldberg that his letter was incorrect and furthermore, ultimate judgment denied her responsibility and authority to protect the health and safety of

District students. The text of Prince's article was, in journalistic terms, well balanced and objective, but the headline writers, who place their pens on stories only moments before they go to print, captioned the reporter's story: "City Schools' Federal Aid is Suspended."[47]

When an agreement was finally worked out between federal officials and District school administrators, both the Star and Post carried articles. The Post article said that some District students would take the objected-to tests but with 43 questions deleted.[48] The Star, however, carried the same story the following day. The article, written by Brockett, was captioned "Questionnaire Left Blank at High Schools."[49] Richard Prince, Brockett's counterpart at the Post, said that they seemed to look for the sensational in whatever was written about. In a May 16 story about a school board meeting the previous night, Brockett began her story by stating that Sizemore told the school board it should stick to policy-making and leave the operation of the city schools to her.[50] Later in the same article Brockett mentioned that the board selected Virginia Morris, a black woman, to become vice president of the body. Morris was eventually to become the president of the board during the summer when board president Barry resigned to run for a seat on the city council. The Washington Post's coverage of the same board meeting was markedly different from that of the Star's. The story, written by Prince, was captioned "Mrs. Morris Elected to D.C. School Board Post."[51] The difference in the two articles was that the Star's article focused on the superintendent with a small section at the bottom reserved for discussion of the Morris election.

Prince, who was later removed from school board coverage because his editors were not satisfied with the "quality of his coverage,"[52] mentioned the controversy at the board meeting much later during his article. Prince said that controversy between the board and Superintendent Sizemore was standard and he saw no need to write about something that everybody knew was going on. He said that he chose to write about things that he considered important to students and the community that the school system was designed to serve.

The summer of 1974 was not as eventful as the previous 8 months had been for the school board and Superintendent Sizemore. With an election for the first elected city council coming up, politics cornered the market on news stories. Also with schools recessed for the summer, there was not much to be written about the schools. Yet in September 1974, the Washington Star had not only attacked Superintendent Sizemore in the written word but it had also attacked her in editorial cartoons. In an August 17, 1974 carricature, cartoonist Bill Garner pictured Sizemore as gritting her teeth at a man representing the school board. Both are holding clubs behind their backs, above a caption that reads, "Now let's not start that again!"[53]

In October when the schools were back into operation, the media coverage of the feud between the elected school board and Superintendent Sizemore occurred once again. Diane Brockett authored an article that would, according to some observers, usually be reserved for the gossip column of a different paper. The article, concerning a "Citizens' Salute to Superintendent Sizemore" (who had been in office for a year), stated that three members of the board of education were not invited to the event because they had been critical of the superintendent.[54] Brockett stated in her article that the three critics of Superintendent Sizemore, Mrs. Hilda Mason, Rev. Raymond B. Kemp and William Treanor (both Kemp and Treanor are whites), were originally not invited.[55] Brockett clenched the implication of the exclusion of whites by including a statement about others invited including the female and Black members of Congress and Mayor Walter E. Washington, who is also Black.

The Washington Star editors carried the

article on the front page of their Metropolitan section, accompanied with banner headlines and a photograph of Superintendent Sizemore.[56] The Washington Post chose not to cover the story.

In November 1974, an election for the school board was held and four members were elected. Among them were two white women, Elizabeth Kane, who was elected as a city-wide candidate, and Carol Schwartz, who represented a predominantly white ward. Both of these women became chief antagonists of Superintendent Sizemore. In a post-election interview with the Washington Post newspaper, both Kane and Schwartz admitted to Washington Post staff writer, Lee Daniels, that Sizemore was an issue in the functioning of the school system.[57]

The Post article said that both Kane and Schwartz agreed that the board would have to monitor Superintendent Sizemore's actions more carefully than it had in the past.[58] It quoted Kane as saying something to the effect that parents are very angry and frustrated about the schools, the irresolution of problems, and the blockages which prevent the solving of school problems.[59] Kane did not say that Sizemore was the "blockage" that she spoke about in her interview, but the implication was there nevertheless. Though Daniels' article covered subjects other than Superintendent Sizemore and the deportment of parents whose children were in public schools, the Washington Post headline writers captioned the article "2 School Board Victors Call Parents 'Angry.'"[60] Though Kane and Schwartz were opposed to Superintendent Sizemore, they could not come out publicly and make statements that were directly critical of the vocal superintendent, who despite her press image had an abundant following among parents, particularly the poor, in the District school system. So the role of chief critic of the superintendent fell to Virginia Morris, who became vice president of the board when Marion Barry was elected to the city council. The spectacle of two Black women fighting each other made it easier for white reporters and white officials to take sides. If either Kane or Schwartz had been elected president of the board, it would have been extremely difficult for them to confront Sizemore publicly. Though Kane and Schwartz could not verbally lambast Sizemore in public, they did make use of the media to wage their dissent. According to Prince, the Star reporter (Diane Brockett) got much of her information that appeared in print from white board members and school administrators.[61]

Mrs. Morris, who had run a Headstart program for the District, began her public criticism of the superintendent in November 1974. Speaking to a gathering of District school instructors, Mrs. Morris indicated that a presentation by the superintendent to the educators was high and mighty.[62]

The school board-superintendent clash continued into 1975 when Mrs. Morris was elected president of the board and Julius Hobson, Jr. was elected vice president. At a board meeting in late January Rev. Raymond B. Kemp, an outspoken critic of the superintendent, described Superintendent Sizemore and her administrative team as not making decisions, not providing leadership, not planning, not being realistic and not running the public schools.[63] Diane Brockett suggested in an article that some members of the school board and administration were not happy with the Morris-Hobson leadership team because they could not handle Superintendent Sizemore.[64]

Though Brockett did not identify the "critics," Prince said during an interview that he believed that the critics of Sizemore were white board members and administrative types. He also said that white parents who were critical of Superintendent Sizemore frequently telephoned editors at the Washington Post venting their personal feelings about the school system and the superintendent. Many whites wanted to see Sizemore removed, Prince said, and they expressed that feeling to white editors and editorial writers. Prince said that the principal editorial staff member who wrote editorials about the school system was Robert Asher, a white, who received a plethora of phone calls from critics of Superintendent Sizemore. His writings about the school system and the superintendent reflected those calls particularly during the dismissal hearings, Prince said.[65]

Animosity between the board and Superintendent Sizemore continued into the month of February when the board rejected her projected budget for FY76. Superintendent Sizemore claimed that the board's redrafting of her budget would hamper her efforts to decentralize the school system, which had been one of her mandates when she was first hired. The Washington Star article indicated that the redrawing of the budget was a part of the board's feud with the superintendent.[66]

Before explaining the intricacies of the $200 million budget, the Star, in its article by Brockett, described Sizemore as sitting quietly reading a Bible through part of the meeting.[67] The Star's depiction of Mrs. Sizemore gave readers the impression that the "feuding Superintendent" was no longer interested now that she could no longer have her way or control the budget.

During much of the month of February, the newspapers devoted their attention to a potential strike involving District school teachers. The dispute between the school board and the Washington Teachers Union dominated headlines, and nearly all that was written about the school system concerned that issue. Little was written about Superintendent Sizemore during that period of time.

In mid-March, the Washington Star reporter, Diane Brockett, surfaced with a story captioned, "Is Supt. Sizemore On the Way Out?"[68] The article, in the paper's Sunday edition (where it had its largest circulation) stated that seven of the school board members wanted to see the superintendent dismissed. The Star account stated that board members felt that Superintendent Sizemore was a nonleader and that she was responsible for the problems affecting the system. A board member quoted by Brockett asked that his identity remain a secret.[69]

The Washington Star article made it clear that all four of the white board members wanted to see Superintendent Sizemore dismissed, and that three Blacks felt that she should go but were reluctant to oust her out because of her significant support among parents and community activists in the District, many of whom had children in the public schools.[70]

This article, which appeared on the first page of their Metropolitan section, did not give Superintendent Sizemore the opportunity to respond until the continuation of its story on another page. And the quote that Brockett and the Washington Star chose to highlight from the superintendent implied that she would not allow the board to fire her unless they paid her.[71] It suggested that the superintendent was solely interested in money and not in the wellbeing of the children. It was clear that a majority of the 11 board members wanted to fire Superintendent Sizemore, but because of a fear that they would be voted out of office in the coming election and that public support would sway against them, they relented. School board members were waiting for a signal from the electorate or from the press that retention of Superintendent Sizemore was not desirable. That signal came on April 4, 1975, when the Washington Post and the Washington Star accused Superintendent Sizemore of being a Black racist who was not fit to run the nation's twelfth largest school system, particularly one located in the nation's capital.

Superintendent Sizemore delivered a speech at the sixth annual conference of the African Heritage Studies Association held in Washington on April 3-6, 1975. In that speech, Mrs. Sizemore spoke on topics from Arnold Toynbee's analysis of the growth of civilizations to Daniel P. Moynihan's work titled "The Politics of a Guaranteed Income." She discussed the roles of Black leaders, past and present, such as Martin Luther King, Jr., Malcolm X, and Elijah Mohammed. She talked about Black elected officials in the nation's capital and the role of the Congress in the running of the city.[72]

In talking about the D.C. public schools, Sizemore mentioned the role of the school board and the role of the superintendent. She also discussed the roles played by Blacks and whites in the city. She talked about some Blacks who defended European modes of thinking and action at the expense of those held by Blacks, and about those whites who sought control of the District and its institutions by the manipulation of Blacks. She also mentioned the plight of poor people in the city, and how their problems are not attended to as well as those of middle class Blacks.[73]

Furthermore, she suggested that there was a racial problem in the District and that whites were attempting to take control of the city that was presently being run by Blacks. Using the D.C. board of education as an example, she talked about the divisions among Black members and how the divisions played into the hands of white manipulators.[74]

Quoting a noted Black writer and historian (Chancellor Williams), she explained that the D.C. situation is puzzling because while there is nothing new about people fighting among themselves, they generally stop if outsiders attack, settle their differences and unite against the common foes. Therefore, she pushed the argument by saying that people in the District of Columbia and those at the conference needed to continue this struggle until that kind of solidarity is won.[75]

The press reaction to the speech was immediate and acerbic. The Washington Star carried a story on the front page of their Metropolitan section captioned "Superintendent Sizemore Assails Whites." Diane Brockett's article said that Sizemore charged Congress with trying to destroy the elected D.C. government by saddling it with a $3 million debt in its first year of operation.[76] The second paragraph of the Star article maintained that Sizemore said that the three Black members of the D.C. board of education's seven member majority are being duped by whites into following a policy that promotes and maintains the idea that Blacks are incompetent and/or inferior.[77]

The very next morning, the Washington Post headlined its Metropolitan section with, "Sizemore Assails Power Structure." The Post's account, written by staff writer Richard Prince, had a similar twist.[78]

Neither the Post nor the Star account made any effort to highlight the intellectual points made by the superintendent during her presentation. Neither article made mention of her summary, the written works of Toynbee, Moynihan, Martin Luther King, Jr., or Malcolm X. The articles did not mention that Superintendent Sizemore was speaking before a gathering of recognized scholars from all across the country who had chosen her as their keynote speaker.

The impression given by the articles was that Sizemore, once again engaging in racial fanaticism, was speaking before a gathering of primitive race mongrels whose chief objective in life was the elimination of white society.

It was not long before the editorial pages of the District's two white dailies spoke on Barbara Sizemore. The Washington Star headlined its editorial "Mrs. Sizemore's Declaration." The Washington Star's editorial account of Superintendent Sizemore's speech said the speech was racist. In fact, the Star editorial, written by a white, accused Sizemore of lying about actions of white board members in regards to race. The editorial said that it had interviewed two white board members whom Mrs. Sizemore had accused of conspiracy against her and a Black school system and believed that their account of events was accurate and that the superintendent was lying.[79]

Soon after Superintendent Sizemore's speech, Post staff writer Richard Prince, who had been covering the District school system for nearly three years, was removed from his assignment and placed on the night police beat, an assignment usually reserved for reporters who fall into disfavor. The working hours were from 6 p.m. in the afternoon until 3 a.m. in the morning. Prince said during an interview that he and Post editors had serious differences about the coverage of the school system and in particular about the handling of the African Heritage Studies Association speech. Prince said that he thought that Sizemore was simply stating how she felt about race in this society and that he found nothing alarming about her statement. He said that his editors differed with him over the point and that was why he was removed.[80] Prince was replaced by Martha Hamilton, a white female reporter, and Lee Daniels, a young Black reporter, who was new to Washington and new to the politics and personalities of the school system.

Throughout Prince's coverage of Sizemore's superintendency, there was a marked difference between the manner in which he covered news events and the manner in which Diane Brockett covered the same stories. Unlike Prince, Brockett was not removed from her post as education writer for the Washington Star after the African Heritage Studies Association speech.

Now that the major papers in the city had spoken, suggesting that the school chief was unfit, board members who were once reluctant to dismiss Superintendent Sizemore now felt that they could move. The editorials acted as a signal from the white power structure.

On May 1, 1975, the board voted in closed session to dismiss the superintendent. The board decided then to draw up a Bill of Particulars against her. The seven board members voting to fire Sizemore included three Blacks, who had resisted pressure from white board members to dismiss the superintendent until after the African Heritage Studies Association speech and the newspaper editorials condemning the superintendent. These included board President Virginia Morris, Vice President Julius Hobson, Jr., and Hilda Mason.

The report that the board had decided to fire Superintendent Sizemore was reported in both the Washington Star and the Washington Post. In both instances, the source of the disclosures was not revealed. The Post account, printed on May 2, the same day that the Star account appeared, said that the majority on the DCBOE had decided to fire Sizemore.[81]

The Washington Post account was written by Martha Hamilton, who had replaced Prince. It is interesting to note that Prince did not always have privileged sources like Diane Brockett always seemed to have on the school board. Immediately after the public discovered that the board had been meeting in secret and had decided to dismiss Superintendent Sizemore, many of her supporters gathered around her. The Washington Star described her supporters as an angry crowd, and described one of the leaders of the group, Mother Ruth Goodwin, as wearing a long dress and headdress with a crucifix on a chain around her neck.[82] To the average reader it appeared that Superintendent Sizemore's supporters were not only racial fanatics but religious zealots in a town that was uncomfortable with religion and whose power structure gave little credence to religious symbolism.

Newspaper coverage of Superintendent Sizemore followed her across the country to Evanston, Illinois, where she delivered a speech at Northwestern University, one of the institutions where she had matriculated. In a Washington Post article penned by Hamilton and Post stringer Joel Weisman, Sizemore was quoted as saying that she would stay on her job until she had done enough so that she would be remembered. The Post article was captioned "Sizemore to Stay on Job." An inch above the major headline was a sidebar, "Vows accomplishments 'They will never forget'."[83] The Washington Star also carried an article about Superintendent Sizemore's speech in Evanston. Generally, it covered much of the material that was covered in the Post article; however, the Star headline writers chose to caption the article "Sizemore Says She Has 6 Job Offers."[84]

At a rally held in a Washington church, entire families and school-age children came to support Superintendent Sizemore. Among those attending the rally was a man by the name of Robert Wooten, who was president of a local PTA. Mr. Wooten said after the rally that he wanted to see Superintendent Sizemore retained and that the rally opened his eyes so he is behind the superintendent 150 percent.[85]

A Washington Post poll published on May 11, 1975 shocked Sizemore's opponents for it showed that 75 percent of the people polled in the District opposed the firing of the superintendent. It also showed that 45 percent of the people making over $18,000.00 per year gave Mrs. Sizemore an unfavorable job rating and that 49 percent of the whites also felt that she was not doing a good job. Contrastingly, 54 percent Black and 43 percent of the respondents making less than $12,000.00 incomes gave her a favorable job performance rating.[86]

The Washington Star made an effort not only to discredit Superintendent Sizemore, but also her supporters and (later, during the dismissal hearings) her attorney of record, DeLong Harris.

On June 1, 1975, the Washington Star devoted

an entire page to the nature of Sizemore supporters. The headline writers wrote "Sizemore Backers: Often Loud, Sometimes Unruly, Always Loyal."[87]

The Washington Star also suggested that employees hired by Mrs. Sizemore were among her supporters and were disruptive and militant. In this case they were referring to Al Gaskins and Peb Ali, both GS-12 coordinators of PACTS, the superintendent's program for involving the community in decision-making in the schools.[88]

Mathews and the Star editors did not mention that highly regarded educators in Washington and from distant parts of the country had supported Superintendent Sizemore and had come to her assistance in Washington. Instead, the paper chose to focus on a group of people whom its editors felt they could imply were unlettered, unacclaimed and lacked decorum.[89] In another article a reporter described the superintendent's April speech as "fiery." It also said that the general public had lost all faith in Superintendent Sizemore after the African Heritage address and that the citizens' reaction was interpreted by the board majority as the signal to dismiss her.[90] Interestingly enough, neither the Star nor the Post felt compelled to ask poor Black people, whose children composed the large majority of the District school population, what they thought of the superintendent. The editors and reporters at the papers decided among themselves and with those people that they regularly talked with, which did not include poor people, that the speech was racist and that the superintendent was dangerous and deranged.

During the hearing stage of the Sizemore controversy, Mathews teamed up with Brockett to deride the superintendent. In an August 1 article, the Washington Star headline writers wrote "Table Talk Delays Start of Hearing on Sizemore Job." The Star article also made an effort to discredit Superintendent Sizemore's attorney of record,

DeLong Harris, when it indicated that Harris was objecting to the arrangement of the tables and to television lights on the stage.[91]

In many instances, quotes and statements by people who supported Superintendent Sizemore during the hearings were not highlighted as were the statements of her detractors. One such example is a statement made by former Baltimore School Superintendent Roland Patterson, who had been dismissed by the school board there, and which appeared at the very end of a Washington Post article. Patterson, who had attended several of the hearings said that many of the charges against Mrs. Sizemore were petty, and many were things that had developed over the course of 30 or 40 years. He chatted with and hugged Superintendent Sizemore after the hearing, mentioning that it would take a Houdini to straighten out the problems of the schools so soon.[92]

In a photograph that accompanied the Post article, Mrs. Sizemore was captured by a Post photographer as looking far off into the distance as her lawyer of record, Harris, and Washington debated a legal point.[93]

Washington Post columnist William Raspberry attended the hearings and wrote an article that suggested that all the school board members, the superintendent, and the judge were tantamount to schoolchildren playing games. The caption of Raspberry's article was "They'll Make Her Stay After School?"[94] Although it was an attempt at humor, it made Superintendent Sizemore, the board of education, and all of those associated with the case appear silly and childish. Raspberry's satire had followed a blistering Post editorial that had appeared on July 30, some five days earlier. In the editorial, which appeared at the top of the paper's editorial page, the Post not only suggested that Superintendent Sizemore was playing games with the school board, but that it was imperative that she leave at once.

Here, the Washington Post stated that educational innovation was not something that the District schools needed. The morning paper suggested that the school system was in desperate need of a technician, an administrator who could see to it that all pencils used in the system had erasers and that all of the system's bus drivers wore the right size caps. Here we have a discussion of whether the school system needed a manager or an educator. Here, too, in its editorial, the paper suggested that the school board should not waste the city's time in conducting a "nationwide search" for another school chief, but that the system should look right in its own backyard and appoint someone.[95] The school board did exactly what the paper suggested; it looked right in its own backyard and selected an administrator, Vincent Reed, to run the nation's twelfth largest school system.

As the result of editorials in the media, Barbara Sizemore herself became the issue, and not her educational philosophy and direction. The papers also made it appear that the major point at issue was a matter of wills between the superintendent and the board president, Virginia Morris, also a Black woman. In an August 7, 1975 article, the Post suggested that Mrs. Sizemore was refusing to leave the school system, even though a majority of the elected school board members wanted to see her removed. In the article written by white reporter Paul Hodge, who was one of many Post reporters who covered the school board situation, the morning newspaper stated that D.C. school board members were continuing their efforts to convince Sizemore to leave office voluntarily.[96]

In another article written by Post staff writer Martha Hamilton, the paper said that three supporters of Sizemore left a school board meeting which forced postponement of hearings on whether she should be fired.[97]

Both of the Post articles left readers with a

picture of an impervious school superintendent who was refusing to leave and who was backed by a gang of disruptive supporters.

During the height of the Superintendent Sizemore-school board controversy, one of the superintendent's sons, Vincent, was arrested for allegedly stealing a street corner sign. Vincent, then 16, made the front page of the Post's Metropolitan section. An unusually long article involving a juvenile who had no previous arrest record, the Post headline writers captioned the second part of the story "Mrs. Sizemore's son is given a lawyer at public expense."98

The Post editorial policy, though not as rustic as that in the Star, was just as damaging to Superintendent Sizemore's effort to retain her position until her three year contract ran out in 1976. In an August 4 editorial, the Post said that Superintendent Sizemore was no longer fit to run the city's school system.99 By the middle of August the editorial page writers at the Star newspaper were beginning to refer to the hearings as the termination hearings of D.C. School Superintendent Barbara A. Sizemore.100 The paper also praised a decision by the board of education to conduct daily hearings.101

With elections for a new school board less than four months away, school board members began to pay more than particular interest in what the newspapers were saying. A message in the Washington Star was rather lucid as it implied that the hearings were purposefully being delayed by a display of petulance.102 Around the same time Washington Star staff writer, Diane Brockett, began to refer to supporters of Superintendent Sizemore on the board of education as minority members.103

Newspaper accounts of the hearings made it appear that the entire event was little more than a carnival. Although angry citizens came out to vent their anger and frustration at the actions

being taken against a superintendent that they
admired and respected, the papers did not bother
to interview any of them. Instead, they focused
on the arrests and statements made by those that
were involved in altercations with the special
security police that were present.

Though Superintendent Sizemore never acknowledged that any of the people attending the hearings
came as a result of a request by her, the papers
labelled all those as Sizemore supporters or
backers.[104] One article which appeared on the
front page of the paper's first section described
how Rev. John Martin of Holy Comforter Baptist
Church was ejected from the school auditorium
while the audience of 55 persons, most of whom
supported Sizemore, shouted against the hearings.[105]

The Washington Post account quoted Rev. John
Martin, whom they referred to as Mr. Martin throughout explaining that he was a preacher. Accompanying
the article was a picture of an angry Rev. John
Martin, his mouth open, and teeth showing, being
pushed down the hall by Black security guards.
Rev. John Martin is also Black. The picture also
appeared on the front page.[106]

The Post article included a second picture
which depicted the arrest of Mr. Al Gaskins, who
was identified as one of the protestors. Gaskins
was also a school board employee and had been identified in earlier newspaper accounts as a supporter of the superintendent.

Also arrested during the incident involving
Rev. John Martin was Yango Sawyer, a supporter of
Superintendent Sizemore, whom the Post described
earlier as being active with an organization of
ex-offenders and as being active in a series of
disruptions of school board meetings called to discuss the firing of Mrs. Sizemore. It also noted
that Rev. John Martin had been involved in at
least one such disruption. The Post account also
suggested that Sizemore's supporters had caused

the school board to make procedural errors during the hearings. It further said that during a June meeting the school board had attempted to correct one of its mistakes but did not do so because the meeting was disrupted by a stink bomb and by Sizemore supporters who shouted at board members and rushed the conference table. The Post account also made mention of the absence of one of Mrs. Sizemore's four supporters on the board, Dr. Therman Evans.[107]

Another Washington Post article that day informed the citizens that Dr. James A. Johnson, an assistant D.C. school superintendent in charge of planning, research, and evaluation, had resigned effective August 29th.[108] The Post did not play a passive role during the hearings. It actively participated.

When Administrative Law Judge Herman T. Benn ruled that the board had improperly acted and that the charges against Superintendent Sizemore were invalid, Post editors wrote that Mr. Benn's ruling was odd, because it contradicted his earlier statements about the charges.[109] It is important to note here that the Post's editorial board at the time of the hearings did not include an administrative lawyer, nor did it include anyone that had any substantive experience as a barrister, yet the paper still felt equipped to offer a legal opinion. Additionally, most of the lawyers that were employed by the Post worked on the corporate side of the newspaper and seldom ventured into the newsroom. The Post editorial went on to say that the superintendent's supporters had disrupted the proceedings so much that she might manage to remain in office until after the November school board elections, that she was politicizing her office instead of running the schools, and that the voters will distinguish between incumbents who acted foolish and those who acted in the interest of education.[110] If we follow the emphases of the previous news articles and editorials, one conclusion to be drawn from this is that the citizens will dump the Sizemore supporters. One interpretation, then, is that this piece of writing contains a not too well concealed threat.

Martha Hamilton, a white reporter and much more sensitive than her counterpart, Diane Brockett at the Washington Star, did cover a speech by Superintendent Sizemore before an annual meeting of District school administrators, where she spoke of the need of confrontation politics in the District school system. She talked about the inability of the school board to properly define its own role, and Hamilton wrote about her remarks characterizing the board as an elected body that does not know what its role is.

Hamilton reported that the administrators applauded Superintendent Sizemore warmly, and that she received two standing ovations when she talked about the need for more political involvement on the part of educators and for increased cooperation between administrators in the various schools and administrators in the central office. Though Hamilton reported the story and the response of the administrators, many of whom had served in the school system for decades, the Post editorial staff did not see fit to comment on it.[111]

Articles such as the one mentioned above received less space in newspapers than did articles in which controversy between factions was prominent. In a Washington Post article written just two days after Superintendent Sizemore's appearance before the educators, a Sizemore supporter on the board was quoted as calling an opponent of the superintendent a "bitch." The Post also indicated that the fact that Mrs. Hilda Mason is married to a white man, Charles Mason, annoys some of the supporters of Mrs. Sizemore. The headline writers at the Post dubbed this section "Veiled Rancor Rises to Surface at Sizemore Ouster Hearings."[112]

During the first day of the resumed dismissal

hearings, there was a fracas, and Washington Post headline writers wrote, "Sizemore Hearings Restart; 3 arrested." The lead of the Post accompanying the article discussed the arrests and not the specifics of the hearings nor why they had to begin once again.

Among the three persons arrested at the first day of the new hearings was a woman named Ruth Pearl, whom the Post identified as a business associate of school board member Simmons.113 Mrs. Simmons was a supporter of Superintendent Sizemore and a frequent critic of media coverage of the hearings against Mrs. Sizemore.

Perhaps one of the more demeaning articles came during the month of September when Post headline writers characterized Superintendent Sizemore's fight for her professional reputation as a competent administrator and educator as a show. The Post, which seldom begins its stories with quotes, began a September 26 article with a quote from Jethro J. Walker, a D.C. resident, who said that the hearing was the best show in town. The Post article ended by describing Mrs. Ruth Goodwin as a pious appearing woman noting that she wears long dresses and headdresses. It further indicated that she prays with the superintendent who was characterized as the Bible-carrying superintendent.114

Earlier in its coverage of Sizemore supporters, the Washington Star described Mrs. Goodwin in a similar fashion. Though persons who supported Superintendent Sizemore were described in detail -- even their personal habits and past experiences -- detractors of the superintendent were referred to by name and never once was there a discussion of their dress or personal histories.

Major daily newspapers also influence public opinion by omission. Often citizens who hold opinions in contravention to those held by papers will send their letters to the editors for publication. Editors select letters and often disregard letters that they deem irresponsible or unacceptable. One such letter, written by Dr. Acklyn Lynch, a former professor at Howard University, the University of Michigan, and the University of Massachusetts, was sent to the Washington Star and to the Washington Post. It did not appear on the editorial pages of those papers. Dr. Lynch, a parent with children in the public schools, had been attending many of the hearing sessions and had not been involved in any disruptions of the process.

The only local publication that chose to publish his letter was the student newspaper at Howard University. His letter was critical of the board majority that wished to fire Superintendent Sizemore. Both major dailies in their editorial policies had been supportive of the board majority. A portion of Dr. Lynch's letter read, "The problem, which we have here, is that the Board has failed to provide effective leadership to the entire system in the way that it has handled the Sizemore affair." He continued:

> One wonders, whether the seven-man majority of the Board, and especially the Chairman and Vice-Chairman, consulted legal advice outside of the Corporation Counsel about the procedural questions [of the hearings], or whether their political judgments were made abstractly without any research or consultation on the matter.[115]

Evidently, the Post and Star editors felt that Dr. Lynch's article was insignificant or simply superintendent-supported propaganda. At any rate, they dismissed it outright by not printing it.

At the conclusion of the hearings, the Post carried a news analysis of the 17 days of testimony. The Post article detailed the charges brought against the superintendent and her defense. Yet the paper could not get away from the linkage that it and the Washington Star had created between Superintendent Sizemore and her "militant" supporters, as the papers had described them.116

After the final day of hearings, the Post carried a news story headlined: "Mrs. Sizemore's Hearings Concluded Much to Relief of Those Involved."117 On Sunday, September 28, the Post featured an editorial entitled "The Sizemore Affair (Cont.)." In that editorial the Washington Post accused Superintendent Sizemore of being the commander-in-chief of those forces that had disrupted school board meetings and threatened the lives and property of school board members. The Post called a statement that Mrs. Sizemore had issued to the general public at a board meeting on August 28 an incitement to racism and a threat to turn the November school board elections into a referendum on whether she should be superintendent of schools.118 However, the Post did print the superintendent's statement so that the public could judge its implications for itself.119

It was a foregone conclusion by the middle of September that Superintendent Sizemore would be dismissed by a majority of the school board members. Yet the criticism by the press of her and her supporters did not abate. The Post on September 15 refuted a statement penned by school board member Barbara Lett Simmons (critical of the paper's coverage of the school board-superintendent conflict) as lies. The Post responded by calling Mrs. Simmons' accusations cheap shots and deceptive. The paper also suggested that Mrs. Simmons reminded them of Richard Nixon in his defense of Supreme Court nominee Harold Carswell.120 This attack on Mrs. Simmons was the most vicious the Post had printed to that date.

Even after Superintendent Sizemore had been dismissed, the Post continued its assault on the woman that they had come to view as a race baiter. In an October 11 editorial, the Post set about criticizing Mrs. Sizemore and lauding Vincent Reed, whom the school board had selected as acting superintendent.[121]

Acting Superintendent Reed made it quite clear publicly that he did not intend to go against the wishes of the school board because he recognized that he was an employee and that the proper role of an employee is to be submissive to the wishes of one's employer, even if the employer may be wrong.

In an October 12 article, the Washington Post headline writers characterized Superintendent Reed as a "strong leader."[122] This article was penned by Post staff writer Martha Hamilton.

On October 25, the Post carried an article written by staff writer Lee Daniels. The article was nothing more than simple coverage of an election debate between three candidates for the school board seat from Ward 5, which Bettie Benjamin, the incumbent and a Sizemore supporter, represented. In his article, Daniels outlined the positions of the candidates and gave a brief history of their community involvement. Daniels was not derisive of Mrs. Benjamin's conduct during the Sizemore affair. He simply identified her as an ardent supporter. Post headline writers did not focus in on the substance of Daniels' article when they titled his piece. Instead, they decided to pen the article "Sizemore Is Issue In Ward 5 Race."[123]

## Conclusion

Suffice it to say that both the Post and Star seemingly were able to create "facts" by the manipulation of opinion printed under a byline. For as William Raspberry of the Washington Post stated to this writer in a telephone interview, reporters are looking for attitudes, not facts. They interview people, gather their data by observing at meetings, and reading the newspaper's file on a topic or under a person's name. Furthermore,

Raspberry said, a columnist is expressing his opinions. He has no data bank and does not gather facts as a researcher does for a scholarly work. He continued by saying that a reporter's data consists of notes from the above sources that you often cannot even read the next day.[124] Thus, we get the kind of reporting discussed in the first part of this section.

In summary, although the newsclips and editorials analyzed are not exhaustive, they are indicative of the negativism propounded by the two dailies. Likewise, they also present evidence that is suggestive of the probability that the negative climate created by the papers might have exacerbated the conflict in superintendent-school board relations. Certainly, one can assume that the newspapers, by publishing editorials raising questions about whether a speech made by the superintendent was racist, inflamed various elements of the public influential with the majority board decision makers and, in turn, precipitated negative board action against her. For, if some board members were hesitant about beginning a process leading toward the termination of the superintendent's contract, as some said in their interview, negative reaction to the speech seemed to have been interpreted as a go-ahead from the powerful forces in the community. Neither the Black mayor of the predominantly Black city council or Congressman Diggs could later halt the process once it began, as will be noted further on. None were powerful enough to influence the board. For the most part, they represented the voice of Black people. Contrastingly, the dailies represented the voice of white people -- white business interests primarily. For in spite of the *Washington Post* poll conducted in the middle of the controversy, which showed the superintendent with 75 percent support among both Black (54%) and whites (23%) in the District, the termination process was not stopped. Significantly, the poll also showed that 45 percent of the persons making over $18,000.00 income per year rated the superintendent unfavorable in terms of how well she was doing her job. Forty-nine percent of the whites felt similarly. That is to say, almost half of the people making a goodly sum of money and almost 50 percent white people were not pleased with the superintendent's job performance. This supports the contention that these were the people with the power in the District.

The data also points up the exceedingly powerful role that the press plays in school policy decision-making. It became quite evident as new members joined the board in November 1974, that several seemed to feel that they had a mandate from the press, not really their ward constituents, to either remove Mrs. Sizemore from the superintendency or suffer defeat in the next election. One interpretation of the wording of the admonition in editorials and news articles is that there was a definite threat that board members who did not obey might also suffer bad press. This possible veiled threat in and of itself helped to shape educational policy in the District.

Chapter X analyzes the factors contributing to the termination of Superintendent Sizemore. As previously stated, the termination process is a significant aspect of the school board's functions.

FOOTNOTES                                    CHAPTER IX

1. *Passow Report*, p. 80.

2. D.C. Federation of Civic Associations 1977 Directory, Washington, D.C.

3. "Minutes of the D.C. Board of Education," Washington, D.C., November 15, 1967, p. 19.

4. Hansen, *Danger in Washington*, p. 207.

5. Constance McLaughlin Green, *Washington-A History of the Capital, 1800-1950*, Vol. II, Princeton University Press, Princeton, New Jersey, 1972, pp. 30-33.

6. Ibid., pp. 175-176.

7. Ibid., p. 215.

8. Ibid., pp. 315-316.

9. Ibid., pp. 437-438.

10. Interview with Hugh Scott, Superintendent of Schools, Washington, D.C., 21 November 1977.

11. "Minutes of the Seventeenth (Stated) Meeting of the Board of Education," Washington, D.C., 15 November 1967, p. 19.

12. Milton Coleman's City Hall Notebook, "The Changing Times at the Board of Trade," *Washington Post District Weekly*, 9 February 1978.

13. This information was taken from a flyer entitled "Highlights of History of D.C. Citizens for Better Public Education, Inc.," June 1975, obtained from files of DCCBPE by the writer.

14. "Minutes of the D.C. Board of Education," Washington, D.C., 17 April 1968 (Enclosure 8).

15. Passow Report, p. 80.

16. "Highlights of the History of D.C. Citizens for Better Public Education."

17. Passow Report, p. 80.

18. "Minutes of the Nineteenth (Stated) Meeting of the Board of Education," Washington, D.C., 16 September 1970, pp. 35-36.

19. "Anne Harrison, Philanthropist, Dies," Washington Post, 13 May 1977.

20. Merlo J. Pusey, Eugene Meyer, New York: Alfred A. Knopf, 1974, p. 337.

21. Ibid., p. 365.

22. Correspondence with attached report, "The D.C. Youth Orchestra Program and the Morale of the Public School Instrumental Music Teachers," to Dr. James T. Guines, Associate Superintendent of Schools, from Barbara White, Representative, Superintendent's Advisory Council, Elementary Instrumental Music Department, and Rosanna B. Saffran, Teacher, Elementary Instrumental Music Department, 16 July 1971.

23. William Delaney and Lynn Dunson, "Hamstrung by Board, Scott says," Washington Star-News, 14 January 1973.

24. Ibid.

25. Richard E. Prince, "Scott Issue Further Divides Board; 2 Members Clash on Racism Charge," Washington Post, 19 January 1973.

26. David Pike, "Board Quizzes 3 Candidates: Challenge Due," Washington Star-News, 28 July 1973.

27. Interview with Richard Prince, *Washington Post* Reporter, Washington, D.C., 15 February 1977.

28. Richard E. Prince, "Selection of School Superintendent Not Going as Planned," *Washington Post*, 18 July 1973.

29. Interview with Richard Prince, *Washington Post* Reporter, Washington, D.C., 15 February 1977.

30. Diane Brockett, "Mrs. Sizemore's View-Schools Sexist, Racist'," *Washington Star-News*, 18 November 1973.

31. Ibid.

32. Andrew Barnes, "Mrs. Sizemore Defends Controversial Ghetto Primer," *Washington Post*, 9 October 1973.

33. Alex Poinsett, "Barbara Sizemore Tackles Job of Running Nation's 12th Largest School System," *Ebony Magazine*, January 1974, p. 102.

34. "Changing Our Schools," *Washington Post*, 7 July 1974.

35. William Raspberry: (1) "Tests Are the Keepers of the Gate," *Washington Post*, 2 September 1974; (2) "Standardized Test and Cultural Bias," *Washington Post*, 4 September 1974; (3) "Teaching the Skills of Test Taking," *Washington Post*, 6 September 1974. See also Davis Burgess, Jr., "Standardized Tests," *Washington Afro-American*, 7 September 1974.

36. Robert Buchanan, "Hawthorne School: Sizemore, Board Clash," *Washington Star-News*, 18 April 1974.

37. Letter of Evaluation from Howard University Team of Educators to Superintendent Sizemore, 3 May 1974.

38. Richard E. Prince, "D.C. Youth Orchestra Contract Renewed," *Washington Post*, 9 July 1974.

39. Ibid.

40. Jacqueline Trescott, "Barbara Sizemore: A Fighter From Way Back," *Washington Star-News*, 8 July 1974.

41. Ibid.

42. Ibid.

43. Diane Brockett, "Face Fund Halt D.C. Schools - 'NO' on Tests," *Washington Star-News*, 25 May 1974.

44. Ibid.

45. Richard E. Prince, "City Schools' Federal Aid Is Suspended," *Washington Post*, 25 May 1974.

46. Ibid.

47. Ibid.

48. Richard E. Prince, "Schools Will Get U.S. Funds," *Washington Post*, 13 June 1974.

49. Diane Brockett, "Questionnaire Left Blank at High Schools," *Washington Star-News*, 14 June 1974.

50. Diane Brockett, "Mrs. Sizemore Lets Go With Verbal Blast at Board," *Washington Star-News*, 16 May 1974.

51. Richard E. Prince, "Mrs. Morris Elected to D.C. School Board Post," *Washington Post*, 16 May 1974.

52. Interview with Richard Prince, *Washington Post* Reporter, Washington, D.C., 15 February 1977.

53. Bill Garner, "Now let's not start that again!," *Washington Star-News*, 17 August 1974.

54. Diane Brockett, "3 Who Weren't Invited to the Sizemore Party," *Washington Star-News*, 23 October 1974.

55. Ibid.

56. Ibid.

57. Lee A. Daniels, "2 School Board Victors Call Parents 'Angry'," *Washington Post*, 7 November 1974.

58. Ibid.

59. Ibid.

60. Ibid.

61. Interview with Richard Prince, *Washington Post* Reporter, Washington, D.C., 15 February 1977.

62. Richard E. Prince, "D.C. Payroll Snarls Rapped by Teachers," *Washington Post*, 5 November 1974.

63. Diane Brockett, "School Board Re-Elects Mrs. Morris and Hobson," *Washington Star-News*, 28 January 1975.

64. Ibid.

65. Interview with Richard Prince, *Washington Post* Reporter, Washington, D.C., 15 February 1977.

66. Diane Brockett, "Panel Dismantles Sizemore Version of School Budget, Writes Its Own," *Washington Star-News*, 11 February 1975.

67. Ibid.

68. Diane Brockett, "Is Supt. Sizemore On the Way Out?," Washington Star, 16 March 1975.

69. Ibid.

70. Ibid.

71. Ibid.

72. Barbara A. Sizemore, "Education: Is Accommodation Enough?," Journal Of Negro Education 44 (Summer 1975), pp. 239-240.

73. Ibid.

74. Ibid.

75. Ibid.

76. Diane Brockett, "Supt. Sizemore Assails Whites," Washington Star, 4 April 1975.

77. Ibid.

78. Richard E. Prince, "Sizemore Assails Power Structure," Washington Post, 5 April 1975.

79. Editorial, "Mrs. Sizemore's Declaration," Washington Star, 9 April 1975.

80. Interview with Richard Prince, Washington Post Reporter, Washington, D.C., 15 February 1977.

81. Martha M. Hamilton, "Board Set to Fire Sizemore," Washington Post, 2 May 1975.

82. John Mathews, "Crowd Angered by Board Action," Washington Star, 2 May 1975.

83. Joel D. Weisman and Martha M. Hamilton, "Sizemore 'to Stay on Job'," Washington Post, 4 May 1975.

84. "Sizemore Says She Has 6 Job Offers," *Washington Star*, 4 May 1975.

85. Lee A. Daniels and Martin Weil, "Sizemore Rally Draws Over 200," *Washington Post*, 5 May 1975.

86. Martha M. Hamilton, "Firing of Sizemore Opposed 3-1 in Poll," *Washington Post*, 11 May 1975.

87. John Mathews, "Sizemore Backers: Often Loud, Sometimes Unruly, Always Loyal," *Washington Star*, 1 June 1975.

88. Ibid.

89. Ibid.

90. "History," *Washington Star*, 1 June 1975.

91. John Mathews and Diane Brockett, "Table Talk Delays Start of Hearing on Sizemore Job," *Washington Star*, 1 August 1975.

92. Martha M. Hamilton, "Case Against Sizemore Is Outlined," *Washington Post*, 5 August 1975.

93. Ibid.

94. William Raspberry, "They'll Make Her Stay After School?," *Washington Post*, 4 August 1975.

95. Editorial, "Some Lessons in the Sizemore Case," *Washington Post*, 30 July, 1975.

96. Paul Hodge, "Sizemore Settlement Pressed," *Washington Post*, 7 August 1975.

97. Martha Hamilton, "Sizemore Group Stages Walk-Out," *Washington Post*, 12 August 1975.

98. "Mrs. Sizemore's Son Is Given A Lawyer at Public Expense," *Washington Post*, 9 August 1975.

99. Editorial, "The Sizemore Hearings and the Schools," Washington Post, 4 August 1975.

100. Editorial, "Sizemore Hearings-get on with them," Washington Star, 14 August 1975.

101. Ibid.

102. Ibid.

103. Diane Brockett, "Daily Hearings On Sizemore Set," Washington Star, 13 August 1975.

104. Martha M. Hamilton, "Police Arrest 4 Supporters of Sizemore," Washington Post, 21 August 1975.

105. Ibid.

106. Ibid.

107. Ibid.

108. Washington Post, 21 August 1975.

109. Editorial, "The Sizemore Affair: Who's in Charge?," Washington Post, 23 August 1975.

110. Ibid.

111. Martha M. Hamilton, "School Chief Defends Her Programs," Washington Post, 28 August 1975.

112. Martha M. Hamilton, "Clashes Flare at Hearings on Sizemore," Washington Post, 30 August 1975.

113. Martha M. Hamilton, "Sizemore Hearings Restart; 3 Arrested," Washington Post, 9 September 1975.

114. Martha M. Hamilton, "Sizemore Show: 'Beats Broadway'," Washington Post, 26 September 1975.

115. Editorial, "Sizemore Supporter," *Hilltop*, September 1975.

116. Martha M. Hamilton, "Sizemore's Fate in Balance After 17 Days of Hearings," *Washington Post*, 28 September 1975.

117. Martha M. Hamilton, "Mrs. Sizemore's Hearings Concluded Much to Relief of Those Involved," *Washington Post*, 27 September 1975.

118. Editorial, "The Sizemore Affair (Cont.)," *Washington Post*, 7 September 1975.

119. Ibid.

120. Editorial, "Mrs. Simmons' Letter," *Washington Post*, 15 September 1975.

121. Editorial, "What Next for the Schools?," *Washington Post*, 11 October 1975.

122. Martha M. Hamilton, "Supt. Reed Seen as a Strong Leader," *Washington Post*, 12 October 1975.

123. Lee A. Daniels, "Sizemore Is Issue in Ward 5 Race," *Washington Post*, 25 October 1975.

124. Telephone interview between writer and William Raspberry, editorial writer of the *Washington Post*, 3 March 1978.

# CHAPTER X

# TERMINATION PROCESS, 1975

### Introduction

Deficiency in the managerial operation of the school system was fully noted and documented from as far back as 1966. Another fact, duly noted in Chapter III, was Hugh Scott's conflict with the board in terms of securing adequate funds for management services. Further, Case 3: Budget/Management (in Chapter VIII) detailed Barbara Sizemore's conflict with the board over securing adequate funds for management services. At least two superintendents struggled to obtain enough funds from the school board to mount an efficient management support system for the D.C. public schools. Both were denied the necessary resources. In the case of Scott, the chairperson of the Committee on School Finance cut his staff by one-third. This was the problem facing Sizemore when she became superintendent. It continued to be a problem for two years of her superintendency and even became exacerbated as the board moved her priorities, which included improving the management system to the "wish" category of "New and Improved Services," and their pet project into the base budget -- for example, the non-legislated early childhood education program. It is significant then that at least 9 of the 17 specifications to support the board's charge of inefficiency on the part of Superintendent Sizemore could be categorized as management matters. Is this then another instance of the DCBOE exercising its most clearly defined and understood power, firing (terminating) a superintendent, by placing blame for its indecision or incorrect decisions on its natural scapegoat, the superintendent?

The budget/management controversy merged into the hearing, climaxing as it did, near the end of the school year. Four of the 17 specifications against the superintendent evolved directly out of the April 7, 1974 board of education meeting. This meeting was held three days after the superintendent spoke at the African Heritage Studies Association conference about the political, racial and class factors influencing decision-making for the public schools in the District.

Each of the three cases, (1) the D.C. Youth Orchestra Program (DCYOP) controversy (June 1974), (2) the General Council dispute (August 1974), and (3) the Budget/Management dispute (September 1974 through May 1975), shows specific instances of steady erosion in superintendent-school board relations during Mrs. Sizemore's tenure as superintendent of the D.C. public school system. As the discussion unfolds, it will be noted that some external as well as internal factors impinged upon the decision-making unit causing a complete break in the relationship between the superintendent and the policy-making majority on the DCBOE.

Although a number of the respondents stated that Allen, Barry and Morris had power because of their positions as president, and Swaim had power because of her position as chairperson of the most powerful committee (Budget and Finance), a close examination of the transcripts reveals that they had power only as long as they could control the majority vote of six. Thus, they jockeyed and negotiated to try to keep control of the votes. Allen did this through sheer force of will and a dominating personality. But then she had an almost unanimous board. Barry was influential because he had strong support of the white financial community as was indicated by the number of his campaign contributors from the business community. But he was not powerful enough to influence board members in their choice of a superintendent of schools.

Likewise, it appeared that Swaim lost in her bid for a city council seat not only because she voted against Sizemore but because she widely circulated a negative letter, dated August 7, 1973,[1] defending her action. Later she circulated a letter of resignation, dated May 31, 1974, in which she not only stated that she was resigning from the board to run for the city council seat from Ward 6, but in which she also indicated that hiring Sizemore was a mistake. To this, Swaim attached a detailed analysis of her very negative assessment of Sizemore's first year in office.[2]

It became even clearer that the president of the DCBOE had to vote with the majority in order to maintain a semblance of power. As indicated in the interview data, Morris' vote pattern shows that when she lost her majority, she switched her position beginning in August 1974 to support the letting of a contract to the Friends of the DCYOP. This was during the time of the seven-member board in the summer of 1974, after Rosenfield, Swaim, Taylor and Barry resigned. Significant also was the fact that on July 12, 1974, Morris assumed the presidency from her role as vice president and Julius Hobson, Jr. was elected vice president.[3] As of the August 13, 1974 meeting, Hobson, Morris and Simmons were still voting against some aspects of negotiating a contract. Notably though, both Hobson and Morris switched their positions by mid-August so that they then pushed for immediacy in the board's renewing the contract with the Friends of the DCYOP.[4] Prior to this, it was Kemp, Treanor, Mason and Evans voting for the renewal of the contract and Simmons, Morris and Hobson voting against the renewal of the contract.[5] This switch in position began the construction of the seven-member majority against the superintendent. From that point on, Hobson's and Morris' decisions were made for them. They did not control the majority. It

controlled them. Therefore, from the end of
August 1974[6] throughout the rest of Sizemore's
tenure, the seven member policy-making majority
began to form, and eventually congealed in February
1975 when sides were chosen on the major issues --
two of which were the FY76 financial plan and the
firing of the superintendent.

As could be noted, Evans switched to become
one of the four who supported the superintendent's
programs when he, along with Benjamin, Simmons and
Warren, signed the Committee on School Finance's
Minority Report of February 19, 1975 on the FY76
budget.[7]

Hobson and Morris never again switched their
positions in support of the superintendent's programs which obviously infuriated their constituencies as displayed in Morris' defeat in her first
bid to be elected (she was originally appointed) to
a school board seat in November 1975. Hobson in
his interview declared that he would not run in
1977 when his term expired.[8]

Hence, it became quite evident that the
majority ruled. The board of education must act as
a board. The legislation states this. Members
cannot act individually, including the president.
Therefore, it became a case of who had the votes.
Morris did not have the votes, but she wanted to
be president, as did Barry, so they both followed
their votes as Hobson said in relation to his and
Morris' case. Significantly then, though it
appeared at first blush that Morris and Hobson were
the leaders because they were so visible in their
positions as president and vice president and he
also in his position as chairperson of the Committee on School Finance, they in fact were followers
of the voting majority on the board. True also,
the plethora of memoranda which moved back and
forth between them and the superintendent and
other administrators would perhaps lead to this
conclusion. Nevertheless, an even closer analysis
reveals that the person who apparently was the

actual "leader" of the four white and three Black board member majority who fired Sizemore was Hilda Howland M. Mason. Mason had the votes. It was she with whom the white board members had to negotiate. It was Mason and her husband who were Morris' biggest contributors as shown in Chapter V. It was she who seemed to serve as the cover for the white board members who did not want it to become obvious that racism was one of the factors in the firing of a Black superintendent in a majority Black and poor city. Neither did they appear to want it understood that the factor of changing the system to make it more responsive to the needs of the 96 percent Black student population was another element in their resistance to Sizemore's programs. April 4, 1975 was not the time to reveal that whites were returning to the city. It was too soon. The white forces had not been gathered nor the plans laid sufficiently just yet. The housing speculators were just moving in and only the young white singles were trickling back from the suburban areas. The big return was to come a few years later.

Therefore, after the April 4, 1975 speech before the African Heritage Studies Association in which Mrs. Sizemore exposed the plan to make D.C. a predominantly white city again, the white business interests again gave direction to the DCBOE through their news organs, the <u>Washington Post</u> and the <u>Washington Star</u>. The policy-setting majority on the DCBOE took heed and proceeded to rid the school system, if not the city, immediately of her presence.

It should again be noted that Mason was married to a white attorney who acted as her research assistant in the performance of her functions on the DCBOE.[9]

It was Mason who made recommendations to the School Finance Committee, which were presented to the board at the April 7, 1975 meeting and which later developed into charges.

As noted in table 10, Mason apparently supplied the board with at least six of the 17 specifications to support the charge of inefficiency against the superintendent. Hobson noted in his interview that he also suggested several specifications, as follows:

> On December 12, 1974, we met to discuss firing the superintendent. We met until 3 a.m. in the morning. I had had it on the budget. If you cannot maintain your management end and don't know how much money you've got, you can't run the system. I don't care what you believe and what you want to do. I think that meeting must have started at 6 o'clock or 7:30 p.m. In that meeting we discussed it, I pushed for the firing then, which is why a lot of people say that the speech that she gave the following April was the reason for her being fired. It may have been the reason to motivate some other people but as far as I was concerned I was ahead of the game in December, and my reasons were management. I pressed it that night and five people, I don't remember who they were, said they would vote to terminate her and two or three others started talking about conditions...and so nothing came out of it. Simmons, Benjamin and Warren said no. As the night wore on people changed sides.... So when it was over, it really wasn't clear what the situation was except that you knew three people were opposed. I led the charge to fire her because of the management piece, but nothing came out of it. It more or less died. If anything, I think the speech in April created an atmosphere for it [the firing]. I think that's what it did. I think... seven people agreeing that the superintendent should be fired started before the speech, but somehow the speech created the atmosphere for it and it started from there....
>
> Mason did a large part of the research looking for various things, but my main concern was management: Quarterly Financial Reports,

TABLE 10

MASON'S RECOMMENDATIONS WHICH EVOLVED INTO CHARGES

| No. | Charge | Mason's Recommendations | Source |
|-----|--------|-------------------------|--------|
| 8 | Failure to Comply with Board Directive to Appoint Administrative Committee, p. 55. | The recommendations were in a motion made by Mrs. Mason which reads as follows: . . . . . . . . . . . . . #3 The Superintendent designate an Administrative Committee to review requests for exemptions from and modifications in the "freeze" on non-personnel expenditures .... | Sixth Special (Emergency) Meeting of the DCBOE, April 7, 1975 |
| 10 | Failure to Comply with Board Directive to submit status report on expenditures, p. 60. | #6 The Administration provide the Board of Education with monthly status reports at the May and June business meetings reflecting the total expenditure applied against the new financial plan and the appropriate balances. | |
| 9 | Failure to provide responses to the Board's questions on the FY 1975 Financial Plan. | Included with #6 - The Administration should be asked to supply answers to the attached questions regarding the March 27 1975 FY75 Financial Status Report (Memo from Mrs. Mason) and to any further questions which other members of the Committee on Finance or Board may raise. | |
| 16 | Failure to Provide Curriculum Development in Fiscal Year 1975 | In answer to the interview question: What items arose as issues and emerged as charges for the termination of the Superintendent's contract?, Hobson replied: "Mason came up with curriculum, equalization, maybe permanent tenure ... | Hobson's Interview on September 28, 1977 |

517

| No. | Charge* | Mason's Recommendations | Source |
|---|---|---|---|
| 1 | Failure to Provide a Plan for Equalization of the Schools | | |
| 14 | Failure to Comply with Board Directive to Make Recommendations on Permanent tenure. | | |

* District of Columbia Board of Education In the Matter of Board of Education v. Barbara A. Sizemore, Superintendent of Schools, Proposed Termination of Contract, Respondent's Answer.

Quarterly Personnel Reports, FY 1976 Financial Plan, Status Report on Expenditures, Quarterly Safety Reports.[10]

It was characteristic of the elected board to operate in conflict with the superintendent of schools. The elected board and Dr. Manning were in conflict. The elected board and Dr. Scott were in conflict. The elected board and Mrs. Sizemore were in conflict. But, more importantly, the elected board was in conflict with each for different reasons. It was very clear from the voluminous transmittals, memos, letters, transcripts, and minutes, that the underlying reason for the conflict with Manning was his slowness in making changes in the school system. The underlying reason for the conflict with Scott was that he did not equalize expenditures or decentralize the school system. But the underlying reason for the conflict with Sizemore was that she did decentralize the system and tried in every way she knew how to change the dynamics of interpersonal relationships through a shortening of the hierarchy, and through the use of the administrative team approach. She also tried to change the educational program from a mono-lingual, mono-cultural, and mono-modal one to a multi-lingual, multi-cultural, and multi-modal one. The boards that Manning and Scott had were decentralization liberal boards that wanted change, whereas the boards that Sizemore had were conservative, anti-decentralization, and anti-change boards.

## Threshold of the Hearing

In all, the charges against Mrs. Sizemore numbered 17. They fell roughly into four specifications: (1) budget/management; (2) personnel; (3) student; and (4) curriculum (see table 11).

As indicated in table 11, 15 of the 17 specifications could be categorized as budget/management matters, one specifically dealt with student matters, and one dealt with curriculum. Of course,

TABLE 11

CHARGES

| \multicolumn{4}{c|}{Management/Budget} | \multicolumn{2}{c|}{Student} | \multicolumn{2}{c}{Curriculum} |
|---|---|---|---|---|---|---|---|
| No. | Charge | No. | Charge | No. | Charge | No. | Charge |
| 1 | Failure to provide a plan for equalization of the schools. | 7 | Failure to provide a timely Annual report. | 15 | Failure to obtain for the Board student comments on proposed rules on students rights and responsibilities and code of conduct. | 16 | Failure to provide curriculum development in Fiscal Year 1975. |
| 2 | Failure to provide quarterly safety reports. | 8 | Failure to comply with Board Directive to appoint administrative committee (non-personnel expenditures). | | | | |
| 3 | Failure to provide and implement adequate personnel hiring controls and failure to maintain hiring within fiscally responsible limits. | 5 | Failure to provide a timely selection procedure for the selection of Regional Superintendents. | | | | |
| 6 | Failure to comply with Board directives concerning Federal Grant proposals. | 14 | Failure to comply with Board directive to make recommendations on permanent tenure. | | | | |
| 9 | Failure to provide responses to the Board's questions on the FY 1975 Financial Plan. | 4 | Failure to fill position as directed by the Board of Education. | | | | |

| Managament/Budget | | Student | | Curriculum | |
|---|---|---|---|---|---|
| No. Charge | No. Charge | No. Charge | No. Charge | No. Charge | No. Charge |
| | 10 Failure to comply with Board Directive to submit status report on expenditures. | | | | |
| 11. Failure to provide quarterly financial reports. | | | | | |
| 12. Failure to provide quarterly personnel reports. | | | | | |
| 14. Failure to comply with Board to provide Fiscal Year 1975 Legislative Proposal. | | | | | |
| 17. Failure to provide report on declining enrollment. | | | | | |

other categorizations could have been made as some matters are a bit fuzzy as to where they might fall, especially in the area of budget/management.

Any number of respondents stressed that primarily management issues were chosen because they were the easiest to prove. Characteristic responses were:

> We were very careful that they would be sustained as charges....(They were primarily management kind of things?) Yeah.[11]

> Primarily management issues.[12]

> (Basically, the management kinds of issues?) Yeah.[13]

Absent from the proposed bill of particulars was any reference to some of the major controversies that arose between the superintendent and the board, including the D.C. Youth Orchestra, the Hawthorne School, the General Counsel dispute, and the April 4, 1975 speech made by the superintendent.

Before examining some of the specific aspects of the hearing, a brief chronology of events is necessary in order to consider significant events leading up to the hearing.

Chronology of the Conflict

April 17, 1974 - Superintendent and board disagreed about contracting with Hawthorne Alternative School over issue of funneling resources of public schools, which should be used to build up instructional services for all students to private sector.[14]

May 15, 1974 - Subcommittee on Federal Grants recommended that administration submit functional statements, organizational charts, and implementation time frames before proposed State Office was staffed and operating.

Viewed by superintendent as administrative details which ought not become conditions for adoption of policy.

- Superintendent presented report to board entitled "Board-Administration Relationships" which spoke to clarifying and delineating relationships, authorities, duties and expectations. Board approved receiving report and referring it to Committee of the Whole for discussion and recommendations.[15]

June 1974 - Superintendent tried to persuade board not to let contract to Friends of the D.C. Youth Orchestra for music services. Issue stemmed from need of public school monies for public school educational services and having no control over programs administered by private organizations.[16]

June 20, 1974 - Memo sent to superintendent and board from D. Cropp concerning schedule for June 25, 1974 to discuss, among other things (1) process of filling interim and permanent positions, and (2) quarterly personnel reports.[17]

August 22, 1974 - Disagreement between superintendent and board president about role of general counsel culminating in directive from board president to superintendent that administrative requests for legal opinion from general counsel should be directed to executive secretary who would establish board staff priorities.[18]

September 6, 1974 - Diane Brockett reported under large heading, "Delay in School Openings Is News to Sizemore," whereas only two schools did not open on time due to legitimate decisions made by regional superintendents, as was their prerogative.[19]

September 24, 1974 - Superintendent and board president met with City Councilman Sterling Tucker to discuss disputed areas in board-superintendent relations.[20]

September 25, 1974 - Superintendent's press release regarding her difficulty in reconciling superintendent's role with that of general counsel of board stating she and president of board will evaluate pertinent materials to clearly delineate roles and relationships of board and superintendent.[21]

- Board president's press release stating school system is faced with a public debate over question of board-superintendent relations and areas of agreement reached.[22]

September 30, 1974 - Superintendent and deputy superintendent for management services presented information on the FY75 and FY76 budgets about which many questions were raised concerning recurring management problems, reorganization and educational programming issues.[23]

October 3, 1974 - Mayor/commissioner announced a freeze on personnel and a budget reduction for FY75 of $3,834,200.00.[24]

October 22, 1974 - Memorandum sent to superintendent from Julius W. Hobson, Jr., chairman, Committee on School Finance requesting answers to six pages of questions on FY76 budget plan.[25]

November 20, 1974 - Board approved statement concerning FY75 financial plan and FY76 budget presented by Morris, requesting: (1) status of all personnel slots as of October 31, 1974; (2) copy of monthly payroll printout for last pay period in October; (3) revised FY75 financial plan, and (4) revised FY76 operating budget. Request had to do with the matter of charges of overhiring.[26]

December 6, 1974 - Board approved School Finance Committee recommendation of appointment of task force to (1) revise FY75 financial plan, (2) look at revised proposed FY76 operating budget, and (3) look at unauthorized and unallowable positions, using 100 percent time of certain key administrators.[27]

December 10, 1974 - Superintendent sent board president memo requesting clarification of use of 100 percent time of key administrators.[28]

December 12, 1974 - Board approved that a special committee of the board be appointed to meet with superintendent to clarify concerns about the board's December 6, 1974 action on the use of 100 percent time of administrative staff.[29]

- Diane Brockett wrote article in the Washington Star stating that board statement was to be delivered to superintendent instructing her once more to appoint six top administrators to task team and, if she failed to do so, a majority of board agreed to fire her and replace her with Vincent Reed, Edward Winner (budget director), Dwight Cropp (executive secretary), or Floretta McKenzie (former deputy superintendent).[30]

- On December 12, 1974, board president sent superintendent memo directing her to comply with directive to appoint members of administration to a task team using 100 percent of their time to advise Committee on School Finance in dealing with budget crisis.[31]

December 15, 1974 - Richard Prince wrote an article in the Washington Post stating that board members took comfort in statement made by superintendent that she recognized board's authority over her to direct implementation of policy which superintendent may consider ill-advised and that if superintendent cannot do so in good conscience then she should resign. Nevertheless, it is within the superintendent's discretion to choose manner of implementation as long as it does not conflict with board action. Furthermore, the superintendent noted in the interview, as reported by Prince, that her contract provides that she may be subject to discharge for adequate cause affecting her character and efficiency but that a hearing on those charges would be held before the school board itself.[32]

December 16, 1974 - Board approved revision of December 6, 1974 directive to superintendent to effect that administrators assigned to task team shall devote necessary time in addition to their regular duties.[33]

January 8, 1975 - Letter sent to board's president from superintendent requesting direction to take in preparing for initial FY76 budget review scheduled for January 14, 1975, since FY76 budget plan submitted to board on October 21, 1974 had not been acted on.[34]

January 22, 1975 - Simmons makes statement on board's inaction on FY75 financial plan.[35]

February 19, 1975 - Board Committee on School Finance task force presented report of the FY76 public school's operating budget. The report was only slightly related to goals and objectives set forth in the 120 Day Report adopted by the board on May 30, 1974.[36] Board members Simmons, Benjamin, Evans and Warren issued a Minority Report in opposition to the budget, stating that it did "irreparable violence to the goals and objectives of decentralization, PACTS process, management services, and programs for Student Services, Curriculum Development, Staff Development, etc.," and prioritized ahead of these was an expanded early childhood program with most of superintendent's program relegated to the New and Improved Services -- a wish category.[37]

April 5, 1975 - Superintendent exposed conspiracy for removing Blacks from the city and, therefore, the school system in a speech presented before the African Heritage Studies Association conference.[38] Media uproar proclaimed superintendent racist.[39]

April 7, 1975 - Board meeting held at which time three actions (decisions) were made which evolved into charges leading to the hearings, namely, (1) the superintendent designate an administrative committee to review exemptions from non-personnel expenditures, (2) administration provide monthly status reports of expenditures, and (3) administration supply answers to Mason's questions on FY75 financial status report.[40]

April 8, 1975 - Superintendent's critic spoke at board meeting.[41]

April 28, 1975 - Superintendent received directive (at home) late Friday, April 25, 1975, to attend meeting on Monday, April 28, 1975 to discuss procedure for evaluating her performance.[42]

- Board adopted president's proposed evaluation document which consisted of 45 items, part of the Charlottesville, Virginia public school instrument taken out of context and separated from instructions for its use[43] (see appendix I).

- Superintendent sent statement to board regarding her interpretation of what transpired at executive session of the board on April 28, 1975, namely that the (1) November 13, 1974 meeting on board-superintendent relations had nothing to do with annual evaluation of her performance; and (2) evaluation of the performance of a superintendent should include:
(a) agreement as to goals and objectives,
(b) an accounting of achievements and failures

in the performance of activities designed to accomplish goals and objectives, (c) whether or not internal or external causes and reasons for non-performance of activities to achieve goals and objectives existed, and (d) comprehension of superintendent's performance in terms of responsibilities under contract.[44]

April 29, 1975 - President of board sent superintendent memorandum of her understanding of what transpired at executive session of April 28, 1975, i.e. (1) discussion of procedure for annual evaluation of superintendent, (2) motion to use five documents (Superintendent's Search, Superintendent's Contract, 120 Day Report, Superintendent's Memorandum of May 15, 1974, and draft of Annual Report), and (3) motion to adopt Morris' proposed evaluation document of April 30, 1975. Vote on first motion was 9 - 1 against; second motion, 6 - 4 against.[45]

April 30, 1975 - Evaluation found superintendent's job performance 60.9 percent unfavorable.

May 1, 1975 - Meeting of Committee of the Whole on Personnel was held, at which time motion passed by board of education to conduct hearings to terminate superintendent.[46]

May 2, 1975 - Letter sent to Splitt, general counsel of the DCBOE, from Cropp, executive secretary to DCBOE, informing him of board action of May 1, 1975 to prepare Bill of Particulars.[47]

May 6, 1975 - City council and mayor sent messages to board of education (1) urging a 60-day moratorium on proceedings to fire superintendent, and (2) announcing an investigation of possible legislation to alter independent status of board. Bill titled "Rational Administration of Public Schools Act" introduced by Councilman Douglas Moore and signed by mayor. Councilman Tucker noted that board "has power to hire and fire the superintendent." Act viewed as threat by some that council could decide to abolish board's present structure and replace elected body with appointed unit. Also noted was that council could initiate legislation, but it would have to be submitted to referendum in Fall election and finally be subject to approval by Congress or amend home rule act.[48]

- Statement made by board president against D.C. city council's declaration of state of emergency and request to delay actions of the board calling attention to court's dismissal, on three occasions earlier in the week, to enjoin board from proceeding with its evaluation meetings. Imputation of political reasons for action.[49]

May 8, 1975 - According to news accounts, 8 council members surveyed said they would not vote for abolition.[50] Board president received letter from Paul B. Salmon, executive director, American Association of School Administrators (AASA), to the effect that since evaluation instrument used was developed by association and results indicated less than satisfactory performance by superintendent, association requested opportunity to review procedures used by board in carrying out evaluation.[51]

May 11, 1975 - <u>Washington Post</u> telephone poll of 306 randomly selected District residents revealed that approximately 75 percent of respondents opposed firing of superintendent.[52]

May 13, 1975 - Board president denied Salmon's request; she questioned sincerity of Salmon since copy of his letter went to city council and mayor. She declared that instrument used was based on AASA instrument, with minor changes but procedures utilized were DCBOE's.[53]

May 21, 1975 - Board meeting held at which time Simmons requested rescheduling of twice-cancelled community meeting to hear from citizens regarding board's method of evaluating and possible attempts to terminate superintendent. She called attention to the May 11 Washington Post poll which indicated citizens' desire to retain superintendent by a margin of 3 to 1.

- Board president stated that purpose of meeting was not to discuss superintendent's evaluation.

- Warren and Evans called attention to difficulty of getting into building because of locked doors and massive security efforts plus request to show identification. Benjamin, Simmons, Warren and Evans implored board president to allow citizens to stand in hallway outside of board room which could only accommodate 115 persons. (Interestingly, media persons and equipment usually consumed large portion of space.)

- After citizens protested direction meeting was taking, board president called for five minute recess, after which she returned and adjourned meeting.[54]

May 28, 1975 - Motion made at board meeting by Warren and seconded by Simmons "That the Board approve the recommendation of the Chairperson, that the Board address itself to finding funds to overcome the distribution of the Student Bill of Rights before the new school year. This board action later developed into charge against superintendent.[55]

May 30, 1975 - DeLong Harris, counsel for superintendent, telephoned board president, requesting to be present at Saturday, May 31, 1975 meeting of the Committee of the Whole on Personnel and received a response of "No, not tommorrow."[56]

May 31, 1975 - DCBOE Committee of the Whole on Personnel with all 11 members present met at 9:00 a.m. with superintendent and Gwendolyn Kimbrough, executive assistant, to receive presentation of Proposed Bill of Particulars.[57]

- Superintendent was sent notice that "Board of Education, pursuant to Section 31-108, D.C. Code, 1973 ed., proposed to terminate your contract, and to remove you from your position of Superintendent of Schools no earlier than 30 days from your receipt of this notice...for cause affecting your efficiency as Superintendent of Schools.... The charge against you is: Neglect of or inattention to your duties as Superintendent and failure to comply with directives and policies of the Board."[58]

- Letter sent to DCBOE by counsel for superintendent requesting same amount of time (approximately 30 days) to prepare refutation of charges used by staff of corporation counsel of the District of Columbia.[59]

- Superintendent sent letter to Cropp requesting to see materials relied on in proposing action to terminate her contract.[60]

June 2, 1975 - Superintendent advised by Cropp that material, upon which charges against superintendent made in May 31, 1975 document rest, would not be available to view until June 4. Letter sent by counsel for superintendent demanding xerox copies of materials or leave for superintendent to have materials copied.[61]

June 16, 1975 - A temporary restraining order against impending hearing of the board was entered by Judge William E. Stewart of the D.C. Superior Court.[62]

June 24, 1975 - Memorandum sent to members, board of education, and superintendent from Dwight Cropp about meetings of the Committee of the

Whole on Personnel scheduled by president for 2:00 p.m., to discuss the procedures and schedule for the hearing requested by the superintendent, at which time Mr. Melvin Washington, assistant corporation counsel, would be present (but superintendent's counsel was denied admittance).[63]

- Special emergency board meeting held at 6:30 p.m. at which time board took action to comply with provisions of the D.C. Administrative Procedures Act, having to do with meeting in emergency sessions. Benjamin, Evans, Simmons and Warren voted No. Kane was absent.[64]

- Board adopted proceedings covering adverse actions included in the Federal Personnel Manual with necessary modifications as outlined by corporation counsel. Evans, Benjamin, Simmons and Warren abstained. Kane was absent.[65]

- Appointment of Judge Herman Benn as Presiding Administrative Law Judge over the hearing. Warren, Evans, Benjamin and Simmons abstained. Kane was absent.[66]

- Adoption of Commissioner's Order 69-694 in order to preserve peace and decorum in hearing facilities in accordance with D.C. Code, paragraph 1-1505(c), Emergency Rulemaking. Evans, Benjamin, Warren and Simmons abstained. Kane was absent.

- Meeting was consistently interrupted by unidentified speaker and a Mrs. Porter, who approached the podium. At this point Mrs. Morris commented, "If you don't get the hell out of my face, I'll...." Mrs. Porter responded "Come on, stand up. Stand up and come around and I will deal with you." As dialogue continued, Morris was accused of building conflict between citizens and security guards by Mr. Yango Sawyer and Mrs. Porter. Audience in unison repeatedly shouted, "No Sizemore, No Schools." Further on, Mr. Yango Sawyer accused Mrs. Morris of duplicity by saying:

> You are doing it for white folks and that is the reason why you keep doing it...you know the guards are Black and you know that we are Black and you know you represent the interest of those poor white Board members. You have always had a confrontation between guards and the Black community.

Interrupting the expressive behavior of the audience, Simmons moved that the audience be allowed to select a spokesman for the community. After resisting this effort, Morris finally accepted the motion.

- Reverend John Martin commented on the ungodly behavior of some board members who would not let the boys and girls in the school system develop to their full potential.

- Subsequently, Benjamin challenged Morris relative to the emergency nature of the rule to remove people from the room if they disturb the proceedings since the rule on public facilities already covered the situation. Morris' explanation pointed to a previous consideration of holding hearing in an air-conditioned facility that did not fall within framework of a public facility. Morris also challenged by Warren and Benjamin relative to necessary items going to committee, a point also dismissed by president of board.

- Motion made that administrative law judge present findings of facts and conclusions of law to board within five working days after the hearing. Benjamin, Simmons, and Warren voted No.

- Motion made and carried that hearing be held at air-conditioned Woodson Senior High School from 1:00 p.m. to 4:30 p.m.; 7:30 p.m. to 10:00 p.m.; 9:00 a.m. to 12:00 noon; and 1:30 p.m. to 4:30 p.m. Specific days to be decided on later.[67]

- Nowhere in transcript does it indicate that board adopted charges, although later it was reported that some board members indicated that such action was taken.[68]

July 2, 1975 - Melvin Washington, counsel for the board, in exchange for superintendent's resignation, offered superintendent through her counsel, DeLong Harris, (1) two $25,000.00 contracts to support research mutually agreeable to board and superintendent, (2) dropping charge and 17 supporting specifications, and (3) agreement to publish and disseminate superintendent's responses to 17 supporting specifications.[69]

July 3, 1975 - Motion made to begin hearing on July 28, 1975, and for duration to meet on Monday and Tuesday, recess on Wednesday and pick up again on Thursday and Friday until hearing completed. Motion carried.

- Motion carried that no member of board testify in behalf or against superintendent but may present affidavit of information for consideration during deliberation by board of evidence prior to reaching decision.[70]

July 18, 1975 - Superintendent filed 113 page response to board's charges and <u>rejected offer of two $25,000.00 contracts if she would resign.</u>* [71]

---

*In order to pursue her due process rights, Mrs. Sizemore and friends raised $10,000.00 which was paid to Attorney DeLong Harris.

July 23, 1975 - Statement made by Congressman Charles C. Diggs, Jr., chairman, committee on the District of Columbia, regarding the school board-school superintendent controversy in the District of Columbia, resulting in five superintendents in 10 years.[72]

July 24, 1975 - Board unanimously adopted revised draft of Chapter X, as amended and as marked up, as proposed rule-making relative to Adverse Personnel Actions.[73]

July 25, 1975 - Judge Stewart issued second order relative to the fact that the court's order of July 1, 1975 provided that Judge Herman Benn serve as Presiding Administrative Law Judge and present Findings of Fact and Conclusions of law in connection with the hearing; and that the language of order was clear and not susceptible to an interpretation whereby he will serve only as conduit of findings suggested by counsel, but will present to the board his own findings. Therefore, the motion of plaintiff for Temporary Restraining Order was denied.[74]

July 28, 29, 31, 1975 - First scheduled hearing was delayed during attempts to reach negotiated settlements.[75]

## First Hearing

August 1, 1975 - Hearing delayed until afternoon when configuration of stage at Woodson High School (site of first hearing) could be agreed upon. Harris complained about media and other lights in his eyes.[76]

- Superintendent's written responses to charges challenged legality of proposed letter (May 31, 1975) to terminate and stated that it was arbitrary and capricious and failed to meet legal cannons (board Rules and the Superintendent's Contract) and precedents for dismissal.

A quorum of the board was present (10 of 11 members).[77]

August 7, 1975 - At Public Hearing on Charges Against Superintendent, arguments presented by Harris indicated that secret (special) meetings were held with notifications sent in the middle of the night or three to four hours before meetings and at least four board members were not fully aware of what was transpiring.[78]

- Administrative Law Judge Herman Benn stated that "even though the action by the board's Committee of the Whole was improper, the board validated it by its own actions" (transcript, p. 469, lines 22-25).

August 12, 1975 - At special meeting of board, three agenda items were dealt with: (1) impact of adverse action on school systems; (2) consideration of vice superintendent's position; and (3) times and dates of the administrative hearing.

- Mason, in near secret session since public had little time to be present on such short notice, moved to reshuffle time and dates of hearing due to cancellations because of conflicting professional previous commitments of Administrative Law Judge Benn. The same consideration was not given the superintendent's counsel who had another engagement on a different day, precluding her having legal counsel on that day of the hearing since, as indicated by her, she had no funds to hire another attorney. Arguments against procedure were offered by Simmons and Warren. Warren, in particular, called attention to implied intent of Mason's motion as follows:

> Likewise, I do not respect those members of the Board...such as the maker of the original motion [Mason] who seeks to camouflage the true intent, which is that

of denying the Superintendent's counsel the right to participate.

Other comments of board members pertained to political ambitions, self-serving schedule of hearing times, interference with opening of school, scheduling at night for convenience of public, media interpretation that the hearings (firing of superintendent) have precedence over management of school system, 28 special meetings since July 1974, and so forth.[79]

August 19, 1975 - Judge Benn presented opinion that morning at 10:00 a.m. that charges were not properly preferred since charges were agreed upon in Committee of the Whole of the board of education and transmitted to superintendent without formal board action (transcript, p. 937, lines 16-19).[80] (Note: Committee of the Whole of the board had been interpreted to mean a sub-unit of the board on the level of all other committees and not on the higher level of the official full board of education.)

- Closed meeting held at 12:30 p.m. Superintendent notified about twelve noon. Morris informed that superintendent was ill and at doctor's office. Board members in attendance were Hobson, Morris, Mason, Kane, Schwartz and Treanor -- six of policy-making majority. Action taken dealt with board's taking under advisement tentative preliminary proposed findings and conclusions with respect to procedure until the conclusion of the hearing, when they may review the entire record.[81]

- Open meeting held at 3:07 p.m. Same motion presented again. Simmons, Warren and Benjamin disagreed with bringing in Judge Benn at such great expense, and then disregarding his ruling only to continue hearing under another judge. Eventually, Hobson recessed meeting until next day.[82]

August 20, 1975 - Board met at 10:51 a.m. to consider Hobson motion made previous day. Mason offered substitute motion. Warren observed that over his protest board accepted Judge Benn based on fact that he was a young, good looking, qualified and highly recommended Black judge without examining previous decisions made by him; now policy-making majority were rejecting his opinion because it was not what they wanted. Benjamin's substitute to the substitute motion was to terminate the hearing on proposed termination of the superintendent's contract, seconded by Simmons. Motion was lost. Resolution approved was Hobson's previous motion with Mason's amendments.[83]

- Simmons suggested change of hearing examiner was due to board's having no further confidence in Benn.[84]

- Mr. Alphonso Gaskins, PACTS coordinator, arrested.[85]

August 25, 1975 - Notice of meetings to be held on August 28, 1975 at 10:30 a.m., 12:30 p.m., and 7:30 p.m., to deal in part with hearing, sent to members of board and superintendent from Cropp.[86]

August 28, 1975 - Board met at 8:00 p.m. to accept action taken at morning meeting to accept ruling of Judge Benn and dismiss him.

- Superintendent raised questions relative to relationship between evaluation and bill of particulars drawn up against her. She also pointed out that her analysis of 17 charges indicated that 12 came out of memoranda from Mason and Kemp. Additionally, superintendent enumerated specific ratings given her by board members (see appendix II). Board president never specifically explained how evaluation was included.

- Superintendent read into record her responses against charges as her first opportunity to do so at a public meeting.

- May 31, 1975 letter to superintendent and bill of particulars against superintendent read by board president and moved for adoption. Motion carried with Kane, Mason, Morris, Schwartz, Kemp and Hobson in favor and Warren, Simmons and Benjamin abstaining.

- Discussion by Warren as to president's selection of Herbert O. Reid as administrative law judge for second hearing, which received no definitive response from board president.

- Reference by Simmons and Warren to the effect that they had not been privy to discussions or secret meetings held by board majority which had participated in drawing up of charges.[87]

August 29, 1975 - Foregoing transmitted to superintendent with attachments of May 31, 1975, plus August 28, 1975 board action (decision).[88]

September 2, 1975 - Members of board and superintendent sent memorandum from Virginia Morris to the effect that new Administrative Law Officer Herbert O. Reid had requested a meeting to present his expectations from the administrative hearings.[89]

September 7, 1975 - Board rules again changed by ruling majority. Quorum consisting of Morris, Hobson, Kane, Kemp, Schwartz and Treanor present. Simmons entered after vote taken on first motion. Revisions follow:

> That paragraph six (6) on page three (3) of the resolution of the Board of Education adopted August 28, 1975, in connection with the Board's proposed "Adverse Personnel Action" to terminate the

contract of employment between the Board of Education and the Superintendent of Schools Barbara A. Sizemore which stated the following:

"(6) Now be it further resolved that whereas the Board intends to move expeditiously to the resolution of any further hearing pursuant to par. 2 of the Superintendent's contract, the evidence produced by either party in the prior proceedings shall become a part of the record of any additional hearing and either party may confront or rebut that evidence during the hearing;"

Is hereby repealed. Vote: Yes - Mr. Treanor, Mrs. Schwartz, Mr. Hobson, Mrs. Kane, Mrs. Morris, and Rev. Kemp; No - No response; Abstentions - Dr. Evans. (Mrs. Simmons entered the room as the vote was being recorded and did not vote).

That the Board of Education, pursuant to the provisions of the D.C. Code, Title 1, Section 1-1505 (c), take the following emergency rulemaking action: Repeal paragraph eight (8) of the emergency rulemaking action taken by the Board at its special meeting on August 28, 1975, which reads as follows: 8. It is the sense of the Board of Education that it is inappropriate for Board members to testify at the hearings, but consistent with the rules of procedure, any member may place into the record by way of deposition on a voluntary basis prior to September 8, 1975, any information that he or she may deem relevant for consideration during the deliberations by the Board of evidence prior to reaching a decision.

Is hereby dissolved and repealed, effective immediately.

Substitute the following language in place of repealed language as a new paragraph eight (8):

9. The determination of the qualifications and competence of all witnesses proposed by the parties shall be made by the administrative law officer, presiding over the hearings.

Vote: Approved Unanimously (Mr. Treanor, Mr. Hobson, Mrs. Morris, Mrs. Kane, Rev. Kemp, Dr. Evans, Mrs. Simmons, Mrs. Schwartz).[90]

Simmons was in favor of changing resolution number 6 of the Resolutions adopted on August 28, 1975, and paragraph number 8 of the Emergency Rules as in violation of the superintendent's contractual rights and/or constitutional rights to due process.

September 8, 1975 - Parties returned to Superior Court for hearing on superintendent's renewed motion for preliminary injunction.

- Dismissal hearing began and continued daily (including Saturdays) for 18 days, concluding with closing arguments on September 30.

- DeLong Harris, superintendent's counsel, protested absence of quorum of the board and that Reid had no authority to convene board meeting; that superintendent had right to hearing before board. As a result, record of presence and absence of board members was kept and read into record at end of each day's session. There was no quorum during most of hearing (see transcripts for records).[91]

September 9, 1975 - Judge Stewart issued order denying superintendent's motion for preliminary injunction. Earlier action brought by board member Simmons and others against Board

President Morris and others to enjoin hearings was denied in Superior Court and motion for an injunction pending appeal was also denied by Court of Appeal.[92]

October 8, 1975 - Reid presented written "Findings and Conclusions" (74 pages) to the Committee of the Whole on Personnel at meeting which began at 2:30 p.m. Reid sustained 13 of the 17 specifications, and concluded that the charge as sustained "constitutes cause affecting the respondent's efficiency as Superintendent of Schools." Mason moved and Hobson seconded that Committee of the Whole accept report of Administrative Hearing Officer Reid. Simmons moved and Warren seconded an amendment to allow members time to put questions to Reid after they had a chance to read the report. Motion was defeated 7-4. Committee then adopted original motion and resolved, by vote of 7-3, to recommend that board terminate superintendent's contract "effective immediately." Second motion was also made by Mason and seconded by Hobson. Motion then passed to convene emergency board meeting on October 9, 1975, at 9:00 a.m.[93] The meeting adjourned at 4:25 p.m.

October 9, 1975 - Meeting convened with all members present. Board adopted Reid's findings and conclusions and voted to dismiss the superintendent as recommended by committee, with Kane, Kemp, Mason, Hobson, Morris, Schwartz and Treanor voting in favor and Warren, Evans, Simmons and Benjamin voting against.[94]

- Before final vote was taken, Simmons noted the following:

> On item 11 and 12 I couldn't help but appreciate (in relation to) quarterly financial reports and personnel quarterly reports...that this Superintendent is the first that has ever submitted either, and

542

I find it interesting that...never having received them from...male superintendents they were never charged with inefficiency. Here we are receiving them for the first time, and...(sic) it is rewarded with the action that I see my colleagues proposing here today.[95]

TABLE 12

Second Hearing[96]

| Charges | Board Reasons for Change | Board Evidence | Superintendent's Refutation | Verdict |
|---|---|---|---|---|
| 1. Failure to provide a plan for equalization of the schools | • Said to have promised new plan on November 14, 1973 but failed to submit plan | • Plan submitted similar to Superintendent Scott's plan, therefore no new plan submitted | • Superintendent proposed in 120 Day Report, approved May 1974, a new Doctrine called "Incommensurability." On September 20, 1974 superintendent sent to board a document entitled "Supporting Arguments for Petitioning the Court to Grant Relief from the Equalization Formula.... Board did not act. | Charge upheld |
|  |  |  | • At its November 14, 1974 meeting the superintendent informed the board that incommensurability would challenge Wright and that she wanted to go back to court. |  |
|  |  |  | • Submitted on November 20, 1974, the Equalization Report for FY75. Board stayed action implicit in report pending additional information. |  |

544

| Charges | Board Reasons for Change | Board Evidence | Superintendent's Refutation | Verdict |
|---|---|---|---|---|
| | | | • In December 1974, she again elaborated the meaning of incommensurability. | |
| | | | • Board action delayed movement of teachers until Board received compliance report developed by administration on January 6, 1975. | |
| | | | • On January 13, 1975 she submitted "Becoming 'Comparable' and 'Equal': Questions and Answers." | |
| 2. Failure to provide quarterly safety reports | • Assured president on January 3, 1974 that quarterly progress reports on Safety and Occupational Health in schools would be submitted for February board meeting. Only initial report submitted on April 17, 1974. | • Dominic Angino, Safety Manager for DCPS testified he submitted monthly safety reports to District Government but was not directed by superintendent to make quarterly reports to Board. | • Specification was predicated upon mere directive from Cropp, not from Board. | Charge upheld. |
| | | | • For FY75 and FY76, the superintendent asked for adequate staffing of the Safety Office. | |
| | | | • On May 31, 1973, April 17, 1975 and August 19, 1974 the board received reports and demands for staffing to meet the Safety Office needs. | |

| Charges | Board Reasons for Change | Board Evidence | Superintendent's Refutation | Verdict |
|---|---|---|---|---|
| | | | On September 18, 1974 the superintendent's staff reported again to the board the needs of Safety. | |
| | | | On December 4, 1974, January 25, March 19, 1975 and April 7, 1975 the superintendent answered individual or board concerns about safety. | |
| | | | No board action addressed the issue of adequate staff. | |
| 3. Failure to provide and implement adequate personnel hiring controls and failure to maintain hiring within fiscally responsible limits. | Failure to maintain adequate personnel and hiring controls which resulted in the filling of positions in excess of funds available as reflected in report submitted on November 13, 1974, entitled Fund Projected Personnel Compensations, October 1, 1974 through June 30, 1975. | November 13, 1974 letter re: 430 excess people on payroll. <br><br> November 19, 1974 memo re: 100 more people paid on November 15, 1974 than on last payroll in October, 1974. <br><br> March 28, 1975 indication of projected $4.6 million budget deficit at current rate of expenditure. | Matters beyond control of superintendent due to outmoded system of personnel hiring controls inherited. <br><br> D.C. public schools has no management information system to match up actual placement with all budget slots as noted by external consultant firm in 1972. <br><br> The school system entered into extraordinary budgetary controls, October, 1974; the Commissioner-Mayor froze the school budget. | Charge upheld. |

| Charges | Board Reasons for Change | Board Evidence | Superintendent's Refutation | Verdict |
|---|---|---|---|---|
| | | | Between October 11, 1974 and December 5, 1974, the superintendent proposed no less than four formal studies to the board to control hiring, to implement a freeze and to have budget savings. Three subsequent reports show sustained effort to manage control and limit school hiring and fiscal spending. | |
| 4. Failure to fill position as directed by board. | Board directed superintendent on October 16, 1974 to fill position of Director of Buildings and Grounds within 60 days. On February 24, 1975, informed Board directive would not be complied with until June 30, 1975. | Fact conceded at p. 36, Respondents Answer.<br><br>Position not filled 60 days after October 16, 1974.<br><br>Position not abolished as contended in Respondent's Answer, p. 36.<br><br>February 24, 1975 informed board she would not comply with directive until after June 30, 1975. | Board approved on July 8, 1974 reorganization plan which included abolition of position of Director of Buildings and Grounds. New similar position substituted and advertised for, person selected, and name submitted to board. Board refused to appoint person.<br><br>Superintendent did not comply with the October 16, 1974 order until after June 30, 1975. She said: "Effective March 1, 1975, nine named persons would continue in their interim assignments (NOT TO EXTEND BEYOND JUNE 30, 1975)." Among those names | Charge upheld. |

547

| Charges | Board Reasons for Charge | Board Evidence | Superintendent's Refutation | Verdict |
|---|---|---|---|---|
| 5. Failure to provide a timely selection procedure for the selection of Regional Superintendents. | Represented to board that procedure for selection of Regional Superintendents would be submitted by October 1, 1974. | A June 5, 1974 and a July 8, 1974 memo indicated procedure would be submitted by October 1, 1974. | was the Acting Director, Buildings and Grounds.<br><br>• On September 30, 1974, superintendent submitted her method of selection.<br><br>• Revised and resubmitted it on November 18, 1974.<br><br>• Board acted on neither plan.<br><br>• On September 18, 1974, in answer to August 19, 1974 letter from board president, and the Executive Board Secretary's letters of September 12, 1974, the superintendent said she "will (appoint)... Regional Superintendents using established procedures for officers ...to be effective ...July 1, 1975." "As soon as the Board...establishes regional Boards and grants to such Boards appropriate governing authority, such Boards...will assume the | • Charge upheld. |

548

| Charges | Board Reasons for Charge | Board Evidence | Superintendent's Refutation | Verdict |
|---|---|---|---|---|
| 6. Failure to comply with board directives concerning Federal Grant proposals. | • For Fiscal Year 1975 no proposals submitted at least 90 days prior to beginning of fiscal year as directed by Board on August 21, 1973.<br><br>• Represented to Board in March 19, 1975 letter that Administration would present report at April meeting. | • Superintendent did submit document, titled Comprehensive Federal Grant Proposals, on June 18, 1975, in response to request. It was not responsive to request and did not satisfy directive. | responsibility... for the appointment of Regional Superintendents." Board did not respond.<br><br>• Superintendent proposed reorganization of the central office on September 8, 1974.<br><br>• Superintendent proposed more comprehensive a plan on November 8, 1974.<br><br>• Board failed to pass the reorganization and vetoed the managerial mechanism to control Federal Grant Proposals.<br><br>• Superintendent gave board "Comprehensive Proposal Flow System," her policy recommendation on the matter on June 18, 1975. | Charge upheld. |
| 7. Failure to provide a timely annual report. | • Annual Report for 1973-74 school year as required by Section 200:3 (n) of Chapter II of the Rules of the Board of Education not submitted. | • Conceded that respondent submitted an annual report for 1973-74 school year yet question remained as to whether report was submitted | • Superintendent supplied periodic portions of the annual report to the board on November 20, 1974 and at other board meetings.<br><br>• In April 1975, | Board failed to present prima facie case to support specification because it demonstrated through practice that time was not of essence. Not sustained. |

549

| Charges | Board Reasons for Charge | Board Evidence | Superintendent's Refutation | Verdict |
|---|---|---|---|---|
| | | in Compliance with Section 200.3 (n) of Chapter II of the Rules of the Board of Education. "...at the close of each school year or as soon thereafter as may be practicable..." Report was 13 months late. | superintendent submitted to board in xerox form, an Annual Report termed 'Draft'. Annual report submitted July 1975 for 73-74 and 74-75. | |
| 8. Failure to comply with board directive to appoint Administration Committee to review the freeze on non-personnel expenditures. | Board directed superintendent on April 7, 1975 to designate Administration Committee to review requests for exceptions and modification in the "freeze" on non-personnel expenditures.... She did not. | Transcript of April 7, 1975 board meeting. | Previous superintendents had not submitted reports at close of school year. At the April 7, 1975 board meeting, Superintendent stated that total school funds then consisted of: (1) uncommitted funds, (2) obligated funds, (3) processed bills not yet obligated, (4) mandatory expenditure. Board by resolution said "go ahead" with commitments in categories (2), (3) and (4). Apply (1) to the projected deficit. This last meant all funds would be spent which meant there was no need for an administrative | Charge upheld. |

550

| Charges | Board Reasons for Charge | Board Evidence | Superintendent's Refutation | Verdict |
|---|---|---|---|---|
| | | | committee to review freeze on non-personnel expenditure monies after board commanded that uncommitted funds would cover projected deficit. | |
| 9. Failure to provide responses to the board's questions on the FY-75 Financial Plan. | Answers to questions not provided as propounded on April 7, 1975. | Letter from Hilda Mason to members of the Committee on School Finance Subject: FY-75 Financial Statement and Projected Deficit Problems purported to have been adopted as board policy in Emergency Meeting of board dated April 7, 1975. | On March 27, 1975, the finance committee of the board received briefing on school budget, spent and unspent funds. All fiscal questions theoretically were answered by the budget actions of board on April 7, 1975. | Charge upheld. |
| | | | Because the April 7, 1975 board action on budget resolved its current status low priority went to answering questions. | |
| | | | Board's Executive Secretary submitted questions on April 8, 1975 with no deadline, reinforcing low priority status. | |
| | | | Board member Mason suggested that board's questions were low priority items on April 7, 1975. | |

| Charges | Board Reasons for Charge | Board Evidence | Superintendent's Refutation | Verdict |
|---|---|---|---|---|
| 10. Failure to comply with board directive to submit status reports on expenditures. | Directed on April 1975 to submit status reports on expenditures which were not provided at May business meeting. | Superintendent did not present at May meeting the Status Reports. | Deputy Superintendent Williams explained staffing problems in his office and over commitments.<br><br>Therefore, board knew questions had low priority to budget crisis.<br><br>April 7, 1975 transcript contains superintendent's argument about involvement in Title I Plan and asked board to set priorities due to lack of staff to do two fiscal reports at the same time. | Charge upheld. |
| 11. Failure to provide Quarterly Financial Reports. | Superintendent's recommendation of March 20 1974 to submit quarterly financial reports adopted but not received except partial on November 13, 1974 .... | Superintendent did not submit financial report to board for second quarter or third quarter of FY75, prior to May 31, 1975. | On March 20, 1974, when Superintendent recommended quarterly fiscal reports and the board adopted it, both knew presenting these reports required additional staff. No staff hired.<br><br>Superintendent produced first quarter report FY75. Mayor's budget freeze occurred during second quarter absorbing limited management staff time. | Charge upheld. |

552

| Charges | Board Reasons for Charge | Board Evidence | Superintendent's Refutation | Verdict |
|---|---|---|---|---|
| | | | · Several budget proposals generated by working 10 to 12 hours per day exhausting staff of four. | |
| | | | · Williams explained on April 7, 1975 staff could produce fiscal reports for budget-crisis planning but not quarterly reports at same time. | |
| | | | · Limited manpower had already produced six financial reports. Previous administration produced only two per year. | |
| 12. Failure to provide quarterly personnel reports. | · Board on June 21, 1967 adopted policy that Personnel Reports would be submitted to board on quarterly basis. Policy communicated to superintendent by memo of April 26, 1974, from Cropp. Except for April 9, 1975 report, none submitted. | · No reports submitted for 4th quarter of FY74 or first and 3rd quarter of FY75. (Respondent's answer, p. 69) *April 26, 1974 memo from Cropp. Action Sheet, Special Meeting of the BOE on July 8, 1974. | · Records show no previous administration submitted personnel reports with any consistency. | · Charge upheld. |
| | | | · Deputy Superintendent on June 13, 1974 advised Committee of the Whole on Personnel that corrective measures were necessary to centralize personnel actions so only an interim report for September would be prepared. | |

| Charges | Board Reasons for Charge | Board Evidence | Superintendent's Refutation | Verdict |
|---|---|---|---|---|
| 13. Failure to comply with board directive to provide FY75 legislative proposal. | Superintendent directed on October 16, 1974 to prepare legislative package for submission commitant with presentation of FY76 budget to include four specific matters. | · Respondent's answer to charge indicated that the report submitted did not incorporate all of the matters requested by the board. | · Regular quarterly reports became a factor in establishing an appropriate mechanism for collecting personnel data, sufficient staff and adequate resources. No board approval for proposition. <br><br> · In lieu of adequate resources ten personnel reports were provided including quarterly reports for 1st, 2nd, and 3rd quarters of FY75. <br><br> · Superintendent informed by memo dated August 22, 1974, by action of the Committee on Board Operations Rules and Policies, that administration develop and submit legislative proposals to board by August 30. <br><br> · Superintendent inquired why superintendent was directed to do this rather than board's general counsel whose job description specified this responsibility. <br><br> · No answer from board ever provided. | Charge upheld. |

| Charges | Board Reasons for Charge | Board Evidence | Superintendent's Refutation | Verdict |
|---|---|---|---|---|
| | | | Nevertheless, superintendent appointed a volunteer committee to assist her. | |
| | | | On January 27, 1975, superintendent submitted to board legislative program for fiscal 1975, 1976, and 1977. | |
| 14. Failure to comply with board directive to make recommendations on permanent tenure. | Board directed on April 17, 1974 for superintendent to make recommendations on permanent tenure. | No evidence provided. | Prolonged debate on their respective authorities engaged in by Hugh Scott and board. | Charge not sustained. |
| | | | Policy developed and adopted by board on June 20, 1973, five months prior to Ms. Sizemore becoming superintendent. | |
| | | | The board's executive secretary in November 1, 1973 memo articulated his concerns about policy to board. | |
| | | | Cropp's memo sent to superintendent on November 19, 1973. | |
| | | | Executive Secretary's memo is being represented as board's directive. | |

555

| Charges | Board Reasons for Charge | Board Evidence | Superintendent's Refutation | Verdict |
|---|---|---|---|---|
| | | | • Superintendent presented her recommendations on March 8, 1974 and approved by board on May 30, 1974. | |
| | | | • Superintendent acted on policy by developing appropriate legislative package including this and approved by board on February 19, 1975. | |
| | | | | • Charge not sustained. |
| 15. Failure to obtain for the board student comments on proposed rules on students' rights and responsibilities and code of conduct. | • August 1974, board adopted Student Bill of Rights and Responsibilities, same not distributed and student input obtained within 75 day comment period. | • At its August 1, 1974 meeting statement made: "This would give the Board enough time to duplicate copies of the Rules for distribution in school assemblies...." 'Comments gathered and submitted but not submitted within 75 day comment period. | • Board promised in August 5, 1974 memo to duplicate copies of Student Bill of Rights and Responsibilities. • Board failed to provide administration printed copies of rules as promised. • Mayor's freeze precluded it as administrative alternative. • Therefore, superintendent accepted administrative proposal to incorporate rules into a short course of study as alternative strategy for implementing board policy. • Students made statements on rules on August 13 and August 20. | |

| Charges | Board Reasons for Charge | Board Evidence | Superintendent's Refutation | Verdict |
|---|---|---|---|---|
| | | | · Students' statements not accepted at these meetings. | |
| | | | · Results of student survey reactions to rules submitted to board on November 25, 1974. | |
| | | | · Board ignored students' reactions. | |
| | | | · Subsequent committee or board discussions have never been held. | |
| 16. Failure to provide curriculum development in FY75. | · In the superintendent's 120 Day Report submitted in March 1974, and accepted and approved by board in May 1974, superintendent stated a reorganization of schools and curriculum in five phases would begin but was not done. | · Board submitted Chapter 2, Section 200.3 (d) of the Board Rules which states: "The Superintendent shall prepare and submit to the Board...complete courses of study to be pursued in the Public Schools of the District of Columbia." | · Overwhelming evidence to support claim that extensive curriculum programs were developed including but not limited to sixteen submitted. | · Charge not sustained. |
| 17. Failure to provide report on declining enrollment. | · Superintendent on March 19, 1975 stated a report on enrollment would be submitted on March 20, 1975 which would release $2.3 million in FY75 to fund improved and innovated | · Report not received on March 20, 1975. Superintendent did send report on June 6, 1975. | · In introductory agency statement for the FY75 budget request, superintendent projected availability of teaching resources due to a smaller projected student enrollment in school year 74-75. | · Charge upheld. |

| Charges | Board Reasons for Charge | Board Evidence | Superintendent's Refutation | Verdict |
|---|---|---|---|---|
| | programs. Did not provide report. | | · In testimony before the House and Senate Subcommittee on Appropriations, superintendent justified retaining those services in FY75 budget by indicating intent to expand pre-kindergarten and kindergarten services; to make teaching services available to students with special needs; and to make additional supportive services available to schools trying to modify the age-graded organizational arrangement.<br><br>· Marion Barry, then president of board and some members were present.<br><br>· In August new board president Morris, after reading the Senate report asked superintendent if she agreed or disagreed with what was printed, and to forward a response if she disagreed.<br><br>· On September 10, 1974 superintendent responded that she fully agreed.<br><br>· Problem reflected not superintendent's | |

| Charges | Board Reasons for Charge | Board Evidence | Superintendent's Refutation | Verdict |
|---------|--------------------------|----------------|-----------------------------|---------|
|         |                          |                | failure to provide report but difficulty of maintaining continuity in a policy making body having a high turnover rate. |         |

### Analysis*

An analysis of the case revealed a number of interesting substantive issues relative to the charge and specifications. No attempt is made to set forth in detail the many pages of testimony and documents presented.

## Selected specifications

### Specification 1 - Equalization[97] --

The Hobson v Hansen decisions of June 19, 1967 and May 25, 1971 resulted from a school segregation suit brought against the superintendent of schools and the D.C. board of education. The remedy imposed by Judge J. Skelly Wright, United States Court of Appeals for the District of Columbia, centered primarily on teacher and pupil assignment and the abolition of optional zones and the track system, with the intent that compliance would equalize overall resources.

On May 19, 1970, an amended motion was filed by Julius Hobson for further relief and enforcement of the decree in that equalization of resources did not occur. This motion requested that the school system be required to equalize expenditures from the regular budget so that per pupil expenditures at each elementary school would not deviate by more than five percent from the average per-pupil expenditures for all elementary schools. Thus, the court in 1971 shifted its attention from total resource equalization to equalization on the basis of teacher salaries and benefits.

From 1967 to 1972, four superintendents, namely Hansen, Manning, Henley, and Scott, encountered difficulty in implementing the Wright decree

---

*Another legal counsel prepared the report from which the legal aspect of this material was drawn. Mrs. Barbara A. Sizemore supplied the writer with this information.

to equalize expenditures. Disruptions due to teacher transfers in an effort to redistribute educational resources continued with no positive effect on educational outcomes. Scott left the superintendency in June 1973 without having solved the equalization problem.

Thus, Sizemore inherited a plan (1) with no clear definition of educational resources, (2) no effective way to allocate school resources, (3) no effective way to prevent school and teacher disruptions, and (4) no definition of how to meet different needs of students. Additionally, she faced the social reality of two more externally imposed constrictions due to the dual compliance of the Waddy decree, to spend additional money for special education, and Title I comparability requirements for federal funds, which forced the school system to show that it provided approximately equal services in all schools using regular budget funds before Title I funds were granted.[98]

Essentially, the Wright decree and Title I requirements differ in the following ways:

1. Personnel affected: Equalization affects elementary teachers and educational aides (except special education teachers) while comparability affects all personnel with the exception of special education and food service workers.

2. Affected schools: Equalization affects elementary schools only, while comparability affects elementary and junior high schools.

3. Grades affected: Equalization affects students in grades pre-kindergarten through grade six while comparability affects students in kindergarten through grade 9.

4. Mean: For purposes of equalization, the

citywide average per pupil cost is used, while for purposes of comparability the average per pupil cost for non Title I schools is used.

5. <u>Comparison</u>: In equalization all schools are compared with the average per pupil costs for all schools. In comparability each Title I school is compared with the average per pupil cost in "non-project schools."

6. <u>Ratio</u>: Pupil-teacher ratio is computed for equalization purposes. However, a total staff-per pupil is computed for purposes of comparability.

7. <u>Salaries</u>: In equalization full salary plus benefits are used while in comparability only base pay is used.[99]

Teachers were redistributed to make the schools both comparable and equal. It was reported in 1975, by all regions but Region I, that the impact on some schools was detrimental to students, teacher morale, and educational programs.

A significant point made by Superintendent Sizemore in the document referred to above was that the underlying philosophy inherent in the comparability rule and the basic assumption of the equalization requirement is in conflict with the heart of the incommensurable philosophy of education propounded by the administration.

In the incommensurability philosophy of education, 'equal' is defined in terms of equity or meeting the educational needs of all children with justice, fairness, and impartiality. Since the needs of children vary, educational programs must vary. Because some educational programs cost more than others, providing programs that cost equal dollars mitigates against providing equity for each child.

Inherent in the Title I requirement is the concept of "fair share," meaning each Title I school gets "at least an equal share" of the budget. The conflict in philosophies is seen in the following assumptions of the concept of comparability:

1. The rule does not focus on the fact that rates of growth and patterns of development among students vary.

2. The rule assumes that equal "imput" can accommodate differential need.

3. The rule denies the premise that every child must be provided equal access to learning situations which build and/or enhance the unique talents, cultures, and languages which he or she brings.[100]

In terms of the equalization requirement, the conflict lies in the assumption that input of approximately equal dollars will result in approximately equal educational outcomes. This disregards the fact that approximately equal dollars will not provide for programs which vary greatly in cost, that are necessary to meet greatly varying educational needs. Thus, Superintendent Sizemore and her key administrators worked on a new commensurable allocation of resources approach which could be offered the court as an alternative to the unacceptable procedure in use.[101] This activity continued up to and through the hearings, with periodic reports being submitted to the board as evidenced by the exhibits submitted to the judge in refutation of the charge inherent in the specification: Failure to Provide a Plan for Equalization of the Schools.

The superintendent's promise was made in a memorandum dated November 14, 1973 to the board:

It is my intention that a new approach to equalization of resources be submitted to the

Board for implementation during the school year 1974-75.

The memorandum further implied that the "new approach to equalization" meant not compliance with the decree, but a petition to the court to modify the decree so that more money could be spent on poor children than on advantaged ones. The board seemingly assumed that when the superintendent said "new approach to" it meant "new plan for." The two are not the same, a point which was not raised by respondent's counsel. In fact, he argued that the proposal to seek relief from the Wright decree was in fact a "new plan."

Further, expressing an intent to do something is not the same as a promise. Respondent's counsel conceded the fact of a promise.

In the face of the overwhelming evidence provided by the respondent of the great hardship entailed in applying the Wright decree, the argument for modifying it could hardly be termed "inefficient." However, it did provide a different view of equalization than the one held by a majority of the board.

Additionally, the testimony, that Sizemore's September 1974 memorandum supporting a petition for relief from the Wright decree was basically the same as her predecessor's June 1973 equalization plan, seems irrelevant.

### Specification 2 - Quarterly Safety Reports --

Ample evidence was provided that the school system had only one safety officer. He had only one assistant for an 8 month period. Mrs. Sizemore testified that the January 31, 1974 promise was understood to depend on the availability of adequate staff which she requested but never received. Two points may be made relative to this specification. First, no evidence was forthcoming that the board relied on the promise. Second, no evidence was presented to show that the information contained in the monthly safety reports could satisfy the board's request for quarterly reports since there was no evidence of what the quarterly reports were to contain.

### Specification 3 - Personnel Hiring Controls --

In the case of personnel hiring controls, Reid made reference to there not being an adequate personnel control system in place prior to May 31, 1975. Inasmuch as there was no evidence as to what "adequate" meant, it seems that the superintendent was under no obligation to meet the board's undefined meaning of the word.

### Specification 4 - Position of Director of Buildings and Grounds --

The position of director of buildings and grounds was abolished in the superintendent's reorganization plan approved in July 1974. On October 16, 1974, a controversy arose after a committee report recommended appointment of a director of buildings and grounds. Obviously the board did not remember that the position was abolished in the superintendent's reorganization plan which they approved in July. This was acknowledged by the board's counsel.[102]

At least three points may be made in respect to this specification. One, no evidence was presented to show that the superintendent could not abolish a position. In fact, paragraph four of the contract gives the superintendent complete freedom "to reorganize the administrative staff." This point was never argued by respondent's counsel.

Second, there is ample evidence to show that the superintendent advertised the job vacancy in August 1974.[103] In March 1975 candidates were interviewed and on May 20, 1975 a candidate was recommended. The board rejected this candidate four days prior to sending the notice letter.

Finally, there is no evidence presented as a basis for the board's construing the routine report of February 24, 1975 as a refusal to comply with the board's directive.

### Specification 5 - Selection Procedure for Regional Superintendents --

In essence, the specification[104] is that the board wanted a selection procedure in which communities could participate and that the superintendent had just filled the slots with central office people on an interim basis.

Two factors may be considered here. First, there was no evidence provided that the board detrimentally relied on the superintendent's representation to submit a permanent selection procedure by October 1, 1974. Second, the regional superintendent slots were filled. Therefore, there is an argument that there was no cause affecting the efficiency of the superintendent.

### Specification 6 - Federal Grant Proposals --

There was ample evidence presented by the superintendent that it was impossible to develop a timetable for submitting federal grant proposals because the staff was over-committed. An impossibility defense seems most feasible here. None was developed by respondent's counsel.

### Specification 9 - Questions on FY-1975 Financial Plan --

The transcript of the April 7, 1975 meeting, as well as much testimony, shows that there were only four qualified accountants -- one had been out sick for five days due to exhaustion as a result of overworking for six to 8 months, and all four were working on the Title I report which required all of their time. Reid's conclusion that the number of accountants budgeted were still employed in April 1975 is unsupported. Therefore, the board's directive to answer the questions was not reasonable under the circumstances. Hence, inefficiency seems not to have been proved by this specification.

<u>Specification 10 - Status Reports on Expenditures</u> --

As in specifications 6 and 9, the impossibility defense could have been used here.

<u>Specification 11 - Quarterly Financial Reports</u> --

Evidence was provided, in the memorandum dated February 21, 1974[105] from the superintendent to the board, that quarterly financial reports be submitted when the capability was developed. In a letter of March 20, 1974, the budget committee reported to the board that it approved the superintendent's recommendation and that the committee and the administration agreed that the capability did not exist for producing detailed financial statements by allotment. The committee's recommendation was adopted at the March 20, 1974 regular meeting.[106]

The superintendent's testimony that Marion Barry, former board president, told her it was the board's responsibility to provide the capability, was stricken on the basis that it was hearsay. Mrs. Sizemore's counsel did not contest that it could be entered as hearsay evidence. Reid construed the board's action as a directive to provide quarterly financial reports, but there is no evidence of this. The evidence points to the fact that this was a goal to be reached when capability was developed. It never was. Therefore, the specification seems not to be supported by the evidence.

Specification 12 - Quarterly Personnel Reports --

Though there was a policy made in 1967 to submit quarterly personnel reports, evidence shows that the policy was never enforced. Yet, on April 26, 1974, the board secretary wrote the superintendent about the policy.[107] The minutes of the May 20, 1974 board meeting, not put in evidence, say the administration promised a personnel report in June. There is no record of a June meeting. Nevertheless, the action sheet[108] of the July 8, 1974 special meeting indicates that the deputy superintendent for management agreed to comply with the request beginning in the fall. Therefore, the first report due, if the action sheet is accurate, would have been for the first quarter of fiscal year 1975 (July 1 - September 30, 1974). Thus, Reid's finding of a failure to file a report for the fourth quarter of fiscal 1974 seems not to be supported.

Specification 17 - Report on Declining Enrollment --

There is no record of the nature of expected content of this report. The superintendent in May 1974 prepared a booklet titled "Q & A" dealing with her testimony before the Senate Subcommittee[109] in which she indicated that due to an expected decline in enrollment during fiscal 1975 $2.3 million would be released for new programs. On August 28, 1974, the board president sent the superintendent a letter asking if she agreed with the statement in the Senate report and, if not, whether or not a response would be forwarded to the board and committee.[110]

The superintendent's response on September 10, 1974 indicated that she agreed with the statement in the Senate report. Thus, the superintendent complied with the request. On October 1, 1974, the "Q & A" booklet containing the testimony was forwarded to the board.[111] On March 11, 1975, the board president wrote the superintendent a letter[112] relating supposed shortcomings, and indicating that on two occasions she had informed the superintendent of several reports required by the Senate Appropriations Sub-committee on the District of Columbia indicating a relationship to the $2.3 million released by declining enrollment to support new and innovative programs. There was no proof at the hearing that this type of report was sought by the Senate Sub-committee.

The specification seemed to deal with the timeliness of the transmittal rather than whether or not the superintendent's response was sufficient. Nevertheless, no proof was given of the board's reliance on the information.

### The Former Deputy Superintendent of Management's Analysis

Dr. James Williams' position is that the termination of Superintendent Barbara Sizemore was based purely on personality conflict and philosophical differences and not really on management concerns. Further, he believes that none of the charges had any basis in fact. In describing the invalidity of those issues emanating out of management which evolved into charges, he had several substantive comments to make which may throw light upon the entire conflict. A few examples should suffice to support his argument.

Personnel control

In his interview Mr. James Williams stated that he began the development of a personnel accounting system under the reorganization plan, which was not completed because he did not have the staff to develop it. Further, he stated that there was controversy developed within his management department. There were staff members who wanted to move in a different direction and used their influence to stymie his plan and slow down the progress of a new system.

He wanted to develop a personnel payroll system that would have given the department control over the assignment of personnel and relate it directly to the payment of personnel control positions and people assignments. This meant literally throwing out the entire system and instituting a different kind of system that he felt not even the top administrators in the system wanted. Williams believed that the top administrators did not want a new system because it would have taken from them the ability to manipulate personnel, staff and salaries without any direct accountability. He felt this was not what most people wanted or had been accustomed to under the system that existed. In the old system there was a certain autonomy in that the assistant superintendents did the hiring and firing and controlled who worked, where they worked, or whether they were qualified or not.

Williams further disclosed that the department of personnel was not really a department of personnel in that the records for employees were not in the department of personnel. They were scattered between the various other departments. Another example Williams gave was that the granting of tenure was dependent on the whim of an assistant superintendent. Hence, a part of his proposal was to bring all personnel matters into the personnel department. Further, Williams stated that he knew that the staff did not want this change and worked to prevent or slow down the development of the whole system.

Another factor, said Williams, which prevented his moving ahead with the changes was the lack of staff to accomplish it. Although his office had the title of Office of Management Services, he did not have the technical staff to do the kind of things that he asked to be done. Noteworthy also, is that the board had not given a date when the personnel control system had to be in place. Further, he mentioned that his reorganization plan, which included a design of a personnel system, predated the over-hiring accusation. It did not come about as a result of over-hiring. The introduction of the idea and the development of the plan rested on his having seen the problem between January and May 1974 and presenting a plan in May 1974, at least a year before the personnel crisis arose. Unfortunately, the board had not provided the resources to complete the implementation of the personnel control system.

Mr. Williams spoke of the person who controlled the budget file and information on the file. In this regard, Mr. Williams stated that there was a controversy between the budget office and the controller's office, in that the two offices did not mesh information.

Therefore, for the above reasons the system was not developed. He found the system that was presented to him inadequate because it had maintained the status quo although in a different manner. It would not have given the office of management financial control, although it would have helped with the count of personnel.

In summing up the discussion, Mr. Williams noted that many people could not understand that you could not place a system within the school system because the system interfaced with the D.C. government. The D.C. government cut the school system's checks. They printed the checks via the federal treasury. Therefore, as Mr. Williams explained, the school system's personnel system had to be compatible with their computer capability. Thus, part of what his reorganization called for was independent computer capacity. The board had no computer capacity; therefore, no personnel system was possible. Williams ended this discussion by pointing out that when information is being manipulated and one is in a position not to be questioned about what you are presenting, it is possible to say you have a system, but not really have one.

In relating the personnel system to the

budget office, Mr. Williams explained that the peculiarity of the budget itself allowed manipulation of number and monies in terms of reporting out data. In this connection, he stated that even though he was unaware of the type of system in place during the new administration, he was aware of what the capacity of the system was and knew that it wasn't such that you could put in a good personnel system.

In discussing the invalidity of the charge regarding quarterly personnel reports, Mr. Williams stated that the board had received them in a timely fashion. In connection with the one report the board built the charge around, he said that it was a report delivered by hand on a night when the board met in the city council chambers in the District building.

## Director of buildings and grounds

In connection with the appointment of a director of buildings and grounds, Mr. Williams pointed out that the administrative reorganization provided for creating two new departments, facilities planning and maintenance. There were problems involved in doing this that the board was aware of. One problem had to do with the fact that an employee could not just be summarily removed from his job (the director). Another problem pertained to locating two competent people to put in charge of the two newly created offices. He emphasized that the original department of buildings and grounds had been abolished and that he was running it as two separate units with an acting director in charge of one of the newly created units. This person had been appointed before the charge was brought against the superintendent. Nonetheless, Williams felt that the person he chose had much to learn.

He further explained that there was difficulty in finding competent people to come to work for the D.C. public schools generally. Although many people had applied for the various positions, few were really competent to handle them and that the competent people from outside the system would not take the jobs. Retired military men were interested but brought a military posture which contributed to what was wrong with management services then.

The status report on expenditures

The information presented by Mr. Williams on this issue was very revealing in terms of how a large organization sometimes works. In this connection, he stated that the board received more status reports on expenditures than they had ever received before. That, in fact, the board had never received full documentation on expenditures in the two or three page reports submitted by previous administrations. The reports submitted by his office were first-time documents on every fund within the school system with the exception of funds that were held locally. He explained that his next plan had to do with getting this money out of the schools. Informed sources had relayed that there were millions of dollars scattered throughout the D.C. schools over which the management services unit had no control.

Additionally, in explaining the invalidity of the charge on quarterly financial reports, Mr. Williams stated that the board was getting total quarterly financial reports. The report was accepted by Mr. Dwight Cropp, Executive Secretary, but never read into the records while a pre-meeting (closed executive session) was being held in the conference room behind the city council chambers. The report was taken and filed, and it was this one report around which the charge was built.

This preceding discussion, coupled with the legal analysis presented, provides enough evidence in relation to the conflict in school superintendent-school board relations to lend credence to the notion that Superintendent Sizemore was fired for reasons other than inefficiency in the performance of her duties.[113]

## Summary

In conclusion, it became clear that seven members of the board, four white and three Black, were determined to terminate the superintendent's contract even as far back as December 1974. The speech before the African Heritage Studies Association and the resulting negative comments alluding to racism made in editorials and newspaper articles propelled this seven-member majority into board action, which was followed by an evaluation based on a hastily designed evaluation process not agreed upon by the superintendent, but nevertheless adopted by the board. Next followed a search for cause for inefficiency on the part of the superintendent by Mason and Kemp, and Hobson primarily, in memoranda, transcripts, D.C. Code, board Rules, and the superintendent's contract, which produced 17 specifications to support the charge. A bill of particulars was drawn up by David Splitt, the board's counsel and the D.C. corporation counsel. The document was hand carried to the superintendent's home late on May 31, 1975. Subsequently, the superintendent prepared a 113-page response to the charges after which an administrative hearing commenced with Herman Benn presiding. Meanwhile, there was pressure from community groups and business enterprises as well as governmental units and the courts to proceed with the termination process or to cease and desist from such action.

Benn's ruling that there was impropriety involved in the procedure for bringing charges against the superintendent led to his release from his contract with the board, at which time the board secured the services of Herbert O. Reid, a former employee. Reid conducted the hearing. This procedure differed from the first hearing which was conducted as a special board meeting with Hobson presiding. The purpose for the change was to prevent the lack of a board quorum hindering the continuation of the hearing. Reid threw out four of the 17 specifications due to overwhelming evidence to the contrary. But in spite of the unsupported nature of 10 of the 13 other charges, he ruled that there was sufficient cause affecting the respondent's efficiency as superintendent of schools. Hence, the board majority voted, without time to review the evidence, to terminate the superintendent's contract.

The superintendent and her counsel went to court three times to obtain due process and received due process. It is interesting to note that the court would only hear pleas for due process, not whether or not an employee is innocent or guilty. The court's concern is with whether or not the employee was treated justly and fairly through due process, in terms of such matters as whether or not the employee's side is heard by a neutral judge. The court refuses to decide whether or not the employee was a good worker for whatever the place of employment was. This is for the employer to decide. The court's interest is strictly in whether or not due process laws or statutes were adhered to. Therefore, by being advised by counsel to go to court before the hearing, it seems possible that the superintendent jeopardized her need to return to court to have the administrative law judge's opinion overturned. In retrospect, it may have been wiser to have proceeded with having the board majority make the decision to terminate the superintendent's contract. Then, the superintendent may have been able to build a case on the basis that due process was denied because she did not have impartial judges to render a decision about her efficiency as superintendent of schools.[114]

Throughout the process of terminating the superintendent, we see operating the external factor of racism, attributed to the superintendent through her speech but actually engaged in by the newspapers and their financial supports -- the business interests in the District which illuminates the community pressure factor as well.

The misuse of the internal organizational factor of board function is revealed (1) through the process used by the board to fire the superintendent, (2) the study of the D.C. Code, the superintendent's contract, board Rules, transcripts and memoranda specifications to support the charge of inefficiency, and (3) the repeated emergency rule change process engaged in by the policy-making majority of the board to restructure the process to fit their predetermined decision to fire the superintendent.

Sexism was displayed in that the female superintendent was required to submit quarterly personnel reports which none of her four male predecessors were required to do.

Simmons, in the September 9, 1975 meeting, called attention to the operation of the external factor of sexism as she revealed that the superintendent's male predecessors were not required to submit quarterly financial or personnel reports. The superintendent had done so without being required to by the board, and was termed inefficient for her efforts.

The type of interest taken in the evaluation by congressmen, the city council and the mayor in their efforts to either abort the evaluation and/or hearing or speed it up might be termed pressure. And certainly the city council's initial consideration of removing the elected status of the board of education, which was totally rejected by the superintendent, might be seen as an aspect of the dependent relationship of the board to those governmental bodies or offices.

Throughout the term of office of the superintendent, approximately 20 months from the issuing of her contract to the issuing of the bill of particulars, there were many occasions when board members took on the role of superintendent and usurped her authority to manage the school system. The three case studies of issues are particularly fertile for providing evidence of how the board tried to impede the superintendent's progress in putting an effective management system in place. Noted also was the conflict in philosophies which came with the changes in board membership, especially after the November 1974 board election when four new board members joined the board, two of whom immediately joined the forces in opposition to the superintendent.

Then, too, the leadership factor is a particularly interesting aspect of the entire situation for though it definitely appeared outwardly that Morris had the reigns, on closer examination a quieter, more subterranean personality, that of Mason, seemed to be pulling the strings.

Further, the internal organizational factor of the superior authority of the board vis-a-vis the authority of the superintendent was indeed pronounced as the board majority engaged in efforts, first, to deny the superintendent due process prerogatives and, then, called upon a colleague, Herbert O. Reid, to press forward with the firing.

Finally, a cursory examination reveals that a plethora of memoranda (at least 141) were sent to Mrs. Sizemore from Mrs. Morris alone, between September 1974 through June 1975. On some days, there were as many as four pieces of correspondence sent requesting information or giving directives, all of which were responded to. It should be noted that this barrage of demands for information came during the critical budget crisis period when the superintendent and her staff were also engaged in day-to-day operations of the school system.

The next chapter will present a brief view of the outcomes in the school system resulting from the board's decision to terminate Mrs. Sizemore as superintendent of the D.C. public schools.

FOOTNOTES                                    CHAPTER X

1. Letter to Friends from Martha S. Swaim, Vice President, Board of Education, 7 August 1973.

2. Letter to the President and Members of the Board of Education from Martha S. Swaim, Member, Board of Education, 31 May 1974, and an attachment, "D.C. Schools As A System," 3 June 1974.

3. "Transcript of the Fifteenth (Special) Board Meeting," Washington, D.C., 15 July 1974, pp. 23-27.

4. Memorandum to Board of Education from Barbara A. Sizemore, Superintendent, re: The D.C. Youth Orchestra Contract, 19 August 1974.

5. "Transcript of A Special Meeting of the Board of Education," Washington, D.C., 13 August 1974, pp. 24, 26, 27.

6. Memorandum to Ms. Barbara A. Sizemore, Superintendent of Schools, from Virginia A. Morris, President, Board of Education, re: D.C. Youth Orchestra Contract, 4 September 1974.

7. "Transcript of the Third (Stated) Meeting of the Board of Education," Washington, D.C., 19 February 1975, pp. 78-92.

8. Interview with Julius Hobson, Jr., D.C. School Board member, 28 September 1977.

9. "Transcript of the Seventeenth (Special) Meeting of the Board of Education," Washington, D.C., 27 June 1973, p. 51.

10. Interview with Julius Hobson, Jr., D.C. Board of Education member, Washington, D.C., 28 September 1977.

11. Interview with William Treanor, D.C. Board of Education member, Washington, D.C., 28 September 1977.

12. Interview with Therman Evans, D.C. Board of Education member, Washington, D.C., 19 October 1977.

13. Interview with Father Raymond Kemp, D.C. Board of Education member, Washington, D.C., 21 November 1977.

14. "Transcript of the Seventh (Stated) Meeting of the Board of Education," Washington, D.C., 17 April 1974, pp. 96-167.

15. "Transcript of A Regular (Stated) Meeting of the Board of Education," Washington, D.C., 15 May 1974, p. 46.

16. See Case Study on DCYOP for voluminous transmittals, memos, legal opinions, letters, etc., which continued around issue.

17. Memorandum to Members, Board of Education/Superintendent, from Dwight S. Cropp, Executive Secretary, re: Board-Superintendent Conference, 20 June 1974.

18. Memorandum to Ms. Barbara A. Sizemore, Superintendent of Schools, from Virginia Morris, President, Board of Education, re: Administrative requests to General Counsel, 22 August 1974. Memorandum to Mrs. Virginia Morris, President, D.C. Board of Education, from Barbara A. Sizemore, Superintendent of Schools, 22 August 1974.

19. Diane Brockett, "Delay in School Openings Is News to Sizemore," Washington Star, 6 September 1974.

20. Statement by Virginia Morris, President, Board of Education, Press Release, "The Board of Education of the District of Columbia: Its Role and Authority," 25 September 1974.

21. Statement by Barbara A. Sizemore, Superintendent, D.C. Public Schools, Press Release, 25 September 1974.

22. Press Release by Virginia Morris, 25 September 1974.

23. "Transcript of the Twentieth (Special) Meeting of the Board of Education," Washington, D.C., 30 September 1974.

24. Memorandum to Public Schools from Comer S. Coppie, Special Assistant to the Mayor-Commissioner for Budget and Financial Management, re: Revised Apportionments and Financial Plans for Fiscal Year 1975, 3 October 1974.

25. Memorandum to Ms. Barbara A. Sizemore, Superintendent of Schools, from Julius W. Hobson, Jr., Chairman, Committee on School Finance, re: FY76 Budget Plan, 22 October 1974.

26. "Transcript of the Twenty-Sixth Meeting of the Board of Education," Washington, D.C., 20 November 1974, p. 210.

27. "Transcript of the Twenty-Seventh (Special) Meeting of the Board of Education," Washington, D.C., 6 December 1974, pp. 1-3A.

28. Memorandum to Virginia Morris, President, Board of Education, from Barbara A. Sizemore, 10 December 1974.

29. "Transcript of An Emergency (Special) Meeting of the Board of Education," Washington, D.C., 12 December 1974.

30. Diane Brockett, "D.C. School Board Issues Ultimatum to Sizemore," Washington Star, 12 December 1974.

31. Letter to Mrs. Barbara A. Sizemore, Superintendent, from Virginia Morris, President, Board of Education, 12 December 1974.

32. Richard E. Prince, "Statement by Mrs. Sizemore Helps Ease Friction With School Board," Washington Post, 15 December 1974.

33. "Transcript of Twenty-Ninth (Special) Meeting of the Board of Education," Washington, D.C., 16 December 1974.

34. Memorandum to Mrs. Virginia Morris, President, Board of Education, from Barbara A. Sizemore, Superintendent, re: FY76 Budget Plan, 8 January 1975.

35. "Transcript of the Thirty-Second (Stated) Meeting of the Board of Education," Washington, D.C., 22 January 1975, pp. 144-146.

36. "Transcript of the Third (Stated) Meeting of the Board of Education," Washington, D.C., 19 February 1975.

37. Ibid.

38. Barbara A. Sizemore, "Education: Is Accommodation Enough?," The Journal of Negro Education 44 (Summer 1975), pp. 233-246.

39. "Mrs. Sizemore's Declaration," Washington Star, 9 April 1975.

40. "Transcript of the Sixth Special (Emergency) Meeting of the Board of Education," Washington, D.C., 7 April 1975.

41. Statement by Richard B. Steinkamp Before the Board of Education of the District of Columbia at its Meeting of 8 April 1975. See also: Lynn Dunson, "Angry Group Shouts Down Sizemore Critic," Washington Star, 9 April 1975.

42. Memorandum to the Board of Education of the District of Columbia from Barbara A. Sizemore, Superintendent of Schools, re: Statement of Barbara A. Sizemore, Superintendent of Schools, Relative to Discussion of the Procedure for the Annual Evaluation of the Superintendent's Performance, 28 April 1975.

43. Memorandum to Mrs. Sizemore from Mr. Cropp, re: Mr. Treanor's motion, 28 April 1975.

44. Memorandum to the Board of Education of the District of Columbia from Barbara A. Sizemore, Superintendent of Schools, re: Statement of Barbara A. Sizemore, Superintendent of Schools, Relative to Discussion of the Procedure for the Annual Evaluation of the Superintendent's Performance, 28 April 1975.

45. Memorandum to Barbara A. Sizemore, Superintendent of Schools, from Virginia Morris, President, Board of Education, re: Executive Session, 28 April 1975.

46. Letter to Mr. David A. Splitt, General Counsel, D.C. Board of Education, from Dwight S. Cropp, Executive Secretary, Board of Education, 2 May 1975.

47. Ibid.

48. A Resolution 1-176 in the City Council of the District of Columbia, 6 May 1975.

49. Statement of President of Board of Education, from Barbara A. Simmons' files, 6 May 1975.

50. Corrie M. Anders and Michael Kiernan, "Most of Council Opposed to Junking School Board," Washington Star, 8 May 1975.

51. Letter to Mrs. Virginia Morris, President, District of Columbia Board of Education, from Paul B. Salmon, Executive Director, American Association of School Administrators, 8 May 1975.

52. "75% in Poll Oppose Firing Supt. Sizemore," Washington Post, 11 May 1975.

53. Letter to Dr. Paul B. Salmon, Executive Director, American Association of School Administrators, from Virginia Morris, President, Board of Education of the District of Columbia, 13 May 1975.

54. "Transcript of a Stated Meeting of the Board of Education," Washington, D.C., 21 May 1975.

55. "Transcript of the Tenth (Continuation of the 8th Stated) Meeting of the Board of Education," Washington, D.C., 28 May 1975, pp. 58-66.

56. Memorandum of Telephone Call to Mrs. Virginia Morris, to Request Permission to be Present at Saturday, May 31 Hearing, from Attorney DeLong Harris, 30 May 1975.

57. Letter to Mrs. Barbara A. Sizemore, Superintendent of Schools, from Virginia Morris, President, Board of Education, Attachment E., 31 May 1975.

58. "Report of the District of Columbia Board of Education's Committee-of-the-Whole on Personnel," 31 May 1975.

59. Letter to D.C. Board of Education, from DeLong Harris, Counsel for Barbara A. Sizemore, Superintendent of Schools, 31 May 1975.

60. Letter to Mr. Dwight Cropp, Executive Secretary, Board of Education, from Barbara A. Sizemore, Superintendent, 2 June 1975.

61. Letter to Dwight S. Cropp, Executive Secretary of the Board of Education, from DeLong Harris, Counsel for Mrs. Barbara A. Sizemore, Superintendent of Schools, re: Mrs. Barbara A. Sizemore, Superintendent of Schools, 2 June 1975.

62. Administrative Hearing Officer's Transmittal to the Board of Education for the District of Columbia, Board of Education of the District of Columbia, Petitioner vs. Barbara A. Sizemore, Superintendent of Schools for the District of Columbia, Respondent, re: Proposed Action by the Board of Education Against Barbara A. Sizemore, 9 September 1975, p. 9.

63. Memorandum to Members, Board of Education, and Superintendent from Dwight S. Cropp, Executive Secretary, re: Meeting of the Committee of the Whole on Personnel, 24 June 1975.

64. "Transcript of the Thirteenth Special (Emergency) Meeting of the Board of Education," Washington, D.C., 24 June 1975, pp. 7-8.

65. Ibid., pp. 9-10.

66. Ibid., pp. 10-15.

67. Ibid., pp. 15-32.

68. "Transcript of Public Hearings on Charges Against Superintendent Sizemore," 7 August 1975, pp. 393-495.

69. Emily Moore, "The Sizemore Controversy Continues," *Power*, July 1975, p. 1. See also: "Big-City School Posts: Can Anyone Hold the Job?," *Education USA* 17 (12 July 1975), p. 259.

70. "Transcript of the Fifteenth (Special) Meeting of the Board of Education," Washington, D.C., 3 July 1975.

71. Diane Brockett, "Sizemore Spurns Cash for Hearing," *Washington Star*, 25 July 1975.

72. Statement of Chairman, Charles C. Diggs, Jr., Regarding The School Board-School Superintendent Controversy in the District of Columbia (Committee on the District of Columbia), U.S. House of Representatives, Washington, D.C., 23 July 1975.

73. "Transcript of the Sixteenth (Special) Meeting of the Board of Education," Washington, D.C., 24 July 1975, pp. 51-65.

74. Superior Court of the District of Columbia, Civil Division, *Barbara A. Sizemore, Plaintiff vs Virginia Morris, et alia, Defendant*, Civil Action No. 5461-75, Order, William Stewart, Jr., Judge, 25 July 1975. Attachment 2 of Administrative Hearing Officer's Transmittal.

75. Administrative Hearing Officer's Transmittal to the Board of Education for the District of Columbia, Board of Education of the District of Columbia, Petitioner vs. Barbara A. Sizemore, Superintendent of Schools for the District of Columbia, Respondent, re: Proposed Adverse Action by the Board of Education Against Barbara A. Sizemore, 19 September 1975, p. 11.

76. Writer's observation of session. See also: Chapter IX.

77. The Superintendent's Responses to the *Committee of the Whole on Personnel Letter*, 31 May 1975, pp. 1-3.

78. "Transcript of Public Hearing on Charges Against Superintendent Sizemore, Washington, D.C., 7 August 1975, pp. 393-473.

79. "Transcript of Seventeenth (Special) Board Meeting," Washington, D.C., 12 August 1975.

80. Administrative Hearing Officer's Transmittal to the Board of Education, District of Columbia, Petitioner, vs. Barbara A. Sizemore, Superintendent of Schools, pp. 11-12.

81. "Transcript of the Board of Education Open Meeting," Washington, D.C., 19 August 1975, pp. 2-8.

82. Ibid., pp. 8-27.

83. "Transcript of the Board of Education Open Meeting," Washington, D.C., 20 August 1975; and Memorandum to Members of the Board of Education, and Superintendent of Schools from Mr. Dwight S. Cropp, Executive Secretary, re: Resolution Approved during the Special Board Meeting on Wednesday, 20 August 1975.

84. Ibid., pp. 67-69.

85. Memorandum to Ms. Barbara A. Sizemore, Superintendent of Schools, from Mrs. Virginia Morris, President, Board of Education, re: Mr. Alphonso Gaskins, PACTS Coordinator, 25 August 1975.

86. Memorandum to Members, Board of Education, and Superintendent, from Dwight S. Cropp, Executive Secretary, re: Notice of Meetings, 25 August 1975.

87. "Transcript of Special Meeting of the Board of Education," Washington, D.C., 28 August 1975.

88. Letter to Mrs. Barbara A. Sizemore, Superintendent of Schools, from Dwight S. Cropp, Executive Secretary, Board of Education, 29 August 1975.

89. Memorandum to D.C. Board of Education and Superintendent from Virginia Morris, 2 September 1975.

90. "Transcript of the Nineteenth (Special) Meeting of the Board of Education," Washington, D.C., 7 September 1975.

91. Memorandum to Barbara A. Sizemore from Michael Nussbaum of Nussbaum and Owen, re: Legal Evaluation of Dismissal of Dr. Barbara A. Sizemore as Superintendent of Schools of the District of Columbia, Washington, D.C., 21 June 1975, pp. 7-8.

92. Ibid., p. 8.

93. "Transcript of A (Special) Meeting of the Board of Education," Washington, D.C., 9 October 1975, pp. 5-9.

94. Ibid., pp. 10-20.

95. Ibid., pp. 16-17.

96. Administrative Hearing Officer's Transmittal to the Board of Education for the District of Columbia, Board of Education of the District of Columbia, Petitioner, vs. Barbara A. Sizemore, Superintendent of Schools for the District of Columbia, Respondent, re: Proposed Adverse Action by the Board of Education Against Barbara A. Sizemore, 9 September 1975; see also Letter to Mrs. Barbara A. Sizemore, Superintendent of Schools from Virginia Morris, President, Board of Education, Attachment E, 31 May 1975; The Superintendent's Response to the Committee of the Whole on Personnel Letter, 31 May 1975. Synopsis of Superintendent's Response to the Committee of the Whole on Personnel Letter, 31 May 1975, 1 August 1975.

97. Hobson v Hansen, 269 F. Supp. 401 (1967); and Hobson v Hansen, 327 F. Supp. 864 (1971).

98. The Superintendent's Response to the Committee of the Whole on Personnel Letter, 31 May 1975, pp. 4-11.

99. Barbara A. Sizemore, "Becoming 'Comparable' and 'Equal' Questions and Answers," January 1975, p. 3.

100. Ibid., p. 5.

101. Ibid., p. 6.

102. Tr. IX 1215. (Tr. means transcript.)

103. Tr. XV 2114-2115.

104. See Pet. Exh. 5.2. (Pet. Exh. means "Petitioner's exhibit.)

105. Pet. Exhs. 11.1 and 11.1.1.

106. "Transcript of the Fifth (Regular) Meeting of the Board of Education," Washington, D.C., 20 March 1974. See also Pet. Exh. 11.2, pp. 14-16.

107. Pet. Exh. 12.2.

108. Resp. Exh. 4.1. (Resp. Exh. means "Respondent's exhibit.)

109. Resp. Exh. 17.2.

110. The letter is referred to in Resp. Exh. 17.1 but is not in evidence.

111. See Resp. Exh. 17.2.1.

112. Pet. Exh. 17.1.

113. Interview with James Williams, Deputy Superintendent, Washington, D.C., 14 December 1977.

114. Interview with Barbara A. Sizemore, Superintendent of Schools, Washington, D.C., 17 April 1978.

# SECTION IV

SUMMARY AND CONCLUSIONS

CHAPTER XI

SCHOOL SYSTEM OUTCOMES

Introduction

This chapter will focus on some outcomes in the school system after the termination of Superintendent Sizemore's contract. Thus, we will again examine some issues that evolved prior to or during Sizemore's administration, which resulted in problems of interference by the school board into administrative matters, to see if this type action continued and, further, to see if and how the issues were resolved.

To recapitulate, the last three superintendents were hired from outside the school system. William Manning was brought in to institute changes which Carl Hansen seemed reluctant to do. Later, some members of the board became disenchanted with Manning's pace in bringing about changes. Hugh Scott was brought in after Manning resigned. His contract was not renewed due in part to the board's displeasure about his budgetary difficulties, his equalization plans, and his failure to decentralize the school system. Sizemore was then hired from outside the school system and city. She implemented a decentralization plan and offered a new concept of equalization for study. But by then the composition of the board had changed three times between October 1973 and October 1975, which meant that Mrs. Sizemore had four boards in two years. This instability in board membership resulted in a change in goals away from decentralization and other innovations propounded by Sizemore.

At least four respondents mentioned the factor of insiders versus outsiders as hampering the smooth relationship between the superintendents and school boards. Although this factor was not listed separately in the design of the model, it was dealt with in the section on changes in superintendents and school board members as this related to changes in goals of the system.

Notably, not only was a superintendent selected from outside the system in 1973, but several of her key administrators were also: two executive assistants, the deputy superintendent of management services, the vice superintendent, and one associate superintendent. Contrasting opinions relative to this phenomenon were offered by four respondents to the interview questions. William Simons, the president of the Washington Teachers Union, felt that the selection of superintendents from outside the school system was a liability because they could not understand the relationship of the DCPS to the Congress.[1]

Napoleon Lewis, a regional superintendent, stated that because Mrs. Barbara Sizemore and Mr. James Williams were both from outside the system they were never able to find out where everything was. He felt that the school system's staff purposely kept information hidden -- that there was collusion among administrators.[2]

Gilbert Diggs, another regional superintendent, said the following when speaking of how Superintendent Sizemore handled the issues that arose during 1973-75:

> I doubt very seriously based on the record of superintendents that anyone could have done better at that time.
>
> This has...caused the city, and the system to resort to saying that probably a person from within the system who understands or who's been here for some time would be able to deal

with those issues, and to appoint that type of person as a superintendent, has developed.

Diggs stated that he has problems with this view since he felt the system should get the best qualified person to solve its problems.[3]

James Williams, who was also at the brunt of the alleged conspiracy, felt that information was being kept from him and the superintendent in terms of two important managerial aspects of the system -- personnel and budget.[4]

Further, one interpretation of the following remarks alleged to have been made by a principal in the system might be that they refer to the comings and goings of outsiders. As reported by the <u>Washington Star</u>, one principal said that he/she has been in the D.C. school system for 10 years and wanted to remain long after Mrs. Sizemore and a few other superintendents leave.[5]

## An Acting Superintendent

At the October 9, 1975 board meeting, at which time Superintendent Sizemore's contract was terminated, Hobson moved that the board take emergency rulemaking action to amend its <u>Rules</u>, Chapter II, Section 200.1, in order to add a provision to designate a person as acting superintendent of schools pending the appointment of a superintendent of schools under D.C. <u>Code</u>, Title 31, Section 31-105. This action was to become effective immediately and remain in effect for no more than 120 days. The motion was seconded by Mason and passed with Treanor, Schwartz, Morris, Hobson, Mason, Kemp and Kane voting in favor, Benjamin and Simmons opposed, and Warren and Evans abstaining.

Hobson then moved that the board designate Vincent E. Reed, associate superintendent, office of State Administration, to be acting superintendent of schools, effective immediately. This motion was seconded by Morris. Evans stressed that the board needed to have respect for the office of the superintendency in order to effectuate a viable superintendent-board relationship. Hence, he said the board must stop the reaction to style versus substance of what is presented which gets the board into all kinds of problems. Further, he stated:

> We cannot have eleven superintendents or twelve, I should say, and this is one of the things that concerns me. We have eleven people on the Board of Education and only one superintendent who is hired, theoretically, to implement the policies that the Board of Education puts together. Now, unfortunately, I think I have seen too much (of) Board Members getting involved in the daily implementation of the school system which creates a problem.... the line between policy and administration is very unclear. But I think that as a Board of Education we have a responsibility to look at that line. We have shied away from that.... If we want to be superintendent, I think we should go through the application procedure to be the same.

Both Benjamin and Simmons tried to get the board to take more time to consider an acting superintendent in a Committee of the Whole on Personnel meeting where there would be time to discuss the qualifications of several possible candidates.

Warren was particularly concerned by this proposed motion also. He stated that:

> ...to move directly from there to another action, the whole action of the acting superintendent, it did so without any prior discussion as has been noted here by other Board members. It did so but say for parliamentary procedure in what was beyond a question an entirely political act.... if it had not been for that technicality, the four Board members, and I say "four" at this point and those who are not a party to what I am about to say,

I ask your forgiveness in advance, who have
not been a part of the discussions with the
media about Mr. Reed, who have not been a part
of what has obviously been some back room
caucus someplace about who the superintendent
will be, the acting superintendent. We have
had no opportunity for questions, discussion
or anything. There have been no consideration
of other people within this system or if
people in the communities that we represent
had indicated a desire based on anticipating
the termination action this morning that
indicated a desire for someone else to be
considered by the Committee of the Whole
during this process. The Whole element of
participatory democracy that we are suppose
to personify for the people of this city who
have been completely eradicated, completely.
Now people talk about and these seven, I am
sorry - this Board talks about being non-
political and concerned about children....
Is it that the people now who shared in the
pre-selection process so convinced? Do they
have some mandate that they are so totally
representative of everybody else in this city
that the rest of us need not participate? If
so, why not take some action to reduce the
membership on the Board to seven?.... It's
an emergency, yes, but it is an emergency
situation that has been created by irresponsible acts in the past just like the one that
is about to be taken....

I would hope though it is in vain that this
action would go back to the Committee of the
Whole and that there would be that discussion....

We are not supposed to prepare the vote based
on what we read in the Washington Star and
the Washington Post. My only knowledge of
Mr. Reed being put forth is in newspaper
report accounts. If the press is going to be
representative of the people, then we should

just go ahead and move to have the elections cancelled and let the press take a poll and based on that poll determine who the superintendent is going to be and save the Board all of the trouble (about) who the Board members are going to be and just do away with the whole process.

Simmons brought up the point that Vincent Reed's shop was in charge of two of the specifications charged to the now former superintendent, and that it seemed inconsistent to her to now put him in charge of the entire school system. Kemp disagreed that Vincent Reed was alone responsible for the problems pointed up by Simmons. Benjamin urged that since it was obvious that Vincent Reed was going to be acting superintendent, the board should act as a united board. Therefore, the vote for Vincent Reed was unanimous.[6]

Acting Superintendent Vincent Reed was given a Memorandum of Understanding between himself and the DCBOE. Aspects of the document most pertinent to this section of the study and corresponding directly to the Sizemore termination hearing are: (1) the development of FY76 and FY77 budgets; (2) the development of an updated, comprehensive K-12 curriculum, which provides a minimum instruction program and options in skill areas; (3) a personnel (position) control system; and (4) the development of an alternative equalization plan for 1976-77, to be coordinated with Title I Comparability and the Waddy decree.[7]

The six specific issues to which we will apply our external and internal factors are: (1) superintendent selection; (2) curriculum; (3) equalization; (4) decentralization; (5) the budget; and (6) the personnel control system.

## Superintendent Selection Process

By March 1976, the board was ready to select

a superintendent. A very interesting superintendent selection procedure was approved of at the March 17, 1976 Committee of the Whole on Personnel meeting which was reported on by the new board president, Therman Evans, at the board meeting that night. The procedure was as follows:

> That the selection process for the appointment of a Superintendent of Schools begin with the question of whether to offer a three-year appointment to the present Acting Superintendent of Schools.

The recommendation to accept this procedure was put in motion by Mrs. Mason and seconded by Mr. Hobson. Mrs. Simmons offered additional language to the motion in the form of an amendment:

> That...the application period remain open for 15 days permitting other qualified candidates who wish to apply to do so.

Warren, Simmons, Benjamin and Evans voted for the amendment, whereas the five consistent opponents of Sizemore were joined by two new board members, Mr. Conrad Smith and Mr. James Featherstone, Jr., to oppose it. A point seemingly lost on these board members, made by Simmons subsequent to this action, was that if the contract were offered to Mr. Reed, it automatically excluded any other candidate from an opportunity to make application or receive consideration. She noted that the process was closed, exclusionary and denied access to others. Furthermore, Simmons explained that the process was not in keeping with the tenets of the Civil Rights Act of 1964, and the Equal Employment Opportunity Act of 1972.

Warren noted that the selection process being considered was highly inconsistent with that used in the past. In this regard, he said that the board had spent an unnecessary amount of money, time and effort and later rejected the superintendent. He stated further that this time the board was proposing to reject even the simplest process of allowing people to apply, reviewing applications, and then making a decision after receiving input from the community other than from those who support the action which is about to take place.

One other significant response to the motion was made by Mrs. Benjamin subsequent to Mr. Hobson's cataloging that the acting superintendent had either accomplished all of the tasks enumerated in the Memorandum of Understanding or that they were in the works. She pointedly clarified, as one example of Mr. Hobson's falsification, that the budget submitted by Mr. Reed was that prepared during Mrs. Sizemore's tenure. After this discussion, the vote was taken with only Mr. Warren voting his opposition to the procedure of beginning the selection process by offering a three year appointment to the position of superintendent of schools to Mr. Vincent Reed.

It should also be noted that in the meeting attention was called to the fact that several community groups or individuals did pressure the board to make a decision or to open up the selection process, namely: Congressman Charles Diggs of Detroit, Voice of Community Informed Expression (VOICE); Capital View Development Corporation; D.C. Citizens for Better Public Education; and Alpha Omega Chapter of Omega Psi Phi Fraternity. Only Congressman Diggs urged that the board not move too hastily in making a selection.[8]

As noted by Mr. Warren, the selection of Mr. Vincent Reed as superintendent of schools in D.C. was vastly different from the last three selection processes that appeared to be more open though wrought with controversy, both healthy and unhealthy. But, then, if we examine various instances of the democratic decision-making process in action, we note that there is usually more controversy permitted than in autocratic, exclusionary, closed systems and procedures. Also, the evidence of history will bear out the fact that systemic structural change is seldom consummated without conflict as is surface change or the maintenance of the status quo. The question then becomes: What changes were proposed and made? And another question raised by Diggs in his interview might be: Now that the books and the people are counted, are the youngsters learning any better?[9]

The next section will examine curriculum changes made in the DCPS since 1975.

## Curriculum

On November 19, 1975, at a stated board meeting, the DCBOE approved Acting Superintendent Vincent Reed's recommendation to affirm two resolutions: (1) that the DCBOE support reading achievement as one of the priorities among the curriculum goals; and (2) that the DCBOE support mathematics achievement also. Both system goals were to be accomplished through short- and long-term educational planning and the allocation of resources.[10]

At the December 17, 1975 board meeting, Superintendent Reed presented a listing of curriculum guides and publications available in all subject fields and those being developed. The listing contained material published from 1948 to 1975.

On November 17, 1976, a proposed junior high school history curriculum was described during the board meeting. This curriculum was developed based on a resolution passed by the board in November 1975, that all junior high school students take a certified course in the history of the District of Columbia.[11]

Superintendent Vincent Reed announced in June 1976 plans to design and implement a competency based curriculum (CBC). The CBC is described in one document as "an individualized, progressive, sequential instructional program based on the use of specific behavioral objectives for which criterion levels of performance have been established and which maximizes the potential of function successfully in life roles."[12]

In another document the CBC is described as a curriculum:

> ...which focuses on performance tasks, the measurable things students are expected to do, and skills acquisition and development. These skills may be classified as analytical communicative, social-political, consumer-producer, and self-actualizing. The operant assumption behind this curriculum approach is that scholastic achievement and successful living depend, to a significant degree, on mastery of these skills.[13]

The CBC thrust will emphasize basic education stressing reading and mathematics. This thrust is in contrast to his predecessor's emphasis on an innovative multi-cultural curriculum that would have de-emphasized European history, music and literature. Reed's emphasis on basics does not stress this thrust.

At the time of this writing (1978-79), a new curriculum emphasizing competency in basic skills has not yet materialized. As late as the Spring of 1978, there has been little substance to Reed's promise. According to an April 1978 news report, Reed indicated that evaluators' reports indicated that substantial changes had to be made in order for the curriculum to be effective.[14]

His latest promise is that the curriculum will more than likely be used system-wide beginning in September 1979.[15]

A series of articles published in the Washington Post in April and May 1978 points to a probability that students in the Washington, D.C. public schools are still having serious problems in learning.[16] Interestingly, board members are not insisting that Mr. Reed produce a curriculum immediately to alleviate the situation. They seem willing to wait indefinitely for the male superintendent to do so, something they were not willing to do for their female superintendent of a few years back. Of course, the supportive position of the board may also be interpreted to mean that board members are more supportive of superintendents selected from inside the school system.

## Equalization

Reed offered no "new" equalization plan to the DCBOE until May 12, 1977. The alternative plan for equalizing educational resources was based on equalizing class size and basic services in all city schools.

The definition of equality used was as follows:

> The proposed Board of Education plan provides for a distribution of instructional resources based on equal treatment for each student.
>
> The definition of equality utilized here refers to sameness or equivalence in number, quantity, measure or degree. Factors to be considered in this proportionate distribution include a definition of student and of resources to be distributed.[17]

In submitting the plan to the board, Superintendent Reed recommended that the board of education request the corporation counsel to petition the court to relinquish further jurisdiction in the case.[18] Essentially, the superintendent was requesting the court to remove itself from the business of education and trust the board and administration to carry out its own plan to equalize basic programs and staffing.

In evaluating the plan, the American Civil Liberties Union (ACLU), which handled Hobson's case, felt that the plan was just an expression of good intentions and that was not good enough after so many years.[19]

Therefore, Judge Wright asked the board to present evidence that the 1971 order had created problems.[20]

On September 19, 1977, Wright signed a new order eliminating salaries as a factor in the equalization arithmetic. The new order states that the pupil-teacher ratio at every elementary school must be within five percent of the city-wide average.

Donald L. Horowitz, whose 1977 study was published by Brookings Institute, stated that though the new equalization formula seems more reasonable since fewer teachers are moved around, there's no evidence that pupil-teacher ratio is any better than per pupil expenditures in predicting performance.[21]

It should also be noted that using class size as the equalization factor instead of teacher salaries was proposed by Superintendent Scott in 1972 when the school system hired Hobson, Sr. as a consultant.[22] The project was never completed.

Again, we have the board supporting its male inside-selected superintendent in an effort which has not really adhered to terms set down in the Memorandum of Understanding which specified the submission of an alternative equalization plan, if alternative is interpreted to mean something new and more viable than the old plan. If it is interpreted to mean just something different than what is current, then, in a sense, Reed has done the job required of him by the board. Much more was required of the female superintendent who preceeded Reed.

## Decentralization

During the decade of the 1960s, some experimental forms of decentralization were implemented:

the Model School Division in 1964, now in Region V; the Adams and Morgan community schools in 1967, now in Region II; and the Anacostia Community Schools Division in 1968, now in Region I. Superintendent William Manning drew up a plan to divide the city into 11 regions over a five year period. This thrust resulted in only the establishment of the Spingarn Instructional Unit. In 1970, Superintendent Hugh J. Scott, responding to a charge from the board of education, initiated a study of decentralization. The study resulted in a May 1971 report, showing six alternative regional patterns and recommending a plan for five decentralized areas. He prepared two other plans between May 1971 and May 1973, neither of which the board took action on. On January 15, 1973, the board of education adopted 10 priority goals for the school system. Included among these goals was decentralization.[23] In spite of all of the above activity toward the goal of decentralization, it remained for Superintendent Barbara A. Sizemore to implement a city-wide decentralization plan in July 1974, in which she established six administrative regions, each with a regional superintendent and staff.

A July 11, 1974 memorandum to all school personnel from Barbara Sizemore, former superintendent of schools, delegated full authority to the regional superintendents over their regions.[24]

The decision-making prerogatives of the regional superintendents changed when Vincent Reed, an insider, was appointed superintendent. Not only did he appoint all of his officers from inside the system, but he redesigned the organizational schema for central administration so that regional superintendents were excluded from top management, as indicated in figure 8. Thus, the authority of the regional superintendents was curtailed and only designated administrative functions and responsibilities were assigned to the regions.[25] Major decisions are no longer made by regional superintendents. They are made by Superintendent Reed and his immediate staff. Directions come from the

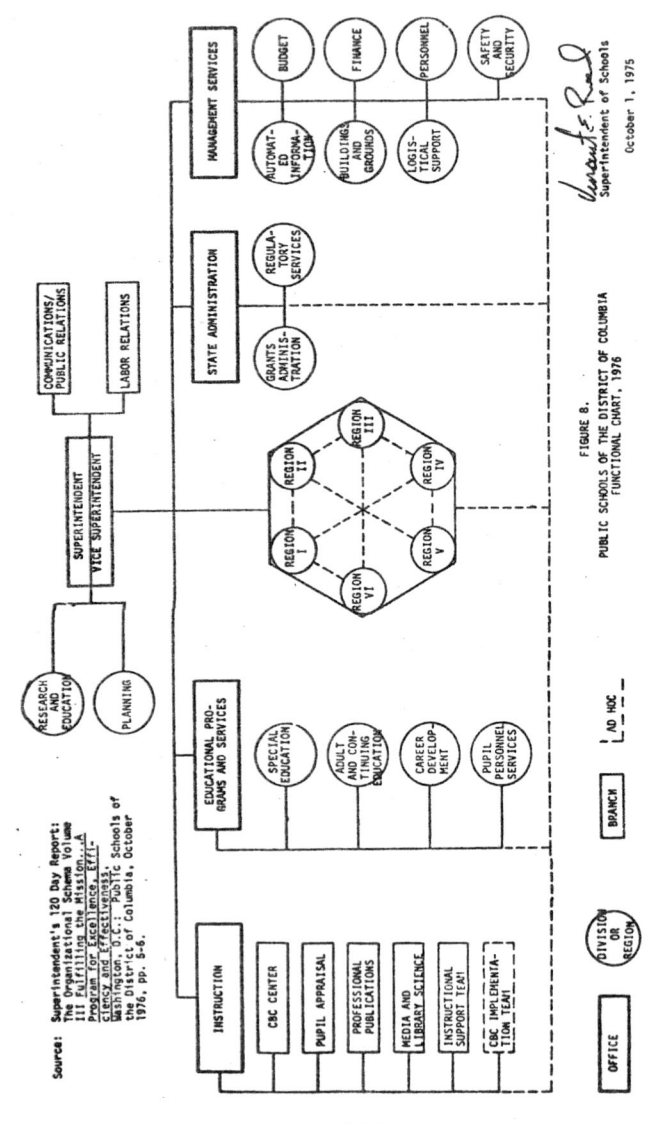

FIGURE 8.
PUBLIC SCHOOLS OF THE DISTRICT OF COLUMBIA
FUNCTIONAL CHART, 1976

central office as to what will be done and how it is going to be done. Regional superintendents simply implement the decisions. The concensus decision-making model introduced by Superintendent Sizemore is no longer in operation, according to at least two of the six regional superintendents interviewed.[26]

Thus, we see that changing the structure of the school system is no longer a board priority, since both the current board and the superintendent are in tune with a change back to the authoritarian, hierarchical arrangement used prior to Superintendent Sizemore's tenure. Nor is changing the decision-making process to a consensus model through the use of an administrative team a priority of the current superintendent and school board.

## Budget[27]

As indicated in Chapters III, VI and VIII, budgetary problems plagued the DCPSS, in part due to problems in the management services area such as: (1) inadequate financial controls; (2) a partial position control system; and (3) the use of different accounting systems by the school system and the District of Columbia government. In spite of these problems, all city agencies had to balance their budgets in line with the requirements of the Antideficiency Act, which made it a violation of the law to end the year with a deficit.[28] Nevertheless, both 1970 and 1971 year end operating fund balances showed a deficit. The 1970 deficit of $198,300.00 was absorbed by the D.C. government and the 1971 deficit of $2,424,140.00 was shifted to the Impact Aid budget. The balance of $435,300.00 in 1972 was achieved through the freeze in January 1972 on all personnel and non-personnel expenditures instituted after a 1971 projected deficit of $3 million dollars was determined. In 1973, there was a savings of $3,637,900.00 in the year end operating fund balance which would have reverted to the treasury of the D.C. government, according to law,[29] if the school system had not transferred impact charges against the regular budget.  As noted, savings in the regular budget reverted to the D.C. government but impact funds could be carried over from one year to the next.  In 1974, the savings dropped to $1,271,600.00.  Superintendent Sizemore proposed to use these savings for staff development by obligating them before June 30, 1974.  Due to the mayor's freeze to prevent a deficit imposed in October 1974, reducing the school budget by $3,834,200.00,[30] there was only a small balance of $24,070.00 left in the 1975 year end operating fund balance.  Thus, the school system was able to use almost all of the money allocated to provide services to children rather than turning a large portion of it back to the D.C. government.

Mrs. Sizemore left the system in October 1975. The following year, the money turned back to the D.C. government at the end of the year again mounted.  In 1976, the year end operating fund balance was $1,342,352.00.  For the short year from July 1, 1976-September 20, 1976, after the change to a new fiscal year beginning October 1, 1976-September 30, 1977, the savings for the D.C. government from the school system's budget was $3,927,657.00.

As was noted in Chapter X, Mrs. Sizemore was involved in termination hearings when school opened in September 1975.  Consequently, she designated Mr. James Williams, deputy superintendent, office of Management Services, as the person in charge of the school system in her absence.[31] Mr. Williams opened school in school year 1974-75 with a balanced budget due to improvements made in management services during Mrs. Sizemore's tenure as superintendent of D.C. schools.  Additionally, many new positions in the management line were not filled due to the reorganization of the central office[32] pending implementation of the new plan. Because the D.C. government office of Budget and Financial Management would not grant exemptions from the mayor's freeze order until the financial plans contained the required reductions, and the DCBOE could not agree on a plan until May 1975, the positions remained vacant for the rest of the school year. Therefore, the new acting superintendent began his tenure with a balanced budget.

At the meeting of June 16, 1976, the committee on School Finance presented a report which included an item concerning the authority of the mayor on the issue of reprogramming funds for personnel and non-personnel items in the FY76 budget. Subsequent to this, the board approved Hobson's motion to the effect that the board should assert its authority to confront the mayor on this issue.[33]

After waiting three months for an opinion from the corporation counsel relating to the mayoral authority over the board of education and the DCPSS, the DCBOE received an opinion on September 13, 1976 which caused them to vote to take the mayor to court.[34] The purpose of this action was to seek judicial determination of the controversy between the board and the mayor of the District with regard to the authority of the board of education to direct expenditures for the public schools and to determine the amounts and purposes for which appropriated funds could be spent. Seemingly, four judgments were filed: (1) Complaint for Declaratory Judgment Injunction; (2) two Motions for Temporary Restraining Order; (3) Motion for Preliminary Injunction; and (4) Memorandum of Points and Authorities in Support of Motions for Temporary Restraining Order and Preliminary Injunction.[35] At the time of this writing, the cases were still awaiting adjudication.[36]

At the September 27, 1976 board meeting, the FY77 operating budget with proposed reductions to accommodate Congressional funding levels was adopted. Notably, funds for the preschool program were not cut. This item was noted by Mrs. Simmons in the following remarks:

> I have very real problems in our not having touched in our educational programs the preschool which is the most expensive education

this school system offers for which we do not have a legal compulsory age responsibility.[37]

Items cut included summer school for a savings of $499,800.00 and 126 classroom teachers for a savings of $2,270,700.00.[38] Thus, Superintendent Reed's priorities seemingly were the priority of the majority members of the board in respect to maintaining the pre-school program at the expense of the regular legally required educational program above the pre-school level. However, this position may or may not be covered in an explanation given by Mr. Reed in his interview when he described the school-by-school budget process. He stated that the local schools decide through a budget committee what teacher services they will buy each year out of their budget allotment.[39] Nevertheless, this explanation may be too simplistic to cover the issue of how you obtain monies short of requesting them in the new and improved service category to conduct innovative educational designs which may more nearly meet the needs of the majority of the students in the D.C. public schools. Seemingly, this was not one of the priority goals of the board, as it was not during Sizemore's tenure when she tried to push forward in the FY76 budget educational programs to make the school system more just to all students.

## Personnel Control System

As indicated earlier in this account, personnel control was a particularly crucial problem in the DCPSS. Hence, a number of efforts were expended to solve it. Several efforts made during the Sizemore administration will be noted as well as the extension, curtailment, and/or changes made in the personnel control system during the Reed administration. The problems stemmed from many causes. One cause was explained by Mr. Ernest Sargent, Director of Finance.

In a February 4, 1974 memorandum from Mr. Sargent to Mr. James Williams, deputy superintendent for Management Services, Sargent explained in some detail one of the main problems. He stated that the D.C. government required the public schools, beginning in fiscal year 1974, to finalize the conversion of a new account code structure, a major change in the financial management system. This finalization process was achieved by the Division of Automated Information Systems (DAIS) through the use of the computer for automated conversion of personnel accounts based on conversion tables submitted by the budget office at an approximately 65 percent accuracy rate. Dummy codes were used in order to meet the conversion deadline. These dummy codes had not been corrected and were therefore invalid. The problem seemed to be that many employees were being paid out of incorrect accounts, and Mr. Sargent was suggesting the use of an audit trail in order to locate them and then to transfer their charges to the correct accounts.

Another problem dealing with personnel, described by Mr. Sargent in his memorandum, had to do with the transfer of a number of elementary schools from the division of Elementary Education to the division of Model Schools without transferring the personnel and related expenditures pertaining to those schools.

A third problem emanated from the appointment of personnel to unauthorized positions, thus causing employees to be paid out of incorrect accounts.

Since Mr. Sargent indicated that the problems, in the main, stemmed from improper coordination and follow-up procedures being used by the various units, he suggested the formation of a task force to provide for coordination and follow-up. The task force was to be composed of representatives of the following units: division of Budget, division of Personnel, Division of Automatic Information Services (DAIS), and the division of Finance.[40]

Subsequent memoranda from Mr. Sargent to Mr. Williams documented specific cases of problems which continued in the personnel control system stemming from the situations described above.[41]

In a March 27, 1974 memorandum to Mr. Williams from Mr. Sargent, he clearly explained the problem of mismatched personnel account codes. He stated:

> As a result of our analysis of a computer listing of employees whose personnel account codes (PAF) do not match those reflected in the Master Payroll file (D.C. Accounting), we discovered the following reasons for this condition:
>
> A. All payroll accounts were initially converted to the '74 budget structure. However, in order to meet the conversion deadline, dummy codes were used in many payroll accounts. There have been subsequent actions to correct the personnel accounting file without instituting corrections in the Master Payroll File.
>
> B. The Division of Automated Information Systems have been providing accountable offices with departmental listings from the personnel accounting system requesting each office to review for any discrepancies and return a copy of the annotated listing to the Position Control Unit to support these changes. However, these changes were not made to the Master Payroll File.
>
> C. The Budget Office, on September 13, 1973, provided all accountable offices with a position authorization list to be compared with the most recent PAF listing to assist them in bringing any errors or inconsistencies to their attention to insure that the PAF was corrected to replace the allotments accurately. Once again, these changes were not made to the Master Payroll File.

In summarizing the problem, Mr. Sargent noted that changes were not made in payroll accounts to reflect PAF file changes made in the DAIS personnel accounts. Thus, invalid codes were still carried by the payroll system causing a mismatch in the two systems. Further, Mr. Sargent noted that the Position Control Unit made corrections of accounts in the PAF file copy used by that office but did not make corrections in copies contained in the Master Payroll File located in the D.C. Accounting Office. Therefore, Sargent requested that all changes initiated by the Position Control Unit be followed up with "Form 275 [IBM punch cards] to correct account codes in the payroll system...." Further, he requested that a listing of the changes be submitted to personnel in order for that unit to correct personnel records.[42]

Following along the line of developing a position control system, Mr. Sargent also wrote to Budget Director Edward G. Winner in May 1974. In his memorandum he explained that in light of the fact that it appeared Mr. Winner had been unable to comprehend the nature and complexity of the problems associated with allotment changes, he was providing a copy of the administrative procedures for position control as an example of what could be developed to resolve the problem.[43] On May 6, 1974, Mr. Sargent wrote again to Mr. Winner suggesting that Mr. Winner not circumvent the funds check system as had been his method. This memorandum followed a March 29, 1974 memorandum which also accused Mr. Winner of circumventing the funds check system.[44]

Again, in a memorandum dated June 3, 1974, Mr. Sargent called Mr. Williams' attention to problems ensuing from the lack of a full position control system in that (1) programs were transferred from one division in the school system to another, and (2) control allotments were changed without related personnel transfers resulting in employees whose positions were transferred but the costs remained still being charged to another account. The point made by Sargent was that even though savings were reflected in certain budget categories, actual savings on a program level were unable to be projected since specific accounts were incorrectly stated. Mr. Sargent's concern apparently had to do with the fact that personnel compensation and benefits were 85 percent of the school system's budget, and that without adequate controls over positions in the system, it was impossible to provide actual obligations and projections to management at the program level.[45]

As discussed in more detail in Chapter VIII, the Mayor-Commissioner's Memorandum #74-164, dated October 3, 1974, and the Mayor-Commissioner's Order #74-202, dated October 2, 1974, sent by the District of Columbia Office of Budget and Financial Management, established a freeze on personnel and other expenditures; reduced the public schools expenditures by $3,834.200.00 for the remainder of fiscal 1975; established estimated reimbursements for pay raises at $11,669,900.00; and established $5,001,400.00 as the estimated amount of absorption of pay raises to be borne by the public schools. This, of course, pushed forward the need for a complete position control system.

Additionally, a projected deficit of $5,407,800.00 was discovered through the projected expenditure analysis. Further, a Department of General Services maintenance work figure of $1.84 to $2.3 million compounded the financial situation and made a position control system absolutely necessary. A November 5, 1974 analysis of the situation revealed that even though large numbers of vacancies existed in the central services and management and were being maintained due to the freeze, problems still existed because of over-expenditures in teaching services. Therefore, the establishment of a personnel control system was a top priority item as indicated by Superintendent Sizemore to Mr. Williams, deputy superintendent of Management Services.[46]

In the summer of 1975, regional superintendents participated in determining procedures for distributing available secondary teacher positions for FY76. Thus, regional superintendents were sent a schedule of position allotment totals to reconcile with the computer listing of individual positions developed by the budget division in terms of specific positions by account code and position number.[47] The budget director, who released this memorandum in August 1975, was appointed deputy superintendent of management under the new superintendent, Vincent Reed. Following through on the design of a position control system begun under Mr. Williams, the budget division proceeded to establish control over positions by indicating that all positions were to be authorized by that division, and that changes, increases or decreases in position allowances of the various departments would be made through the budget division.[48]

Complete control over the personnel system has not been accomplished, however, as the payroll file is still maintained by the District Accounting Office, and is therefore not within the control of the school system. The system in use by the school system can identify discrepancies and make corrections, but the corrections are entered on the payroll by the D.C. Accounting Office and the school system has no control over this operation.[49]

Interestingly, when asked the question: "What were your perceptions of the goals of the superintendent, and how many of these goals do you believe were actually achieved during Sizemore's administration?," Gilbert Diggs, former regional superintendent, responded:

> There is no question that in terms of processes or designs to achieve the goals being set in motion...many of them were well on their way. For example, the goal to establish a real personnel accounting system was practically eighty-five percent complete... and that one did ultimately get to what I would consider to be ninety-five to ninety-eight percent at the present time.[50]

Apparently, to at least one of the key administrators during the Sizemore years, the personnel system now in place was initiated then and was operating with 85 percent accuracy prior to the Reed years. From this and the other information presented here, it can be deduced that, given adequate time in office, Sizemore would have improved the management mess through her innovations there as well as changed the instructional program to fit the human growth and development needs of the students in the public school system. Board interference in the day-to-day operation of the school system, in part, through the usurpation of Sizemore's budgetary authority by the Committee on School Finance, hampered her efforts. No such action was imposed on the current male superintendent selected from inside the school system.

## Summary

This chapter has discussed six crucial decisions made by the DCBOE and two of its superintendents of schools: Sizemore and Reed. These decisions were: (1) superintendent selection of Mr. Vincent Reed as acting superintendent and then as school superintendent; (2) equalization; (3) curriculum; (4) decentralization; (5) budget; and (6) personnel control system. The information presented followed actions begun during the Sizemore administration and continued or discontinued during the Reed administration in order to provide a comparison of superintendent-school board relations after the termination of Sizemore as superintendent of the DCPSS.

It was noted that historically some members of the DCBOE grappled with whether to select a superintendent from inside the school system or outside the system in order to bring about changes. In the final analysis the Anita Allen board in 1968 selected William Manning from outside the city. Subsequently, the DCBOE became displeased with his slow pace at making changes. Consequently, he was relieved of his duties as school superintendent and the board again sought through a nationwide search another superintendent. In 1971, they brought in Dr. Hugh Scott, a young Black man from Detroit, Michigan, who eventually presented the board with at least three decentralization plans. None pleased the board in time for it to seek to continue his services as superintendent. Therefore, a third search for an outsider ensued in 1973 amid much agitation and pressure. Resultingly, a female with many years of administrative experience in the Chicago public school system was selected. This was an historical event since the selection of Mrs. Barbara A. Sizemore as superintendent of the DCPSS marked the first time a Black female was superintendent of a large urban school system.

When Mrs. Sizemore made changes in the school system despite the vastness of its problems, she encountered severe criticism from some of the monied interests in the District through their organs, the <u>Washington Star</u> and the <u>Washington Post</u>, both of which suggested a change in superintendents might be the new course of action to follow. Some board members took their direction from the newspapers, especially after the April 4, 1975, speech Mrs. Sizemore gave before the African Heritage Studies Association conferees, in which she exposed the plan of big business interests in the District to take back the city from the Blacks, who comprised 72 percent of the population, and out of this majority had elected a Black mayor and a majority Black city council. Her passion over the displacement of Blacks by whites in the District through housing speculation, however, was not representative of the placid nature of the majority of board members about this. Hence, soon after the speech, a process to terminate Mrs. Sizemore was set in motion which concluded in October 1975. Subsequently, the DCBOE appointed Vincent Reed, an insider, as acting superintendent. In the Spring of 1976 without benefit of a nationwide search he was appointed superintendent of the DCPSS.

Although Mrs. Sizemore was pushed to offer a new equalization plan early in her tenure as superintendent of schools, and was in the process of arriving at such through the study of the concept of incommensurability, she was not supported in this effort by the DCBOE. Later, she was charged with not offering a new plan for equalizing the resources of the school system. Contrastingly, Mr. Reed, though appointed in October 1975, did not come up with a plan until May 1977, and it was more a request to Judge Wright to be left alone than it was a new plan of equalization. The board supported him in this action. Obviously, a new plan was not what the DCBOE desired.

In the area of curriculum development in the District schools, there was a shift away from the monolingual, monocultural European emphasis. There was a change toward a multicultural, multilingual thrust using all four symbol systems: words, notes, numbers and images, based on the assumption that human beings are different. They grow and develop at different rates and according to different patterns and therefore need multi-age, multi-level and multi-model groupings. They learn in different ways, and therefore must have available to them all four symbol systems, not just words. Art, media (images), mathematics (numbers), and music (notes) are just as valuable as tools for learning for some children as are words for some other children.[51] This, then, was a part of the thrust during the Sizemore years.

Seemingly, the pendulum has swung back again to the basics with the competency based curriculum thrust introduced by Reed, reminiscent of the Clark Plan (AAP) of 1968-70. The notion of "back to the basics" implies an end to such things as open classrooms where students are permitted to learn in their own way. It implies a stress on competence in reading, writing, computing, and other basic skills with a curtailment on such nonacademic electives as music and art, two particularly important symbol systems for Black students. Further, it implies a reliance on standardized tests and textbooks to support a norm referenced curriculum which has not helped Black and poor children learn because they do not conform to the norm upon which these tests are referenced. They are not white and the majority are not middle class.[52]

Indeed, it has also been reported that test vocabularies and illustrations are geared toward white middle class cultures.[53]

Another author succinctly sums up in somewhat comic fashion the deep seated problems he had with standardized tests. He artfully explains that anyone who: makes subtle distinctions, thinks broadly, is an original thinker, sees unusual relationships among things, is unique, is better at using a concept than naming it, is not middle class, is confused by misleading and crowded graphic layouts, cannot follow confused test directions, or is frightened by the test, will be severely penalized by these tests.[54]

Even Christopher Jencks, a Harvard sociologist on leave at the University of California at Santa Barbara, and author of Inequality: A Reassessment of the Effect of Family and School in America, acknowledges that the schools are not turning out huge numbers of "functional illiterates" and that today's students are not doing worse in the "basics" -- the three Rs. Jencks states that, according to the National Assessment of Educational Progress reports, the 9-year olds examined about every four years improved in both reading and writing between 1970 and 1974 while high school S.A.T. scores have been falling. The point Jencks seems to be making is that it is not back to the basics which is needed, but back to the complex skills of comprehension and critical thinking.[55]

Chuck Stone, former ETS Director of Minority Affairs from 1973-76, informs us that Educational Testing Services (ETS), a small company in 1947, developed into a $250 million monopoly after the College Entrance Examination Board hired ETS to develop test items and norm the SAT tests. ETS also controls the development and construction of other nationally distributed tests: GRE, ATGSB, ASPT, NTE, LSAT, FSE and TOEFL.[56] He describes ETS as a "testing mafia." He also emphasized that Blacks at ETS found pervasive racism in test construction.[57] Naturally, the testmakers are not going to acknowledge the uselessness of their creations in the learning process, especially for minority and poor persons.

Further, a report, titled <u>The Reign of ETS: The Corporation That Makes Up Minds</u> authored by Allan Nairm for consumer advocate Ralph Nader, said that the Scholastic Aptitude Test (SAT) and other admissions tests constructed by the Educational Testing Service (ETS) did little to predict academic performance in school.[58]

Robert Williams, a Black psychologist, and the Association of Black Psychologists have both consistently pointed up the unfairness of using norm referenced tests which decide who goes to college, gets the better jobs, and has the power.[59]

Notwithstanding the critical analysis of the test aspects of the competency based curriculum presented above, when the D.C. public schools open in the Fall of 1978, the new structured curriculum, noted as competency-based, will be instituted in 30 of the city's 168 regular schools to teach reading, writing, and mathematics. Furthermore, it will include norm referenced tests that students must pass before they can move ahead to new work.[60] So again, the DCPSS has come full circle "back to the basics."

Another innovation brought to fruition during the Sizemore two years is being slowly stripped from the D.C. public school system during the Reed administration, as was noted in the preceding section. The new design of the system excludes regional superintendents from the decision-making core of administrators.

Budgetary data certainly pointed up that no money was reprogrammed for decentralization and testimony on the budget during Committee on School Finance meetings, as well as board meetings, corroborate the fact that Mrs. Sizemore's last board rejected the concept of flattening the pyramidal arrangement of administrators. So, too, did the memorandum of understanding between Vincent Reed and the DCBOE stipulate that he appoint a vice superintendent post haste.

It was shown that Mrs. Sizemore used almost all of the money allocated to the school system to mount programs to help students learn. This could especially be seen in the year end operating fund balance of $24,070.00 left in 1975. Both her predecessor and Mr. Reed who followed her left upward of a million dollars or more money to be turned back to the D.C. government. Here again, one might assume that change was rejected by the DCBOE and a return to the status quo was the order of the day. Furthermore, it was noted that in spite of the numerous budget crises which occurred during 1975, Mrs. Sizemore and her deputy manager, Mr. James Williams, left the school system in the black so that the new superintendent was able to begin his tenure with a balanced budget, a factor attributed to Mr. Reed's astuteness but actually performed by the Sizemore-Williams team. In contrast, Mr. Reed and the current board had to resort to the courts to redress their grievance against the mayor and city council relative to control over the budget.

Some editorials would lead one to assume that Mr. Reed stepped into a chaotic management situation and with one sweep of his magic wand made it all blow away. One such indicated that Reed reduced payroll errors by almost 90 percent in a matter of months.[61] Another suggested that Reed cleared up great administrative problems and mistakes in 14 months.[62] Perhaps his female predecessor might have done as well without harrassment and with more board support.

Interestingly, issue seems not to be taken about the fact that the students are performing badly since the superintendent acknowledges it, but praise is given for clearing up management and personnel problems. These would have cleared up in the natural course of events over time anyway since the present superintendent was simply following through on designs and procedures put in place by the former superintendent, as the data show.

In brief, we have examined board and superintendent actions which occurred as an outcome of Mrs. Sizemore's termination as superintendent of the DCPSS. We have noted a reversal of some of the innovations made during her tenure. We have also noted credit given to her successor for management changes instituted during her administration. In all, we have noted that her firing was politically oriented and in actual fact had little or nothing to do with poor management skills as the newspapers and her opponents on the board and in the city led the citizens to believe.

In summary, it was noted that the external factors of the colonial status of the District and the school system -- racism, classism and group pressure -- did in fact impact on the decision-making unit, pressuring it to make political decisions which were not in the best interest of the majority of the students in the school system. So, too, did such internal factors as the process for making decisions, the structure of the decision-making unit and its functions, as well as membership changes on the board and motivations had an effect on the system. Likewise, a change in superintendents from an outsider to an insider affected school system goals and relationships between people. Noted in regard to the above was the change in how the board operated vis-a-vis the superintendent. The board changed from a conflicted entity to a more or less acquiescing and placid entity since there was no longer present in the decision-making unit a driving force to change the status quo to cause the school system to fit the needs of all of the children in attendance.

Notably, the school board and the current superintendent are still subject to external controls imposed by the Congress, the city council and the mayor, especially in the area of budget constraints. A recent conflict has developed between the mayor, the city council and the school system in the area of budget. This pressure point has not changed. Nevertheless, one can conjecture as to whether the approach employed by Mrs. Sizemore of pointing the finger at the real culprit, the Congress, is the more reasonable approach to get at the larger issue of not enough money to adequately operate a viable school system. Are the present board and the superintendent diverting the public's attention from the elephant to the mouse as it blames the people with little control over the vast resources of this country or even this city, the Black mayor and the majority Black city council, by instituting a law suit against them? Is this really the answer to the basic problem of the colonial status of the city government and hence the school system?

The desires of big business interests in the District are apparently now satisfied. The editorials and news articles, for the most part, are supportive of the present superintendent. But, then, why shouldn't they be, since he is moving the school system back to the pre-Sizemore years? In this regard, too, we note that community pressure from many of the influential groups in the community has abated, though we do note a faint pressure from some parents on the decision-making unit to reconsider giving services to the Hawthorne Alternative (private) School.

The external factor of sexism has been seen in operation as the male superintendent has not been held accountable for the immediate implementation of a new curriculum. Even approximately three years after his original appointment, one is not completely in place. In less than two years into her superintendency, Mrs. Sizemore was charged with not having provided for curriculum development. This charge was not supported by the overwhelming evidence to the contrary presented at the hearings. So even the apparently former employee of the board, Administrative Law Judge Herbert O. Reid, had to concede this point in his deliberations.

Neither was Mr. Reed, the male superintendent, held accountable for providing a new equalization plan. He was instructed in the Memorandum of Understanding to present an alternative equalization plan, a subtle but significant difference. Therefore, Reed offered a plan actually pursued to some extent by Superintendent Hugh Scott which, as indicated by authorities in the field, is no more viable than that presently being used.

The personnel control system being used is not radically different from that used prior to Reed's tenure, though the decision-making prerogative shifted from the instructional line to the management line under the budget officer. Needless-to-say, the male superintendent was supported in his efforts to rigidify the system, whereas the female superintendent's attempts to flex up the structure were aborted by the majority on her board.

As noted, there is a return to the more rigid hierarchical administrative structure where the consensus model used by the administrative team has been abandoned and the decision-making prerogatives distributed on the regional level have been recalled to central administration. There is even some evidence that the regions are being dismantled. The above points to a change in the functions of the regional superintendents. They are now a funnel through which administrative decisions made at the top reach the local administrative unit.

Thus, we see how a change in terms of the internal factor of administrative structure also changes the relationships of the people operating within the system. The majority of the board and the present superintendent seem satisfied with this "new" old arrangement.

New goals instituted by Superintendent Vincent Reed also changed the direction of the educational program to a deemphasis on a more just model to a reemphasis of more of the same, to wit, back to the basics. So, not only did the new superintendent return the administrative structure to its former rigidity with the blessings of the majority on the board, he also returned the curriculum to its prior rigid format which portends continued failure for the majority student population. This is, in this writer's view, blatant racism in operation. It is unconscionable to continue to perpetuate failure in the schools by continuing to use an obsolete, European model with its accompanying oppressive tests, and then to say that minority children have failed the work because they are not like those in control of the design of educational programs; that is, they have not been through the cloning process; they are not exact duplicates in looks, in learning styles, in customs, in history, of those in control of the world.

Therefore, we must consider the possibility of the impact of self-serving interests in the form of political ambitions and the acquisition of money through higher paying positions, as a partial motivation for the sell-out of Black interests by other Blacks.

Chapter XII presents the findings of the study and conclusions derived from the findings.

FOOTNOTES — CHAPTER XI

1. Interview with William Simons, President, D.C. Teachers Union, Washington, D.C., 29 November 1977.

2. Interview with Napoleon Lewis, Regional Superintendent, Washington, D.C., 9 October 1977.

3. Interview with Gilbert Diggs, D.C. Board of Education member, Washington, D.C., 30 September 1977.

4. Interview with James Williams, Deputy Superintendent, Washington, D.C., 14 December 1977.

5. John Matthews, "School Rift Doesn't Bother Status Quo," Washington Star, 11 May 1975.

6. "Transcript of the Twenty-Third (Special) Meeting of the Board of Education," Washington, D.C., 9 October 1975, pp. 23-41.

7. Memorandum to Mrs. Virginia Morris, President, Board of Education from Mr. John Warren, Member, Board of Education, re: Document of Understanding Between the Board and Mr. Reed, 17 November 1975 with draft copy of Memorandum of Understanding Between the District of Columbia Board of Education and the Acting Superintendent of Schools.

8. "Transcript of the Fourth (Stated) Meeting of the D.C. Board of Education," Washington, D.C., 17 March 1976.

9. Interview with Gilbert Diggs, Regional Superintendent, Washington, D.C., 30 September 1977.

10. "Transcript of the Twenty-Fifth Meeting of the D.C. Board of Education," Washington, D.C., 19 November 1975, pp. 72-75.

11. "Transcript of the Fifteenth (Stated) Meeting of the D.C. Board of Education," Washington, D.C., 17 November 1976, pp. 11-23.

12. Vincent E. Reed, Superintendent of Schools, Alternative Plan for Equalizing Educational Resources (Washington, D.C.: Public Schools of the District of Columbia, May 1977), p. 18.

13. Vincent E. Reed, Meeting the Challenge - Annual Report of the Public Schools of the District of Columbia for 1976 (Washington, D.C.: Division of Communications and Public Relations, 1976), p. 25; see also: Vincent E. Reed, A Design for A Competency-Based Curriculum - Pre-Kindergarten - Grade Twelve, (Washington, D.C.: Public Schools of the District of Columbia, April 1976), p. 1.

14. Lawrence Feinberg, "D.C. Competency Curriculum Delayed," Washington Post, 8 April 1978.

15. Ibid.

16. Juan Williams, "Secret of a Senior Classman: He Doesn't Know How to Read," Washington Post, 30 April 1978. See also: Juan Williams, "Teaching: 'It's a Little Harder' Every Year," Washington Post, 3 May 1978; and Juan Williams, "Educators Seek Ways to Unravel Problems," Washington Post, 4 May 1978.

17. Vincent E. Reed, Superintendent of Schools, Alternative Plan for Equalizing Educational Resources, Washington, D.C.: Public Schools of the District of Columbia, May 1977, p. 5.

18. Memorandum to the Board of Education from Vincent E. Reed, Superintendent of Schools, 12 May 1977, p. 2.

19. Lawrence Feinberg, "Schools Told to Detail Wright Decree Problems," Washington Post, 7 August 1977.

20. Ibid.

21. Lawrence Feinberg, "Transfers of Teachers Drop in D.C.," *Washington Post*, 6 February 1978.

22. "Minutes of the Second Session of the Seventeenth (Special) Meeting of the Board of Education," Washington, D.C., 19 July 1972, pp. 43-44.

23. "Goals of the Board of Education," Washington, D.C. Public Schools of the District of Columbia, 15 January 1972, pp. 1-2.

24. Memorandum to All School Personnel from Barbara A. Sizemore, Superintendent of Schools, re: Decentralization, 11 July 1974.

25. Vincent E. Reed, *Decentralization Report Phase II*, Washington, D.C.: Public Schools of the District of Columbia, 28 May 1976, p. 4.

26. Interviews with Gary Freeman, Regional Superintendent, 6 October 1977, and Margaret Labat, Regional Superintendent, 18 November 1977.

27. For a more complete discussion, see Barbara A. Sizemore, "The Politics of Decentralization: A Case Study of the D.C. Public Schools, 1973-1976," Doctoral dissertation, University of Chicago, 1979.

28. *U.S. Code*, Title 31--Section 665, *D.C. Code*, Title 47-105.

29. *D.C. Code*, Title I-310.

30. Commissioner's Memorandum 74-164, 3 October 1974. See also: Letter to the DCBOE regarding the FY75 Expenditure Plan (Revision III), from Barbara A. Sizemore, Superintendent of Schools, 5 December 1974.

31. Memorandum to Mr. Julius W. Hobson, Jr., Vice President, Board of Education, from Barbara A. Sizemore, Superintendent of Schools, 7 August 1975.

32. James L. Williams, <u>Administrative Reorganization and Major Responsibilities of Management Services of the DCPS</u>, Part I, Washington, D.C.: DCPS, May 1974.

33. "Report of the Committee on School Finance to the Board of Education of the District of Columbia," 16 June 1976. See also: "Transcript of the Eighth (Stated) Meeting of the D.C. Board of Education," Washington, D.C., 16 June 1976, pp. 163-168.

34. "Transcript of the Eleventh (Stated) Meeting of the Board of Education," Washington, D.C., 15 September 1976, pp. 40-46.

35. Motion for Preliminary Injunction and Memorandum of Points and Authorities in Support of Motions for Temporary Restraining Order and Preliminary Injunction, 1976.

36. Telephone conversation between writer and Barbara Simmons, D.C. School Board member, Washington, D.C., 2 October 1978.

37. "Transcript of the Twelfth Special (Emergency) Meeting of the D.C. Board of Education," Washington, D.C., 27 September 1976, p. 37.

38. Ibid., p. 30.

39. Interview with Vincent Reed, Superintendent of D.C. Public Schools, Washington, D.C., 5 December 1977.

40. Memorandum to Mr. James L. Williams, Deputy Superintendent for Management Services, from Ernest E. Sargent, Director of Finance, re: Financial Management in the School System

Requires Proper Coordination and Adequate Follow-Up Procedures, 4 February 1974.

41. Memorandum to Mr. James L. Williams, Deputy Superintendent for Management Services, from Ernest E. Sargent, Director of Finance, 20 February 1974; Memorandum to Mr. James L. Williams, Deputy Superintendent, from Ernest E. Sargent, Director of Finance, re: Status of Appropriation Report as of 31 January, 1 March 1974.

42. Memorandum to Mr. James L. Williams, Deputy Superintendent, from Ernest E. Sargent, Director of Finance, re: Mismatched Personnel Account Codes, 27 March 1974.

43. Memorandum to Mr. Edward G. Winner, Director of Budget, from Ernest E. Sargent, Director of Finance, re: Allotment Changes, 10 May 1974.

44. Memorandum to Mr. Edward Winner, Budget Director, from Ernest E. Sargent, Director of Finance, re: Your Memorandum dated 29 April 1974 - Allotment Changes, 6 May 1974.

45. Memorandum to Mr. James L. Williams, from Ernest E. Sargent, Director of Finance, re: FY74 Reprogramming, 3 June 1974.

46. Memorandum to Mr. James L. Williams, Deputy Superintendent, from Barbara A. Sizemore, Superintendent of Schools, re: Position Control, 20 March 1975.

47. Memorandum to Regional Superintendents from Edward G. Winner, Budget Director, re: Secondary Teaching Position Allotments: FY76, 6 August 1975.

48. See Barbara A. Sizemore, "The Politics of Decentralization: A Case Study of the D.C. Public Schools, 1973-1976," Doctoral dissertation, University of Chicago, 1979.

49. Letter to Mrs. Barbara A. Sizemore from Edward G. Winner, Deputy Superintendent, 31 May 1977, and sent to this writer by Mrs. Sizemore.

50. Interview with Gilbert Diggs, Regional Superintendent, Washington, D.C., 30 September 1977.

51. Barbara A. Sizemore, Superintendent's 120-Day Report, Washington, D.C.: Public Schools of the District of Columbia, March 1974.

52. Statement by Barbara A. Sizemore, "A Retreat From Progress: Back to the Basics?," read at a DCBOE community meeting, undated (a copy given to this writer by Barbara Simmons is ink dated 3 December 1975).

53. "What's Wrong with Standardized Testing?," Today's Education, March-April 1977, p. 37.

54. Edwin F. Taylor, "The Looking-Glass World of Testing," Ibid., p. 42.

55. Christopher Jencks, "The Wrong Answer for Schools is: Back to Basics," Washington Post, 19 February 1978.

56. Chuck Stone, "A Black Paper: Standardized Tests: True or False," The Black Collegian (November/December 1975), pp. 44-56. Reference to this article appears in Barbara A. Sizemore, "A Retreat from Progress: Back to the Basics?"

57. "350 Attend Conference on Testing Reform Strategies," The Testing Digest, Spring 1980, p. 13.

58. Steve Solomon, "The Nader Report on ETS," Ibid., p. 9.

59. Robert L. Williams, "The Politics of I.Q., Racism and Power," The Journal of Afro-American Issues 3 (Winter 1975), p. 1.

Reference to this article appears in Barbara A. Sizemore, "A Retreat from Progress: Back to the Basics?"

60. Lawrence Feinberg and Lily Ju-li Dow, "Schools Open Next Thursday," Washington Post, 31 August 1978.

61. Editorial, "Vincent Reed and The Three Rs," Washington Post, 14 September 1976.

62. Lawrence Feinberg, "D.C. Schools: A Time For Optimism," Washington Post, 3 January 1977.

CHAPTER XII

SUMMARY AND CONCLUSIONS

## Introduction

Six questions were posed in Chapter II of the study, to which the answers were explored in the data collected and analyzed. The essential questions considered were:

1. What is policy-making within the framework of superintendent-school board relations?

2. What is administration within the framework of superintendent-school board relations?

3. What factors precipitated conflict between the policy makers and the central administration of the DCPS system?

    a. Who were the major actors in the conflict between the superintendent and the board of education?

    b. Out of what educational issues did the conflict evolve?

    c. What intervening social, political and/or economic factors compounded the conflict?

    d. What external pressures impinged on the decision-making unit to compound the conflict?

4. What policy evolved?

5. How was the conflict resolved?

6. What were the outcomes of the change in policy?

In exploring question three above, we used seven propositions to help clarify the examination of the issues involved in the conflict. The seven propositions used for exploratory purposes were:

1. If the school board has a dependency relationship with an agency of higher authoity, it will establish an adversarial relationship with the superintendent and use rules and regulations to maintain control of school superintendents.

2. If there are drastic changes in the socioeconomic condition of the student body resulting in rapid changes in superintendents and school board members, goals will shift causing strain in superintendent-school board relations.

3. If school board members see their loyalties as being with big business interests in the community, they will succumb to these pressures and make decisions acceptable to big business interests rather than to their historically powerless poor constituents, even when they are of the same racial group.

4. If change is desired, school board members will select superintendents from outside the school system. Conversely, if maintenance of the status quo is desired, school board members will select superintendents from inside the system.

5. If school board members view their school board positions as a steppingstone to

higher political offices, they will make political decisions rather than educational ones.

6. If school board members are confused about their role, they will usurp the prerogatives of the superintendent and interfere with the day-to-day operation of the school system rather than focus on making policy decisions.

7. If there is sexism in the school system, school board members will require more from a female superintendent than from a male superintendent.

## What is policy-making within the framework of superintendent-school board relations?

As indicated in Chapter II sociologists Kaplan, C. Wright Mills and Bierstedt seem to feel that power is inherent in the ability to make decisions which have major consequences. Certainly the fact was established throughout the study that each board was involved in making policy decisions which committed the school system to a certain direction in the spending priorities as, for example, in terms of which programs were supported, who was hired, how staff was deployed, and what equipment and materials were purchased. Proof of this point certainly was observed in the fight that Hugh Scott and his board had over the appointment of a management assistant and the controversy over the plan to eliminate administrators because of the $3.7 million projected deficit discussed in Chapter III. More proof was offered in Chapter IV as could be observed in regard to the appointment of additional board staff out of Title V funds even though Superintendent Scott objected to this use of school system funds as did Mattie Taylor, a board member who felt that these funds could be better used for positions on the superintendent's staff. Certainly the opposition to Hansen's track plan and his subsequent resignation because of the opposition discussed in Chapter V is proof of the board's power to make decisions about which programs to fund and who to retain. Also, the termination of Hansen, the hiring and termination of Manning, Scott and Sizemore, as discussed specifically in Chapters V and IX, are further proof that policy decisions made by the various boards committed the school system to a certain direction in the use of funds in terms of programs, staff and so on. And, certainly if more proof is still needed, the entire discussion in Chapter VIII regarding the DCYOP case, the General Counsel dispute and the budget/management dispute provides overwhelming evidence of this point.

## What is administration within the framework of superintendent-school board relations?

Evidence was offered from Getzels and Allison in Chapter I that even though it is often said that the board makes policy and the superintendent executes it, it is seldom this cut and dried since board members seek the help of superintendents in formulating policy. Superintendents, in fact, furnish information to the board and recommend policy. Simon points up the ambiguity of the concept of authority. He says that authority to make policy decisions is usually vested in boards of education and administration usually focuses on processes and methods of getting the job done. Simon acknowledged though that operationally decision-making involves both deciding and doing as noted in Chapter II, titled "An Outline of a Theory."

In Chapter IV, titled "Authority, Function, Structure," it was noted that Section 31-103 of the D.C. Code calls attention to the fact that the board determines questions of general policy relating to the schools, appoints the executive officers, defines their duties, and directs expenditures. Elsewhere in the Code, it says that the board may delegate specific authority for the superintendent to act. The problem with the DCBOE, it was proved, was that it was hard for board members to delegate specific authority in certain matters to superintendents to handle the day-to-day operation of the school system.

Both the documentation taken from transcripts, minutes, memoranda and interview data provides absolute proof that the DCBOE never clearly defined for itself where to draw the line between policy-making and administration. For instance, in the matter of implementing the Ten Priority Goals discussed in Chapter V, some board members and Superintendent Scott expressed concern about whether he would be given authority to act on the goals once they were approved. In fact, board members Cassell and Barry had problems with giving the superintendent authority to reprogram or redirect funds. In Chapter VII, titled "Board Profiles, Motives, Leadership Styles, Role Conflict, Membership Change," it was shown that Hobson, Sr. felt that unless the school administration changed, board members needed to become experts in administration as well as in policy-making. Superintendent Scott expressed the need to have school board rules make a clearer distinction between policy and administration. He presented several instances where he felt that the school board interfered in matters which were administrative such as making major insertions, deletions and changes in curriculum documents, reducing support services to the school's music program, and shifting these funds to the DCYOP. Board members Hobson, Jr. and Tirana, James Williams, former deputy superintendent, and Superintendent Reed revealed in interview data that they believed the board interfered in the day-to-day operation of the schools. Kemp believed that the board had to monitor the administration because the parents he represented did not respect the difference between policy and administration. Martha Swaim also expressed the opinion that board members must become involved in administration. She presented several cases in a Bulletin Board article to support her contention. The minutes of the January 17, 1973 board meeting revealed that several citizens were also of the opinion that the board interfered in administration. And certainly Barbara Sizemore and several board members made frequent references to the board's interference in administration as revealed in Chapter VIII, "Case Studies of the Decision-Making Process - 1973-75." All of the above provided overwhelming evidence of this problem.

<u>What factors precipitated conflict between the policy-makers and the central administration of the DCPS system?</u>

Data in the study spoke to who the major actors were, the educational issues out of which the conflict evolved, the intervening social, political and economic factors which compounded the conflict and the external pressures which compounded the conflict. Focus on the seven propositions will also help us see more clearly the evidence provided.

The major actors in our study are the superintendents, administrative officers, and school board members. Secondary actors include groups, organizations and individual citizens in the District. The tertiary level of characters may be said to include the mayor, city council and the courts.

Evidence offered in Chapter VIII proved that in Sizemore's case the DCYOP was of paramount importance in the conflict and in a sense hardened the board's attitude against the superintendent. The attitude was so set that whatever she proposed subsequently, as described in the case study of the budget/management dispute, was rejected by those Black board members who seemingly were influenced by the monied interests in the District such as Barry, Mason, Hobson, Jr. and Morris (Chapters VII, VIII and IX), and the white board members. These board members were also determined to maintain the status quo in the system, despite the approximately 96 percent Black student population,

for the returning middle class whites and some
Blacks as substantiated by the data in this chapter.

Decentralization was another significant educational issue which caused conflict in Scott's situation because he moved too slowly. The data in Chapter VI speaks for itself. Decentralization was again the issue in Sizemore's case because she moved too swiftly. Data in Chapter VIII shows conclusively that her budget plan of 1976 to support decentralization was rejected by the board.

Dependent relationship --

Social, political and/or economic factors did intervene to compound the conflict in school superintendent-school board relations. It was adequately proved in Chapter III, "Race, Class, Sex, and Colonial Status," that the board was powerless in terms of control of its finances, which really decided which programs would or would not be supported. The data confirmed that the mayor and the city council determined what the school system's budget would be in total dollars. This determination decided the limits of the budget even before it got to the congressional committees. The data suggested that this frustration experienced by the city governing unit seeped down to envelop the school board thus frustrating them into using board rules and regulations to control how the superintendents used the funds allocated.

Racism --

Data presented in Chapter III also proved that race was a factor in all matters, and that taken collectively the several incidents and situations -- such as the Marian Anderson incident, threats to reduce appropriations for District schools after distribution of the Intergroup Education Handbook in 1947, the maintenance of a segregated school system until 1954, Hansen's track system, the racial altercation at the stadium on Thanksgiving Day in 1962, the need for the Hobson v

Hansen case and so forth -- all translate into racism. The data show that this factor certainly disrupted the relationship Superintendent Hansen had with his Black board members and some liberal white ones. The factor of classism was evident in terms of the vast number of poor Blacks, in particular, who were relegated to the lowest educational track.

Racism became evident in the opinions and actions of some board members during the superintendent selection process for Scott and Sizemore as discussed in Chapter V. As for instance, Swaim's August 7, 1973 letter is expressive in her non-support of Sizemore. It also reveals her preference for a person who had decentralized, thus successfully eliminating all of the Black candidates.

The European thrust which totally excluded any Black musical expression of the DCYOP and the location of the program in the whiter section of the District was thought to have racist overtones by Superintendent Sizemore. This was expressed in her testimony at the July 2, 1974 special meeting of the board, analyzed in Chapter VIII. Data in that chapter document how this educational program, in particular, caused conflict in superintendent-school board relations.

As indicated in Chapter VI, titled "Goal Setting," drastic changes in the socio-economic condition of the student body resulted in rapid changes in superintendents and school board members. These changes caused shifts in the school system's goals causing strain in superintendent-school board relations as reflected in the shift from Hansen's Track System, and the Clark Plan (AAP) left for Scott to implement. We see evidence of this again in Scott's decentralization effort as well as Sizemore's administrative decentralization into six regions. The change in goals was also reflected in Sizemore's efforts to change the curriculum as described in Chapters V and VIII.

It was proved also that these goals changed as school board members changed starting with the increase of Black members on the school board in 1967 when for the first time in the history of the DCPSS, the board was majority Black. Right away this Black majority began agitating to eliminate the track system which caused conflict with white Superintendent Hansen as authenticated with data in Chapter III. Sizemore had four boards in two years. Goals shifted from an emphasis on decentralization and other changes in order to maintain the status quo. Data in Chapter VIII substantiate this.

Sexism --

Sexism was noted in the data provided about the selection of principals in Chapter III, titled "Race, Class, Sex, and Colonial Status." Chapter V, titled "Selection and Termination Processes - 1969-73," revealed data that some board members definitely preferred a male superintendent. Therefore, it might be deduced that the fact that Sizemore was a female may have been a problem for those board members.

Pressure and influence --

Data provided in Chapter VII, titled "Board Profile, Motives, Leadership Styles, Role Conflict, Membership Changes," support the observation that it might be possible to infer that large contributors to a politician's campaign expect to be able to influence the way that politician votes on issues of concern to the contributors. In light of this, then, we might assume that Barry, for example, was influenced by big business contributors to maintain the contract with the Friends of the DCYOP and to give public school money away to other private enterprises. Kemp, Treanor, Mason and Swaim, who also received contributions from the business sector, might also have been influenced to support the contract with the Friends group. And even Morris might have eventually been influenced by

Mason who contributed to her campaign. Therefore, we may deduce that if school board members see their loyalties as being with big business interests in the community, they will make decisions acceptable to big business interests, rather than to their historically powerless poor constituents, even when they are of the same racial group. Mason and Morris are Black.

Chapter IX, titled, "Group Pressures on the Decision-Making Process--1973-75," bears witness to the fact that outside pressures in the form of Congress, the White House, the courts, influential community groups and the press impinged on the decision-making unit to compound the conflict. That chapter contained overwhelming evidence to this effect.

Role conflict --

Data in Chapter VII also substantiate that role conflict existed in terms of the relationship which D.C. board members had with their superintendents. Information on this point is covered to some extent in the section of that chapter on "Administration." A very specific instance of this was discussed in Chapter VIII, titled "Case Studies of the Decision-Making Process--1973-75." Here, reference was made to the withdrawal of the budgetary process from the purview of the superintendent. Authority to do so was given to a board committee. This usurped administrative authority and prerogatives inherent in the position of superintendent and rendered the superintendent without leadership authority. Superintendent Sizemore's authority to deal directly with the corporation counsel was also withdrawn by the president of the board, Virginia Morris. These incidents prove the point that if school board members are confused about their role, they will usurp the prerogatives of the superintendent and interfere with the day-to-day operation of the school system rather than focus on making policy decisions.

Motives --

As early as 1967 a Washington Afro-American article pointed to political maneuvering as seeming more important than the problem of education. Reference to political maneuvering was noted in the board minutes of February 12, 1969. Citizens at the January 17, 1973 board meeting also spoke to this issue.

Data from interviews with several board members presented in Chapter IV in regard to how decisions were made show clearly that many felt that other board members made political rather than educational decisions. Taylor and Hobson spoke of this in the case of Barry. Hobson spotlighted Mason and Kane as engaging in politics. Hobson and Simmons spoke to the political maneuvering of Morris. And Warren felt Evans engaged in politics when making committee assignments.

Chapter VII also documents, with interview data and data obtained from school board election campaign contribution folders, enough information for us to draw some conclusions about the motives of citizens in seeking membership on the DCBOE. Interview data provided by seven board members revealed that they joined the school board for altruistic reasons. Nonetheless, the subsequent behavior of some board members revealed that there may have been other reasons. In fact, at the January 20, 1974 meeting some voiced their objection to having to resign from the board before running for another office. Again, it was pointed up in Chapter VII that Evans, Cassell and Taylor opinioned in their interview that the Barry board was highly political and that Barry was especially so. Kemp expressed the opinion that in Morris' time the board was more political. The fact that Barry spent more than $17,000.00 and Mason $7,000.00 for their school board campaigns is significant. The average amount spent for at-large seats was $5,000.00. At least six board members did campaign for a higher office. Barry,

Swaim, Rosenfield, Mason, Kane and Morris all ran for another political office. Barry, Swaim, Mason and Kane were elected to the city council. Barry also ran for and became mayor of the District of Columbia.

Thus the data provide conclusive evidence that some school board members may have viewed their school board positions as a steppingstone to a higher political office, and therefore may have made political decisions rather than educational ones.

Outsiders vs. insiders --

The data provided in Chapter V, titled "Selection and Termination Process--1969-73," confirm the fact that board members chose outsiders when they wanted changes to occur in the system. These outsiders were Manning, Scott and Sizemore. Data presented in Chapter XI, titled "School System Outcomes," confirm the fact that when board members wanted to maintain the status quo they selected an insider as superintendent. This insider was Reed.

The interview data also recorded in Chapter V provide the opinions of two regional superintendents: Napoleon Lewis and Gilbert Diggs. Both believe that the fact that Sizemore was an outsider accounted for much of her trouble.

What policy evolved?

The policy which evolved from the conflict was to maintain the status quo as revealed by data in Chapter VIII, titled "Case Studies of the Decision-Making Process--1973-75." The case study about the budget/management dispute denotes the change from providing funds for decentralization and curriculum changes to the maintenance of the obsolete administrative structure and the mono-lingual, mono-cultural curriculum.

How was the conflict resolved?

Resolution of the conflict came in the form of the firing of Superintendent Sizemore focused upon in Chapter X, titled "Termination Process, 1975." Evidence was presented which documented the cunning way Mason and Hobson searched the minutes and transcripts for evidence of board policy not yet completed by Sizemore. Also in this regard, Morris rushed through a bogus evaluation process based on items in an instrument designed for a situation in another school system. The result, of course, was the start of the process to fire the superintendent soon after Sizemore made a speech in April 1975 revealing the plan of whites to take back the city. Sizemore was consequently fired in October 1975 after a long dismissal hearing.

What were the outcomes of the change in policy?

Chapter XI, titled "School System Outcomes," presented data which proved that the new superintendent, Vincent Reed, implemented a traditional curriculum noted as CBC with a back to basics thrust, and an equalization approach which was the same as Scott's in 1972. He also returned to a centralized administrative structure by maintaining the form of the six regions but removing the authority given to regional superintendents by Mrs. Sizemore.

Curriculum innovations made or proposed by Sizemore no longer exist or some that exist are no longer recognizable. Needless to say though, many of the internal management improvements which Sizemore and Williams made were claimed by the new administration.

Finally, Mrs. Sizemore came into the superintendency of the DCPSS when there was a legacy of confusion in the relationship between the school board and the school superintendent. Confusion still remains in that relationship. Sizemore performed her task of changing the system while she was employed. She was a catalyst for change. If this is true, and according to the evidence it is, then she fulfilled her mandate from the board that appointed her in 1973. And, as Sizemore said in her initial public interview, any process of change causes disruption. Unfortunately, some of the people who thought they wanted change saw that it upset their political wishes and therefore reneged on their original commitment.

A very fundamental question began to emerge during the administrations prior to Sizemore's and arose to the crest of the wave between 1973-75. This question was: why change the District school system to benefit the Black poor? -- especially since the intention of the whites was to take back the city from the over 70 percent Black majority. An analysis of a number of news articles between 1976 and 1978 clarified this issue. For instance, one article indicated that a theorist on the recovery of American cities proposed that poor people in the cities be moved away from the center, so as to clear the area for white collar workers employed downtown.[1] A second article indicated that even though suburbanites were getting about one-half of the special public works pay checks provided to relieve unemployment in the District of Columbia, city officials maintained that the program was successful for city residents.[2] Obviously, city officials are not too concerned about the poor. A third article informs the public that inner city neighborhoods are again becoming fashionable places in which to live as middle class professionals return from the suburbs.[3] It is clear again that few love the poor. A fourth article explains that blockbusting in the District means that whites are moving into Black neighborhoods, and that it is no longer a trickle but a surge created by real estate brokers, absentee land owners and the District government.[4] A fifth article indicates that people in the city feel that there is a trend to push people out of their neighborhoods as upper and middle income people, especially whites, move back into the inner city.[5]

Lastly, for purposes here, another article deals with three choices which the District leaders have. The first choice briefly discussed suggests that the concerns of the haves can be ignored and the city therefore abandoned to the have-nots, making it all Black and entirely dependent financially on the federal government. The second choice suggests that the poor can be driven out by cutting back on public services and giving the affluent a tax break. Thirdly, there is the choice of finding a formula to ensure a mix of the poor, the middle income and the rich.[6] Interestingly, these news articles were now saying the same thing that Sizemore predicted in 1975.

It was she who was the siren which awakened the Black poor in 1975 as to what their fate might be in the District. Therefore, she had to be discredited and removed. She had to be silenced. The April 1975 speech was too soon to warn the people, and by the time Black people really woke up to what was happening to them, large numbers of them had already been removed from the city by one means or another. Barbara Sizemore's conclusions and assertions were a vision of what could be if fundamental changes were made and given a chance to work. Her successor's conclusions and assertions and educational program built upon the status quo, is a reflection of <u>what exists</u>.

Sizemore was in the center of a controversy that extended way beyond that of the DCBOE. She was the center of a controversy that had polarized the entire community into two opposing camps of a power contest for the control of the District. When she tried to tighten her administrative control over the DCPSS as part of the strategy in a fight to change the school system and make it responsive to poor Black children, she involved herself in a web of power that extended far beyond the school system and out into the city. This, then, exploded into a political struggle with the powerful white business interests. Only a few Black people were even aware of what was happening and lent their support to her effort to make the District school system a model for the nation. This was the first step in making the District, a city 72 percent Black, a showcase of how people power could transform a corrupt city into a place where justice for all prevailed. In this endeavor, Barbara Sizemore took on not only the DCBOE but the city government and the Congress. Unfortunately, her troops ran scared and took cover in the camps of the oppressors. Therefore, it is necessary for anyone studying the D.C. public school situation, especially during 1973-75, to recognize and deal with the larger political ramifications of the situation and not just try to examine the educational issues in isolation of the external environmental factors that impacted on the school system.

The confusion in superintendent-school board relations in Washington, D.C. may stem from the fact that a new model in school governance has evolved. Traditionally, the structure under which school districts operated was vertical. In essence, the board of education was primarily a policy-making body. The board hired a superintendent to administer the school. The authority was more or less clear.

Today, the structure is similar to a "federalized" model with three components: (1) the board of education; (2) the superintendent; and (3) the quasi-judicial. As can be noted in the study, the board takes on many aspects of a legislative body (the Congress). It views the superintendent and the administrative staff as the "executive branch" (the President). Examples of the activity engaged in by the third branch, the quasi-judicial, and its effects on the day-to-day operation of the school system are the court orders, i.e. the 1954 Supreme Court decision on desegregation of schools, the Wright decree on equalization of educational resources and the Waddy decree on special education. Other examples include the citizen advisory groups and other interest groups such as the

Friends of the DCYOP and the DCCBPE.

Actually, the DCBOE took on a new role when it became an elected body. Between 1971 and 1975, board candidates spent an aggregate amount in excess of $167,000.00 for their campaigns to be elected to a nonpaying position.

Obviously, those who gave generously to school board members' campaigns often feel candidates owe their special interests some special consideration as, for example, board of trade members, some of whom are, or their wives are, members of DCCBPE or perhaps involved in some way in the DCYOP.

Further, the DCBOE behaves as if it were a legislative body with its own staff which is independent of the established administrative structure. Note the conflict between Splitt, the board's lawyer, and Superintendent Sizemore as to their respective authority in the DCYOP case. Additionally, the board has standing committees that have a direct voice in the day-to-day operational decisions of the school system -- for example, the Committee on Educational Programs, appointed in 1975 under Morris, whose duties concerned curriculum in terms of what was taught and how it was taught. As noted, the DCBOE also conducts legislative hearings on matters of concern to the public. Further, as Swaim and Kemp indicated in Chapter II, when parents call board members the complaint is often handled personally rather than referred to the superintendent as was done in the past.

School board meetings are held much more frequently than in the past; for example, there are the monthly regularly stated board meetings, the monthly community meetings, and closed sessions, in addition to committee meetings. In this new style of school governance, the role of a board member is very time-consuming. Often his/her role also brings a high degree of visibility as in the case of Barry, Swaim, Morris and Kane, in particular. This, then, makes the role of school board member very attractive for those members who are politically ambitious for other elected positions. As previously noted, Barry and Mason were elected to the city council and Barry later became mayor. Kane recently was elected to the city council. Both Rosenfield and Swaim campaigned for the city council but did not win. Morris campaigned for an Advisory Neighborhood Council seat and lost.

The situation described above caused conflict in superintendent-school board relations in D.C. Some board members played to the grandstand rather than functioning as advocates for the youngsters in the school as the superintendent did.

Indeed, the board generally avoids the label "rubber stamp" by playing an adversarial role. They interrogate the superintendent and school administrators regarding recommendations brought to them through the committee structure. This posturing as independent thinkers for the benefit of their constituencies brings about discord in superintendent-school board relations as, for example, in the budget/management case in regard to the allocation of money by the board majority to the non-legislated pre-kindergarten classes rather than to the board-adopted policy of decentralizing the school system through the adoption of the <u>120 Day Report</u>.

And even though the administration presents various options for board approval as in the DCYOP case, in regard to use of the $150,500.00, and the budget/management case in regard to elimination of the budgetary problems brought about by the mayor's freeze of 1974, the board accepted neither option in either case, but proposed its own solutions which did not take into account all of the problems involved. Thus, dissension in the policy-making unit became the rule rather than the exception in 1973-75. Therefore, this new role of the board of education or new style of governance generally has not thus far been eliminated of its dysfunctional aspects enough for it to be useful in the DCPS system.[7]

Some suggestions which may help this new style of governance to be less an impetus for confrontation for confrontation's sake are these offered next.

## Alternative Strategies

### Elect the superintendent

First, in recognition of the force of politics in the educational enterprise, it seems reasonable to suggest that superintendents be elected by the citizens to operate a school system to their liking.[8] Naturally, when this is no longer the case, the citizens can then vote the superintendent out of office as they now do board members. It becomes more and more clear as we examine in-depth the decision-making process in school systems such as the D.C. one, that it is not so much an educational leader being called for as it is a politician -- one who can manipulate, negotiate, and compromise on principles. What seems needed is a person who can spend time talking to everyone, which naturally consumes any time for in-depth consideration of educational theory and practice, any consideration of human growth and development, any consideration of the benefits of including ethnic content in curricula, any thought of how children fail and why, and any consideration of the oppression of standardized tests normed on white middle-class children and unrelated to the learnings of poor Black children.

The politically chosen superintendent would then have eons of time to lunch with Congressmen, Senators or their aides, city government officials, or others, to obtain adequate funds and, perhaps, even surplus funds to finance status quo programs.

On the other hand, we can paint another scenario -- this one a more positive reflection of a superintendent elected by the citizens. The election process would certainly move the superintendent out from under the hammer of board members.

They would be on a par with each other. Then, the
superintendent would not have to operate under the
threat of the board's firing. An educationally
inclined politically selected superintendent could
then make changes whether they were entirely concurred with by the majority members of the board or
not and take her or his chances with the citizens
at the next election. There would be room within
the role of superintendent to respond to citizens'
desires when it was found that the majority of the
board was in fact representing the powerful business
interests in a community. Even this approach to
the selection of a superintendent has a two-edged
sword though. In a majority white community, the
superintendent elected might always be white and
might always be attuned to the interests of white
and affluent citizens to the exclusion of poor and
minority citizens. But there is still the very
real possibility that in a community predominantly
Black and poor, like Washington, D.C., the citizens
may seek a different solution to their educational
problems. Thus, the election process would give
them an opportunity to exercise this right. The
point in all of this is to give the people another
option which may prove to be more beneficial to
their needs.

Clarify roles and responsibilities

A second recommendation growing out of this
case study of superintendent-school board relations
has to do with the ambiguities inherent in the
roles and responsibilities of the D.C. board of
education and the superintendent of schools. An
advisory commission on Educational Law Revision
was established by the DCBOE in 1975. The board
received their report dated November 2, 1976, which
spoke to the issue of board operations, policies,
rules and legislation. The recommendations of the
commission are being recommended here for adoption
by school systems with similar problems. Commission members noted that in the absence of a clearly
defined statement of roles and responsibilities,
there was room for misunderstanding and confusion

within the D.C. public school system. Hence, the commission dealt specifically with Title 31 of the D.C. Code and the D.C. Administrative Procedures Act.

In reference to Title 31 of the D.C. Code, it was noted that the Code was poorly organized, ambiguous, archaic in some of its provisions, and failed to require a system of accountability for school officials. Therefore, the commission recommended the following: (1) code organization; (2) differentiated and well-defined legislative functions of the board and administrative/executive functions of the superintendent; (3) description of specific powers with respect to personnel; (4) description of a system of accountability; and (5) revisions to reflect recent changes in educational legislation.

Recommendations were also made to ensure that the board complied with the mandates of the D.C. Administrative Procedures Act.

Section II of the commission's report dealt specifically with the subject of this study -- board-superintendent relations. In this regard, it was noted that "no formal policy exists which clearly delineates the roles and responsibilities of the Board of Education (or) Superintendent in relation to each other." In essence, the commission recommended that the legislation of policies is the function of the board and the execution of those policies is the responsibility of the superintendent. It was noted that administrative decisions were within the purview of the superintendent, that the superintendent may ask for guidance from the board but was obligated to keep the board informed with respect to matters of operation. Noted also was the superintendent's role in assisting the board in changing or setting new policies through the preparation of new statements or recommendations in line with new problems or changed circumstances. In this regard, it was noted that the board was obligated to consider the opinions of the superintendent in its deliberations.

In the area of superintendent evaluation, another area dealt with in this study, it was recommended that a formal procedure be implemented based on mutually agreed-upon criteria, a procedure not adhered to in the Sizemore termination process.

Additionally, the commission recommended that a code of ethics be adopted and disseminated by the board against which board members and the public could evaluate their performance.

One very real problem also pointed up in this study was the information requests of individual board members. The commission's report stated as follows: "Currently, no system for the prioritization and processing of these 'constituent-related' information requests made by individual Board members exists." Also dealt with were "agenda-related" information requests. Reasonable procedures were recommended for handling both of these problem areas. For the former, the pertinent recommendation allowed the superintendent to establish procedures for handling them. For the latter, board approval had to be secured before requests could be acted upon.

In the area of community involvement, the commission's recommendations included: (1) the issuance of a statement by the board at the beginning of the year informing the public of the goals and objectives of the school system; (2) the use of the local media; (3) the presentation of a joint statement by the board and superintendent on the "State of the Schools" at the end of each school year; (4) the dissemination of an information handbook; (5) the use of the ombudsman concept to respond to the needs of students, parents and staff; (6) the use of the Anacostia school board as a possible model to develop a policy with regard to local school boards; (7) the restructure of board meeting agendas so that educational issues appear early in the meeting; and (8) the continuance of regional and community board meetings, the 21-member planning committee for building programs, school-by-school budgeting, and the publication of board agendas in advance.

The critical area of intergovernmental relations was also dealt with. Of particular relevance to this study was the commission's recommendation relative to the employment of independent counsel by the board. The commission agreed that a continued investigation of this possibility was necessary. Nonetheless, it did not deal with the more critical issue of legal counsel for the board and a separate legal counsel for the superintendent which arose in 1974.[9] Perhaps this is because the present superintendent is allowed his own separate legal counsel.

## Eliminate ambiguities between school codes, the chief executive's contract and actual practice

An interview with the most recent former superintendent of the D.C. public schools, Mrs. Barbara A. Sizemore, revealed some ambiguities and inconsistencies between the D.C. Code, Title 31, the superintendent's contract, and actual practice.[10] For example, she pointed out that the superintendent was not as free to hire personnel as it appeared at first blush. Paragraph 4 of the superintendent's contract reads:

> The Superintendent will have complete freedom to organize, reorganize, and arrange the administrative and supervisory staff, including instruction and business affairs, which in her judgment best serves the District of Columbia Public Schools. The responsibility for selection, placement, and transfer of personnel shall be vested in the Superintendent subject to approval by the Board.[11]

Board action of June 21, 1967, amended on October 18, 1967, delegated to the superintendent authority to appoint, promote, reassign, and process resignations of employees up to and including grades TSA-9* (Teachers' Salary Act) and GS-11 (General).[12] On the surface, it appears that any new superintendent has the power to appoint 98 percent of the staff. Actually though, at least 90 percent of those personnel was subject to union contract which the superintendent had to abide by. This certainly curtailed any firing of entrenched personnel and the rehiring of replacements since teachers and officers were guaranteed a grievance process through the board's contract with the unions. Therefore, in a very real sense, a superintendent's power was severely restricted by the board's agreement with the unions since union contracts supersede board policy. It is, therefore, recommended that union contracts and board policy be consistent.

Stabilize board membership

A third recommendation deals with stabilizing board membership so that the board does not constantly "re-invent the wheel." It might be that board members may be required to serve out their term of office, except in cases of illness or some other extreme circumstance, as a condition for election to the board. This will provide more continuity in policymaking and relations with the superintendent. It was noted in the study that board-superintendent relations conferences were not engaged in on a regular basis, as indicated in paragraph seven of the superintendent's contract.[13] A part of the problem seemed to stem from the fact that the board became involved in constantly replacing members who had left for either sickness, job requirements, running for city

---

*Includes teachers and other employees on the TSA-15 line up to assistant principals at TSA-8 as noted in Pub. Law 92-518, 92nd Congress, H. R. 16965, October 21, 1972, pp. 5-6.

council seats, or lack of funds to continue to serve. Added to the above was the normal process of running for reelection. Thus, in the case of Sizemore, the majority of conferences dealing with superintendent-school board relations were held after the majority of the board was determined to fire her.

## Remove ambiguities within the superintendent's contract

Another problem, which arose during the Sizemore administration and which needs to be dealt with, has to do with paragraph 10 of the superintendent's contract relative to attending appropriate professional meetings,[14] and paragraph three relative to undertaking consultative work, speaking engagements, writing, lecturing, or other professional duties and obligations.[15] Interestingly, the 1973 board sought a superintendent well-known for her scholarly pursuits, professional writing and lecturing capabilities -- one of the giants in the field of urban education. And then the board president of 1974, Virginia Morris, seemingly sought to circumscribe and even to abort Sizemore's continued service to the field in these areas.[16] Obviously, a clearer statement needs to be included in a superintendent's contract or the matter needs to be discussed with all members of the board, not just the board president who may have a less than broad view of the matter due to her/his personal interests and/or background, personal ambitions or even jealousy. Perhaps, then, such an avalanche of correspondence as Sizemore received would not be necessary about the matter of speaking engagements and attending professional meetings.

## Clearly define "control" of the school system

In summary, it is absolutely essential that a board of education not tell a superintendent how to carry out policy after the board sets it. Therefore, Title 31, Chapter 1, Section 101, of the

D.C. Code, which states that the control of the public schools of the District of Columbia is vested in the board of education, must not be interpreted in such a broad sense as to mean that the board will run the schools, will administer the schools. If the practice continues, as it occurred during the Sizemore administration, it leaves the superintendent in the untenable position of trying to implement board policy in the way the board says it must be done. Then if the procedure is unsuccessful, the superintendent has to take the blame -- be the scapegoat for the board's errors. Therefore, it is recommended that "control" be clearly defined to exclude the method of implementation of board policy.

FOOTNOTES                           CHAPTER XII


1.  Ernest Holsendolph, "Shift of Poor Urged Out
    of Center Cities," New York Times, 28 September 1976.

2.  Jack Eisen, "Suburbanites Get 51 Pct. of Jobs
    in D.C. Program," Washington Post, 23 June
    1978.

3.  David E. Anderson, "Neighborhood Movement
    Seeking Clout, Strategy," Washington Post,
    24 June 1978.

4.  R. J. Turner, "The Changing Face of D.C.
    Neighborhoods," Washington Post, 24 June 1978.

5.  Arlene Knighten, "Blacks Forced Out of D.C.,"
    Hilltop, Howard University, 2 December 1977.

6.  John Sansing, "Can Whites Survive in D.C. or
    Are We Going Toward a 'Chocolate City' and
    Vanilla Suburbs?," Washingtonian, October 1976.

7.  Some ideas in this section were triggered by
    a paper written by George C. Garver, "Changing
    Styles of School Governance," January 17, 1977,
    unpublished.

8.  A solution suggested by Mrs. Sizemore in her
    interview of 16 April 1978. See also: Bernard Watson, "Interview: Barbara Sizemore,"
    Cross Reference, May/June 1978, p. 236.

9.  Advisory Commission on Educational Law-
    Revision, Interim Report of the Advisory Commission on Educational Law Revision, Washington, D.C., 2 November 1976.

10. Interview with Barbara A. Sizemore, Superintendent of Schools, Washington, D.C., 16 April
    1978.

11. D.C. Public School System, The Superintendent's Contract, 6 September 1973, p. 2.

12. Memorandum to the Board of Education from Hilda Howland M. Mason, re: Delegation of Personnel Authority to the Superintendent, 16 June 1974.

13. D.C. Public School System, The Superintendent's Contract, 6 September 1973, p. 3.

14. Ibid., p. 4.

15. Ibid., p. 2.

16. See correspondence to Mrs. Virginia Morris, President, Board of Education, from Barbara A. Sizemore, Superintendent of Schools, 11 October 1974; Letter to Mrs. Barbara A. Sizemore, Superintendent of Schools, from Virginia Morris, President, 24 February 1975; Letter to Mrs. Virginia M. Morris, President, Board of Education, from Barbara A. Sizemore, Superintendent of Schools, 25 February 1975. Memorandum to Mrs. Virginia Morris, President, Board of Education, from Barbara A. Sizemore, Superintendent of Schools, 10 March 1975; Letter to Ms. Barbara A. Sizemore, Superintendent of Schools, from Virginia Morris, President, Board of Education, 11 March 1975. Memorandum to the Board of Education of the District of Columbia, from Barbara A. Sizemore, Superintendent of Schools, re: Response to Board President's Correspondence dated 11 March 1975, 19 March 1975. Memorandum to Barbara A. Sizemore, Superintendent of Schools, from Virginia Morris, President, Board of Education, re: Your Memorandum dated 24 June 1975, Relative to Requesting Clarification of Sick Leave in Advance, 24 June 1975; Memorandum to Mrs. Virginia Morris, President, Board of Education, from Barbara A. Sizemore, Superintendent of Schools, from Virginia Morris, President, Board of Education, re: Leave

Status as of 23 June 1975, 24 June 1975.
Memorandum to Ms. Barbara A. Sizemore, Superintendent of Schools, from Mrs. Virginia Morris, President, Board of Education, re: Leave status as of 23 June 1975, 23 June 1975. Memorandum to Mrs. Virginia Morris, President, Board of Education, from Ms. Barbara A. Sizemore, Superintendent, re: Leave status on 23 June 1975, 24 June 1975.

EPILOGUE

One synthesis of the data analyzed in the preceding pages and based on what is currently happening in the District and in the DCPSS, and which was also actually predicted by Barbara A. Sizemore when she was superintendent, can be illustrated in the form of a model. But first, let us review what Mrs. Sizemore said.

In her April 1975 speech, Mrs. Sizemore clearly described the situation when she said the following:

> Supported by the former Black Board President now a member of the City Council, this former Vice President of the Board of Education initiated a program which has become the blueprint for the actions of the present policy-making majority of the D.C. Board of Education: (1) the abolition of tenure so that the Black Administrators and Black teachers can be removed more easily upon the return of whites to the city; (2) the contracting out of sizeable sums of money to white organizations and institutions for services to Black students especially in areas where Black expertise is superior, i.e. dropouts and music; (3) the election of supporters of this viewpoint to the school board; (4) promotion and maintenance of the idea that Blacks are incompetent and/or inferior; (5) the rotation of the superintendency so that there will be no continuity of effort toward the improvement of the quality of education for the Black poor; and (6) the prevention of any change in the age-graded, monolingual, monocultural

hierarchical structure of the public schools which benefits affluent whites of European descent.[1]

Predictably, all of the above and much more have occurred in the D.C. public school system as the policy-making majority on the school board and the current superintendent, Vincent Reed, have systematically and seemingly in a reasonable fashion moved to concretize the design described by Mrs. Sizemore three years ago. The situation facing us can be encapsulated in the following political schema of education in the District in 1978.

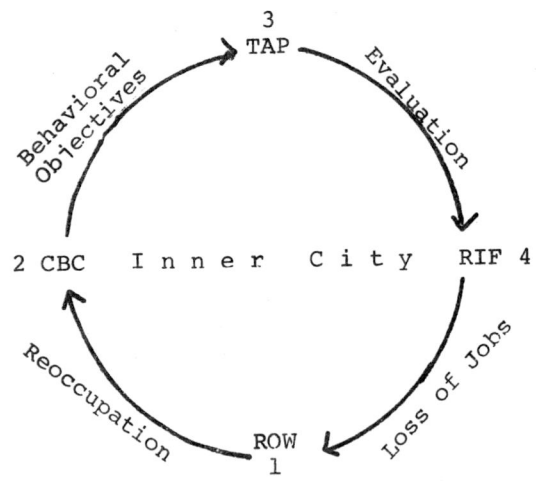

```
              3
              TAP
    Behavioral        Evaluation
    Objectives
2 CBC    I n n e r    C i t y    RIF 4
    Reoccupation      Loss of Jobs
              ROW
              1
```

ROW = Return Of Whites
CBC = Competency Based Curriculum
TAP = Teacher Appraisal Process
RIF = Reduction In Force

FIGURE 9

Design of Theory of Reoccupation

The above model (figure 9) is the design of a cyclic theory based on the belief or idea that whites will reclaim the inner city and the schools. Therefore, they must systematically and subtly remove Blacks from positions of (pseudo) power and leadership as administrators and teachers as well. Thus, whites have encouraged and supported Blacks in a school system design that will diminish the Black administrative and teaching staff with little or no real recourse for its victims. First, in 1976 came the introduction of a curriculum design based on the emotion ladden principles of accountability to dupe Black parents into believing that those in power are properly looking out for the right to a quality education for their children. The "back to the basics" curriculum program incorporates behavioral objectives set up by the teachers to waylay the claim that they are imposed from without so that uninitiated teachers can hang themselves. Then, in the fall of 1978, the Teacher Appraisal Process (TAP) was introduced as the next step in the conspiracy. Naturally, if a teacher does not achieve the behavioral objectives she/he set for her/him, the evaluation will be low. The third link in the chain around the teacher's economic future is presented in the form of a Reduction In Force (RIF) procedure which can easily be construed to mean an opportunity to get rid of "ineffective" teachers, by their own admission. Teachers were not able to effectively and efficiently bring students up to the behavioral objectives they themselves set and which were tested by the oppressive standardized tests, which they themselves accepted without protest as a necessary part of the "new" curriculum thrust. The clincher becomes the hiring of effective teachers after Black teachers have vacated the positions. Naturally, these will be white teachers since the curriculum is Anglo-Saxon Protestant oriented, more of the children will be white, and the complexion of the evaluators (supervisors, administrators) will have changed. And again, as in the integration myth where Blacks lost their jobs in the 60s, Blacks will have cut their own throats through their duplicity and acquiescence to the accountability myth.

Overlayed on this design is the present smokescreen of no union contract. Teachers are emotionally involved in this action as was displayed at the Wednesday night school board meeting of September 19, 1978, which I and my class in Conceptual Cases attended. Pickets at the board of education office and angry teachers chanting in unison, "no contract, no work," "no CBC, no ABCs," "Strike vote on Monday," were all a part of the scenario. Their emotions were so charged that they failed to see the more subtle design. The teachers failed to see that contract or no contract, they will not have jobs since their protector, the union, has also been duped by the accountability myth of competency-based curriculum and the Teacher Appraisal Process package.

Nor can these D.C. teachers see a pattern in what is happening in their U.S.A. (United States of America) so similar to what happened in that other U.S.A. (Union of South Africa) where Blacks live on the outer perimeters of the city and whites occupy the choice land within. Similarly, Blacks are being pushed to the outer rim of the large urban centers in the United States of America and whites are trooping back inside to the center of the cities and acquiring properties through their scouts, the real estate speculators, who are surveying the "enemies" camp and finding it unprotected.

And certainly, we must add one other factor to a description of the model, home rule, that is, real home rule and voting rights which the more astute among District residents know is probably not going to come until whites are in the majority (1) in the city, (2) in the city government, (3) on the school board, and (4) in the administrative and teaching positions, in the school in order to protect their white progeny, just now trickling back into the schools, but who will probably flood back by the mid 1980s.

One final item. The <u>colonial model</u> suggests that the dominant institutions of the city which are white-controlled work for the pacification of the Black masses. In part, their satisfaction with Superintendent Reed rests on the "peace" of the school system. But pacification is not necessarily education. It most often serves the interests of the ruling elite. Where basic change occurs, it is most often disruptive and the responsible person or persons are the scapegoat(s) for reactionaries.

FOOTNOTES — EPILOGUE

1. Barbara A. Sizemore, "Education: Is Accomodation Enough?," *The Journal of Negro Education* 44 (Summer 1975), pp. 239-240.

# APPENDIX 1

EVALUATION DOCUMENT

# MEMO OFFICE OF THE DISTRICT OF COLUMBIA BOARD OF EDUCATION

DATE: April 28, 1975

TO: Mrs. Sizemore

FROM: Mr. Cropp *A.S.C.*

SUBJECT: Mr. Treanor's Motion

"That the Board adopt Mrs. Morris' proposed evaluation document as the instrument for use on Wednesday."

Vote— 6 yes and 4 no

**BOARD OF EDUCATION OF THE DISTRICT OF COLUMBIA**
PRESIDENTIAL BUILDING
415 TWELFTH STREET, N. W.
WASHINGTON, D. C. 20004

MARION BARRY, JR., PRESIDENT
MARTHA S. SWAIM, VICE PRESIDENT
CHARLES I. CASSELL
JAMES E. COATES
RAYMOND B. KEMP
HILDA HOWLAND M. MASON
DELORES E. PRYDE
ALBERT A. ROSENFIELD
MATTIE G. TAYLOR
BARDYL R. TIRANA
EVIE M. WASHINGTON

DWIGHT S. CROPP
EXECUTIVE SECRETARY

## THE SUPERINTENDENT'S CONTRACT

It is hereby agreed by and between the Board of Education of the District of Columbia located in Washington, D. C. (hereinafter called the Board) and Ms. Barbara A. Sizemore (hereinafter called the Superintendent) that the said Board in accordance with its action as found in the minutes of the meeting held on the 7th day of August, 1973, has and does hereby employ the said Ms. Barbara A. Sizemore as Superintendent for a 3 year period commencing October 1, 1973. Both parties agree that said employee shall perform the duties of the Superintendent in and for the public schools in said District as prescribed by the District of Columbia Code and by the rules and regulations and/or any forthcoming amendments applicable thereto made thereunder by the Board of Education of the District of Columbia.

**WITNESSETH**

1. In consideration of a salary of $39,500 per annum plus such increases as are authorized by Public Law 92-518, 86 Stat. 1005, or by subsequent legislation, said Superintendent agrees to perform faithfully the duties of Superintendent and to serve as Executive Officer of the Board. The annual salary shall be paid in equal installments in accordance with law governing payment of other professional staff members in the School System. The Board expresses its commitment to seek a salary for the Superintendent that is comparable to the salary paid superintendents in other large urban area school districts.

2. Throughout the term of this contract the Superintendent shall be subject to discharge for adequate cause affecting her character and efficiency as Superintendent, provided, however, that the Board does not arbitrarily or capriciously call for her dismissal and that the Superintendent shall have the right to written charges, notice of hearing, and a fair hearing before the Board. If the Superintendent chooses to be accompanied by legal counsel at the hearing, she will assume the cost of legal Counsel.

3. Throughout the life of this contract the Board of Education authorizes the Superintendent to serve as the State Superintendent for the District of Columbia. The Superintendent hereby agrees to devote her time, skill, labor, and attention to said employment during the term of her contract, provided, however, that the Superintendent, by agreement with the Board, may undertake consultative work, speaking engagements, writing, lecturing, or other professional duties and obligations which may be outside the scope of her employment but are permissible under the laws of the District of Columbia.

4. The Superintendent will have complete freedom to organize, reorganize, and arrange the administrative and supervisory staff, including instruction and business affairs, which in her judgment best serves the District of Columbia Public Schools. The responsibility for selection, placement, and transfer of personnel shall be vested in the Superintendent subject to approval by the Board; and the Board, individually and collectively, will refer promptly all criticisms, complaints, and suggestions called to its attention to the Superintendent for study, action, and/or recommendation.

5. The Superintendent does hereby agree to have a comprehensive medical examination once each year; that a statement certifying to the physical competency of the Superintendent shall be filed with the Executive Secretary of the Board and treated as confidential information by the Board, cost of said medical examination to be borne by the Board.

6. The Board shall provide the Superintendent with transportation required in the performance of her official duties during her employment under this contract or shall provide her with mileage at the prevailing government rate. The Board will actively seek any additional authority or funds necessary to meet these requirements.

7. The Board shall provide the Superintendent with periodic opportunities to discuss Superintendent-Board relationships and shall provide for an annual conference for the purpose of discussing the performance of the Superintendent.

8. The Superintendent shall receive 26 days of vacation leave annually exclusive of legal holidays and shall be entitled to 13 days of sick leave annually. Earned leave shall be cumulative to the extent provided by law or Board rules or regulations applicable to other administrative employees.

9. The Board, at the request of the Superintendent and in accordance with Public Law 92-281, April 26, 1972, shall withhold and transfer an amount of salary each pay period, said amount to be determined by the Superintendent, permitting the Superintendent to participate if she so desires, in a tax-deferred annuity program of her choosing. Retirement benefits shall be provided for in the District of Columbia Teachers Retirement System established by law. Participation in such plan is mandatory.

Page Three

10. It shall be within the Superintendent's scope of employment to attend appropriate professional meetings. The Board expects the Superintendent to continue her professional development and expects her to participate in relevant learning experiences and will, accordingly, approve reasonable amounts for this purpose in the annual budget request.

11. The Board shall reimburse the Superintendent for expenses reasonably incurred in moving her family, furniture, household goods, and related personal belongings from Chicago, Illinois, to Washington, D. C., according to the rules and schedules established by the Administrator of General Services.

12. The Board agrees to notify the Superintendent in writing of its intention not to renew this contract at least 180 days prior to the termination date herein. Failure to do so will automatically renew this contract. Conversely, the Superintendent agrees to notify the Board, at least 180 days in advance, of her intention to terminate her employment with the Board upon the expiration of the initial contract.

13. The Superintendent shall receive life insurance and health benefits coverage, terminal pay, and other personal benefits accorded to other personal benefits accorded to other professional employees of the Board. Any improvements in fringe benefits as may be authorized by law or statute will automatically apply to the Superintendent.

14. The Board and the Superintendent respectively shall fulfill all aspects of this contract, any exception thereto being by mutual consent of the Board and the Superintendent.

Dated this sixth day of September, 1973.

_____  
Superintendent

_____  
President, Board of Education

_____  
Executive Secretary  
Board of Education

Subscribed and sworn to before me this sixth day of _____
September, 1973.

_____  
Notary Public, D.C.

My Commission Expires September 1, 1975

April 28, 1975

CONFIDENTIAL
NOT FOR RELEASE
TO THE PRESS

TO: The Board of Education of the
District of Columbia

Ladies and Gentlemen:

STATEMENT OF BARBARA A. SIZEMORE, SUPERINTENDENT OF SCHOOLS RELATIVE TO DISCUSSION OF THE PROCEDURE FOR THE ANNUAL EVALUATION OF THE SUPERINTENDENT'S PERFORMANCE

### Preliminary Statement

Sometimes subsequent to 10:00 o'clock the night of April 25, 1975, a copy of the Memorandum of the President of the Board of Education, dated April 25, 1975, was deposited in the mail slot of my home, which by its terms required my presence at an Executive Session of the Board of Education to be held at 1:30 o'clock P.M., Monday, April 28, 1975. Pursuant to that request I appear. I have deemed it wise to reduce to writing my understanding of the purpose of the meeting and, more importantly, the matters presented for discussion in the Session and, therefore, beg your leave to present to you the within statement in lieu of any oral dialogue save that I, as your employee, am perfectly amenable to reasonable interrogation upon questions that are germaine to the purpose of the Executive Session.

### Matters Contained in the Notice of April 25, 1975

The notice advises that I should be prepared to move ahead in the area of discussing the procedure for the annual evaluation of the Superintendent's performance, "In accordance with discussions during the Board/Superintendent Conference on November 13, 1974...". I, of course, am unprepared to "move ahead" in accordance with the discussions during the Board/Superintendent Conference of November 13, 1974, for a number of reasons:

1. My best recollection is that annual evaluation of the Superintendent's performance was most briefly discussed in more or less general terms without anything dispositive being stated by any Board Member present or by the Superintendent, but from the discussion I came to the conclusion that at some date in the near future the Board would take up the matter.

2. My recollection is that there was no secretary present at the November 13, 1974, conference, nor was any tape recording or any transcript of any sort made of this meeting, nor was any resolution of any sort passed.

3. On November 13, 1974, the Board consisted of seven (7) members, all of whom were not present; the new members not having been sworn as of that date.

4. I did not then understand, nor do I now understand, that the November 13, 1974, conference had anything at all to do with performance of the Board's duty under Paragraph Seven (7) of my contract with respect to an annual evaluation of my performance. This conference was called, as I understand it, for the purpose of discussing Board-Superintendent Relations.

### Procedure for Annual Evaluation of the Superintendent's Performance

I assume that the possible purpose of causing my attendance at this Executive Session was to obtain from me some of my ideas as to procedure. It is hoped that you will not view it as being presumptuous when I tender to you my ideas. This I do in full recognition of the fact that evaluation is primarily a Board function. I believe that your procedure for evaluating the performance of a Superintendent should include these factors:

1. There must be an agreement as to goals and objectives.

2. There must be an accounting of achievements and failures in the performance of activities designed to accomplish the goals and objectives.

3. A consideration of whether or not there existed internal or external causes and reasons for non-performance of activities to achieve the goals and objectives.

4. A comprehension of the Superintendents' performance in terms of her responsibilities under the contract dated September 6, 1973.

5. The annual report of the Superintendent is commended to you as a critique. (A draft copy of this report will be available to each Board Member today, if at all possible and, if not, on or before May 2, 1975).

Respectfully submitted,

Barbara A. Sizemore
Superintendent of Schools

Members of the Board of Education
of the District of Columbia

Ladies and Gentlemen:

Introduction: Evaluation of the Superintendent of Schools is an important responsibility which must be handled well and efficiently by a Board of Education. There is really nothing new about a Board of Education evaluating its Superintendent. With the ever growing demand for more accountability of public officials, many Boards have moved from the informal verbal type of evaluation toward the more formalized written evaluation.

In developing this evaluative instrument much reliance was placed upon a document forwarded by our Superintendent to the Board on Sept. 10, 1973, "Performance Evaluation of School Superintendent" by William J. Ellena. Also, there was an attempt to incorporate pertinent elements from the following documents: (1) "Superintendent Search," April 1973; (2) "Superintendent's 120 Day Report," March 1974; (3) "The Superintendent's Contract," September 1973; and (4) "Superintendent's Memorandum-Board/Administration Relationships," May 15, 1974.

Scoring Instructions: An attempt has been made to organize the Superintendent's responsibilities in six categories. Each Board member is asked to rate the Superintendent on each of the items cited in each of the categories. Each Board member is to submit his/her evaluation form to the Executive Secretary within twenty-four hours of issuance. Upon receiving all forms, the Executive Secretary will then tally the results and provide a composite score. The Superintendent and each Board member will be given a copy of the results. The Superintendent will not be given the questionnaires from individual Board members or be informed as to how any individual answered the questions.

Board members are encouraged to include any additional written comments on the blank sheets attached.

# EVALUATION FORM

**Scoring Instructions:** Please assess the Superintendent's performance by placing a check (✓) in the appropriate column. Your appraisal is a serious and responsible assignment. The Superintendent wants to know her level of performance as perceived by the Board.

| Areas of Responsibility | Unsatisfactory | Satisfactory | Commendable | Comment |
|---|---|---|---|---|
| **A. Relationships with the Board** | | | | |
| 1. Keeps the Board informed on issues, needs and operation of the School System. | | | | |
| 2. Offers professional advice to the Board on items requiring Board action, with appropriate recommendations based on thorough study and analysis. | | | | |
| 3. Interprets and executes the intent of Board Policy. | | | | |
| 4. Seeks and accepts constructive criticism of her work. | | | | |
| 5. Supports Board Policy and actions to the public and staff. | | | | |
| 6. Has a harmonious working relationship with the Board. | | | | |
| 7. Understands her role in administration of Board Policy, makes recommendations for employment or promotion of personnel in writing and with supporting data, and accepts responsibility for her recommendations. If the recommendation is questioned by the Board, she finds another person to recommend. | | | | |
| 8. Accepts her responsibility for maintaining liaison between the Board and personnel, working toward a high degree of understanding and respect between the staff and the Board and the Board and the staff. | | | | |

| Areas of Responsibility | Unsatisfactory | Satisfactory | Commendable | Comment |
|---|---|---|---|---|
| Relationships with the Board continued | | | | |
| 9. Remains impartial toward the Board, treating all Board members alike. | | | | |
| 10. Refrains from criticism of individual or group members of the Board. | | | | |
| 11. Goes immediately and directly to the Board when she feels an honest, objective difference of opinion exists between her and any or all members of the Board, in an earnest effort to resolve such difference immediately. | | | | |
| 12. Feels free to maintain her opposition to matters under discussion by the Board until an official decision has been reached, after which time she supports the views of the Board as long as she remains in its employ. | | | | |
| B. Community Relationships | | | | |
| 13. Gains respect and support of the community on the conduct of the school operation. | | | | |
| 14. Solicits and gives attention to problems and opinions of all groups and individuals. | | | | |
| 15. Develops friendly and cooperative relationships with the media. | | | | |
| 16. Participates actively in community life and affairs. | | | | |
| 17. Achieves status as a community leader in public education. | | | | |
| 18. Works effectively with public and private agencies. | | | | |
| C. Staff and Personnel Relationships | | | | |
| 19. Develops and executes sound personnel procedures and practices. | | | | |
| 20. Delegates authority to staff members appropriate to the position each holds. | | | | |

| Areas of Responsibility | Unsatisfactory | Satisfactory | Commendable | Comment |
|---|---|---|---|---|
| **Staff and Personnel Relationships** continued | | | | |
| 21. Recruits and assigns the best available personnel in terms of their competencies. | | | | |
| 22. Takes an active role in development of salary schedules for all personnel, and recommends to the Board the levels which, within budgetary limitations, will best serve the interests of the District. | | | | |
| 23. At the direction of the Board, meets and confers with the employee associations representing to the best of her ability and understanding the interest and will of the Board. | | | | |
| D. **Educational Leadership** | | | | |
| 24. Understands and keeps informed regarding all aspects of the instructional program. | | | | |
| 25. Implements the District's philosophy of education. | | | | |
| 26. Participates with staff, Board, and community in studying and developing curriculum improvement. | | | | |
| 27. Organizes a planned program of staff evaluation and improvement. | | | | |
| 28. Provides democratic procedures in curriculum work, utilizing the abilities and talents of the entire professional staff and lay people of the community. | | | | |
| 29. Inspires others to highest professional standards. | | | | |
| E. **Business and Finance** | | | | |
| 30. Keeps informed on needs of the school program – plants, facilities, equipment, and supplies. | | | | |
| 31. Supervises operations, insisting on competent and efficient performance. | | | | |

| Areas of Responsibility | Unsatisfactory | Satisfactory | Commendable | Comment |
|---|---|---|---|---|
| **Business and Finance continued** | | | | |
| 32. Determines that funds are spent wisely, and adequate control and accounting are maintained. | | | | |
| 33. Evaluates financial needs and makes recommendations for adequate financing. | | | | |
| **F. Personal Qualities** | | | | |
| 34. Maintains high standards of ethics, honesty, and integrity in all professional matters. | | | | |
| 35. Earns respect and standing among her professional colleagues. | | | | |
| 36. Devotes her time and energy effectively to her job. | | | | |
| 37. Retains sensitivity to people and ability to relate well with the diverse elements of our international city. | | | | |
| 38. Exhibits the skill and willingness needed to anticipate and resolve conflict whenever possible, while minimizing disruption to the teaching and learning processes. | | | | |
| 39. Demonstrates the capability to command the respect of the community and capability of relating effectively with external forces on the local and federal levels. | | | | |
| 40. Exercises good judgment and the democratic processes in arriving at decisions. | | | | |
| 41. Possesses and maintains the health and energy necessary to meet the responsibilities of her position. | | | | |
| 42. Maintains poise and emotional stability in the full range of her professional activities. | | | | |
| 43. Uses language effectively in dealing with staff members, the Board, and the public. | | | | |
| **Personal Qualities continued** | | | | |
| 44. Writes clearly and concisely. | | | | |
| 45. Thinks well on her feet when faced with an unexpected or disturbing turn of events in a large group meeting. | | | | |

## COMPOSITE PROFILE OF EVALUATION OF SUPERINTENDENT BY THE BOARD OF EDUCATION
### (TO BE COMPLETED BY THE EXECUTIVE SECRETARY)

|         | Unsatisfactory | Satisfactory | Commendable |
|---------|----------------|--------------|-------------|
| Item 1  |                |              |             |
| Item 2  |                |              |             |
| Item 3  |                |              |             |
| Item 4  |                |              |             |
| Item 5  |                |              |             |
| Item 6  |                |              |             |
| Item 7  |                |              |             |
| Item 8  |                |              |             |
| Item 9  |                |              |             |
| Item 10 |                |              |             |
| Item 11 |                |              |             |
| Item 12 |                |              |             |
| Item 13 |                |              |             |
| Item 14 |                |              |             |
| Item 15 |                |              |             |
| Item 16 |                |              |             |
| Item 17 |                |              |             |
| Item 18 |                |              |             |
| Item 19 |                |              |             |
| Item 20 |                |              |             |
| Item 21 |                |              |             |
| Item 22 |                |              |             |
| Item 23 |                |              |             |
| Item 24 |                |              |             |
| Item 25 |                |              |             |
| Item 26 |                |              |             |
| Item 27 |                |              |             |
| Item 28 |                |              |             |
| Item 29 |                |              |             |
| Item 30 |                |              |             |
| Item 31 |                |              |             |
| Item 32 |                |              |             |
| Item 33 |                |              |             |
| Item 34 |                |              |             |
| Item 35 |                |              |             |
| Item 36 |                |              |             |
| Item 37 |                |              |             |
| Item 38 |                |              |             |
| Item 39 |                |              |             |
| Item 40 |                |              |             |
| Item 41 |                |              |             |
| Item 42 |                |              |             |
| Item 43 |                |              |             |
| Item 44 |                |              |             |
| Item 45 |                |              |             |
| TOTAL   |                | TOTAL        | TOTAL       |
| PERCENTAGE |             | PERCENTAGE   | PERCENTAGE  |

# MEMO

**OFFICE OF THE DISTRICT OF COLUMBIA BOARD OF EDUCATION**

DATE: April 29, 1975

TO : Barbara A. Sizemore
Superintendent of Schools

FROM : Virginia Morris, President
Board of Education

SUBJECT : Executive Session, April 28, 1975

On Monday, April 28, 1975, the Board of Education met with you for the purpose of discussing "the procedure for the annual evaluation of the Superintendent's performance." During the meeting, there was extensive discussion on the process, proposed criteria, and documents passed out during the meeting. I offered a proposed evaluation instrument for the consideration of the Board and Superintendent. There was further discussion about the role to be played by the Superintendent in the development of the evaluation process (goals, objectives, criteria, etc.).

As a result of the extensive discussion, the Board approved the following motions:

### Hobson's Substitute Motion

"I move that the five documents (Superintendent's Search, Superintendent's Contract, 120 Day Report, Superintendent's Memorandum of May 15, 1974, and the Draft of the Annual Report) be utilized and that the Superintendent make a presentation to the Board at 9:00 a.m., Wednesday, April 30, 1975." Mr. Treanor seconded.

Mrs. Kane's amendment - "add the proposed (Mrs. Morris') evaluation form to the list." Mr. Treanor seconded.

Vote: Yes - 9; No - 1

### Treanor's Motion

"I move that the board adopt Mrs. Morris' proposed evaluation document as the instrument for use on Wednesday." Mrs. Schwartz seconded.

**Vote:** Yes - 6; No - 4

Pursuant to these actions, the Board and Superintendent are scheduled to meet in Executive Session at 9:00 a.m., Wednesday, April 30, 1975, for the purpose of continuing the discussion from Monday's meeting. The meeting will be held in the Board Room.

Your cooperation is very much appreciated.

cc: Board Members
Mr. Cropp

Attachment U

## BOARD OF EDUCATION OF THE DISTRICT OF COLUMBIA
**PRESIDENTIAL BUILDING**
**415 TWELFTH STREET, N. W.**
**WASHINGTON, D. C. 20004**

VIRGINIA MORRIS, PRESIDENT
JULIUS W. HOBSON, JR., VICE PRESIDENT
BETTIE G. BENJAMIN
THERMAN E. EVANS
ELIZABETH KANE
RAYMOND B. KEMP
HILDA HOWLAND M. MASON
CAROL L. SCHWARTZ
BARBARA LETT SIMMONS
WILLIAM W. TREANOR
JOHN E. WARREN

DWIGHT S. CROPP
EXECUTIVE SECRETARY

DAVID A. SPLITT
GENERAL COUNSEL

May 2, 1975

Mr. David A. Splitt
General Counsel
D. C. Board of Education
415 Twelfth Street, N. W.
Washington, D. C. 20004

Dear Mr. Splitt:

I am transmitting for your immediate attention and action the motion passed by the Board of Education in the meeting of the Committee of the Whole on Personnel on Thursday, May 1, 1975:

### MOTION:

WHEREAS the Board of Education of the District of Columbia is charged by law with the responsibility for the control of the Public Schools of the District of Columbia; and

WHEREAS the Board of Education is charged by law with the responsibility for the appointment and removal of the Superintendent of Schools of the District of Columbia; and

WHEREAS the Superintendent of Schools is an employee of the Board of Education; and

WHEREAS the Board of Education has determined that the performance of the present Superintendent of Schools has not been satisfactory; and

WHEREAS the Board of Education must exercise its discretion on matters affecting the employment of the Superintendent of Schools in compliance with the Code of Laws of the District of Columbia, the Rules of the Board of Education, the rights of the Superintendent under the law and her contract, and in the public interest;

Mr. David A. Splitt            -2-         May 2, 1975
General Counsel

BE IT THEREFORE RESOLVED -

    THAT the Board of Education hereby directs its General Counsel, in cooperation with the Corporation Counsel of the District of Columbia, to prepare such documents as may be necessary for the Board of Education to proceed pursuant to Title 31, Section 31-108 of the Code of Laws of the District of Columbia, and further to make recommendations to the Board of Education as may be necessary in order to carry out such procedures within the framework of the Code of Laws of the District of Columbia, the Rules of the Board of Education, and the rights of the Superintendent of Schools under the law and her contract; and further

    THAT the Board directs that such documents and recommendations be presented to the Board for review and action at a meeting of the Committee of the Whole on Personnel to be held on Monday, May 5, 1975, at 2:00 p.m. in the Board meeting room.

                                   Sincerely,

                                   Dwight S. Cropp
                                   Executive Secretary
                                   Board of Education

DSC:mab
cc: Board Members

Attachment A

# MEMO
### OFFICE OF THE DISTRICT OF COLUMBIA BOARD OF EDUCATION

DATE: May 29, 1975

TO : Members, Board of Education

FROM : Dwight S. Cropp
Executive Secretary

SUBJECT : Meeting of the Committee of the Whole on Personnel

    The President of the Board of Education has scheduled a meeting of the Committee of the Whole on Personnel at 9:00 a.m., on Saturday, May 31, 1975, in the Board meeting room. The agenda of this meeting is as follows:

        Presentation of the proposed, "Bill of Particulars"

    I am attaching for your review, a copy of the letter of transmittal from Mr. David Splitt, General Counsel to the Board, and a copy of the proposed Bill of Particulars. These documents should be treated as confidential and should not be released for public discussion. The President of the Board has indicated that the meeting of the Committee of the Whole may possibly result in the issuance of a public statement by the Board of Education.

Attachment

cc: Mr. Splitt

Attachment B

**BOARD OF EDUCATION OF THE DISTRICT OF COLUMBIA**
PRESIDENTIAL BUILDING
415 TWELFTH STREET, N. W.
WASHINGTON, D. C. 20004

**VIRGINIA MORRIS, PRESIDENT**
**JULIUS W. HOBSON, JR., VICE PRESIDENT**
**BETTIE G. BENJAMIN**
**THERMAN E. EVANS**
**ELIZABETH KANE**
**RAYMOND B. KEMP**
**HILDA HOWLAND M. MASON**
**CAROL L. SCHWARTZ**
**BARBARA LETT SIMMONS**
**WILLIAM W. TREANOR**
**JOHN E. WARREN**

**DWIGHT S. CROPP**
**EXECUTIVE SECRETARY**

**DAVID A. SPLITT**
**GENERAL COUNSEL**

May 29, 1975

Memorandum to: Mrs. Barbara A. Sizemore
Superintendent of Schools

From: Mr. Dwight S. Cropp
Executive Secretary

Subject: Meeting of the Committee of the Whole on Personnel

The President of the Board of Education has scheduled a meeting of the Committee of the Whole on Personnel at 9:00 a.m., Saturday, May 31, 1975, in the Board Meeting Room.

The Agenda is as follows:

. Presentation of the proposed "Bill of Particulars"

DSC:mab
cc: Board Members
Mr. David A. Splitt

Attachment C

## BOARD OF EDUCATION OF THE DISTRICT OF COLUMBIA
PRESIDENTIAL BUILDING
415 TWELFTH STREET, N. W.
WASHINGTON, D. C. 20004

RECEIVED
1975 ...

VIRGINIA MORRIS, PRESIDENT
JULIUS W. HOBSON, JR., VICE PRESIDENT
BETTIE C. BENJAMIN
THERMAN E. EVANS
ELIZABETH KANE
RAYMOND E. KEMP
HILDA HOWLAND M. MASON
CAROL I. SCHWARTZ
BARBARA LETT SIMMONS
WILLIAM W. TREANOR
JOHN E. WARREN

DWIGHT S. CROPP
EXECUTIVE SECRETARY

DAVID A. SPLITT
GENERAL COUNSEL

May 29, 1975

Mr. Dwight S. Cropp
Executive Secretary
D. C. Board of Education
415 Twelfth Street, N.W.
Washington, D. C. 20004

Dear Mr. Cropp:

Pursuant to the direction of the Board of Education transmitted to this office by your memorandum of May 2, 1975, the attached document has been prepared for the consideration of the Board.

Working in cooperation with the Office of the Corporation Counsel, this office has prepared the attached notice of proposed adverse action to remove Barbara A. Sizemore from the office of Superintendent of Schools and terminate the contract between her and the Board of Education. The notice of proposed adverse action is based upon seventeen (17) specific grounds, contained therein, and includes notification of the right to submit written responses to the charges, the right to request a hearing and the right to choose an open or closed hearing, the right to retain counsel for such a hearing, and the right to request leave with pay in order to answer the charges or prepare for a hearing.

In further response to the Board's directive, the following recommendations are made for procedures to follow in the consideration of the attached document:

    1) After receiving a copy of the attached document, each Board member should carefully review each charge and specification.

    2) After sufficient time for review, the Board should meet in closed session to consider the charges and specifications. After full and due consideration, the Board should determine whether it shall adopt any or all of the specified charges.

Page Two

   3) After determining which, if any, of the charges it shall adopt, the Board should then determine whether or not the charges adopted constitute grounds for further action by the Board. If the Board determines that action is warranted, it should then determine the form of such proposed action; i.e., censure, suspension, termination, or some other form of sanction.

   4) If the Board determines that it shall take adverse action based upon the adopted charges, it should then adopt a final form of notice of adverse action and make delivery of such notice upon the Superintendent.

Subsequent to its consideration and deliberations, if the Board should determine to proceed with an adverse action requiring further procedural steps, this office is prepared, in cooperation with the Office of the Corporation Counsel, to advise the Board on any required procedures.

Sincerely,

David A. Splitt
General Counsel
D. C. Board of Education

Attachment
cc: The Corporation Counsel

**BOARD OF EDUCATION OF THE DISTRICT OF COLUMBIA**
PRESIDENTIAL BUILDING
415 TWELFTH STREET, N. W.
WASHINGTON, D. C. 20004

VIRGINIA MORRIS, PRESIDENT
JULIUS W. HOBSON, JR., VICE PRESIDENT
BETTIE G. BENJAMIN
THERMAN E. EVANS
ELIZABETH KANE
RAYMOND B. KEMP
HILDA HOWLAND M. MASON
CAROL L. SCHWARTZ
BARBARA LETT SIMMONS
WILLIAM W. TREANOR
JOHN E. WARREN

DWIGHT S. CROPP
EXECUTIVE SECRETARY

DAVID A. SPLITT
GENERAL COUNSEL

May 31, 1975

## Report of the District of Columbia Board of Education's Committee-of-the-Whole on Personnel

### Members Present:

Mrs. Virginia Morris, President
Mr. Julius Hobson, Vice President
Mrs. Bettie G. Benjamin
Dr. Therman E. Evans
Mrs. Elizabeth Kane
Rev. Raymond B. Kemp
Mrs. Hilda Howland M. Mason
Mrs. Carol L. Schwartz
Mrs. Barbara Lett Simmons
Mr. William W. Treanor
Mr. John E. Warren

### Administration Present:

Mrs. Barbara A. Sizemore, Superintendent
Ms. Gwendolyn Kimbrough, Exec. Asst. to

### Board Staff:

Mr. Dwight Cropp, Exec. Sec.
Mr. Joseph C. Browne, Bd. Reporter

### Summary of Discussion:

A meeting of the Committee-of-the-Whole on Personnel was called by the President of the Board of Education on Saturday, May 31, 1975 at 9:00 a. m., in the Board meeting room. The Agenda consisted of the "Presentation of the Proposed Bill of Particulars."

Mrs. Morris read into the record the contents of the following:

. Memorandum to Board Members dated May 29, 1975; (Attachment A)

. Memorandum to the Superintendent dated May 29, 1975; (Attachment B)

. Memorandum from Mr. David Splitt to Mr. Dwight Cropp dated May 29, 1975 (Attachment C)

- 2 -

. **Memorandum** from Mr. Cropp to Mr. Splitt dated May 2, 1975;
(Attachment D)

. **Draft letter** of proposed Bill of Particulars to Mrs. Sizemore.
(Attachment E)

After a lengthy discussion, the Committee-of-the-Whole on Personnel adopted the letter to Mrs. Sizemore, as amended and corrected, dated May 31, 1975; the letter to be sent to Mrs. Sizemore immediately.

The Committee-of-the-Whole on Personnel recommends approval of this report by the Board of Education."

Virginia Morris, President

Julius Hobson, Jr., Vice Pres.

Bettie Benjamin

Therman E. Evans

Elizabeth Kane

Raymond B. Kemp

Hilda H. M. Mason

Carol L. Schwartz

Barbara Lett Simmons

William Treanor

John E. Warren

Attachment E

May 31, 1975

Mrs. Barbara A. Sizemore
Superintendent of Schools
Room 1209
415 12th Street, N.W.
Washington, D.C.

Dear Mrs. Sizemore:

This is notice that the Board of Education, pursuant to Section 31-108, D.C. Code, 1973 ed., proposes to terminate your contract, and to remove you from your position of Superintendent of Schools no earlier than 30 days from your receipt of this notice. It is proposed that you be removed for cause affecting your efficiency as Superintendent of Schools, and to thereby terminate the contract dated September 6, 1973 between the Board of Education and Barbara A. Sizemore.

The charge against you is: Neglect of or inattention to your duties as Superintendent and failure to comply with directives and policies of the Board.

The reasons supporting this charge are as follows:

1. Failure to provide a plan for equalization of the schools.

On November 14, 1973, you represented to the Board that you would develop a new plan to equalize the distribution of resources in connection with Judge Wright's decree in Hobson v. Hansen. You further represented that said plan would be submitted to the Board in time for implementation during the 1974-75 school year. You have failed, or neglected to, submit said plan.

2. Failure to provide quarterly safety reports.

On January 3, 1974, you assured the then President of the Board of Education that quarterly progress reports on Safety and Occupational Health in the D.C. Schools will be submitted to the Board.

Except for an initial report dated April 17, 1974, you have failed, or neglected, to submit or cause to be submitted, such quarterly safety reports.

3. Failure to provide and implement adequate personnel hiring controls and failure to maintain hiring within fiscally responsible limits.

You did fail to maintain adequate personnel and hiring controls, which failure resulted in the filling of positions in excess of funds available as reflected in the report submitted to the Board by you on November 13, 1974, entitled General Fund Projected Personnel Compensations, October 1, 1974 through June 30, 1975.

4. Failure to fill position as directed by the Board.

On October 16, 1974, the Board directed that you fill the position of Director of Buildings and Grounds (Assistant Superintendent) with a probationary appointment within 60 days. You failed or neglected to make such appointment within the time prescribed. Further, on February 24, 1975, you informed the Board that you would not comply with this directive until June 30, 1975.

5. Failure to provide a timely selection procedure for the selection of Regional Superintendents.

At the meeting of the Board of Education of July 8, 1974, you represented to the Board that you would submit a procedure for the selection of Regional Superintendents by October 1, 1974. You have failed, or neglected, to provide to the Board the said procedures.

6. Failure to comply with Board directives concerning Federal Grant proposals.

On August 21, 1973, in order to provide for timely consideration of Federal Grant proposals, the Board directed "that the Budget Office certify all Federal budgets and that the Board be provided with activity and time frames for Fiscal Year 1975 at least 90 days prior to the beginning of the fiscal year." For Fiscal Year 1975 no proposals were submitted to the Board in accordance with the time requirements so specified.

By letter dated March 19, 1975, you represented to the President of the Board that in connection with Federal Grant proposals for Fiscal Year 1976, "the Administration will present a report to the Board at the April meeting. The report will include a proposal flow emanating from both State and other offices. It will also include a systematic design and recommendations for Board consideration to ensure an orderly flow of submissions to the Board consistent with the granting agencies' guidelines and calendar." You have failed, or neglected to submit such a report at the April meeting.

7. Failure to provide a timely annual report.

You failed or neglected to submit to the Board the annual report for the 1973-74 school year as required by Section 200.3(n) of Chapter II of the Rules of the Board of Education.

    8. Failure to comply with Board directive to appoint Administration Committee.

On April 7, 1975, the Board directed you to designate an Administration Committee for the purpose of reviewing requests for exceptions and modifications in the "freeze" on non-personnel expenditures, and further provided that such Committee was to meet on a weekly basis and present its recommendations to the Board's Committee on School Finance. You have failed or neglected to designate such an Administration Committee.

    9. Failure to provide responses to the Board's questions on the FY-1975 Financial Plan.

On April 7, 1975, the Board propounded to you certain questions regarding the FY-1975 projected financial status report. You have failed, or neglected, to supply the Board with the answers to such questions.

    10. Failure to comply with Board directive to submit status reports on expenditures.

On April 7, 1975, the Board directed that you provide the Board with status reports reflecting total expenditures applied against the new financial plan, and the appropriate balances. You were required to submit the first such report at the May business meeting, and you have failed, or neglected, to submit such report.

11. Failure to provide Quarterly Financial Reports.

On March 20, 1974, the Board adopted your recommendation that quarterly financial reports be presented to the Board. Other than a partial financial report submitted on November 13, 1974 for the first quarter Fiscal Year 1975 (July 1, 1974 - September 30, 1974), you have failed, or neglected, to submit such financial reports, for Fiscal Year 1975.

12. Failure to provide quarterly personnel reports.

Except for a report submitted on April 9, 1975, for the second quarter, Fiscal Year 1975 (October 1 - December 31, 1974), you have failed, or neglected, to file with the Board quarterly reports on the status of school personnel as required by the policy of the Board of Education adopted June 21, 1967.

13. Failure to comply with Board directive to provide FY-75 legislative proposal.

On October 16, 1974, the Board of Education directed you to prepare a legislative and reorganizational package for submission concomitant with the presentation of the FY-76 Budget. This package was to include the following:

    a) phased-in school system control of contracts related to building construction.

    b) total control of major maintenance and repairs for the school system by the school system.

    c) positions and costs to implement these new controls.

    d) such information as is necessary to convince the Council and the Congress that such controls are needed by the school system.

You have failed or neglected to prepare or cause to be prepared such a legislative package.

    14. Failure to comply with Board directive to make recommendations on permanent tenure.

On April 17, 1974, the Board directed you to prepare and make recommendations to the Board on permanent tenure. You have failed or neglected to provide such recommendations to the Board.

    15. Failure to obtain for the Board student comments on proposed rules on students' rights and responsibilities and code of conduct.

In August, 1974, the Board adopted proposed rules, including the Student Bill of Rights and Responsibilities and the Student Code of Conduct. The Board action included a comment period of 75 days for the purpose of allowing students to get copies of the rules and for the various student governments in the schools to hold seminars and vote on the rules and provide the Board with the results of such student votes. You failed or neglected to carry out the directive of the Board with regard to obtaining student input on these rules.

16. Failure to provide curriculum development in FY-1975.

In March, 1974, you submitted to the Board The Superintendent's 120-Day Report, which was accepted and approved by the Board in May, 1974. In that Report, you stated that you would initiate a reorganization of schools and curriculum in five phases. In part, the first phase, which was to be completed in FY-1975, included development of curriculum in the Pre-K through Grade 4 (Primary) block in the areas of language, mathematics, music, art, science, and social studies. You have failed or neglected to provide such curriculum development to the Board in accordance with the Rules of the Board of Education, Chapter 2, Section 200.3(d).

17. Failure to provide report on declining enrollment.

On March 19, 1975, you represented to the Board that you would provide a report on March 20, 1975 on declining enrollment in the D.C. Public Schools which would release $2.3 million in FY-75 to fund improved and innovative programs.

You have failed or neglected to provide such report.

You have the right to answer these charges, in writing, if you wish, and may submit affidavits in support of your answer. You will be allowed 10 (business) days from the date of your receipt of this notice to submit your written answer. Your written reply, if any, should be addressed to the Executive Secretary, Board of Education, Room 1205, Presidential Building, 415 12th Street, N.W., Washington, D.C.

You may also answer these charges personally by requesting a hearing before the Board of Education on these charges. A request for such a hearing must be made in writing to the Board of Education and received no later than the close of business on June 16, 1975.

Should a hearing be requested, as provided herein, such hearing shall be held at a place and time to be established by the Board of Education. Such hearing will be open to the public unless you specifically request in writing that such hearing be closed to the public. You have the right to be represented by counsel of your choosing at such hearing. The cost of such legal representation, however, must be borne by you.

Pending final action by the Board of Education on the proposed removal and termination, as provided herein, you are and shall continue to be the Superintendent of Schools of the District of Columbia; provided that you may be permitted to take a leave of absence with pay in order to prepare and answer the charges or to prepare for a hearing on the proposed removal and termination, as provided herein.

You may review the material relied on in proposing this action by contacting the Executive Secretary of the Board of Education. The material may be reviewed by you or your representative in Room 1205 of the Presidential Building, 415 12th Street, N.W., Washington, D.C.

Very truly yours,

President
Board of Education

*Proposed*
5-31-75
*[initials]*

Mrs. Barbara A. Sizemore
Superintendent of Schools
Room 1209
415 12th Street, N.W.
Washington, D.C.

Dear Mrs. Sizemore:

  This is notice that the Board of Education, pursuant to Section 31-108, D.C. Code, 1973 ed., proposes to terminate your contract, and to remove you from your position of Superintendent of Schools no earlier than 30 days from your receipt of this notice. It is proposed that you be removed for cause affecting your efficiency as Superintendent of Schools, and to thereby terminate the contract dated September 6, 1973 between the Board of Education and Barbara A. Sizemore.

  The charge against you is: Neglect of or inattention to your duties as Superintendent and failure to comply with directives and policies of the Board.

  The reasons supporting this charge are as follows:

  1. Failure to provide a plan for equalization of the schools.

  On November 13, 1973, you represented to the Board that would develop a new plan to equalize the distribution of resources in connection with Judge Wright's decree in <u>Hobson</u> v. <u>Hansen</u>. You further represented that said plan would be submitted to the Board in time for implementation during the 1974-75 school year. You have failed, or neglected to, submit said plan.

2. Failure to provide quarterly safety reports.

On January 3, 1974, you assured the then President of the Board of Education that quarterly progress reports on Safety and Occupational Health in the D.C. Schools will be submitted to the Board.

Except for an initial report dated April 17, 1974, you have failed, or neglected, to submit or cause to be submitted, such quarterly safety reports.

3. Failure to provide and implement adequate personnel hiring controls and failure to maintain hiring within fiscally responsible limits.

You did fail to maintain adequate personnel and hiring controls, which failure resulted in the filling of positions in excess of funds available as reflected in the report submitted to the Board by you on November 13, 1974, entitled General Fund Projected Personnel Compensations, October 1, 1974 through June 30, 1975.

4. Failure to fill position as directed by the Board.

On October 16, 1974, the Board directed that you fill the position of Director of Buildings and Grounds (Assistant Superintendent) with a probationary appointment within 60 days. You failed or neglected to make such appointment within the time prescribed. Further, on February 24, 1975, you informed the Board that you would not comply with this directive until June 30, 1975.

5. Failure to provide a timely selection procedure for the selection of Regional Superintendents.

At the meeting of the Board of Education of July 8, 1974, you represented to the Board that you would submit a procedure for the selection of Regional Superintendents by October 1, 1974. You have failed, or neglected, to provide to the Board the said procedures.

6. Failure to comply with Board directives concerning Federal Grant proposals.

On August 21, 1973, in order to provide for timely consideration of Federal Grant proposals, the Board directed "that the Budget Office certify all Federal budgets and that the Board be provided with activity and time frames for Fiscal Year 1975 at least 90 days prior to the beginning of the fiscal year." For Fiscal Year 1975 no proposals were submitted to the Board in accordance with the time requirements so specified.

By letter dated March 19, 1975, you represented to the President of the Board that in connection with Federal Grant proposals for Fiscal Year 1976, "the Administration will present a report to the Board at the April meeting. The report will include a proposal flow emanating from both State and other offices. It will also include a systematic design and recommendations for Board consideration to ensure an orderly flow of submissions to the Board consistent with the granting agencies' guidelines and calendar." You have failed, or neglected to submit such a report at the April meeting.

7. Failure to provide a timely annual report.

You failed or neglected to submit to the Board the annual report for the 1973-74 school year as required by Section 200.3 (n) of Chapter II of the Rules of the Board of Education.

8. Failure to comply with Board directive to appoint Administration Committee.

On April 7, 1975, the Board directed you to designate an Administration Committee for the purpose of reviewing requests for exceptions and modifications in the "freeze" on non-personnel expenditures, and further provided that such Committee was to meet on a weekly basis and present its recommendations to the Board's Committee on School Finance. You have failed or neglected to designate such an Administration Committee.

9. Failure to provide responses to the Board's questions on the FY-1975 Financial Plan.

On April 7, 1975, the Board propounded to you certain questions regarding the FY-1975 projected financial status report. You have failed, or neglected, to supply the Board with the answers to such questions.

10. Failure to comply with Board directive to submit status reports on expenditures.

On April 7, 1975, the Board directed that you provide the Board with status reports reflecting total expenditures applied against the new financial plan, and the appropriate balances. You were required to submit the first such report at the May business meeting, and you have failed, or neglected, to submit such report.

11. Failure to provide Quarterly Financial Reports.

On March 20, 1974, the Board adopted your recommendation that quarterly financial reports be presented to the Board. Other than a partial financial report submitted on November 13, 1974 for the first quarter Fiscal Year 1975 (July 1, 1974 - September 30, 1974), you have failed, or neglected, to submit such financial reports.

12. Failure to provide quarterly personnel reports.

Except for a report submitted on April 9, 1975, for the second quarter, Fiscal Year 1975 (October 1 - December 31, 1974), you have failed, or neglected, to file with the Board quarterly reports on the status of school personnel as required by the policy of the Board of Education adopted June 21, 1967.

13. Failure to comply with Board directive to provide FY-75 legislative proposal.

On October 16, 1974, the Board of Education directed you to prepare a legislative and reorganizational package for submission concomitant with the presentation of the FY-76 Budget. This package was to include the following:

    a) phased-in school system control of contracts related to building construction.

- 5 -

    b) total control of major maintenance and repairs for the school system by the school system.

    c) positions and costs to implement these new controls.

    d) such information as is necessary to convince the Council and the Congress that such controls are needed by the school system.

You have failed or neglected to prepare or cause to be prepared such a legislative package.

    14. Failure to comply with Board directive to make recommendations on permanent tenure.

On April 17, 1974, the Board directed you to prepare and make recommendations to the Board on permanent tenure. You have failed or neglected to provide such recommendations to the Board.

    15. Failure to obtain for the Board student comments on proposed rules on students' rights and responsibilities and code of conduct.

In August, 1974, the Board adopted proposed rules, including the Student Bill of Rights and Responsibilities and the Student Code of Conduct. The Board action included a comment period of 75 days for the purpose of allowing students to get copies of the rules and for the various student governments in the schools to hold seminars and vote on the rules and provide the Board with the results of such student votes. You failed or neglected to carry out the directive of the Board with regard to obtaining student input on these rules.

16. Failure to provide curriculum development in FY-1975.

In March, 1974, you submitted to the Boart The Superintendent's 120-Day Report, which was accepted and approved by the Board in May, 1974. In that Report, you stated that you would initiate a reorganization of schools and curriculum in five phases. In part, the first phase, which was to be completed in FY-1975, included development of curriculum in the Pre-K through Grade 4 (Primary) block in the areas of language, mathematics, music, art, science, and social studies. You have failed or neglected to provide such curriculum development to the Board in accordance with the Rules of the Board of Education, Chapter 2, Section 200.3(d).

17. Failure to provide report on declining enrollment.

On March 19, 1975, you represented to the Board that you would provide a report on March 20, 1975 on declining enrollment in the D.C. Public Schools which would release $2.3 million in FY-75 to fund improved and innovative programs.

You have failed or neglected to provide such report.

You have the right to answer these charges, in writing, if you wish, and may submit affidavits in support of your answer. You will be allowed 10 calendar days from the date of your receipt of this notice to submit your written answer. Your written reply, if any, should be addressed to the Executive Secretary, Board of Education, Room 1215, Presidential Building, 415 12th Street, N.W., Washington, D.C.

- 7 -

# APPENDIX II

# SUPERINTENDENT'S RATING

Transcript of the D.C. Board of Education
Meeting of August 28, 1975

MRS. SIMMONS: I didn't know that was the game. He was set up to do that.

CHRMN MORRIS: Your name was not listed. If you wish to speak following Mrs. Sizemore, then I will call on you.

MRS. SIMMONS: Very good. I certainly would like to.

CHRMN MORRIS: You called my name and I said "Mrs. Simmons", and in the meantime I was looking at Mrs. Sizemore. Mrs. Sizemore?

SUPT SIZEMORE: "The Superintendent denies neglect or inattention to her duties. The Superintendent denies failure to comply with Board directives and policies. Each subsequent answer that I have given to you represents the Superintendent's response to the allegations made against her on May 31, 1975 on negligence to duty or failure to perform Board directives." The Superintendent finds very little correlation between this letter of proposed charges and the discussion that I had with the Board on the evaluation and finds no relationship between that evaluation and these charges. The evaluation as it was explained to me by the Board Members who participated in that conference was that the evaluation was to comply with the Board's responsibility to evaluate the Superintendent and that the resolution for the issuing of these charges grew out of that evaluation. Therefore, I think it is only reasonable and logical for me to expect some correlation between the evaluation and these charges.

Finding none my question then remains as to how these charges were brought about and from whence they came. In my analysis of these charges I find that most of them, some 12, come out of memorandum from Mrs. Mason and Father Kemp. Since that is not analysis I would like to know at this time Madam President if I am privileged to have an answer, as to how the other Board members participated in the issuing of these charges?

CHRMN MORRIS: Mrs. Sizemore, I believe the questions you are raising were discussed in the Committee of the Whole and after a lengthy discussion the Committee of the Whole adopted the May 31 document. Mrs. Simmons?

SUPT SIZEMORE: Mrs. Morris, I am not finished.

CHRMN MORRIS: I am sorry.

SUPT SIZEMORE: On the evaluation form if you recall, the areas of responsibility on which I was rated are as follows:

 1. KEEPS THE BOARD INFORMED ON ISSUES, NEEDS AND OPERATION OF THE SCHOOL SYSTEM.

I received seven unsatisfactory, no satisfactory and four commendable.

 2. OFFERS PROFESSIONAL ADVICE TO THE BOARD ON ITEMS REQUIRING BOARD ACTION WITH APPROPRIATE RECOMMENDATIONS BASED ON THOROUGH STUDY AND ANALYSIS.

I received seven unsatisfactory, no satisfactory and three commendable.

 3. INTERPRETS AND EXECUTES THE INTENT OF BOARD POLICY.

I received seven unsatisfactory and four commendable.

 4. SEEKS AND ACCEPTS CONSTRUCTIVE CRITICISM OF HER WORK.

I received seven unsatisfactory, one satisfactory and three commendable.

 5. SUPPORT TO BOARD POLICY AND ACTIONS TO THE PUBLIC AND STAFF.

I received seven unsatisfactory and three commendable.

 6. HAS A HARMONIOUS WORKING RELATIONSHIP WITH THE BOARD.

I received seven unsatisfactory and three commendable.

7. UNDERSTANDS HER ROLE IN ADMINISTRATION OF BOARD POLICY; MAKES RECOMMENDATIONS FOR EMPLOYMENT OR PROMOTION OF PERSONNEL IN WRITING AND WITH SUPPORTING DATE AND ACCEPTS RESPONSIBILITY FOR HER RECOMMENDATIONS. IF THE RECOMMENDATION IS QUESTIONED BY THE BOARD, SHE FINDS ANOTHER PERSON TO RECOMMEND.

I received six unsatisfactory, two satisfactory and three commendable.

8. ACCEPTS HER RESPONSIBILITY FOR MAINTAINING LIAISON BETWEEN THE BOARD AND PERSONNEL WORKING TOWARDS A HIGHER DEGREE AND UNDERSTANDING AND RESPECT BETWEEN THE STAFF AND THE BOARD AND THE BOARD AND THE STAFF.

I received seven unsatisfactory and four commendable.

These are in areas of responsibility with relationship with the Board.

9. REMAINS IMPARTIAL TOWARDS THE BOARD TREATING ALL BOARD MEMBERS ALIKE.

I received seven unsatisfactory, and four commendable.

10. REFRAINS FROM CRITICISM OF INDIVIDUAL OR GROUP MEMBERS OF THE BOARD.

I received seven unsatisfactory and three commendable.

11. GOES IMMEDIATELY AND DIRECTLY TO THE BOARD WHEN SHE FEELS AN HONES, OBJECTIVE DIFFERENCE OF OPINION EXISTS BETWEEN HER AND ANY OR ALL MEMBERS OF THE BOARD, IN AN EARNEST EFFORT TO RESOLVE SUCH DIFFERENCE IMMEDIATELY.

I received seven unsatisfactory and four commendable.

12. FEELS FREE TO MAINTAIN HER OPPOSITION TO MATTERS UNDER DISCUSSION BY THE BOARD UNTIL AN OFFICIAL DECISION HAS BEEN REACHED, AFTER WHICH TIME SHE SUPPORTS THE VIEWS OF THE BOARD AS LONG AS SHE REMAINS IN ITS EMPLOY.

I received seven unsatisfactory and four commendable.

Community Relationships

13. GAINS RESPECT AND SUPPORT OF THE COMMUNITY ON THE CONDUCT OF THE SCHOOL OPERATION.

I received seven unsatisfactory, one satisfactory and three commendabl.

14. SOLICITS AND GIVES ATTENTION TO PROBLEMS AND OPINIONS OF ALL GROUPS AND INDIVIDUALS.

I received seven unsatisfactory and four commendable.

15. DEVELOPS FRIENDLY, AND COOPERATIVE RELATIONSHIPS WITH THE MEDIA.

I received seven unsatisfactory and three commendable.

16. PARTICIPATES ACTIVELY IN COMMUNITY LIFE AND AFFAIRS.

I received six unsatisfactory, one satisfactory and four commendable.

17. ACHIEVES STATUS AS A COMMUNITY LEADER IN PUBLIC EDUCATION.

I received seven unsatisfactory, one satisfactory and three commendable.

18. WORKS EFFECTIVELY WITH PUBLIC AND PRIVATE AGENCIES.

I received seven unsatisfactory and four commendable.

Staff and Personnel Relationships

19. DEVELOPS AND EXECUTES SOUND PERSONNEL PROCEDURES AND PRACTICES.

I received seven unsatisfactory, one satisfactory and three commendable.

20. DELEGATES AUTHORITY TO STAFF MEMBERS APPROPRIATE TO THE POSITION EACH HOLDS.

I received six unsatisfactory and three commendable.

21. RECRUITS AND ASSIGNS THE BEST AVAILABLE PERSONNEL IN TERMS OF THEIR COMPETENCIES.

I received seven unsatisfactory and four commendable.

22. TAKES AN ACTIVE ROLE IN DEVELOPMENT OF SALARY SCHEDULES FOR ALL PERSONNEL, AND RECOMMENDS TO THE BOARD THE LEVELS WHICH, WITHIN BUDGETARY LIMITATIONS, WILL BEST SERVE THE INTERESTS OF THE DISTRICT.

I received seven unsatisfactory and four commendable.

23. AT THE DIRECTION OF THE BOARD, MEETS AND CONFERS WITH THE EMPLOYEE ASSOCIATIONS REPRESENTING TO THE BEST OF HER ABILITY AND UNDERSTANDING THE INTEREST AND WILL OF THE BOARD.

I received six unsatisfactory, one satisfactory and three commendable.

Educational Leadership

24. UNDERSTANDS AND KEEPS INFORMED REGARDING ALL ASPECTS OF THE INSTRUCTIONAL PROGRAM.

I received six unsatisfactory, one satisfactory and three commendable.

25. IMPLEMENTS THE DISTRICT'S PHILOSOPHY OF EDUCATION.

I received unsatisfactory and three commendable.

26. PARTICIPATES WITH STAFF, BOARD, AND COMMUNITY IN STUDYING AND DEVELOPING CURRICULUM IMPROVEMENT.

I received six unsatisfactory, one satisfactory and four commendable.

27. ORGANIZES A PLANNED PROGRAM OF STAFF EVALUATION AND IMPROVEMENT.

I received seven unsatisfactory and three commendable.

28. PROVIDES DEMOCRATIC PROCEDURES IN CURRICULUM WORK, UTILIZING THE ABILITIES AND TALENTS OF THE ENTIRE PROFESSIONAL STAFF AND LAY PEOPLE OF THE COMMUNITY.

I received seven unsatisfactory and four commendable.

29. INSPIRES OTHERS TO HIGHEST PROFESSIONAL STANDARDS.

I received seven unsatisfactory and three commendable.

Business and Finance

30. KEEPS INFORMED ON NEEDS OF THE SCHOOL PROGRAM – PLANTS, FACILITIES, EQUIPMENT, AND SUPPLIES.

I received seven unsatisfactory and four commendable.

31. SUPERVISES OPERATIONS, INSISTING ON COMPETENT AND EFFICIENT PERFORMANCE.

I received seven unsatisfactory and four commendable.

32. DETERMINES THAT FUNDS ARE SPENT WISELY, AND ADEQUATE CONTROL AND ACCOUNTING ARE MAINTAINED.

I received seven unsatisfactory and four commendable.

33. EVALUATES FINANCIAL NEEDS AND MAKES RECOMMENDATIONS FOR ADEQUATE FINANCING.

I received seven unsatisfactory and three commendable.

This is under Personal Qualities.

34. MAINTAINS HIGH STANDARDS OF ETHICS, HONESTY, AND INTEGRITY IN ALL PROFESSIONAL MATTERS.

I received seven unsatisfactory and four commendable

35. EARNS RESPECT AND STANDING AMONG HER PROFESSIONAL COLLEAGUES.

I received seven unsatisfactory and four commendable.

36. DEVOTES HER TIME AND ENERGY EFFECTIVELY TO HER JOB.

I received seven unsatisfactory and four commendable.

37. RETAINS SENSITIVITY TO PEOPLE AND ABILITY TO RELATE WELL WITH THE DIVERSE ELEMENTS OF OUR INTERNATIONAL CITY.

I received seven unsatisfactory and four commendable.

38. EXHIBITS THE SKILL AND WILLINGNESS NEEDED TO ANTICIPATE AND RESOLVE CONFLICT WHENEVER POSSIBLE WHILE MINIMIZING DISRUPTION TO THE TEACHING AND LEARNING PROCESSES.

I received seven unsatisfactory and three commendable.

39. DEMONSTRATES THE CAPABILITY TO COMMAND THE RESPECT OF THE COMMUNITY AND CAPABILITY OF RELATING EFFECTIVELY WITH EXTERNAL FORCES ON THE LOCAL AND FEDERAL LEVELS.

I received seven unsatisfactory and three commendable.

40. EXERCISES GOOD JUDGMENT AND THE DEMOCRATIC PROCESSES IN ARRIVING AT DECISIONS.

I received seven unsatisfactory and four commendable.

41. POSSESSES AND MAINTAINS THE HEALTH AND ENERGY NECESSARY TO MEET THE RESPONSIBILITIES OF HER POSITION.

I received three unsatisfactory, four satisfactory and four commendable.

42. MAINTAINS POISE AND EMOTIONAL STABILITY IN THE FULL RANGE OF HER PROFESSIONAL ACTIVITIES.

I received seven unsatisfactory and four commendable.

43. USES LANGUAGE EFFECTIVELY IN DEALING WITH STAFF MEMBERS, THE BOARD, AND THE PUBLIC.

I received seven unsatisfactory and four commendable.

44. WRITES CLEARLY AND CONCISELY.

I received seven unsatisfactory and four commendable.

45. THINKS WELL ON HER FEET WHEN FACED WITH AN UNEXPECTED OR DISTURBING TURN OF EVENTS IN A LARGE GROUP MEETING.

I received seven unsatisfactory and four commendable.

46. DEVELOPS GOOD STAFF MORALE AND LOYALTY TO THE ORGANIZATION.

I received seven unsatisfactory and four commendable.

47. TREATS ALL PERSONNEL FAIRLY, WITHOUT FAVORITISM OR DISCRIMINATION, WHILE INSISTING ON PERFORMANCE OF DUTIES.

I received seven unsatisfactory and four commendable.

48. ENCOURAGES PARTICIPATION OF APPROPRIATE STAFF MEMBERS AND GROUPS IN PLANNING, PROCEDURES, AND POLICY INTERPRETATION.

I received seven unsatisfactory and three commendable.

49. DEFENDS PRINCIPLE AND CONVICTION IN THE FACT OF PRESSURE AND PARTISAN INFLUENCE.

I received two unsatisfactory, five satisfactory and four commendable.

50. DEMONSTRATES HER ABILITY TO WORK WELL WITH INDIVIDUALS AND GROUPS.

I received seven unsatisfactory and four commendable.

The total for this evaluation was 335 unsatisfactory, 19 satisfactory and 181 commendable. The basis of the percentage If I recall the meeting correctly, there were 60.9 percent unsatisfactory, 3.4 percent satisfactory and 32.9 percent commendable, and on the basis on this unsatisfactory evaluation the Board passed a resolution to issue the charges to me. As I repeat and as you can very well see, there is very little relationship between the charges issued to me in the evaluation. Most of the charges come from Business and Finance section if you will notice -- and issued memoranda sent to me by Mrs. Mason and Father Kemp.

In the evaluation sessions which ensued on May 1, however, there was little discussion of those memoranda except as of that April 7 meeting. As I recall correctly, there was some discussion from each of these people about my relationship at certain meetings and under certain circumstances. One of the concerns as I recall that Mrs. Mason had was about a meeting of December, 1973 when some lawyers, which I had asked her to bring to the meeting, were thrown out of that meeting because the meeting was to be a closed meeting and Mr. Mason was one of those people. As I recall, I am not certain as to how that concern is addressed in these charges and that is only one example of the many things that were discussed in that meeting, Madam President, which do not appear in these charges. My question still is Madam President, how do these charges relate to my evaluation and how were they arrived in lieu of the discussion that we had when we talked about this evaluation?

CHRMN MORRIS: Mrs. Sizemore, I believe the report before us is on the May 31 letter. Now, all of the data that you have read into the record, and I certainly did not interfere or interrupt at the time you were reading it, is quite alright. But you will recall as every other member that at the time of that evaluation we did indeed pass the motion which directed the General Counsel and the Corporation Counsel to set forth a Bill of Particulars. We dealt with certain specific documents and we did not include the evaluation instrument as such but all of the data and the items that had been pulled together. Now, if there is a request for those items, I believe everything that we dealt with in setting forth the Bill of Particulars we have discussed at length and the purpose of this particular motion is to approve the Committee of the Whole's report which was dated May 31.

SUPT SIZEMORE: Am I to understand Madam President that there is no relationship between the evaluation which took place April 28, 30 and May 1 and these charges?

CHRMN MORRIS: All of those are a portion of a total package. I believe we have previously discussed that Mrs. Sizemore.

SUPT SIZEMORE: I am sorry Madam President.

CHRMN MORRIS: I said all of that is a part of a total package and a total package was dealt with in terms of the establishment of the Bill of Particulars. We set forth specific areas that would be covered in this. We have discussed this at length and we have held massive discussions on it and this is a report on the May 31 letter.

SUPT SIZEMORE: But I don't recall seeing five of those items in the evaluation in these charges. I don't see nothing about my being about to write concisely in these charges.

CHRMN MORRIS: Well, Mrs. Sizemore, this is not the first time that this document has been discussed and I believe those very same questions were raised. They are a matter of record, and at this time I wish to have the question addressed to the May 31 document which is the item that is before us.

SUPT SIZEMORE: Madam President, this is my first opportunity to --

(QUESTIONS WERE FURTHER PROPOUNDED TO MRS. MORRIS BY MRS. SIZEMORE)

A: -- No Mrs. Sizemore. This is not your first opportunity.

Q: Madam President, this is my first opportunity to address --

A: (Interposing): -- Mrs. Sizemore, we held many sessions on this during the month of April. We started in December and you were given an opportunity to discuss this document.

Q: May 31?

A: You were given an opportunity to discuss it.

Q: I am sorry -- the May 31 document?

A: May 31, yes --

Q: No, no.

A: (continuing): -- and you left the meeting because you did not have an attorney.

Q: Therefore, this public board meeting is my first opportunity. Mrs. Mason, may I talk please? Madam President are you recognizing me or Mrs. Mason?

A: I am addressing my remarks to your response.

At the time we held the May 31 meeting you will recall and I believe the record will -- (pounding the gavel) May we please have quietness. I am asking Board Members as well as members of the audience.

Mrs. Sizemore, on the May 31 meeting at the time this document was presented on the Committee of the Whole you were given an opportunity to speak, and if you will recall, you did not remain at the meeting because of your desire to have an attorney. However,

718

this letter has been submitted to you and we do indeed have a very lengthy response from you on every single issue including exhibits.

Q: That's correct. But we are doing this all over again now to make it legal. So this is my first opportunity in this new legal process to question the relationship between the evaluation which took place April 28, 30 and May 1 and the drawing up of these charges. This was my only opportunity to do that Madam President.

A: Thank you Mrs. Sizemore. I believe Mrs. Simmons -- where is Mrs. Simmons? Mrs. Simmons had requested --

MRS. SIMMONS: --I am here.

CHRMN MORRIS: Okay. You are on.

MRS. SIMMONS: Thank you Madam President. Madam President first I would like to say that the report as you read it and I am sure you would want it to be accurate and I am sure you would want it to be complete. So I just call to your attention that the meeting on May 31 here list one at large Board Member name Barbara Lett Simmons as present. I have in front of me the transcript labeled, "The Official Transcript" where I am not listed as present, yet on page 19 which is the first page following your reading into the record all of the memoranda that you referred to -- the first inquiry was a point of clarification made by one Mrs. Simmons who was not present.

CHRMN MORRIS: (interposing): -- Who came in later.

MRS. SIMMONS: The fact is that this was not transcribed before I arrived.

# APPENDIX III

## INTERVIEW SCHEDULE

INTERVIEW SURVEY--D.C. BOARD OF EDUCATION MEMBERS 1973-1975

THIS CASE STUDY WILL BE AN INDEPTH EXAMINATION OF FACTORS IMPINGING ON THE DECISION-MAKING PROCESS IN SCHOOL BOARD-SUPERINTENDENT RELATIONS THROUGH A MODEL OF SUPERINTENDENT-SCHOOL BOARD CONFLICT DESIGNED BY THIS WRITER.

THE PRIMARY RESEARCH TECHNIQUE WILL BE THE FIELD STUDY APPROACH. OBSERVATION, SCHOOL BOARD MEETINGS AND COMMITTEE MEETING MINUTES AND TRANSCRIPTS, SCHOOL BOARD HEARING TRANSCRIPTS, MEMORANDA, REPORTS AND RECORDS FROM THE SCHOOL SYSTEM, RELATED AGENCIES, THE FEDERAL GOVERNMENT AND NEWSPAPERS WILL BE USED TO INVESTIGATE THE FACTORS IMPINGING ON THE DECISION-MAKING PROCESS WHICH LED TO CONFLICT IN SUPERINTENDENT-SCHOOL BOARD RELATIONS. SEMI-STRUCTURED INTERVIEWS WILL BE CONDUCTED WITH KEY PARTICIPANTS.

THIS RESEARCH IS UNDERTAKEN WITH THE BELIEF THAT AS A RESULT OF THE OBSERVATIONS AND INQUIRIES MADE, SIGNIFICANT INFORMATION WILL BE REVEALED TO UNDERSTAND MORE CLEARLY THE NATURE OF CONFLICTS BETWEEN BOARDS OF EDUCATION AND SUPERINTENDENTS VIS A VIS POLICY MAKING AND IMPLEMENTATION.

1. When did you serve on the school board or become an administrator in the D.C. Public School System?

2. What was your occupation before you became a school board member or administrator in the D.C.P.S.?

3. What became your occupation when you left the D.C.P.S. System?

4. What is your definition of the role of a D.C.B.O.E. member? Are there any exceptions to your definition? If so, what are they?

5. How do/did you perceive of your role in a majority black, majority female school system serving majority poor children?

6. To what extent do you see yourself as a representative of your electoral constituency or of the city in general?

7. Did the instability of the DCBOE membership affect the goals of the system. If so, in what ways?

8. What were the goals of the D.C.B.O.E. and in your opinion how many of these goals were actually achieved?

9. What procedure did the D.C.B.O.E. use to execute its functions?

10. What were the power and status resources of the D.C.B.O.E.?

11. Of the issues listed on this paper, do you feel that any issues were major problems? They are ordered by date and the listing has no other significance. Please describe the nature of the problem, the participants, and the outcome?

12. How did the D.C.B.O.E. handle the issues that arose during 1973-1975? What positions were staked out, what bargaining took place, and what values were traded?

13. What items arose as issues and emerged as charges for the termination of the Superintendent's contract? Why do you think some issues did not become charges?

14. Do you feel that the school board has enough control over policies? How would you improve the school board's voice?

15. Who were the most powerful and influential school board members during 1973-1975? Why do you think these people were influential? Over what issue(s) did they have influence?

16. What community groups had great influence over decisions made by the school board? Which issues did these groups influence?

17. What is your definition of the D.C. Superintendency?

18. How stable has the superintendenty been? Did this effect the goals of the system? If so, in what ways?

19. What were your perceptions of the goals of the superintendent and how many of these goals do you believe were actually achieved?

20. What are your perceptions of the functions (tasks, duties and responsibilities) of the D.C. Superintendent? How did the superintendent execute administrative functions?

21. What were the power and status resources of the superintendency?

22. What was your opinion of how the superintendent handled the issues that arose during 1973-1975? What positions were staked out, what bargaining took place, and what values were traded?

23. Who were the most powerful and influential administrators in the school system? Why do you think these people were influential? Over what issues did they have influence?

24. Do you feel that the superintendent had enough control over policies? How would you improve the superintendent's voice?

25. What community groups had great influence over decisions made by the superintendent? Which issues did these groups influence?

26. What were the critical administrative problems that you saw in the school system?

27. Would you care to make any comments about the decision making process engaged in by the D.C.B.O.E. and the superintendent of schools that were not covered in this interview?

## ISSUES

| | |
|---|---|
| .the superintendency search and selection | Aug. 73 |
| .Burroughs Elementary School Dispute | Oct. 73 |
| .Pomeroy and Erie School Dispute | Nov. 73 |
| .Cozette Carter Tenure Dispute | Nov. 73 |
| .Mills vs. DCBOE (Waddy Decree) Complaint | Dec. 73 |
| .Hobson vs. Hansen (Wright Decree) Complaint | Dec. 73 |
| .Student Identification Dispute | Jan. 74 |
| .Weatherless Elementary School Dispute | Feb. 74 |
| .120 Day Report Controversy | Mar. 74 |
| .Hawthorne Alternative School Dispute | Apr. 74 |
| .Administrative Reorganization Controversy | May 74 |
| .D.C. Youth Orchestra Controversy | June 74 |
| .Staff Development Controversy | July 74 |
| .Decentralization Dispute | July 74 |
| .General Counsel Dispute | Aug. 74 |
| .CSO Union Contract Impasse | Aug. 74 |
| .WTU Union Contract Impasse | Aug. 74 |
| .Opening of Schools Problems | Sept. 74 |
| .Teacher Payroll Problems | Sept. 74 |
| .Mayor's Freeze | Oct. 74 |
| .Overhiring /Budget Deficit | Nov. 74 |
| .Hobson Task Force Dispute | Nov. 74 |
| .FY 76 Budget/FY 75 Financial Plan | Dec. 74 |
| .Title I Comparability/Wright Decree | Dec. 74 |
| .AHSA Speech Controversy | Apr. 75 |
| .Superintendent's Evaluation | Apr. 75 |
| .Hearings on Termination of Contract | July 75 |

# BIBLIOGRAPHY

BIBLIOGRAPHY

BOOKS

Baldridge, Victor and Deal, Terrence E. Managing
   Change in Educational Organizations. Berkeley,
California: McCutchan Publishing Corporation, 1975.

Banks, James A., ed. Teaching Ethnic Studies:
   Concepts and Strategies. 43rd Yearbook.
   Washington, D.C.: National Council for the
   Social Studies, 1973.

Barnard, Chester I. The Functions of the Executive.
   Cambridge, Mass.: Harvard University Press,
   1968.

Cunningham, Luvern L. Governing Schools - New
   Approaches to Old Issues. Columbus, Ohio:
   Charles E. Merrill Publishing Company, 1971.

Frazier, E. Franklin. Black Bourgeoisie: The Rise
   of a New Middle Class in the United States.
   Glencoe, Illinois: The Free Press, 1957.

Getzels, Jacob W., Lipman, James M., and Campbell,
   Roald F. Educational Administration as a
   Social Process - Theory, Research, Practice.
   New York: Harper and Row, Publishers, 1968.

Green, Constance McLaughlin. The Secret City - A
   History of Race Relations in the Nation's
   Capital. Princeton, N.J.: Princeton Univer-
   sity Press, 1967.

Gross, Neal. Who Runs Our Schools? New York:
   Wiley, 1975.

Hansen, Carl F. *Danger in Washington - The Story of My Twenty Years in the Public Schools in the Nation's Capital.* West Nyack: Parker Publishing Company, Inc., 1968.

_____. *The Amidon Elementary School - A Successful Demonstration in Basic Education.* Englewood Cliffs, N.J.: Prentice-Hall, Inc., 1962.

_____. *The Four Track Curriculum for Today's High Schools.* Englewood Cliffs, N.J.: Prentice-Hall, Inc., 1964.

Hamphill, John K., Griffiths, Daniel E., and Frederiksen, Norman. *Administrative Performance and Personality: A Study of the Principal in a Simulated Elementary School.* New York: Bureau of Publications, Teachers College, Columbia University, 1962.

Himes, Joseph S. *Racial Conflict in American Society.* Columbus, Ohio: Charles E. Merrill Publishing Company, 1973.

Lenski, Gerhard. *Power and Privilege.* New York: McGraw-Hill, 1967.

Moore, Rev. Douglas E. *The Buying and Selling of the D.C. City Council.* Washington, D.C.: Rev. Douglas E. Moore, 1978.

Lasswell, Harold D. and Kaplan, Abraham. *Power and Society.* New Haven: Yale University Press, 1950.

Morgenthau, Hans. *Politics Among Nations.* New York: Alfred A. Knoff, 1966.

Park, Robert E. and Burgess, Ernest. *Introduction to the Science of Sociology.* Chicago: University of Chicago Press, 1921.

Passow, A. Harry. *Toward Creating a Model Urban School System: A Study of the Washington, D.C. Public School*. New York: Teachers College, Columbia University, 1967.

Pusey, Merlo J. *Eugene Meyer*. New York: Alfred A. Knoff, 1974.

Rosenthal, Allen. *Governing Education*. Garden City, New York: Anchor Books, 1969.

Sexton, Patricia. *Women in Education*. Bloomington, Indiana: Phi Delta Kappa Educational Foundation, 1976.

Sestak, Michael E. and Fredrich, David D. "The Principal's Role in School-Community Relations," *Selected Articles for Elementary School Principals*. Washington, D.C.: Department of Elementary School Principals, National Education Association, 1968.

Simon, Herbert A. *Administrative Behavior - A Study of Decision-Making Processes in Administrative Organizations*. Glencoe, Ill.: The Free Press, 1957.

_____. *Models of Man*. New York: John Wiley and Sons, Inc., 1956.

Staples, Robert. *Introduction to Black Sociology*. New York: McGraw-Hill Book Company, 1976.

## JOURNALS AND MAGAZINES

"Big-City School Posts: Can Anyone Hold the Job?" *Education USA*, 17, 21 July 1975, p. 259.

Billingsley, Amy and Nagle, Pat. "An Interview with Barbara Sizemore," *Bulletin Board*, February 1974, pp. 2-4.

Cleaver, Eldridge. "Education and Revolution." *The Black Scholar* 1 (November 1969), p. 46.

Dale, Charlene T. "Women are Still Missing Persons in Administrative and Supervisory Jobs." *Educational Leadership* 31, November 1973, pp. 123-27.

"The Dysfunctions of Public Education," *The Black Child Advocate*, November 1974, p. 6.

"Educators Discuss Board-Superintendent Relations in District," *Bulletin Board*, December 1974, pp. 1, 2 and 5.

Friedman, Betty and West, Anne Grant. "Sex Bias: The Built-in Mentality that Maims the Public Schools." *American School Board Journal* 159, October 1971, pp. 16-20.

Gregg, Russell T. and Knezevich, Stephen J. "The Superintendent: What Makes Him What He Is." *American School Board Journal* 158, June 1971, pp. 12-17.

Grobman, Hulda and Hines, Vynce A., "What Makes a Good Principal?" *Bulletin of the National Association of Secondary School Principals* 40, November 1956, pp. 5-16.

Hunter, Mary R., "Looking for a Superperson," *Bulletin Board*, April 1977, pp. 7-9.

_____. "Looking for a Superperson, Part II: Barbara A. Sizemore - 1973-75," *Bulletin Board*, May 1977, pp. 3-6.

"Interview: Barbara Sizemore," *Black Books Bulletin* 2, Winter 1974, pp. 50-59.

Malone, Louise, "D.C. School Budget - FY'75," *Bulletin Board*, April 1974, pp. 1, 2 and 5.

"The New Budget What Will Happen to the Schools?" *Bulletin Board*, 5 September 1972, pp. 1-3.

Poinsett, Alex. "Barbara Sizemore Tackles Job of Running Nation's 12th Largest School System,"

*Ebony Magazine.* January 1974, p. 102.

Sansing, John, "Can Whites Survive in D.C. or Are We Going Toward a 'Chocolate City' and 'Vanilla Suburbs'?", *Washingtonian*, October 1976, p. 37.

"The School Board: Who Does What, Why and With Whom," *Bulletin Board*, May 1974, p. 3.

Sizemore, Barbara A. "Education: Is Accommodation Enough?", *The Journal of Negro Education* 44, Summer 1975, pp. 233-246.

_____. "Education and Justice Through PACTS," *Comment*, November 1973, pp. 1-8.

_____. "The Four M Curriculum: A Way to Shape The Future," *The Journal of Negro Education* 48, Summer 1979, pp. 341-356.

Solomon, Steve. "The Nader Report on ETS," *The Testing Digest*, Spring 1980, p. 37.

Stone, Chuck. "A Black Paper: Standardized Tests: True or False." *The Black Collegian* 6, November/December 1975, pp. 44-56.

Taylor, Edwin F. "The Looking Glass World of Testing," *Today's Education*, March-April 1977, p. 42.

"350 Attend Conference on Testing Reform Strategies," *The Testing Digest*, Spring 1980, p. 13.

"Voter Information," *Bulletin Board*, August-September, 1973, p. 1.

Watson, Bernard, "Interview: Barbara Sizemore," *Cross Reference* 1, May/June 1978, p. 236.

"What's Wrong with Standardized Testing," *Today's Education*, March-April 1977, p. 37.

Wiles, Kimball and Gross, Hulda. "Principals As Leaders," <u>Nations Schools</u> 56, October 1955, p. 75.

Williams, Robert L., "The Politics of I.Q., Racism and Power," <u>The Journal of Afro-American Issues</u> 3, Winter 1975, p. 1.

NEWSPAPERS

<u>Hilltop</u>, September 1975, 2 December 1977.

<u>New York Times</u>, 28 September 1976.

<u>Power</u>, August 1975.

<u>Washington Afro-American</u>, 1 July and 2 October 1967; 30 March 1968; 4 March and 7 September 1974.

<u>Washington Daily News</u>, 1 September 1967; 21 January 1972.

<u>Washington Post</u>, 19 March 1967; 6 July 1968; 20 January, 15 February, 31 March, 26 April, 13 June and 24 October 1972; 19 January, 18 July and 9 October 1973; 16 May, 25 May, 13 June, 7 July, 9 July, 2 September, 4 September, 6 September, 5 November, 7 November and 15 December 1974; 5 April, 2 May, 4 May, 5 May, 11 May, 30 July, 4 August, 5 August, 7 August, 9 August, 12 August, 21 August, 23 August, 28 August, 30 August, 7 September, 9 September, 15 September, 26 September, 27 September, 28 September, 11 October, 12 October and 25 October 1975; 14 September 1976; 3 January, 13 May, 7 July, 7 August and 12 August 1977; 30 January, 6 February, 9 February, 19 February, 23 March, 8 April, 30 April, 3 May, 4 May, 23 June, 24 June and 31 August 1978.

<u>Washington Star</u>, 1 October, 4 October, 25 October and 25 April 1967; 5 January 1968; January, 2 February and 9 May 1972; 14 January, 28 July and 18 November 1973; 18 April, 28 May, 14

June, 8 July, 17 August, 6 September, 23 October and 12 December 1974; 28 January, 11 February, 16 March, 4 April, 9 April, 2 May, 8 May, 11 May, 1 June, 1 August, 13 August and 14 August 1975; 25 January 1976.

COURT CASES

Hobson v. Hansen, 269F. Supp. 401 (1967).

Hobson v. Hansen, 327F. Supp. 844 (1971).

Superior Court of the District of Columbia, Civil Division, Barbara A. Sizemore, Plaintiff v. Virginia Morris, et alia, Defendant, Civil Action No. 5461-75, Order, William Steward, Jr., Judge, 25 July 1975.

PUBLIC DOCUMENTS

U.S. Government Documents and Publications

U.S. Bureau of the Census; Current Population Reports Series P-23, No. 67. "Population Estimates by Race for States: July 1, 1973 and 1975," Washington, D.C.: U.S. Government Printing Office, 1978.

U.S. Bureau of the Census; Statistical Abstract of the United States, 98th Edition, Washington, D.C.: U.S. Government Printing Office.

U.S. Congress, House of Representatives; Public Law No. 90-292, 90th Congress, H.R. 13042, 22 April 1968.

D.C. Government Documents and Publications

Washington, Walter E., Mayor. Ten Years Since April 4, 1968: A Decade of Progress for the District of Columbia - A Report to the People, The District of Columbia. Washington, D.C., 4 April 1978.

A Compilation of Laws Relating to Elections, Election Campaigns, Lobbying and Conflict of Interest in the District of Columbia, Washington, D.C.: District of Columbia Board of Elections and Ethics, Office of General Counsel, District Building, April 1977.

Government of the District of Columbia, Board of Elections, Washington, D.C. Hilda Howland Campaign Committee, "Report of Campaign Contributions, 12 November 1977; "Report of Receipts and Expenditures for a Candidate," 10 October 1975; "Report of Receipts and Expenditures for a Candidate," 20 October 1975; "Report of Receipts and Expenditures for a Candidate," 30 October 1975; "Report of Campaign Contributions," 23 November 1971

_____. The Committee to Re-elect John Warren, "Report of Receipts and Expenditures for a Committee," 25 October 1976, January 1975, 10 October 1975, 24 October 1975, 10 December 1975, 17 October 1974

_____. Citizens to Re-elect Bettie Benjamin, "Report of Receipts and Expenditures for a Committee," 15 October 1975, 20 October 1975.

_____. The Carol Schwartz for School Board Committee, "Report of Receipts and Expenditures for a Committee, 21 October 1974, 30 October 1974, 10 December 1974, 31 January 1975.

_____. Citizens for Virginia Morris, "Report of Receipts and Expenditures," 29 October 1975, 10 December 1975.

_____. Citizens for Kane, "Report of Receipts and Expenditures for a Committee," 15 October 1975, 10 December 1975.

_____. Raymond B. Kemp, Ward 1. "Report of Campaign Contributions," 3 January 1971.

_____. Dr. Therman Evans' Campaign Fund, "Report of Campaign Contributions," 28 January 1974.

_____. Bill Treanor Campaign Committee, "Report of Campaign Contributions," 1 November 1973, 23 November 1973, 29 January 1974.

_____. Campaign folder, Memorandum to Thornell Page from Marion Barry, 6 May 1973.

_____. Albert A. Rosenfield, "Report of Campaign Contributions," 31 October 1973, 10 December 1973.

_____. Martha S. Swaim, "Report of Campaign Contributions," 7 January 1972.

_____. Citizen's Coalition for Cassell, "Report of Campaign Contributions,' 1 November 1973.

_____. Marion Barry for School Board, "Report of Campaign Contributions, 3 December 1971.

_____. Delores Pryde for Board of Education, "Report of Campaign Contributions," Accounting period September through 5 December 1971.

_____. Ward 5 Committee for Mattie G. Taylor, "Report of Campaign Contributions," 20 December 1971.

Hanson, Royce and Bernard H. Ross, <u>Governing the District of Columbia: An Introduction</u>, Washington, D.C.: Washington Center for Metropolitan Studies, January 1971.

1975 Population Estimates City-Wards-Anc's Census Tracts for Washington, D.C., Washington, D.C.: Government of the District of Columbia Municipal Planning Office, May 1977.

1976 Population Estimates Provisional City-Wards for Washington, D.C.: Government of the District of Columbia Municipal Planning Office, November 1977.

Washington, D.C., <u>D.C. Code</u> (1968 and 1973).

<u>Report of the Special Committee on Group Activities of the District of Columbia</u>, 8 January 1963.

### D. C. Board of Education Documents and Publications

Administrative Hearing Officer's Transmittal to the Board of Education for the District of Columbia, Board of Education of the District of Columbia, Petitioner vs. Barbara A. Sizemore, Superintendent of Schools for the District of Columbia, Respondent, re: Proposed Adverse Action By the Board of Education Against Barbara A. Sizemore, 9 September 1975.

"Background for Workshop on Education - School Decentralization and Community Involvement," League of Women Voters, 18 March 1970.

Bellamy, Wilbur, Coordinator, Resource Professional Program, 1972-1973 Progress Report Resource Professional Program, D.C. Youth Orchestra Program, Music Department, Public Schools of the District of Columbia, 30 June 1973.

Board of Education, "Goals of the Board of Education," Washington, D.C.: Public Schools of the District of Columbia, 15 January 1973, mimeographed paper.

Cropp, Dwight S., Executive Secretary, "Report of the Joint Committee on Educational Programs and Student Services and Community Involvement," 12 August 1974.

D.C. Board of Education, Committee Structure, mimeographed, Washington, D.C., 1975-76.

D.C. Board of Education. Rules of the Board of Education, Washington, D.C.: D.C. Public Schools, 1971.

_____. Rules of the Board of Education, Washington, D.C., D.C. Public Schools, Revised through 22 January 1975.

_____. "Statement to friends from Martha Swaim re: Barbara A. Sizemore as Superintendent," 7 August 1973.

D.C. Federation of Civic Associations 1977 Directory, Washington, D.C.

D.C. Public School System. Superintendent's Contract, Washington, D.C.: D.C. Public School System, 6 September 1973.

Equal Employment Opportunity Commission, "Elementary-Secondary Staff Information," EEO-5, 1 October 1977.

ESAA Grant Proposal, Component B., 1974.

Fantini, Mario D., Young, Milton A., and Douglas, Freda. A Design for a New and Relevant System of Education for Fort Lincoln New Town, Washington, D.C.: D.C. Schools and Ford Foundation, 15 August 1958.

Freeman, Gary. Region VI Progress Report, 1974-75. Washington, D.C.: District of Columbia Public Schools, July 1975.

Gullatee, Latinee, Committee Chairman, "Report of the Committee on Elementary Instrumental Music," 25 August 1972.

Government of the District of Columbia, Bureau of Procurement, Department of Public Schools, Negotiated Services Contract, 24 September 1973.

Interim Report of the Advisory Commission on Educational Law Revision, Washington, D.C.: D.C. Public School System, 2 November 1976.

McLain, Lyn, Director, D.C. Youth Orchestra Program, "Brief Report of Incident of Saturday, 23 March 1974," 26 March 1974.

Manning, William R. (Superintendent). Major Activities, 1968, mimeographed.

Memorandum of Understanding Between D.C. Board of Education and Superintendent of Schools, 15 March 1972.

Model School Division. <u>Model School Division: A Report to the Board of Education</u>. Washington, D.C.: District of Columbia Public Schools, June 1967.

Motion for Preliminary Injunction and Memorandum of Points and Authorities in Support of Motion for Temporary Restraining Order and Preliminary Injunction, 1976.

<u>The People of the District of Columbia: A Demographic Social, Economic and Physical Profile of the District of Columbia and Its Nine Service Areas</u>, Washington, D.C.: Office of Planning, 1973.

Petition signed by 22 persons and submitted to Superintendent Scott, Marion Barry, other administrators and some citizens, 8 September 1972.

Position Description, Special Assistant, D.C. Board of Education, Position Control, 31 May 1973.

The Public Schools of the District of Columbia. <u>The Board of Education Administrative and Supervisory Staff Directory</u>, Washington, D.C., 1969.

Presumably draft of statement to Mrs. Mason's 5 July 1974 memo, from Superintendent Sizemore, unsigned, undated.

Reed, Vincent E. A Design for A Competency-Based Curriculum-Pre-Kindergarten-Grade Twelve, Washington, D.C.: Public Schools of the District of Columbia, April 1976.

_____. Superintendent of Schools. Alternative Plan for Equalizing Educational Resources, Washington, D.C.: Public Schools of the District of Columbia, May 1977.

_____. Decentralization Report Phase II, Washington, D.C.: Public Schools of the District of Columbia, 28 May 1976.

_____. Meeting the Challenge-Annual Report of the Public Schools of the District of Columbia for 1976, Washington, D.C.: Division of Communications and Public Relations, 1976.

Report from Committee on Student Services and Community Involvement, Chairman, Julius Hobson, Jr. "Report on the Joint Committees on Educational Programs and Student Services and Community Involvement," 17 September 1974.

Report of the District of Columbia Board of Education's Committee of the Whole on Personnel, 31 May 1975.

Response to Educational Needs Report, Washington, D.C.: District of Columbia Public Schools, August 1972.

Scott, Hugh J. The Superintendent's Annual Report. Washington, D.C.: District of Columbia Public Schools, December, 1971.

_____. Superintendent's Identification of Tasks Resource Needs and Prerequisite Actions Associated with the Ten Priority Goals of the

Board of Education: A Planning Document.
Washington, D.C.: District of Columbia
Public Schools, February 1973.

_____. The Superintendent's 120-Day Report.
Washington, D.C., District of Columbia Public
Schools, 17 February 1971.

_____. "Proposed Administrative Reorganization of the D.C. Public School System,"
Reorganization Summary, District of Columbia
Public Schools, 5 May 1971.

Sizemore, Barbara A., Superintendent of Schools,
"Become 'Comparable' and 'Equal': Questions
and Answers," January 1975.

_____. Superintendent of Schools Reorganization of Central Office, Washington, D.C.:
Public Schools of the District of Columbia,
8 November 1974.

_____. The Superintendent's 120-Day Report.
Washington, D.C.: District of Columbia Public
Schools, March 1974.

Statement of Barbara A. Sizemore, "A Retreat From
Progress: Back to the Basics?," read at a
DCBOE community meeting, undated; copy from
Barbara Simmons' file dated in handwriting as
3 December 1975.

_____, Superintendent, D.C. Public Schools,
Press Release, 25 September 1974.

Statement of Chairman, Charles C. Diggs, Jr.,
Regarding The School-Board-School Superintendent Controversy in the District of Columbia
Committee on the District of Columbia, U.S.
House of Representatives, Washington, D.C.,
23 July 1975.

Statement by Richard B. Steinkemp Before the Board
of Education of the District of Columbia at
Its Meeting of 8 April 1975.

Statement by Virginia Morris, President, Board of
    Education, Press Release, "The Board of Educa-
    tion of the District of Columbia: Its Role and
    Authority," 25 September 1974.

Statement of President of the Board of Education,
    from Barbara A. Simmons' files, 6 May 1975.

Strayer, George D. *The Report of a Survey of the
    Public Schools of the District of Columbia*,
    Washington, D.C.: Government Printing Office,
    1949.

Summary of Membership for All School Levels by Race,
    Washington, D.C.: Division of Research and
    Evaluation, 20 October 1960 through 21 October
    1976.

Synopsis of Superintendent's Response to the Commit-
    tee of the Whole on Personnel Letter, 31 May
    1975, 1 August 1975.

Taylor, Hortense, Chairman, Proposal Committee,
    "Toward a Comprehensive Music Education Program
    of Quality for the Public Schools of Washington,
    D.C.--K-12," 18 July 1972.

*The Superintendent's Annual Report: School Year
    1970-71*, Washington, D.C.: District of Colum-
    bia Public Schools, December 1971.

The Superintendent's Response to the Committee of
    the Whole on Personnel Letter, 31 May 1975.

The Respondent's Answer submitted to the DCBOE in
    compliance with the specifications of the
    charges brought against the Superintendent,
    Barbara A. Sizemore, 25 June 1975.

Williams, James L., Deputy Superintendent, *Adminis-
    trative Reorganization and Major Responsibili-
    ties of Management Services of the District of
    Columbia Public Schools*--Part I, Washington,
    D.C.: DCPS, May 1974.

CORRESPONDENCE

Correspondence with attached report, "The D.C.
Youth Orchestra Program and the Morale of the
Public School Instrumental Music Teachers," to
Dr. James T. Guines, Associate Superintendent of
Schools, from Barbara White, Representative,
Superintendent's Advisory Council, Elementary
Instrumental Music Department, and Rosanna B.
Saffran, Teacher, Elementary Instrumental
Music Department, 16 July 1971.

_____ to Mr. Delroy L. Cornick, Director,
Department of Budget and Legislation, DCPS,
from Mrs. Paul D. Gable, Supervising Director,
Music Department, and Lyn G. McLain, Director,
D.C.Y.O.P., 9 October 1970.

_____ to Barbara A. Sizemore, Superintendent
of Schools, from Myrtle Morris, President, re:
Friends of the DCYOP, 22 May 1974.

_____ to Mrs. Virginia Morris, President, Board
of Education, from Barbara A. Sizemore, 19
September 1974.

Memorandum from Claudette E. Helms, Director of
Personnel, New Salary Scales for TSA and GS
Personnel, DCPSS, Division of Personnel,
11 October 1978.

Letter to Mrs. Barbara A. Sizemore from Edward G.
Winner, Deputy Superintendent, 31 May 1977.

_____ to Mrs. Barbara A. Sizemore from Virginia
Morris, President, DCBOE, 24 February 1975.

_____ to Mrs. Virginia M. Morris, President,
DCBOE, from Barbara A. Sizemore, Superintendent,
25 February 1975.

_____ to Barbara A. Sizemore, Superintendent,
from Virginia Morris, President, DCBOE, 11
March 1975.

_____ to David A. Splitt, General Council, DCBOE, from Dwight S. Cropp, Executive Secretary, DCBOE, 2 May 1975.

_____ to Virginia Morris, President, DCBOE, from Paul B. Salmon, Executive Director, American Association of School Administrators, 8 May 1975.

_____ to Paul B. Salmon, Executive Director, American Association of School Administrators, from Virginia Morris, President, DCBOE, 13 May 1975.

_____ to DCBOE from DeLong Harris, Counsel for Barbara A. Sizemore, Superintendent, DCPSS, 31 May 1975.

_____ to Superintendent Sizemore, from DCBOE President Virginia Morris, Attachment E, 31 May 1975.

_____ to Dwight S. Cropp, Executive Secretary, DCBOE, from DeLong Harris, Counsel for Superintendent Sizemore, re: Mrs. Barbara A. Sizemore, Superintendent of Schools, 2 June 1975.

_____ to Superintendent Sizemore from Dwight S. Cropp, Executive Secretary, DCBOE, 29 August 1975.

_____ to Superintendent Sizemore, from James E. Hall, Junior Band Director, 26 March 1974.

_____ to Floretta McKenzie, Deputy Superintendent, from Juanita Thompson, President, Junior Band Boosters, 4 April 1974.

_____ to Lyn McLain, Teacher, from Floretta D. McKenzie, Deputy Superintendent, 4 April 1974.

_____ of Evaluation to Superintendent Sizemore from Howard University Team of Educators, 3 May 1974.

_____ to the President and Members of the DCBOE from Martha S. Swaim, Member, DCBOE, 31 May 1974.

_____ to Myrtle C. Morris, President, from James T. Guines, Associate Superintendent, re: Friends of the DCYOP, 31 May 1974.

_____ to the President and Members, DCBOE, from Martha S. Swaim, Member, DCBOE, 31 May 1974, and an attachment, "D.C. Schools As a System," 3 June 1974.

_____ to Richard L. Hurlbut, Chief, Tuition Act Enforcement Branch, from Lyn McLain, Director, DCYOP, 4 June 1974.

_____ of Intent, Myrtle C. Morris, President, Friends of the DCYOP, 9 July 1974.

_____ from Relford Patterson, Ph.D. Chairman, Department of Music, Howard University, 10 July 1974.

_____ to Lyn McLain, Director, DCYOP, from Richard L. Hurlbut, Chief, Tuition Act Enforcement Branch, DCPSS, re: Payment of Tuition, 15 July 1974.

_____ to Superintendent Sizemore, DCPSS, from President Myrtle C. Morris, Friends of the DCYOP, Inc., 29 July 1974.

_____ to Superintendent Sizemore, from Dwight S. Cropp, Executive Secretary, DCBOE, 2 August 1974.

_____ to Superintendent Sizemore, from Reverend Raymond B. Kemp, Member, DCBOE, 14 August 1974.

_____ to Superintendent Sizemore, DCPSS, from Edward Maguire, Chief Negotiator, Friends of the DCYOP, Inc., and Dr. James Johnson, Chief Negotiator, DCPSS, 17 August 1974.

_____ to Rev. Raymond B. Kemp, Member, DCBOE, from Superintendent Sizemore, 23 August 1974.

_____ to President Virginia Morris, DCBOE, from Superintendent Sizemore, 10 September 1974.

_____ to President Virginia Morris, DCBOE, from Superintendent Sizemore, 13 November 1974.

_____ to the DCBOE regarding the FY75 Expenditure Plan (Revision III), from Superintendent Sizemore, 5 December 1974.

_____ to Superintendent Sizemore, from Dwight S. Cropp, Executive Secretary, 9 December 1974.

_____ to Superintendent Sizemore, DCPSS, from President Virginia Morris, DCBOE, 12 December 1974.

_____ to Superintendent Sizemore, from President Morris, 12 December 1974.

_____ to Friends of the DCYOP, from Martha S. Swaim, Vice President, DCBOE, 7 August 1973.

Memorandum to DCBOE President Morris, from Superintendent Sizemore, DCPSS, re: FY76 Budget Plan, 8 January 1975.

_____ to the DCBOE from Superintendent Sizemore, 10 January 1975.

_____ to Superintendent Sizemore, from Executive Secretary Dwight S. Cropp, DCBOE, re: Establishment of FY 1976 Budget Base Figure, 10 January 1975.

_____ to DCBOE President Virginia Morris, from Superintendent Sizemore, re: Opening Statement to Accompany the D.C. Public Schools FY76 Budget, 16 January 1975.

_____ to DCBOE, from Superintendent Sizemore, re: FY76 Budget Concerns, 19 February 1975.

_____ to President Virginia Morris, DCBOE, from Superintendent Barbara A. Sizemore, 10 March 1975.

_____ to the DCBOE from Superintendent Sizemore, re: Response to Board President's Correspondence dated 11 March 1975, 19 March 1975.

_____ to the Citizenry from DCBOE President Virginia Morris, re: A Statement on the Role of the General Counsel to the Board of Education, 19 March 1975.

_____ to Deputy Superintendent James L. Williams, from Superintendent Sizemore, re: Position Control, 20 March 1975.

_____ to the DCBOE from Superintendent Sizemore, re: Statement of Barbara A. Sizemore, Superintendent of Schools, Relative to Discussion of the Procedure for the Annual Evaluation of the Superintendent's Performance, 28 April 1975.

_____ to Mrs. Sizemore from Mr. Cropp, re: Mr. Treanor's Motion, 28 April 1975.

_____ to Superintendent Sizemore, from President Virginia Morris, DCBOE, re: Executive Session, 28 April 1975.

_____ of Telephone Call to Mrs. Virginia Morris, to Request Permission to be Present at Saturday, 31 May Hearing, from Attorney DeLong Harris, 30 May 1975.

_____ to Barbara A. Sizemore from Michael Nussbaum of Nussbaum and Owen, re: Legal Evaluation of Dismissal of Dr. Barbara A. Sizemore as Superintendent of Schools of the District of Columbia, Washington, D.C., 21 June 1975.

_____ to Barbara A. Sizemore, Superintendent of Schools, from President Virginia Morris, DCBOE, re: Leave Status as of 23 June 1975, 24 June 1975.

_____ to Superintendent Sizemore from DCBOE President Morris, re: Your Memorandum dated 24 June 1975, Relative to Requesting Clarification of Sick Leave in Advance, 24 June 1975.

_____ to DCBOE Members, and Superintendent, from Dwight S. Cropp, Executive Secretary, re: Meeting of the Committee of the Whole on Personnel, 24 June 1975.

_____ to DCBOE President Morris, from Superintendent Sizemore, re: Leave Status on 23 June 1975, 24 June 1975.

_____ to DCBOE President Morris, from Superintendent Sizemore, 24 June 1975.

_____ to Regional Superintendents from Budget Director Edward G. Winner, re: Secondary Teaching Position Allotments: FY1976, 6 August 1975.

_____ to DCBOE Vice President Julius W. Hobson, Jr., from Superintendent Barbara A. Sizemore, 7 August 1975.

_____ to DCBOE Members, and Superintendent, from Executive Secretary Cropp, re: Resolution Approved during the Special Meeting of 20 August 1975.

_____ to DCBOE Members and Superintendent, from Executive Secretary Cropp, re: Notice of Meetings, 25 August 1975.

_____ to Superintendent Sizemore, from DCBOE President Morris, re: Mr. Alphonso Gaskins, PACTS Coordinator, 25 August 1975.

_____ to DCBOE and Superintendent from Virginia Morris, 2 September 1975.

_____ to DCBOE President Morris, from DCBOE Member John E. Warren, re: Document of Understanding Between the Board and Mr. Reed, 17 November 1975, with draft copy of Memorandum of Understanding Between the District of Columbia Board of Education and the Acting Superintendent of Schools.

_____ to Deputy Superintendent James L. Williams, from Ernest E. Sargent, Director of Finance, re: Financial Management in the School System Requires Proper Coordination and Adequate Follow-Up Procedures, 4 February 1974.

_____ to Deputy Superintendent for Management Services James L. Williams, from Director of Finance Ernest E. Sargent, 20 February 1974.

_____ to To Whom It May Concern, from DCYOP, Junior Band Percussion Section, 23 February 1974.

_____ to President Myrtle Morris, Friends of the DCYOP, from DCYOP Director Lyn McLain, re: Attached memo from Mr. Bellamy, February 28, 1974 re: The Junior Band Situation, 27 February 1974.

_____ to Deputy Superintendent James L. Williams, from Director of Finance Ernest E. Sargent, re: Status of Appropriation Report as of 31 January, 1 March 1974.

_____ to Executive Secretary Dwight S. Cropp, from Albert A. Rosenfield, re: Committee Structure, Washington, D.C. Public Schools, 25 March 1974 and 26 March 1974.

_____ to Parents of Junior Band Students from Assistant Director Wilbur Bellamy, re: Junior Band Rehearsals, 27 March 1973.

_____ to Deputy Superintendent James L. Williams, from Director of Finance Ernest E. Sargent, re: Mismatched Personnel Account Codes, 27 March, 1974.

_____ to Deputy Superintendent Floretta McKenzie, from Security Director Edgar B. Dews, Jr., re: "Assault-D.C. Youth Orchestra Program, Coolidge High School," 28 March 1974.

_____ to Lyn McLain from Wilbur Bellamy, re: Junior Band Rehearsal (2 April 1974), 5 April 1974.

_____ to Superintendent Barbara A. Sizemore, from Deputy Superintendent Floretta D. McKenzie, re: Altercation at Coolidge High School; D.C. Youth Orchestra Program, 5 April 1974.

_____ to Deputy Superintendent James L. Williams, from Deputy Superintendent Floretta D. McKenzie, 23 April 1974.

_____ to DCYOP Assistant Director Wilbur Bellamy, from DCYOP Director Lyn McLain, re: Enrollment Breakdown (1973-74) Winter Season--September-June, 29 April 1974.

_____ to Budget Director Edward Winner from Director of Finance Ernest E. Sargent, re: Your Memorandum dated 29 April 1974 - Allotment Changes, 6 May 1974.

_____ to Budget Director Edward G. Winner, from Director of Finance Ernest E. Sargent, re: Allotment Changes, 10 May 1974.

_____ to Chairman William Treanor, and Members Martha S. Swaim, Mattie G. Taylor, Committee on Board Operations. Rules and Policies, from Executive Secretary Dwight S. Cropp, re: "Referral of document 'Duties of the General Counsel to the Board of Education'", to Committee, 13 May 1974.

_____ to DCBOE from Superintendent Barbara A. Sizemore, re: General Counsel to the Board of Education, 15 May 1974.

_____ to Hortense Taylor, Department of Music, from Associate Superintendent James T. Guines, re: Future Arrangements for the DCYOP, 15 May 1974.

_____ to Parents, from Assistant Director Wilbur Bellamy, DCYOP, 24 May 1974.

_____ to Superintendent Sizemore and Deputy Superintendent McKenzie, from Associate Superintendent James T. Guines, 31 May 1974.

_____ to James L. Williams, from Director of Finance Ernest E. Sargent, re: FY 1974 Reprogramming, 3 June 1974.

_____ to DCBOE Member Hilda Howland M. Mason, from Superintendent Sizemore, re: <u>120-Day Report</u>, 4 June 1974.

_____ to DCBOE from Hilda Howland M. Mason, re: Delegation of Personnel Authority to the Superintendent, 16 June 1974.

_____ to DCBOE Members and Superintendent, from Executive Secretary Dwight S. Cropp, re: Board-Superintendent Conference, 20 June 1974.

_____ to DCBOE from DCBOE Member Hilda Howland M. Mason, re: Applications of the D.C. Non-Resident Tuition Act to the DCYOP, 5 July 1974.

_____ to DCBOE Members, from DCBOE President Marion Barry, Jr., re: Youth Orchestra Contract, 8 July 1974.

_____ to the DCBOE, from Superintendent Sizemore, re: Report to the DCYOP, 8 July 1974.

_____ to Superintendent from Executive Secretary Cropp, 10 July 1974.

_____ to All School Personnel from Superintendent Sizemore, re: Decentralization, 11 July 1974.

_____ to Superintendent Sizemore from General Counsel David A. Splitt, re: Negotiated Services Contract (74-75), 25 July 1974.

_____ to DCBOE from Superintendent Sizemore, re: DCYOP, 1 August 1974.

_____ to Associate Superintendent Dr. James Johnson, Planning, Research and Evaluation, and Deputy Superintendent James L. Williams, Management Services, from Superintendent Sizemore, 7 August 1974.

_____ to Mrs. Sizemore and Dr. Guines from Dick Hurlbut, re: DCYOP Contractural Agreement, 10 August 1974.

_____ to Superintendent Sizemore from Deputy Superintendent Williams (reply), 12 August 1974.

_____ to DCBOE from Superintendent Sizemore, re: Statement on Contracting, 13 August 1974.

_____ to James L. Williams from Superintendent Sizemore, 16 August 1974.

_____ to DCBOE from Superintendent Sizemore, re DCYOP Contract, 19 August 1974.

_____ to Superintendent Sizemore from President Morris, DCBOE, re: Administrative Requests to General Counsel, 22 August 1974.

_____ to DCBOE President Morris from Superintendent Sizemore, 22 August 1974.

_____ to DCBOE President Morris, from Superintendent Sizemore, 23 August 1974, with attached memorandum to Elementary School Principals from Deputy Superintendent Floretta D. McKenzie, re: Teacher Service Allotment: Regular Budget FY75, 29 March 1974.

_____ to DCBOE Executive Secretary Cropp, from Superintendent Sizemore, re: "Transmittal of Draft of Proposed D.C. Youth Orchestra Contract Prepared on D.C. Government Negotiated Services Contract Forms, 26 August 1974.

_____ to Superintendent Sizemore from DCBOE President Morris, re: "D.C. Youth Orchestra Contract," 29 August 1974.

_____ to DCBOE President Morris, from Superintendent Sizemore, re: "D.C. Youth Orchestra Contract," 30 August 1974.

_____ to Deputy Superintendent Guines, from Superintendent Sizemore, re: DCYOP Youth Chorale, 3 September 1974.

_____ to Superintendent Sizemore from Deputy Superintendent Williams, re: FY75 Financial Plan, 30 September 1974; and Commissioner's Memorandum 74-139 to Public Schools from Comer S. Coppie, Special Assistant to the Mayor-Commissioner for Budget and Financial Plans for Fiscal Year 1975 Appropriated Funds, 3 September 1974.

_____ to Superintendent Sizemore from DCBOE President Morris, re: D.C. Youth Orchestra Contract, 4 September 1974.

_____ to Superintendent Sizemore from Associate Superintendent Guines, 4 September 1974.

_____ to Executive Staff from Superintendent Sizemore, re: 1976 Budget Proposals, 6 September, 1974, and 4 September 1974 memorandum attached.

_____ to Superintendent Sizemore from Associate Superintendent Guines, 6 September 1974.

_____ to DCBOE President Virginia Morris, from Superintendent Barbara A. Sizemore, re: "D.C. Youth Orchestra Program," 9 September 1974.

_____ to DCBOE from Superintendent Sizemore, re: Negotiated Services Contracts, 18 September 1974.

_____ to DCBOE from Superintendent Sizemore, re: 1975 Legislative Program: Addendum Number I, 3 October 1974.

_____ to DCBOE from Special Assistant to the Mayor-Commissioner for Budget and Financial Management, Comer S. Coppie, re: Revised Apportionments and Financial Plans for Fiscal Year 1975, 3 October 1974.

Letter to President Myrtle C. Morris, Friends of the DCYOP, Inc., from Executive Assistant to the Superintendent J. Weldon Green, 3 October 1974.

Memorandum to DCPSS Superintendent Sizemore, from Acting Material Management Officer, D.C., General Services, Material Management, Government of the District of Columbia, re: Proposed Negotiated Services Contract 0477-AA-NS-N-5-GA, The Friends of the DCYOP, Inc., 7 October 1974.

Correspondence to DCBOE President Virginia Morris from Superintendent Sizemore, 11 October 1974.

Memorandum to DCBOE from Superintendent Sizemore, re: FY1976 Operating Budget, 21 October 1974.

_____ to Superintendent Sizemore, from Chairman Julius W. Hobson, Jr., Committee on School Finance, re: FY76 Budget Plan, 22 October 1974.

_____ to Superintendent Sizemore from Deputy Superintendent Williams, re: Projected FY 1975 Expenditure Requirements, 11 November 1974.

_____ to DCBOE President Morris, from Superintendent Sizemore, 12 November, 13 November 1974.

_____ to Superintendent Sizemore, from Deputy Superintendent Williams, re: Revision of FY75 Financial Plan, 19 November 1974.

_____ to Superintendent Sizemore, from Julius W. Hobson, Jr., re: Status of D.C. Youth Orchestra Contract, 9 December 1974.

_____ to Superintendent Sizemore, from DCBOE President Morris, re: Status of the DCYOP Contract, 13 December 1974.

_____ to DCBOE Member Julius W. Hobson, Jr., from Superintendent Sizemore, re: Status of the DCYOP Contract, 13 December 1974.

_____ to DCBOE Members and Superintendent, from Executive Secretary Cropp, re: Special Meeting of Board on 16 December 1974, 16 December 1974.

_____ to Superintendent Sizemore, from DCBOE President Morris, re: DCYOP Contract, 19 December 1974.

_____ to DCBOE President Morris, from Superintendent Sizemore, 24 December 1974.

_____ to Deputy Superintendent Williams, from Director of Finance Ernest E. Sargent, re: Revised Financial Report as of 31 December 1973.

_____ to DCBOE of Superintendent Hugh J. Scott, re: The DCYOP, 19 July 1972.

_____ to Assistant Superintendent William Bedford, from Paul D. Gable, Supervising Director, Music Department and DCYOP Director Lyn G. McLain, 9 October 1970.

_____ from President Marian S. Banner, Friends of the DCYOP, 17 September 1969.

ACTION SHEETS, JOURNALS, MINUTES AND TRANSCRIPTS

D.C. Public School System, Washington, D.C., D.C. Board of Education, Action Sheet, (Special) Meeting of 16 December 1974.

_____, Journal, Index to the Transcript of the Eighteenth (Special) Meeting of 13 August 1974.

_____ Minutes of the Twelfth (Stated) Meeting of 19 June 1974.

_____, Minutes of the Twenty-Fifth (Stated) Meeting of 9 January 1973.

_____, Minutes of the Thirty-Sixth (Special) Meeting of 11 January 1973.

_____, Minutes of the Thirty-Seventh (Stated) Meeting of 17 January 1973.

_____, Minutes of the Third (Stated) Meeting of 21 February 1973.

_____, Minutes of the Fifth (Special) Meeting of 14 March 1973.

_____, Minutes of the Sixth (Stated) Meeting of 21 March 1973.

_____, Minutes of the Thirteenth (Business) Meeting of 4 June 1973.

_____, Minutes of the Sixteenth (Stated) Meeting of 20 June 1973.

_____, Minutes of the Nineteenth (Special) Meeting of 25 July 1973.

_____, Minutes of the Twenty-First (Special) Meeting of 7 August 1973.

_____, Minutes of the Twenty-Second (Special) Meeting of 21 August 1973.

_____, Minutes of the Twenty-Fifth (Community) Meeting of 3 October 1973.

_____, Minutes of the Thirty-First (Community) Meeting of 6 December 1973.

_____, Minutes of the Twenty-Fifth (Stated) Meeting of 19 January 1972.

_____, Minutes of the Second (Special) Meeting of 9 February 1972.

_____, Minutes of the Third (Stated) Meeting of 16 February 1972.

_____, Minutes of the Fifth (Stated) Meeting of 15 March 1972 and 16 March 1972.

_____, Minutes of the Seventh (Stated) Meeting of 19 April 1972.

_____, Minutes of the Eighth (Special) Meeting of 25 April 1972.

_____, Minutes of the Tenth (Stated) Meeting of 23 May 1972.

_____, Minutes of 21 June 1972.

_____, Minutes of the Second Session of the Seventeenth (Special) Meeting of 19 July 1972.

_____, Minutes of the First (Organizational) Meeting of 25 January 1971.

_____ Minutes of the Fourth (Stated) Meeting of 17 February 1971.

_____, Minutes of the Eighth (Stated) Meeting of 17 March 1971.

_____, Minutes of the Eleventh (Stated) Meeting of 19 May 1971.

_____, Minutes of the Twelfth (Stated) Meeting of 9 June 1971.

_____, Minutes of the Fourteenth (Special) Meeting of 12 July 1971.

_____, Minutes of the Sixteenth (Special) Meeting of 12 August 1971.

_____, Minutes of the Seventeenth (Special) Meeting of 30 August 1971.

_____, Minutes of the Twenty-First (Stated) Meeting of 20 October 1971.

_____, Minutes of the Twenty-Third (Stated) Meeting of 17 November 1971.

_____, Minutes of the Forty-Seventh (Stated) Meeting of 21 January 1970.

_____, Minutes of the First (Organizational) Meeting of 26 January 1970.

_____, Minutes of the Fourth (Stated) Meeting of 18 February 1970.

_____, Minutes of the Fifth (Special) Meeting of 12 March 1970.

_____, Minutes of the Tenth (Stated) Meeting of 20 May 1970.

_____, Minutes of the Eleventh (Special) Meeting of 27 May 1970.

_____, Minutes of the Twelfth (Stated) Meeting of 17 June 1970.

_____, Minutes of the Fourteenth (Special) Meeting of 13 July 1970.

_____, Minutes of the Fifteenth (Special) Meeting of 24 July 1970.

_____, Minutes of the Sixteenth (Special) Meeting of 30 July 1970.

_____, Minutes of the Eighteenth (Special) Meeting of 31 August 1970.

_____, Minutes of the Nineteenth (Stated) Meeting of 16 September 1970.

_____, Minutes of the Twenty-Second (Stated) Meeting of 21 October 1970.

_____, Minutes of the First (Organizational) Meeting of 27 January 1969.

_____, Minutes of the Third (Special) Meeting of 12 February 1969.

_____, Minutes of the Fifth (Special) Meeting of 24 February 1969.

_____, Minutes of the Twenty-Fourth (Community) Meeting of 24 June 1969.

_____, Minutes of the Twenty-Sixth (Special) Meeting of 2 July 1969.

_____, Minutes of the Thirty-Second (Stated) Meeting of 17 September 1969.

_____, Minutes of the Thirty-Seventh (Stated) Meeting of 16 October 1969.

_____, Minutes of the Fortieth (Stated) Meeting of 19 November 1969.

_____, Minutes of the Forty-Third (Special) Meeting of 3 December, 1969.

_____, Minutes of the Forty-Fifth (Stated) Meeting of 17 December 1969.

_____, Minutes of the Twenty-Seventh (Stated) Meeting of 21 February 1968.

_____, Minutes of the Thirteenth (Stated) Meeting of 20 March 1968.

_____, Minutes of 17 April 1968.

_____, Minutes of the Thirty-Fourth (Special) Meeting of 25 April 1968.

_____, Minutes of the Third (Special) Meeting of 15 July 1968.

_____, Minutes of the Ninth (Stated and the Reconvened) Meeting of 18 September 1968 and Reconvened, 26 September 1968.

_____, Minutes of the Twenty-Seventh (Special) Meeting of 26 June 1967.

_____, Minutes of the Seventeenth (Stated) Meeting of 15 November 1967.

_____, Minutes of the Tenth (Stated) Meeting of 16 February 1966.

_____, Minutes of the Eleventh (Stated) Meeting of 16 March 1966.

_____, Minutes of the Twelfth (Stated) Meeting of 20 April 1966.

_____, Minutes of the Fourteenth (Stated) Meeting of 18 May 1966.

_____, Minutes of the Tenth (Stated) Meeting of 1964-1965, 17 March 1965.

_____, Minutes of the Twelfth (Special) Meeting of 22 April 1965.

_____, Minutes of the Thirteenth (Stated) Meeting of 19 May 1965.

_____, Minutes of the Fourteenth (Postponed) Meeting of 23 June 1965.

_____, Minutes of the Fourth (Postponed) Meeting of 22 September 1965.

_____, Minutes of the Seventeenth (Stated) Meeting of 1963-1964, 17 June 1964.

_____, Minutes of the Eleventh (Special) Meeting of 1962-1963, 21 February 1963.

_____, Transcript of the Fourth (Stated) Meeting of 17 March 1976.

_____, Transcript of the Eighth (Stated) Meeting of 16 June 1976.

_____, Transcript of the Eleventh (Stated) Meeting of 15 September 1976.

_____, Transcript of the Twelfth Special (Emergency) Meeting of 27 September 1976.

_____, Transcript of the Fifteenth (Stated) Meeting of 17 November 1976.

_____, Transcript of the Thirty-Second (Stated) Meeting of 22 January 1975.

_____, Transcript of the Third (Stated) Meeting of 19 February 1975.

_____, Transcript of the Fifth (Stated) Meeting of 19 March 1975.

_____, Transcript of the Sixth Special (Emergency) Meeting of 7 April 1975.

_____, Transcript of the Seventh Meeting of 16 April 1975.

_____, Transcript of a Stated Meeting of 21 May 1975.

_____, Transcript of the Tenth (Continuation of the 8th Stated) Meeting of 28 May 1975.

_____, Transcript of the Thirteenth Special (Emergency) Meeting of 24 June 1975.

_____, Transcript of the Fifteenth (Special) Meeting of 3 July 1975.

_____, Transcript of the Sixteenth (Special) Meeting of 24 July 1975.

_____, Transcript of Public Hearings on Charges Against Superintendent Sizemore, 7 August 1975.

_____, Transcript of the Seventeenth (Special) Board Meeting of 12 August 1975.

_____, Transcript of Open Meeting of 19 August 1975.

_____, Transcript of Open Meeting of 20 August 1975.

_____, Transcript of Special Meeting of 28 August 1975.

_____, Transcript of the Nineteenth (Special) Meeting of 7 September 1975.

_____, Transcript of the Twenty-Third (Special) Meeting of 9 October 1975.

_____, Transcript of the Twenty-Fifth Meeting of 19 November 1975.

_____, Transcript of the Continuation Meeting of 16 January 1974 (Stated), 21 January 1974.

_____, Transcript of the Fifth Regular Meeting of 20 March 1974.

_____, Transcript of the Seventh Stated Meeting of 17 April 1974.

_____, Transcript of the Stated Meeting of 15 May 1974.

_____, Transcript of the Third Annual Meeting for Students of 14 June 1974.

_____, Transcript of the Twelfth (Stated) Meeting of 19 June 1974.

_____, Transcript of the Thirteenth (Special) Meeting of 2 July 1974.

_____, Transcript of the Fourteenth (Special) Meeting of 8 July 1974.

_____, Transcript of the Fifteenth (Special) Meeting of 15 July 1974.

_____, Transcript of the Special Meeting of 1 August 1974.

_____, Transcript of A Special Meeting, 13 August 1974.

Statement by Julius W. Hobson, Jr., 18 September 1974, attached to Transcript of the Nineteenth (Stated) Meeting of 18 September 1974.

D.C. Public School System, Washington, D.C., D.C. Board of Education, Transcript of the Twentieth (Special) Meeting of 30 September 1974.

_____, Transcript of the Twenty-Fourth (Stated) Meeting of 16 October 1974.

_____, Transcript of the Twenty-Fifth (Special) Meeting of 22 October 1974.

_____, Transcript of the Twenty-Sixth Meeting of 20 November 1974.

_____, Transcript of the Twenty-Sixth (Special) Continuation Meeting of 2 December 1974.

_____, Transcript of An Emergency (Special) Meeting of 6 December 1974.

_____, Transcript of the Committee on School Finance Meeting of 6 December 1974.

_____, Transcript of the Twenty-Seventh (Special) Meeting of 6 December 1974.

_____, Transcript of An Emergency (Special) Meeting of 12 December 1974.

_____, Transcript of the Twenty-Ninth (Special) Meeting of 16 December 1974.

_____, Transcript of the Twenty-Fourth (Stated) Meeting of 18 December 1974.

_____, Transcript of the Second (Community) Meeting of 7 February 1973.

_____, Transcript of the Fourth (Community) Meeting of 7 March 1973.

_____, Transcript of the Seventh (Special) Meeting of 26 March 1973.

_____, Transcript of the Twelfth (Stated) Meeting of 16 May 1973.

_____, Transcript of the Seventeenth (Special) Meeting of 27 June 1973.

_____, Transcript of the Eighteenth (Special) Meeting of 12 July 1973.

_____, Transcript of the Twenty-Third (Special) Meeting of 5 September 1973.

_____, Transcript of the Twenty-Sixth (Stated) Meeting of 17 October 1973.

_____, Transcript of a (Special) Meeting of 4 December 1973.

_____, Transcript of the Thirty-Second (Stated) Meeting of 19 December 1973.

_____, Transcript of the Thirty-Seventh (Stated) Meeting of 17 January 1972.

_____, Transcript of the Thirty-Second (Stated) Meeting of 21 November 1972.

DOCTORAL DISSERTATIONS

Allison, Howard D. "Professional and Lay Influences on School Board Decision-Making." Doctoral dissertation, University of Chicago, 1965.

Bowman, Thomas R. "The Participation of the Superintendent in School Board Decision-Making." Doctoral dissertation, University of Chicago, 1962.

Hencley, S.P. "A Topology of Conflict Between School Superintendents and Their Reference Groups." Doctoral dissertation, University of Chicago, 1960.

McCarty, Donald J. "Motives for Seeking School Board Membership." Doctoral dissertation, University of Chicago, 1959.

Morsink, Helen M. "The Leader Behavior of Men and Women Secondary School Principals." Doctoral dissertation, Central Michigan University, 1968.

Sizemore, Barbara A. "The Politics of Decentralization: A Case Study of the D.C. Public Schools, 1973-76." Doctoral dissertation, University of Chicago, 1979.

INTERVIEWS

Personal interview, Charles Cassell, Washington, D.C., 5 October 1977.

Donaldson, Andrew, Tapes of interview held by the D.C. Board of Education, Washington, D.C., finalist for the D.C. Superintendency, 30 July 1973.

Personal interview, Luther Elliott, Washington, D.C., 20 October 1977.

_____, Therman Evans, Washington, D.C., 19 October 1977.

_____, Gary Freeman, Washington, D.C., 6 October 1977.

_____, Ruth Goodwin, Washington, D.C., 6 May 1978.

_____, Kenneth Haskins, Washington, D.C., 22 November 1977.

_____, Julius Hobson, Jr., Washington, D.C., 28 September 1977.

_____, Raymond Kemp, Washington, D.C., 21 November 1977.

_____, Margaret Labat, Washington, D.C., 18 November 1977.

_____, Napoleon Lewis, Washington, D.C., 9 October 1977.

_____, Virginia Morris, Washington, D.C., 11 October 1977.

Minor, John, Tapes of interview held by the DCBOE, Washington, D.C., Finalist for the D.C. Superintendency, 28 July 1973.

Personal interview, Richard Prince, Washington, D.C., 15 February 1977; conducted by Joe Green, former Washington Post newsman.

_____, Delores Pryde, Washington, D.C., 23 October 1977.

_____, Vincent Reed, Washington, D.C., 5 December 1977.

_____, William Rice, Washington, D.C., 21 September 1977.

_____, Hugh Scott, Washington, D.C., 21 November 1977.

_____, William Simon, Washington, D.C., 29 November 1977.

_____, Barbara L. Simmons, Washington, D.C., 20 September 1977.

_____, Barbara A. Sizemore, Washington, D.C., 17 April 1978 and tape of 31 July 1973.

_____, Conrad Smith, Washington, D.C., 17 October 1977.

_____, Mattie Taylor, Washington, D.C., 6 October 1977.

Telephone conversation between writer and Barbara Simmons, D.C. School Board member, 2 November 1978.

Telephone interview between writer and William Raspberry, editorial writer of the Washington Post, 3 March 1978.

Personal interview, Bardyl Tirana, Washington, D.C., 27 September 1977.

_____, William Treanor, Washington, D.C., 28 September 1977.

_____, John Warren, Washington, D.C., 27 September 1977.

_____, Evie Washington, Washington, D.C., 12 October 1977.

_____, James Williams, Chicago, Illinois, 14 December 1977.

OTHER SOURCES

CBS News broadcast, 20 January 1978.

"Highlights of History of D.C. Citizens for Better Public Education, Inc.," June 1975, obtained from files of DCCBPE by the writer.

Sizemore, Barbara A. "Is there Still Room for the Black School?" Washington, D.C.: Sixth Annual Research Conference, Howard University, June 1978, pp. 1-24 (mimeographed).

_____. "Quality Education and the Black Community." Address at the Institute of the Black World, Inc., Atlanta, Georgia, January 1976. Tape available at the Institute.

# INDEX

INDEX

## A

Academic Achievement Plan, 139, 184-190, 207, 212, 616, 638. See also Clark Plan
Acting Superintendents, 130, 133-134, 149, 372, 498-499, 593-596
Adams Community School, 151, 197-198, 226, 603
Administration, and the budget/management dispute, 371-413; and the D.C. Youth Orchestra Program, 310-352, 475, 523; and the general counsel, 353-360; as an issue, 4, 24, 636; D.C. Board of Education, interference in, 3, 98, 111, 139, 189, 224, 268-276, 349-350, 400-404, 422-423, 463, 478, 523, 576-577, 634-636; of Clark Plan, 187; Scott's interpretation of, 268-269; Sizemore's interpretation of, 356
Administration reorganization controversy, 379-390
Administrative Team Concept, 152, 264-266, 361-362, 381-382, 397-399, 481, 519, 605, 622
Adverse action, 18, 688. See Termination
African Heritage Studies Association, 10, 114, 409-410, 412, 425, 483, 486-487, 489, 512, 515-516, 527, 574-575, 615
Ali, Peb, 489
Allen, Anita Ford, 61, 89-90, 92-93, 97-99, 101, 106, 111, 118, 130-133, 135, 138, 186, 189-190, 196, 225-226, 228-230, 232, 243, 256-258, 266, 289, 292-293, 512, 614
Alexander, Benjamin, 61, 130, 133, 196
Allen, Thomas, 246
Alexander, Harry T., 143-144, 146
Alexander, Muriel, 89, 131, 135, 186, 257
Allison, Howard, 6, 13, 634
Alternative Educational Programs, 10; as board priority, 378; D.C. Youth Orchestra Program, 310-352; Hawthorne Alternative School, 225, 339, 345, 416-421, 423, 472-473, 475, 522, 723
American Association of School Administrators, 166, 464
Anacostia Community School Project, 151, 198-200, 380, 603
Anders, Corrie M., 583
Anderson, David E., 657
Anderson, L. V., 173
Anderson, Marian, 55, 637
Angino, Dominic, 545
Anthony, Lewis, 140, 242, 274-275
Appointed status, DCBOE, 89
Appointment, D.C. school superintendents, 86-87
Asher, Robert, 482
Authoritarian leadership behavior, 17, 19, 232-233, 256-258, 293, 419, 425
Authority, and the D.C. Youth Orchestra Program, 333; and the Code, 634-635; and the general counsel, 360; as conflict issue, 11; in budget/management matters, 365-366, 377, 422-423; of local school boards, 152, 193-199, 201; of the D.C. Board of Education, 76, 85-87, 139, 285-286, 671; of the D.C. school superintendent, 87, 139-140, 356, 525; under decentralization, 379-382, 548; withdrawal from the D.C. school superintendent, 309-430

## B

Baldridge, Victor, 39
Banks, James A., 40
Banner, Marian S., 320, 431
Barnard, Chester, 26, 38
Barnes, Andrew, 504
Barry, Marion, 25, 27, 73-75, 90-91, 93-94, 97-98, 100-101, 106, 111, 138-140, 142-143, 145, 147-150, 164, 166, 190, 223-224, 226, 228, 237, 241, 243-244, 246-249, 252-255, 257-258, 266, 277, 292-293, 297, 332-335, 338-340, 342, 352, 355, 372-373, 417-420, 424, 432, 451, 464-466, 468, 474-475, 478, 480, 512-514, 558, 567, 635-636, 639, 641-642,

647-648, 670, 672
Bellamy, Wilbur, 324-325, 327, 329-330, 432-433
Bedford, William 325, 431
Benjamin, Bettie G., 95-96, 234-235, 238, 251, 253, 277, 298, 396, 401, 403, 407-408, 412, 424, 499, 514, 516, 526, 530, 532-533, 537-539, 542, 593-594, 596-598, 683, 686-687, 689-690
Benn, Herman T., 116, 494, 532, 535-538, 574
Beveridge, Albert J., 247
"Bill of Particulars," 685-686, 690, 715-716
Billingsley, Amy, 180
Billingsley, Andrew, 143
Binswanger, Robert, 199
Blaine, Anita McCormick, 454-455
Blaine, James G., 454
Board of Election and Ethics, 9
Board of Trade. See Metropolitan Washington Board of Trade
Board/superintendent relations, and conferences, 187-188, 671, 673-674; guidelines for, 137; meetings of, 527-528; superintendent's memorandum of, 523, 675
Bolling v Sharpe, 21, 55, 446
Bowman, Thomas R., 38
Branch, Essie, 469
Brockett, Diane, 343, 379, 399, 404, 423, 441, 443, 469, 477-479, 481-483, 485-487, 489, 492, 495, 504-509, 523, 525, 597, 581, 584
Brooks, Betty, 9
Brown, Carter J., 248
Brown, H. Rap, 44
Brown, Joseph C., 689
Brown, Oliver E., 143
Brown v Board of Education of Topeka, Kansas, 55
Buchanan, Robert, 504
Budget/management, and stated board policy, 405-406, 425; and Sizemore's termination, 511; and personnel control, 366-368; as charge, 520-521; as conflict issue, 10, 139, 289; bifurcation of, 5; budget, 365-366, 377-390, 396-408, 422, 517, 520, 527, 551, 554, 559, 723; management, 362-365; mayor's freeze, 390-391, 524, 546, 552, 556, 723; problems in, 139, 286, 368-371, 420, 422-425, 524; school system organization, 361-362; sequence of events in conflict, 371-413;

Sizemore's administration, philosophy of, 360
Burgess, David, Jr., 504
Burgess, Ernest W., 39
Burguden, Bernie, Jr., 247
Byrd, Ricardo, 143

C

Cafritz, William, 255, 322
Cain, Vincent, 492
Campaign contributions, 245-256, 512, 639-641
Campbell, Roald F., 13, 38
Carmichael, Stokeley, 44
Carswell, Harold, 498
Carter, Cozette, 723
Cassell, Charles I., 75-76, 83, 90, 93, 98-99, 106, 118, 124-125, 134-136, 138-139, 143, 146-150, 156, 160, 162-164, 166, 176, 179, 185-186, 189, 225, 229, 237, 244, 249-250, 252-254, 257, 277, 286, 289-290, 296, 298, 300, 355, 372-373, 451, 458, 465-466, 475, 635, 641, 670
Change, and decentralization, 191-207, 378-399, 425; and Hansen's administration, 132, 289; and Scott's administration, 189, 289; and Sizemore's selection, 159-161, 643-646; as introduced by Sizemore, 406, 615-620; financing of, 360-410; in control of D.C. Youth Orchestra Program, 325-352, 376; in equalization concept, 388-390; in established board policy, 405-406, 425; in goals, 181-213, 291, 468, 596, 623; in school board membership, 3, 11, 277-284, 291; in school board procedure, 101, 646-648; in superintendents, 3, 291; in values, 278-279, 291; of power bases, in decision-making, 259
Charges, termination, and hearings, 526-577; and management matters, 511; and H. Mason, 515-517; and memorandum to Sizemore, 691-705; and proposed adverse action, 687-688; and the Washington Post, 497; categorization of, 519-522; development of, 515-519; emergence of, 353, 360, 376, 386-388, 396-397, 408-412, 422; specifications of, 519-569, 596
Citizens decentralization plan, 205-207, 227, 420
City wards
Ward 1, 48, 50, 225, 229, 236,

325
Ward 2, 48, 50, 53-55, 225, 231, 325
Ward 3, 50-51, 53-54, 226, 230, 234, 270, 325, 332, 416, 457
Ward 4, 50-51, 53-54, 227, 270, 325
Ward 5, 50, 52-54, 224, 235, 247, 325
Ward 6, 50, 52-55, 227-228, 235, 325, 332, 457, 513
Ward 7, 50, 52-54, 230, 232, 237, 325, 332
Ward 8, 50, 53-54, 228, 233, 325, 332, 416, 424
Clark, Kenneth, 139-140, 161, 184-189, 207, 212, 224, 289, 292, 453-454, 616, 638
Clark Plan, 181, 184-190, 207, 212, 224, 292, 453, 616, 638. See also Academic Achievement Plan
Class conflict, and the Morgan Community School Project, 194-195. See also Classism
Classism, and Hansen, 129, 290; and population shifts, 285; and the budget, 406; and the Citizen's Decentralization Plan, 206, 227; and the D.C. Youth Orchestra Program, 334, 416-417
Cleaver, Eldridge, 40
Closed sessions, DCBOE. See Executive sessions
Coates, James, 72, 89-90, 97, 134-136, 143, 163-164, 166, 186, 199, 208, 211, 228, 237, 243, 257, 277, 355, 463, 670
Coleman, Milton, 295, 300, 502
Colonial status, 4, 17, 19-20, 35-36, 43, 64, 66-78, 285-288, 365-366, 372, 413, 415-416, 424, 426, 467, 592, 607, 620-622, 639, 661-665. See also Dependent relationship; Governmental dominance
Committee structure, DCBOE, 92-106, 119, 648
Competency based curriculum (CBC), 599-601, 616, 643
Composition, D.C. Board of Education, 27, 88, 119
Conduct at board meetings, and dismissal hearings, 495-496, 522-523, 527, 532-533, 567, 573-574; and use of police, 118-119, 530
Conflict issues, 3, 4, 18, 20, 24, 72-74, 78, 309-430, 631-633. See also Conflict in superintendent-school board relations
Conflict, superintendent-school board relations, and budget/management problems, 139, 360-430, 524; and D.C. Youth Orchestra Program, 310-352, 475, 523; and decentralization, 190-192; and equalization, 208-210; and general counsel, 353-360, 523-524; and politics, 242-243; and track system, 129; chronology of, 522-543; in Hansen's administration, 128-129; in Manning's administration, 131-134, 196, 268, 519; in political theory, 11; in Scott's administration, 139-142, 186-190, 203-204, 208-210, 268-270, 519; in Sizemore's administration, 206, 309-430, 478-501, 519-577; issues in, 10; summary of, 636-642
Contract, superintendent, on authority, 167, 565; on discharge, 167; on due process rights, 128; on duties and responsibilities, 670-672; on evaluation, 168; on superintendent-school board relations, 167; on termination, 670, 675
Control, and budget matters, 365-374, 390-392; and D.C. Youth Orchestra Program, 317-319, 333-335, 338-339, 344-346, 418, 445, 523; and equalization, 58-59; and general counsel, 353-354; and public schools, 127, 288, 372-373, 683; and school board majority votes, 513-515; and sub units in school system, 191-207; and superintendent, 86, 101-102
Cook, George F., 448
Coppie, Comer S., 441-442
Cornick, Delroy, 72, 320, 431
Corning, Hobart M., 57
Cropp, Dwight S., 9, 117, 123, 340, 342-343, 355, 402, 434-436, 439, 443, 523, 525, 528, 531, 538, 545, 553, 555, 573, 579, 582, 584, 586, 669-670, 672, 682-687, 689-690
Cunningham, Luvern L., 26, 38, 237, 295
Curriculum, and decentralization, 192, 198, 202; and Scott, 185, 190, 426, 616, 635; and Sizemore, 171, 259, 309-352, 378, 406, 409-410, 416-417, 425, 471, 517, 519-520, 526, 557, 596, 616, 697; and Reed, 599-601, 614, 616-618, 623, 642-643, 662-663

## D

Dale, Charlene T., 36, 41
Daniels, Lee A., 486, 499, 506, 508, 510
Danzansky, Joseph, 143, 144-145, 147-148, 155, 451
Davis, James C., 445
Davis, Melvin, 45
Deal, Terrence E., 39
D.C. Code, and recommendations to improve, 651; and ambiguities in, 653; on advertising for supplies or services, 338, 341; on appointment of superintendent, 127, 593; on conduct at public meetings, 532; on control of public schools, 117, 655-656; on delegation of authority, 634; on policy matters, 85, 127, 634; on termination of superintendent, 127-128, 531, 683-684, 691, 699
Decentralization, and changes in goals, 282, 393, 591; and Citizen's Decentralization Plan, 108, 420; and conflict with board goals, 378-394, 519; and the D.C. Citizens for Better Public Education, 453-454; and financing of, 373, 376, 380-382, 391-394, 406-420, 526; and Hansen, 183; and implementation, 110, 190-206, 260, 266, 376, 378; and local control, 191-207; and management services, 361-362; and Manning, 130; and PACTS, 5; and Reed, 602-605; and school board members, 224-230, 232, 234; and Scott, 139; and superintendent selection, 151-152; of the hiring function, 397-398
Decision-making process, and board members, 103; and decentralization, 380-382, 393; and inclusive nature of, 259, 265-266; and the general counsel dispute, 358, 523-524; and local school boards, 152, 193, 201; and partial recentralization, 603-605, 622; and superintendent exclusion from, 102; and superintendent selection and termination, 127-172; broadening of, 5; case studies of, 309-430; disruption of, 10, 11; examination of, 7; explanation of, 104-105
D.C. Citizens for Better Public Education, Inc. (DCCBPE), 9, 60, 225, 232, 234, 236, 246-247, 249, 255, 335, 373-374, 452-460, 598, 647

D.C. Youth Orchestra Program, and events leading to conflict; as conflict issue, 10; as private enterprise, 420; as trade off in decision-making process, 105-106; control of, 317-319, 333-335, 338-339, 344-346, 418, 445; explanation of, 310-311; history of, 310-325, 455-456; in Sizemore's termination, 513-514, 522-523; problems in, 311-325, 416-421, 423
D.C. Self-Government and Governmental Reorganization Act, 66-67, 415. See also Home Rule
Delaney, William, 82, 295, 503
Dennard, Cleveland, 143-144
Dependent relationship, 36, 632, 637. See also Colonial status
Desegregation, 55-59, 77, 311-316, 325-327, 336
Dews, Edgar, Jr., 328, 433
Diggs, Charles, 460, 467, 500, 535, 585, 598-599
Diggs, Gilbert A., 110, 263, 265-266, 302, 460, 592-593, 613, 624, 629, 642
Dismissal hearings, 5, 519-569; "Bill of Particulars" for, 528; events leading up to, 522-535; first hearing, 535-543; second hearing, 544-559
Doherty, Subuola O., 62
Dolce, Carl, 130
Donaldson, Andrew G., 150, 152, 155, 163, 177, 290, 464
Donaldson, Ivanhoe, 150, 246
Douglas, Freda, 218
Dugas, Julian, 61, 131
Dunbar, Leslie, 130
Duncan, John, 46
Dunson, Lynn, 503, 582
Duties, superintendent, in contract 403; in evaluation document, 676-679; to obey the board, 403
Dwan, Ralph H., 247

## E

Eagleton, Thomas, 467
Eaton, David, 246
Educational programs, and Hansen, 128-129, 182-184; and Reed, 599-601; and Scott, 139, 184-190; and Sizemore, 152-172; changes in, 289; summary of, 616-618
Eisen, Jack, 657
Elected school board act, 21, 68, 89, 130, 131
Ellena, William J., 675

Elliott, Luther, Jr., 109, 292, 304, 459
England, Richard, 247
Epilogue, 661-665
Epstein, Lionel C., 247
Equalization, and the D.C. Citizens for Better Public Education, 453-454, 456; D.C. Youth Orchestra Program, 341; and Hansen, 128-129; and pressure, 446; and Reed, 601-602; and Scott, 138, 181, 207-212; and Sizemore, 379, 388-390, 396, 517, 520, 544, 560-564, 566-567, 591, 596, 601-602, 614, 616, 643, 691; as conflict issue, 368; origin of, 58-60, 62. See also Hobson v Hansen; Title I Comparability/Wright Decree
Evaluation, superintendent, 5, 167-168, 527-528, 669-718
Evans, Therman, 93-94, 96-97, 104, 106, 124, 234, 238, 241, 244, 251-254, 256, 258, 267, 277, 293, 297-298, 301, 303, 333-334, 338, 340, 342-344, 346, 358, 388, 407-408, 412, 424, 458, 494, 513-514, 526, 530, 532, 540-542, 579, 593, 597, 641, 683, 686-687, 689-690
Executive Sessions, and board members' concern, 113, 412; and dismissal hearings, 532, 673-674, 681-682, 715; and superintendent's evaluation, 527-528, 681-682; explanation of, 112-113; in budget/management dispute, 403-404; in superintendent selection, 135, 151; use of, 102-103, 115-117
Executive Study Group, 129-130, 362
External factors, 11, 17-23, 37, 43-78, 156, 273, 285-290, 413, 426, 445-501, 528, 596, 620-621, 646

## F

Fantini, Mario, 201, 218
Fauntroy, Walter, 224, 246-247, 254
Featherstone, James, Jr., 277, 597
Federation of Civic Associations, 144, 147-148, 447-448, 457-459, 460
Feinberg, Lawrence W., 79, 82, 220, 625-626, 630
Fitzgerald, Jean, 247
Folger, Betsy, 247
Fort Lincoln New Town, 130, 200-202, 234, 246
Frazier, E. Franklin, 34, 40
Frederiksen, Norman, 36, 41

Freeman, Gary, 110-111, 218, 292, 304, 459, 626
Frerich, David D., 33, 40
Friedan, Betty, 36, 41
Friends of the D.C. Youth Orchestra Program, 255-256, 311, 316, 319-320, 324-328, 330-331, 334-335, 337-339, 341, 343-344, 346-347, 350-351, 417-419, 447, 455-460, 513, 523, 639, 646
Functions, D.C. Board of Education, and goal setting, 181-213; and superintendent selection and termination, 127-172; and the D.C. Code, 651; as factor in conflict, 11, 17, 19, 23; execution of, 99-106; explanation of, 85, 87-88; in superintendent' contract, 670-672; non-functioning of, 139-140
Function, Superintendent, as factor in conflict, 11; explanation of, 88; in contract, 671-672
FY76 budget/FY75 financial plan, 377-390, 396-408, 422, 517, 520, 524, 527, 551, 554, 558, 723

## G

Garner, Bill, 479, 506
Garver, George C., 657
Gaskins, Alphonso, 489, 493, 538, 586
Gatslon, Jolan W., 246
Gay, Geneva, 35, 40
Gerstin, Marvin, 246, 254
Getzels, Jacob W., 5-6, 13, 38-39, 237, 276-280, 295, 303, 634
Glover, Charles, 448
Gable, Paul D., 311, 316, 431
General Counsel dispute, and administrative requests, 347-348; and authority, 421, 428; and charge, 422, 512, 522; and role conflict, 524; introduction of problem, 353; sequence of events, 355-360; statement of the problem, 353-355
Goal setting, and change, 181-213, 278-284, 368-410, 591; and Reed, 596; and Scott, 139-141, 420; and Sizemore, 152, 166, 278, 368-410; and the budget, 368-410, 512; as factor in conflict, 11, 186-189; as school board function 11
Goldberg, Herman R., 477
Goodwin, Ruth, 9, 141, 274, 335, 343, 434, 487, 496
Governmental dominance, 17, 19, 285-288. See also Colonial status

Green, Constance, 44, 79, 216, 502
Green, Joe, 461
Gregg, Russell, 41
Griffiths, Arthuro, 274
Griffiths, Daniel E., 36, 41
Grobman, Hulda Gross, 36, 41
Gross, Neal, 6, 13, 31, 38, 267, 302
Guines, James T., 313-314, 323-324, 328, 330-331, 343, 348-349, 431, 433-435, 437, 456, 503
Gullatee, Latinee, 431

## H

Hancock, Edward, 89-90, 135, 186, 207-208, 230, 257
Hagan, Theodore, Jr., 246, 255
Hahn, Gilbert, 72, 82
Hall, James E., 324, 327-330, 337, 418, 433
Hamilton, Martha, 486-488, 491, 495, 499, 507-510
Hamilton, West A., 57, 182
Hannan, William T., Sr., 248
Hansen, Carl F., 55, 57-62, 77, 79, 95, 128-129, 172-173, 181-183, 191, 207, 212, 214-215, 279, 289-292, 294, 341, 360, 362, 368, 396-397, 446, 448, 452, 502, 560, 587, 591, 633, 637-639, 691, 699, 723
Hanson, Royce, 81
Harris, DeLong, 353, 488, 490, 530, 534, 535-536, 541, 583-584
Harrison, Anne (Nancy) Blaine, 454, 503. See also Harrison, Nancy
Harrison, Gilbert, 455
Harrison, Nancy, 452, 455. See also Harrison, Anne Blaine
Hart, George L., 61
Haskins, Kenneth, 108, 150, 152, 160-161, 178, 194, 226, 262, 283, 301, 304, 393, 407, 459
Haworth, Ellis, 162
Hawthorne Alternative School, 225, 339, 345, 423, 473, 475, 522, 621
Hay, Ramond G., 249
Haynes, Euphemia, 61, 113-114, 128, 131, 133, 182-183, 194, 196, 296
Hechinger, John E., 246, 248, 250-252, 254, 255
Helms, Claudette E., 80
Hemphill, John K., 36, 41
Hencley, S. P., 39
Henley, Benjamin, 73, 130-131, 133-134, 181, 194, 204, 320, 331, 560
Hewlett, Everett A., 61, 130, 133
Hicks, Louise, 27
Hilts, Phil, 82

Himes, Joseph S., 32, 40
Hines, Vynce, 36, 41
Hobson, Julius, W., Jr., 93, 95-98, 100, 102-103, 105-106, 124-125, 231, 233, 237, 253, 257-258, 263, 270-271, 277, 280, 300-302, 304, 332-335, 338-340, 342-344, 346, 351, 358, 368, 392-393, 397-398, 400-401, 407-408, 412, 422, 424-425, 428, 437-438, 442, 456, 458, 481, 487, 506, 513-514, 516-517, 524, 537-542, 560, 574, 578, 580, 593, 597-598, 601, 607, 627, 635-636, 641, 643, 681, 683, 686-687, 689-690
Hobson, Julius W., Sr., 60, 89, 91, 95, 128, 131-134, 144-145, 160, 173, 191, 207, 209, 212, 227, 268, 272, 289, 292, 341, 360, 368, 396-397, 446, 452, 560, 587, 602, 635, 637, 699, 723
Hobson Task Force (Team) dispute, 10, 368, 400-404, 424, 428-430, 525-526, 723
Hobson v Hansen (Wright Decree) (decision), 21, 59-60, 95, 115, 128, 137, 191, 207-209, 341, 360, 368, 396-397, 452-453, 560-561, 564, 616, 637, 646, 691, 699, 723. See also Equalization; Title I Comparability/Wright Decree
Hodge, Paul, 491, 508
Hoffman, Ellen, 219
Holsendolph, Ernest, 657
Home Rule, 66-67, 77, 243, 285-288, 415, 449, 664
Hoover, Edgar J., 43, 44
Horowitz, Donald L., 602
Horsky, Charles, 452
Howard, Pamela, 121
Hunter, Mary, 9, 173, 177
Hurd, James D., 247
Hurlbut, Richard L., 248-249, 340, 343, 348, 434, 435

## I

Ianni, Francis, 130
Influence, 31, 227, 372, 387, 399, 404, 423, 445-501, 621, 639-640. See also Pressure groups
Insiders vs Outsiders, and the D.C. Youth Orchestra Program, 312-313, 315, 324, 326, 416; and race, 484; and superintendent-school board relations, 592; and superintendent selection, 22, 34, 37, 132, 157, 278-279, 291, 591-593, 601-603, 614-615, 620, 632, 642

Integration. See Desegregation
Interference in administration, 3-4, 98-99, 111, 139, 187, 189, 208-209, 224, 258, 263-277, 291-292, 309-430, 478, 523, 591, 594, 614, 633, 635-636, 640, 650-651
Internal factors, 11, 17-23, 37, 78, 85-120, 127-172, 181-213, 223-284, 290-294, 309-430, 511-577, 596, 620, 623

## J

Jarvis, Areatha, 248
Jencks, Christopher, 617, 629
Jenkins, Harriette, 150
Johnson, Dorothy, 109
Johnson, James A., 249, 343, 346, 387-388, 436, 441, 494
Johnson, Lyndon B., 43, 89, 198, 200-201
Johnson, Mordecai W., 57-59, 182
Jones, Theresa, 140

## K

Kane, Elizabeth, 95-96, 98, 101, 103, 235-236, 238, 241, 252-254, 277, 292-293, 298, 305, 396, 401, 407-408, 412, 424-425, 456-457, 459, 480-481, 532, 537, 539-542, 593, 641-642, 647-648, 681, 683, 686-687, 689-690
Kane, Noel W., 249
Kay, Walter, 247
Kemp, Raymond B., 91, 93, 95-98, 139, 148, 163-164, 190, 211, 225, 231, 237, 244, 248, 253-256, 272-273, 286, 296-297, 302, 332, 335, 338-340, 342-346, 348, 355, 358-359, 373, 386-387, 390, 393, 397-399, 401, 404, 407-408, 412, 420, 423-424, 436-437, 457, 459, 479, 481, 513, 538-542, 574, 579, 593, 596, 635, 639, 641, 647, 670, 683, 686-687, 689-690, 709, 715
Kennedy, John F., 43, 191
Kiernan, Michael, 583
Kimbrough, Gwendolyn, 348, 531, 689
Kinard, John R., 143, 144, 151, 464-465
King, Jeanne, 9
King, Martin Luther, Jr., 43-44, 484-485
Knezevich, Stephen J., 41
Knighten, Arlene, 657
Kenny, Charles F., 150. See also Kenny, William

Kenny, William, 162, 163. See also, Kenny, Charles F.

## L

Labat, Margaret, 109, 110-111, 126, 260-261, 282, 301, 304, 459, 626
Leadership styles/behavior, and community pressure, 497; as factor in conflict, 11, 17, 19, 23; of Allen, 232, 256-257, 293; of Barry, 257-258, 293, 419; of Morris, 232, 256-258, 293, 425; of Reed, 262-263; of Scott, 183-189, 288, 293; of Sizemore, 258-267, 293
Lenski, Gerhard, 39
Leventon, Melvin, 249
Lewis, Napoleon, 109, 110, 459, 592, 624, 642
Lewis, Robert T., 247
Lincoln, Abraham, 471
Linowes, Robert, 451
Lipham, James, 13, 38
Local school budgeting, 365. See also School-by-school budgeting
Lucy, Bill, 246
Lynch, Acklyn, 497

## M

McAndrew, Gordon O., 130-131
McCarty, Donald J., 28-29, 38-39, 238-239, 295
McCormick, Cyrus, 452, 454
McCoy, Rhody, 135
McGuire, Michael, 248
McKenzie, Floretta Dukes, 108-109, 149, 164, 328-330, 372, 433-434, 441, 525
McLain, Lyn G., 317, 324, 327-329, 340, 349, 418-419, 431-435
McLendon, Preston K., 57, 182
McMillan, John C., 68
McNamara, Robert, 452
McWilliams, Jimmie, 206
Management ability vs educational leadership, 157-159, 463, 465, 491
Management Review Report, 362-363
Malone, Louise, 335, 440
Maguire, Edward, 346, 436
Manning, William, 68, 128-133, 172-173, 191, 194, 196-197, 201, 212, 217, 242, 268, 279, 291, 294, 519, 560, 591, 603, 614, 634, 642
Marland, Sidney P., 199
Martin, Charles, 473
Martin, John, 493, 533

Mason, Charles N., Jr., 226, 231, 237-238, 241, 244, 248-250, 252, 254, 495, 715
Mason, Hilda Howland, 28, 75, 91, 93, 95-97, 101, 103, 108, 142-143, 146, 156, 163-164, 166, 190, 206, 225-227, 248-256, 271, 286, 292-293, 293, 332-335, 338-340, 342-344, 346, 355, 358-359, 386-388, 393, 401, 407-408, 411-412, 416, 418-420, 424-425, 458, 479, 487, 495, 513, 515-517, 527, 536-539, 542, 551, 574, 577, 593, 597, 636, 639-643, 648, 653, 670, 683, 686-687, 689-690, 709, 715, 717
Matthews, John, 173, 489, 507-508, 624
Mayor's freeze, 390-391, 524, 546-547, 552, 556, 72
Membership changes, DCBOE, 17, 19, 181, 277-282, 284, 290-292, 414, 416, 577, 591, 620, 632, 635, 639, 654-655
Metropolitan Washington Board of Trade, 145, 246, 255, 322, 363, 448-452, 457-460, 465
Meyer, Agnes, 420, 452, 455
Meyer, Bill, 455
Meyer, Eugene, 420, 452, 455, 503
Meyer, Eugene and Agnes, Foundation, 108, 420, 452, 455, 457
Milgram, Morris, 249
Millard, Wilbur, 211
Mills, C. Wright, 25, 633, 723
Minor, John, 150, 152, 163-164, 177, 290, 464
Mitchell, Jeff, 247
Model School Division, 151, 191-194, 361, 380, 447, 603, 609
Mohammed, Elijah, 484
Moody, George, 150
Moore, Douglas, 528
Moore, Emily, 584
Moore, Irna, 82, 174
Morgan Community School, 130, 151, 194-197, 448, 603
Morgenthau, Hans, 40
Morris, Myrtle C., 328, 330-331, 340-341, 432-435
Morris, Virginia, 93-95, 97-98, 100, 102-104, 106, 111, 118, 231-232, 237-238, 244, 250, 253-254, 256-258, 271, 277, 280, 292-294, 298, 304, 333-335, 338-340, 342-343, 346-347, 351-352, 358-359, 375-376, 393-396, 399-404, 407-408, 411-412, 420-425, 436-439, 441-443, 458, 478, 480-481, 487, 491, 505-506, 512-515, 524, 532-533, 537, 539-542, 558, 577, 579-587, 593, 624, 636, 639-643, 647-648, 655, 658-659, 669, 681-683, 686-687, 689-690, 698, 708-709, 716-718
Morse, Helen, 452
Morsink, Helen M., 36, 41
Motivation. See Motives
Motives, 11, 17, 19, 29, 233-245, 281, 291-293, 416, 641-642
Moynihan, Daniel P., 434-435

N

Nairm, Allan, 618
Nagle, Pat, 130
National Education Association (NEA), 60
Nelsen Commission Report, 362-363, 446, 453
Newell, Philip, 246, 249, 255
Newmyer, A., 247
Nixon, Richard M., 147, 202, 498
Nussbaum, Michael, 587

O

Ohl, Pete T., 82
120 Day Report, and Academic Achievement Plan, 137; and decentralization, 111, 205; and Scott, 187-188, 205; and Sizemore, 284, 338, 352, 379-380, 387, 405-406, 417, 422-423, 526, 675, 681, 697
Opening of school problems, 375, 379, 523, 723
Organic Act of 1906, 67, 71
Orr, Alexander, 472-473
Orr, Eleanor, 472-473
Outcomes, School System, 18, 20, 591-623
Overhiring/budget deficit, 395-399

P

PACTS process, 152, 168, 171, 202, 207, 227, 234, 345, 393, 406, 417, 426, 526, 538
Page, Thornell, 297
Park, Robert E., 39
Passow, A. Harry, 57, 60, 68, 81, 86, 92, 106, 123, 125, 129-130, 139, 183, 185, 214, 362, 446, 452, 454, 502-503
Patterson, Relford, 340, 435
Patterson, Roland, 3, 490
Pearl, Ruth, 148, 496

Personnel control system, and charges, 408-409, 546-547, 565, 568-572; and overhiring/budget deficit, 395-399, 546-547; and school-by-school budget, 366; and Reed, 608-614, 622; and Waterhouse Report, 286, 364; description of, 366-368
Peter Mills, et al, v Board of Education, et al, 97, 139, 723. See also Waddy Decree (decision)
Philosophy, Sizemore, 152-154, 168-171, 360, 373-399, 468-472
Pike, David, 503
Pinkett, Flaxie, 452
Pitts, Cornelius C., 247
Poinsett, Alex, 504
Policy versus implementation. See Interference in administration
Policy-making, and Clark, 185-186; and community pressure, 30, 445-501; and scheduling, 388; and the budget/management dispute, 377-413; and the corporation counsel, 355-360, 634; and the D.C. Youth Orchestra Program, 331-352, 634; and non-implementation, 139-140; and school board procedure, 99-106; and school board role, 267-277, 633; as conflict point, 30, 414-415; outcome of, 642
Politics, among school board members, 100, 106, 244-245, 291, 421-422; and the D.C. Youth Orchestra Program, 351-352; in education, 30, 153, 140, 241, 446; in superintendent selection process, 145-143, 156; school board members as politicians, 101, 103-104, 105, 138, 227, 232, 236, 240-245, 247, 255, 281, 419, 423, 464, 474-475, 513, 623, 641-642
Political conflict, theory of, 17-37
Pollard, Alfonso, 332
Population in the District, 30, 44-55, 135-136, 245, 279, 288, 409, 415, 500, 515, 615, 644-646; in the school system, 47-49, 56, 69, 135, 183-184, 278, 288, 337, 374, 409, 415, 424, 426-427, 446, 471, 515, 636-637, 644
Position control system. See Personnel control system
Powell, Adam C., 235
Power, and community groups, 445-501; and the D.C. Youth Orchestra Program, 344-345; and the District government, 285-288; and the Finance Committee, 228; and local school boards, 152; and the D.C. Board of Education; and the superintendent, 101-102, 424

Pressure, as factor in conflict, 11, 639; of Clark's study group, 184-190; of city council and mayor, 528, 576; of community groups, 447-501, 598, 621; of congressional and White House interest, 191, 198, 200-201, 445-446, 500, 535, 576, 598; of court decisions, 207; of federal agencies, 199-200; of newspapers, 157, 290, 372, 387, 399, 461-501, 527; of Passow's study group, 183-184
Price-Waterhouse Report, 204, 286, 362-364, 446
Principal selection, 151, 204-205
Prince, Richard, 465, 477-478, 481-482, 485-487, 503-507, 525-526, 581
Procedures, D.C. Board of Education, 98-106, 112-114
Profiles, D.C. Board of Education, 223-237
Pryde, Delores E., 77, 83, 91, 156-157, 163-164, 178, 190, 210, 230, 232, 237, 250, 253, 258, 277, 280, 295-296, 298, 300, 303, 352, 458, 670
Pucinski, Roman C., 446
Pupil Personnel Field Centers, 203
Purvis, Charles, 448
Pusey, Merlo J., 503

## R

Race, and control of Blacks, 484-486; and school board constituents, 33, 44-55, 135-136, 279, 288, 409, 415, 500, 515, 615, 644-646; of school board members, 223-237, 280; and superintendent selection, 130, 134, 136, 161-162, 164, 463; and the "Citizens Salute to Superintendent Sizemore" 479-430; and the D.C. Youth Orchestra Program, 315, 326-327; as disruptive factors, 56, 140, 288
Racial conflict, 31-34, 183-184, 285
Racism, and the D.C. Youth Orchestra Program, 332, 334-336, 416-419; and the District newspapers, 468-473, 485; and the general counsel dispute, 421; and the

781

Metropolitan Washington Board of Trade, 449; and Scott's retention, 140-141; and superintendent-school board relations, 3; and the track system, 129, 183-184; as factor in conflict, 11, 637-638
Raspberry, William, 472, 490, 499-500, 504, 508, 510
Recommendations (Alternative Strategies), 649-656
Reed, Vincent E., 34, 111-112, 231, 236-237, 261-265, 267, 275, 282, 303, 357-358, 460, 491, 498-499, 510, 525, 593, 595-604, 608, 613-616, 619, 622-627, 630, 635, 642-643, 662, 665
Reid, Herbert O., 75, 539, 541, 542, 556, 567-568, 574-575, 577, 622
Responsibility, D.C. Board of Education, 76, 135, 145, 670-672
Rhodes, George, 136
Riecks, John H., 130
Rice, William, 109, 111, 126, 199, 265, 266, 282, 301-302, 304, 460
Rigbey, John J., 247
Riles, Wilson C., 130-131
Roberts, Gloria K., 182
Robinson, Floyd, 329
Robinson, Gerald, 246
Role conflict, and superintendent-school board relations, 98-99, 268-276, 349-350, 424, 463, 495, 640; as factor in conflict, 5-6, 11, 17-19, 22-23; explanation of, 29-30; some examples of, 400-404, 422-423
Role confusion, 30, 276-277. See also Interference in administration
Roots, Nelson, 89, 134-135, 147, 186, 197, 198, 225, 242, 257, 447
Rosenfield, Albert A., 89, 90-91, 93-94, 98, 123, 133-135, 138, 140, 142-143, 148, 163-164, 186, 189, 196, 198, 209, 225-226, 234, 238, 248, 253, 257, 277, 286, 292-293, 297, 335, 338-339, 342, 352, 372-373, 424, 463, 475, 513, 642, 648, 670
Rosenthal, Allen, 30, 39
Ross, Bernard H., 81
Roxborough, Claude, 355
Rules, D. C. Board of Education, 86, 94, 166, 233, 356, 382, 400, 421, 535, 557, 574, 576, 593, 683-684

## S

Saffran, Rosanna B., 312-314, 431, 503
Saks, Isadore, 448
Salmon, Paul B., 583
Sansing, John, 657
Sargent, Ernest E., 608-612, 627-628
Sawyer, Yango, 493, 533
School-by-school budgeting, 151, 203-204, 228, 366, 608. See also Local school budgeting
Schwartz, Carol L., 95-97, 233, 237, 251, 253, 277, 298, 396, 399, 401, 407-408, 412, 424, 480-481, 537, 539-542, 593, 682-683, 686-687, 689-690
Scott, Hugh, 9, 34, 69, 71-74, 78, 81-82, 98, 107, 119-120, 123, 128, 134, 136-142, 149, 151, 172, 174-176, 181, 186-191, 199, 202-212, 215, 219, 224-225, 228-230, 257-258, 261, 267-270, 276, 279, 285-286, 289, 291-295, 300, 302, 321, 323-325, 350, 368, 371, 420, 422, 430-432, 450-451, 456, 460, 462-464, 502, 511, 519, 544, 555, 560, 591, 602-603, 615, 622, 633-635, 637-638, 642-643
Selection, superintendent, 99, 116, 120, 127-172, 229, 451, 465-466, 513, 593-599, 614-615, 638-639, 642
Sessions, John A., 89, 130-134, 196
Sestak, Michael E., 33, 40
Sexism, and general counsel dispute, 421; and school board expectations 37; and superintendent-school board relations, 43; and superintendent selection, 146, 156-157, 290; and superintendent termination, 542-543, 576, 602, 621-622; as factor in conflict, 11, 17, 19 22, 639; definition of, 35; in the D.C. public school system, 62-63, 65; in educational administration, 62; Sizemore's view of, 468, 476
Sexton, Patricia, 35, 41
Shackelton, Polly, 246, 248, 250, 254
Simon, Herbert, 25-26, 31, 38-39, 634
Simons, William, 459, 592, 624
Simmons, Barbara Lett, 93-96, 102, 114, 124, 143-144, 146, 148-149, 231, 238, 249-250, 252-253, 262, 277, 280, 298, 301, 303, 333-336, 339-340, 342-344, 346, 358, 391,

400-401, 407-408, 412, 419-420, 424, 459, 496, 498, 510, 513-514, 516, 526, 530, 532-533, 536-542, 576, 582, 593-594, 596-597, 607, 627, 629, 641, 683, 686-687, 689-690, 708, 718
Simpson, Edith B., 247
Sisco, Jean H. 246, 255
Sizemore, Barbara A., 3, 9, 34, 94, 98, 102-103, 108-112, 114, 119-120, 150, 152-161, 163-166, 168-172, 177-181, 190, 199-202, 206, 213, 216, 218, 220, 224-228, 231-236, 254, 258-260, 262-264, 266-267, 278-280, 282, 284-286, 290-291, 293-295, 300-301, 328-333, 337, 340-353, 356-358, 360-361, 368, 371, 373, 375, 377-385, 387-389, 392-395, 397, 402-405, 408, 410-411, 420-421, 423, 425, 430, 433-444, 456, 460, 462, 464-499, 501, 504-515, 518-519, 523, 533-534, 540, 555, 560-564, 567, 569, 573, 577-588, 591-593, 596-598, 603, 605-606, 608, 612-622, 626-630, 634, 636-640, 642-647, 652-653, 655-659, 661-662, 666, 669-670, 672-674, 681, 686-687, 689-691, 699, 708-709, 716-718
Smith, Conrad P., 236, 238, 459, 597
Smith, Samuel F. H., 247, 249
Smuck, Carl C., 182
Socioeconomic characteristics, school board members, 237-238
Sole source contract, 341, 344-346, 350
Solomon, Steve, 629
Spingarn Instruction Unit, 202-203, 380, 603
Splitt, David A., 107, 231, 248, 254, 341, 347, 355, 359, 421, 435, 528, 574, 582, 683-690
Staff, D.C. Board of Education, 106-107
Staff, superintendent, 108-112
Staples, Robert, 31, 39-40
Steele, Louise, 182-183
Steinkamp, Richard B., 582
Stern, Phillip, 247
Stewart, William E., 531, 535, 541, 585
Stone, Avatus, 246
Stone, Chuck, 617, 629
Strayer, George D., 67, 81, 92, 139, 445
Strayer Report (study), 67, 92, 139, 445
Street, Victoria, 271

Structure, D.C. Board of Education, 11, 17-19, 23, 27, 73, 85, 88-107
Structure, superintendent's office, as factor in conflict, 11: staff of, 108-112
Stults, Ann, 130, 196
Sullivan, Neil C., 130
Superintendent selection, of Hansen, 128-129; of Manning, 128-134; of Scott, 128, 134-142; of Sizemore, 142-168, 451, 464-466; of Reed, 491, 596-598; as school board function, 11, 127-172
Swaim, Martha, 74, 89, 91, 93-94, 97, 135, 139, 142-143, 148, 156-157, 159, 161-164, 178-179, 185-186, 190, 199, 210-211, 227-229, 241, 250, 253-257, 273-274, 277, 286, 290, 292-293, 298, 333-335, 338-340, 342, 352-353, 355, 362, 370, 373, 418-420, 424, 430, 439-440, 456, 465-466, 474-475, 512-513, 578, 635, 638-639, 642, 647-648, 670
Sylvester, Ed., 247
Symington, Lloyd, 247, 255

T

Taylor, Edwin F., 629
Taylor, Hortense P., 324, 331, 343, 431, 434
Taylor, Mattie G., 89-90, 93-94, 100-101, 106-107, 113-114, 124-125, 135, 139-140, 142-143, 146, 156, 163-164, 166, 186, 189, 208, 211, 224, 229, 235, 237, 243, 247-248, 253-254, 259, 277, 280, 296-297, 301, 304, 333-334, 342, 355, 419, 424, 439, 458, 513, 633, 641, 670
Teacher payroll problems, 723
Termination, analysis of, 560-574; as school board function, 11, 127-172; as resolution of conflict, 643; "Bill of Particulars," 685-686, 690, 715-716; documents for, 669-718; of Hansen, 129; of Manning, 135; of Scott, 138-142; of Sizemore, 404, 422, 486-498, 511-577
Terrell, Robert, 448
Thompson, Juanita, 329, 337, 433
Thompson, Lewis and Associates, 208
Thornton, Alvin, 239, 296
Tirana, Bardyl, 71-72, 76, 83, 90, 99, 124, 134-135, 156, 163-164, 185-187, 190, 225, 229-230, 237, 248, 250, 252, 257, 259-260, 271,

277, 280, 286, 295, 301-302, 304, 355, 458, 635, 670
Title I Comparability/Wright Decree, 552, 566-567
Toynbee, Arnold, 483, 485
Track System, 57-58, 60, 77, 128, 181-184, 191, 292, 560, 637-639
Treanor, John H., 89
Treanor, William, 93-96, 98, 103, 134, 230-231, 238, 250, 252-256, 258, 264, 280, 296, 298, 300-301, 303, 333-335, 338-340, 342-344, 346, 352, 355, 358-359, 407-408, 412, 420, 424, 439, 458, 473, 479, 513, 537, 539-542, 579, 582, 593, 639, 660, 681-683, 686-687, 689-690
Trescott, Jacqueline, 476, 505
Tucker, Sterling, 213-224, 523
Turner, R. J., 657

## U

Unique relationship between Congress, city council, mayor, the courts and/or the school board, 20, 66-73, 426. See also Colonial status
United Planning Organization (UPO), 447, 457

## V

Valentine, Paul W., 300
Vincent, Harry, 247

## W

Waddy Decree (decision), 139, 360, 446, 453, 561, 596, 646. See also Peter Mills, et al, v Board of Education, et al
Waddy, Joseph P., 139, 360, 446, 453, 561, 596, 646. See also Waddy Decree
Walker, Jethro J., 496
Ward 1, 48, 50, 225, 229, 236, 325
Ward 2, 48, 51, 53-55, 225, 231, 325
Ward 3, 50-51, 53-54, 226, 230, 234, 270, 325, 332, 416, 457
Ward 4, 50-51, 53-54, 227, 270, 325
Ward 5, 50, 52-54, 224, 235, 247, 325
Ward 6, 50, 52-55, 227-228, 235, 325, 332, 457, 513
Ward 7, 50, 52-54, 230, 232, 237, 325, 332
Ward 8, 50, 53-54, 228, 233, 325, 332, 416, 424
Washington Board of Trade. See Metropolitan Washington Board of Trade
Warner, Brainard, 448
Warren, John E., 95-97, 106, 114, 124-125, 235, 241, 251, 253, 277, 296, 298, 396, 399, 401, 407-408, 412, 424, 458, 514, 516, 526, 530, 532-533, 536-539, 542, 593-594, 597-598, 624, 641, 683, 686-687, 689-690
Washington, Evie M., 90, 134-135, 143, 148, 163-164, 186, 190, 225-226, 237, 248, 253, 257-258, 295, 298, 300, 355, 458, 670
Washington, George, 471
Washington, Melvin, 490, 532, 534
Washington Post, 8, 227, 423, 448, 455, 461, 463, 465-466, 469, 471-472, 474-478, 480, 483, 485-500, 515, 525, 530, 595-596, 600, 615
Washington Star, 68, 128, 227, 375, 379, 399, 404, 423, 461, 463, 467-469, 473-479, 481-485, 487-489, 492, 495-499, 515, 525, 593, 595-596, 615
Washington, Walter E., 68, 81, 304, 479
Weaver, Margo, 143
Weil, Martin, 508
Weisman, Joel D., 488, 507
West, Anne Grant, 36, 41
Whedbee, Michael, 248
Wheeler, Robert, 136
White, Barbara, 312-314, 431, 503
Wiles, Kimball, 36, 41
Wilkins, Beriah, 448
Williams, Chancellor, 484
Williams, James L., 97, 109, 266, 275, 281, 303-304, 362, 364, 377, 382, 386-388, 391, 395-399, 408, 411-412, 440-442, 444, 459, 552-553, 569-573, 588, 592-593, 606, 608-613, 619, 624, 627-628, 635, 643
Williams, Juan, 625
Williams, Robert L., 618, 629
Williams, Smallwood, 55
Williams, Wesley S., 183, 191, 216
Wilmer, Cutler and Pickering, 71
Wilson, Woodrow, 449
Wingate, Richard E., 350-351
Winner, Edward G., 97, 372-373, 525, 611, 628-629
Wirtz, Willard, 250
Wolf, Simon, 448
Woodson, Minnie Shumate, 236-237, 271

Woodward, S.W., 448
Wooten, Robert, 488
Wornley, James T., 448
Wright, J. Skelly, 60, 63, 115,
 131, 137, 207-209, 292, 341, 360,
 368, 396-397, 446, 452-453, 544,
 560-561, 564, 602, 616, 625, 646,
 691, 699. See also Hobson v
 Hansen
Wright, Joseph, 247

## X

X, Malcolm, 484-485

## Y

Yochelson, Irving B., 182
Young, Milton A., 201, 218

## Z

Zeonarias, Jerrold R., 191

ABOUT THE AUTHOR

Nancy Levi Arnez, A.B., Morgan State University; M.A., Columbia University; Ed.D., Columbia University; Graduate Professor. Specialization: Educational Administration. Dr. Arnez is a former Associate Dean and Acting Dean of the School of Education, Howard University. She has also served as Director of the Center for Inner City Studies, a dean-like position, at Northeastern Illinois University; as an associate professor and director of Student Teaching at Morgan State University; as a consultant for the Maryland State Board of Higher Education; the National Institute of Education; the California Commission on Teacher Preparation; and National Follow-Through. While at the Center for Inner City Studies, Northeastern Illinois University, between 1966 and 1973, Dr. Arnez was instrumental in securing over $2,000,000 worth of Grants to operate a Master's Degree fellowship program for prospective teachers, an Experienced Teacher Fellowship Program, a Career Opportunity Program and a Follow Through Program. In this connection, she conceptualized an early Childhood Education Program for National Follow Through which was implemented in California, Kansas, Ohio and Chicago. Also, while Director of the Center for Inner City Studies, Dr. Arnez and her colleagues designed multicultural, interdisciplinary undergraduate and graduate programs for social workers, policemen, teachers, paraprofessionals and social agency workers in the inner city.

At Howard University, Dr. Arnez assisted with the development of a doctoral program in Educational Administration and during 1978-79 completed research on the superintendency of the D.C. Public School System between October 1973-75, funded by Spencer Foundation and AAUW, exploring the issues of policy-making and the administration of policy. In 1977 Dr. Arnez along with Dr. Charles Martin and Dr. Bessie Howard completed a research study entitled,

"Racism and Sexism in Children's Books in Two Inner City Libraries." In 1980, she wrote a manual titled <u>Administrative Issues in the Implementation of the Response to Educational Needs Project (RENP)</u> for the National Institute of Education.

Additionally, Dr. Arnez is the author of over 100 poems, peer-reviewed articles, chapters in books, book reviews and books. She is currently writing non-racist and non-sexist children's stories.